THE AVENGERS

D1192755

KREE-SKRULL WAR

Neal Adams
COVER ART

Neal Adams
Steve Buccellato
COVER COLOR

JG and Comicraft's
Eric Eng Wong
DESIGN

Mikhail Bortnik
COVER and
INTERIOR
TOUCH-UP

Jessica Schwartz
EDITORIAL/PRODUCTION
ASSITANT

Matty Ryan
ASSITANT EDITOR

Ben Abernathy
COLLECTIONS EDITOR

Bernadette Thomas
MANUFACTURING MANAGER

Bob Greenberger
DIRECTOR: EDITORIAL
OPERATIONS

Joe Quesada
EDITOR IN CHEIF

Bill Jemas
PRESIDENT

INTRODUCTION:
NEAL ADAMS

"THE ONLY GOOD ALIEN..."
CHAPTER ONE

"JUDGMENT DAY"
CHAPTER TWO

"TAKE ONE GIANT
STEP...BACKWARD!"
CHAPTER TWO

"ALL THINGS MUST END!"
CHAPTER THREE

"THIS BEACHHEAD EARTH"
CHAPTER FOUR

"MORE THAN INHUMAN!"
CHAPTER FIVE

"SOMETHING INHUMAN
THIS WAY COMES!"
CHAPTER SIX

"ANDROMEDA SWARM!"
CHAPTER SEVEN

"GODHOOD'S END!"
CHAPTER EIGHT

AFTERWORD:
ROY THOMAS

AVENGERS® KREE-SKRULL WAR Contains material originally published in magazine form as AVENGERS Vol. 1, #'s 89-97. Published by MARVEL COMICS, a division of MARVEL ENTERPRISES, INC. Lou Gioia, Executive Vice-President, Publishing. Bob Greenberger, Director, Editorial Operations. Stan Lee, Chairman Emeritus. OFFICE OF PUBLICATION: 387 PARK AVENUE SOUTH, NEW YORK, N.Y. 10016. Copyright © 1971, 1972, 2000 and 2001 Marvel Characters, Inc. All rights reserved. No similarity between any of the names, characters, persons, and/or institutions in this magazine with those of any living or dead person or institution is intended, and any such similarity which may exist is purely coincidental. This periodical may not be sold except by authorized dealers and is sold subject to the condition that it shall not be sold or distributed with any part of its cover or markings removed, nor in a mutilated condition. AVENGERS (including all prominent characters featured in this issue and the distinctive likenesses thereof) is a registered trademark of MARVEL CHARACTERS, INC. No part of this book may be printed or reproduced in any manner without the written permission of the publisher. Printed in CANADA. Second Printing: July, 2001. ISBN # 0-7851-0745-2. GST #R127032852. MARVEL COMICS is a division of MARVEL ENTERPRISES, INC. Peter Cuneo, Chief Executive Officer; Avi Arad, Chief Creative Officer.   10 9 8 7 6 5 4 3 2

THREE COWS SHOT ME DOWN

Okay, it deserves an explanation.

Actually, when you read this book the reason for the Vision's line on the cover will be quite evident.

So, this is written for those few people who must know what's up... before they read the book. If you're one of those, here goes.

When I was invited onto the Avengers, I had to play "catch-up" on where we were in the story. Roy, the continuing writer on the series, told me he'd originally had in mind a kind of back-story of a Kree-Skrull War, but the story had kind of wandered off the track on this particular theme. I could, he told me, pick up the Kree-Skrull War idea or go on to something else.

Well, the Kree-Skrull War idea was just to my liking. I asked if we could work pretty much like we did on X-Men; Roy said okay, and we were off.

Where to begin the story? We needed to begin with an opening salvo of misdeeds by the Skrulls... or the Kree.

Then I remembered Jack Kirby's first Skrull story... way back when... four Skrulls, shape-shifters, had battled the Fantastic Four. Of course, the F.F. won. But what do you do with - and how do you get rid of - shape-shifters? Can't jail or kill them. What do you do?

Jack and Stan had Reed Richards super-hypnotize the four Skrulls and told them they were cows. And so they would spend their lives lowing in the fields and eating grass.

But as fate would have it, when the cows-in-the-field frame was drawn by Jack, for some reason, he drew only three cows.

I called Roy and told him I'd like to use these cows/Skrulls to begin the story. Roy knew the very story and frame. He also knew there were only three cows, not four. So he suggested we could use the fourth Skrull as a foil and make him the politician or some such. He'd be the one Skrull that escaped. Now I could use the three cows as an opening gun. So I had the Vision stagger into Avengers Mansion all messed up... necessitating the now-legendary trip through the Vision's body by Ant-Man and his ants, Crosby, Stills and Nash.

The title of the beginning book would be "Three Cows Shot Me Down." So I wrote it on the bottom of that page as a suggested title.

I guess Roy felt it was a frivolous title for the opening salvo of a big epic project like this. He named the story "This Beachhead Earth." A good title. But in my mind that story would ever be titled "Three Cows Shot Me Down."

Now, many years later, Marvel asked me to do a new cover for the collection.

So... what was I to do? I picked the moment before Vision burst through the door of Avengers' Mansion. The moment when he actually said, "Three Cows Shot Me Down," and called for help.

I sincerely would have loved to finish that story... it would have been a grand romp. Please... enjoy... everything in this book.

NEAL ADAMS · 6·2000

P.S. Uh... on the cover. Are we looking at the Vision through the door and it's a reflection of the rest... or are we looking at the Avengers through the door and a reflection of the Vision...?

CHAPTER ONE

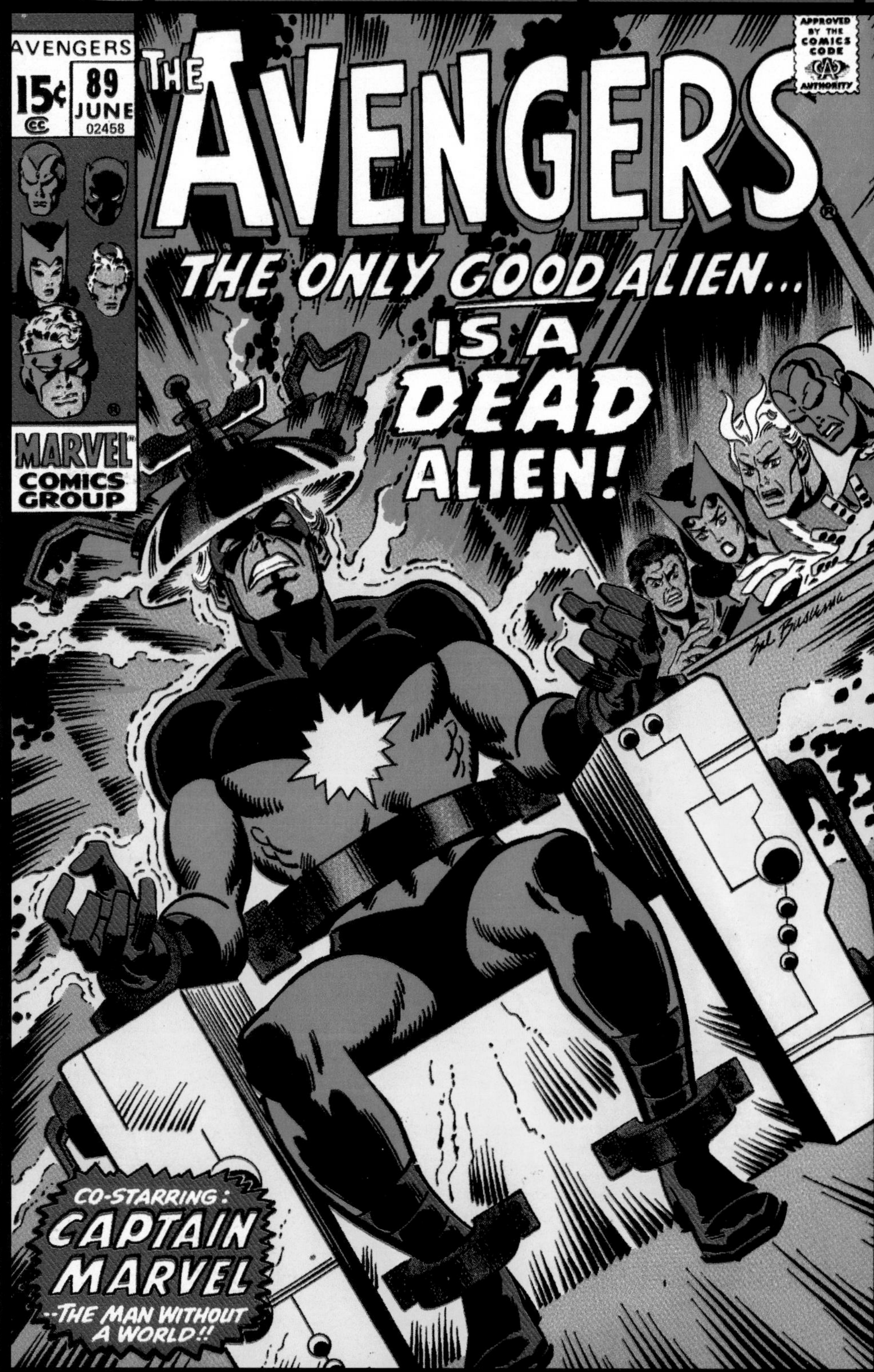
AVENGERS
15¢
89
JUNE
02458
THE AVENGERS
APPROVED BY THE COMICS CODE AUTHORITY
THE ONLY GOOD ALIEN...
IS A DEAD ALIEN!
MARVEL COMICS GROUP
CO-STARRING:
CAPTAIN MARVEL
--THE MAN WITHOUT A WORLD!!

THE ONLY GOOD ALIEN...

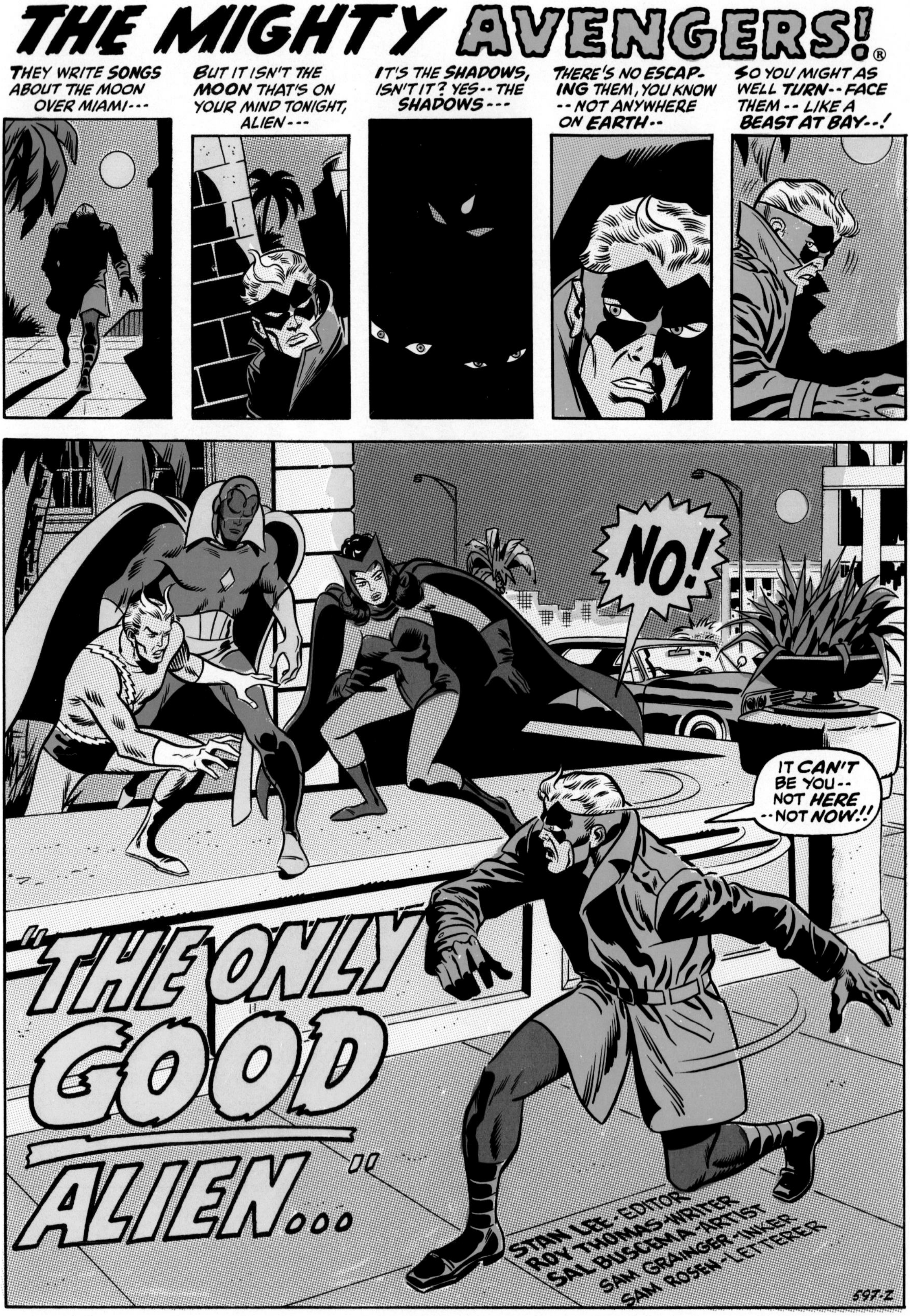
THE MIGHTY AVENGERS!®
THEY WRITE SONGS ABOUT THE MOON OVER MIAMI---
BUT IT ISN'T THE MOON THAT'S ON YOUR MIND TONIGHT, ALIEN---
IT'S THE SHADOWS, ISN'T IT? YES-- THE SHADOWS---
THERE'S NO ESCAPING THEM, YOU KNOW -- NOT ANYWHERE ON EARTH--
SO YOU MIGHT AS WELL TURN-- FACE THEM -- LIKE A BEAST AT BAY--!
NO!
IT CAN'T BE YOU-- NOT HERE --NOT NOW!!
"THE ONLY GOOD ALIEN..."
STAN LEE-EDITOR
ROY THOMAS-WRITER
SAL BUSCEMA-ARTIST
SAM GRAINGER-INKER
SAM ROSEN-LETTERER
597-2

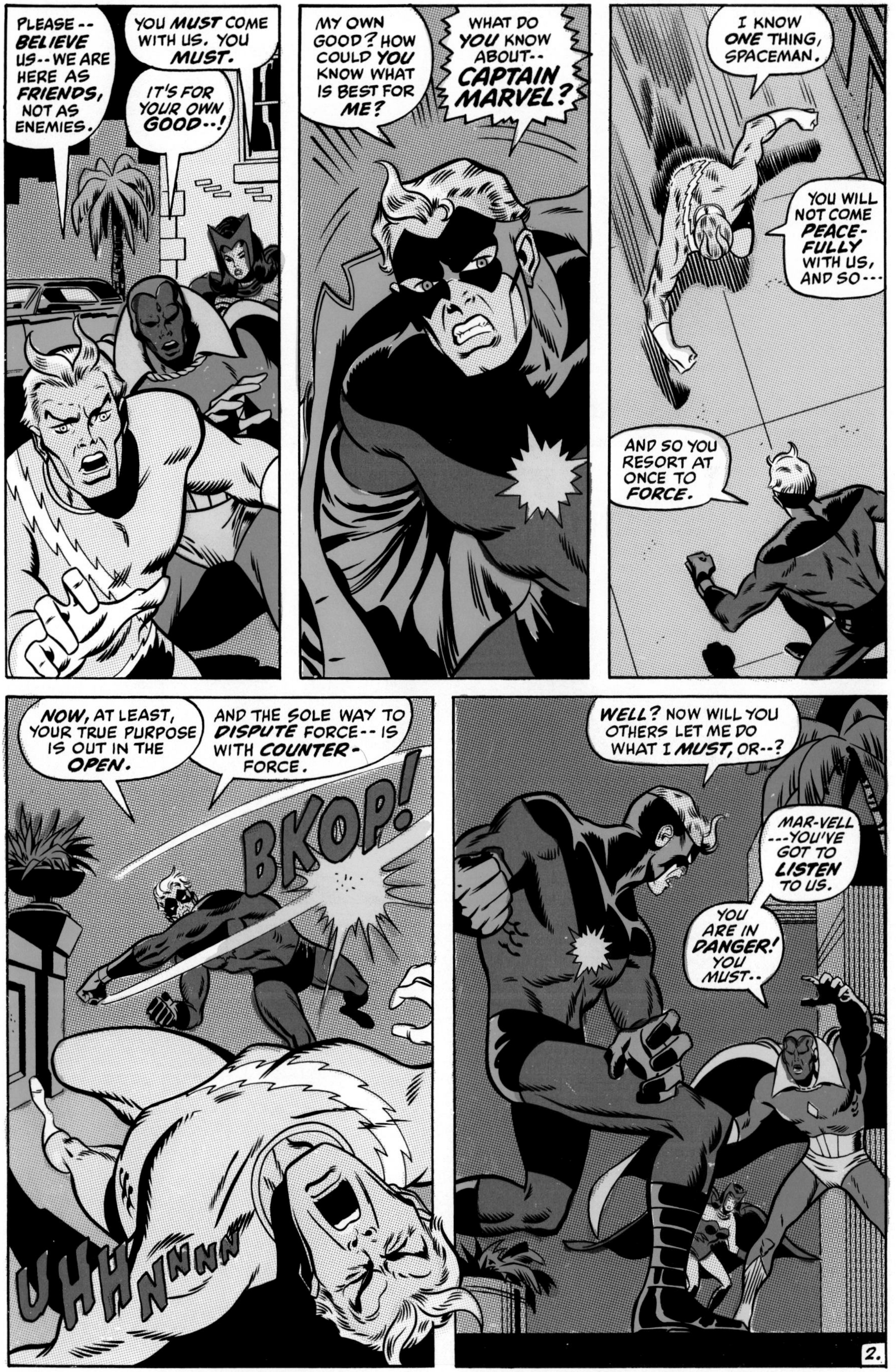
PLEASE -- BELIEVE US -- WE ARE HERE AS FRIENDS, NOT AS ENEMIES.
YOU MUST COME WITH US. YOU MUST.
IT'S FOR YOUR OWN GOOD--!
MY OWN GOOD? HOW COULD YOU KNOW WHAT IS BEST FOR ME?
WHAT DO YOU KNOW ABOUT-- CAPTAIN MARVEL?
I KNOW ONE THING, SPACEMAN.
YOU WILL NOT COME PEACE-FULLY WITH US, AND SO---
AND SO YOU RESORT AT ONCE TO FORCE.
NOW, AT LEAST, YOUR TRUE PURPOSE IS OUT IN THE OPEN.
AND THE SOLE WAY TO DISPUTE FORCE -- IS WITH COUNTER-FORCE.
BKOP!
UHHNNNN
WELL? NOW WILL YOU OTHERS LET ME DO WHAT I MUST, OR--?
MAR-VELL---YOU'VE GOT TO LISTEN TO US.
YOU ARE IN DANGER! YOU MUST..
2.

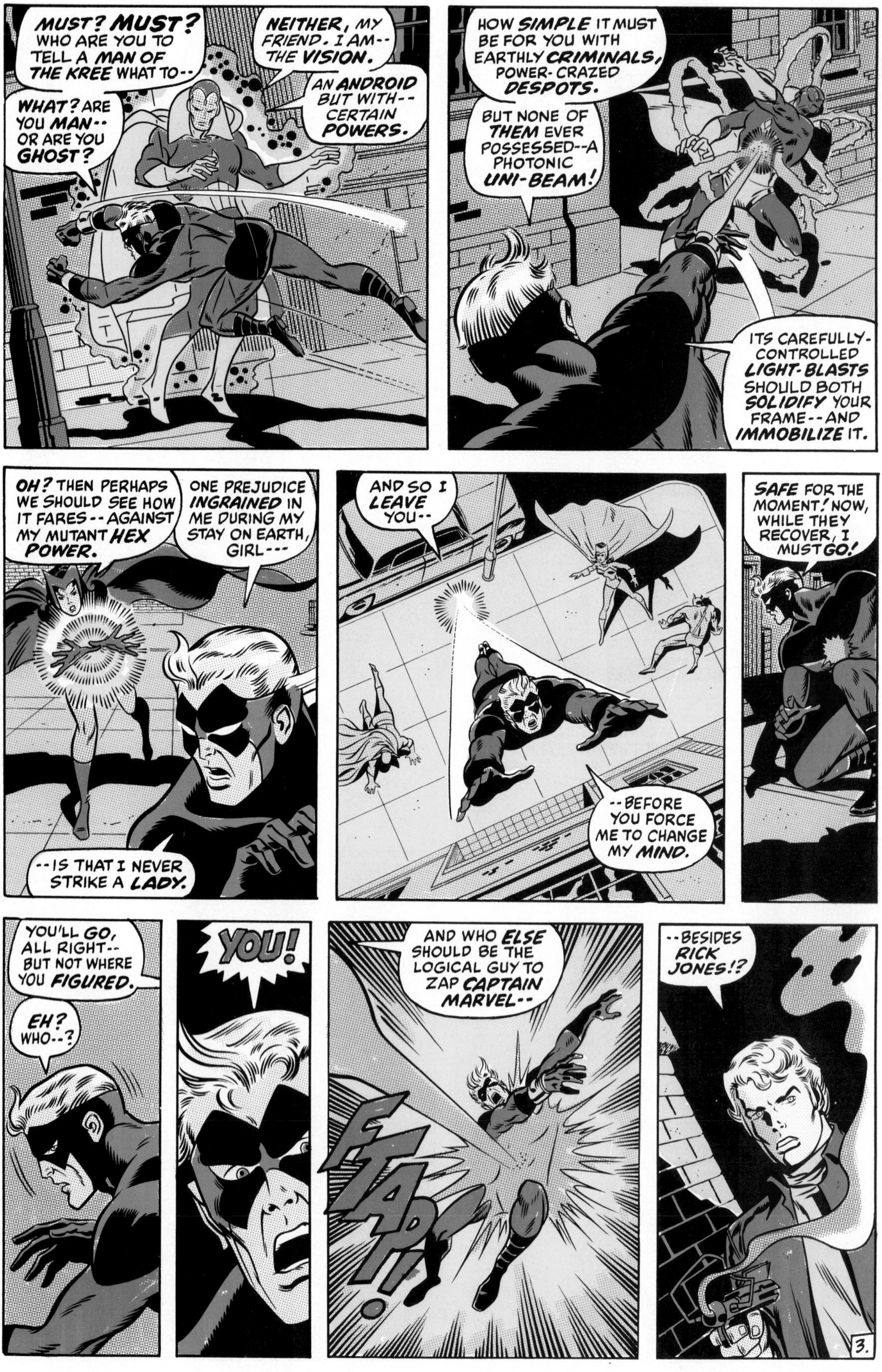
MUST? MUST? WHO ARE YOU TO TELL A MAN OF THE KREE WHAT TO--
WHAT? ARE YOU MAN-- OR ARE YOU GHOST?
NEITHER, MY FRIEND. I AM-- THE VISION.
AN ANDROID BUT WITH-- CERTAIN POWERS.
HOW SIMPLE IT MUST BE FOR YOU WITH EARTHLY CRIMINALS, POWER-CRAZED DESPOTS.
BUT NONE OF THEM EVER POSSESSED--A PHOTONIC UNI-BEAM!
ITS CAREFULLY-CONTROLLED LIGHT-BLASTS SHOULD BOTH SOLIDIFY YOUR FRAME--AND IMMOBILIZE IT.
OH? THEN PERHAPS WE SHOULD SEE HOW IT FARES--AGAINST MY MUTANT HEX POWER.
ONE PREJUDICE INGRAINED IN ME DURING MY STAY ON EARTH, GIRL---
--IS THAT I NEVER STRIKE A LADY.
AND SO I LEAVE YOU--
--BEFORE YOU FORCE ME TO CHANGE MY MIND.
SAFE FOR THE MOMENT! NOW, WHILE THEY RECOVER, I MUST GO!
YOU'LL GO, ALL RIGHT-- BUT NOT WHERE YOU FIGURED.
EH? WHO--?
YOU!
AND WHO ELSE SHOULD BE THE LOGICAL GUY TO ZAP CAPTAIN MARVEL--
FTAP!!
--BESIDES RICK JONES!?
3.

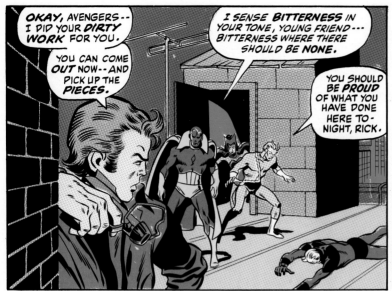

OKAY, AVENGERS-- I DID YOUR *DIRTY WORK* FOR YOU.

YOU CAN COME *OUT* NOW-- AND PICK UP THE *PIECES*.

I SENSE *BITTERNESS* IN YOUR TONE, YOUNG FRIEND--- BITTERNESS WHERE THERE SHOULD BE *NONE*.

YOU SHOULD BE *PROUD* OF WHAT YOU HAVE DONE HERE TO-NIGHT, RICK.

YEAH, OKAY-- SO I'M *PROUD*.

NOW LET'S *GO*, BEFORE I *TOSS* MY *COOKIES*, HUH?

LUCK WAS *WITH* US. NO ONE STUMBLED ACROSS OUR *QUINJET* HERE IN THIS *PARK*.

GOOD. IF THE AUTHORITIES FOUND MAR-VELL JUST NOW, THERE WOULD BE QUESTIONS... *RED TAPE...*

AND WE MUSTN'T EVEN THINK OF HOW *DISASTROUS* THAT WOULD BE-- BOTH FOR *MAR-VELL...*

-- AND FOR THE *WORLD!*

YOU SEEM STRANGELY *SILENT*, WANDA. IS SOME-THING--?

I WAS MERELY THINKING-- THIS MAN IS AN *ALIEN...* MAROONED HERE FROM A DISTANT *STAR*--

-- WHILE PIETRO AND I ARE *MUTANTS*-- NO MORE AT HOME ON EARTH THAN *HE!*

WE ARE ALL *STRANGERS*-- IN A *STRANGE* LAND.

HE SAYS *NOTHING*, THIS MAN-ROBOT. FOR, WANDA HAS HER *BRO-THER*-- AND EVEN MAR-VELL, HIS *MEMORIES*.

BUT WHAT HAS AN *ANDROID*-- SAVE THE EMPTINESS OF THE *PRESENT*, AND THE DREAD OF ENDLESS *TOMORROWS?*

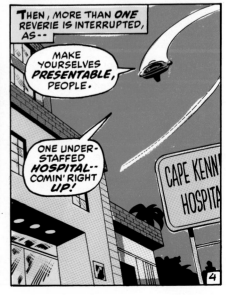

THEN, MORE THAN *ONE* REVERIE IS INTERRUPTED, AS--

MAKE YOURSELVES *PRESENTABLE*, PEOPLE.

ONE UNDER-STAFFED *HOSPITAL*-- COMIN' RIGHT *UP!*

CAPE KENN HOSPITA

4

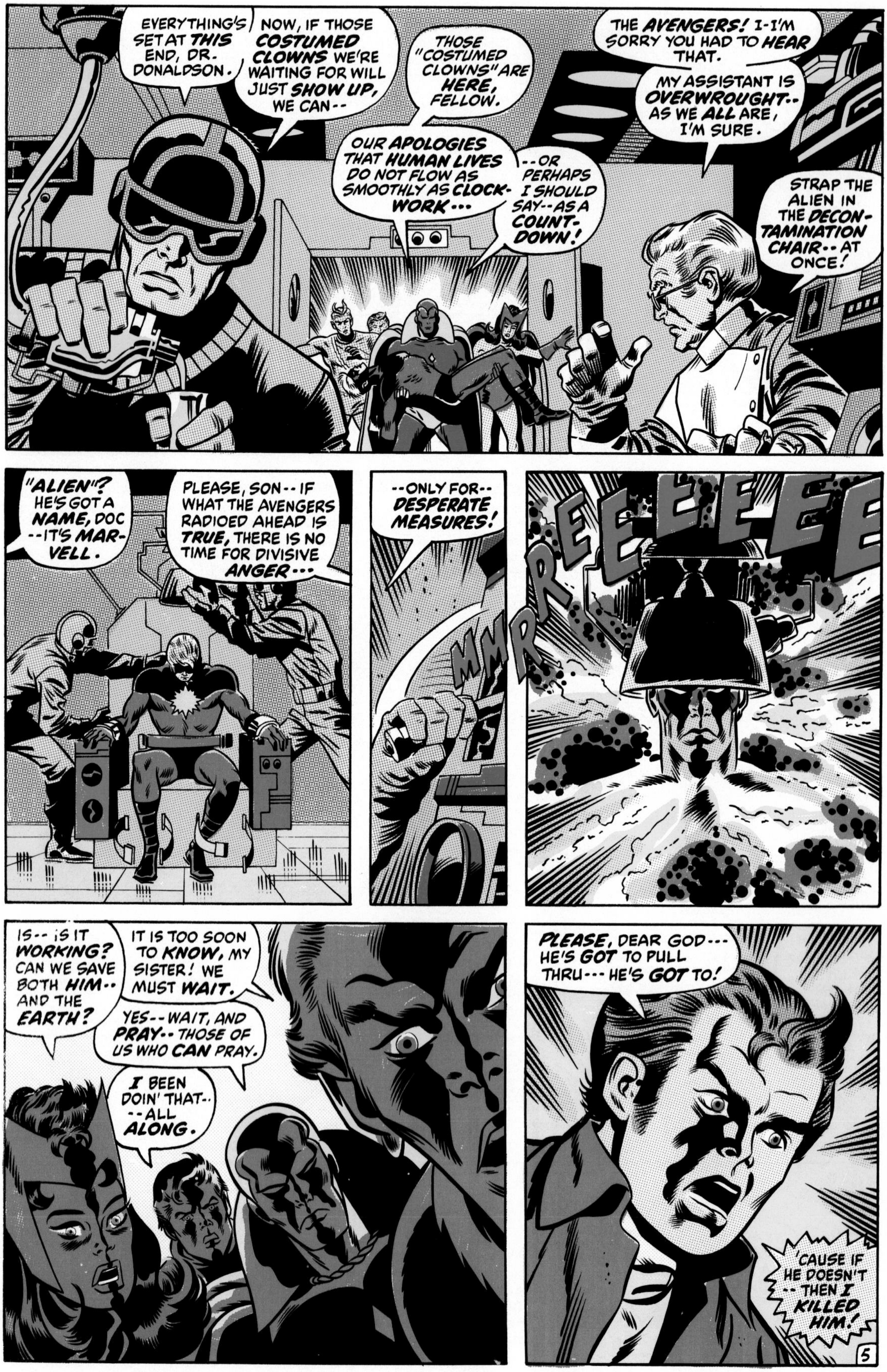
EVERYTHING'S SET AT THIS END, DR. DONALDSON.
NOW, IF THOSE COSTUMED CLOWNS WE'RE WAITING FOR WILL JUST SHOW UP, WE CAN--
THOSE "COSTUMED CLOWNS" ARE HERE, FELLOW.
OUR APOLOGIES THAT HUMAN LIVES DO NOT FLOW AS SMOOTHLY AS CLOCK-WORK...
--OR PERHAPS I SHOULD SAY--AS A COUNT-DOWN!
THE AVENGERS! I-I'M SORRY YOU HAD TO HEAR THAT.
MY ASSISTANT IS OVERWROUGHT--AS WE ALL ARE, I'M SURE.
STRAP THE ALIEN IN THE DECON-TAMINATION CHAIR--AT ONCE!
"ALIEN"? HE'S GOT A NAME, DOC--IT'S MAR-VELL.
PLEASE, SON--IF WHAT THE AVENGERS RADIOED AHEAD IS TRUE, THERE IS NO TIME FOR DIVISIVE ANGER...
--ONLY FOR--DESPERATE MEASURES!
MMRREEEEEE
IS--IS IT WORKING? CAN WE SAVE BOTH HIM--AND THE EARTH?
IT IS TOO SOON TO KNOW, MY SISTER! WE MUST WAIT.
YES--WAIT, AND PRAY--THOSE OF US WHO CAN PRAY.
I BEEN DOIN' THAT----ALL ALONG.
PLEASE, DEAR GOD---HE'S GOT TO PULL THRU---HE'S GOT TO!
'CAUSE IF HE DOESN'T--THEN I KILLED HIM!

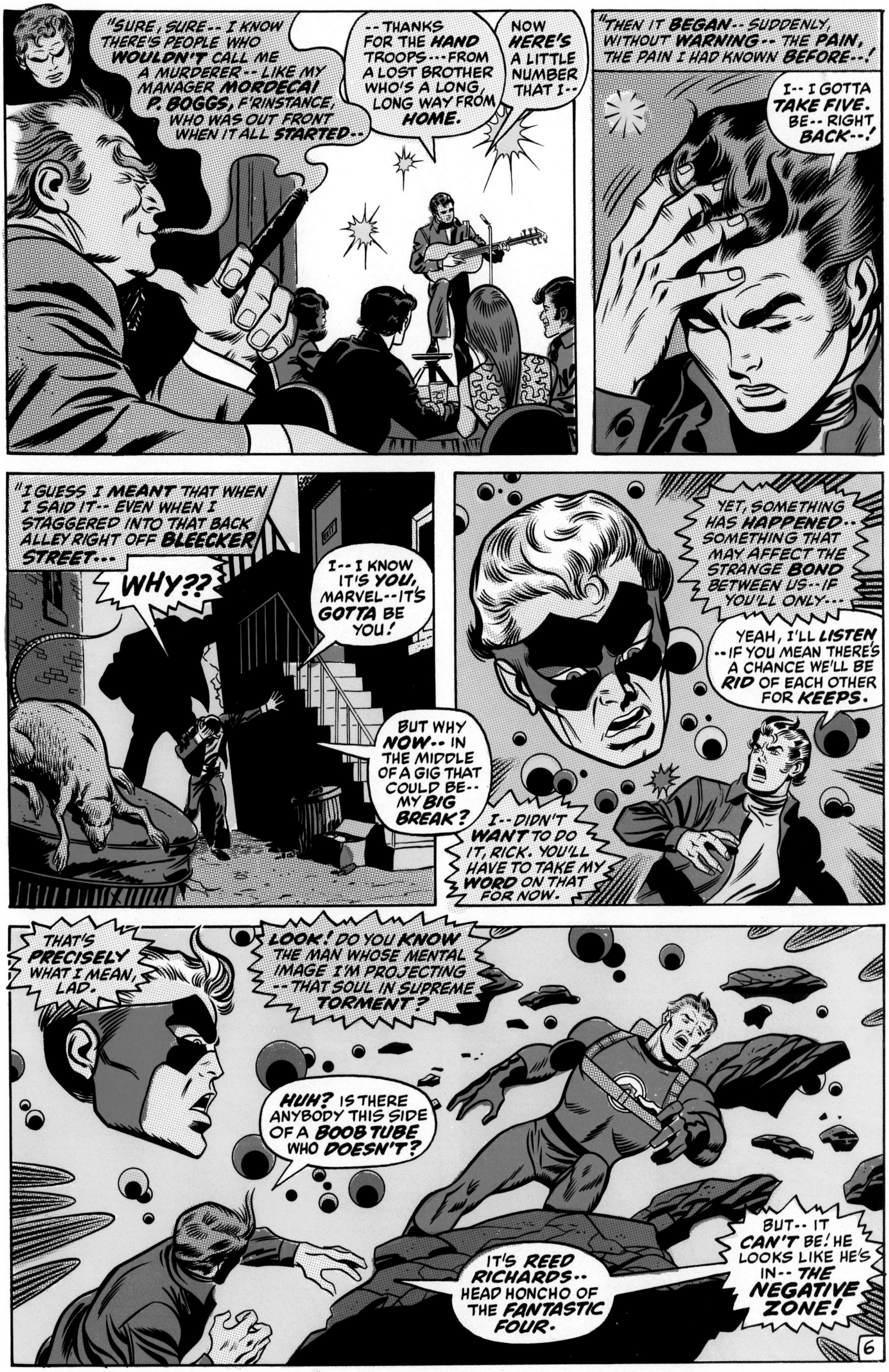
"SURE, SURE-- I KNOW THERE'S PEOPLE WHO WOULDN'T CALL ME A MURDERER-- LIKE MY MANAGER MORDECAI P. BOGGS, F'RINSTANCE, WHO WAS OUT FRONT WHEN IT ALL STARTED--
--THANKS FOR THE HAND TROOPS---FROM A LOST BROTHER WHO'S A LONG, LONG WAY FROM HOME.
NOW HERE'S A LITTLE NUMBER THAT I--
"THEN IT BEGAN-- SUDDENLY, WITHOUT WARNING-- THE PAIN, THE PAIN I HAD KNOWN BEFORE--!
I-- I GOTTA TAKE FIVE. BE-- RIGHT BACK--!
"I GUESS I MEANT THAT WHEN I SAID IT-- EVEN WHEN I STAGGERED INTO THAT BACK ALLEY RIGHT OFF BLEECKER STREET--
WHY??
I-- I KNOW IT'S YOU, MARVEL--IT'S GOTTA BE YOU!
BUT WHY NOW-- IN THE MIDDLE OF A GIG THAT COULD BE-- MY BIG BREAK?
YET, SOMETHING HAS HAPPENED-- SOMETHING THAT MAY AFFECT THE STRANGE BOND BETWEEN US-- IF YOU'LL ONLY--
YEAH, I'LL LISTEN --IF YOU MEAN THERE'S A CHANCE WE'LL BE RID OF EACH OTHER FOR KEEPS.
I--DIDN'T WANT TO DO IT, RICK. YOU'LL HAVE TO TAKE MY WORD ON THAT FOR NOW.
THAT'S PRECISELY WHAT I MEAN, LAD.
LOOK! DO YOU KNOW THE MAN WHOSE MENTAL IMAGE I'M PROJECTING --THAT SOUL IN SUPREME TORMENT?
HUH? IS THERE ANYBODY THIS SIDE OF A BOOB TUBE WHO DOESN'T?
IT'S REED RICHARDS-- HEAD HONCHO OF THE FANTASTIC FOUR.
BUT-- IT CAN'T BE! HE LOOKS LIKE HE'S IN-- THE NEGATIVE ZONE!
EXIT
6

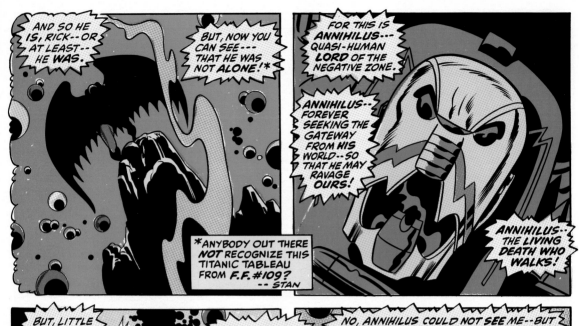

AND SO HE IS, RICK-- OR AT LEAST-- HE WAS.

BUT, NOW YOU CAN SEE--- THAT HE WAS NOT ALONE!*

FOR THIS IS ANNIHILUS--- QUASI-HUMAN **LORD** OF THE NEGATIVE ZONE.

ANNIHILUS-- FOREVER SEEKING THE GATEWAY FROM HIS WORLD-- SO THAT HE MAY RAVAGE **OURS!**

*ANYBODY OUT THERE *NOT* RECOGNIZE THIS TITANIC TABLEAU FROM *F.F. #109?* -- STAN

ANNIHILUS-- THE **LIVING DEATH** WHO **WALKS!**

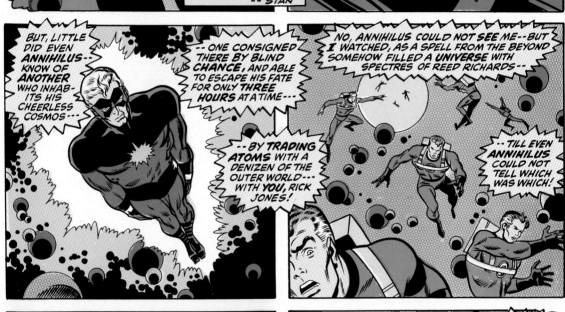

BUT, LITTLE DID EVEN **ANNIHILUS** KNOW OF **ANOTHER** WHO INHABITS HIS CHEERLESS COSMOS---

--ONE CONSIGNED THERE BY BLIND **CHANCE,** AND ABLE TO ESCAPE HIS FATE FOR ONLY **THREE HOURS** AT A TIME---

--BY TRADING **ATOMS** WITH A DENIZEN OF THE OUTER WORLD-- WITH **YOU,** RICK JONES!

NO, ANNIHILUS COULD NOT SEE ME--BUT **I** WATCHED, AS A SPELL FROM THE BEYOND SOMEHOW FILLED A UNIVERSE WITH SPECTRES OF REED RICHARDS--

--TILL EVEN **ANNIHILUS** COULD NOT TELL WHICH WAS WHICH!

ONLY **THEN** COULD THE MASTER SCIENTIST MAKE HIS HEADLONG LEAP TOWARD A **HOLE** WHICH BRIEFLY YAWNED BETWEEN **THIS** COSMOS AND YOUR **OWN**---

--A PINPRICK OF LIGHT AND ENERGY WHICH LASTED BUT LONG ENOUGH FOR RICHARDS TO PASS **THRU** IT--

--LEAVING ME MORE **ALONE,** EVEN MORE DESOLATE THAN **BEFORE!**

--AND THEN WAS **GONE**---

7.

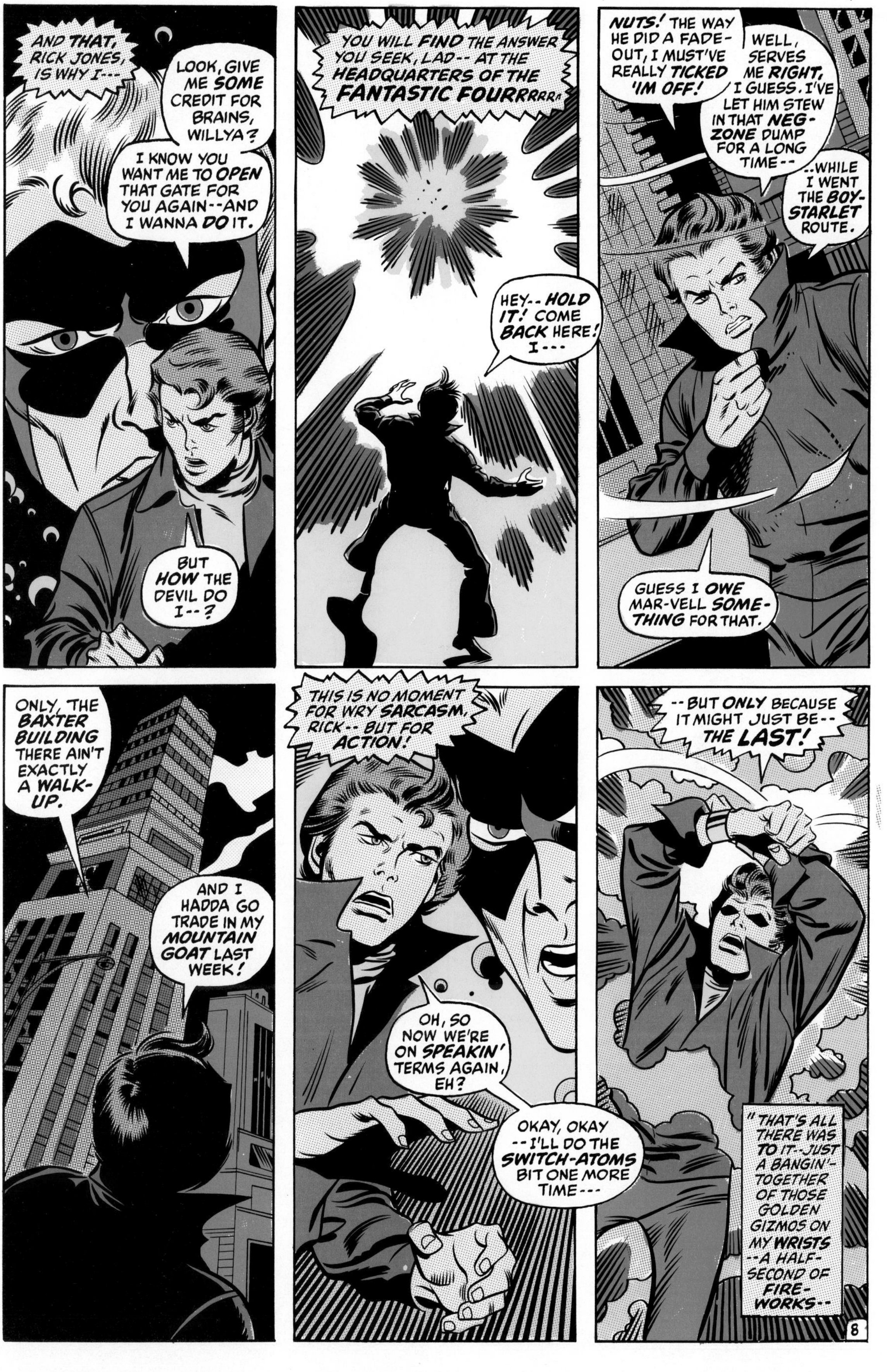

AND THAT, RICK JONES, IS WHY I---
LOOK, GIVE ME SOME CREDIT FOR BRAINS, WILLYA?
I KNOW YOU WANT ME TO OPEN THAT GATE FOR YOU AGAIN--AND I WANNA DO IT.
BUT HOW THE DEVIL DO I--?
YOU WILL FIND THE ANSWER YOU SEEK, LAD-- AT THE HEADQUARTERS OF THE FANTASTIC FOURRRRR
HEY-- HOLD IT! COME BACK HERE! I---
NUTS! THE WAY HE DID A FADE-OUT, I MUST'VE REALLY TICKED 'IM OFF!
WELL, SERVES ME RIGHT, I GUESS. I'VE LET HIM STEW IN THAT NEG-ZONE DUMP FOR A LONG TIME--
..WHILE I WENT THE BOY-STARLET ROUTE.
GUESS I OWE MAR-VELL SOMETHING FOR THAT.
ONLY, THE BAXTER BUILDING THERE AIN'T EXACTLY A WALK-UP.
AND I HADDA GO TRADE IN MY MOUNTAIN GOAT LAST WEEK!
THIS IS NO MOMENT FOR WRY SARCASM, RICK-- BUT FOR ACTION!
OH, SO NOW WE'RE ON SPEAKIN' TERMS AGAIN, EH?
OKAY, OKAY --I'LL DO THE SWITCH-ATOMS BIT ONE MORE TIME---
--BUT ONLY BECAUSE IT MIGHT JUST BE-- THE LAST!
"THAT'S ALL THERE WAS TO IT-JUST A BANGIN'-TOGETHER OF THOSE GOLDEN GIZMOS ON MY WRISTS --A HALF-SECOND OF FIRE-WORKS--

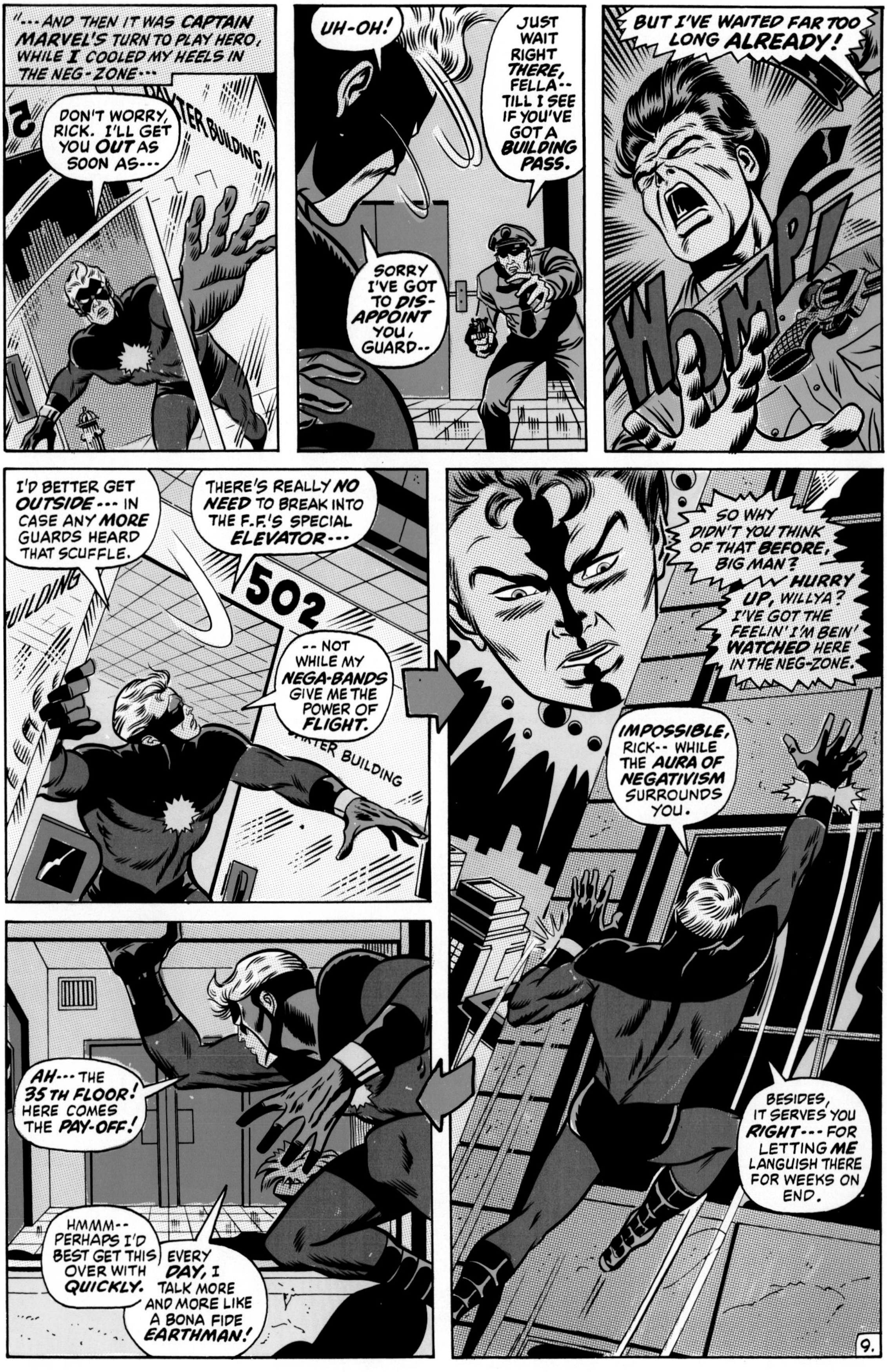
"--- AND THEN IT WAS CAPTAIN MARVEL'S TURN TO PLAY HERO, WHILE I COOLED MY HEELS IN THE NEG-ZONE---
DON'T WORRY, RICK. I'LL GET YOU OUT AS SOON AS---
BAXTER BUILDING
UH-OH!
JUST WAIT RIGHT THERE, FELLA-- TILL I SEE IF YOU'VE GOT A BUILDING PASS.
SORRY I'VE GOT TO DIS-APPOINT YOU, GUARD--
BUT I'VE WAITED FAR TOO LONG ALREADY!
WOMP!
I'D BETTER GET OUTSIDE--- IN CASE ANY MORE GUARDS HEARD THAT SCUFFLE.
THERE'S REALLY NO NEED TO BREAK INTO THE F.F.'S SPECIAL ELEVATOR---
502
-- NOT WHILE MY NEGA-BANDS GIVE ME THE POWER OF FLIGHT.
BAXTER BUILDING
SO WHY DIDN'T YOU THINK OF THAT BEFORE, BIG MAN?
HURRY UP, WILLYA? I'VE GOT THE FEELIN' I'M BEIN' WATCHED HERE IN THE NEG-ZONE.
IMPOSSIBLE, RICK-- WHILE THE AURA OF NEGATIVISM SURROUNDS YOU.
BESIDES, IT SERVES YOU RIGHT--- FOR LETTING ME LANGUISH THERE FOR WEEKS ON END.
AH--- THE 35TH FLOOR! HERE COMES THE PAY-OFF!
HMMM-- PERHAPS I'D BEST GET THIS OVER WITH QUICKLY.
EVERY DAY, I TALK MORE AND MORE LIKE A BONA FIDE EARTHMAN!
9.

STEEL-- LOCKED-- AND THREE INCHES *THICK*, AT LEAST.

BUT THEN, I HARDLY EXPECTED A *WEL-COME MAT!*

ALL I NEED --- IS-- THE BAREST *FINGER-HOLD* ---

---*JUST-- A --- FINGER-HOLD* ---

--- AND I SHALL *PREVAIL!*

SKRUTTTTCH!

THAT MADE ENOUGH NOISE TO WAKE UP THE *DEAD*-- LET ALONE A *SUPERHERO.*

SO THE F.F. MUST BE *GONE*-- AS I GUESSED FROM THE ABSENCE OF *LIGHTS.*

NOW--- TO *WORK!*

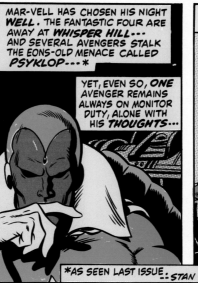

MAR-VELL HAS CHOSEN HIS NIGHT *WELL*. THE FANTASTIC FOUR ARE AWAY AT *WHISPER HILL*--- AND SEVERAL AVENGERS STALK THE EONS-OLD MENACE CALLED *PSYKLOP*---*

YET, EVEN SO, *ONE* AVENGER REMAINS ALWAYS ON MONITOR DUTY, ALONE WITH HIS *THOUGHTS*---

*AS SEEN LAST ISSUE. --STAN

-- SO THAT HE IS NEARLY *RELIEVED* WHEN ---

THE SIGNAL--- FROM THE *BAXTER BUILDING!*

THEN, WHAT THE F.F. FEARED--- HAS COME *TRUE!*

BREEP BREEP

10

SOMEONE HAS MADE A *FORCED* ENTRY INTO THEIR QUARTERS.

REED RICHARDS SAID HIS WIFE HAD A *PREMONITION* OF SUCH A THING HAPPENING TONIGHT---

BUT I HAVE ALWAYS BEEN *DISDAINFUL* OF SUCH HUMAN FEELINGS--UNTIL *NOW.*

CALLING PIETRO-- CALLING WANDA--- *F.F. ALERT!*

PROCEED AS PLANNED TO QUINJET AREA-- REPEAT, PROC

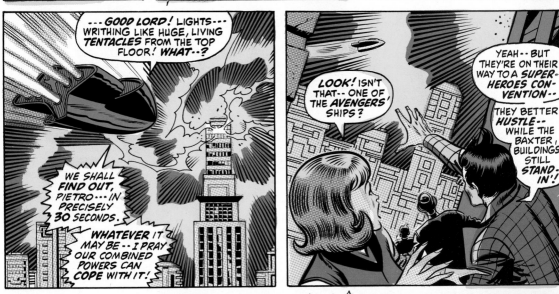

---*GOOD LORD!* LIGHTS--- WRITHING LIKE HUGE, LIVING *TENTACLES* FROM THE TOP FLOOR! *WHAT--?*

WE SHALL *FIND OUT,* PIETRO--- IN PRECISELY *30 SECONDS.*

WHATEVER IT MAY BE-- I PRAY OUR COMBINED POWERS CAN *COPE* WITH IT!

LOOK! ISN'T THAT-- ONE OF THE *AVENGERS'* SHIPS?

YEAH-- BUT THEY'RE ON THEIR WAY TO A *SUPER- HEROES* CON- VENTION--

THEY BETTER *HUSTLE--* WHILE THE BAXTER BUILDINGS STILL *STAND- IN'!*

BLAST IT! I THOUGHT MY *KREE TRAINING* WOULD ALLOW ME TO MASTER *ANY* EARTHIAN INVENTION IN *MOMENTS.*

BUT REED RICHARDS' *GENIUS* IS FAR BEYOND ANY I HAVE ENCOUNTERED ON THIS PLANET.

STILL-- I THINK I *HAVE* IT NOW.

YOU-- BETTER DO MORE THAN *THINK,* STAR- MAN---

--'CAUSE I CAN STILL FEEL *EYES* BORIN' RIGHT INTO ME --INTO MY *SOUL!*

HURRY, MAN-- *HURRY!!*

IT WILL TAKE SEVERAL SECONDS FOR THE MACHINE TO *BUILD* POWER, RICK.

THEN-- YOU MUST *LEAP* FOR YOUR LIFE-- FOR THE GATEWAY WILL REMAIN OPEN FOR ONLY A FEW *MOMENTS!*

11.

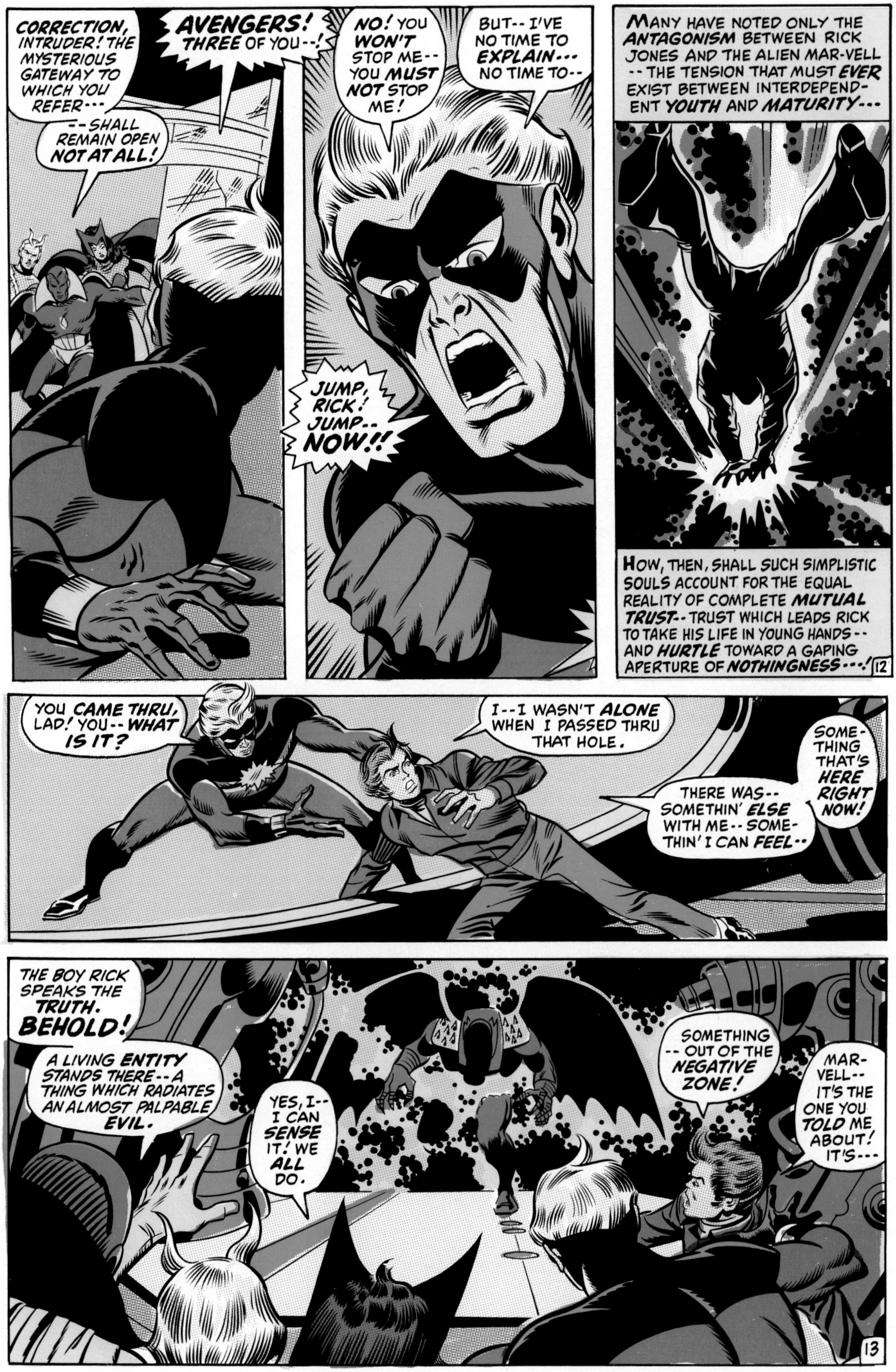
CORRECTION, INTRUDER! THE MYSTERIOUS GATEWAY TO WHICH YOU REFER---
--SHALL REMAIN OPEN NOT AT ALL!
AVENGERS! THREE OF YOU--!
NO! YOU WON'T STOP ME-- YOU MUST NOT STOP ME!
BUT-- I'VE NO TIME TO EXPLAIN--- NO TIME TO--
JUMP, RICK! JUMP-- NOW!!
MANY HAVE NOTED ONLY THE ANTAGONISM BETWEEN RICK JONES AND THE ALIEN MAR-VELL --THE TENSION THAT MUST EVER EXIST BETWEEN INTERDEPENDENT YOUTH AND MATURITY---
HOW, THEN, SHALL SUCH SIMPLISTIC SOULS ACCOUNT FOR THE EQUAL REALITY OF COMPLETE MUTUAL TRUST-- TRUST WHICH LEADS RICK TO TAKE HIS LIFE IN YOUNG HANDS-- AND HURTLE TOWARD A GAPING APERTURE OF NOTHINGNESS---!
12
YOU CAME THRU, LAD! YOU-- WHAT IS IT?
I--I WASN'T ALONE WHEN I PASSED THRU THAT HOLE.
THERE WAS-- SOMETHIN' ELSE WITH ME-- SOMETHIN' I CAN FEEL--
SOMETHING THAT'S HERE RIGHT NOW!
THE BOY RICK SPEAKS THE TRUTH. BEHOLD!
A LIVING ENTITY STANDS THERE--A THING WHICH RADIATES AN ALMOST PALPABLE EVIL.
YES, I--I CAN SENSE IT! WE ALL DO.
SOMETHING --OUT OF THE NEGATIVE ZONE!
MAR-VELL-- IT'S THE ONE YOU TOLD ME ABOUT! IT'S---
13

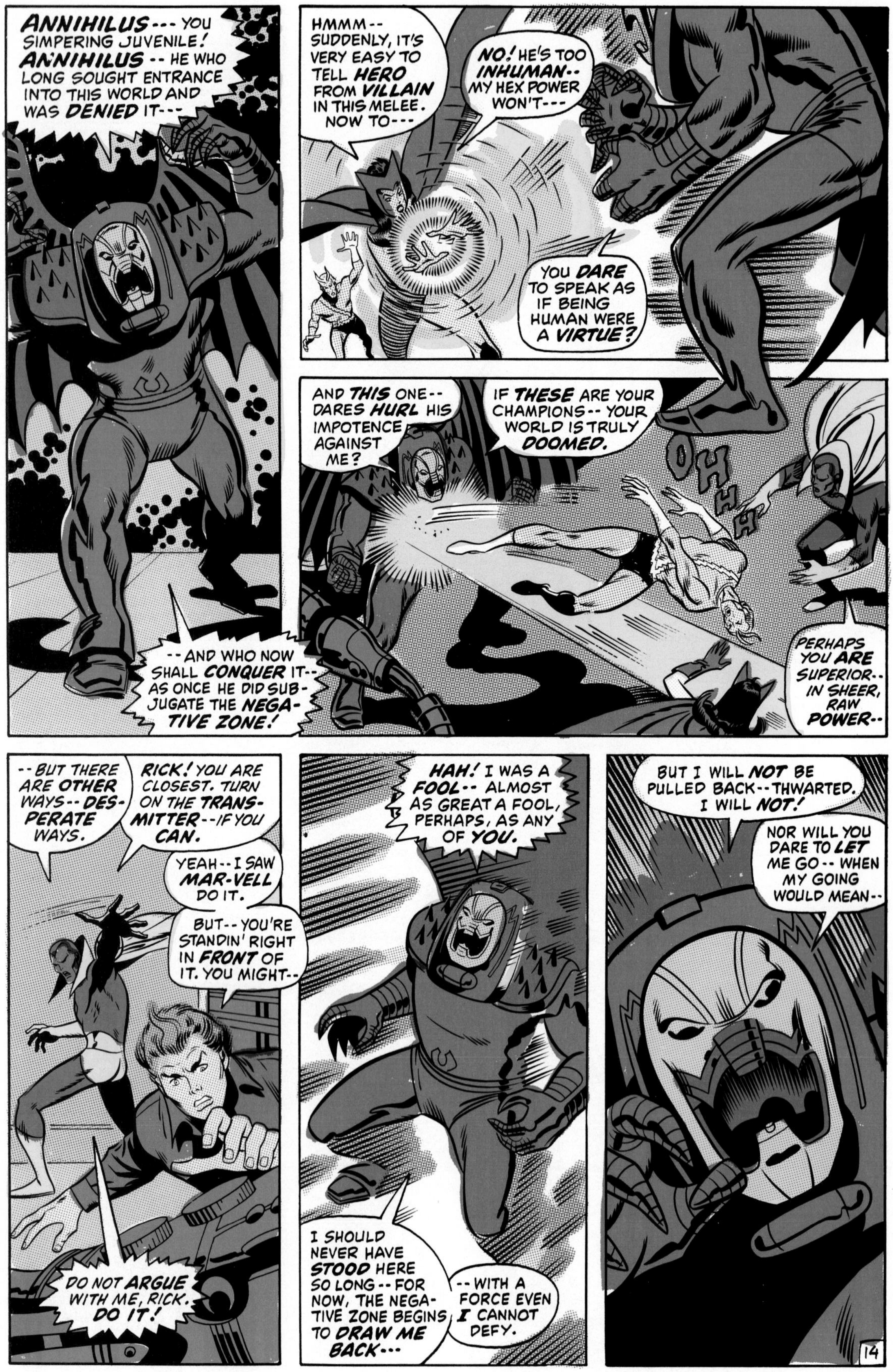
ANNIHILUS--- YOU SIMPERING JUVENILE! ANNIHILUS -- HE WHO LONG SOUGHT ENTRANCE INTO THIS WORLD AND WAS DENIED IT---
--AND WHO NOW SHALL CONQUER IT-- AS ONCE HE DID SUBJUGATE THE NEGATIVE ZONE!
HMMM-- SUDDENLY, IT'S VERY EASY TO TELL HERO FROM VILLAIN IN THIS MELEE. NOW TO---
NO! HE'S TOO INHUMAN-- MY HEX POWER WON'T---
YOU DARE TO SPEAK AS IF BEING HUMAN WERE A VIRTUE?
AND THIS ONE-- DARES HURL HIS IMPOTENCE AGAINST ME?
IF THESE ARE YOUR CHAMPIONS-- YOUR WORLD IS TRULY DOOMED.
OHHHH
PERHAPS YOU ARE SUPERIOR-- IN SHEER, RAW POWER--
--BUT THERE ARE OTHER WAYS-- DESPERATE WAYS.
RICK! YOU ARE CLOSEST. TURN ON THE TRANSMITTER--IF YOU CAN.
YEAH--I SAW MAR-VELL DO IT.
BUT--YOU'RE STANDIN' RIGHT IN FRONT OF IT. YOU MIGHT--
DO NOT ARGUE WITH ME, RICK. DO IT!
HAH! I WAS A FOOL-- ALMOST AS GREAT A FOOL, PERHAPS, AS ANY OF YOU.
I SHOULD NEVER HAVE STOOD HERE SO LONG--FOR NOW, THE NEGATIVE ZONE BEGINS TO DRAW ME BACK---
--WITH A FORCE EVEN I CANNOT DEFY.
BUT I WILL NOT BE PULLED BACK--THWARTED. I WILL NOT!
NOR WILL YOU DARE TO LET ME GO-- WHEN MY GOING WOULD MEAN--
14

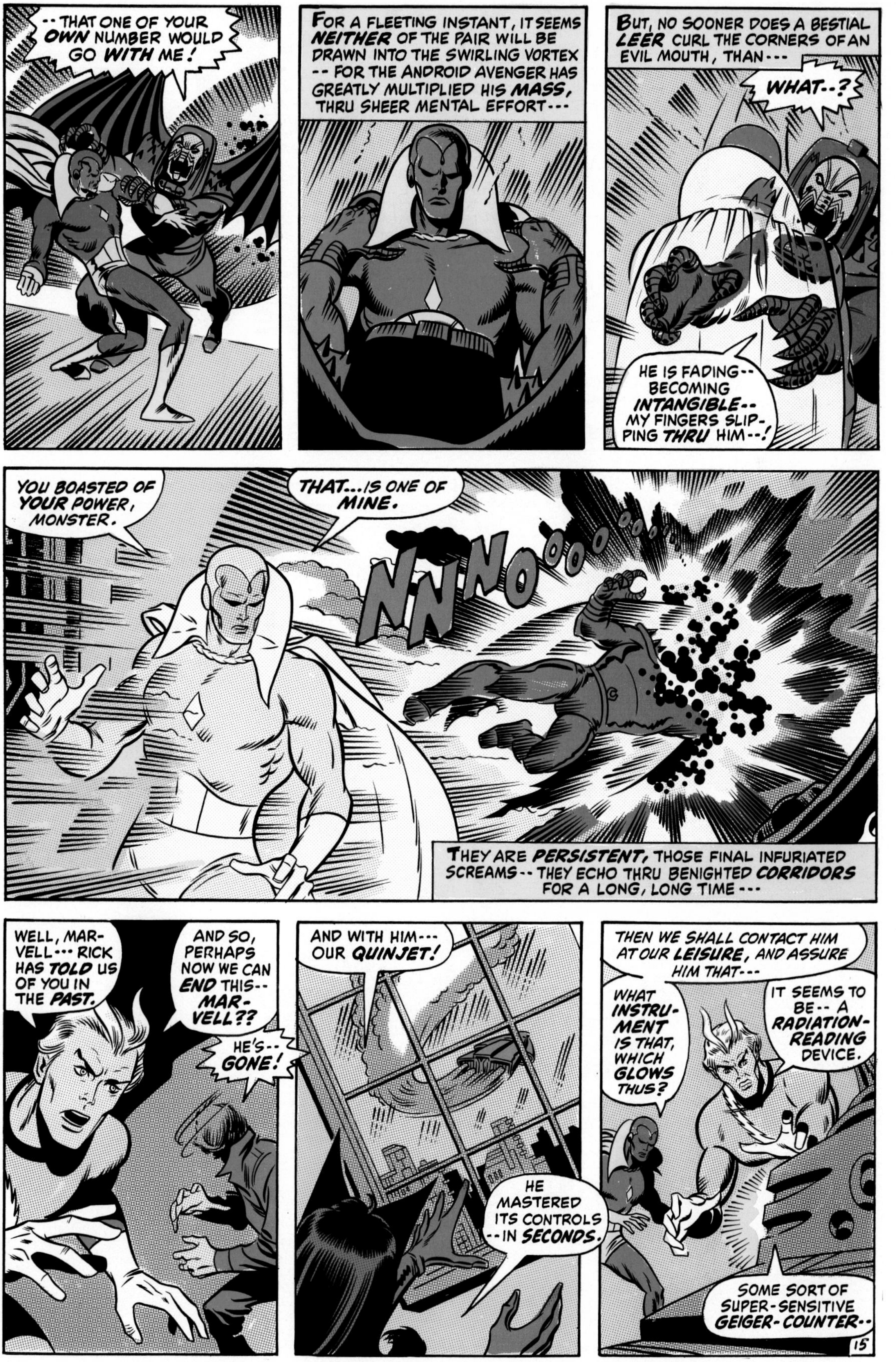

--THAT ONE OF YOUR OWN NUMBER WOULD GO WITH ME!
FOR A FLEETING INSTANT, IT SEEMS NEITHER OF THE PAIR WILL BE DRAWN INTO THE SWIRLING VORTEX -- FOR THE ANDROID AVENGER HAS GREATLY MULTIPLIED HIS MASS, THRU SHEER MENTAL EFFORT---
BUT, NO SOONER DOES A BESTIAL LEER CURL THE CORNERS OF AN EVIL MOUTH, THAN---
WHAT--?
HE IS FADING-- BECOMING INTANGIBLE-- MY FINGERS SLIP-PING THRU HIM--!
YOU BOASTED OF YOUR POWER, MONSTER.
THAT...IS ONE OF MINE.
NNNOOOOOO
THEY ARE PERSISTENT, THOSE FINAL INFURIATED SCREAMS-- THEY ECHO THRU BENIGHTED CORRIDORS FOR A LONG, LONG TIME---
WELL, MAR-VELL--- RICK HAS TOLD US OF YOU IN THE PAST.
AND SO, PERHAPS NOW WE CAN END THIS-- MAR-VELL??
HE'S-- GONE!
AND WITH HIM--- OUR QUINJET!
HE MASTERED ITS CONTROLS --IN SECONDS.
THEN WE SHALL CONTACT HIM AT OUR LEISURE, AND ASSURE HIM THAT---
WHAT INSTRU-MENT IS THAT, WHICH GLOWS THUS?
IT SEEMS TO BE-- A RADIATION-READING DEVICE.
SOME SORT OF SUPER-SENSITIVE GEIGER-COUNTER--

-- AND IT SEEMS TO BE *GOING WILD!*

NO! IT'S DYING NOW--

BUT-- THAT'S WHERE *MAR-VELL* WAS STANDING!

THEN, *YOU* THINK--

-- THAT HE *PICKED UP* SOMETHING, DURING ALL THE WEEKS I LET 'IM SIMMER IN THE *NEG-ZONE.*

RADIATION, MAYBE, THAT MIGHT *KILL* 'IM!

OR WHICH MIGHT BUILD INTO AN EVENTUAL *CHAIN REACTION--* WHICH MIGHT DESTROY ALL THE WORLD.

TELL ME, RICK-- FOR I THINK I'VE *GUESSED* THE BOND BETWEEN YOU-- WHAT WAS MARVEL'S PREVIOUS *TIME LIMIT* FOR REMAINING ON *EARTH?*

NO MORE THAN *THREE* HOURS.

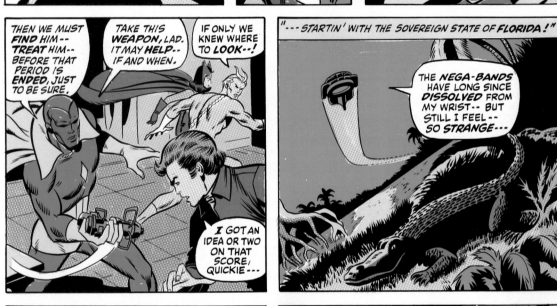

THEN WE MUST *FIND* HIM-- *TREAT* HIM-- BEFORE THAT PERIOD IS *ENDED*, JUST TO BE SURE.

TAKE THIS *WEAPON*, LAD. IT MAY *HELP--* IF AND WHEN.

IF ONLY WE KNEW WHERE TO *LOOK--!*

I GOT AN IDEA OR TWO ON THAT SCORE, *QUICKIE---*

"--- STARTIN' WITH THE SOVEREIGN STATE OF *FLORIDA!*"

THE *NEGA-BANDS* HAVE LONG SINCE *DISSOLVED* FROM MY WRIST-- BUT STILL I FEEL-- SO *STRANGE---*

BUT-- MUST MAKE IT TO THE *CAPE---* COMMANDEER A *ROCKET---* THEN TRY TO MODIFY IT TO---

WHAT? THE SHIP IS *FALTERING--* LOSING ALTITUDE--

FOOL THAT I AM! THE FUEL-GAUGE READS-- *EMPTY!*

BUT *NOTHING* WILL STOP ME-- NOW THAT I'M SO *CLOSE.*

I CAN *FLY* NO LONGER-- BUT, IN THIS PLANET'S LESSER GRAVITY, I CAN STILL *LEAP.*

AND, A *UNI-BEAM BLASTER* I ONCE HID NEAR HERE WILL HELP ME REACH MY ULTIMATE *DESTINATION--*

16

-- WHICH IS NOTHING **LESS** THAN-- **-- THE KREE GALAXY!**

--BUT HE NEVER **REACHED** THE STARS, DID HE, AVENGERS?

WE BROUGHT 'IM DOWN TO EARTH-- LIKE A WOUNDED **SPARROW.**

YOU DID-- WHAT **HAD** TO BE DONE, RICK JONES. NOW **WATCH!**

THE MACHINE IS **HUMMING** -- THE DRAINING-OFF PROCESS IS **BEGUN.**

LET IT **WORK,** DEAR LORD--

-- **PLEASE** LET IT WORK!

WE'VE DRAINED OFF--- **SOME** OF THE RADIATION, DOC.

BUT THERE'S **MORE** -- AND WE'VE USED UP NEARLY ALL OUR **POWER.**

AMAZING! THE NEGA-RADIATION IS FAR MORE **POWERFUL** THAN WE IMAGINED.

BUT-- IF THE DECONTAMINATION ISN'T **TOTAL** -- THE RADIATION WILL **BUILD UP** ALL OVER AGAIN-- **FEED** UPON ITSELF, UNTIL---

NO! WE **MUST** FIND ANOTHER POWER SOURCE-- SOMEHOW--

WOULD-- **SOLAR POWER** BE SUFFICIENT?

IT SURE **WOULD** -- BUT **WHERE**..?

FROM **ME,** DOCTOR.

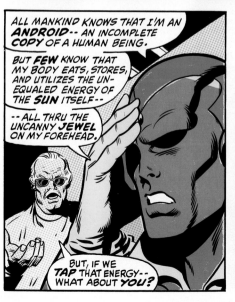

ALL MANKIND KNOWS THAT I'M AN **ANDROID** -- AN INCOMPLETE **COPY** OF A HUMAN BEING.

BUT **FEW** KNOW THAT MY BODY EATS, STORES, AND UTILIZES THE UNEQUALED ENERGY OF THE **SUN** ITSELF--

-- ALL THRU THE UNCANNY **JEWEL** ON MY FOREHEAD.

BUT, IF WE **TAP** THAT ENERGY-- WHAT ABOUT **YOU?**

I WILL HAVE TO TAKE MY **CHANCES,** DR. DONALDSON.

IF THE **NEGA-POWER** WITHIN CAPTAIN MARVEL BUILDS TO A **CRITICAL MASS**...

THERE WILL BE **NO** CHANCE--- FOR **ANY** OF US!

17

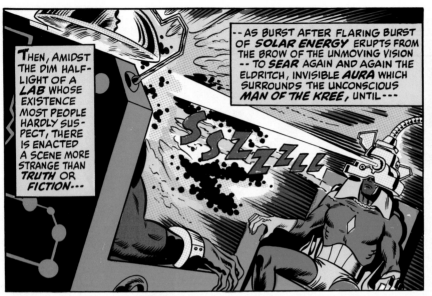

THEN, AMIDST THE DIM HALF-LIGHT OF A *LAB* WHOSE EXISTENCE MOST PEOPLE HARDLY SUSPECT, THERE IS ENACTED A SCENE MORE STRANGE THAN *TRUTH* OR *FICTION*---

--AS BURST AFTER FLARING BURST OF *SOLAR ENERGY* ERUPTS FROM THE BROW OF THE UNMOVING VISION -- TO *SEAR* AGAIN AND AGAIN THE ELDRITCH, INVISIBLE *AURA* WHICH SURROUNDS THE UNCONSCIOUS *MAN OF THE KREE*, UNTIL---

SSSZZZLL

STOP! THAT IS *ENOUGH.*

ANY *MORE*-- MIGHT KILL THEM *BOTH!*

THEY BOTH SEEM -- SO TERRIBLY *STILL*, DOC.

ARE THEY--?

THEY WILL BOTH *SURVIVE*-- IF I HAVE CALCULATED *CORRECTLY.*

I ONLY PRAY-- THAT I *HAVE.*

DR. HENRY PYM HAS OFTEN TOLD US OF HOW YOU ONCE *WORKED* TOGETHER --- -- AND OF HOW HE HAS *COMPLETE CONFIDENCE* IN YOUR JUDGMENT.

I SAW THE VISION *BREATHIN!* OR WHATEVER HE DOES --

COULD *WE*, THEN, HAVE *LESS?*

BUT *MARVELL*-- LOOKED SO *STILL* -- HE --

COME, RICK. WE CAN DO *NOTHING* NOW.

YEAH -- BUT WE'VE DONE *ENOUGH*, AIN'T WE?

MAYBE --- *TOO MUCH.*

AND NOW-- HE MAY *NEVER* SEE IT AGAIN!

ALL MAR-VELL WANTED -- WAS TO MAKE IT BACK TO THE WORLD WHERE HE WAS *BORN*--

THERE ARE THINGS YOU *CANNOT KNOW*, RICK JONES -- THINGS TRANSPIRING MORE *LIGHT YEARS* FROM EARTH THAN MAN MAY *COUNT*--

BUT, IF *YOU* KNEW THEM --IF *MARVELL* KNEW THEM -- YOU WOULD BOTH WISH YOU HAD NEVER HEARD OF -- THE *KREE GALAXY!*

18

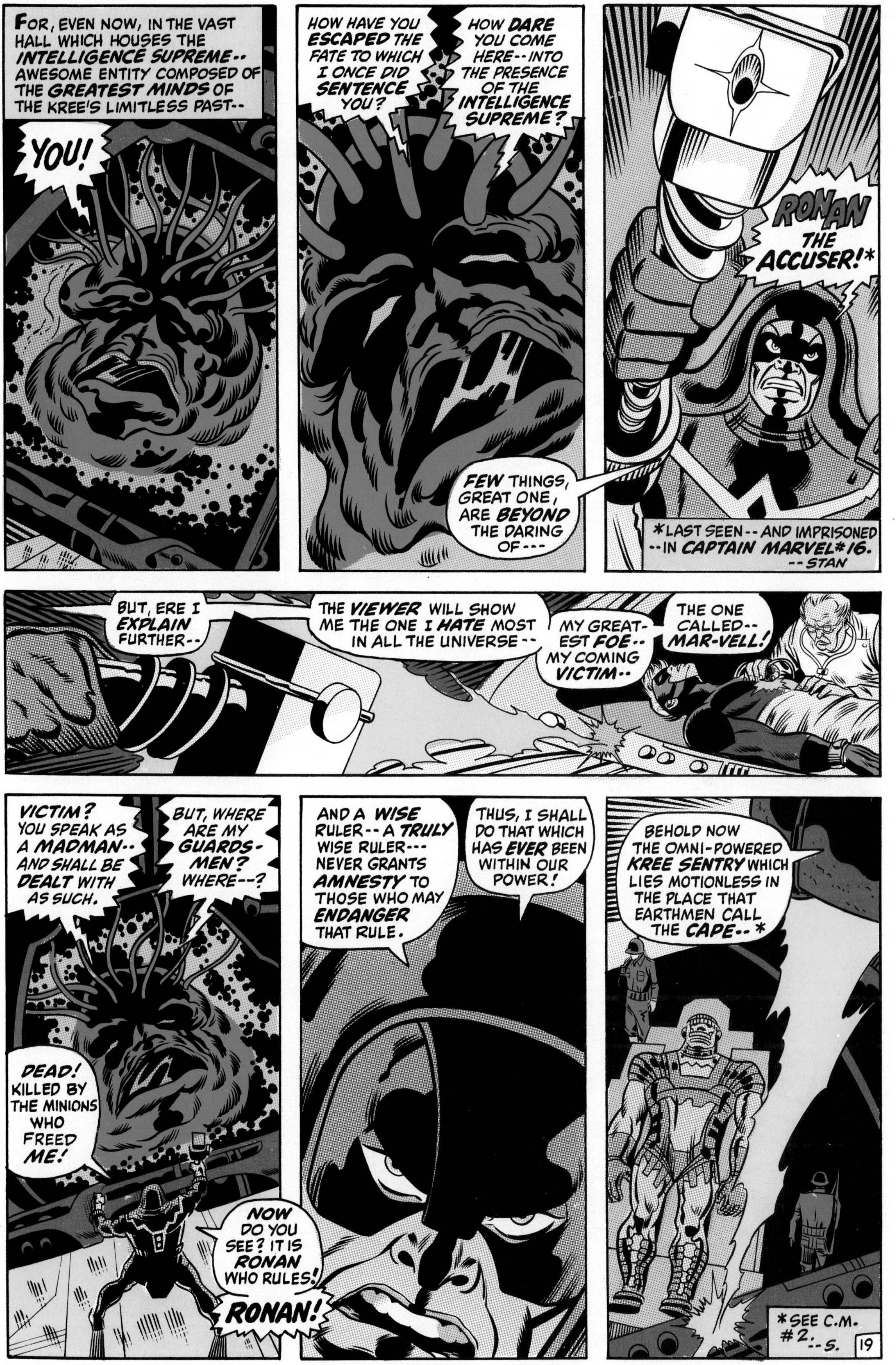

FOR, EVEN NOW, IN THE VAST HALL WHICH HOUSES THE INTELLIGENCE SUPREME-- AWESOME ENTITY COMPOSED OF THE GREATEST MINDS OF THE KREE'S LIMITLESS PAST--
YOU!
HOW HAVE YOU ESCAPED THE FATE TO WHICH I ONCE DID SENTENCE YOU?
HOW DARE YOU COME HERE--INTO THE PRESENCE OF THE INTELLIGENCE SUPREME?
FEW THINGS, GREAT ONE, ARE BEYOND THE DARING OF---
RONAN THE ACCUSER!*
*LAST SEEN--AND IMPRISONED --IN CAPTAIN MARVEL #16. --STAN
BUT, ERE I EXPLAIN FURTHER--
THE VIEWER WILL SHOW ME THE ONE I HATE MOST IN ALL THE UNIVERSE--
MY GREATEST FOE-- MY COMING VICTIM--
THE ONE CALLED-- MAR-VELL!
VICTIM? YOU SPEAK AS A MADMAN-- AND SHALL BE DEALT WITH AS SUCH.
BUT, WHERE ARE MY GUARDSMEN? WHERE--?
DEAD! KILLED BY THE MINIONS WHO FREED ME!
NOW DO YOU SEE? IT IS RONAN WHO RULES!
RONAN!
AND A WISE RULER-- A TRULY WISE RULER--- NEVER GRANTS AMNESTY TO THOSE WHO MAY ENDANGER THAT RULE.
THUS, I SHALL DO THAT WHICH HAS EVER BEEN WITHIN OUR POWER!
BEHOLD NOW THE OMNI-POWERED KREE SENTRY WHICH LIES MOTIONLESS IN THE PLACE THAT EARTHMEN CALL THE CAPE--*
*SEE C.M. #2. --S.
19

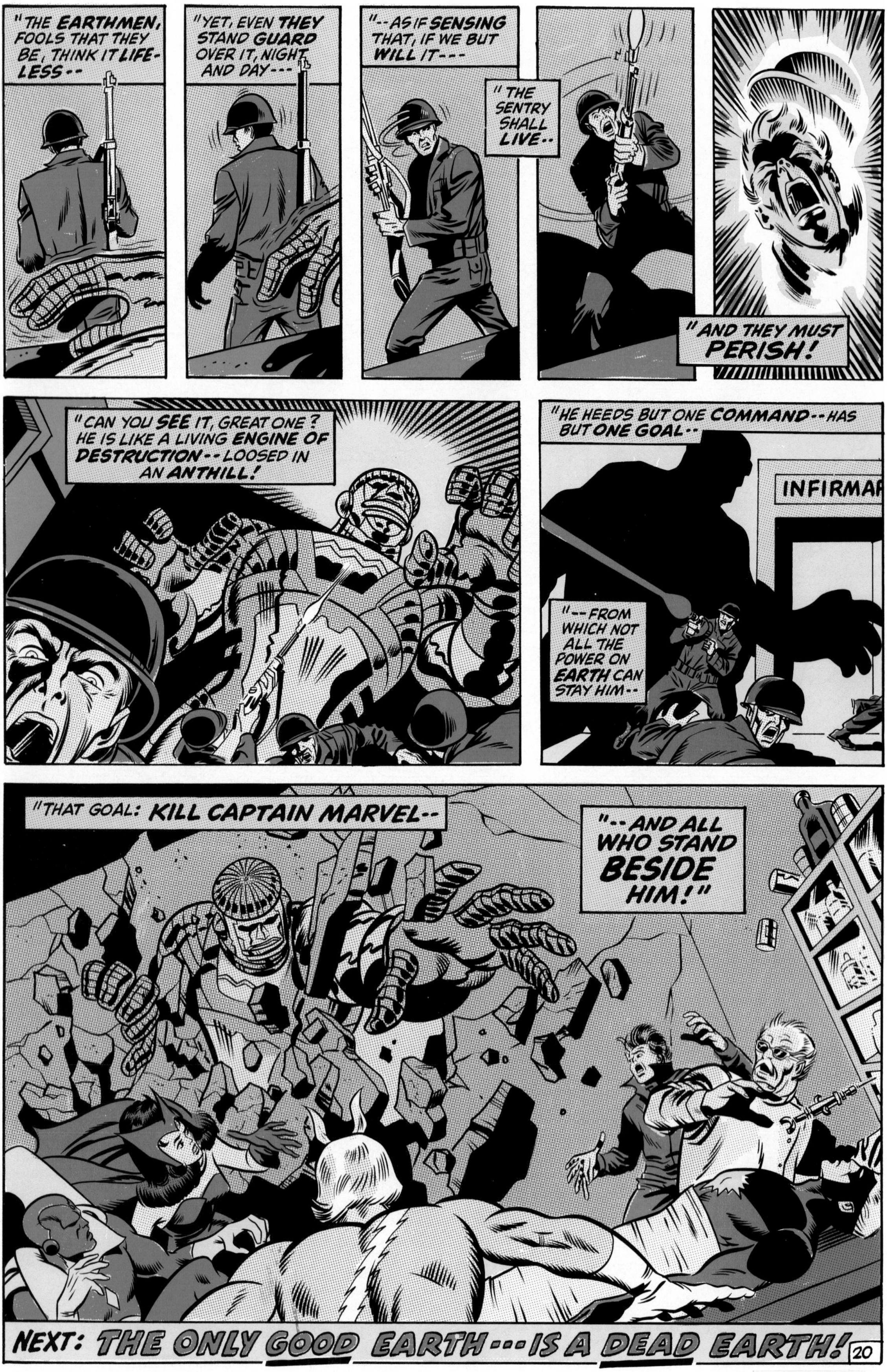
"THE EARTHMEN, FOOLS THAT THEY BE, THINK IT LIFE-LESS--
"YET, EVEN THEY STAND GUARD OVER IT, NIGHT AND DAY---
"--AS IF SENSING THAT, IF WE BUT WILL IT---
"THE SENTRY SHALL LIVE--
"AND THEY MUST PERISH!
"CAN YOU SEE IT, GREAT ONE? HE IS LIKE A LIVING ENGINE OF DESTRUCTION--LOOSED IN AN ANTHILL!
"HE HEEDS BUT ONE COMMAND--HAS BUT ONE GOAL--
INFIRMAR
"--FROM WHICH NOT ALL THE POWER ON EARTH CAN STAY HIM--
"THAT GOAL: KILL CAPTAIN MARVEL--
"--AND ALL WHO STAND BESIDE HIM!"
NEXT: THE ONLY GOOD EARTH---IS A DEAD EARTH!

CHAPTER TWO

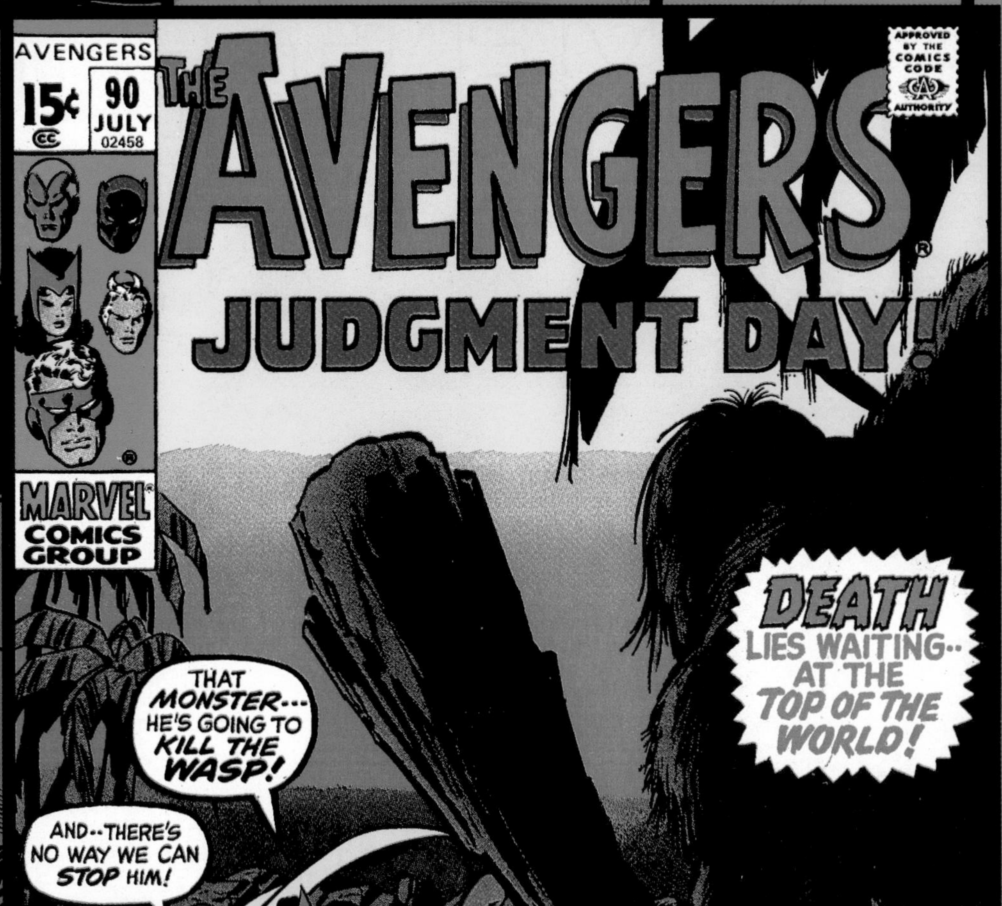

AVENGERS
15¢
90
JULY
02458
APPROVED BY THE COMICS CODE AUTHORITY
THE AVENGERS
JUDGMENT DAY!
MARVEL COMICS GROUP
DEATH LIES WAITING.. AT THE TOP OF THE WORLD!
THAT MONSTER--- HE'S GOING TO KILL THE WASP!
AND--THERE'S NO WAY WE CAN STOP HIM!
BUT--WE'VE GOT TO TRY! WE'VE GOT TO!!

JUDGMENT DAY

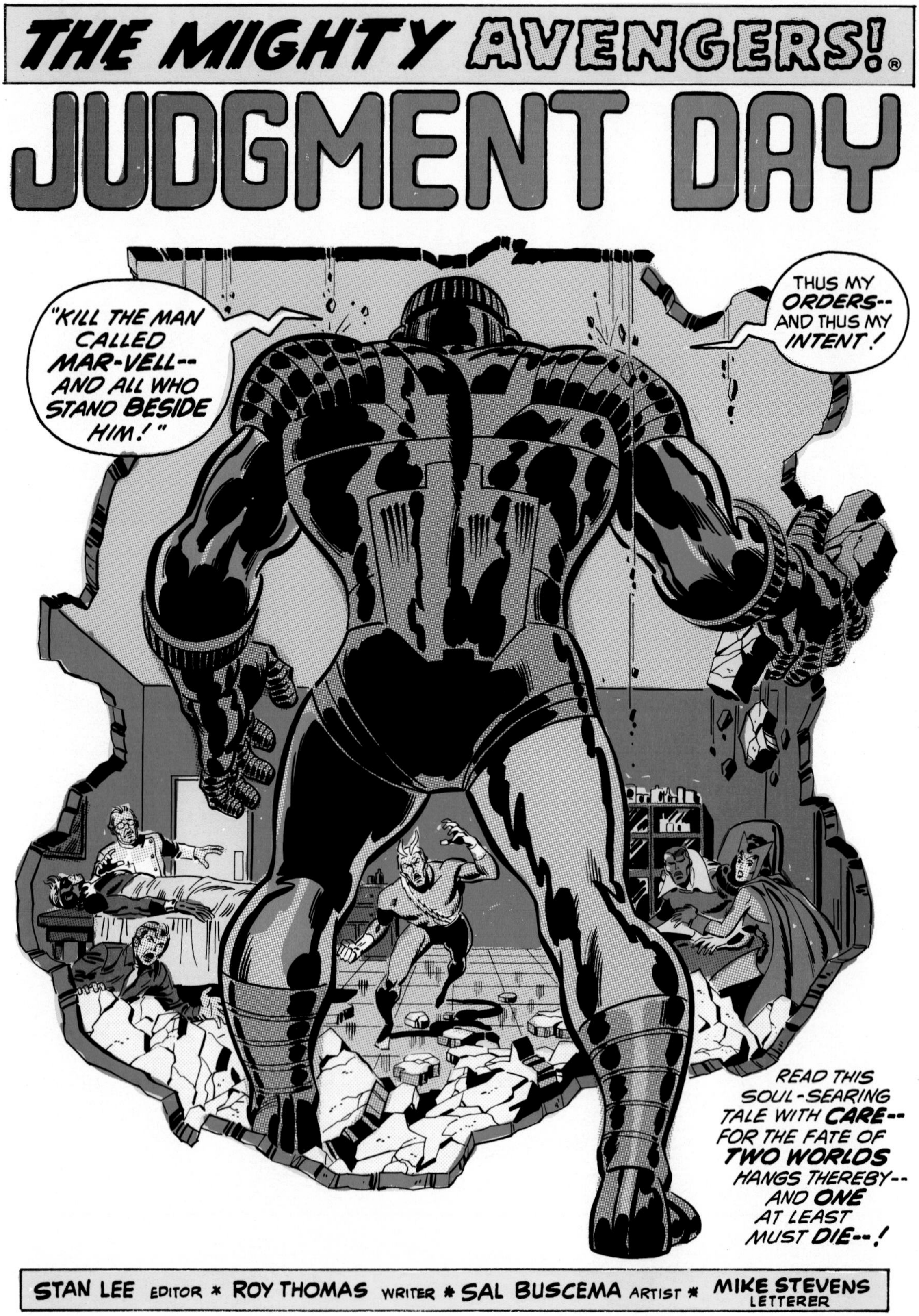
THE MIGHTY AVENGERS!®
JUDGMENT DAY
"KILL THE MAN CALLED MAR-VELL-- AND ALL WHO STAND BESIDE HIM!"
THUS MY ORDERS-- AND THUS MY INTENT!
READ THIS SOUL-SEARING TALE WITH CARE-- FOR THE FATE OF TWO WORLDS HANGS THEREBY-- AND ONE AT LEAST MUST DIE--!
STAN LEE EDITOR * ROY THOMAS WRITER * SAL BUSCEMA ARTIST * MIKE STEVENS LETTERER

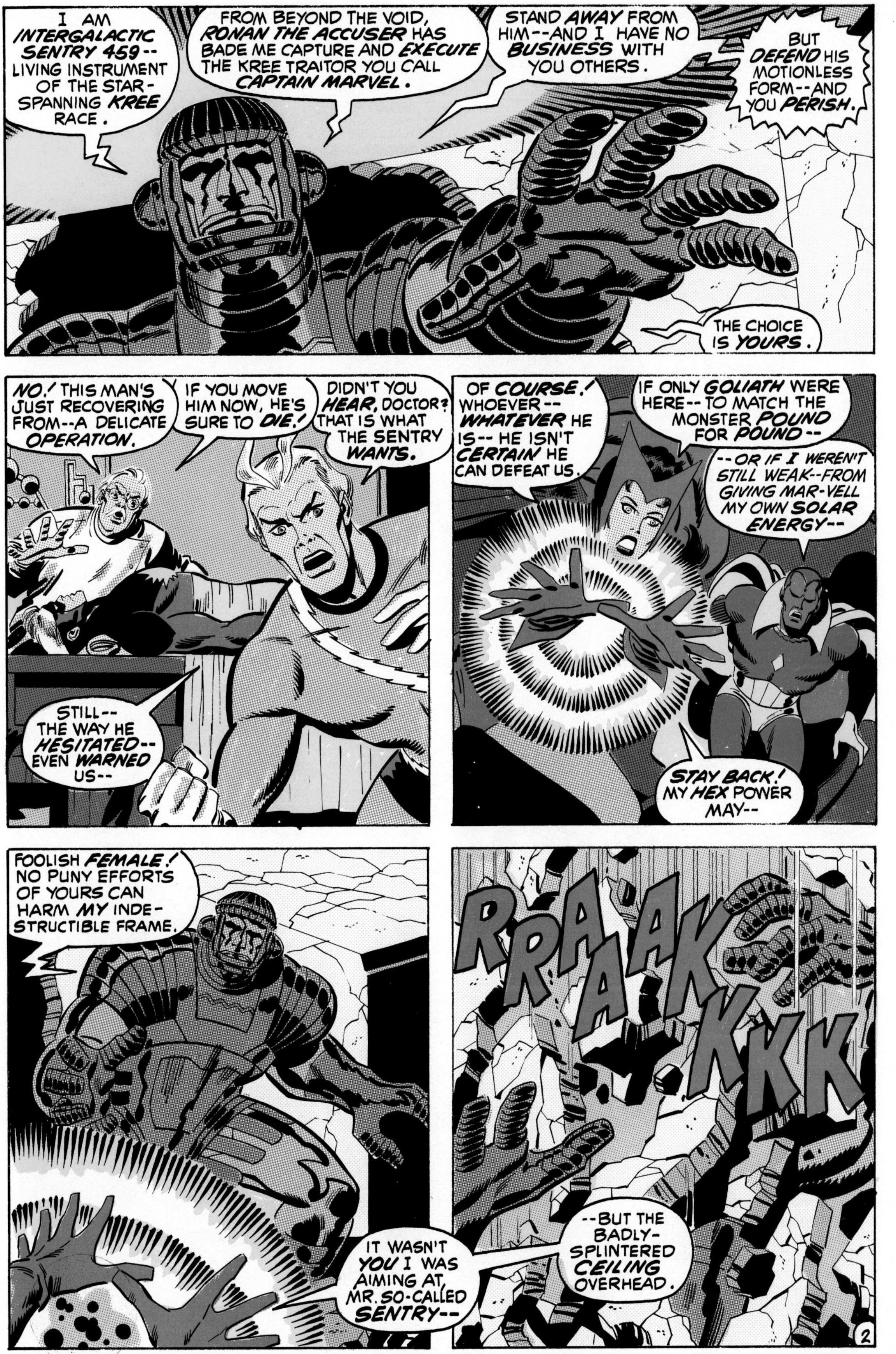
I AM INTERGALACTIC SENTRY 459 -- LIVING INSTRUMENT OF THE STAR-SPANNING KREE RACE.
FROM BEYOND THE VOID, RONAN THE ACCUSER HAS BADE ME CAPTURE AND EXECUTE THE KREE TRAITOR YOU CALL CAPTAIN MARVEL.
STAND AWAY FROM HIM--AND I HAVE NO BUSINESS WITH YOU OTHERS.
BUT DEFEND HIS MOTIONLESS FORM--AND YOU PERISH.
THE CHOICE IS YOURS.
NO! THIS MAN'S JUST RECOVERING FROM--A DELICATE OPERATION.
IF YOU MOVE HIM NOW, HE'S SURE TO DIE!
DIDN'T YOU HEAR, DOCTOR? THAT IS WHAT THE SENTRY WANTS.
STILL-- THE WAY HE HESITATED-- EVEN WARNED US--
OF COURSE! WHOEVER-- WHATEVER HE IS-- HE ISN'T CERTAIN HE CAN DEFEAT US.
IF ONLY GOLIATH WERE HERE-- TO MATCH THE MONSTER POUND FOR POUND--
--OR IF I WEREN'T STILL WEAK--FROM GIVING MAR-VELL MY OWN SOLAR ENERGY--
STAY BACK! MY HEX POWER MAY--
FOOLISH FEMALE! NO PUNY EFFORTS OF YOURS CAN HARM MY INDE-STRUCTIBLE FRAME.
RRAAK RAAK AKKK
IT WASN'T YOU I WAS AIMING AT, MR. SO-CALLED SENTRY--
--BUT THE BADLY-SPLINTERED CEILING OVERHEAD.
2

YET, *AVENGERS*, TOO, MAY ERR -- AND SO, EVEN AS GREAT FRAGMENTS STILL *FALL* FROM ABOVE --

FAAAN-TASTIC!

HE'S SHAKIN' IT ALL *OFF--* LIKE A DUCK SHEDS WATER.

YOU HAVE *MADE* YOUR CHOICE, EARTHLINGS-- AND NOW--

AND *NOW*, ROBOT--THOUGH YOU SURVIVED A RAIN OF STONE AND *MORTAR--*

WE SHALL SEE HOW YOU FARE AGAINST *ANOTHER* TYPE OF ASSAULT--NAMELY--

-- THE --

-- LIGHTNING --

-- FISTS --

-- OF --

QUICKSILVER!

ARRHH

YOU *OFFEND* MY SPACE-SPAWNED MASTERS, HUMAN-- BY TERMING ME A MERE *ROBOT.*

I AM A LIVING *SENTRY--* MIGHTY SERVANT OF THE SUPREME *KREE.*

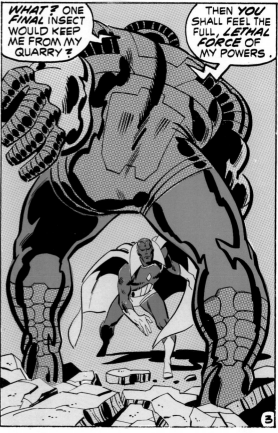

WHAT? ONE *FINAL* INSECT WOULD KEEP ME FROM MY QUARRY?

THEN *YOU* SHALL FEEL THE FULL, *LETHAL FORCE* OF MY POWERS.

3

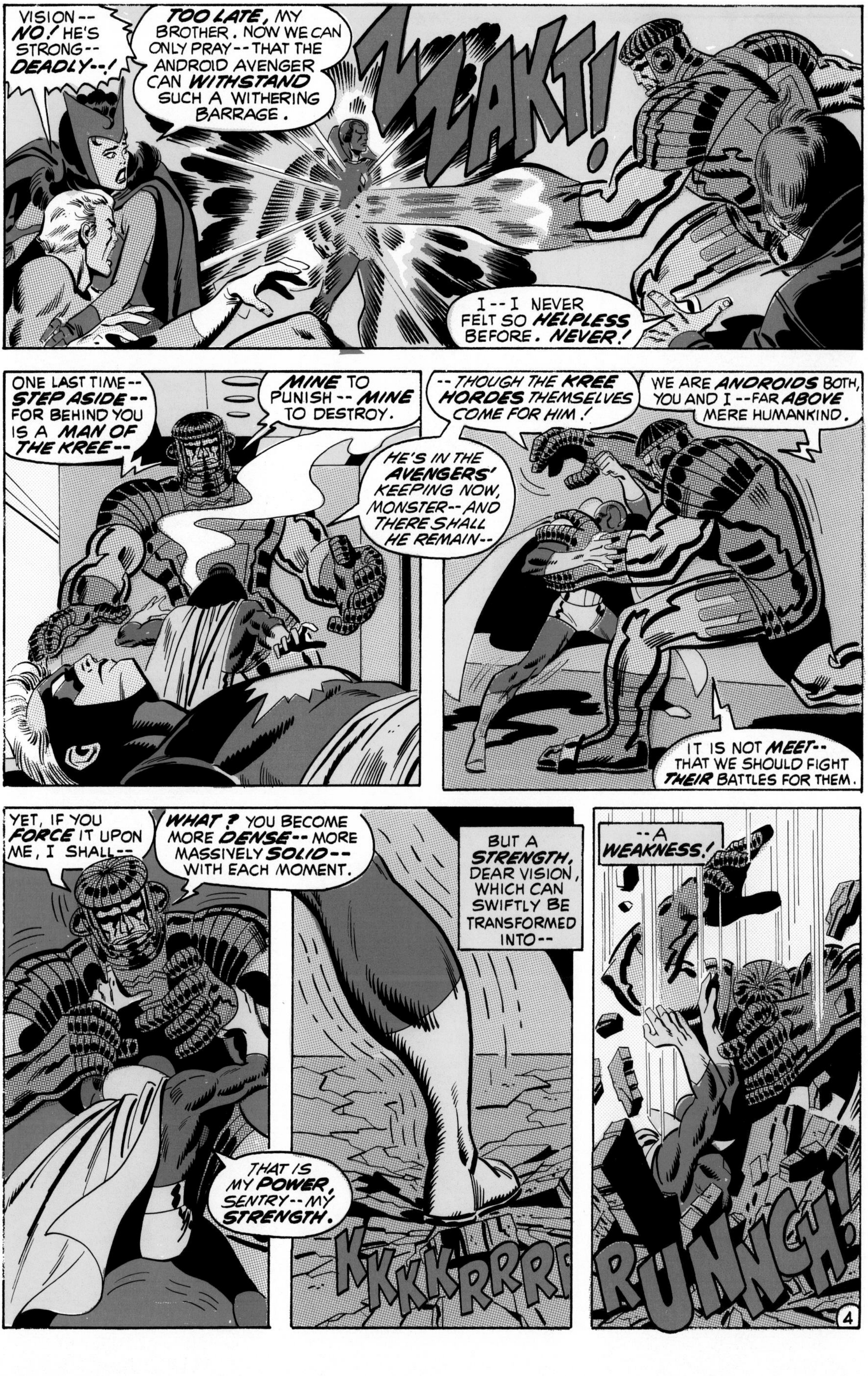
VISION -- NO! HE'S STRONG -- DEADLY--!
TOO LATE, MY BROTHER. NOW WE CAN ONLY PRAY -- THAT THE ANDROID AVENGER CAN WITHSTAND SUCH A WITHERING BARRAGE.
ZZZAKT!
I -- I NEVER FELT SO HELPLESS BEFORE. NEVER!
ONE LAST TIME -- STEP ASIDE -- FOR BEHIND YOU IS A MAN OF THE KREE --
MINE TO PUNISH -- MINE TO DESTROY.
HE'S IN THE AVENGERS' KEEPING NOW, MONSTER -- AND THERE SHALL HE REMAIN --
-- THOUGH THE KREE HORDES THEMSELVES COME FOR HIM!
WE ARE ANDROIDS BOTH, YOU AND I -- FAR ABOVE MERE HUMANKIND.
IT IS NOT MEET -- THAT WE SHOULD FIGHT THEIR BATTLES FOR THEM.
YET, IF YOU FORCE IT UPON ME, I SHALL --
WHAT? YOU BECOME MORE DENSE -- MORE MASSIVELY SOLID -- WITH EACH MOMENT.
THAT IS MY POWER, SENTRY -- MY STRENGTH.
KKKKRRRR
BUT A STRENGTH, DEAR VISION, WHICH CAN SWIFTLY BE TRANSFORMED INTO --
-- A WEAKNESS!
RUNNCH!

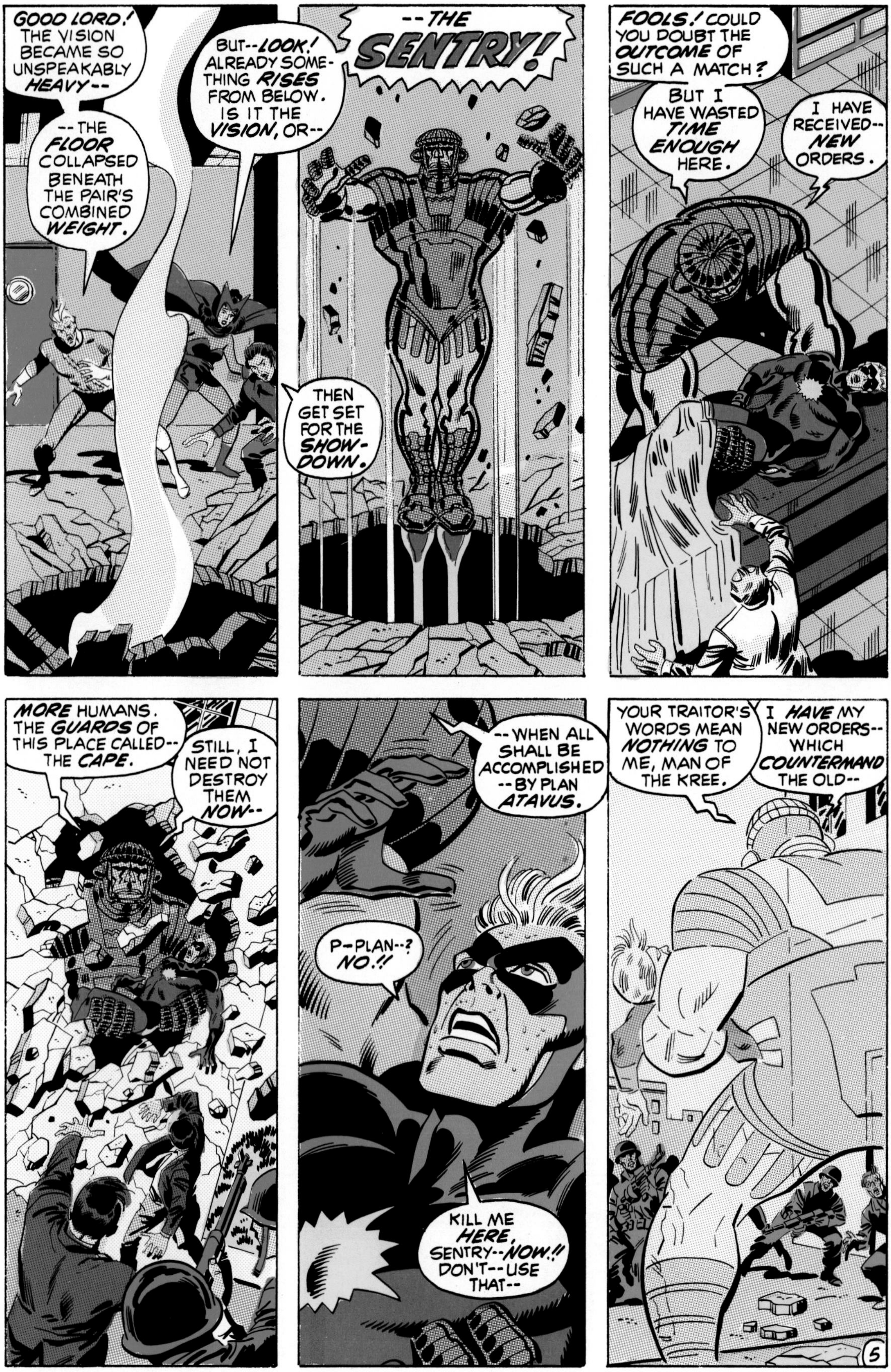
GOOD LORD! THE VISION BECAME SO UNSPEAKABLY HEAVY--
--THE FLOOR COLLAPSED BENEATH THE PAIR'S COMBINED WEIGHT.
BUT--LOOK! ALREADY SOMETHING RISES FROM BELOW. IS IT THE VISION, OR--
THEN GET SET FOR THE SHOW-DOWN.
--THE SENTRY!
FOOLS! COULD YOU DOUBT THE OUTCOME OF SUCH A MATCH?
BUT I HAVE WASTED TIME ENOUGH HERE.
I HAVE RECEIVED--NEW ORDERS.
MORE HUMANS. THE GUARDS OF THIS PLACE CALLED--THE CAPE.
STILL, I NEED NOT DESTROY THEM NOW--
--WHEN ALL SHALL BE ACCOMPLISHED--BY PLAN ATAVUS.
P-PLAN--? NO.!!
KILL ME HERE, SENTRY--NOW!! DON'T--USE THAT--
YOUR TRAITOR'S WORDS MEAN NOTHING TO ME, MAN OF THE KREE.
I HAVE MY NEW ORDERS--WHICH COUNTERMAND THE OLD--

--AND I GO TO *FULFILL* THEM--!

THEY'RE *GONE*-- BOTH OF THEM.

BUT--*WHERE?* RICK, DID MAR-VELL EVER TELL YOU OF-- A *PLAN ATAVUS?*

NOT A *WORD,* QUICKIE. 'COURSE, HE NEVER TOLD ME A KREE SENTRY COULD JUST UP AND *VANISH,* EITHER--

--BUT IT *DID.*

WELL, WE CAN DO NOTHING MORE *HERE.* ARE YOU COMING, MY SISTER?

YES, PIETRO, BUT-- THE *VISION*--

--*IS HERE,* WANDA--AND APPRECIATIVE OF YOUR *CONCERN.*

WEAKENED AS I WAS--IT TOOK A MOMENT TO *RECOVER* FROM THE SENTRY'S ONSLAUGHT.

AVENGERS--WAIT! I MUST SPEAK WITH YOU.

I FEAR WE'RE IN A *HURRY,* MISS--

I'M CAROL DANVERS--HEAD OF CAPE SECURITY.

YOU'RE NOT THE *ONLY* ONES.

I MUST HAVE A FULL *REPORT* FROM EACH OF YOU--ON WHAT JUST HAPPENED.

BUT-- WE MUST *GO*--!

OH? WHERE TO? HOW DO YOU PURSUE SOMETHING THAT-- *DISAPPEARS?*

SHE HAS A *POINT* THERE, AVENGER.

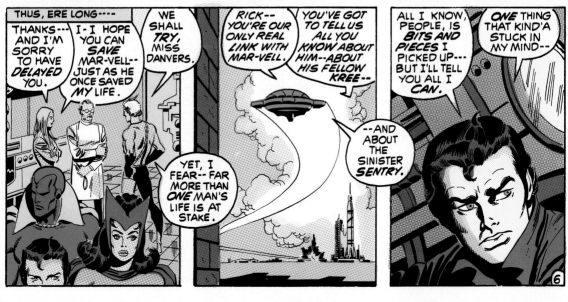

THUS, ERE LONG----

THANKS--- I-I HOPE YOU CAN *SAVE* MAR-VELL-- JUST AS HE ONCE SAVED MY LIFE.

AND I'M SORRY TO HAVE *DELAYED* YOU.

WE SHALL *TRY,* MISS DANVERS.

YET, I FEAR-- FAR MORE THAN *ONE* MAN'S LIFE IS AT STAKE.

RICK-- YOU'RE OUR ONLY REAL *LINK* WITH MAR-VELL.

YOU'VE GOT TO TELL US ALL YOU *KNOW* ABOUT HIM--ABOUT HIS FELLOW *KREE*--

--AND ABOUT THE SINISTER *SENTRY.*

ALL I KNOW, PEOPLE, IS *BITS AND PIECES* I PICKED UP--- BUT I'LL TELL YOU ALL I *CAN.*

ONE THING THAT KIND'A STUCK IN MY MIND--

6

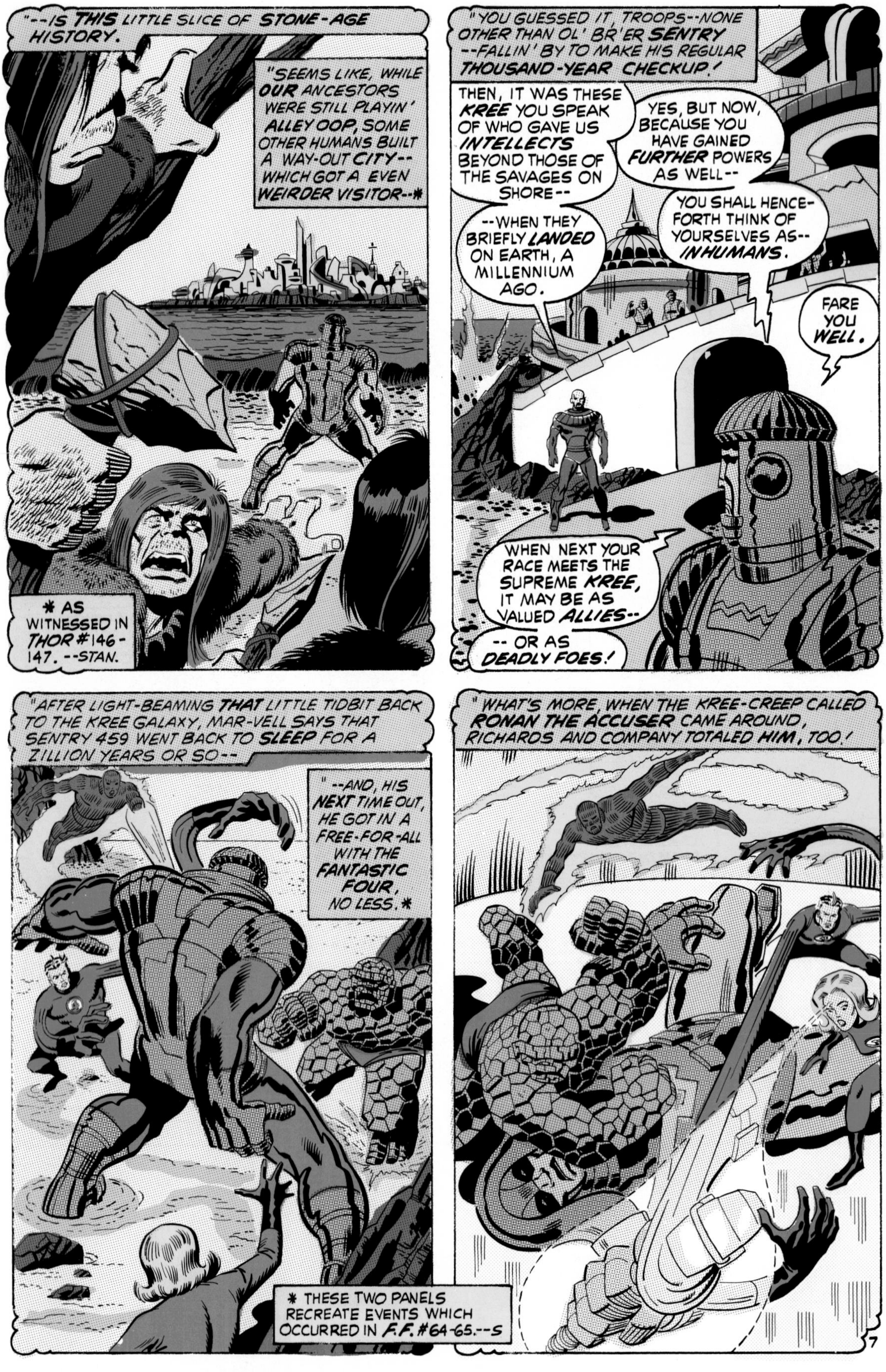
"--IS THIS LITTLE SLICE OF STONE-AGE HISTORY.
"SEEMS LIKE, WHILE OUR ANCESTORS WERE STILL PLAYIN' ALLEY OOP, SOME OTHER HUMANS BUILT A WAY-OUT CITY-- WHICH GOT A EVEN WEIRDER VISITOR--*
* AS WITNESSED IN THOR #146-147. --STAN.
"YOU GUESSED IT, TROOPS--NONE OTHER THAN OL' BR'ER SENTRY --FALLIN' BY TO MAKE HIS REGULAR THOUSAND-YEAR CHECKUP!
THEN, IT WAS THESE KREE YOU SPEAK OF WHO GAVE US INTELLECTS BEYOND THOSE OF THE SAVAGES ON SHORE--
--WHEN THEY BRIEFLY LANDED ON EARTH, A MILLENNIUM AGO.
YES, BUT NOW, BECAUSE YOU HAVE GAINED FURTHER POWERS AS WELL--
YOU SHALL HENCEFORTH THINK OF YOURSELVES AS-- INHUMANS.
FARE YOU WELL.
WHEN NEXT YOUR RACE MEETS THE SUPREME KREE, IT MAY BE AS VALUED ALLIES--
-- OR AS DEADLY FOES!
"AFTER LIGHT-BEAMING THAT LITTLE TIDBIT BACK TO THE KREE GALAXY, MAR-VELL SAYS THAT SENTRY 459 WENT BACK TO SLEEP FOR A ZILLION YEARS OR SO--
" --AND, HIS NEXT TIME OUT, HE GOT IN A FREE-FOR-ALL WITH THE FANTASTIC FOUR, NO LESS.*
"WHAT'S MORE, WHEN THE KREE-CREEP CALLED RONAN THE ACCUSER CAME AROUND, RICHARDS AND COMPANY TOTALED HIM, TOO!
* THESE TWO PANELS RECREATE EVENTS WHICH OCCURRED IN F.F. #64-65.--S
7

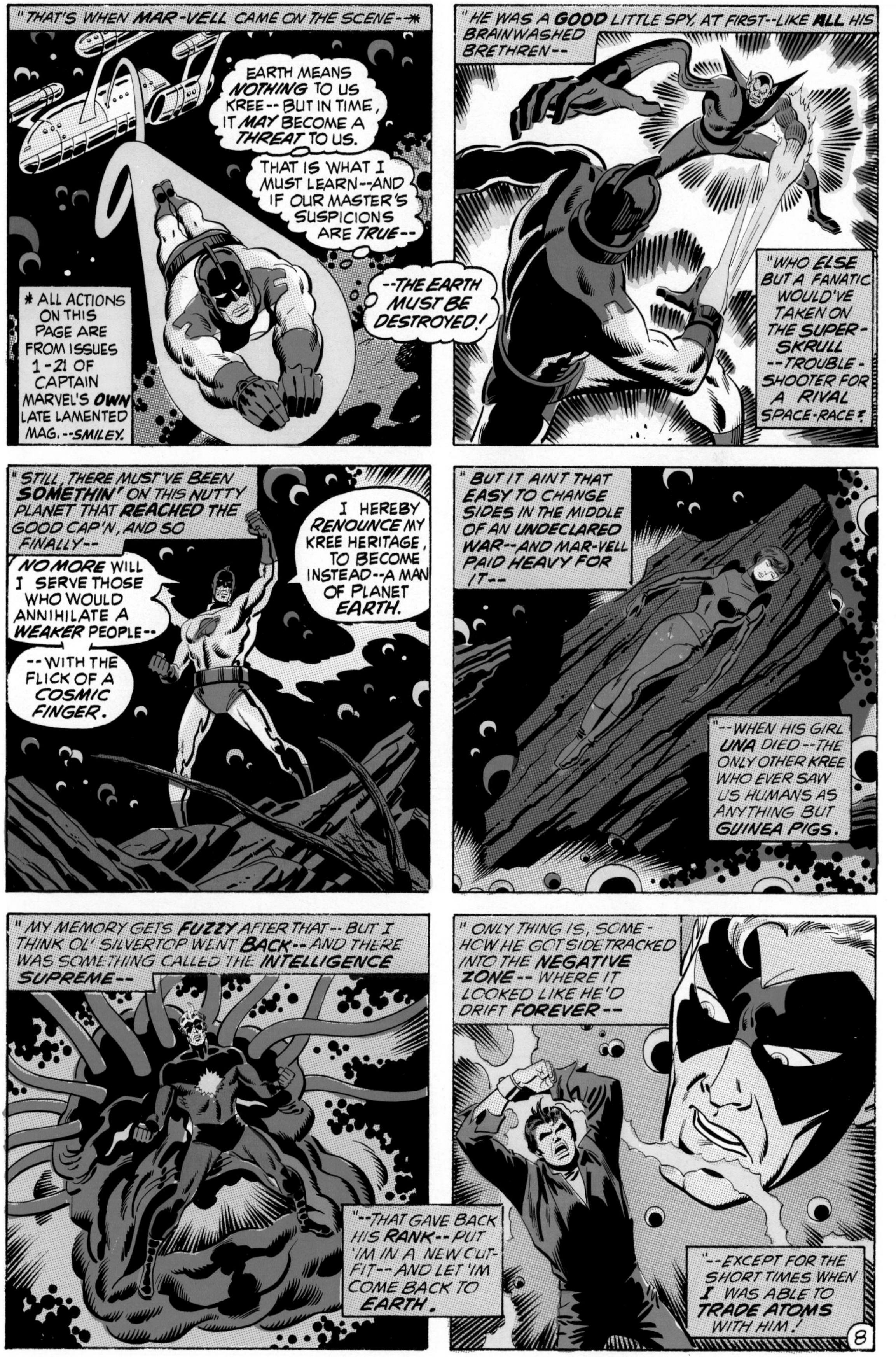
"THAT'S WHEN MAR-VELL CAME ON THE SCENE--*
EARTH MEANS NOTHING TO US KREE-- BUT IN TIME, IT MAY BECOME A THREAT TO US.
THAT IS WHAT I MUST LEARN--AND IF OUR MASTER'S SUSPICIONS ARE TRUE--
--THE EARTH MUST BE DESTROYED!
* ALL ACTIONS ON THIS PAGE ARE FROM ISSUES 1-21 OF CAPTAIN MARVEL'S OWN LATE LAMENTED MAG. --SMILEY.
"HE WAS A GOOD LITTLE SPY, AT FIRST--LIKE ALL HIS BRAINWASHED BRETHREN--
"WHO ELSE BUT A FANATIC WOULD'VE TAKEN ON THE SUPER-SKRULL --TROUBLE-SHOOTER FOR A RIVAL SPACE-RACE?
"STILL, THERE MUST'VE BEEN SOMETHIN' ON THIS NUTTY PLANET THAT REACHED THE GOOD CAP'N, AND SO FINALLY--
NO MORE WILL I SERVE THOSE WHO WOULD ANNIHILATE A WEAKER PEOPLE--
--WITH THE FLICK OF A COSMIC FINGER.
I HEREBY RENOUNCE MY KREE HERITAGE, TO BECOME INSTEAD--A MAN OF PLANET EARTH.
"BUT IT AINT THAT EASY TO CHANGE SIDES IN THE MIDDLE OF AN UNDECLARED WAR--AND MAR-VELL PAID HEAVY FOR IT--
"--WHEN HIS GIRL UNA DIED--THE ONLY OTHER KREE WHO EVER SAW US HUMANS AS ANYTHING BUT GUINEA PIGS.
"MY MEMORY GETS FUZZY AFTER THAT-- BUT I THINK OL' SILVERTOP WENT BACK--AND THERE WAS SOMETHING CALLED THE INTELLIGENCE SUPREME--
"--THAT GAVE BACK HIS RANK-- PUT 'IM IN A NEW OUT-FIT--AND LET 'IM COME BACK TO EARTH.
"ONLY THING IS, SOME-HOW HE GOT SIDETRACKED INTO THE NEGATIVE ZONE-- WHERE IT LOOKED LIKE HE'D DRIFT FOREVER--
"--EXCEPT FOR THE SHORT TIMES WHEN I WAS ABLE TO TRADE ATOMS WITH HIM!

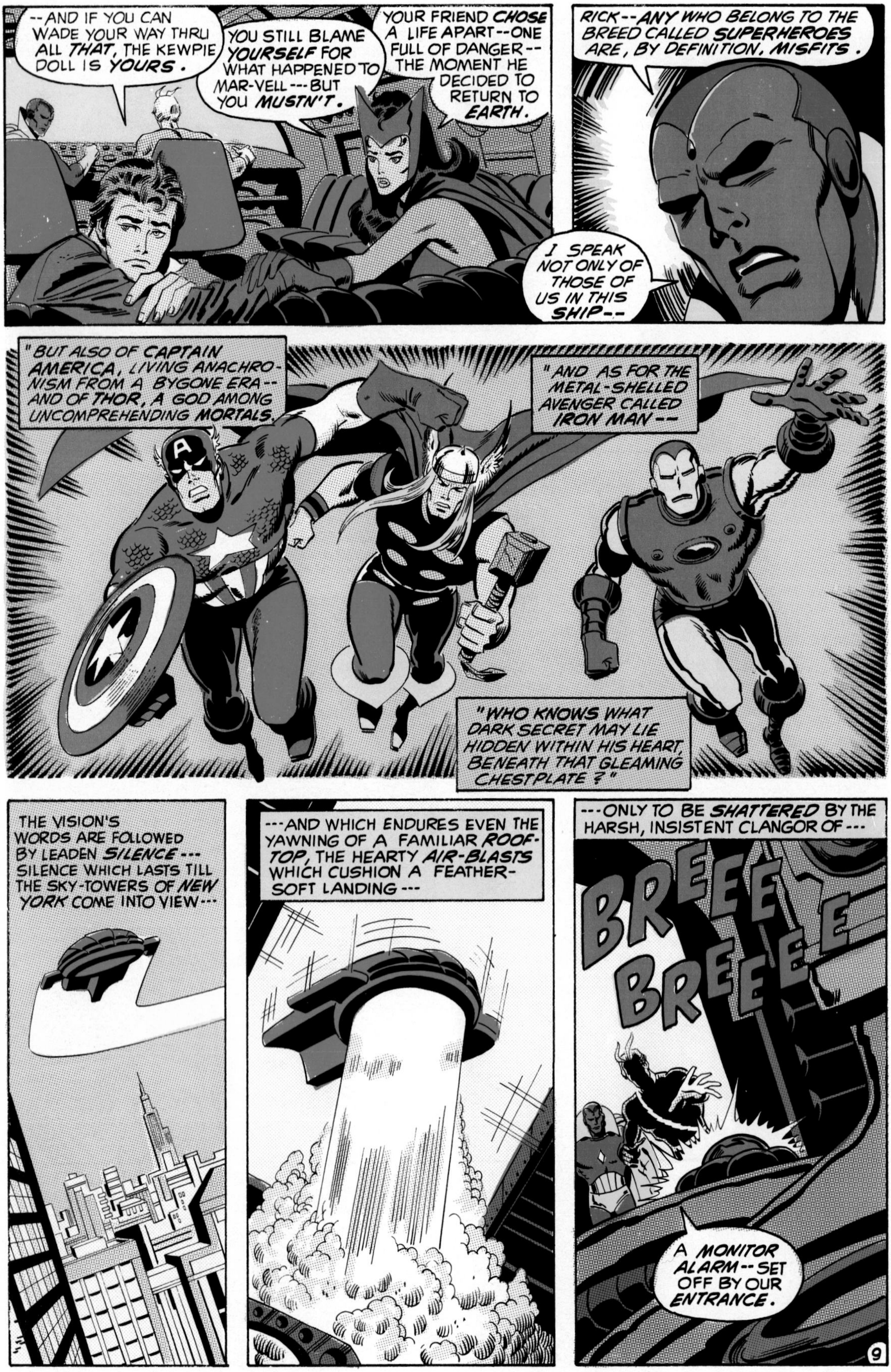
--AND IF YOU CAN WADE YOUR WAY THRU ALL THAT, THE KEWPIE DOLL IS YOURS.
YOU STILL BLAME YOURSELF FOR WHAT HAPPENED TO MAR-VELL---BUT YOU MUSTN'T.
YOUR FRIEND CHOSE A LIFE APART--ONE FULL OF DANGER--THE MOMENT HE DECIDED TO RETURN TO EARTH.
RICK--ANY WHO BELONG TO THE BREED CALLED SUPERHEROES ARE, BY DEFINITION, MISFITS.
I SPEAK NOT ONLY OF THOSE OF US IN THIS SHIP--
"BUT ALSO OF CAPTAIN AMERICA, LIVING ANACHRONISM FROM A BYGONE ERA--AND OF THOR, A GOD AMONG UNCOMPREHENDING MORTALS.
"AND AS FOR THE METAL-SHELLED AVENGER CALLED IRON MAN--
"WHO KNOWS WHAT DARK SECRET MAY LIE HIDDEN WITHIN HIS HEART, BENEATH THAT GLEAMING CHESTPLATE?"
THE VISION'S WORDS ARE FOLLOWED BY LEADEN SILENCE---SILENCE WHICH LASTS TILL THE SKY-TOWERS OF NEW YORK COME INTO VIEW---
---AND WHICH ENDURES EVEN THE YAWNING OF A FAMILIAR ROOF-TOP, THE HEARTY AIR-BLASTS WHICH CUSHION A FEATHER-SOFT LANDING---
---ONLY TO BE SHATTERED BY THE HARSH, INSISTENT CLANGOR OF---
BREEE
BREEEE
A MONITOR ALARM--SET OFF BY OUR ENTRANCE.
9

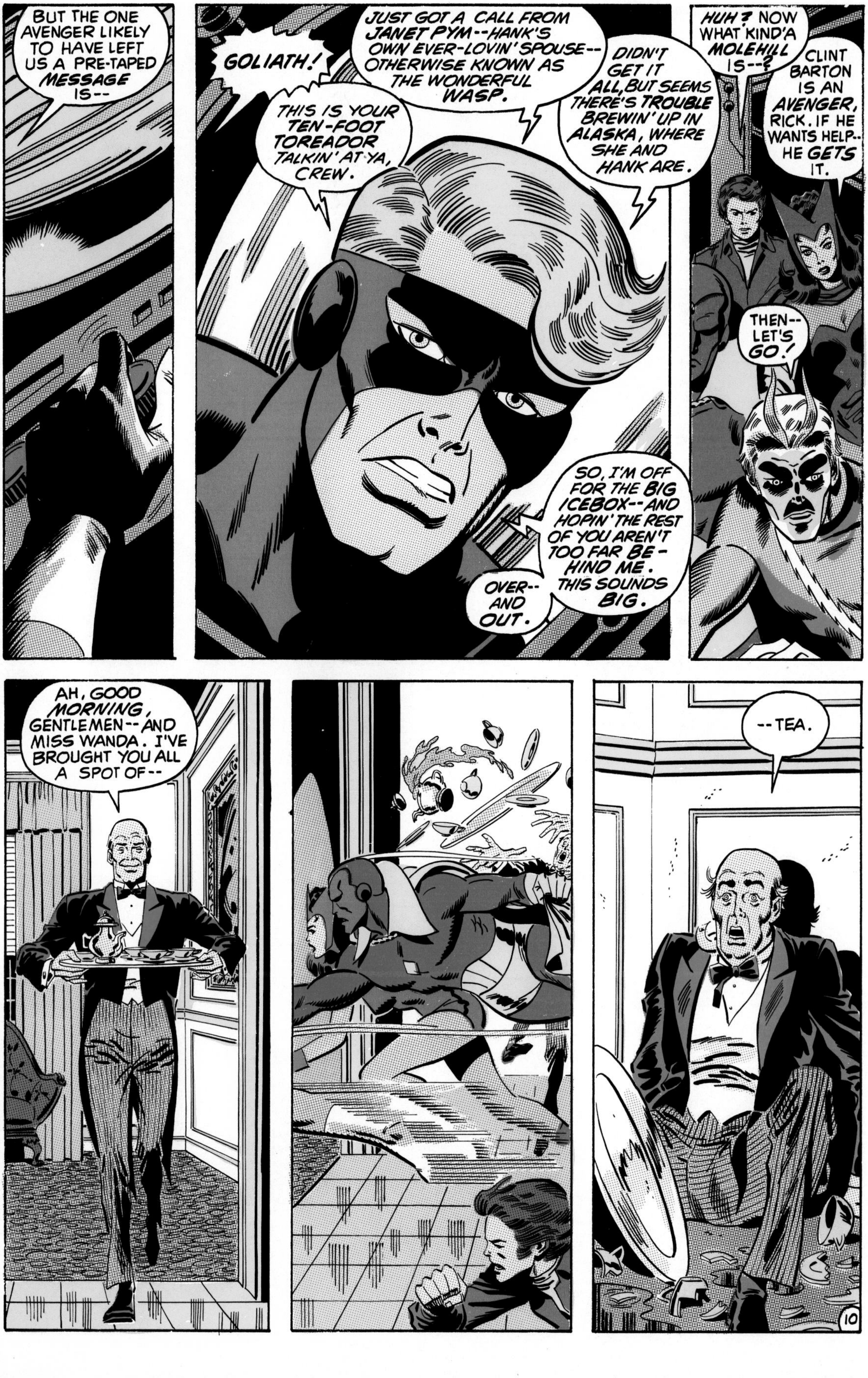

BUT THE ONE AVENGER LIKELY TO HAVE LEFT US A PRE-TAPED MESSAGE IS--
GOLIATH!
JUST GOT A CALL FROM JANET PYM--HANK'S OWN EVER-LOVIN' SPOUSE--OTHERWISE KNOWN AS THE WONDERFUL WASP.
THIS IS YOUR TEN-FOOT TOREADOR TALKIN' AT YA, CREW.
DIDN'T GET IT ALL, BUT SEEMS THERE'S TROUBLE BREWIN' UP IN ALASKA, WHERE SHE AND HANK ARE.
SO, I'M OFF FOR THE BIG ICEBOX--AND HOPIN' THE REST OF YOU AREN'T TOO FAR BE-HIND ME. THIS SOUNDS BIG.
OVER--AND OUT.
HUH? NOW WHAT KIND'A MOLEHILL IS--?
CLINT BARTON IS AN AVENGER, RICK. IF HE WANTS HELP--HE GETS IT.
THEN--LET'S GO!
AH, GOOD MORNING, GENTLEMEN--AND MISS WANDA. I'VE BROUGHT YOU ALL A SPOT OF--
--TEA.

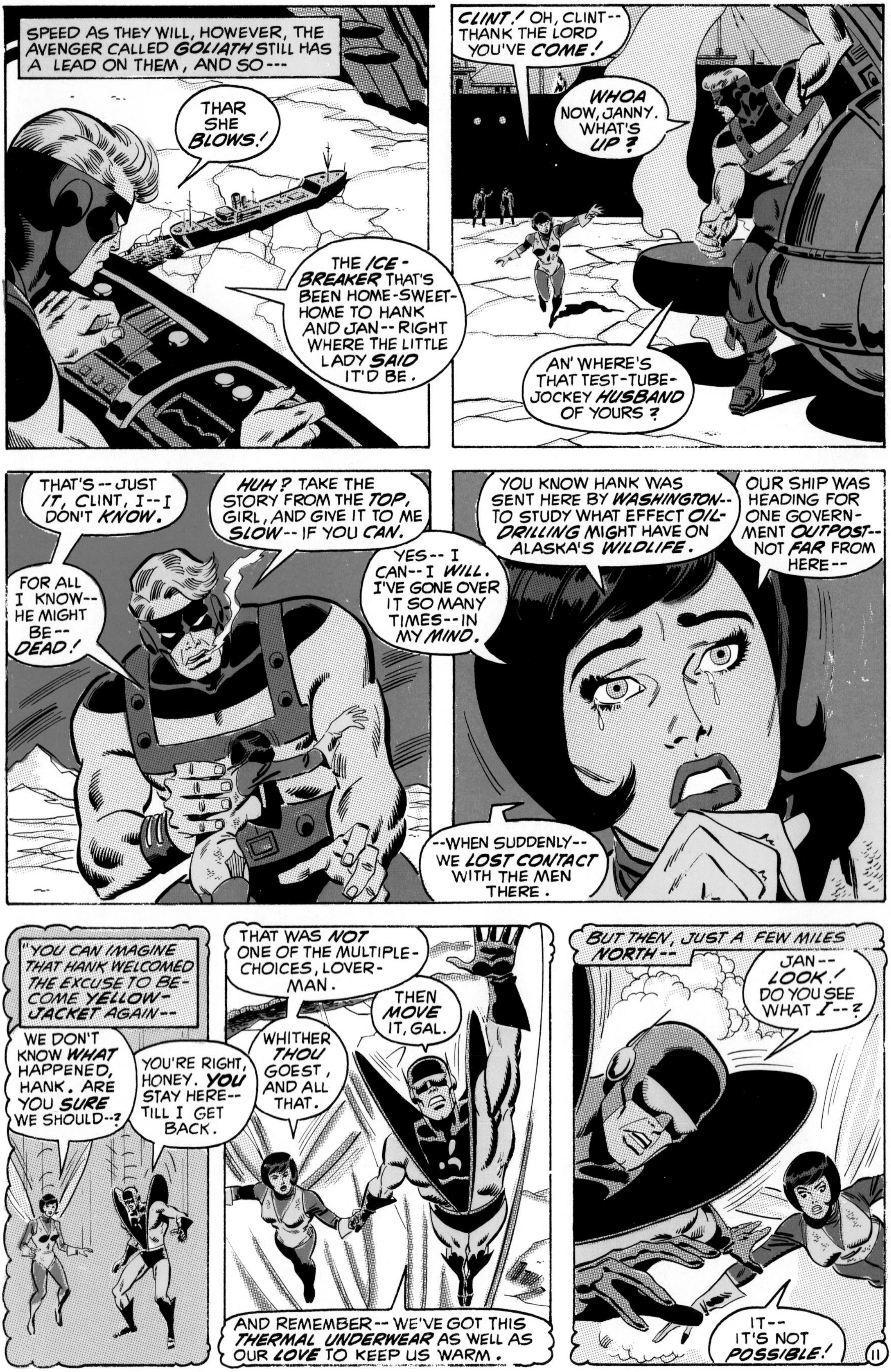
SPEED AS THEY WILL, HOWEVER, THE AVENGER CALLED GOLIATH STILL HAS A LEAD ON THEM, AND SO---
THAR SHE BLOWS!
THE ICE-BREAKER THAT'S BEEN HOME-SWEET-HOME TO HANK AND JAN -- RIGHT WHERE THE LITTLE LADY SAID IT'D BE.
CLINT! OH, CLINT -- THANK THE LORD YOU'VE COME!
WHOA NOW, JANNY. WHAT'S UP?
AN' WHERE'S THAT TEST-TUBE-JOCKEY HUSBAND OF YOURS?
THAT'S -- JUST IT, CLINT, I -- I DON'T KNOW.
FOR ALL I KNOW -- HE MIGHT BE -- DEAD!
HUH? TAKE THE STORY FROM THE TOP, GIRL, AND GIVE IT TO ME SLOW -- IF YOU CAN.
YES -- I CAN -- I WILL. I'VE GONE OVER IT SO MANY TIMES -- IN MY MIND.
YOU KNOW HANK WAS SENT HERE BY WASHINGTON -- TO STUDY WHAT EFFECT OIL-DRILLING MIGHT HAVE ON ALASKA'S WILDLIFE.
OUR SHIP WAS HEADING FOR ONE GOVERNMENT OUTPOST -- NOT FAR FROM HERE --
--WHEN SUDDENLY -- WE LOST CONTACT WITH THE MEN THERE.
"YOU CAN IMAGINE THAT HANK WELCOMED THE EXCUSE TO BECOME YELLOWJACKET AGAIN --
WE DON'T KNOW WHAT HAPPENED, HANK. ARE YOU SURE WE SHOULD--?
YOU'RE RIGHT, HONEY. YOU STAY HERE -- TILL I GET BACK.
THAT WAS NOT ONE OF THE MULTIPLE-CHOICES, LOVER-MAN.
WHITHER THOU GOEST, AND ALL THAT.
THEN MOVE IT, GAL.
AND REMEMBER -- WE'VE GOT THIS THERMAL UNDERWEAR AS WELL AS OUR LOVE TO KEEP US WARM.
BUT THEN, JUST A FEW MILES NORTH --
JAN -- LOOK! DO YOU SEE WHAT I --?
IT -- IT'S NOT POSSIBLE!
11

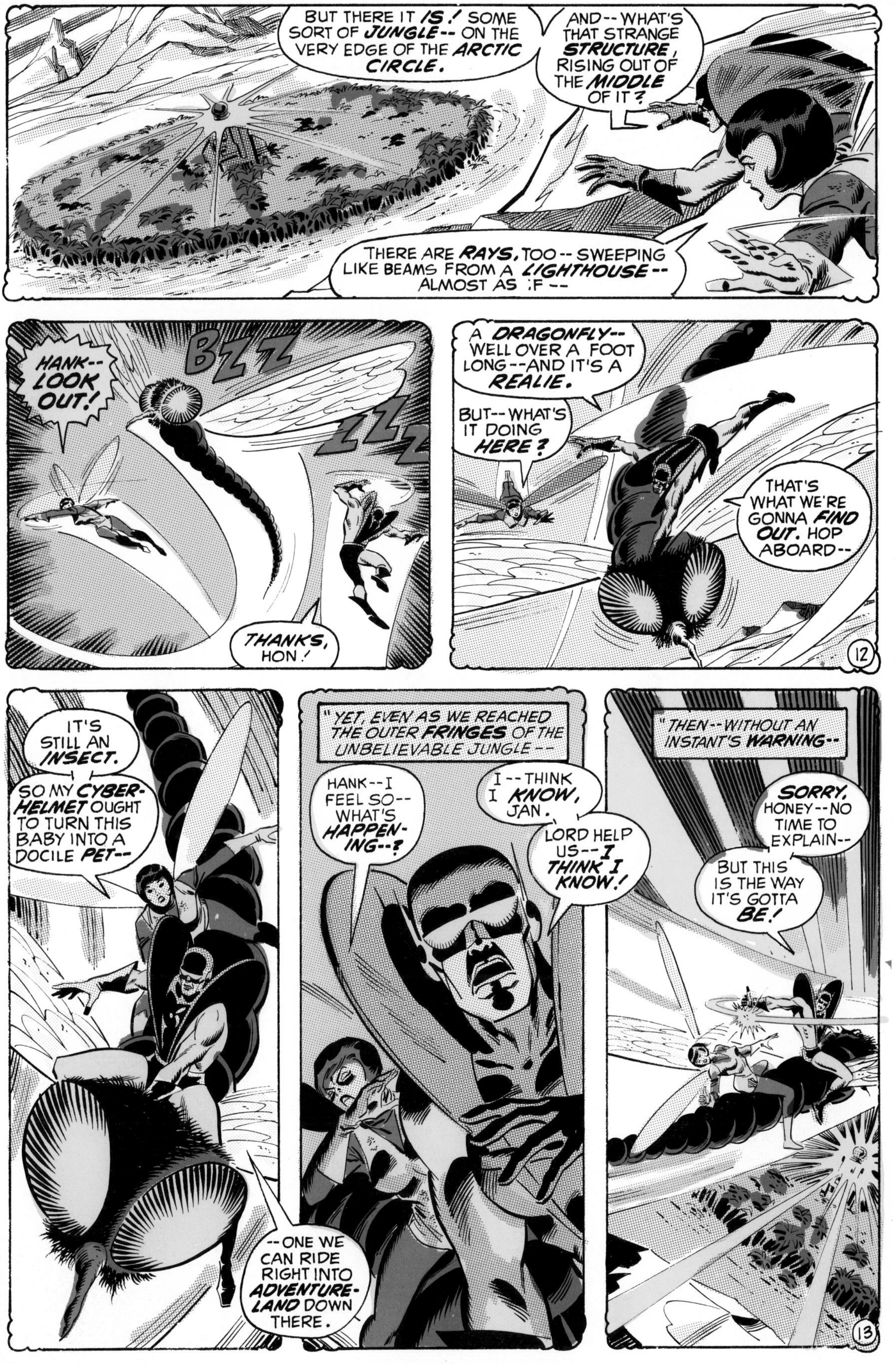
BUT THERE IT IS! SOME SORT OF JUNGLE-- ON THE VERY EDGE OF THE ARCTIC CIRCLE.
AND--WHAT'S THAT STRANGE STRUCTURE, RISING OUT OF THE MIDDLE OF IT?
THERE ARE RAYS, TOO--SWEEPING LIKE BEAMS FROM A LIGHTHOUSE-- ALMOST AS IF --
HANK-- LOOK OUT!
BZZ
ZZZ
THANKS, HON!
A DRAGONFLY-- WELL OVER A FOOT LONG--AND IT'S A REALIE.
BUT--WHAT'S IT DOING HERE?
THAT'S WHAT WE'RE GONNA FIND OUT. HOP ABOARD--
12
IT'S STILL AN INSECT.
SO MY CYBER-HELMET OUGHT TO TURN THIS BABY INTO A DOCILE PET--
--ONE WE CAN RIDE RIGHT INTO ADVENTURE-LAND DOWN THERE.
"YET, EVEN AS WE REACHED THE OUTER FRINGES OF THE UNBELIEVABLE JUNGLE--
HANK--I FEEL SO-- WHAT'S HAPPEN-ING--?
I--THINK I KNOW, JAN.
LORD HELP US--I THINK I KNOW!
"THEN--WITHOUT AN INSTANT'S WARNING--
SORRY, HONEY--NO TIME TO EXPLAIN--
BUT THIS IS THE WAY IT'S GOTTA BE!
13

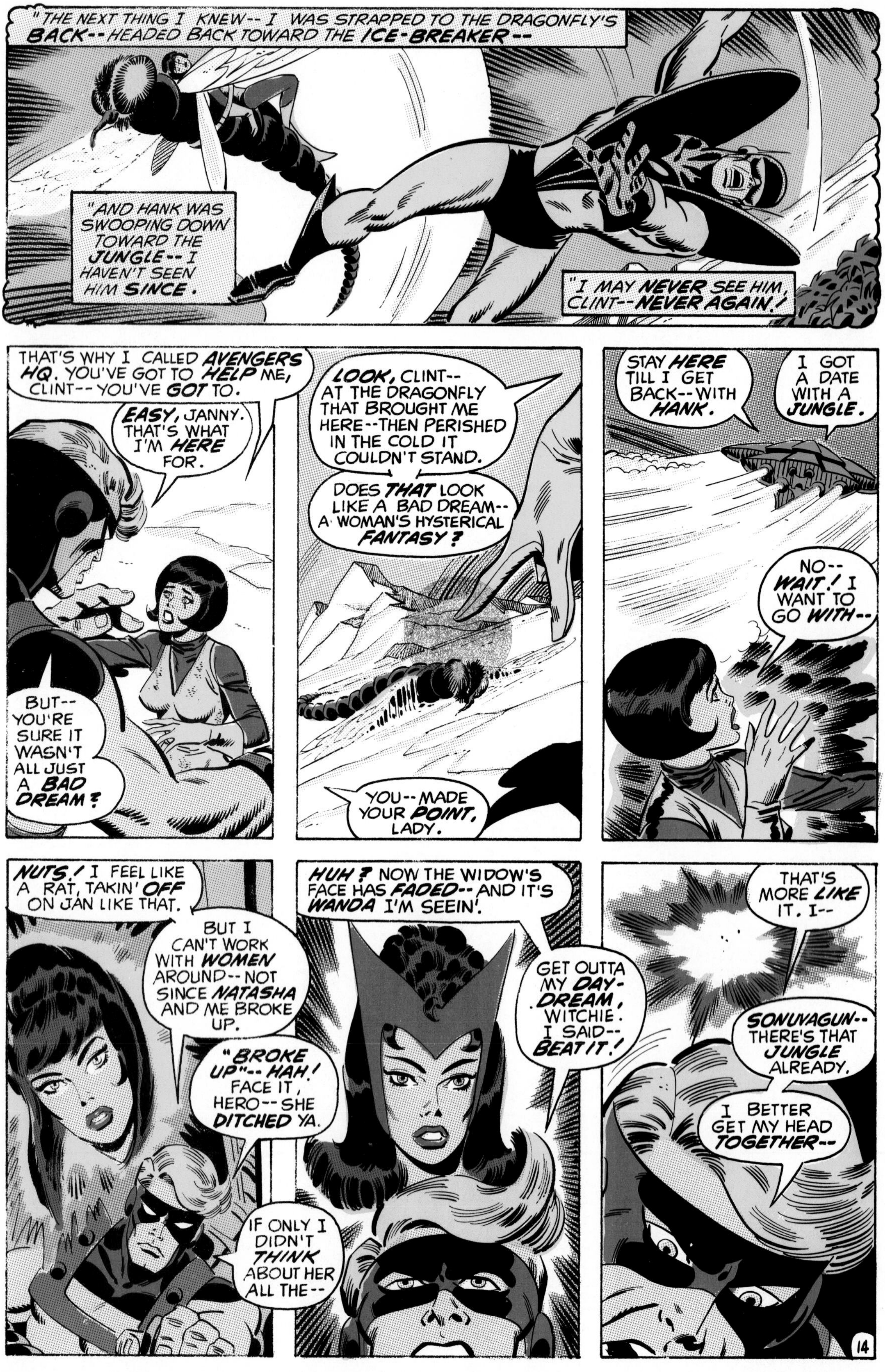
"THE NEXT THING I KNEW-- I WAS STRAPPED TO THE DRAGONFLY'S BACK-- HEADED BACK TOWARD THE ICE-BREAKER--
"AND HANK WAS SWOOPING DOWN TOWARD THE JUNGLE-- I HAVEN'T SEEN HIM SINCE.
"I MAY NEVER SEE HIM, CLINT-- NEVER AGAIN!
THAT'S WHY I CALLED AVENGERS HQ. YOU'VE GOT TO HELP ME, CLINT-- YOU'VE GOT TO.
EASY, JANNY. THAT'S WHAT I'M HERE FOR.
BUT-- YOU'RE SURE IT WASN'T ALL JUST A BAD DREAM?
LOOK, CLINT-- AT THE DRAGONFLY THAT BROUGHT ME HERE--THEN PERISHED IN THE COLD IT COULDN'T STAND.
DOES THAT LOOK LIKE A BAD DREAM-- A WOMAN'S HYSTERICAL FANTASY?
YOU--MADE YOUR POINT, LADY.
STAY HERE TILL I GET BACK--WITH HANK.
I GOT A DATE WITH A JUNGLE.
NO-- WAIT! I WANT TO GO WITH--
NUTS! I FEEL LIKE A RAT, TAKIN' OFF ON JAN LIKE THAT.
BUT I CAN'T WORK WITH WOMEN AROUND--NOT SINCE NATASHA AND ME BROKE UP.
"BROKE UP"--HAH! FACE IT, HERO--SHE DITCHED YA.
IF ONLY I DIDN'T THINK ABOUT HER ALL THE--
HUH? NOW THE WIDOW'S FACE HAS FADED-- AND IT'S WANDA I'M SEEIN'.
GET OUTTA MY DAY-DREAM, WITCHIE. I SAID-- BEAT IT!
THAT'S MORE LIKE IT. I--
SONUVAGUN-- THERE'S THAT JUNGLE ALREADY.
I BETTER GET MY HEAD TOGETHER--

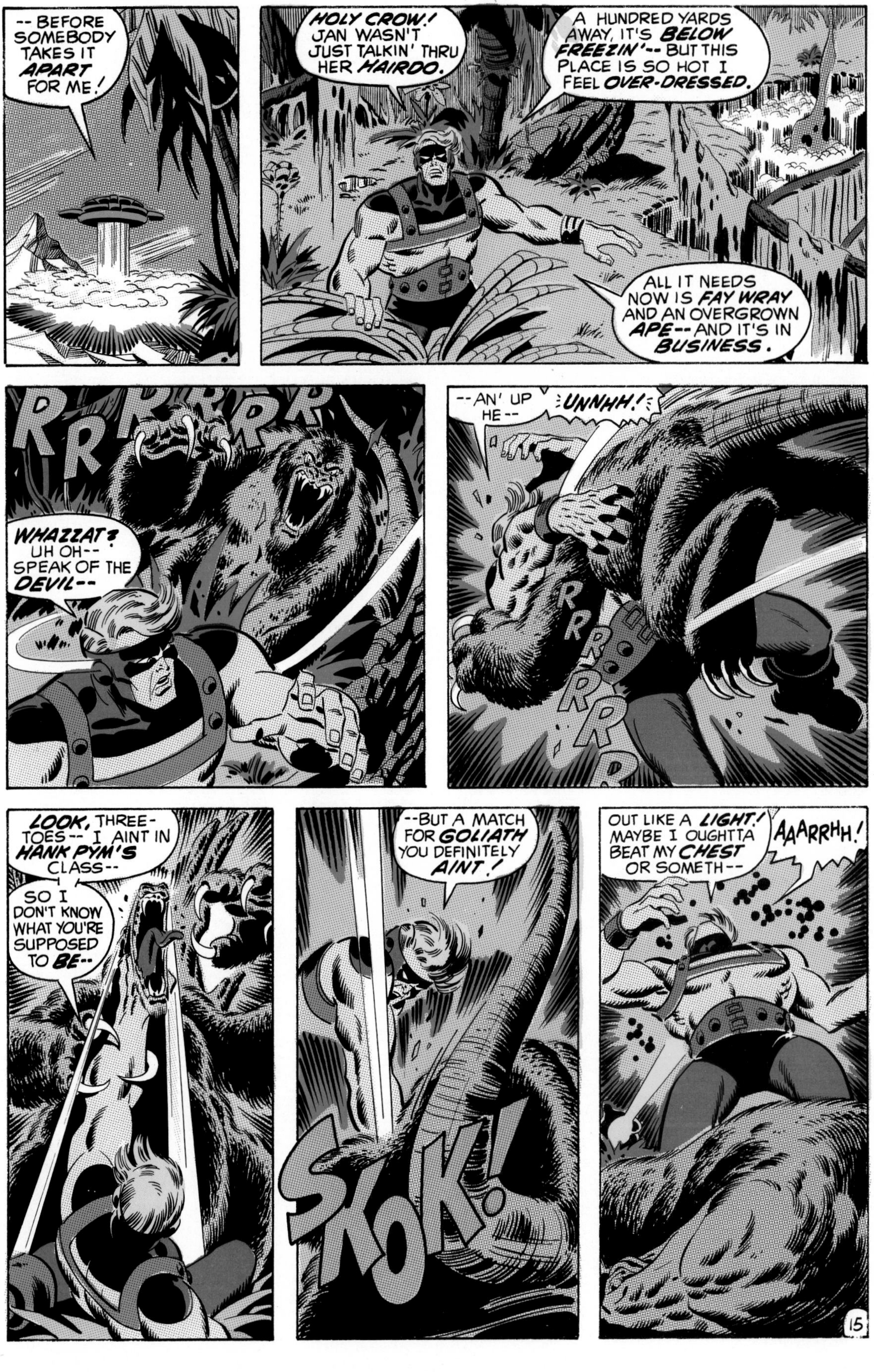
-- BEFORE SOMEBODY TAKES IT APART FOR ME!
HOLY CROW! JAN WASN'T JUST TALKIN' THRU HER HAIRDO.
A HUNDRED YARDS AWAY, IT'S BELOW FREEZIN'-- BUT THIS PLACE IS SO HOT I FEEL OVER-DRESSED.
ALL IT NEEDS NOW IS FAY WRAY AND AN OVERGROWN APE-- AND IT'S IN BUSINESS.
RRRRRR
WHAZZAT? UH OH-- SPEAK OF THE DEVIL--
--AN' UP HE--
UNNHH!
RRRRRR
LOOK, THREE-TOES-- I AINT IN HANK PYM'S CLASS--
SO I DON'T KNOW WHAT YOU'RE SUPPOSED TO BE--
--BUT A MATCH FOR GOLIATH YOU DEFINITELY AINT!
SOK!
OUT LIKE A LIGHT! MAYBE I OUGHTTA BEAT MY CHEST OR SOMETH--
AAARRHH!
15

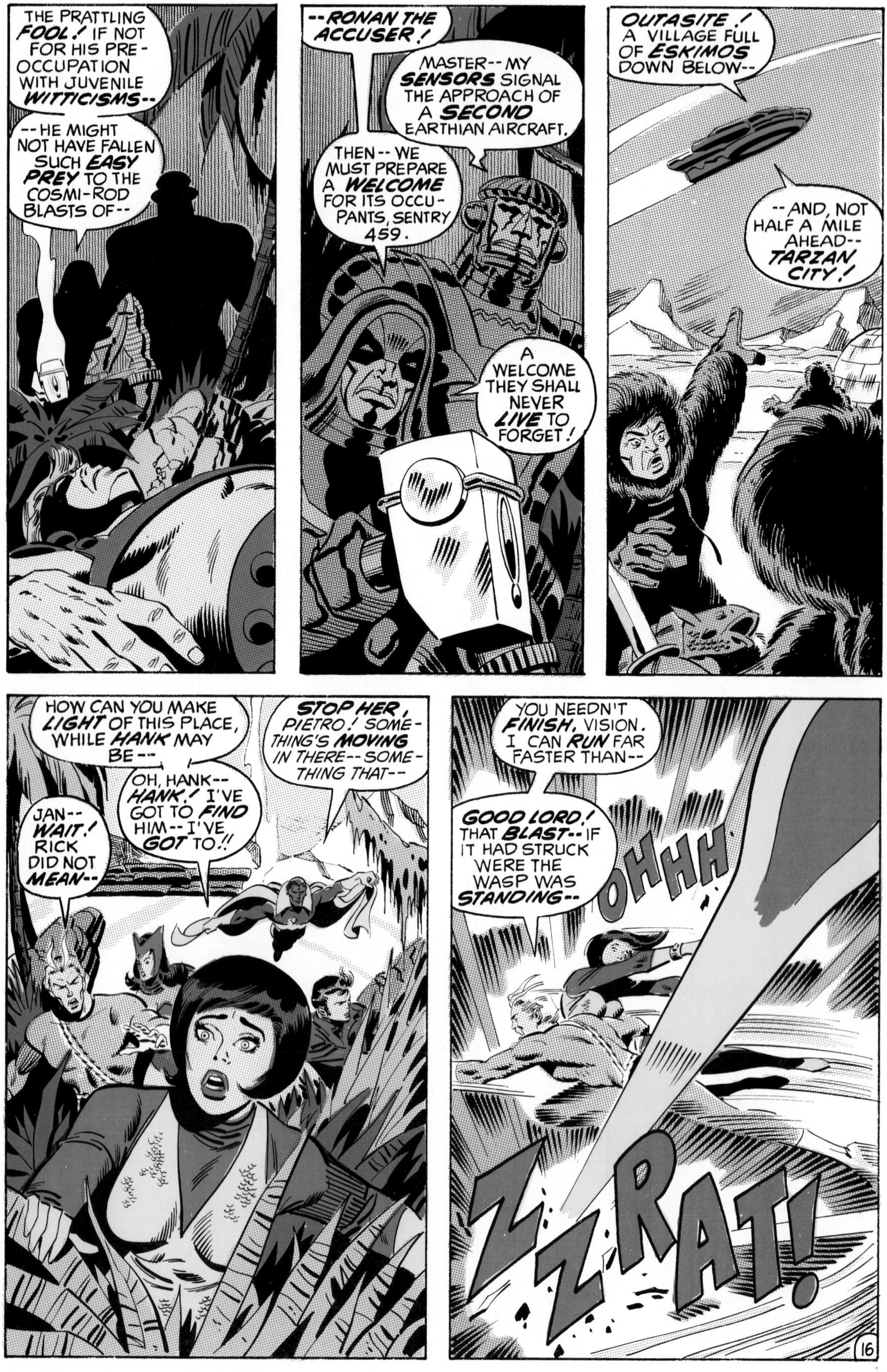

THE PRATTLING FOOL! IF NOT FOR HIS PRE-OCCUPATION WITH JUVENILE WITTICISMS--
--HE MIGHT NOT HAVE FALLEN SUCH EASY PREY TO THE COSMI-ROD BLASTS OF--
--RONAN THE ACCUSER!
MASTER-- MY SENSORS SIGNAL THE APPROACH OF A SECOND EARTHIAN AIRCRAFT.
THEN-- WE MUST PREPARE A WELCOME FOR ITS OCCU-PANTS, SENTRY 459.
A WELCOME THEY SHALL NEVER LIVE TO FORGET!
OUTASITE! A VILLAGE FULL OF ESKIMOS DOWN BELOW--
--AND, NOT HALF A MILE AHEAD-- TARZAN CITY!
HOW CAN YOU MAKE LIGHT OF THIS PLACE, WHILE HANK MAY BE--
OH, HANK-- HANK! I'VE GOT TO FIND HIM-- I'VE GOT TO!!
JAN-- WAIT! RICK DID NOT MEAN--
STOP HER, PIETRO! SOME-THING'S MOVING IN THERE-- SOME-THING THAT--
YOU NEEDN'T FINISH, VISION. I CAN RUN FAR FASTER THAN--
GOOD LORD! THAT BLAST-- IF IT HAD STRUCK WERE THE WASP WAS STANDING--
OHHH
ZZRAT!
16

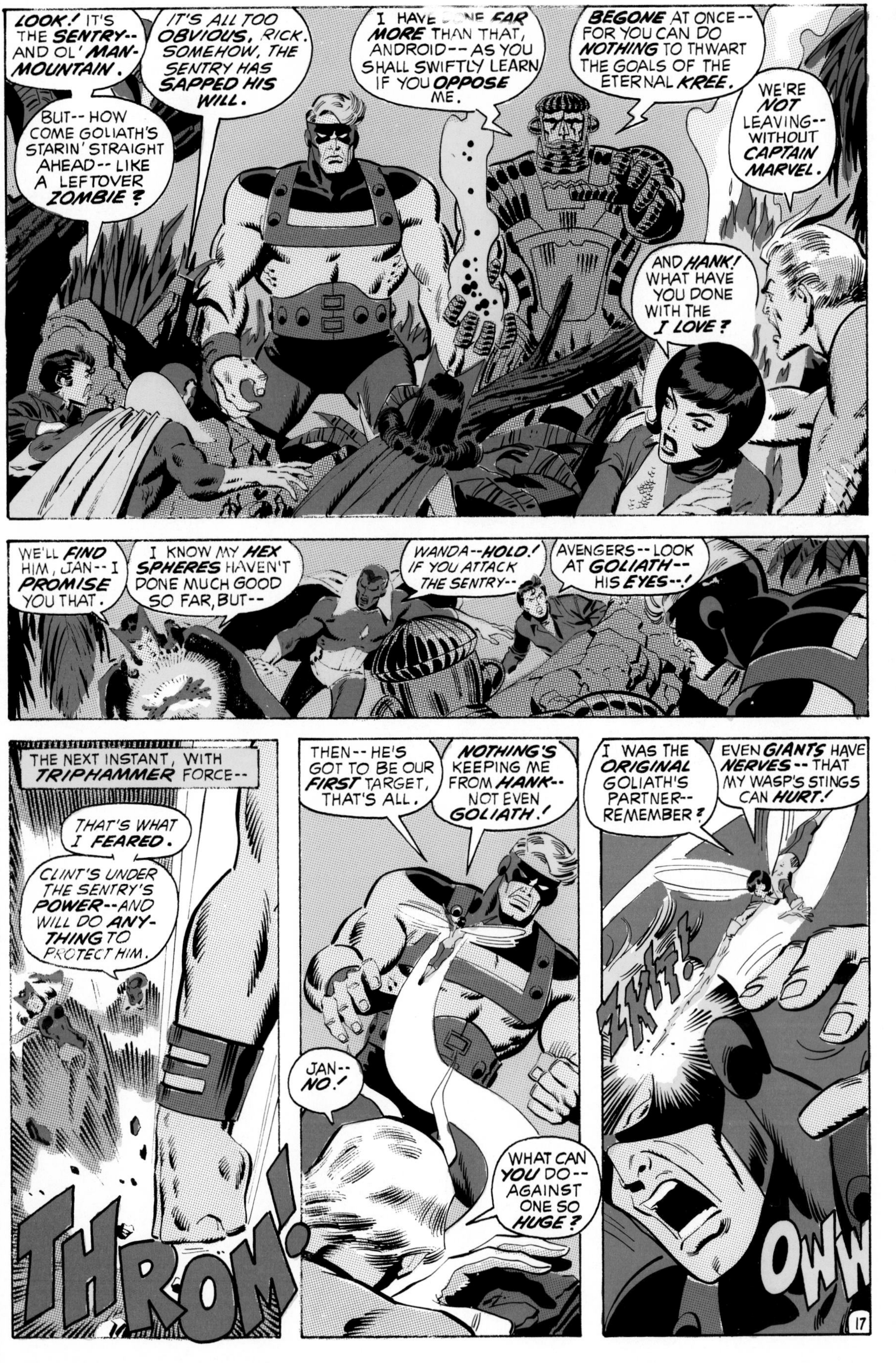
LOOK! IT'S THE SENTRY-- AND OL' MAN-MOUNTAIN.
BUT-- HOW COME GOLIATH'S STARIN' STRAIGHT AHEAD-- LIKE A LEFTOVER ZOMBIE?
IT'S ALL TOO OBVIOUS, RICK. SOMEHOW, THE SENTRY HAS SAPPED HIS WILL.
I HAVE DONE FAR MORE THAN THAT, ANDROID-- AS YOU SHALL SWIFTLY LEARN IF YOU OPPOSE ME.
BEGONE AT ONCE-- FOR YOU CAN DO NOTHING TO THWART THE GOALS OF THE ETERNAL KREE.
WE'RE NOT LEAVING-- WITHOUT CAPTAIN MARVEL.
AND HANK! WHAT HAVE YOU DONE WITH THE I LOVE?
WE'LL FIND HIM, JAN-- I PROMISE YOU THAT.
I KNOW MY HEX SPHERES HAVEN'T DONE MUCH GOOD SO FAR, BUT--
WANDA--HOLD! IF YOU ATTACK THE SENTRY--
AVENGERS-- LOOK AT GOLIATH-- HIS EYES--!
THE NEXT INSTANT, WITH TRIPHAMMER FORCE--
THAT'S WHAT I FEARED.
CLINT'S UNDER THE SENTRY'S POWER--AND WILL DO ANYTHING TO PROTECT HIM.
THROM!
THEN-- HE'S GOT TO BE OUR FIRST TARGET, THAT'S ALL.
NOTHING'S KEEPING ME FROM HANK-- NOT EVEN GOLIATH!
JAN-- NO!
WHAT CAN YOU DO-- AGAINST ONE SO HUGE?
I WAS THE ORIGINAL GOLIATH'S PARTNER-- REMEMBER?
EVEN GIANTS HAVE NERVES-- THAT MY WASP'S STINGS CAN HURT!
ZKKT!
OWW

HIGH-POCKETS IS *RATTLED*— BUT WHAT ABOUT— *?*

PERHAPS— THIS *BOULDER*— CAN BUY US *TIME*, RICK.

IF I WERE AN *EMOTIONAL* CREATURE, ANDROID—

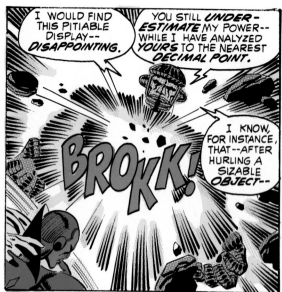

I WOULD FIND THIS PITIABLE DISPLAY— *DISAPPOINTING.*

YOU STILL *UNDER-ESTIMATE* MY POWER— WHILE I HAVE ANALYZED *YOURS* TO THE NEAREST *DECIMAL POINT.*

I KNOW, FOR INSTANCE, THAT—AFTER HURLING A *SIZABLE OBJECT*—

BROKK!

—IT WILL TAKE YOU *5.073 SECONDS* TO BECOME ONCE MORE INTANGIBLE.

AR RRHH

TIME ENOUGH FOR ME TO *WEAKEN* YOU— WITH A BURST THAT WOULD *KILL* A LESSER BEING.

THE VISION'S *HURT.* WE MUST *HELP* HIM.!

BUT— WE DARE NOT TURN OUR BACKS ON *GOLIATH.*

NO— IT IS HARDLY NECESSARY TO *IGNORE* CLINT BARTON—

MERELY TO SUFFER A MOMENT'S *DISTRACTION* IS SUFFICIENT FOR A *MAMMOTH HAND* TO CLEAVE THE HOT, MUGGY AIR—

AND, THOUGH IT IS A *WASP-SIZED AVENGER* WHO IS STRUCK BY MASSIVE FLAILING KNUCKLES—

—IT IS A *NORMAL-SIZED GIRL* WHO FALLS TO EARTH—LIKE A *WOUNDED STARLING.* ⑱

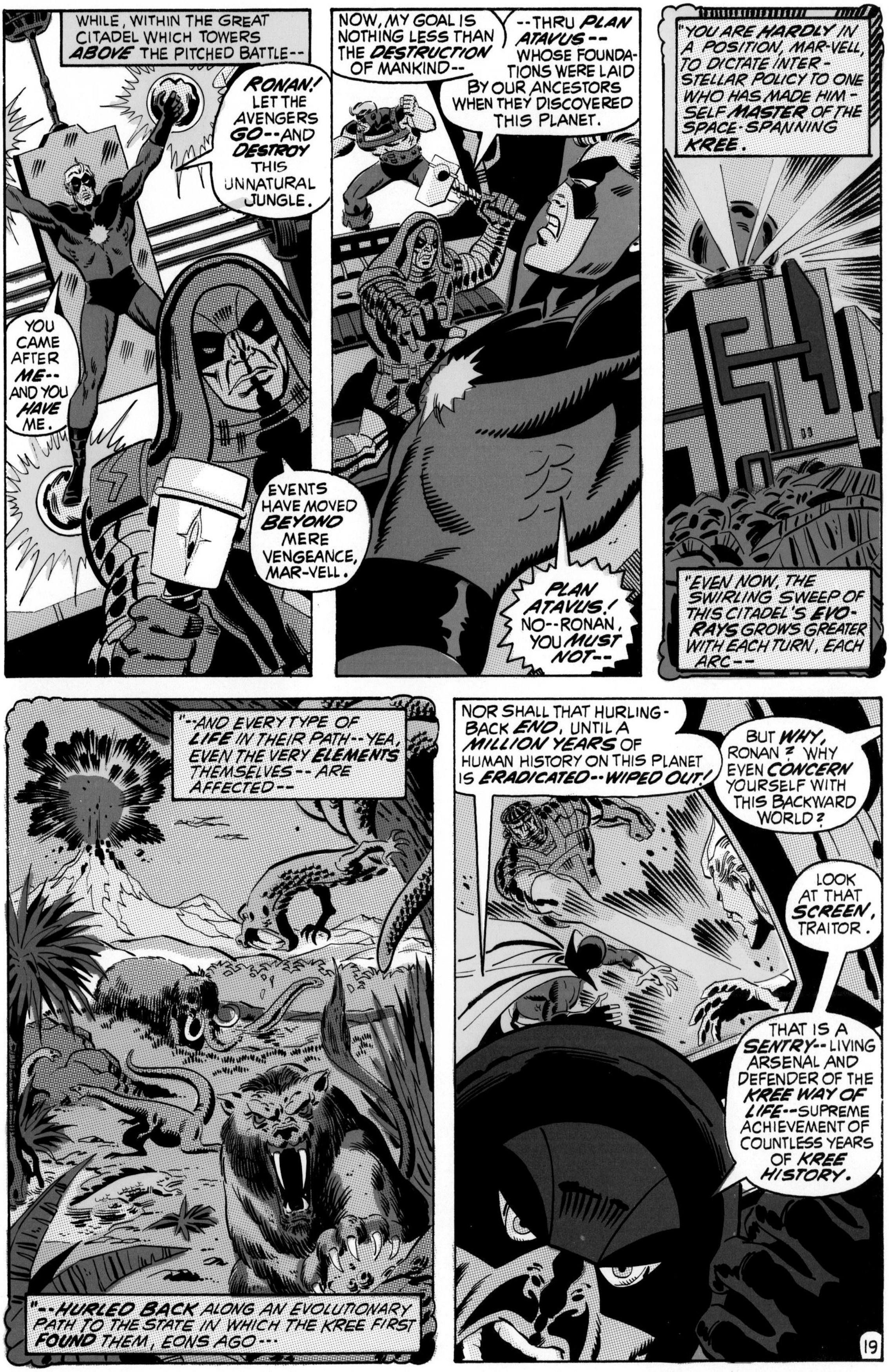

WHILE, WITHIN THE GREAT CITADEL WHICH TOWERS ABOVE THE PITCHED BATTLE--
RONAN! LET THE AVENGERS GO--AND DESTROY THIS UNNATURAL JUNGLE.
YOU CAME AFTER ME--AND YOU HAVE ME.
EVENTS HAVE MOVED BEYOND MERE VENGEANCE, MAR-VELL.
NOW, MY GOAL IS NOTHING LESS THAN THE DESTRUCTION OF MANKIND--
--THRU PLAN ATAVUS--WHOSE FOUNDATIONS WERE LAID BY OUR ANCESTORS WHEN THEY DISCOVERED THIS PLANET.
PLAN ATAVUS! NO--RONAN, YOU MUST NOT--
"YOU ARE HARDLY IN A POSITION, MAR-VELL, TO DICTATE INTER-STELLAR POLICY TO ONE WHO HAS MADE HIMSELF MASTER OF THE SPACE-SPANNING KREE.
"EVEN NOW, THE SWIRLING SWEEP OF THIS CITADEL'S EVO-RAYS GROWS GREATER WITH EACH TURN, EACH ARC--
"--AND EVERY TYPE OF LIFE IN THEIR PATH--YEA, EVEN THE VERY ELEMENTS THEMSELVES--ARE AFFECTED--
"--HURLED BACK ALONG AN EVOLUTIONARY PATH TO THE STATE IN WHICH THE KREE FIRST FOUND THEM, EONS AGO--
NOR SHALL THAT HURLING-BACK END, UNTIL A MILLION YEARS OF HUMAN HISTORY ON THIS PLANET IS ERADICATED--WIPED OUT!
BUT WHY, RONAN? WHY EVEN CONCERN YOURSELF WITH THIS BACKWARD WORLD?
LOOK AT THAT SCREEN, TRAITOR.
THAT IS A SENTRY--LIVING ARSENAL AND DEFENDER OF THE KREE WAY OF LIFE--SUPREME ACHIEVEMENT OF COUNTLESS YEARS OF KREE HISTORY.

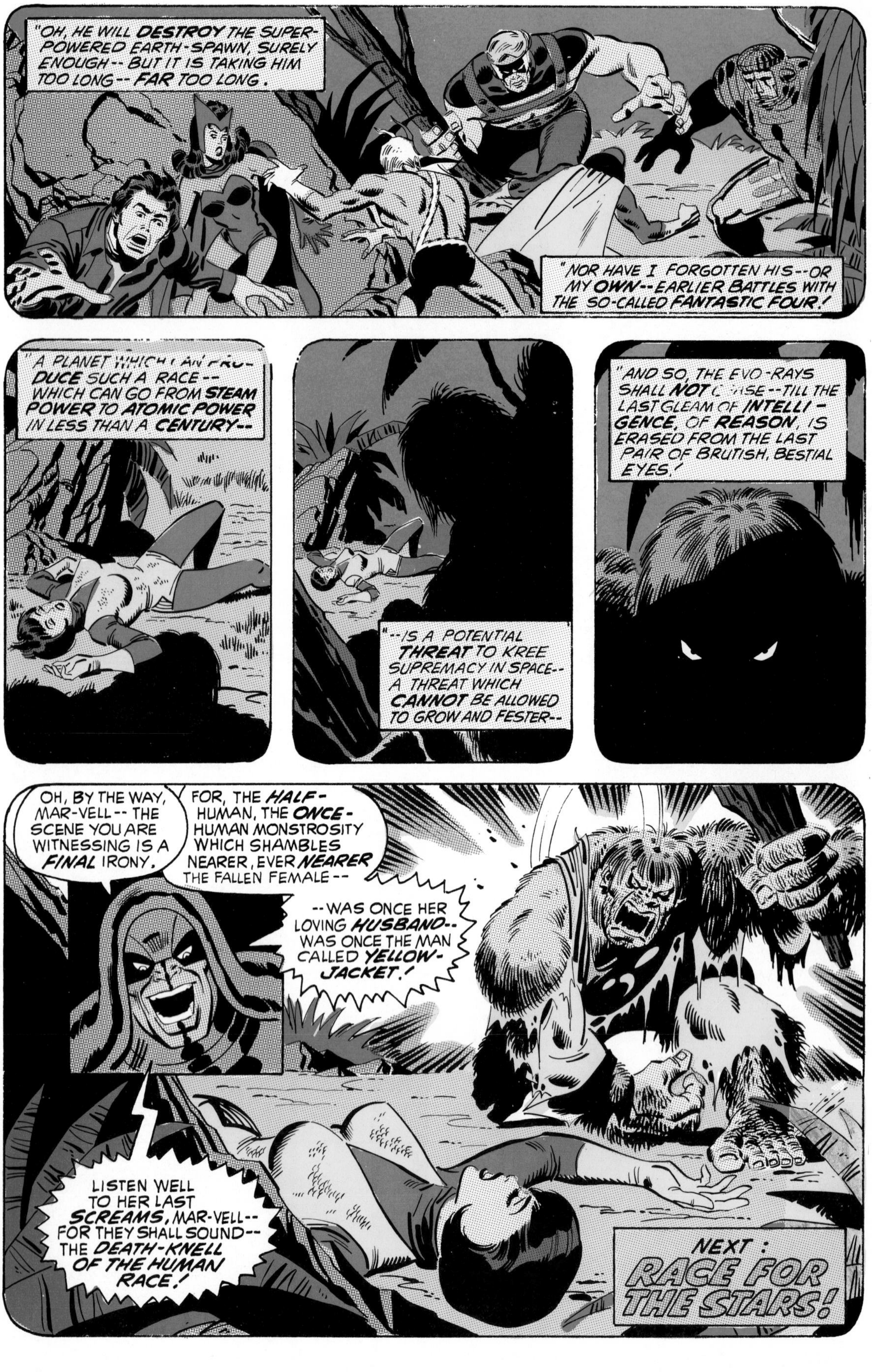
"OH, HE WILL DESTROY THE SUPER-POWERED EARTH-SPAWN, SURELY ENOUGH -- BUT IT IS TAKING HIM TOO LONG -- FAR TOO LONG.
"NOR HAVE I FORGOTTEN HIS -- OR MY OWN -- EARLIER BATTLES WITH THE SO-CALLED FANTASTIC FOUR!
"A PLANET WHICH CAN PRO-DUCE SUCH A RACE -- WHICH CAN GO FROM STEAM POWER TO ATOMIC POWER IN LESS THAN A CENTURY --
"-- IS A POTENTIAL THREAT TO KREE SUPREMACY IN SPACE -- A THREAT WHICH CANNOT BE ALLOWED TO GROW AND FESTER --
"AND SO, THE EVO-RAYS SHALL NOT CEASE -- TILL THE LAST GLEAM OF INTELLI-GENCE, OF REASON, IS ERASED FROM THE LAST PAIR OF BRUTISH, BESTIAL EYES!
OH, BY THE WAY, MAR-VELL -- THE SCENE YOU ARE WITNESSING IS A FINAL IRONY.
FOR, THE HALF-HUMAN, THE ONCE-HUMAN MONSTROSITY WHICH SHAMBLES NEARER, EVER NEARER THE FALLEN FEMALE --
-- WAS ONCE HER LOVING HUSBAND -- WAS ONCE THE MAN CALLED YELLOW-JACKET!
LISTEN WELL TO HER LAST SCREAMS, MAR-VELL -- FOR THEY SHALL SOUND -- THE DEATH-KNELL OF THE HUMAN RACE!
NEXT: RACE FOR THE STARS!

CHAPTER THREE

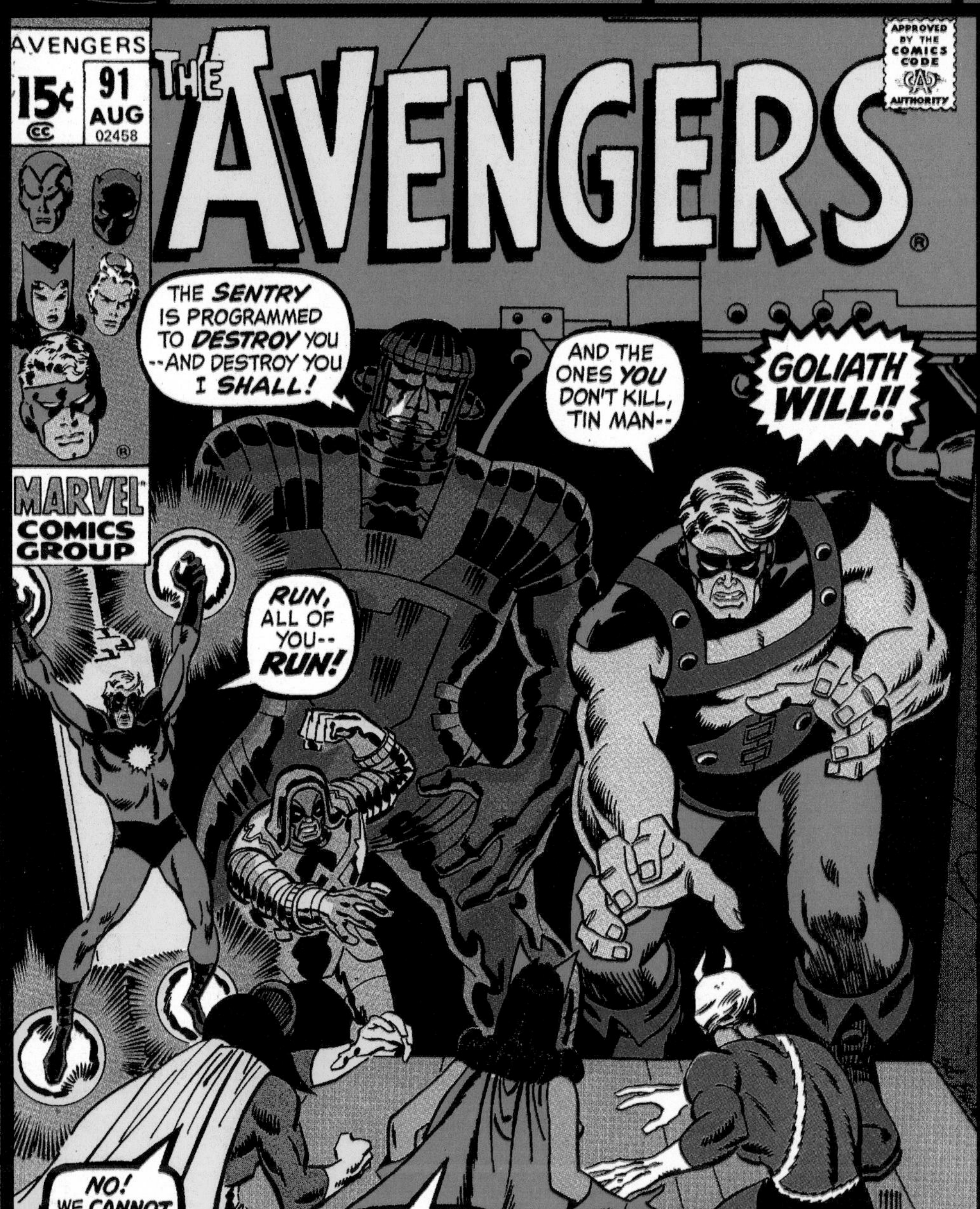
AVENGERS
15¢
CC
91
AUG
02458
THE AVENGERS ®
APPROVED BY THE COMICS CODE CA AUTHORITY
MARVEL COMICS GROUP
THE SENTRY IS PROGRAMMED TO DESTROY YOU --AND DESTROY YOU I SHALL!
AND THE ONES YOU DON'T KILL, TIN MAN--
GOLIATH WILL!!
RUN, ALL OF YOU-- RUN!
NO! WE CANNOT FLEE--WE DARE NOT!
IT'S AVENGER VS. AVENGER-- --- TO THE DEATH!
AND THE PRIZE IS-- THE PLANET EARTH!!

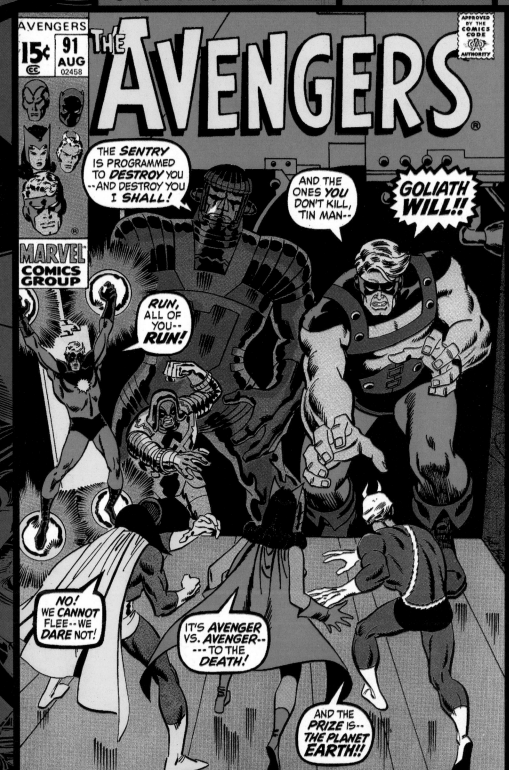

TAKE ONE GIANT STEP... BACKWARD!

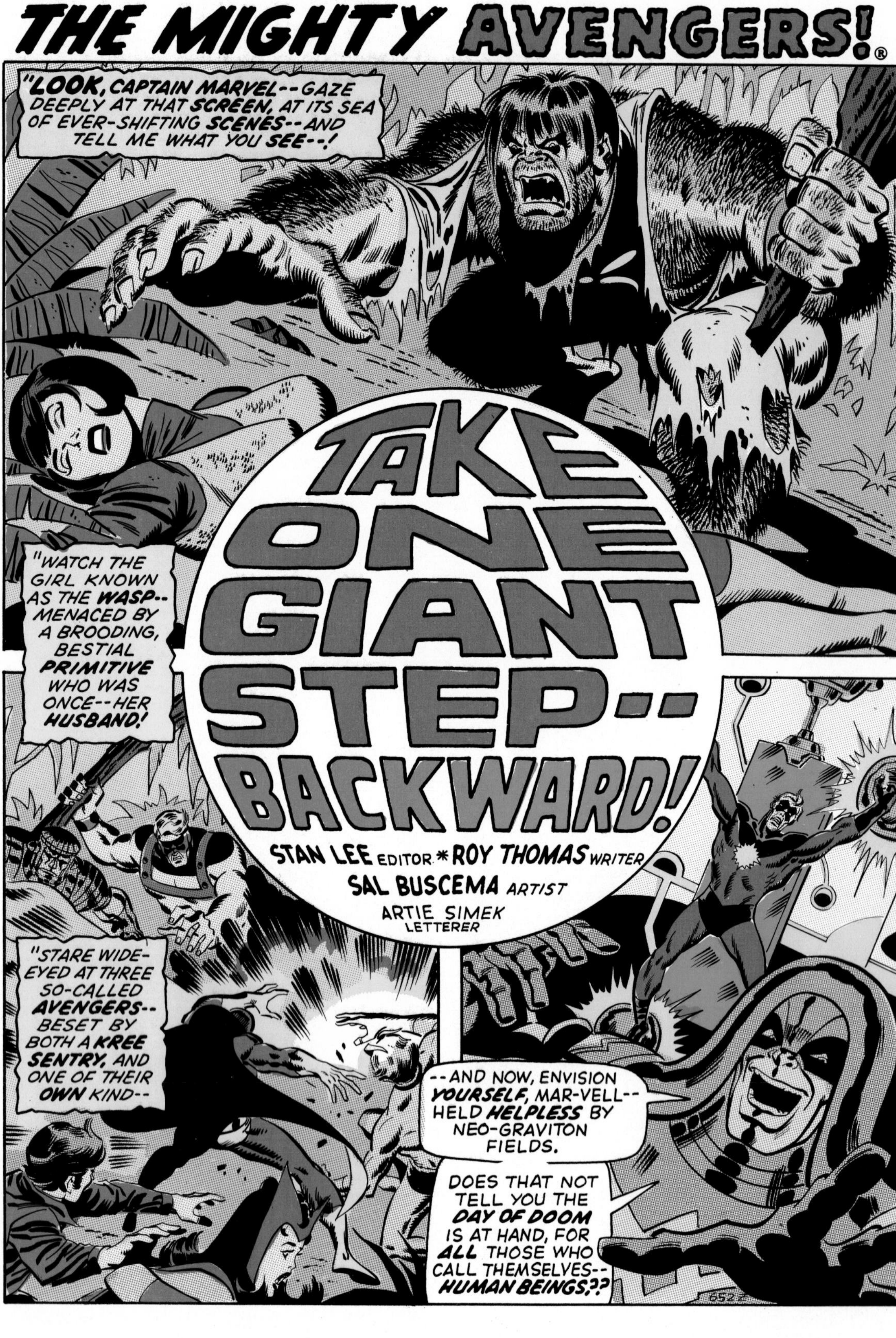
THE MIGHTY AVENGERS!®
"LOOK, CAPTAIN MARVEL--GAZE DEEPLY AT THAT SCREEN, AT ITS SEA OF EVER-SHIFTING SCENES--AND TELL ME WHAT YOU SEE--!
"WATCH THE GIRL KNOWN AS THE WASP--MENACED BY A BROODING, BESTIAL PRIMITIVE WHO WAS ONCE--HER HUSBAND!
TAKE ONE GIANT STEP.. BACKWARD!
STAN LEE EDITOR * ROY THOMAS WRITER
SAL BUSCEMA ARTIST
ARTIE SIMEK LETTERER
"STARE WIDE-EYED AT THREE SO-CALLED AVENGERS--BESET BY BOTH A KREE SENTRY, AND ONE OF THEIR OWN KIND--
--AND NOW, ENVISION YOURSELF, MAR-VELL--HELD HELPLESS BY NEO-GRAVITON FIELDS.
DOES THAT NOT TELL YOU THE DAY OF DOOM IS AT HAND, FOR ALL THOSE WHO CALL THEMSELVES--HUMAN BEINGS??

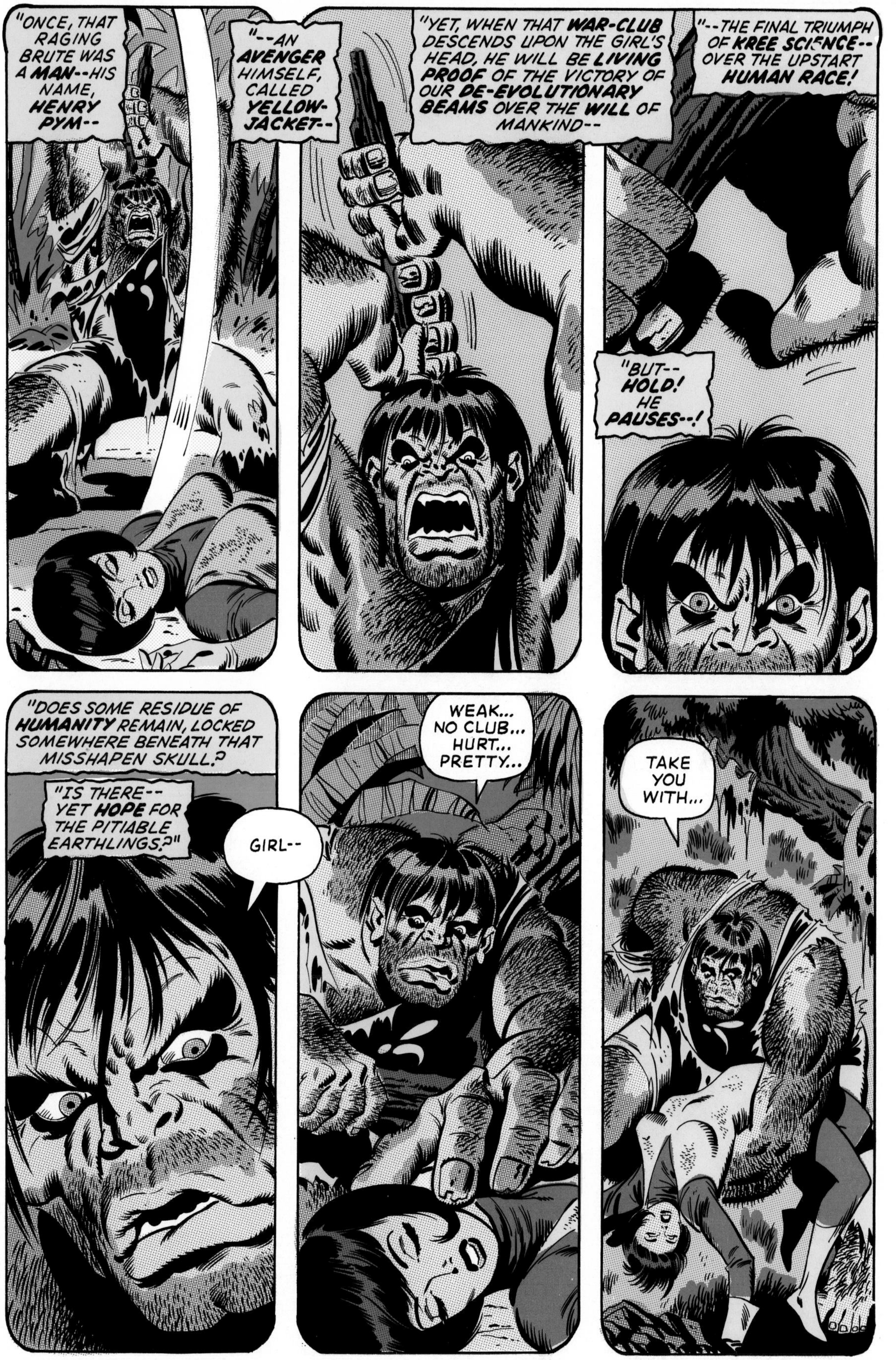
"ONCE, THAT RAGING BRUTE WAS A MAN--HIS NAME, HENRY PYM--
"--AN AVENGER HIMSELF, CALLED YELLOW-JACKET--
"YET, WHEN THAT WAR-CLUB DESCENDS UPON THE GIRL'S HEAD, HE WILL BE LIVING PROOF OF THE VICTORY OF OUR DE-EVOLUTIONARY BEAMS OVER THE WILL OF MANKIND--
"--THE FINAL TRIUMPH OF KREE SCIENCE--OVER THE UPSTART HUMAN RACE!
"BUT--HOLD! HE PAUSES--!
"DOES SOME RESIDUE OF HUMANITY REMAIN, LOCKED SOMEWHERE BENEATH THAT MISSHAPEN SKULL?
"IS THERE--YET HOPE FOR THE PITIABLE EARTHLINGS?"
GIRL--
WEAK... NO CLUB... HURT... PRETTY...
TAKE YOU WITH...

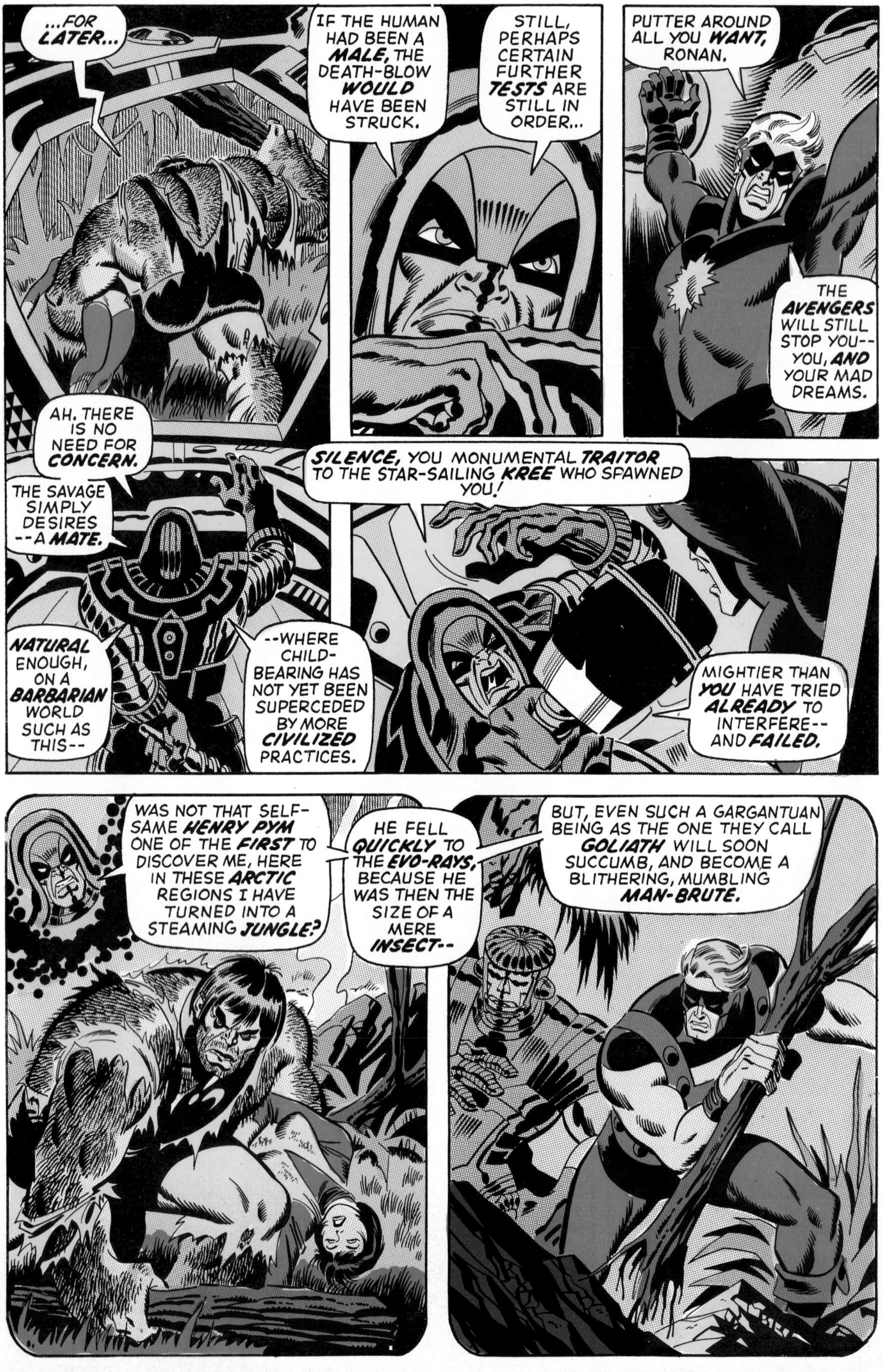

...FOR LATER...
IF THE HUMAN HAD BEEN A MALE, THE DEATH-BLOW WOULD HAVE BEEN STRUCK.
STILL, PERHAPS CERTAIN FURTHER TESTS ARE STILL IN ORDER...
PUTTER AROUND ALL YOU WANT, RONAN.
THE AVENGERS WILL STILL STOP YOU--YOU, AND YOUR MAD DREAMS.
AH. THERE IS NO NEED FOR CONCERN.
THE SAVAGE SIMPLY DESIRES --A MATE.
NATURAL ENOUGH, ON A BARBARIAN WORLD SUCH AS THIS--
--WHERE CHILD-BEARING HAS NOT YET BEEN SUPERCEDED BY MORE CIVILIZED PRACTICES.
SILENCE, YOU MONUMENTAL TRAITOR TO THE STAR-SAILING KREE WHO SPAWNED YOU!
MIGHTIER THAN YOU HAVE TRIED ALREADY TO INTERFERE--AND FAILED.
WAS NOT THAT SELF-SAME HENRY PYM ONE OF THE FIRST TO DISCOVER ME, HERE IN THESE ARCTIC REGIONS I HAVE TURNED INTO A STEAMING JUNGLE?
HE FELL QUICKLY TO THE EVO-RAYS, BECAUSE HE WAS THEN THE SIZE OF A MERE INSECT--
BUT, EVEN SUCH A GARGANTUAN BEING AS THE ONE THEY CALL GOLIATH WILL SOON SUCCUMB, AND BECOME A BLITHERING, MUMBLING MAN-BRUTE.

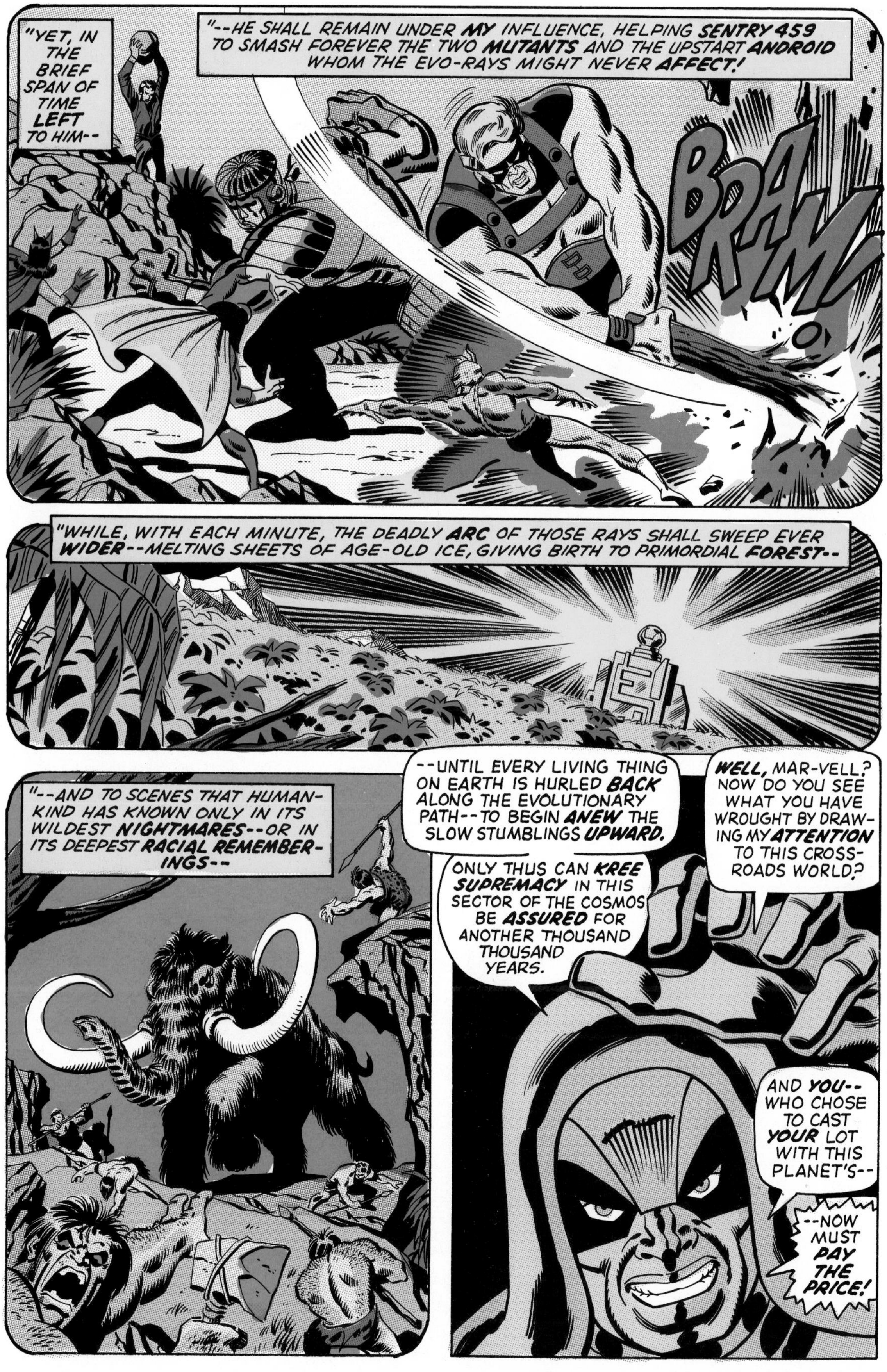
"YET, IN THE BRIEF SPAN OF TIME LEFT TO HIM--
"--HE SHALL REMAIN UNDER MY INFLUENCE, HELPING SENTRY 459 TO SMASH FOREVER THE TWO MUTANTS AND THE UPSTART ANDROID WHOM THE EVO-RAYS MIGHT NEVER AFFECT!
BRAM!
"WHILE, WITH EACH MINUTE, THE DEADLY ARC OF THOSE RAYS SHALL SWEEP EVER WIDER--MELTING SHEETS OF AGE-OLD ICE, GIVING BIRTH TO PRIMORDIAL FOREST--
"--AND TO SCENES THAT HUMAN-KIND HAS KNOWN ONLY IN ITS WILDEST NIGHTMARES--OR IN ITS DEEPEST RACIAL REMEMBER-INGS--
--UNTIL EVERY LIVING THING ON EARTH IS HURLED BACK ALONG THE EVOLUTIONARY PATH--TO BEGIN ANEW THE SLOW STUMBLINGS UPWARD.
ONLY THUS CAN KREE SUPREMACY IN THIS SECTOR OF THE COSMOS BE ASSURED FOR ANOTHER THOUSAND THOUSAND YEARS.
WELL, MAR-VELL? NOW DO YOU SEE WHAT YOU HAVE WROUGHT BY DRAWING MY ATTENTION TO THIS CROSS-ROADS WORLD?
AND YOU--WHO CHOSE TO CAST YOUR LOT WITH THIS PLANET'S--
--NOW MUST PAY THE PRICE!

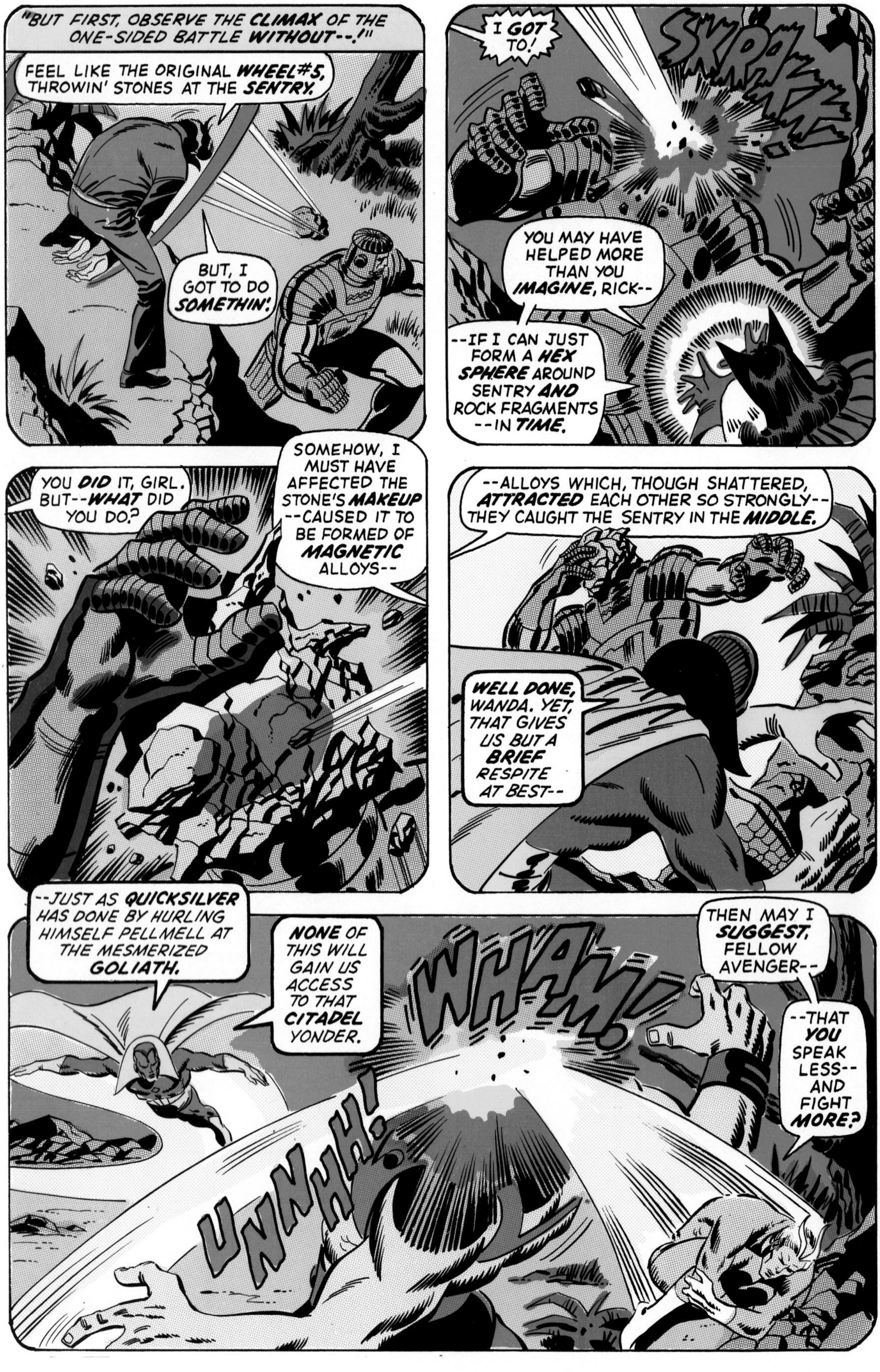
"BUT FIRST, OBSERVE THE CLIMAX OF THE ONE-SIDED BATTLE WITHOUT--!"
FEEL LIKE THE ORIGINAL WHEEL#5, THROWIN' STONES AT THE SENTRY.
BUT, I GOT TO DO SOMETHIN'.
I GOT TO!
SKRAK
YOU MAY HAVE HELPED MORE THAN YOU IMAGINE, RICK--
--IF I CAN JUST FORM A HEX SPHERE AROUND SENTRY AND ROCK FRAGMENTS --IN TIME.
YOU DID IT, GIRL. BUT--WHAT DID YOU DO?
SOMEHOW, I MUST HAVE AFFECTED THE STONE'S MAKEUP --CAUSED IT TO BE FORMED OF MAGNETIC ALLOYS--
--ALLOYS WHICH, THOUGH SHATTERED, ATTRACTED EACH OTHER SO STRONGLY-- THEY CAUGHT THE SENTRY IN THE MIDDLE.
WELL DONE, WANDA. YET, THAT GIVES US BUT A BRIEF RESPITE AT BEST--
--JUST AS QUICKSILVER HAS DONE BY HURLING HIMSELF PELLMELL AT THE MESMERIZED GOLIATH.
NONE OF THIS WILL GAIN US ACCESS TO THAT CITADEL YONDER.
WHAM!
THEN MAY I SUGGEST, FELLOW AVENGER--
--THAT YOU SPEAK LESS-- AND FIGHT MORE?
UNNHH!

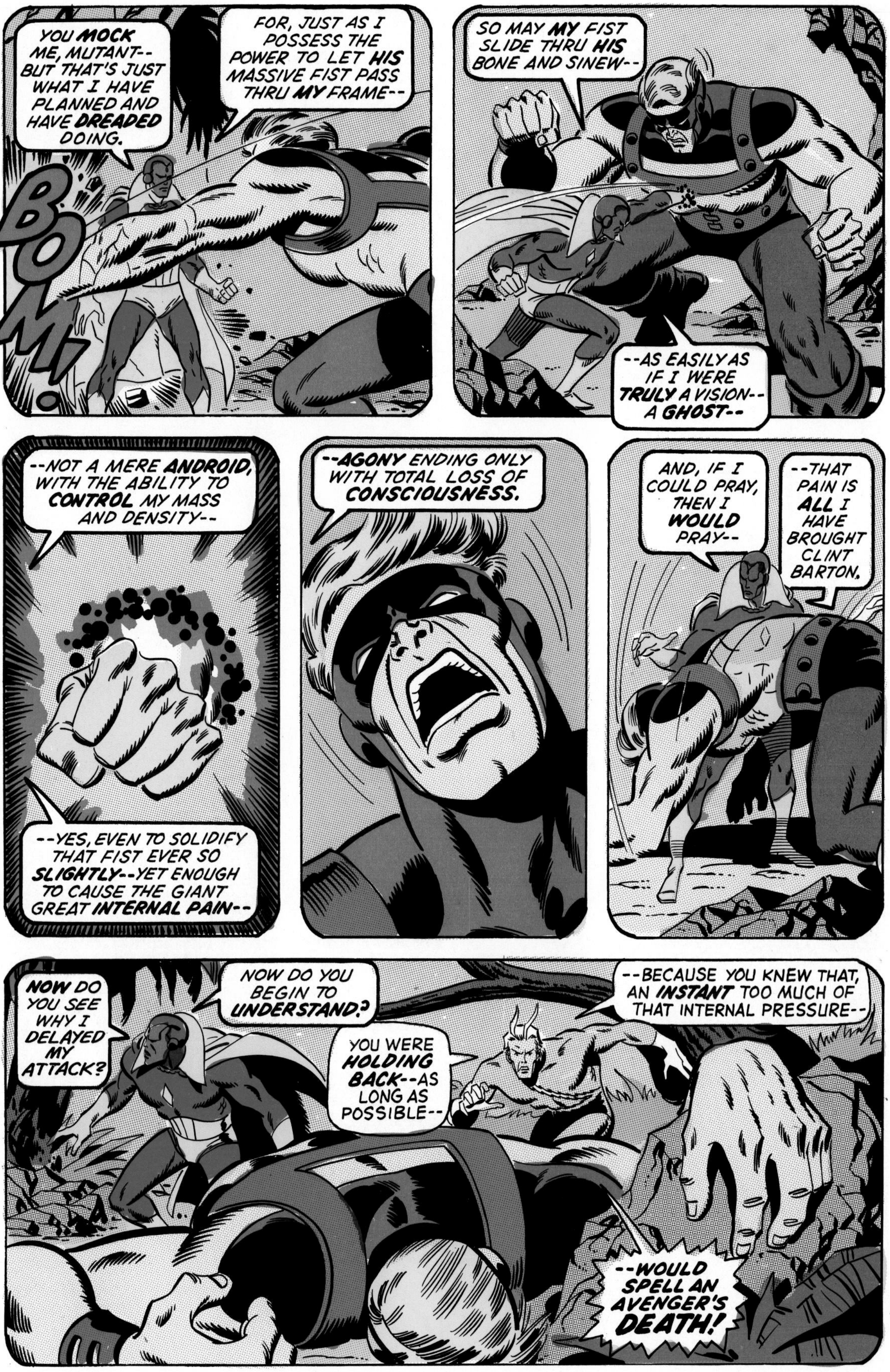
YOU MOCK ME, MUTANT-- BUT THAT'S JUST WHAT I HAVE PLANNED AND HAVE DREADED DOING.
BOOM!
FOR, JUST AS I POSSESS THE POWER TO LET HIS MASSIVE FIST PASS THRU MY FRAME--
SO MAY MY FIST SLIDE THRU HIS BONE AND SINEW--
--AS EASILY AS IF I WERE TRULY A VISION-- A GHOST--
--NOT A MERE ANDROID, WITH THE ABILITY TO CONTROL MY MASS AND DENSITY--
--YES, EVEN TO SOLIDIFY THAT FIST EVER SO SLIGHTLY--YET ENOUGH TO CAUSE THE GIANT GREAT INTERNAL PAIN--
--AGONY ENDING ONLY WITH TOTAL LOSS OF CONSCIOUSNESS.
AND, IF I COULD PRAY, THEN I WOULD PRAY--
--THAT PAIN IS ALL I HAVE BROUGHT CLINT BARTON.
NOW DO YOU SEE WHY I DELAYED MY ATTACK?
NOW DO YOU BEGIN TO UNDERSTAND?
YOU WERE HOLDING BACK--AS LONG AS POSSIBLE--
--BECAUSE YOU KNEW THAT, AN INSTANT TOO MUCH OF THAT INTERNAL PRESSURE--
--WOULD SPELL AN AVENGER'S DEATH!

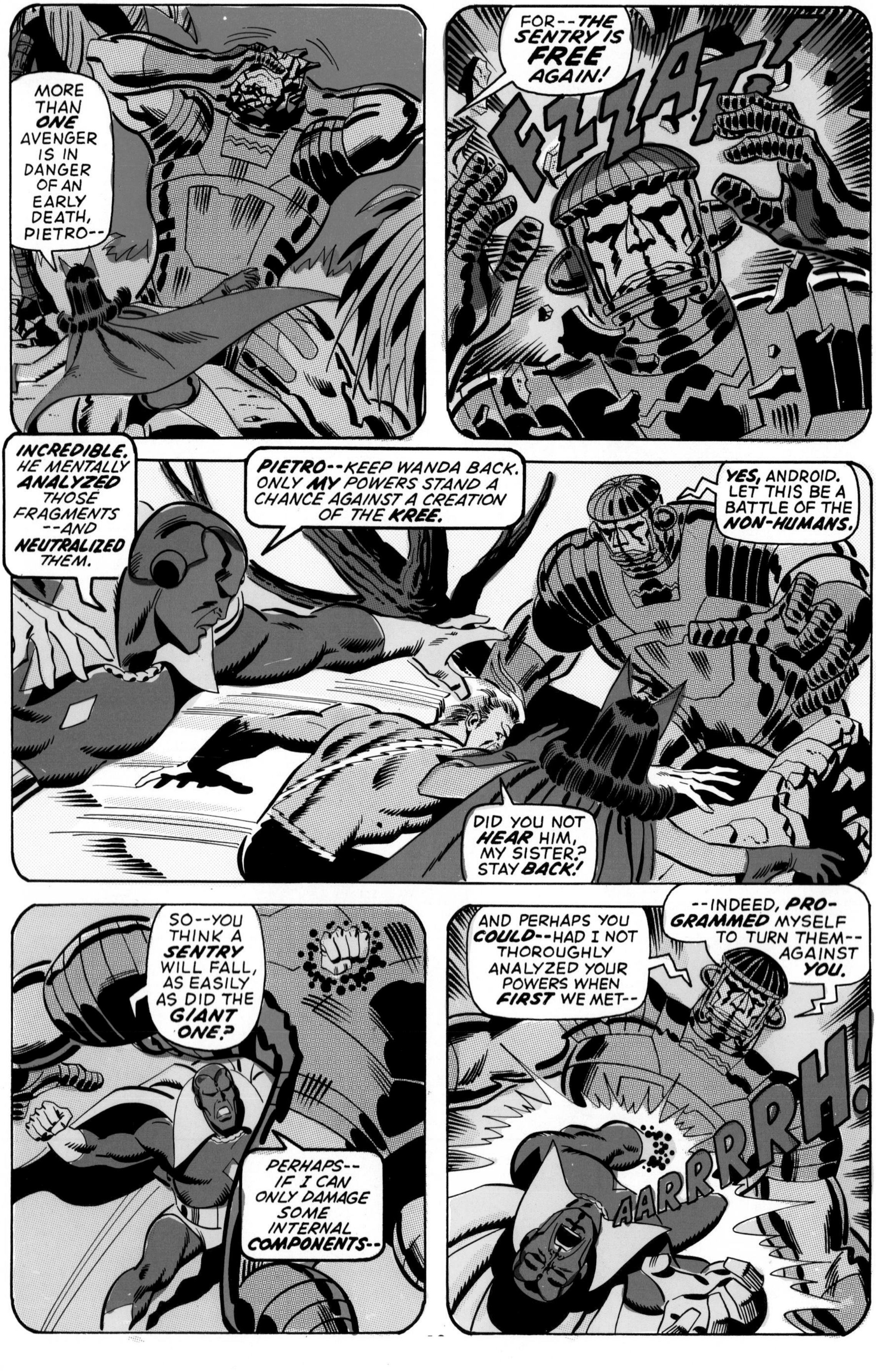

MORE THAN ONE AVENGER IS IN DANGER OF AN EARLY DEATH, PIETRO--
FOR--THE SENTRY IS FREE AGAIN!
FZZZAT!
INCREDIBLE. HE MENTALLY ANALYZED THOSE FRAGMENTS --AND NEUTRALIZED THEM.
PIETRO--KEEP WANDA BACK. ONLY MY POWERS STAND A CHANCE AGAINST A CREATION OF THE KREE.
YES, ANDROID. LET THIS BE A BATTLE OF THE NON-HUMANS.
DID YOU NOT HEAR HIM, MY SISTER? STAY BACK!
SO--YOU THINK A SENTRY WILL FALL, AS EASILY AS DID THE GIANT ONE?
PERHAPS-- IF I CAN ONLY DAMAGE SOME INTERNAL COMPONENTS--
AND PERHAPS YOU COULD--HAD I NOT THOROUGHLY ANALYZED YOUR POWERS WHEN FIRST WE MET--
--INDEED, PRO-GRAMMED MYSELF TO TURN THEM-- AGAINST YOU.
AARRRRRH!

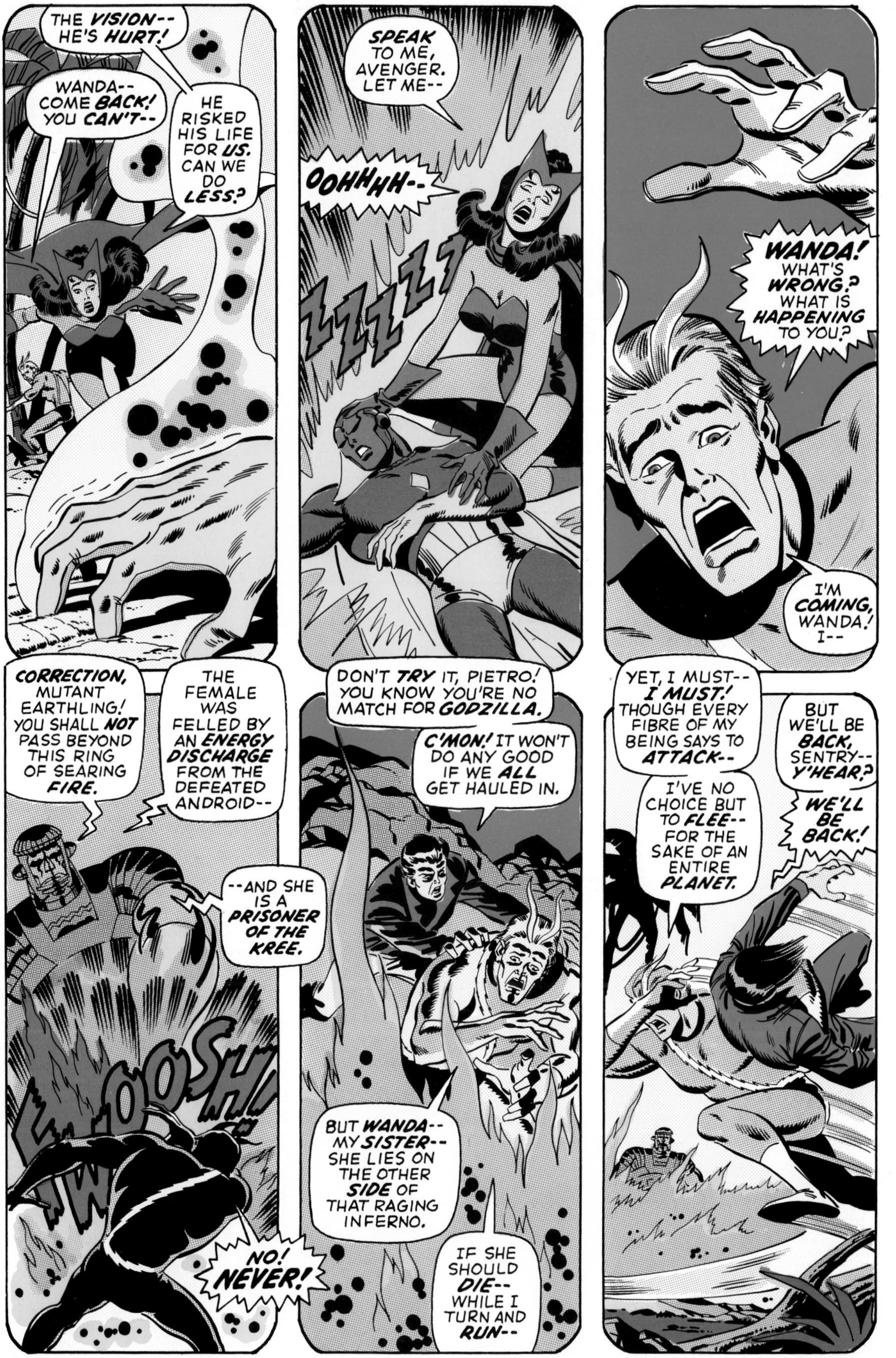
THE VISION-- HE'S HURT!
WANDA-- COME BACK! YOU CAN'T--
HE RISKED HIS LIFE FOR US. CAN WE DO LESS?
SPEAK TO ME, AVENGER. LET ME--
OOHHHHH--
ZZZZZT
WANDA! WHAT'S WRONG? WHAT IS HAPPENING TO YOU?
I'M COMING, WANDA! I--
CORRECTION, MUTANT EARTHLING! YOU SHALL NOT PASS BEYOND THIS RING OF SEARING FIRE.
THE FEMALE WAS FELLED BY AN ENERGY DISCHARGE FROM THE DEFEATED ANDROID--
--AND SHE IS A PRISONER OF THE KREE.
WHOOSH!
NO! NEVER!
DON'T TRY IT, PIETRO! YOU KNOW YOU'RE NO MATCH FOR GODZILLA.
C'MON! IT WON'T DO ANY GOOD IF WE ALL GET HAULED IN.
BUT WANDA-- MY SISTER-- SHE LIES ON THE OTHER SIDE OF THAT RAGING INFERNO.
IF SHE SHOULD DIE-- WHILE I TURN AND RUN--
YET, I MUST-- I MUST! THOUGH EVERY FIBRE OF MY BEING SAYS TO ATTACK--
I'VE NO CHOICE BUT TO FLEE-- FOR THE SAKE OF AN ENTIRE PLANET.
BUT WE'LL BE BACK, SENTRY-- Y'HEAR?
WE'LL BE BACK!

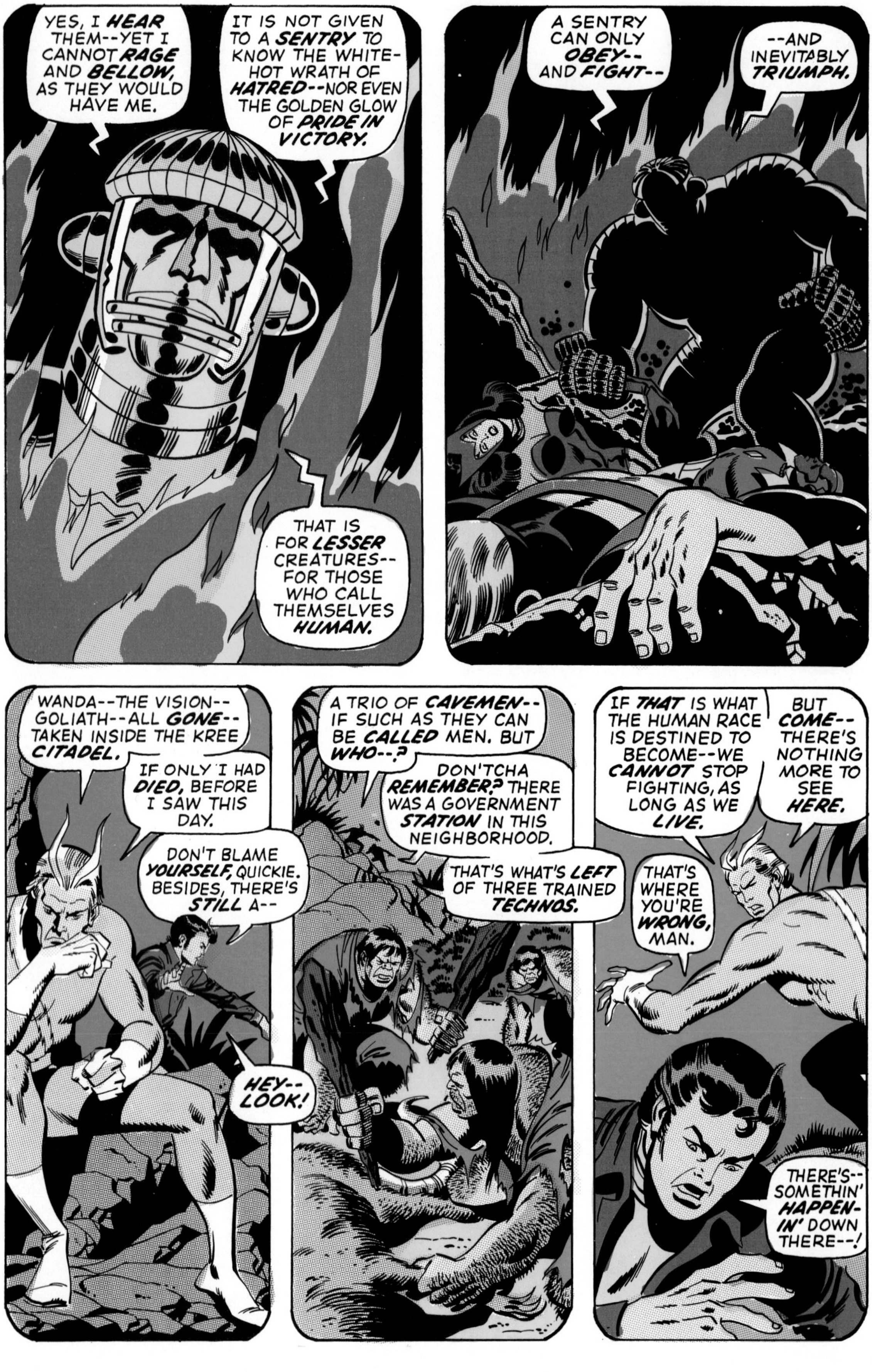

YES, I HEAR THEM--YET I CANNOT RAGE AND BELLOW, AS THEY WOULD HAVE ME.
IT IS NOT GIVEN TO A SENTRY TO KNOW THE WHITE-HOT WRATH OF HATRED--NOR EVEN THE GOLDEN GLOW OF PRIDE IN VICTORY.
THAT IS FOR LESSER CREATURES--FOR THOSE WHO CALL THEMSELVES HUMAN.
A SENTRY CAN ONLY OBEY--AND FIGHT--
--AND INEVITABLY TRIUMPH.
WANDA--THE VISION--GOLIATH--ALL GONE--TAKEN INSIDE THE KREE CITADEL.
IF ONLY I HAD DIED, BEFORE I SAW THIS DAY.
DON'T BLAME YOURSELF, QUICKIE. BESIDES, THERE'S STILL A--
HEY--LOOK!
A TRIO OF CAVEMEN--IF SUCH AS THEY CAN BE CALLED MEN. BUT WHO--?
DON'TCHA REMEMBER? THERE WAS A GOVERNMENT STATION IN THIS NEIGHBORHOOD.
THAT'S WHAT'S LEFT OF THREE TRAINED TECHNOS.
IF THAT IS WHAT THE HUMAN RACE IS DESTINED TO BECOME--WE CANNOT STOP FIGHTING, AS LONG AS WE LIVE.
BUT COME--THERE'S NOTHING MORE TO SEE HERE.
THAT'S WHERE YOU'RE WRONG, MAN.
THERE'S--SOMETHIN' HAPPEN-IN' DOWN THERE--!

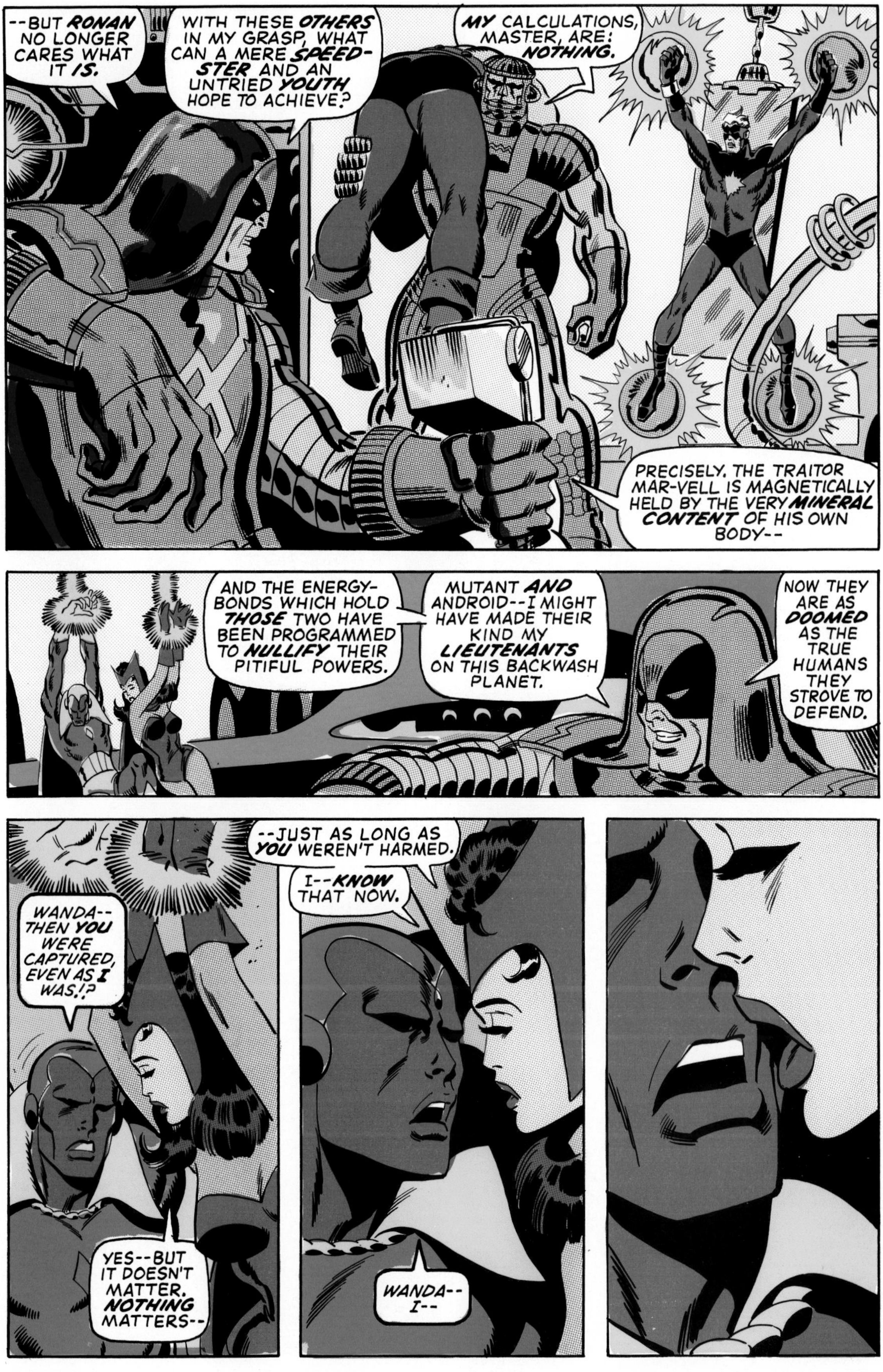
--BUT RONAN NO LONGER CARES WHAT IT IS.
WITH THESE OTHERS IN MY GRASP, WHAT CAN A MERE SPEED-STER AND AN UNTRIED YOUTH HOPE TO ACHIEVE?
MY CALCULATIONS, MASTER, ARE: NOTHING.
PRECISELY. THE TRAITOR MAR-VELL IS MAGNETICALLY HELD BY THE VERY MINERAL CONTENT OF HIS OWN BODY--
AND THE ENERGY-BONDS WHICH HOLD THOSE TWO HAVE BEEN PROGRAMMED TO NULLIFY THEIR PITIFUL POWERS.
MUTANT AND ANDROID--I MIGHT HAVE MADE THEIR KIND MY LIEUTENANTS ON THIS BACKWASH PLANET.
NOW THEY ARE AS DOOMED AS THE TRUE HUMANS THEY STROVE TO DEFEND.
WANDA--THEN YOU WERE CAPTURED, EVEN AS I WAS.!?
YES--BUT IT DOESN'T MATTER. NOTHING MATTERS--
--JUST AS LONG AS YOU WEREN'T HARMED.
I--KNOW THAT NOW.
WANDA--I--

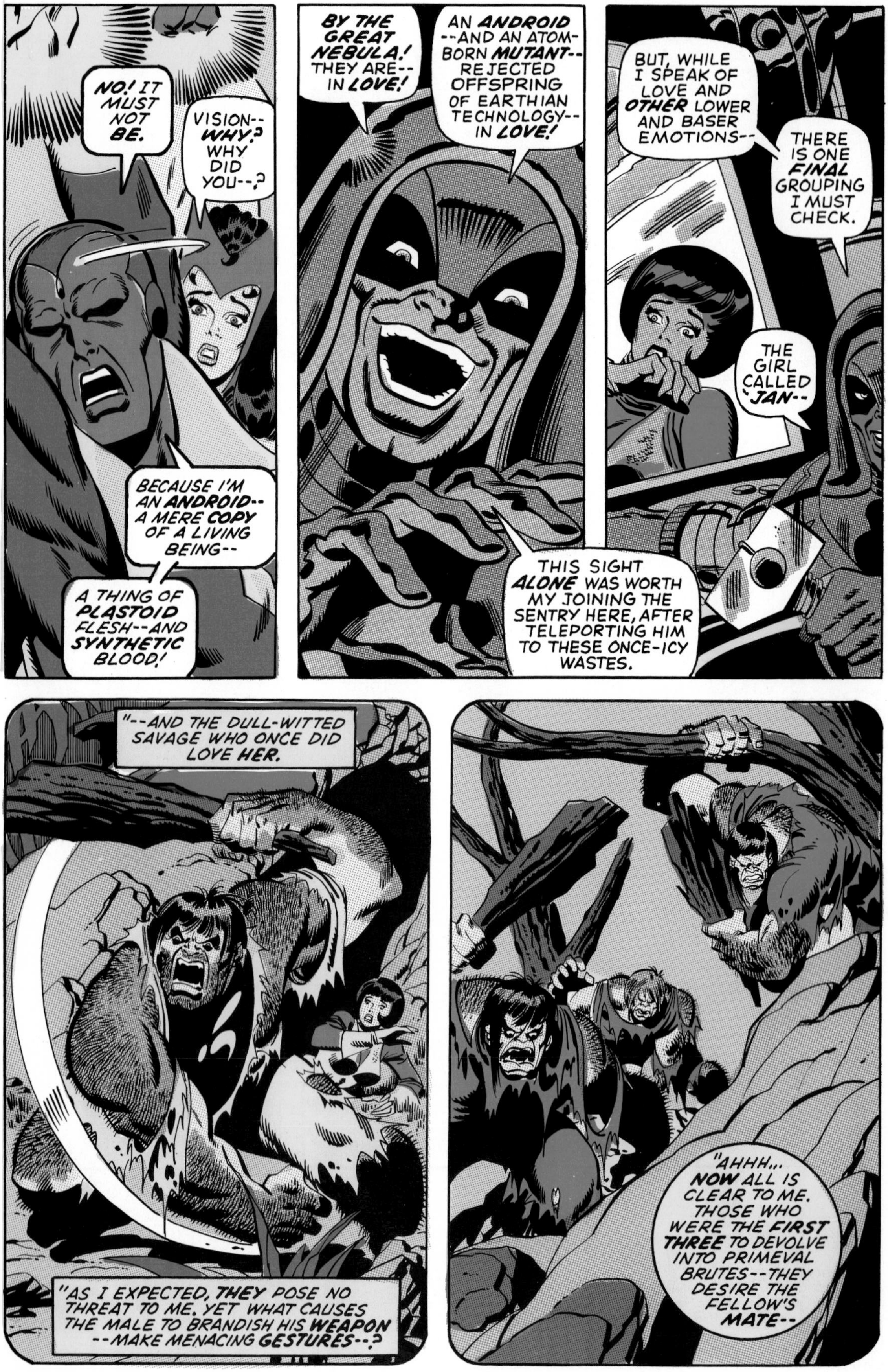
NO! IT MUST NOT BE.
VISION--WHY? WHY DID YOU--?
BECAUSE I'M AN ANDROID--A MERE COPY OF A LIVING BEING--
A THING OF PLASTOID FLESH--AND SYNTHETIC BLOOD!
BY THE GREAT NEBULA! THEY ARE--IN LOVE!
AN ANDROID--AND AN ATOM-BORN MUTANT--REJECTED OFFSPRING OF EARTHIAN TECHNOLOGY--IN LOVE!
THIS SIGHT ALONE WAS WORTH MY JOINING THE SENTRY HERE, AFTER TELEPORTING HIM TO THESE ONCE-ICY WASTES.
BUT, WHILE I SPEAK OF LOVE AND OTHER LOWER AND BASER EMOTIONS--
THERE IS ONE FINAL GROUPING I MUST CHECK.
THE GIRL CALLED "JAN--
"--AND THE DULL-WITTED SAVAGE WHO ONCE DID LOVE HER.
"AS I EXPECTED, THEY POSE NO THREAT TO ME. YET WHAT CAUSES THE MALE TO BRANDISH HIS WEAPON--MAKE MENACING GESTURES--?
"AHHH... NOW ALL IS CLEAR TO ME. THOSE WHO WERE THE FIRST THREE TO DEVOLVE INTO PRIMEVAL BRUTES--THEY DESIRE THE FELLOW'S MATE--

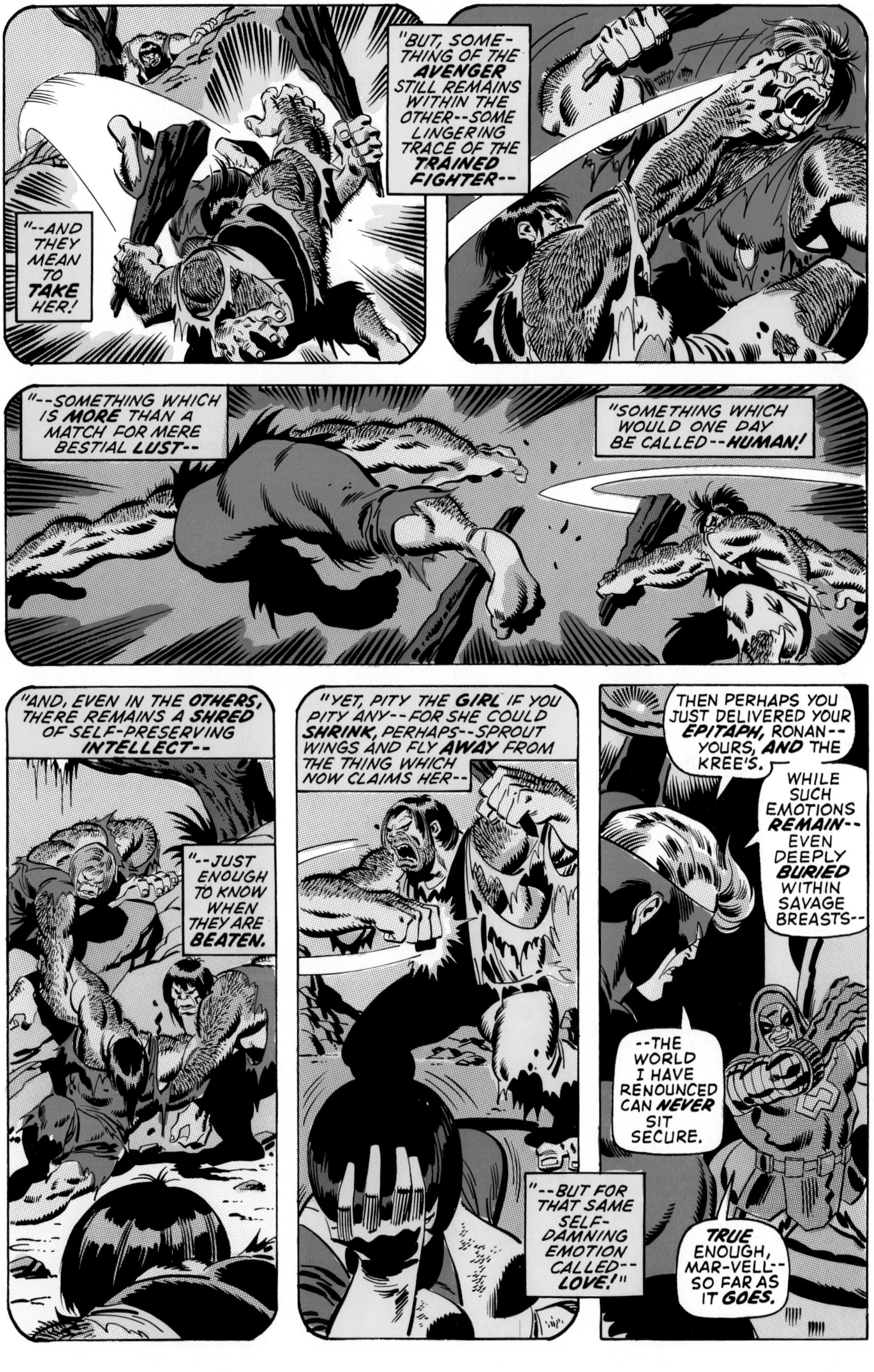
"BUT, SOMETHING OF THE AVENGER STILL REMAINS WITHIN THE OTHER--SOME LINGERING TRACE OF THE TRAINED FIGHTER--
"--AND THEY MEAN TO TAKE HER!
"--SOMETHING WHICH IS MORE THAN A MATCH FOR MERE BESTIAL LUST--
"SOMETHING WHICH WOULD ONE DAY BE CALLED--HUMAN!
"AND, EVEN IN THE OTHERS, THERE REMAINS A SHRED OF SELF-PRESERVING INTELLECT--
"--JUST ENOUGH TO KNOW WHEN THEY ARE BEATEN.
"YET, PITY THE GIRL IF YOU PITY ANY--FOR SHE COULD SHRINK, PERHAPS--SPROUT WINGS AND FLY AWAY FROM THE THING WHICH NOW CLAIMS HER--
"--BUT FOR THAT SAME SELF-DAMNING EMOTION CALLED--LOVE!"
THEN PERHAPS YOU JUST DELIVERED YOUR EPITAPH, RONAN--YOURS, AND THE KREE'S.
WHILE SUCH EMOTIONS REMAIN--EVEN DEEPLY BURIED WITHIN SAVAGE BREASTS--
--THE WORLD I HAVE RENOUNCED CAN NEVER SIT SECURE.
TRUE ENOUGH, MAR-VELL--SO FAR AS IT GOES.

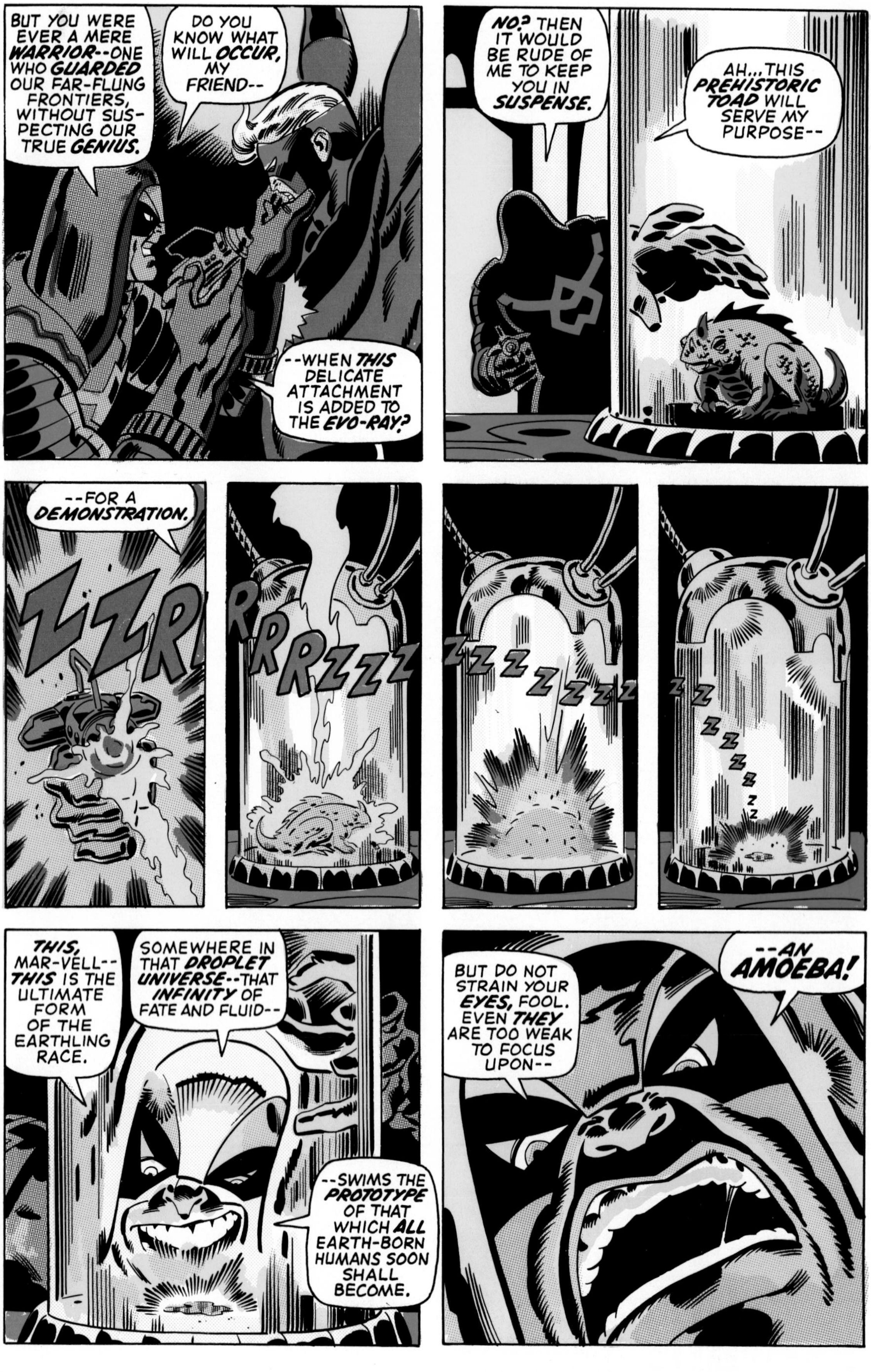
BUT YOU WERE EVER A MERE WARRIOR--ONE WHO GUARDED OUR FAR-FLUNG FRONTIERS, WITHOUT SUSPECTING OUR TRUE GENIUS.
DO YOU KNOW WHAT WILL OCCUR, MY FRIEND--
--WHEN THIS DELICATE ATTACHMENT IS ADDED TO THE EVO-RAY?
NO? THEN IT WOULD BE RUDE OF ME TO KEEP YOU IN SUSPENSE.
AH...THIS PREHISTORIC TOAD WILL SERVE MY PURPOSE--
--FOR A DEMONSTRATION.
ZZRRRRRZZZZ
ZZZZZZZZ
ZZZZZZZ
THIS, MAR-VELL--THIS IS THE ULTIMATE FORM OF THE EARTHLING RACE.
SOMEWHERE IN THAT DROPLET UNIVERSE--THAT INFINITY OF FATE AND FLUID--
--SWIMS THE PROTOTYPE OF THAT WHICH ALL EARTH-BORN HUMANS SOON SHALL BECOME.
BUT DO NOT STRAIN YOUR EYES, FOOL. EVEN THEY ARE TOO WEAK TO FOCUS UPON--
--AN AMOEBA!

SO, *STRAIN* ALL YOU WANT, MY *DEAR* CAPTAIN--

AYE, *CRY OUT* LOUD ENOUGH TO BE HEARD IN THE FAR-OFF *KREE GALAXY* ITSELF--

MANKIND IS NONETHELESS *DOOMED*-- DOOMED TO RETURN TO THE MUCK AND THE MIRE!

...*COME, RICK.* HERE IS THE CITADEL OF OUR HATED *ENEMY.*

WE CAN'T GET IN *THERE.* THE PLACE IS TIGHT AS A *DRUM.*

WE *WILL* GET IN. WE *MUST* GET IN.

FOR THE SAKE OF MY *SISTER*-- FOR THE SAKE OF THE *WORLD.*

AHH... THIS METAL *BAR....!*

THERE ARE THOSE WHO THINK MY MUTANT SPEED A *USELESS* WEAPON --A MERE TRICK GOOD FOR CARRY- ING *MESSAGES,* AND NOTHING MORE.

TODAY WE SHALL SEE--

--IF IT MAY BE *FAR, FAR MORE!!*

*FAAAN-*TASTIC!

ZZZZZZZZZZZZZZZZZZZ

iRAT!

HE PLOWED THAT BAR THRU THE WALL LIKE A *STRAW* THRU A TREE IN A *HURRICANE*--

--OR THE *GREEN BAY PACKERS* THRU A *HIGH SCHOOL DEFENSE!*

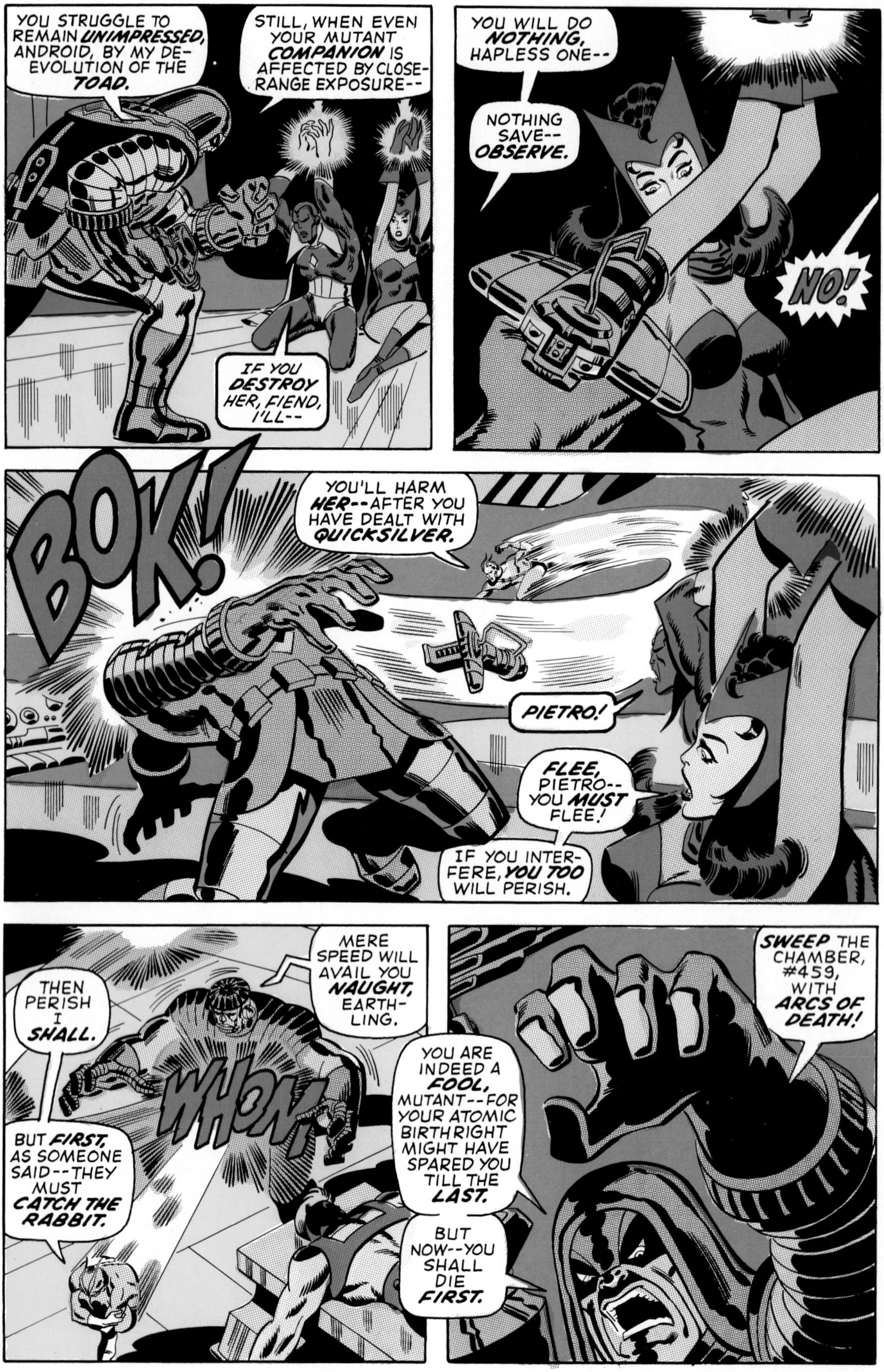
YOU STRUGGLE TO REMAIN UNIMPRESSED, ANDROID, BY MY DE-EVOLUTION OF THE TOAD.
STILL, WHEN EVEN YOUR MUTANT COMPANION IS AFFECTED BY CLOSE-RANGE EXPOSURE--
IF YOU DESTROY HER, FIEND, I'LL--
YOU WILL DO NOTHING, HAPLESS ONE--
NOTHING SAVE-- OBSERVE.
NO!
BOK!
YOU'LL HARM HER--AFTER YOU HAVE DEALT WITH QUICKSILVER.
PIETRO!
FLEE, PIETRO-- YOU MUST FLEE!
IF YOU INTER-FERE, YOU TOO WILL PERISH.
THEN PERISH I SHALL.
MERE SPEED WILL AVAIL YOU NAUGHT, EARTH-LING.
WHOM!
BUT FIRST, AS SOMEONE SAID--THEY MUST CATCH THE RABBIT.
YOU ARE INDEED A FOOL, MUTANT--FOR YOUR ATOMIC BIRTHRIGHT MIGHT HAVE SPARED YOU TILL THE LAST.
BUT NOW--YOU SHALL DIE FIRST.
SWEEP THE CHAMBER, #459, WITH ARCS OF DEATH!

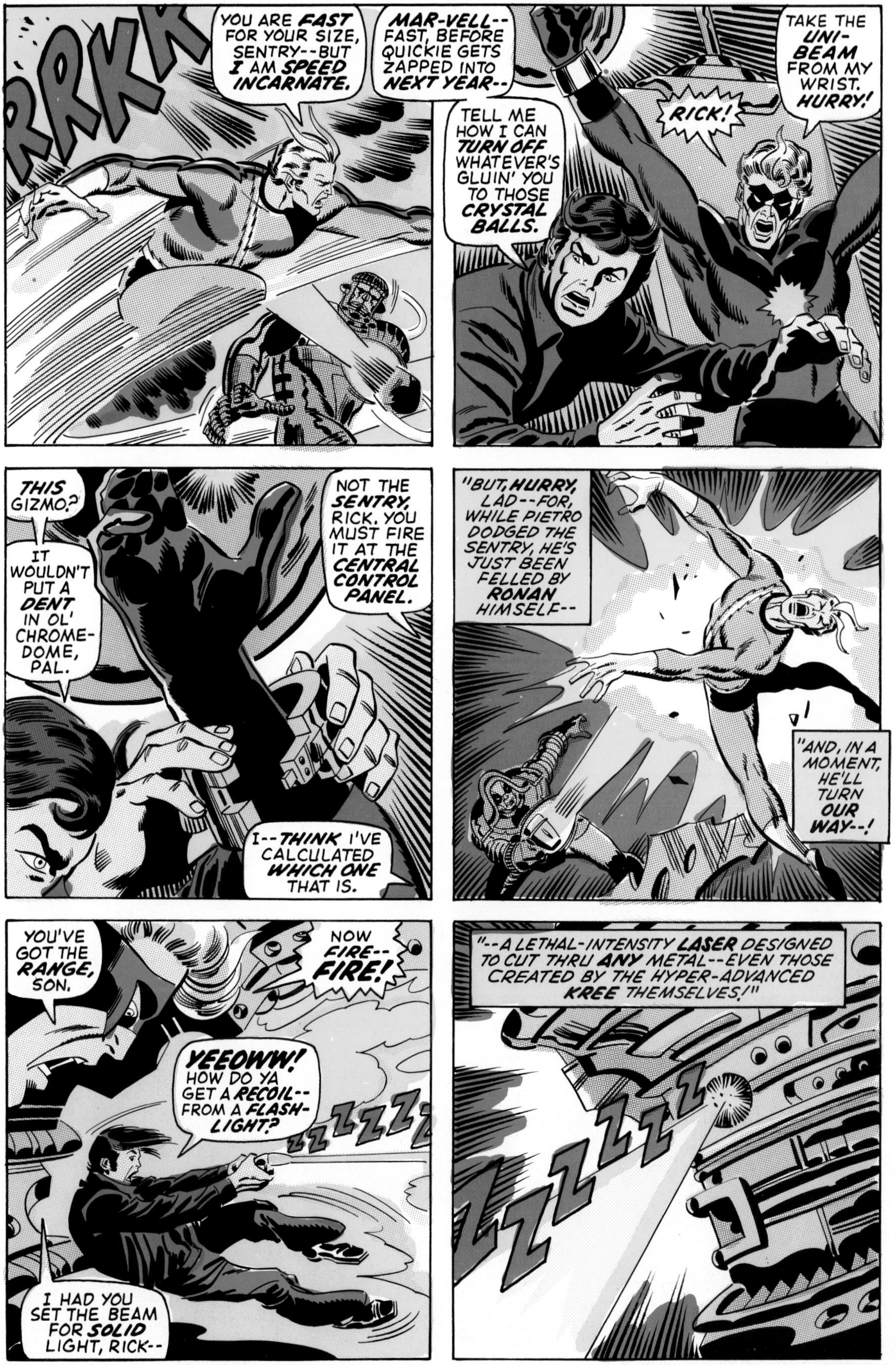
RRKK
YOU ARE FAST FOR YOUR SIZE, SENTRY--BUT I AM SPEED INCARNATE.
MAR-VELL--FAST, BEFORE QUICKIE GETS ZAPPED INTO NEXT YEAR--
TELL ME HOW I CAN TURN OFF WHATEVER'S GLUIN' YOU TO THOSE CRYSTAL BALLS.
RICK!
TAKE THE UNI-BEAM FROM MY WRIST. HURRY!
THIS GIZMO?
IT WOULDN'T PUT A DENT IN OL' CHROME-DOME, PAL.
NOT THE SENTRY, RICK. YOU MUST FIRE IT AT THE CENTRAL CONTROL PANEL.
I--THINK I'VE CALCULATED WHICH ONE THAT IS.
"BUT, HURRY, LAD--FOR, WHILE PIETRO DODGED THE SENTRY, HE'S JUST BEEN FELLED BY RONAN HIMSELF--
"AND, IN A MOMENT, HE'LL TURN OUR WAY--!
YOU'VE GOT THE RANGE, SON.
NOW FIRE--FIRE!
YEEOWW! HOW DO YA GET A RECOIL--FROM A FLASH-LIGHT?
ZZZZZZ
I HAD YOU SET THE BEAM FOR SOLID LIGHT, RICK--
"--A LETHAL-INTENSITY LASER DESIGNED TO CUT THRU ANY METAL--EVEN THOSE CREATED BY THE HYPER-ADVANCED KREE THEMSELVES!"
ZZZZZZZZZ

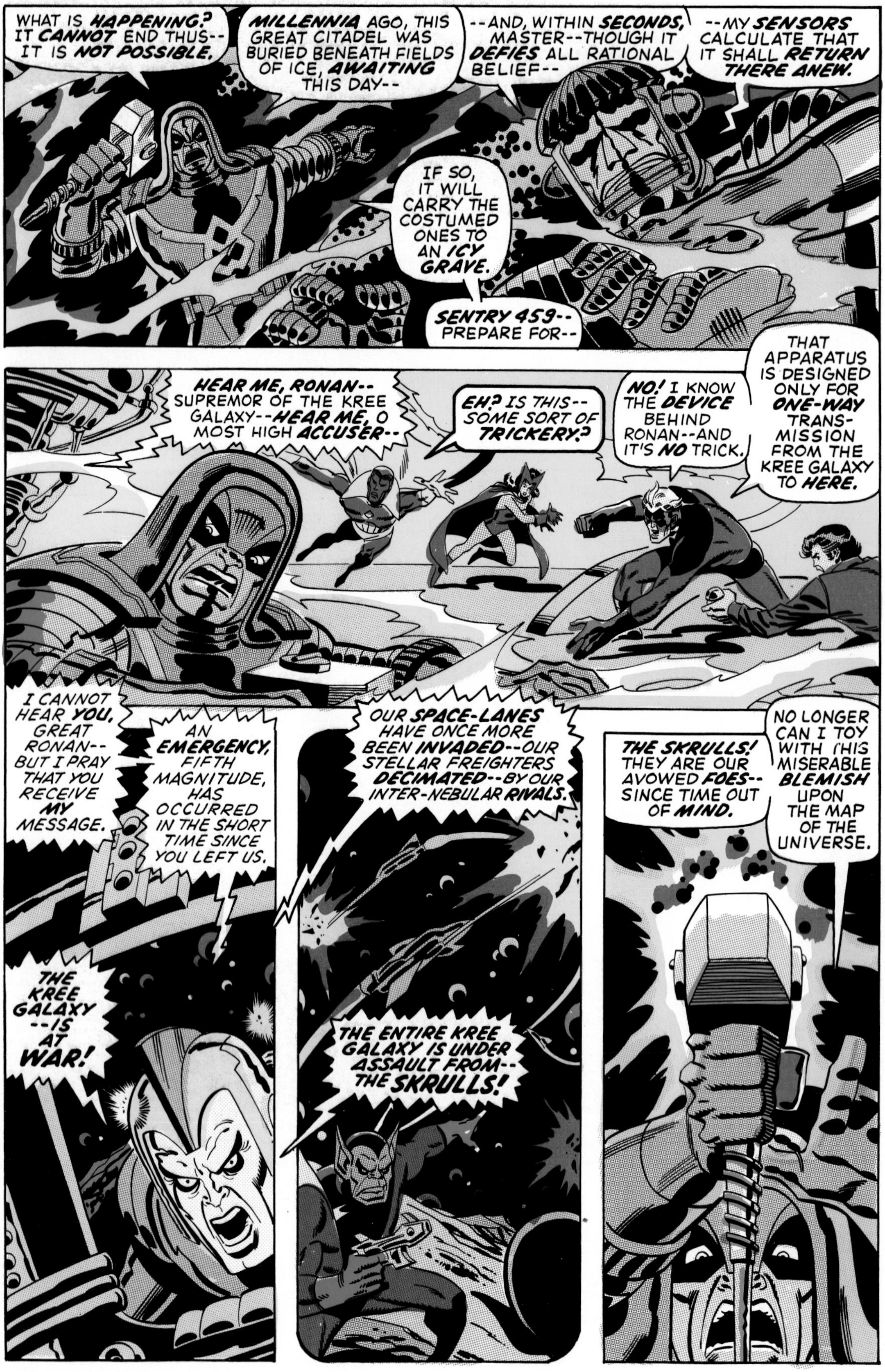
WHAT IS HAPPENING? IT CANNOT END THUS-- IT IS NOT POSSIBLE.
MILLENNIA AGO, THIS GREAT CITADEL WAS BURIED BENEATH FIELDS OF ICE, AWAITING THIS DAY--
--AND, WITHIN SECONDS, MASTER--THOUGH IT DEFIES ALL RATIONAL BELIEF--
--MY SENSORS CALCULATE THAT IT SHALL RETURN THERE ANEW.
IF SO, IT WILL CARRY THE COSTUMED ONES TO AN ICY GRAVE.
SENTRY 459-- PREPARE FOR--
HEAR ME, RONAN-- SUPREMOR OF THE KREE GALAXY--HEAR ME, O MOST HIGH ACCUSER--
EH? IS THIS-- SOME SORT OF TRICKERY?
NO! I KNOW THE DEVICE BEHIND RONAN--AND IT'S NO TRICK.
THAT APPARATUS IS DESIGNED ONLY FOR ONE-WAY TRANSMISSION FROM THE KREE GALAXY TO HERE.
I CANNOT HEAR YOU, GREAT RONAN-- BUT I PRAY THAT YOU RECEIVE MY MESSAGE.
AN EMERGENCY, FIFTH MAGNITUDE, HAS OCCURRED IN THE SHORT TIME SINCE YOU LEFT US.
THE KREE GALAXY --IS AT WAR!
OUR SPACE-LANES HAVE ONCE MORE BEEN INVADED--OUR STELLAR FREIGHTERS DECIMATED--BY OUR INTER-NEBULAR RIVALS.
THE ENTIRE KREE GALAXY IS UNDER ASSAULT FROM-- THE SKRULLS!
THE SKRULLS! THEY ARE OUR AVOWED FOES-- SINCE TIME OUT OF MIND.
NO LONGER CAN I TOY WITH THIS MISERABLE BLEMISH UPON THE MAP OF THE UNIVERSE.

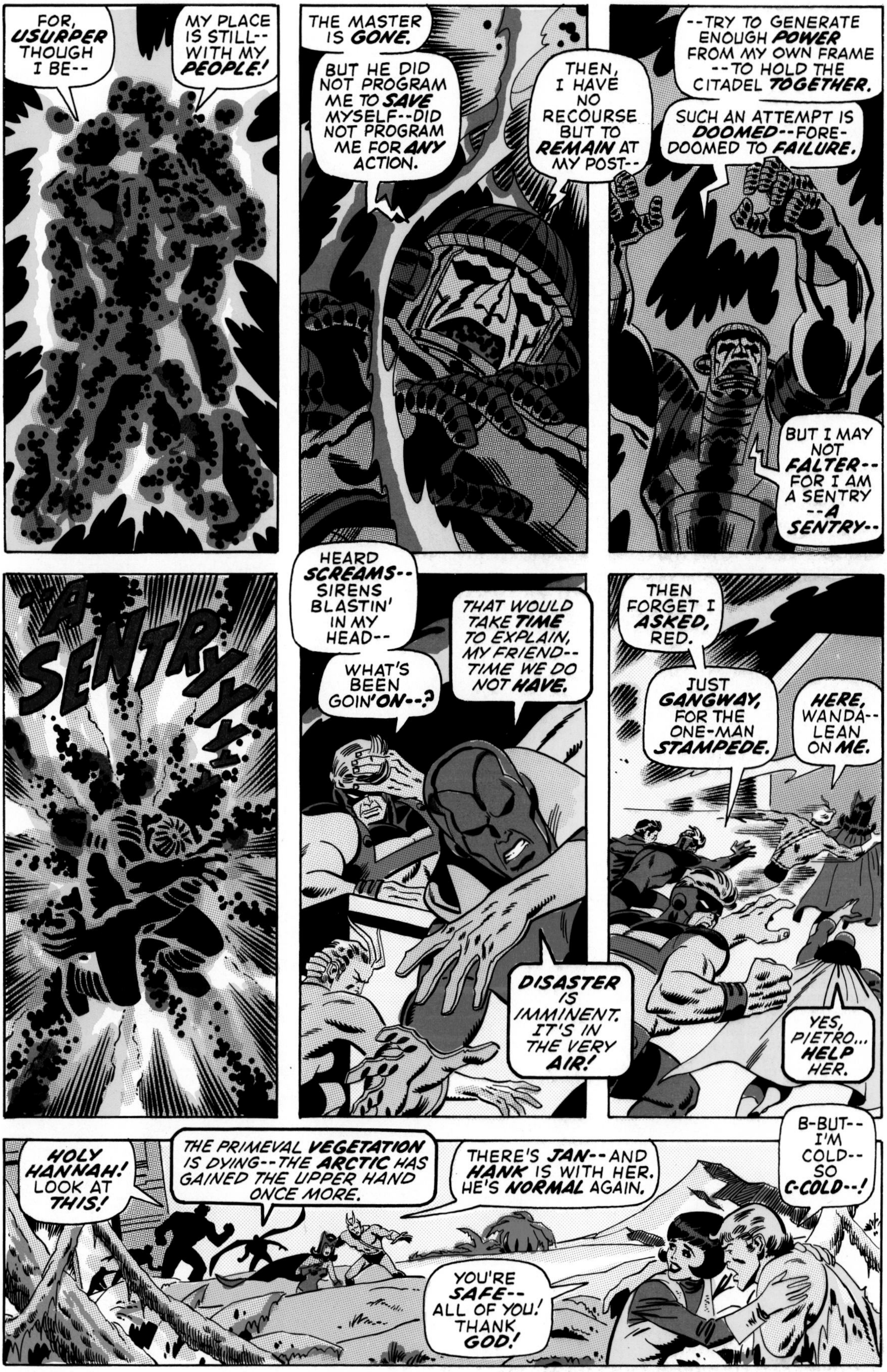
FOR, USURPER THOUGH I BE--
MY PLACE IS STILL-- WITH MY PEOPLE!
THE MASTER IS GONE.
BUT HE DID NOT PROGRAM ME TO SAVE MYSELF--DID NOT PROGRAM ME FOR ANY ACTION.
THEN, I HAVE NO RECOURSE BUT TO REMAIN AT MY POST--
--TRY TO GENERATE ENOUGH POWER FROM MY OWN FRAME --TO HOLD THE CITADEL TOGETHER.
SUCH AN ATTEMPT IS DOOMED--FORE-DOOMED TO FAILURE.
BUT I MAY NOT FALTER--FOR I AM A SENTRY --A SENTRY--
--A SENTRYY!
HEARD SCREAMS--SIRENS BLASTIN' IN MY HEAD--
WHAT'S BEEN GOIN' ON--?
THAT WOULD TAKE TIME TO EXPLAIN, MY FRIEND--TIME WE DO NOT HAVE.
DISASTER IS IMMINENT. IT'S IN THE VERY AIR!
THEN FORGET I ASKED, RED.
JUST GANGWAY, FOR THE ONE-MAN STAMPEDE.
HERE, WANDA--LEAN ON ME.
YES, PIETRO... HELP HER.
HOLY HANNAH! LOOK AT THIS!
THE PRIMEVAL VEGETATION IS DYING--THE ARCTIC HAS GAINED THE UPPER HAND ONCE MORE.
THERE'S JAN--AND HANK IS WITH HER. HE'S NORMAL AGAIN.
B-BUT--I'M COLD--SO C-COLD--!
YOU'RE SAFE--ALL OF YOU! THANK GOD!

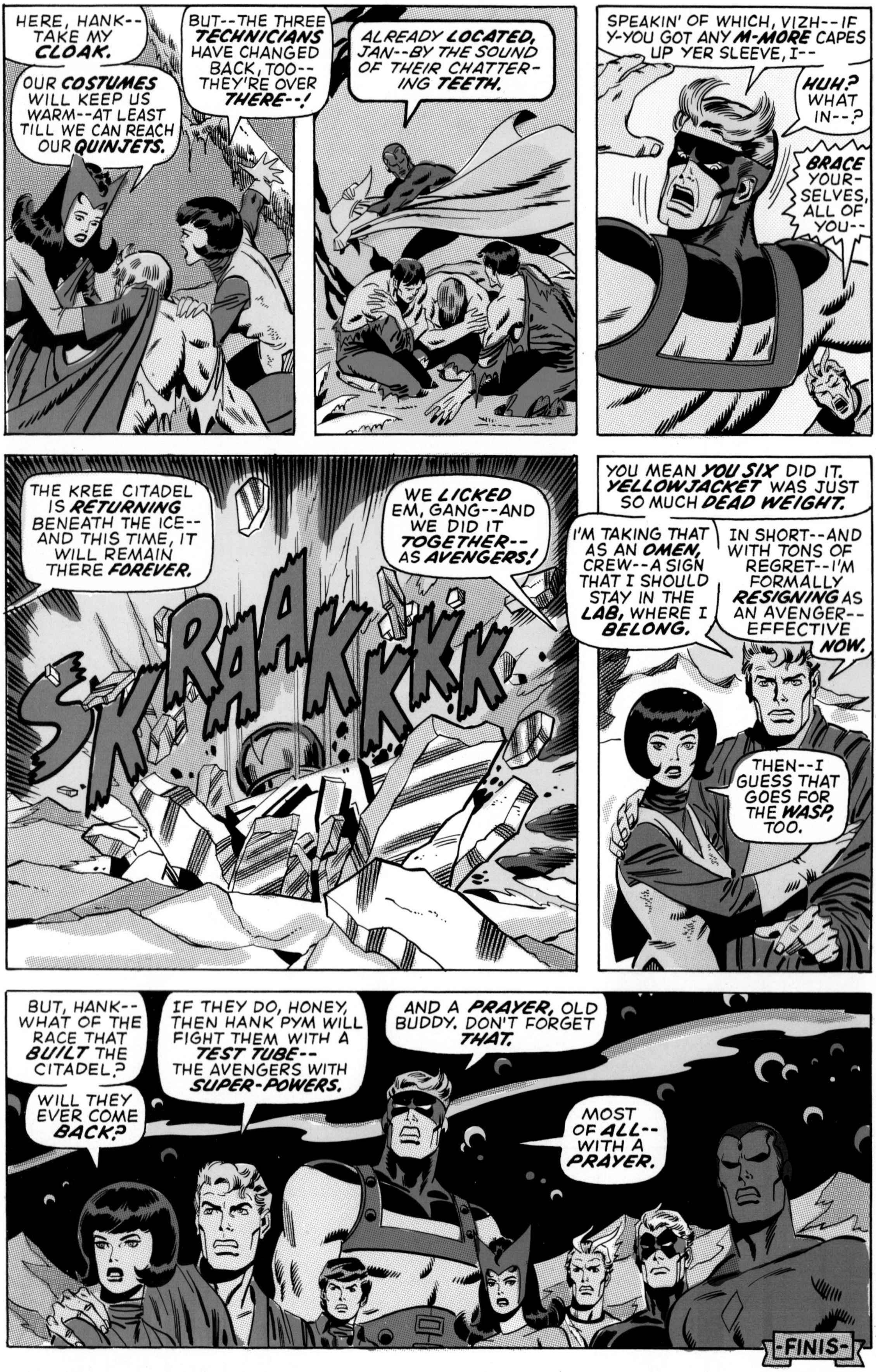
HERE, HANK--TAKE MY CLOAK.
OUR COSTUMES WILL KEEP US WARM--AT LEAST TILL WE CAN REACH OUR QUINJETS.
BUT--THE THREE TECHNICIANS HAVE CHANGED BACK, TOO--THEY'RE OVER THERE--!
ALREADY LOCATED, JAN--BY THE SOUND OF THEIR CHATTERING TEETH.
SPEAKIN' OF WHICH, VIZH--IF Y-YOU GOT ANY M-MORE CAPES UP YER SLEEVE, I--
HUH? WHAT IN--?
BRACE YOURSELVES, ALL OF YOU--
THE KREE CITADEL IS RETURNING BENEATH THE ICE--AND THIS TIME, IT WILL REMAIN THERE FOREVER.
WE LICKED EM, GANG--AND WE DID IT TOGETHER--AS AVENGERS!
SKRAAKKKK
YOU MEAN YOU SIX DID IT. YELLOWJACKET WAS JUST SO MUCH DEAD WEIGHT.
I'M TAKING THAT AS AN OMEN, CREW--A SIGN THAT I SHOULD STAY IN THE LAB, WHERE I BELONG.
IN SHORT--AND WITH TONS OF REGRET--I'M FORMALLY RESIGNING AS AN AVENGER--EFFECTIVE NOW.
THEN--I GUESS THAT GOES FOR THE WASP, TOO.
BUT, HANK--WHAT OF THE RACE THAT BUILT THE CITADEL?
WILL THEY EVER COME BACK?
IF THEY DO, HONEY, THEN HANK PYM WILL FIGHT THEM WITH A TEST TUBE--THE AVENGERS WITH SUPER-POWERS.
AND A PRAYER, OLD BUDDY. DON'T FORGET THAT.
MOST OF ALL--WITH A PRAYER.
-FINIS-

CHAPTER FOUR

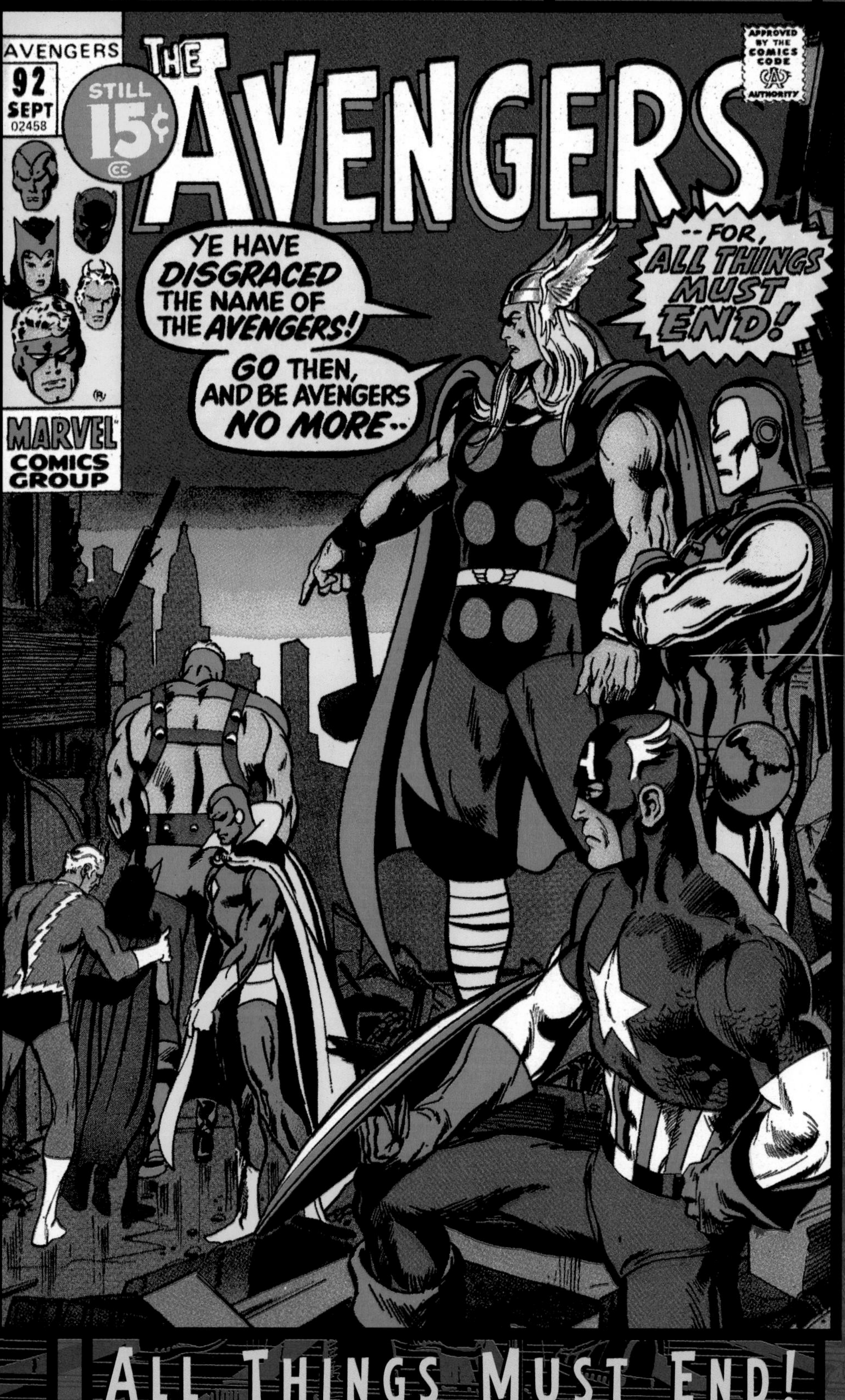
AVENGERS
92
SEPT
02458
STILL 15¢
THE AVENGERS
APPROVED BY THE COMICS CODE AUTHORITY
YE HAVE DISGRACED THE NAME OF THE AVENGERS!
GO THEN, AND BE AVENGERS NO MORE..
--FOR, ALL THINGS MUST END!
MARVEL COMICS GROUP

ALL THINGS MUST END!

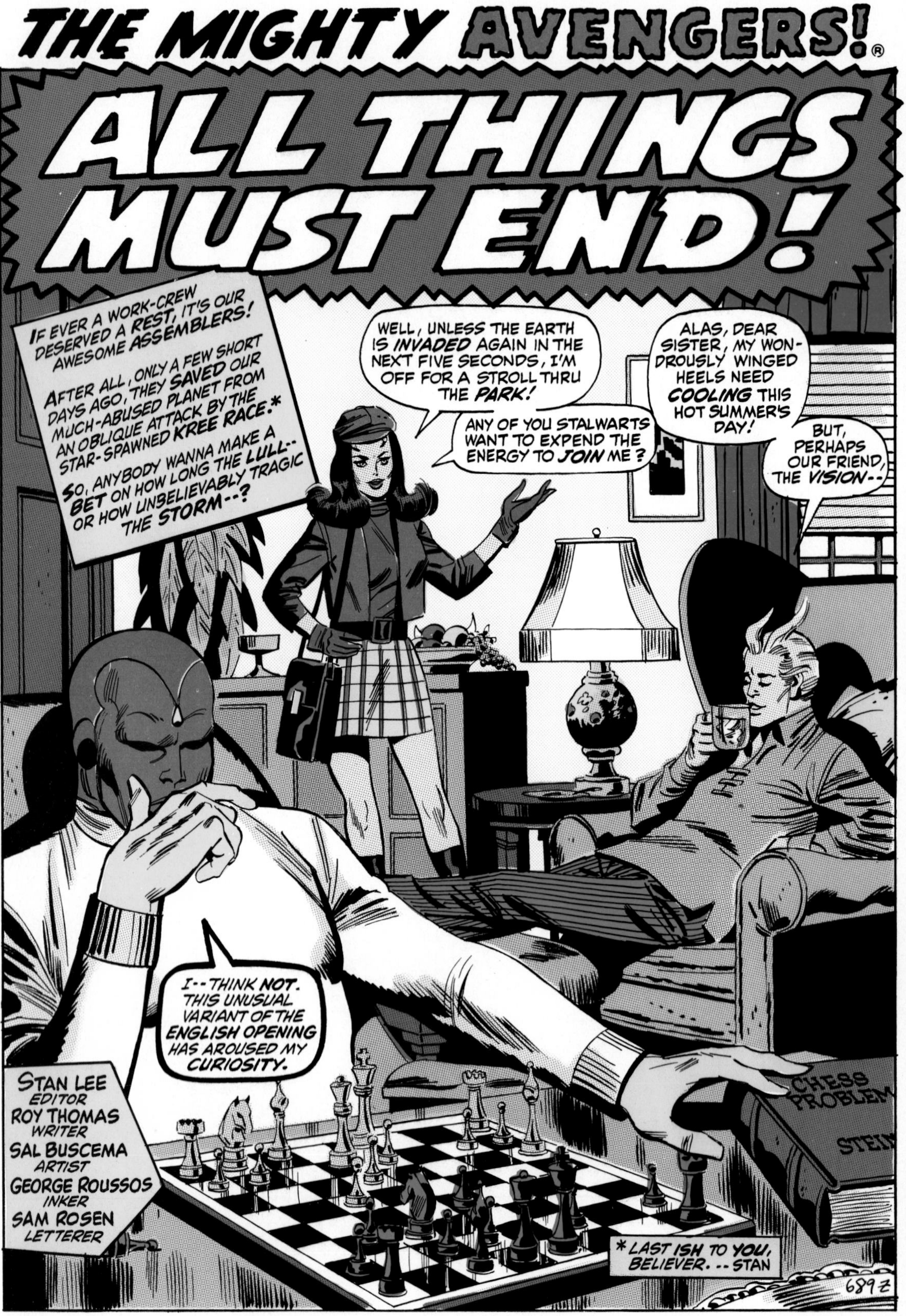
THE MIGHTY AVENGERS!®
ALL THINGS MUST END!
IF EVER A WORK-CREW DESERVED A REST, IT'S OUR AWESOME ASSEMBLERS!
AFTER ALL, ONLY A FEW SHORT DAYS AGO, THEY SAVED OUR MUCH-ABUSED PLANET FROM AN OBLIQUE ATTACK BY THE STAR-SPAWNED KREE RACE.*
SO, ANYBODY WANNA MAKE A BET ON HOW LONG THE LULL-- OR HOW UNBELIEVABLY TRAGIC THE STORM--?
WELL, UNLESS THE EARTH IS INVADED AGAIN IN THE NEXT FIVE SECONDS, I'M OFF FOR A STROLL THRU THE PARK!
ANY OF YOU STALWARTS WANT TO EXPEND THE ENERGY TO JOIN ME?
ALAS, DEAR SISTER, MY WONDROUSLY WINGED HEELS NEED COOLING THIS HOT SUMMER'S DAY!
BUT, PERHAPS OUR FRIEND, THE VISION--
I--THINK NOT. THIS UNUSUAL VARIANT OF THE ENGLISH OPENING HAS AROUSED MY CURIOSITY.
CHESS PROBLEM
STEIN
STAN LEE EDITOR
ROY THOMAS WRITER
SAL BUSCEMA ARTIST
GEORGE ROUSSOS INKER
SAM ROSEN LETTERER
*LAST ISH TO YOU, BELIEVER. --STAN
689 Z

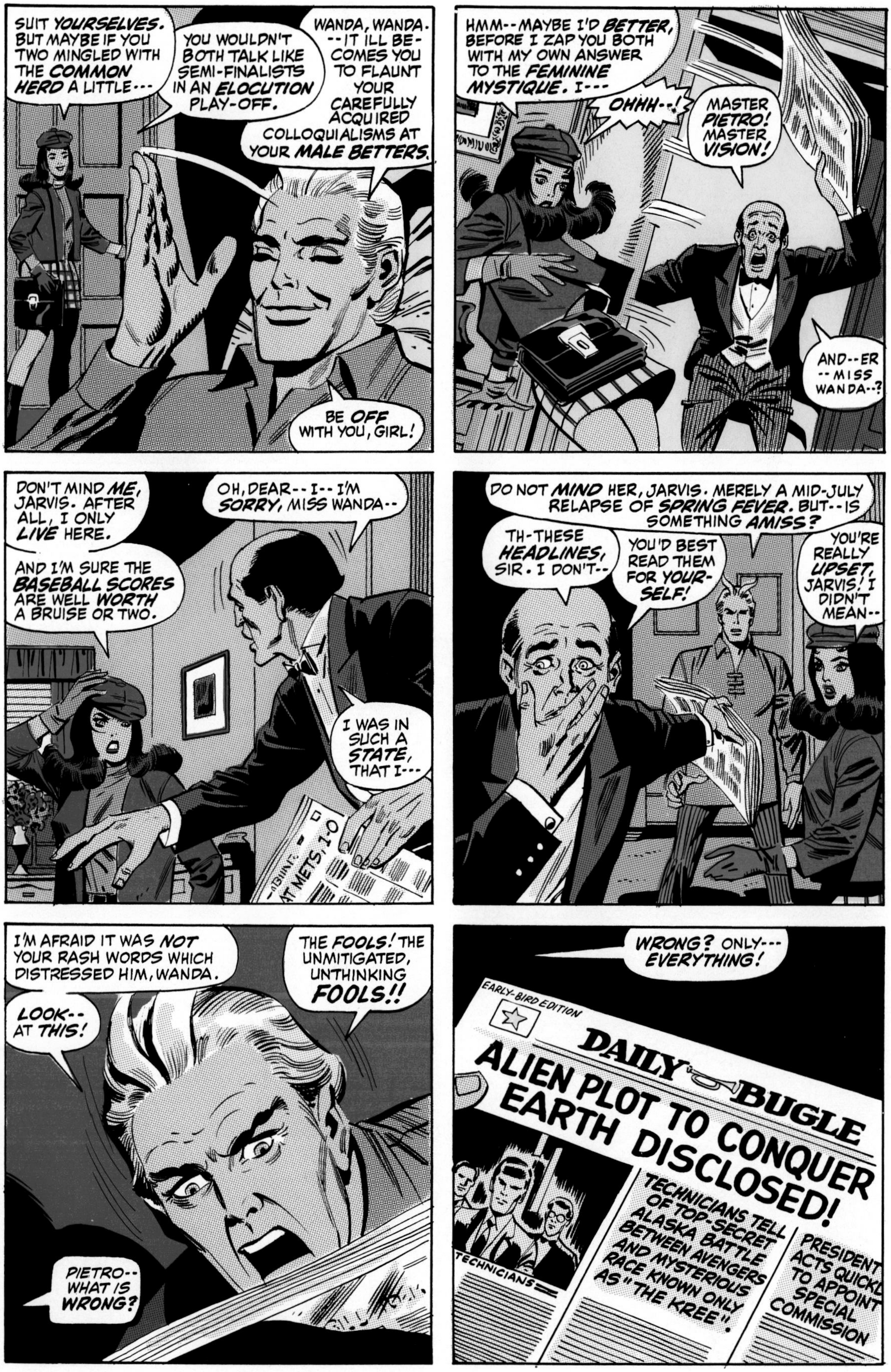
SUIT YOURSELVES. BUT MAYBE IF YOU TWO MINGLED WITH THE COMMON HERD A LITTLE---
YOU WOULDN'T BOTH TALK LIKE SEMI-FINALISTS IN AN ELOCUTION PLAY-OFF.
WANDA, WANDA--IT ILL BE-COMES YOU TO FLAUNT YOUR CAREFULLY ACQUIRED COLLOQUIALISMS AT YOUR MALE BETTERS.
BE OFF WITH YOU, GIRL!
HMM--MAYBE I'D BETTER, BEFORE I ZAP YOU BOTH WITH MY OWN ANSWER TO THE FEMININE MYSTIQUE. I---
OHHH--!
MASTER PIETRO! MASTER VISION!
AND--ER --MISS WANDA--?
DON'T MIND ME, JARVIS. AFTER ALL, I ONLY LIVE HERE.
AND I'M SURE THE BASEBALL SCORES ARE WELL WORTH A BRUISE OR TWO.
OH, DEAR-- I-- I'M SORRY, MISS WANDA--
I WAS IN SUCH A STATE, THAT I---
AT METS, 1-0
DO NOT MIND HER, JARVIS. MERELY A MID-JULY RELAPSE OF SPRING FEVER. BUT--IS SOMETHING AMISS?
TH-THESE HEADLINES, SIR. I DON'T--
YOU'D BEST READ THEM FOR YOUR-SELF!
YOU'RE REALLY UPSET, JARVIS! I DIDN'T MEAN--
I'M AFRAID IT WAS NOT YOUR RASH WORDS WHICH DISTRESSED HIM, WANDA.
LOOK--AT THIS!
THE FOOLS! THE UNMITIGATED, UNTHINKING FOOLS!!
PIETRO--WHAT IS WRONG?
WRONG? ONLY---EVERYTHING!
EARLY-BIRD EDITION
DAILY BUGLE
ALIEN PLOT TO CONQUER EARTH DISCLOSED!
TECHNICIANS TELL OF TOP-SECRET ALASKA BATTLE BETWEEN AVENGERS AND MYSTERIOUS RACE KNOWN ONLY AS "THE KREE".
TECHNICIANS
PRESIDENT ACTS QUICKL TO APPOINT SPECIAL COMMISSION

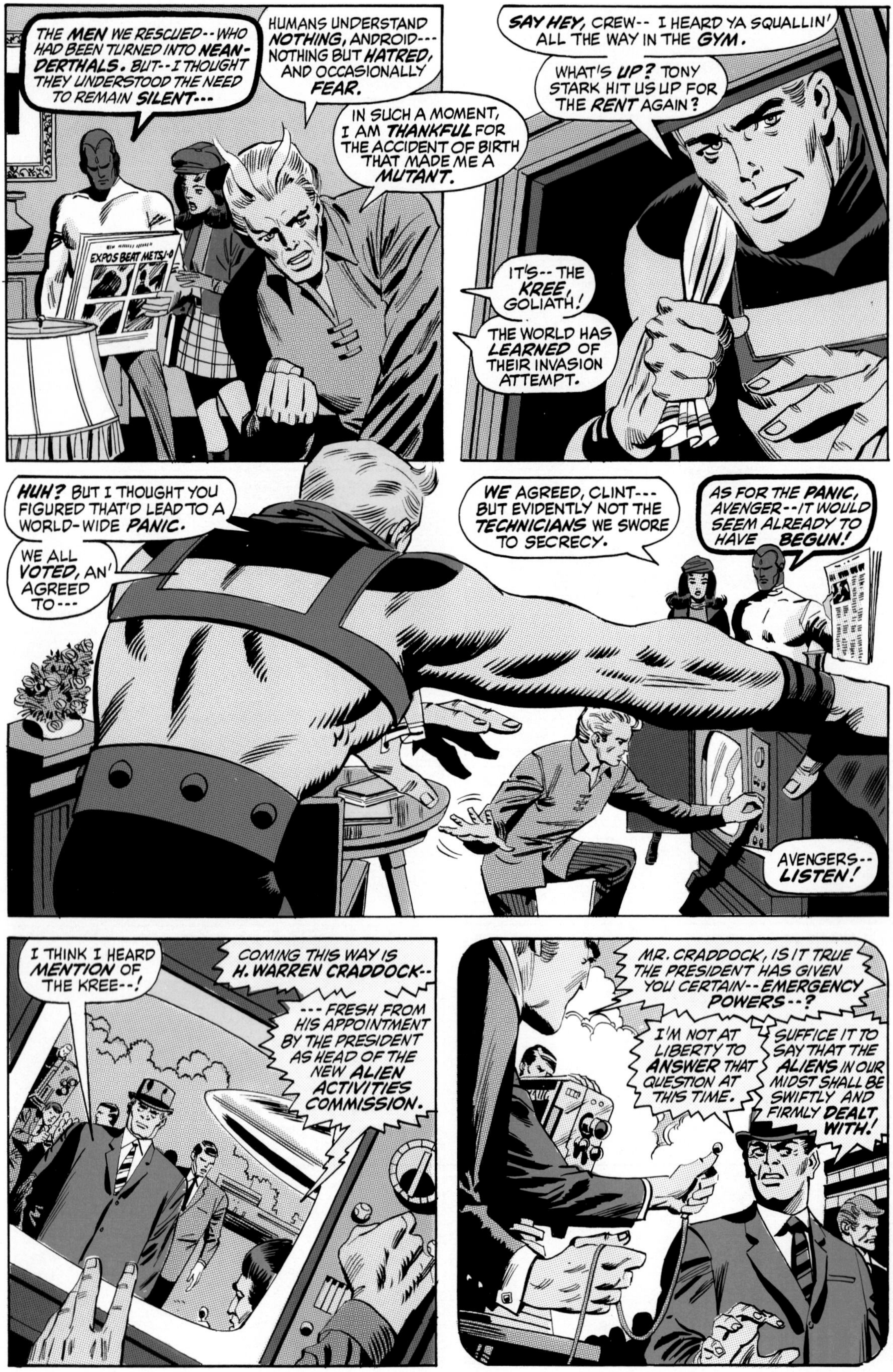
THE MEN WE RESCUED--WHO HAD BEEN TURNED INTO NEANDERTHALS. BUT--I THOUGHT THEY UNDERSTOOD THE NEED TO REMAIN SILENT---
HUMANS UNDERSTAND NOTHING, ANDROID--- NOTHING BUT HATRED, AND OCCASIONALLY FEAR.
IN SUCH A MOMENT, I AM THANKFUL FOR THE ACCIDENT OF BIRTH THAT MADE ME A MUTANT.
EXPOS BEAT METS 1-0
SAY HEY, CREW-- I HEARD YA SQUALLIN' ALL THE WAY IN THE GYM.
WHAT'S UP? TONY STARK HIT US UP FOR THE RENT AGAIN?
IT'S-- THE KREE, GOLIATH!
THE WORLD HAS LEARNED OF THEIR INVASION ATTEMPT.
HUH? BUT I THOUGHT YOU FIGURED THAT'D LEAD TO A WORLD-WIDE PANIC.
WE ALL VOTED, AN' AGREED TO---
WE AGREED, CLINT--- BUT EVIDENTLY NOT THE TECHNICIANS WE SWORE TO SECRECY.
AS FOR THE PANIC, AVENGER--IT WOULD SEEM ALREADY TO HAVE BEGUN!
AVENGERS-- LISTEN!
I THINK I HEARD MENTION OF THE KREE--!
COMING THIS WAY IS H. WARREN CRADDOCK--
--- FRESH FROM HIS APPOINTMENT BY THE PRESIDENT AS HEAD OF THE NEW ALIEN ACTIVITIES COMMISSION.
MR. CRADDOCK, IS IT TRUE THE PRESIDENT HAS GIVEN YOU CERTAIN--EMERGENCY POWERS--?
I'M NOT AT LIBERTY TO ANSWER THAT QUESTION AT THIS TIME.
SUFFICE IT TO SAY THAT THE ALIENS IN OUR MIDST SHALL BE SWIFTLY AND FIRMLY DEALT WITH!

IS THERE ANYTHING YOU CAN *TELL* US ABOUT THOSE ALIENS?

SO FAR THERE'S BEEN LITTLE BUT *RUMORS*...

NOR DO I INTEND TO *ADD* TO THE PUBLIC *HYSTERIA* BY GIVING OUT *CLASSIFIED* INFORMATION.

SIR, THERE'VE *ALSO* BEEN REPORTS THAT THE MASKED MAN CALLED *CAPTAIN MARVEL* IS ONE OF THESE ALIENS.

YES-- I'VE *HEARD* THOSE RUMORS.

WHAT *ABOUT* THIS--AND THE FACT THAT THE FAMOUS *AVENGERS* SEEM TO HAVE BE-FRIENDED HIM?

STILL, I *CAN* TELL YOU THAT IT INVOLVED AN AGE-OLD *CITADEL*, IN THE HEART OF THE *NORTH*---

--WHICH CAME CLOSE TO TURNING BACK THE TIDE OF *EVOLUTION* BY A *BILLION* YEARS!

I ACCUSE THE AVENGERS OF *NOTHING*, MIND YOU---

BUT, I HAVE IN MY POSSESSION A LIST OF *153* "MODEL CITIZENS" WHO ARE ACTUALLY *ALIEN SPIES.*

AND-- YOU CAN *QUOTE* ME ON THIS, BOYS--- I INTEND TO *FERRET THEM OUT*---

--NO MATTER *WHERE* THEIR TRAIL MAY LEAD---

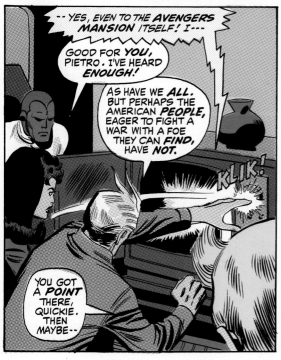

-- YES, EVEN TO THE AVENGERS MANSION *ITSELF!* I---

GOOD FOR *YOU*, PIETRO. I'VE HEARD *ENOUGH!*

AS HAVE WE *ALL.* BUT PERHAPS THE AMERICAN *PEOPLE*, EAGER TO FIGHT A WAR WITH A FOE THEY CAN *FIND*, HAVE *NOT.*

KLIK!

YOU GOT A *POINT* THERE, QUICKIE. THEN MAYBE--

THEN *MAYBE*, AVENGERS--

--*CAPTAIN MARVEL* SHOULD GIVE HIMSELF *UP!*

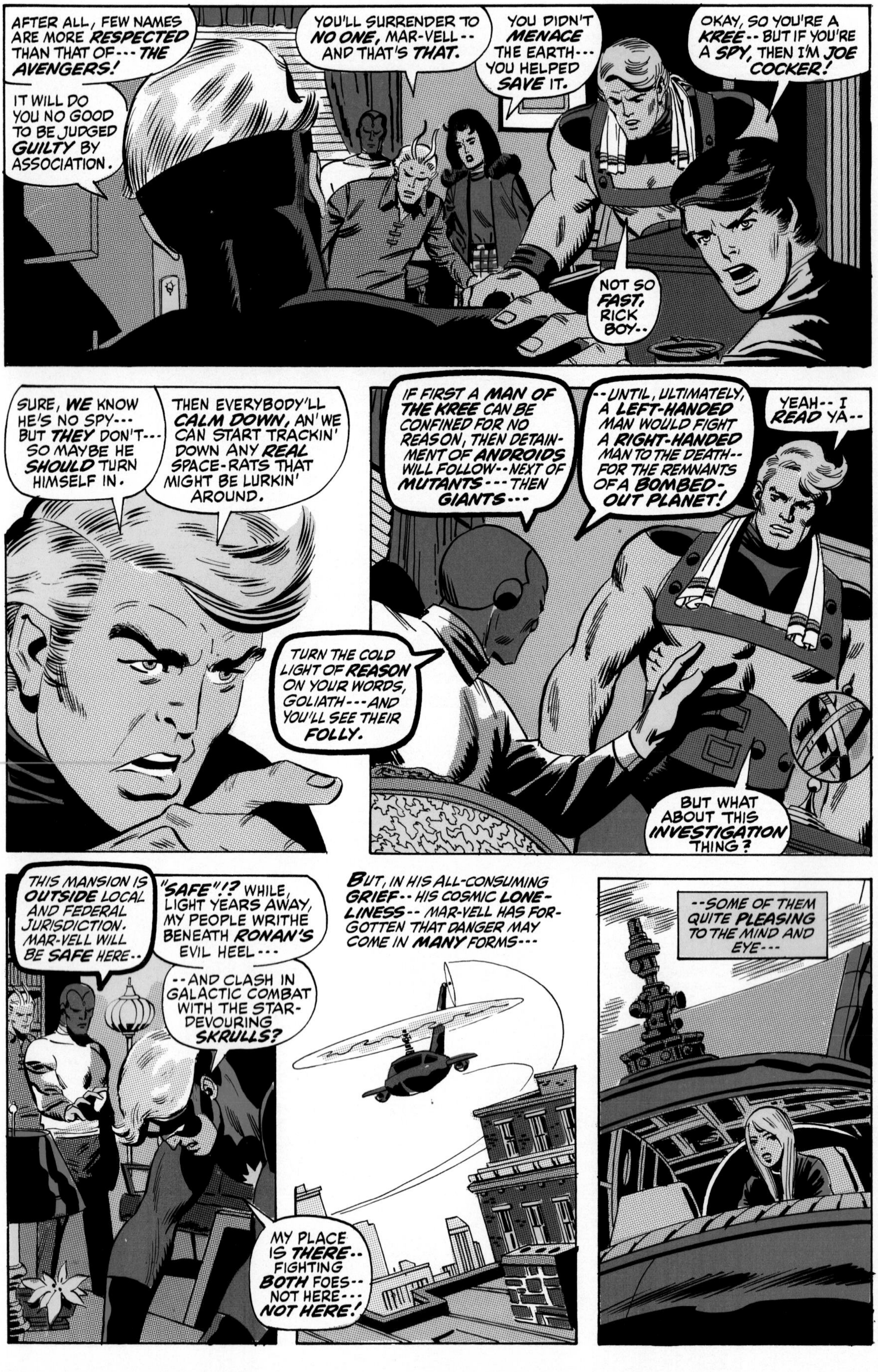
AFTER ALL, FEW NAMES ARE MORE RESPECTED THAN THAT OF--- THE AVENGERS!
IT WILL DO YOU NO GOOD TO BE JUDGED GUILTY BY ASSOCIATION.
YOU'LL SURRENDER TO NO ONE, MAR-VELL-- AND THAT'S THAT.
YOU DIDN'T MENACE THE EARTH--- YOU HELPED SAVE IT.
OKAY, SO YOU'RE A KREE-- BUT IF YOU'RE A SPY, THEN I'M JOE COCKER!
NOT SO FAST, RICK BOY--
SURE, WE KNOW HE'S NO SPY--- BUT THEY DON'T--- SO MAYBE HE SHOULD TURN HIMSELF IN.
THEN EVERYBODY'LL CALM DOWN, AN' WE CAN START TRACKIN' DOWN ANY REAL SPACE-RATS THAT MIGHT BE LURKIN' AROUND.
IF FIRST A MAN OF THE KREE CAN BE CONFINED FOR NO REASON, THEN DETAINMENT OF ANDROIDS WILL FOLLOW-- NEXT OF MUTANTS--- THEN GIANTS---
--UNTIL, ULTIMATELY, A LEFT-HANDED MAN WOULD FIGHT A RIGHT-HANDED MAN TO THE DEATH-- FOR THE REMNANTS OF A BOMBED-OUT PLANET!
YEAH-- I READ YA--
TURN THE COLD LIGHT OF REASON ON YOUR WORDS, GOLIATH---AND YOU'LL SEE THEIR FOLLY.
BUT WHAT ABOUT THIS INVESTIGATION THING?
THIS MANSION IS OUTSIDE LOCAL AND FEDERAL JURISDICTION. MAR-VELL WILL BE SAFE HERE--
"SAFE"!? WHILE, LIGHT YEARS AWAY, MY PEOPLE WRITHE BENEATH RONAN'S EVIL HEEL---
--AND CLASH IN GALACTIC COMBAT WITH THE STAR-DEVOURING SKRULLS?
MY PLACE IS THERE-- FIGHTING BOTH FOES-- NOT HERE--- NOT HERE!
BUT, IN HIS ALL-CONSUMING GRIEF-- HIS COSMIC LONELINESS-- MAR-VELL HAS FORGOTTEN THAT DANGER MAY COME IN MANY FORMS---
--SOME OF THEM QUITE PLEASING TO THE MIND AND EYE---

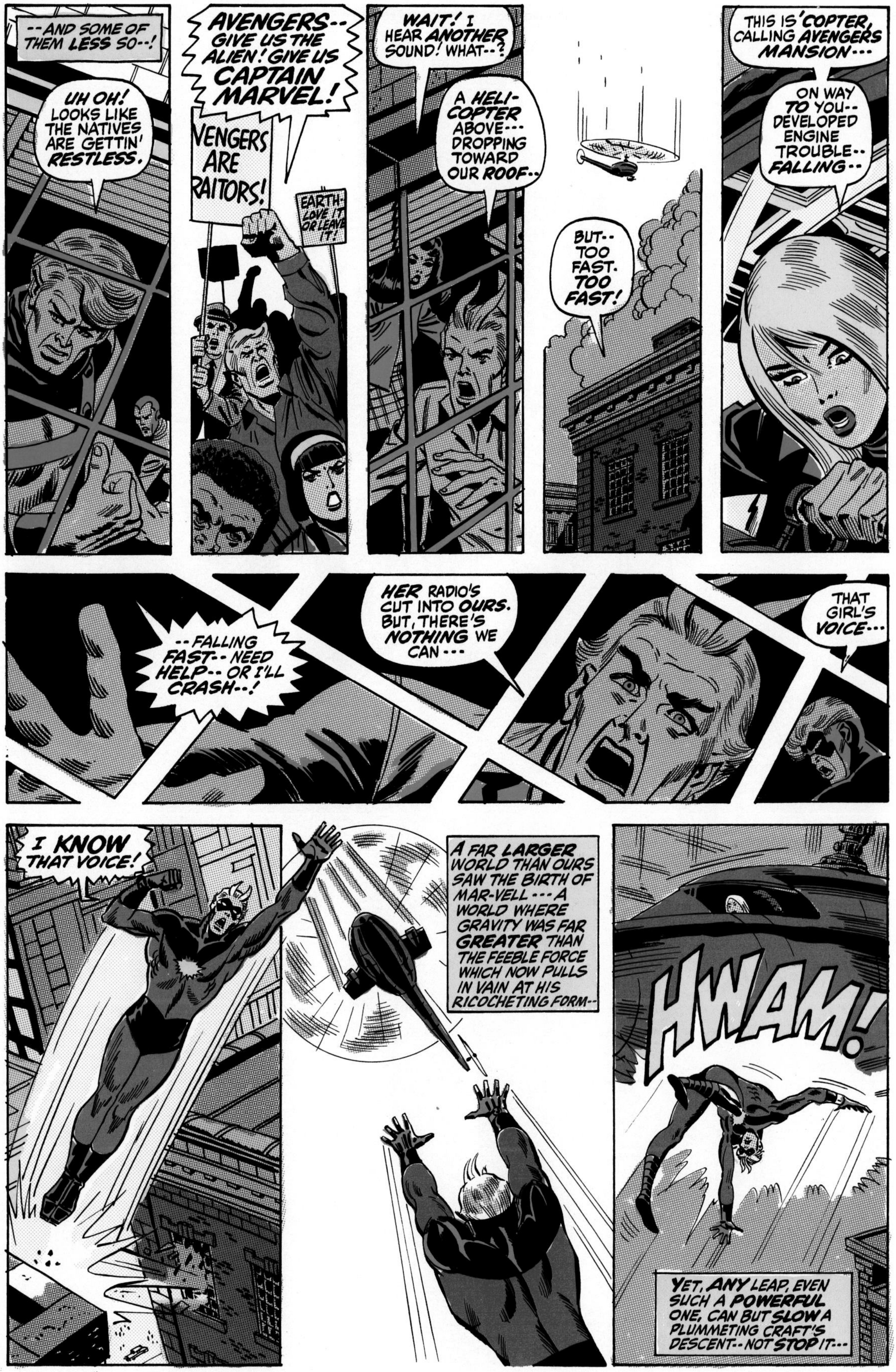
--AND SOME OF THEM LESS SO--!
UH OH! LOOKS LIKE THE NATIVES ARE GETTIN' RESTLESS.
AVENGERS--GIVE US THE ALIEN! GIVE US CAPTAIN MARVEL!
VENGERS ARE RAITORS!
EARTH-LOVE IT OR LEAVE IT!
WAIT! I HEAR ANOTHER SOUND! WHAT--?
A HELI-COPTER ABOVE---DROPPING TOWARD OUR ROOF--
BUT--TOO FAST. TOO FAST!
THIS IS 'COPTER, CALLING AVENGERS MANSION---
ON WAY TO YOU--DEVELOPED ENGINE TROUBLE--FALLING--
--FALLING FAST--NEED HELP--OR I'LL CRASH--!
HER RADIO'S CUT INTO OURS. BUT, THERE'S NOTHING WE CAN---
THAT GIRL'S VOICE---
I KNOW THAT VOICE!
A FAR LARGER WORLD THAN OURS SAW THE BIRTH OF MAR-VELL---A WORLD WHERE GRAVITY WAS FAR GREATER THAN THE FEEBLE FORCE WHICH NOW PULLS IN VAIN AT HIS RICOCHETING FORM--
HWAM!
YET, ANY LEAP, EVEN SUCH A POWERFUL ONE, CAN BUT SLOW A PLUMMETING CRAFT'S DESCENT--NOT STOP IT---

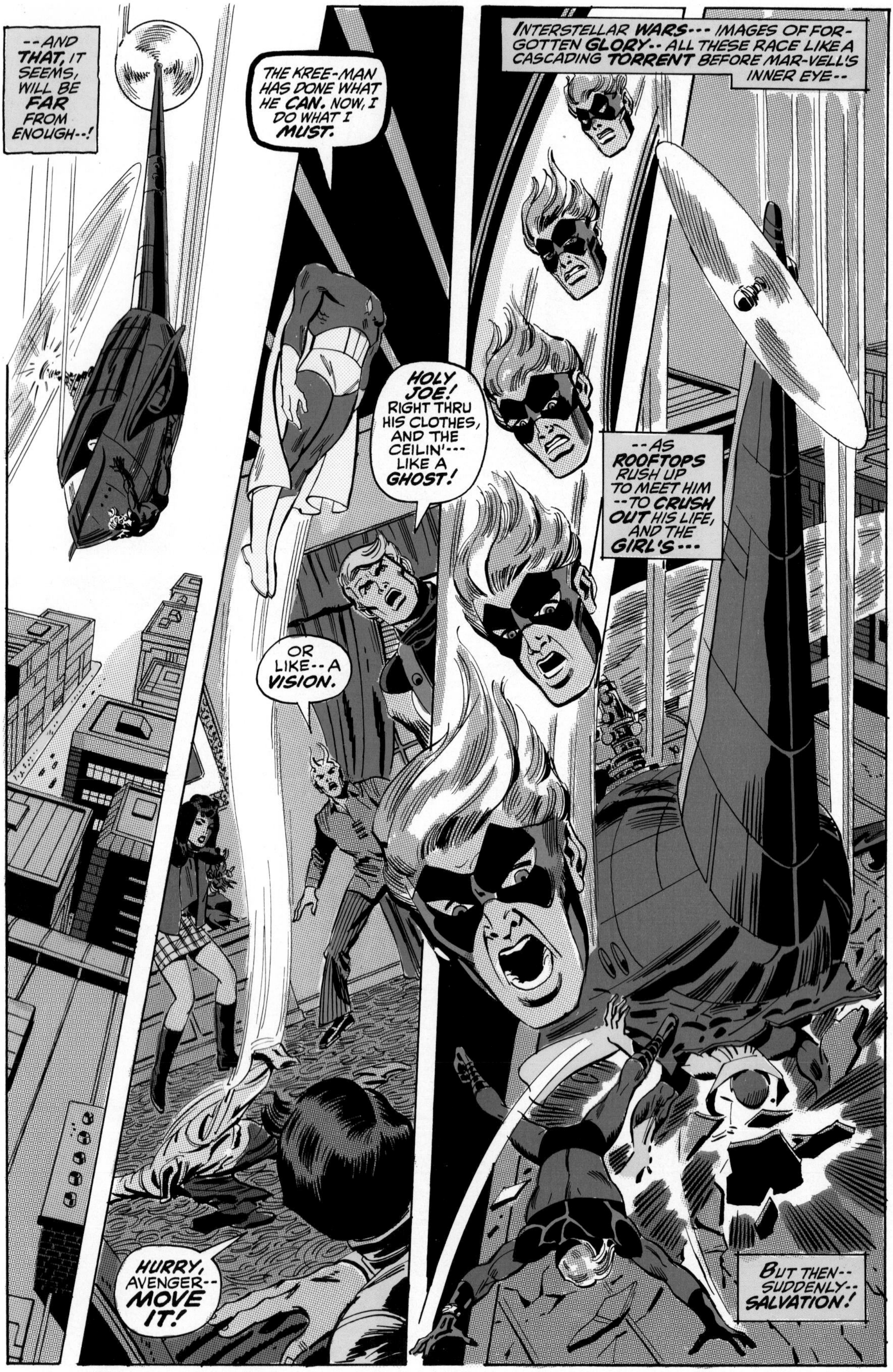
--AND THAT, IT SEEMS, WILL BE FAR FROM ENOUGH--!
HURRY, AVENGER--MOVE IT!
THE KREE-MAN HAS DONE WHAT HE CAN. NOW, I DO WHAT I MUST.
HOLY JOE! RIGHT THRU HIS CLOTHES, AND THE CEILIN'--- LIKE A GHOST!
OR LIKE--A VISION.
INTERSTELLAR WARS--- IMAGES OF FORGOTTEN GLORY-- ALL THESE RACE LIKE A CASCADING TORRENT BEFORE MAR-VELL'S INNER EYE--
--AS ROOFTOPS RUSH UP TO MEET HIM --TO CRUSH OUT HIS LIFE, AND THE GIRL'S---
BUT THEN-- SUDDENLY-- SALVATION!

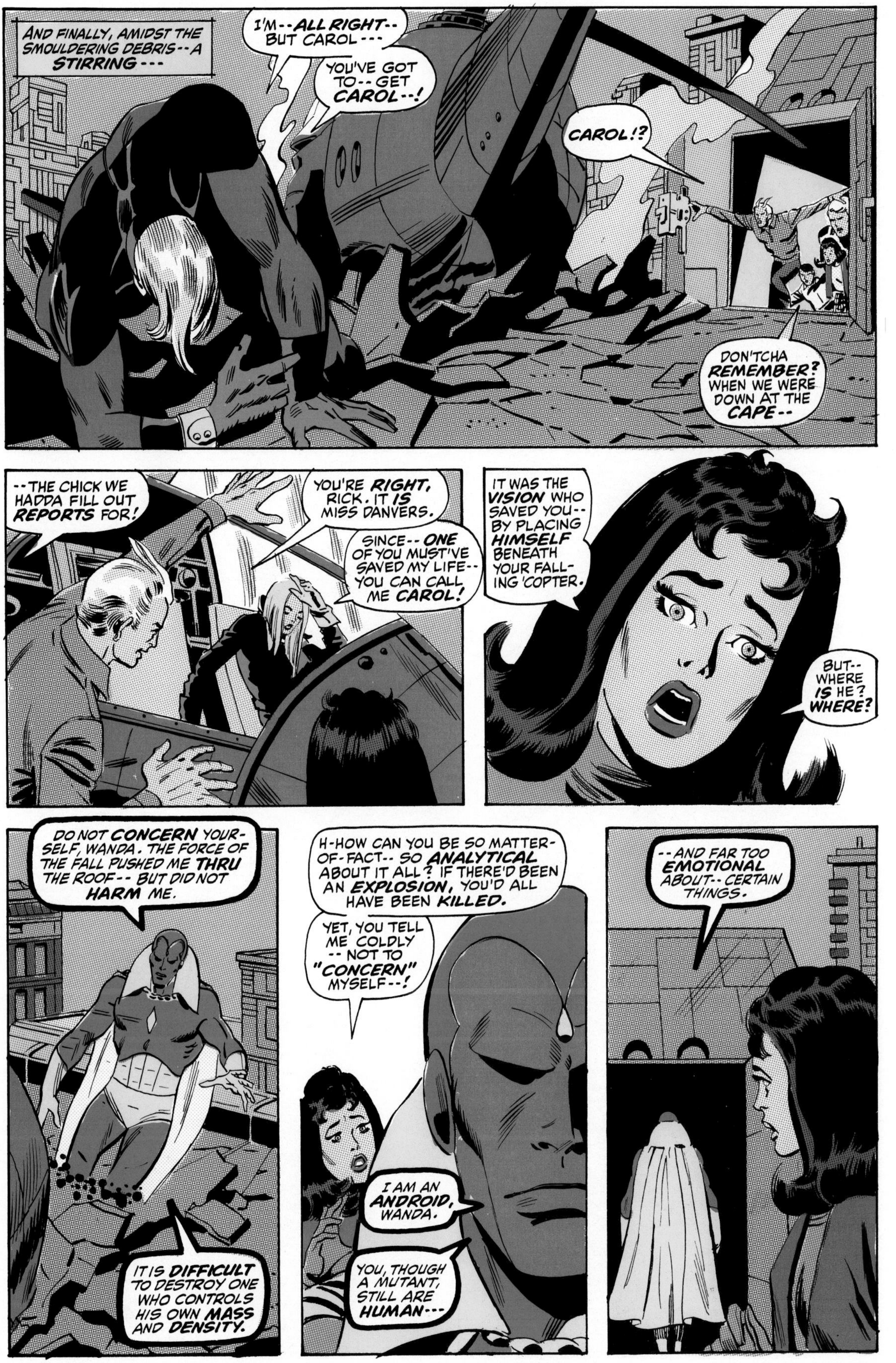
AND FINALLY, AMIDST THE SMOULDERING DEBRIS--A STIRRING---
I'M--ALL RIGHT--BUT CAROL---
YOU'VE GOT TO--GET CAROL--!
CAROL!?
DON'TCHA REMEMBER? WHEN WE WERE DOWN AT THE CAPE--
--THE CHICK WE HADDA FILL OUT REPORTS FOR!
YOU'RE RIGHT, RICK. IT IS MISS DANVERS.
SINCE--ONE OF YOU MUST'VE SAVED MY LIFE--YOU CAN CALL ME CAROL!
IT WAS THE VISION WHO SAVED YOU--BY PLACING HIMSELF BENEATH YOUR FALLING 'COPTER.
BUT--WHERE IS HE? WHERE?
DO NOT CONCERN YOURSELF, WANDA. THE FORCE OF THE FALL PUSHED ME THRU THE ROOF--BUT DID NOT HARM ME.
IT IS DIFFICULT TO DESTROY ONE WHO CONTROLS HIS OWN MASS AND DENSITY.
H-HOW CAN YOU BE SO MATTER-OF-FACT--SO ANALYTICAL ABOUT IT ALL? IF THERE'D BEEN AN EXPLOSION, YOU'D ALL HAVE BEEN KILLED.
YET, YOU TELL ME COLDLY--NOT TO "CONCERN" MYSELF--!
I AM AN ANDROID, WANDA.
YOU, THOUGH A MUTANT, STILL ARE HUMAN---
--AND FAR TOO EMOTIONAL ABOUT--CERTAIN THINGS.

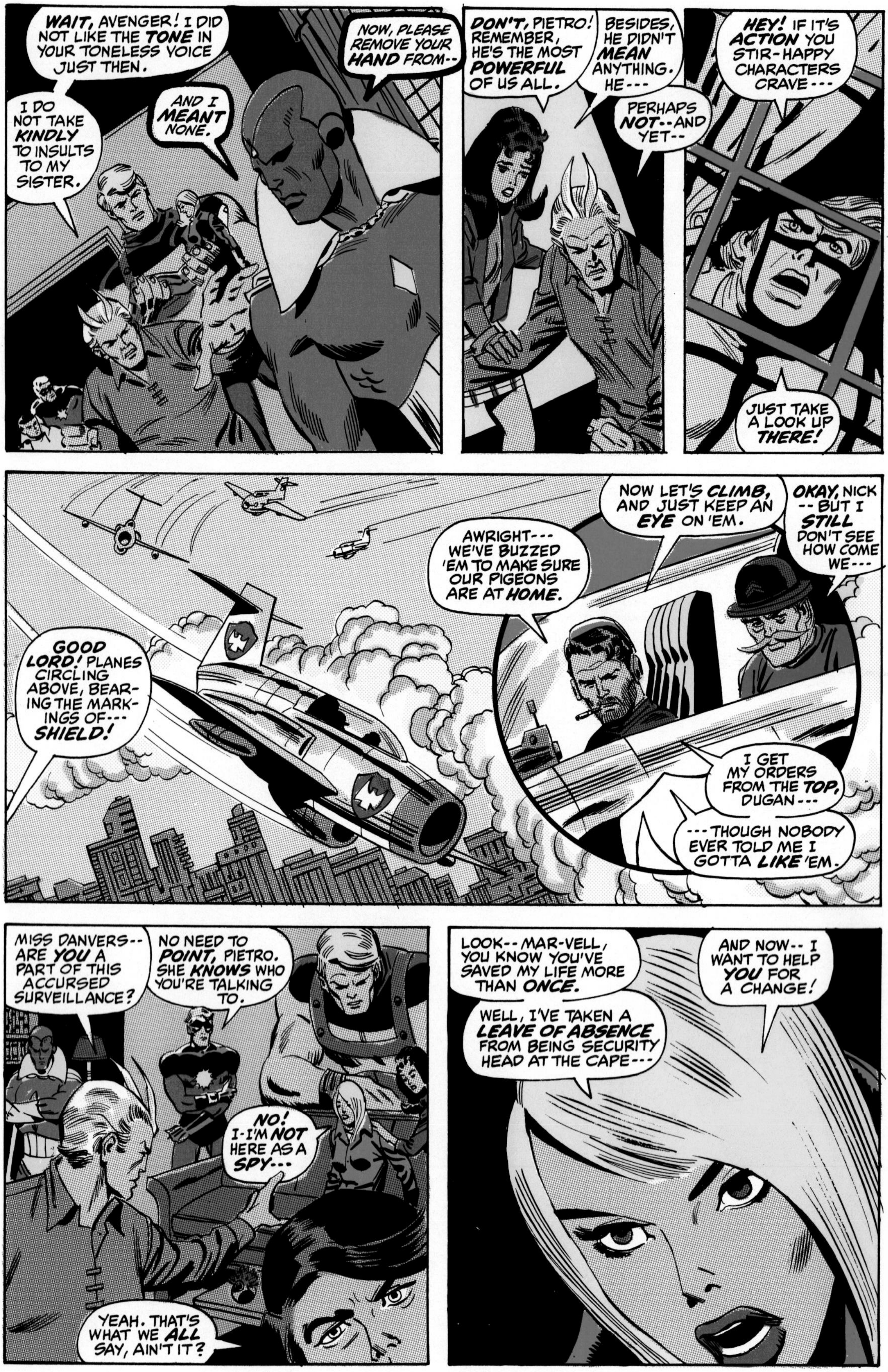
WAIT, AVENGER! I DID NOT LIKE THE TONE IN YOUR TONELESS VOICE JUST THEN.
I DO NOT TAKE KINDLY TO INSULTS TO MY SISTER.
AND I MEANT NONE.
NOW, PLEASE REMOVE YOUR HAND FROM--
DON'T, PIETRO! REMEMBER, HE'S THE MOST POWERFUL OF US ALL.
BESIDES, HE DIDN'T MEAN ANYTHING. HE---
PERHAPS NOT--AND YET--
HEY! IF IT'S ACTION YOU STIR-HAPPY CHARACTERS CRAVE---
JUST TAKE A LOOK UP THERE!
GOOD LORD! PLANES CIRCLING ABOVE, BEARING THE MARKINGS OF--- SHIELD!
AWRIGHT--- WE'VE BUZZED 'EM TO MAKE SURE OUR PIGEONS ARE AT HOME.
NOW LET'S CLIMB, AND JUST KEEP AN EYE ON 'EM.
OKAY, NICK -- BUT I STILL DON'T SEE HOW COME WE---
I GET MY ORDERS FROM THE TOP, DUGAN---
---THOUGH NOBODY EVER TOLD ME I GOTTA LIKE 'EM.
MISS DANVERS-- ARE YOU A PART OF THIS ACCURSED SURVEILLANCE?
NO NEED TO POINT, PIETRO. SHE KNOWS WHO YOU'RE TALKING TO.
NO! I-I'M NOT HERE AS A SPY...
YEAH. THAT'S WHAT WE ALL SAY, AIN'T IT?
LOOK-- MAR-VELL, YOU KNOW YOU'VE SAVED MY LIFE MORE THAN ONCE.
WELL, I'VE TAKEN A LEAVE OF ABSENCE FROM BEING SECURITY HEAD AT THE CAPE---
AND NOW-- I WANT TO HELP YOU FOR A CHANGE!

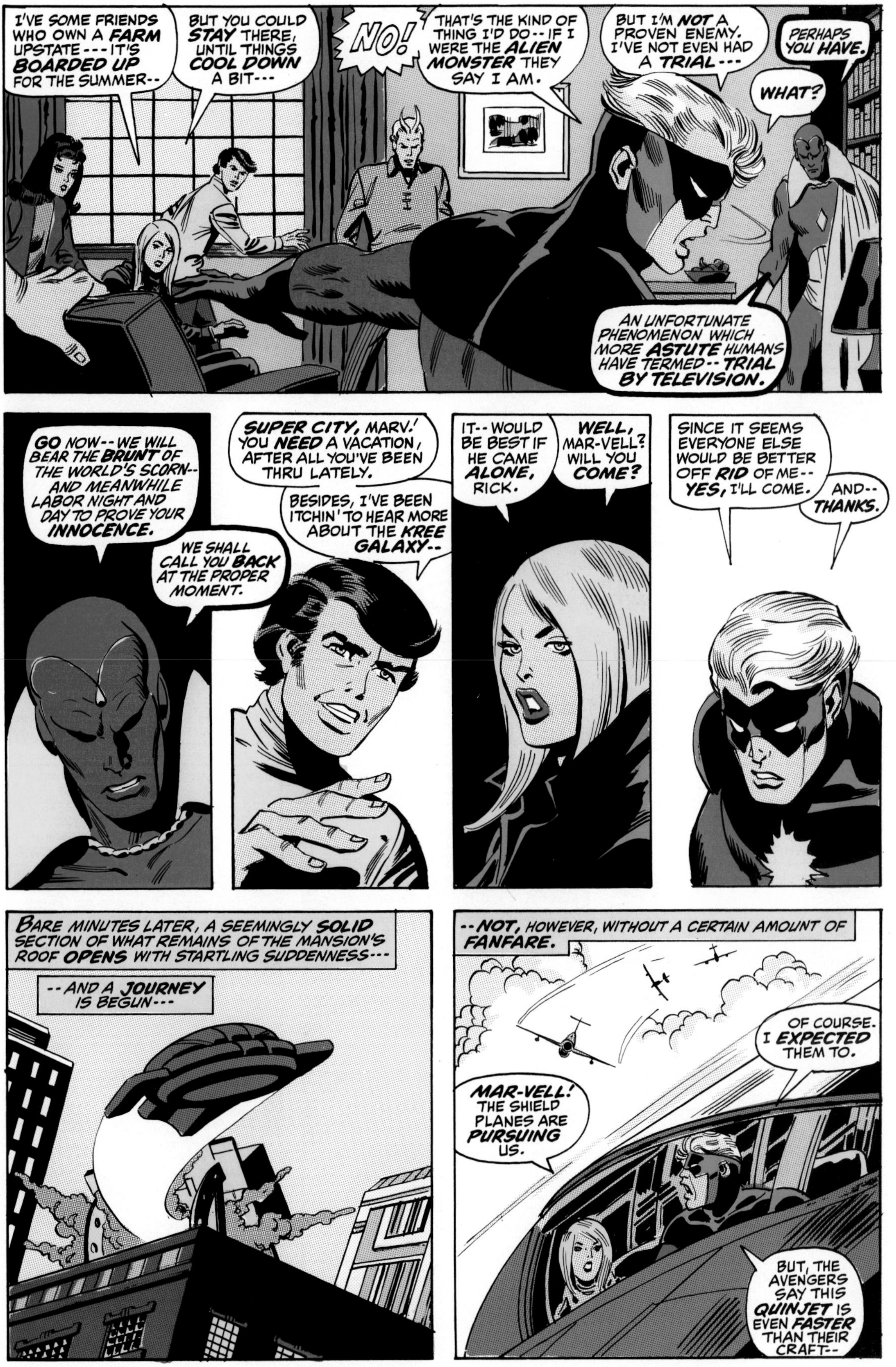
I'VE SOME FRIENDS WHO OWN A FARM UPSTATE---IT'S BOARDED UP FOR THE SUMMER--
BUT YOU COULD STAY THERE, UNTIL THINGS COOL DOWN A BIT---
NO!
THAT'S THE KIND OF THING I'D DO--IF I WERE THE ALIEN MONSTER THEY SAY I AM.
BUT I'M NOT A PROVEN ENEMY. I'VE NOT EVEN HAD A TRIAL---
PERHAPS YOU HAVE.
WHAT?
AN UNFORTUNATE PHENOMENON WHICH MORE ASTUTE HUMANS HAVE TERMED--TRIAL BY TELEVISION.
GO NOW--WE WILL BEAR THE BRUNT OF THE WORLD'S SCORN--AND MEANWHILE LABOR NIGHT AND DAY TO PROVE YOUR INNOCENCE.
WE SHALL CALL YOU BACK AT THE PROPER MOMENT.
SUPER CITY, MARV.! YOU NEED A VACATION, AFTER ALL YOU'VE BEEN THRU LATELY.
BESIDES, I'VE BEEN ITCHIN' TO HEAR MORE ABOUT THE KREE GALAXY--
IT--WOULD BE BEST IF HE CAME ALONE, RICK.
WELL, MAR-VELL? WILL YOU COME?
SINCE IT SEEMS EVERYONE ELSE WOULD BE BETTER OFF RID OF ME--YES, I'LL COME.
AND--THANKS.
BARE MINUTES LATER, A SEEMINGLY SOLID SECTION OF WHAT REMAINS OF THE MANSION'S ROOF OPENS WITH STARTLING SUDDENNESS---
--AND A JOURNEY IS BEGUN---
--NOT, HOWEVER, WITHOUT A CERTAIN AMOUNT OF FANFARE.
MAR-VELL! THE SHIELD PLANES ARE PURSUING US.
OF COURSE. I EXPECTED THEM TO.
BUT, THE AVENGERS SAY THIS QUINJET IS EVEN FASTER THAN THEIR CRAFT--

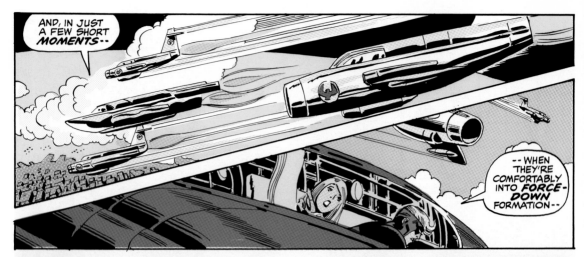

AND, IN JUST A FEW SHORT **MOMENTS**--

-- WHEN THEY'RE COMFORTABLY INTO **FORCE-DOWN** FORMATION--

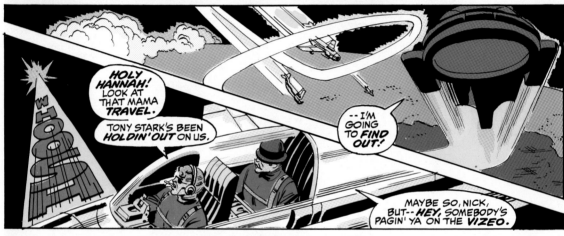

WHOOOM

HOLY HANNAH! LOOK AT THAT MAMA **TRAVEL.**

TONY STARK'S BEEN **HOLDIN' OUT** ON US.

-- I'M GOING TO **FIND OUT!**

MAYBE SO, NICK, BUT-- **HEY**, SOMEBODY'S PAGIN' YA ON THE **VIZEO.**

I HEAR IT, I **HEAR** IT.

WELL, WOTTA SURPRISE. **H.W. CRADDOCK**, IN GLORIOUS BLACK'N' WHITE.

DON'T SWEET-TALK **ME**, FURY. I'LL HAVE YOUR **JOB** FOR THIS OUTRAGE.

YOU **WANT** IT-- YOU **GOT** IT.

NOW, WHAT OUTRAGE YOU **TALKIN'** ABOUT?

I'VE BEEN **MONITORING** YOU-- AND I THINK YOU **DELIBERATELY** LEFT HIM A HOLE TO ESCAPE.

YOU KNOW I WANT TO **IMPOUND** ALL PROVEN TRAITORS--

PROVE, **SHMOOVE.** MARVEL AIN'T EVEN BEEN **CHARGED** WITH NOTHIN' YET.

OVER-- AN' **OUT.**

HEY, FURY-- WHY **DID** YOU ORDER SUCH A **LOOSE** FORMATION?

I GOT A LOOK AT SOME OF OUR JAPANESE-AMERICAN **RELOCATION CENTERS,** BACK DURING THE **BIG ONE.**

SAW WHAT THEY **DO** TO MEN-- ON **BOTH** SIDES OF THE BARBED WIRE.

SO, I DIDN'T DO THAT FOR **MARVEL,** YA OLD **WALRUS.**

I DID IT FOR-- **AMERICA!**

KLIK!

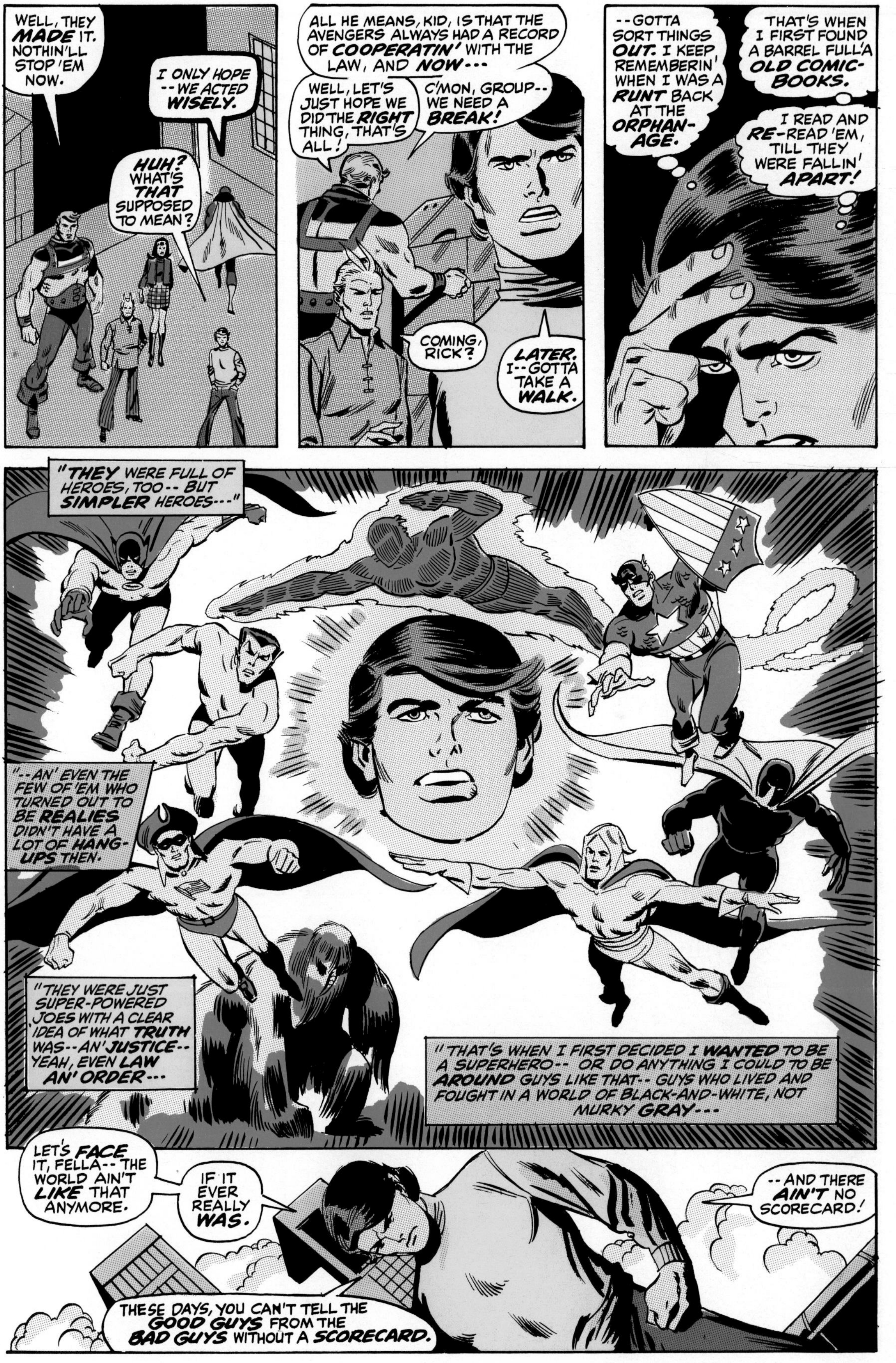
WELL, THEY MADE IT. NOTHIN'LL STOP 'EM NOW.
I ONLY HOPE --WE ACTED WISELY.
HUH? WHAT'S THAT SUPPOSED TO MEAN?
ALL HE MEANS, KID, IS THAT THE AVENGERS ALWAYS HAD A RECORD OF COOPERATIN' WITH THE LAW, AND NOW---
WELL, LET'S JUST HOPE WE DID THE RIGHT THING, THAT'S ALL!
C'MON, GROUP-- WE NEED A BREAK!
COMING, RICK?
LATER. I--GOTTA TAKE A WALK.
--GOTTA SORT THINGS OUT. I KEEP REMEMBERIN' WHEN I WAS A RUNT BACK AT THE ORPHAN-AGE.
THAT'S WHEN I FIRST FOUND A BARREL FULL'A OLD COMIC-BOOKS.
I READ AND RE-READ 'EM, TILL THEY WERE FALLIN' APART!
"THEY WERE FULL OF HEROES, TOO-- BUT SIMPLER HEROES---"
"--AN' EVEN THE FEW OF 'EM WHO TURNED OUT TO BE REALIES DIDN'T HAVE A LOT OF HANG-UPS THEN.
"THEY WERE JUST SUPER-POWERED JOES WITH A CLEAR IDEA OF WHAT TRUTH WAS--AN' JUSTICE-- YEAH, EVEN LAW AN' ORDER---
"THAT'S WHEN I FIRST DECIDED I WANTED TO BE A SUPERHERO-- OR DO ANYTHING I COULD TO BE AROUND GUYS LIKE THAT-- GUYS WHO LIVED AND FOUGHT IN A WORLD OF BLACK-AND-WHITE, NOT MURKY GRAY---
LET'S FACE IT, FELLA-- THE WORLD AIN'T LIKE THAT ANYMORE.
IF IT EVER REALLY WAS.
--AND THERE AIN'T NO SCORECARD!
THESE DAYS, YOU CAN'T TELL THE GOOD GUYS FROM THE BAD GUYS WITHOUT A SCORECARD.

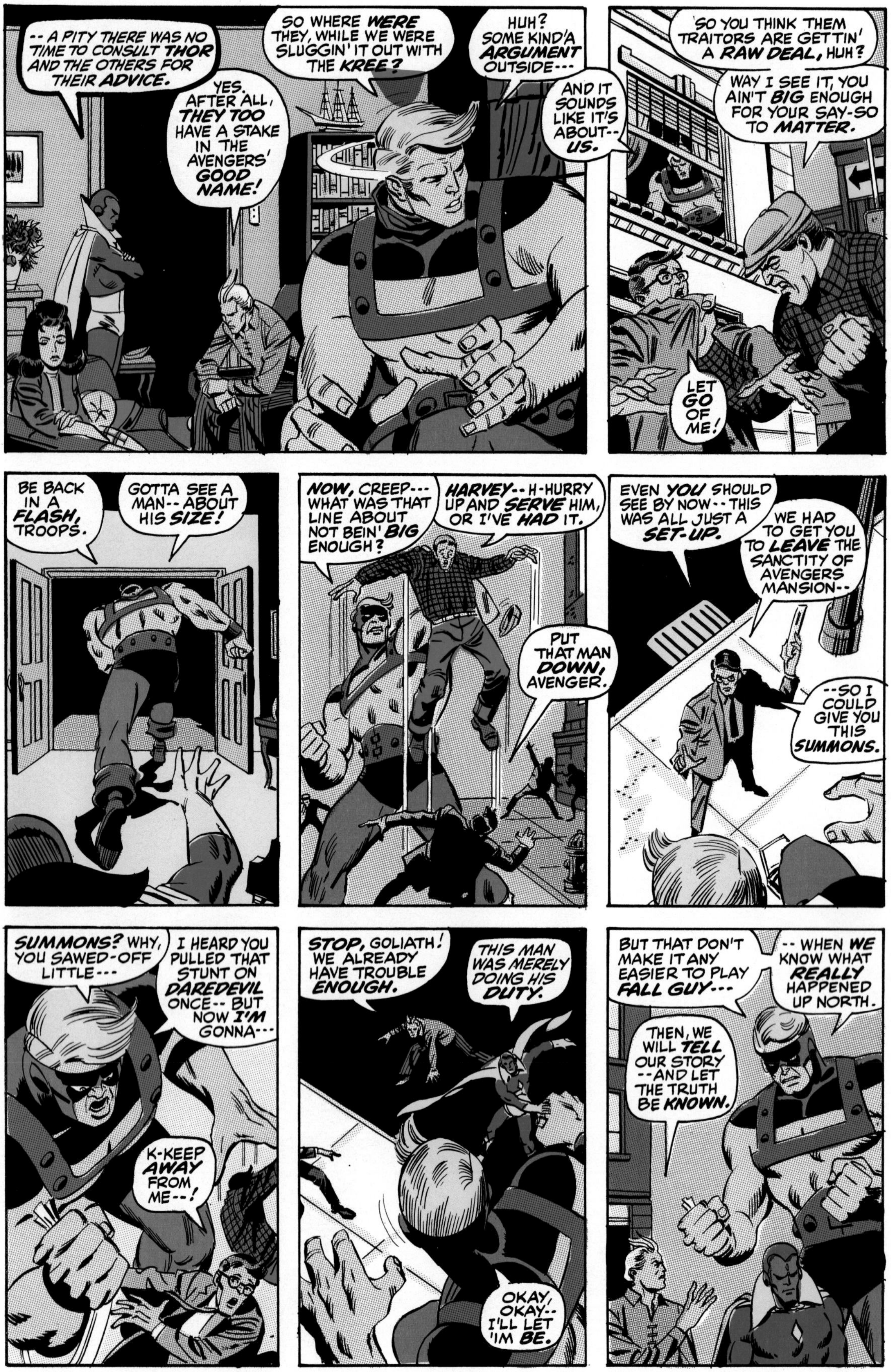

-- A PITY THERE WAS NO TIME TO CONSULT THOR AND THE OTHERS FOR THEIR ADVICE.
YES. AFTER ALL, THEY TOO HAVE A STAKE IN THE AVENGERS' GOOD NAME!
SO WHERE WERE THEY, WHILE WE WERE SLUGGIN' IT OUT WITH THE KREE?
HUH? SOME KIND'A ARGUMENT OUTSIDE---
AND IT SOUNDS LIKE IT'S ABOUT-- US.
'SO YOU THINK THEM TRAITORS ARE GETTIN' A RAW DEAL, HUH?
WAY I SEE IT, YOU AIN'T BIG ENOUGH FOR YOUR SAY-SO TO MATTER.
LET GO OF ME!
BE BACK IN A FLASH, TROOPS.
GOTTA SEE A MAN-- ABOUT HIS SIZE!
NOW, CREEP--- WHAT WAS THAT LINE ABOUT NOT BEIN' BIG ENOUGH?
HARVEY-- H-HURRY UP AND SERVE HIM, OR I'VE HAD IT.
PUT THAT MAN DOWN, AVENGER.
EVEN YOU SHOULD SEE BY NOW-- THIS WAS ALL JUST A SET-UP.
WE HAD TO GET YOU TO LEAVE THE SANCTITY OF AVENGERS MANSION--
--SO I COULD GIVE YOU THIS SUMMONS.
SUMMONS? WHY, YOU SAWED-OFF LITTLE---
I HEARD YOU PULLED THAT STUNT ON DAREDEVIL ONCE-- BUT NOW I'M GONNA---
K-KEEP AWAY FROM ME--!
STOP, GOLIATH! WE ALREADY HAVE TROUBLE ENOUGH.
THIS MAN WAS MERELY DOING HIS DUTY.
OKAY, OKAY-- I'LL LET 'IM BE.
BUT THAT DON'T MAKE IT ANY EASIER TO PLAY FALL GUY---
-- WHEN WE KNOW WHAT REALLY HAPPENED UP NORTH.
THEN, WE WILL TELL OUR STORY --AND LET THE TRUTH BE KNOWN.

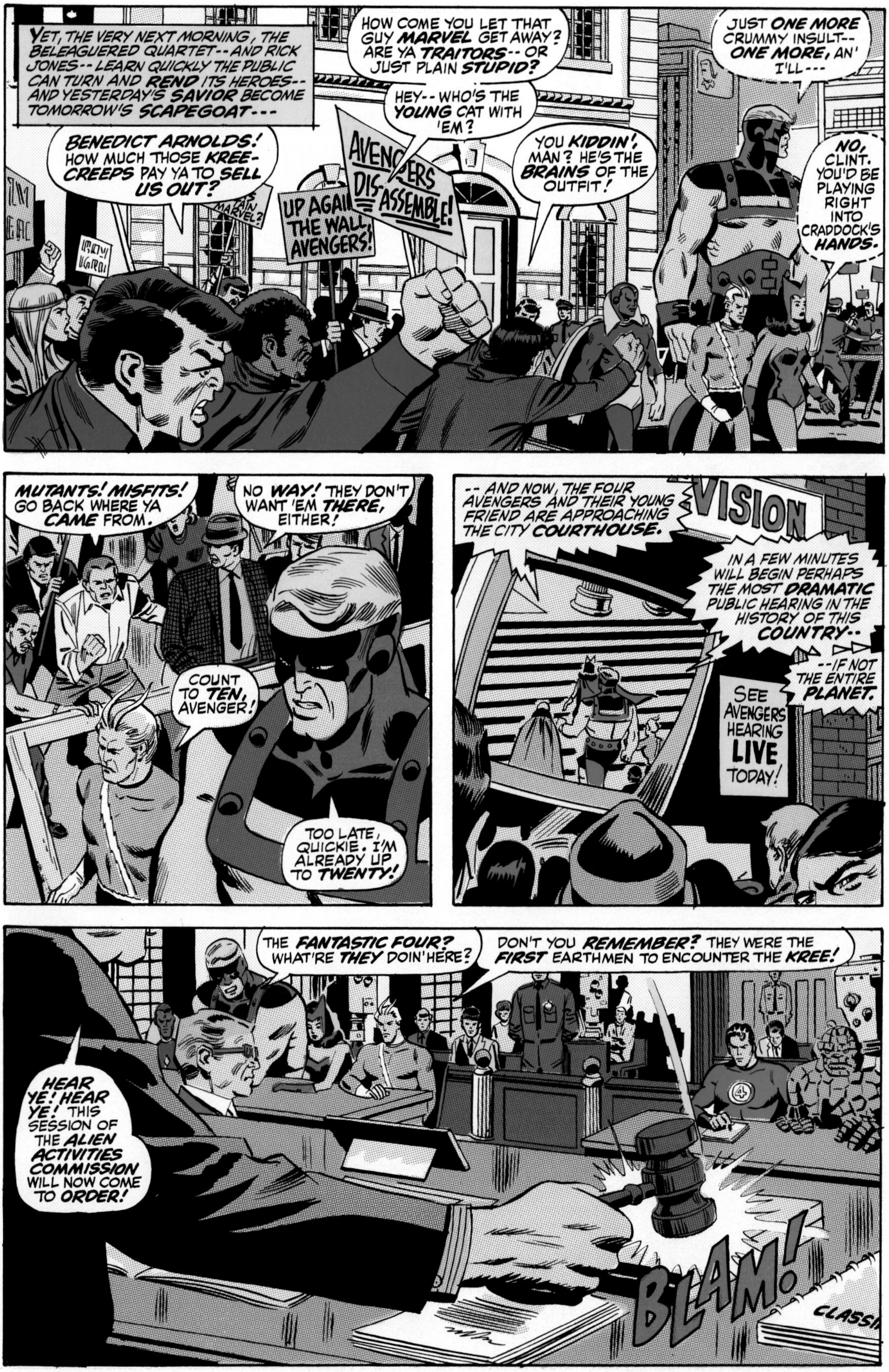

YET, THE VERY NEXT MORNING, THE BELEAGUERED QUARTET -- AND RICK JONES -- LEARN QUICKLY THE PUBLIC CAN TURN AND REND ITS HEROES -- AND YESTERDAY'S SAVIOR BECOME TOMORROW'S SCAPEGOAT---
HOW COME YOU LET THAT GUY MARVEL GET AWAY? ARE YA TRAITORS -- OR JUST PLAIN STUPID?
BENEDICT ARNOLDS! HOW MUCH THOSE KREE-CREEPS PAY YA TO SELL US OUT?
HEY -- WHO'S THE YOUNG CAT WITH 'EM?
YOU KIDDIN', MAN? HE'S THE BRAINS OF THE OUTFIT!
JUST ONE MORE CRUMMY INSULT -- ONE MORE, AN' I'LL---
NO, CLINT. YOU'D BE PLAYING RIGHT INTO CRADDOCK'S HANDS.
DIS-ASSEMBLE!
THE WALL AVENGERS!
MUTANTS! MISFITS! GO BACK WHERE YA CAME FROM.
NO WAY! THEY DON'T WANT 'EM THERE, EITHER!
COUNT TO TEN, AVENGER!
TOO LATE, QUICKIE. I'M ALREADY UP TO TWENTY!
-- AND NOW, THE FOUR AVENGERS AND THEIR YOUNG FRIEND ARE APPROACHING THE CITY COURTHOUSE.
VISION
IN A FEW MINUTES WILL BEGIN PERHAPS THE MOST DRAMATIC PUBLIC HEARING IN THE HISTORY OF THIS COUNTRY--
--IF NOT THE ENTIRE PLANET.
SEE AVENGERS HEARING LIVE TODAY!
THE FANTASTIC FOUR? WHAT'RE THEY DOIN' HERE?
DON'T YOU REMEMBER? THEY WERE THE FIRST EARTHMEN TO ENCOUNTER THE KREE!
HEAR YE! HEAR YE! THIS SESSION OF THE ALIEN ACTIVITIES COMMISSION WILL NOW COME TO ORDER!
BLAM!

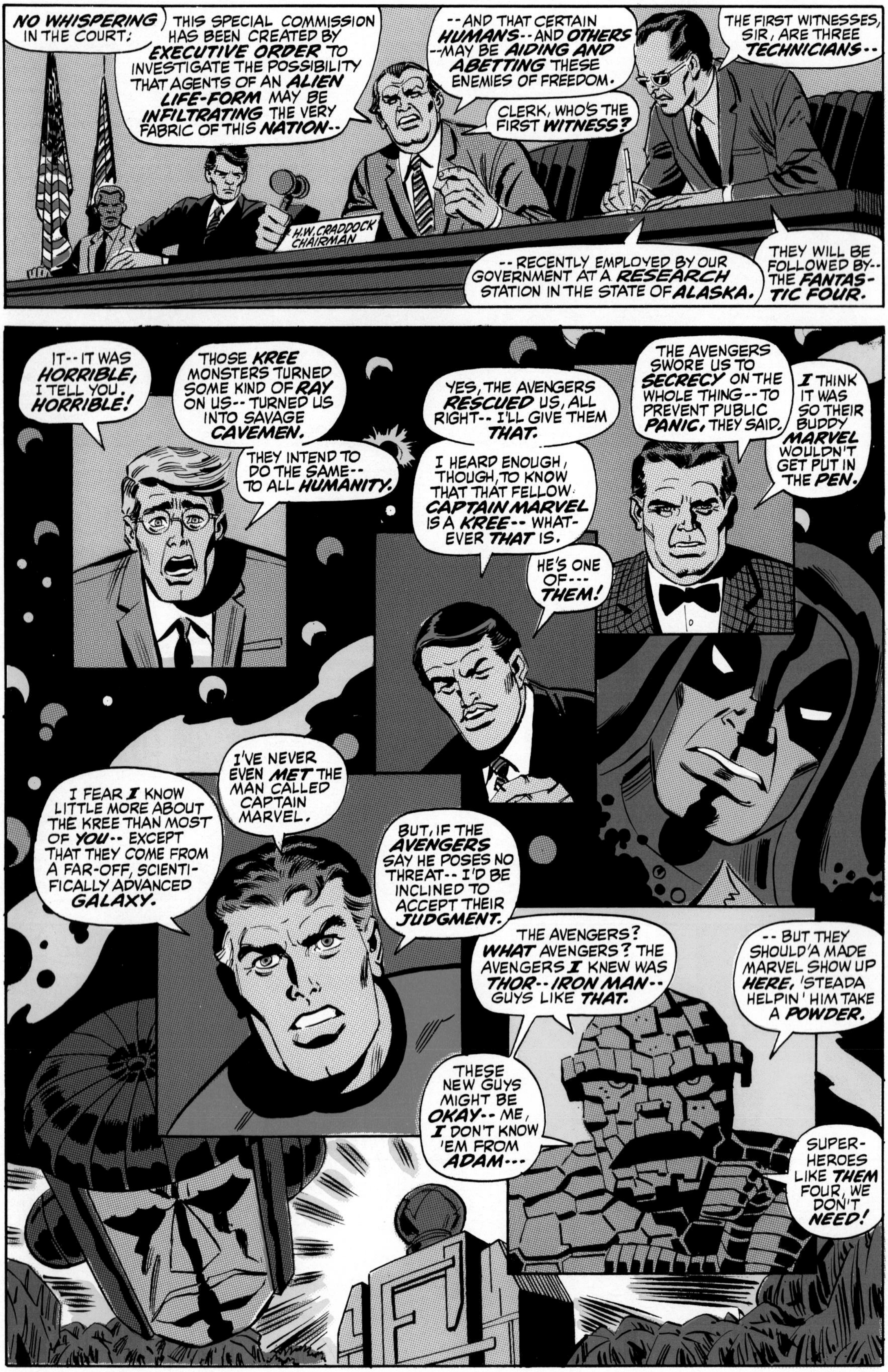
NO WHISPERING IN THE COURT!
THIS SPECIAL COMMISSION HAS BEEN CREATED BY EXECUTIVE ORDER TO INVESTIGATE THE POSSIBILITY THAT AGENTS OF AN ALIEN LIFE-FORM MAY BE INFILTRATING THE VERY FABRIC OF THIS NATION--
--AND THAT CERTAIN HUMANS--AND OTHERS--MAY BE AIDING AND ABETTING THESE ENEMIES OF FREEDOM.
CLERK, WHO'S THE FIRST WITNESS?
THE FIRST WITNESSES, SIR, ARE THREE TECHNICIANS--
--RECENTLY EMPLOYED BY OUR GOVERNMENT AT A RESEARCH STATION IN THE STATE OF ALASKA.
THEY WILL BE FOLLOWED BY--THE FANTASTIC FOUR.
H.W. CRADDOCK CHAIRMAN
IT--IT WAS HORRIBLE, I TELL YOU. HORRIBLE!
THOSE KREE MONSTERS TURNED SOME KIND OF RAY ON US--TURNED US INTO SAVAGE CAVEMEN.
THEY INTEND TO DO THE SAME--TO ALL HUMANITY.
YES, THE AVENGERS RESCUED US, ALL RIGHT--I'LL GIVE THEM THAT.
I HEARD ENOUGH, THOUGH, TO KNOW THAT THAT FELLOW CAPTAIN MARVEL IS A KREE--WHATEVER THAT IS.
HE'S ONE OF---THEM!
THE AVENGERS SWORE US TO SECRECY ON THE WHOLE THING--TO PREVENT PUBLIC PANIC, THEY SAID.
I THINK IT WAS SO THEIR BUDDY MARVEL WOULDN'T GET PUT IN THE PEN.
I FEAR I KNOW LITTLE MORE ABOUT THE KREE THAN MOST OF YOU--EXCEPT THAT THEY COME FROM A FAR-OFF, SCIENTIFICALLY ADVANCED GALAXY.
I'VE NEVER EVEN MET THE MAN CALLED CAPTAIN MARVEL.
BUT, IF THE AVENGERS SAY HE POSES NO THREAT--I'D BE INCLINED TO ACCEPT THEIR JUDGMENT.
THE AVENGERS? WHAT AVENGERS? THE AVENGERS I KNEW WAS THOR--IRON MAN--GUYS LIKE THAT.
--BUT THEY SHOULD'A MADE MARVEL SHOW UP HERE, 'STEADA HELPIN' HIM TAKE A POWDER.
THESE NEW GUYS MIGHT BE OKAY--ME, I DON'T KNOW 'EM FROM ADAM---
SUPER-HEROES LIKE THEM FOUR, WE DON'T NEED!

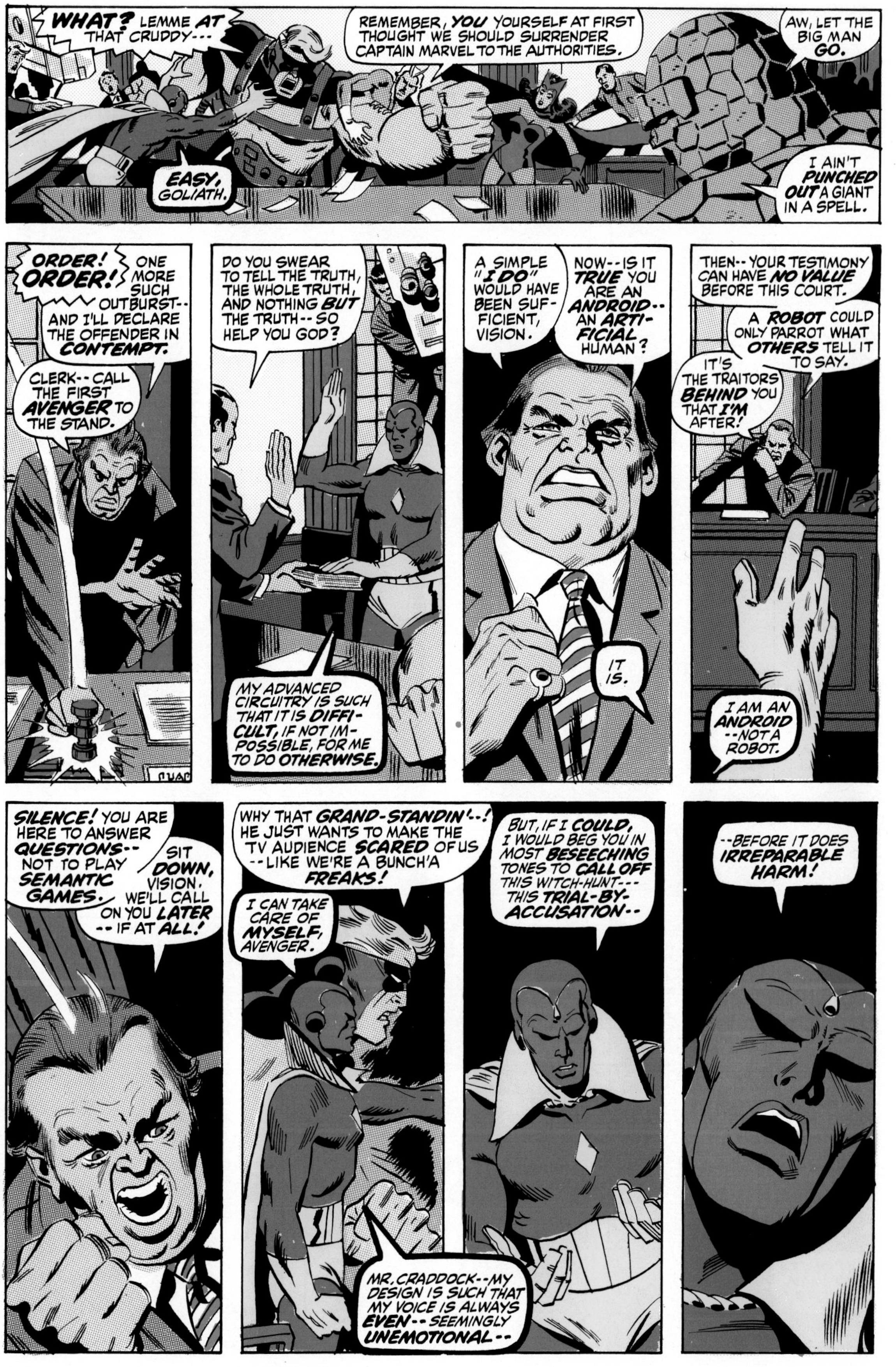
WHAT? LEMME AT THAT CRUDDY---
REMEMBER, YOU YOURSELF AT FIRST THOUGHT WE SHOULD SURRENDER CAPTAIN MARVEL TO THE AUTHORITIES.
AW, LET THE BIG MAN GO.
EASY, GOLIATH.
I AIN'T PUNCHED OUT A GIANT IN A SPELL.
ORDER! ORDER!
ONE MORE SUCH OUTBURST-- AND I'LL DECLARE THE OFFENDER IN CONTEMPT.
CLERK-- CALL THE FIRST AVENGER TO THE STAND.
DO YOU SWEAR TO TELL THE TRUTH, THE WHOLE TRUTH, AND NOTHING BUT THE TRUTH-- SO HELP YOU GOD?
MY ADVANCED CIRCUITRY IS SUCH THAT IT IS DIFFI-CULT, IF NOT IM-POSSIBLE, FOR ME TO DO OTHERWISE.
A SIMPLE "I DO" WOULD HAVE BEEN SUF-FICIENT, VISION.
NOW-- IS IT TRUE YOU ARE AN ANDROID-- AN ARTI-FICIAL HUMAN?
IT IS.
THEN-- YOUR TESTIMONY CAN HAVE NO VALUE BEFORE THIS COURT.
A ROBOT COULD ONLY PARROT WHAT OTHERS TELL IT TO SAY.
IT'S THE TRAITORS BEHIND YOU THAT I'M AFTER!
I AM AN ANDROID --NOT A ROBOT.
SILENCE! YOU ARE HERE TO ANSWER QUESTIONS-- NOT TO PLAY SEMANTIC GAMES.
SIT DOWN, VISION. WE'LL CALL ON YOU LATER -- IF AT ALL!
WHY THAT GRAND-STANDIN'--! HE JUST WANTS TO MAKE THE TV AUDIENCE SCARED OF US -- LIKE WE'RE A BUNCH'A FREAKS!
I CAN TAKE CARE OF MYSELF, AVENGER.
MR. CRADDOCK-- MY DESIGN IS SUCH THAT MY VOICE IS ALWAYS EVEN-- SEEMINGLY UNEMOTIONAL--
BUT, IF I COULD, I WOULD BEG YOU IN MOST BESEECHING TONES TO CALL OFF THIS WITCH-HUNT--- THIS TRIAL-BY-ACCUSATION--
--BEFORE IT DOES IRREPARABLE HARM!

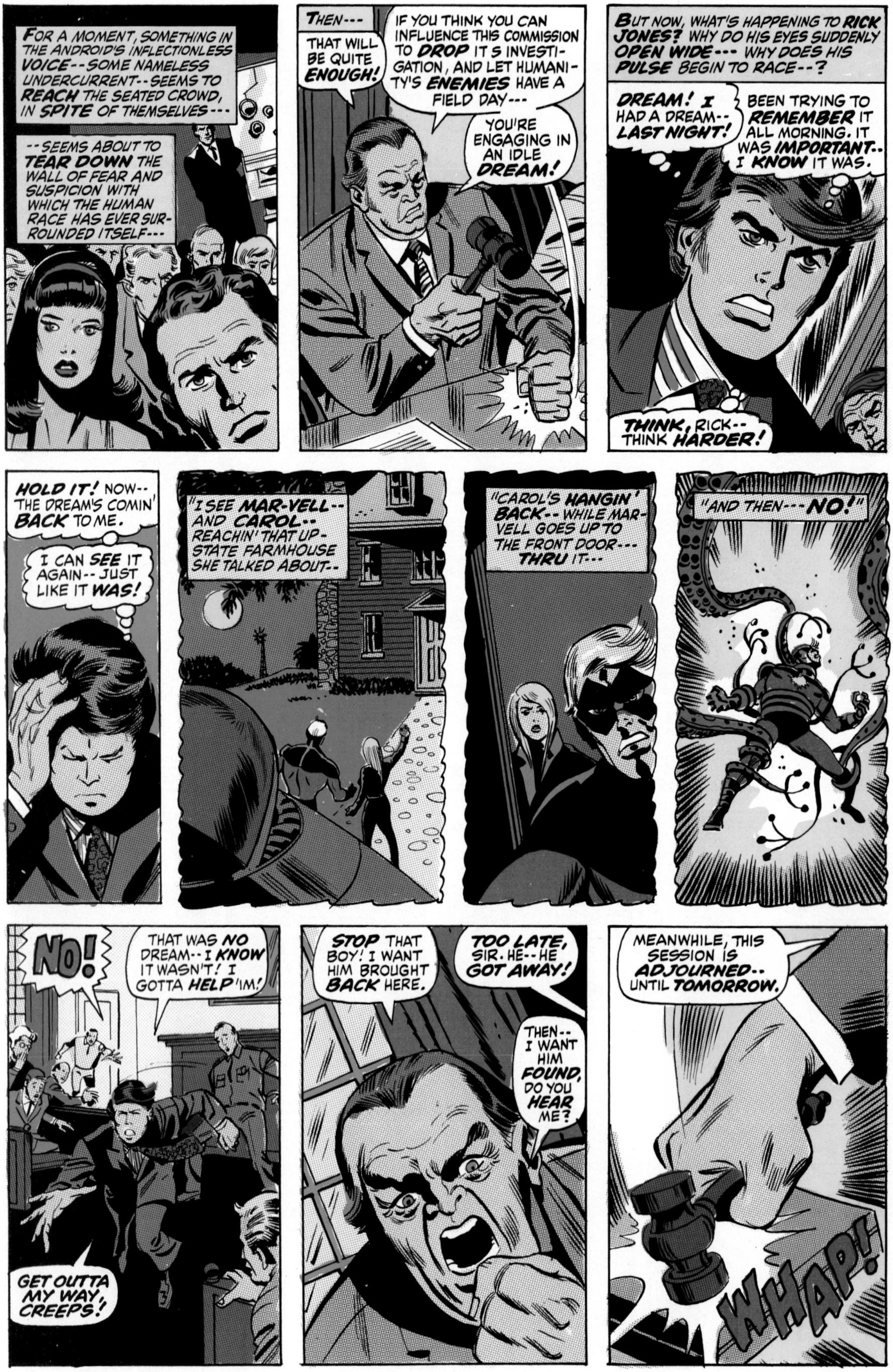

FOR A MOMENT, SOMETHING IN THE ANDROID'S INFLECTIONLESS VOICE--SOME NAMELESS UNDERCURRENT--SEEMS TO REACH THE SEATED CROWD, IN SPITE OF THEMSELVES---
--SEEMS ABOUT TO TEAR DOWN THE WALL OF FEAR AND SUSPICION WITH WHICH THE HUMAN RACE HAS EVER SURROUNDED ITSELF---
THEN---
THAT WILL BE QUITE ENOUGH!
IF YOU THINK YOU CAN INFLUENCE THIS COMMISSION TO DROP IT'S INVESTIGATION, AND LET HUMANITY'S ENEMIES HAVE A FIELD DAY---
YOU'RE ENGAGING IN AN IDLE DREAM!
BUT NOW, WHAT'S HAPPENING TO RICK JONES? WHY DO HIS EYES SUDDENLY OPEN WIDE--- WHY DOES HIS PULSE BEGIN TO RACE--?
DREAM! I HAD A DREAM--LAST NIGHT!
BEEN TRYING TO REMEMBER IT ALL MORNING. IT WAS IMPORTANT--I KNOW IT WAS.
THINK, RICK--THINK HARDER!
HOLD IT! NOW--THE DREAM'S COMIN' BACK TO ME.
I CAN SEE IT AGAIN--JUST LIKE IT WAS!
"I SEE MAR-VELL--AND CAROL--REACHIN' THAT UP-STATE FARMHOUSE SHE TALKED ABOUT--
"CAROL'S HANGIN' BACK--WHILE MAR-VELL GOES UP TO THE FRONT DOOR---THRU IT---
"AND THEN---NO!"
NO!
THAT WAS NO DREAM--I KNOW IT WASN'T! I GOTTA HELP 'IM!
GET OUTTA MY WAY, CREEPS!
STOP THAT BOY! I WANT HIM BROUGHT BACK HERE.
TOO LATE, SIR. HE--HE GOT AWAY!
THEN--I WANT HIM FOUND, DO YOU HEAR ME?
MEANWHILE, THIS SESSION IS ADJOURNED--UNTIL TOMORROW.
WHAP!

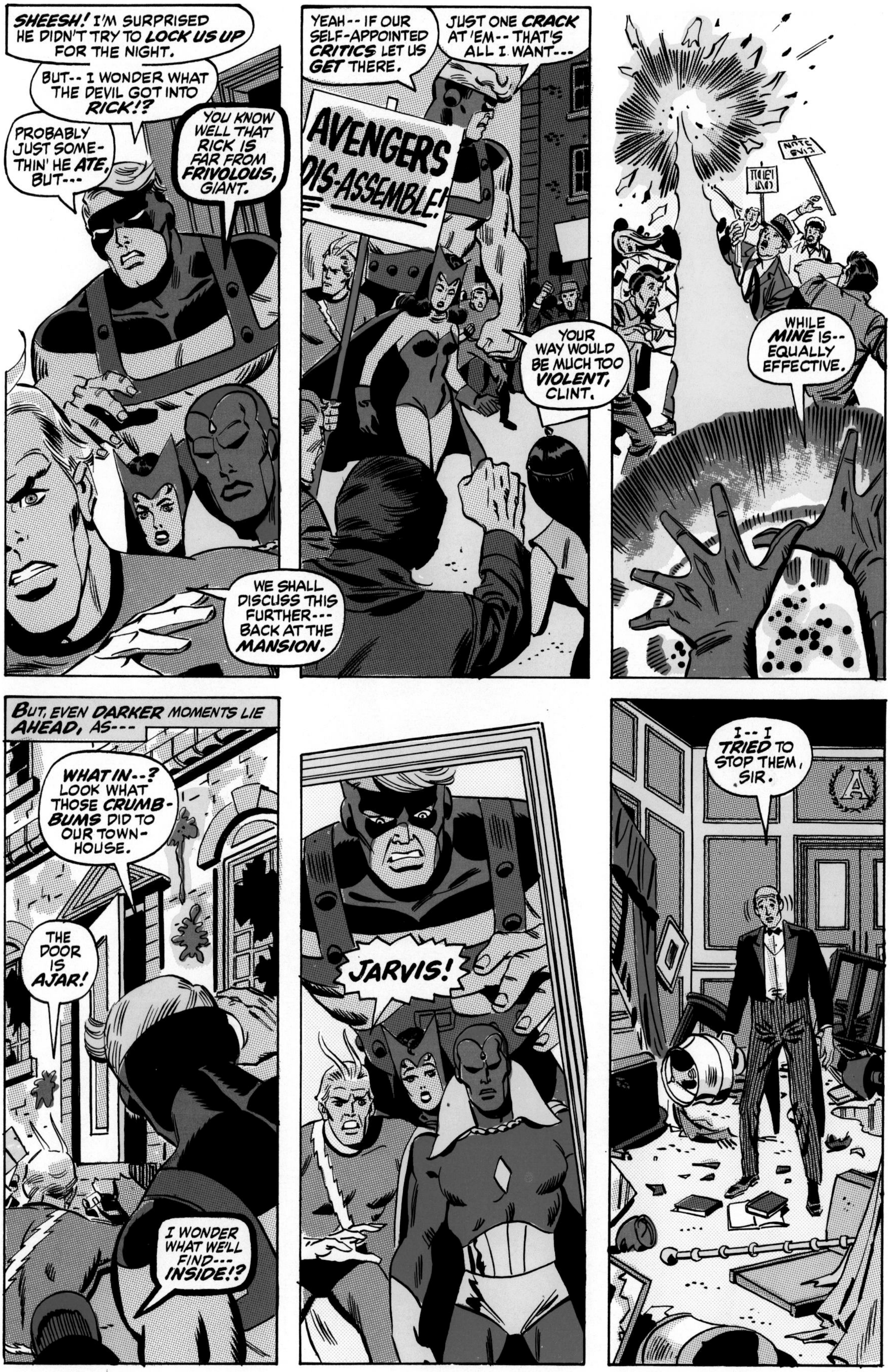
SHEESH! I'M SURPRISED HE DIDN'T TRY TO LOCK US UP FOR THE NIGHT.
BUT-- I WONDER WHAT THE DEVIL GOT INTO RICK!?
PROBABLY JUST SOME-THIN' HE ATE, BUT---
YOU KNOW WELL THAT RICK IS FAR FROM FRIVOLOUS, GIANT.
WE SHALL DISCUSS THIS FURTHER--- BACK AT THE MANSION.
YEAH-- IF OUR SELF-APPOINTED CRITICS LET US GET THERE.
JUST ONE CRACK AT 'EM-- THAT'S ALL I WANT---
AVENGERS DIS-ASSEMBLE!
YOUR WAY WOULD BE MUCH TOO VIOLENT, CLINT.
WHILE MINE IS-- EQUALLY EFFECTIVE.
BUT, EVEN DARKER MOMENTS LIE AHEAD, AS---
WHAT IN--? LOOK WHAT THOSE CRUMB-BUMS DID TO OUR TOWN-HOUSE.
THE DOOR IS AJAR!
I WONDER WHAT WE'LL FIND--- INSIDE!?
JARVIS!
I-- I TRIED TO STOP THEM, SIR.

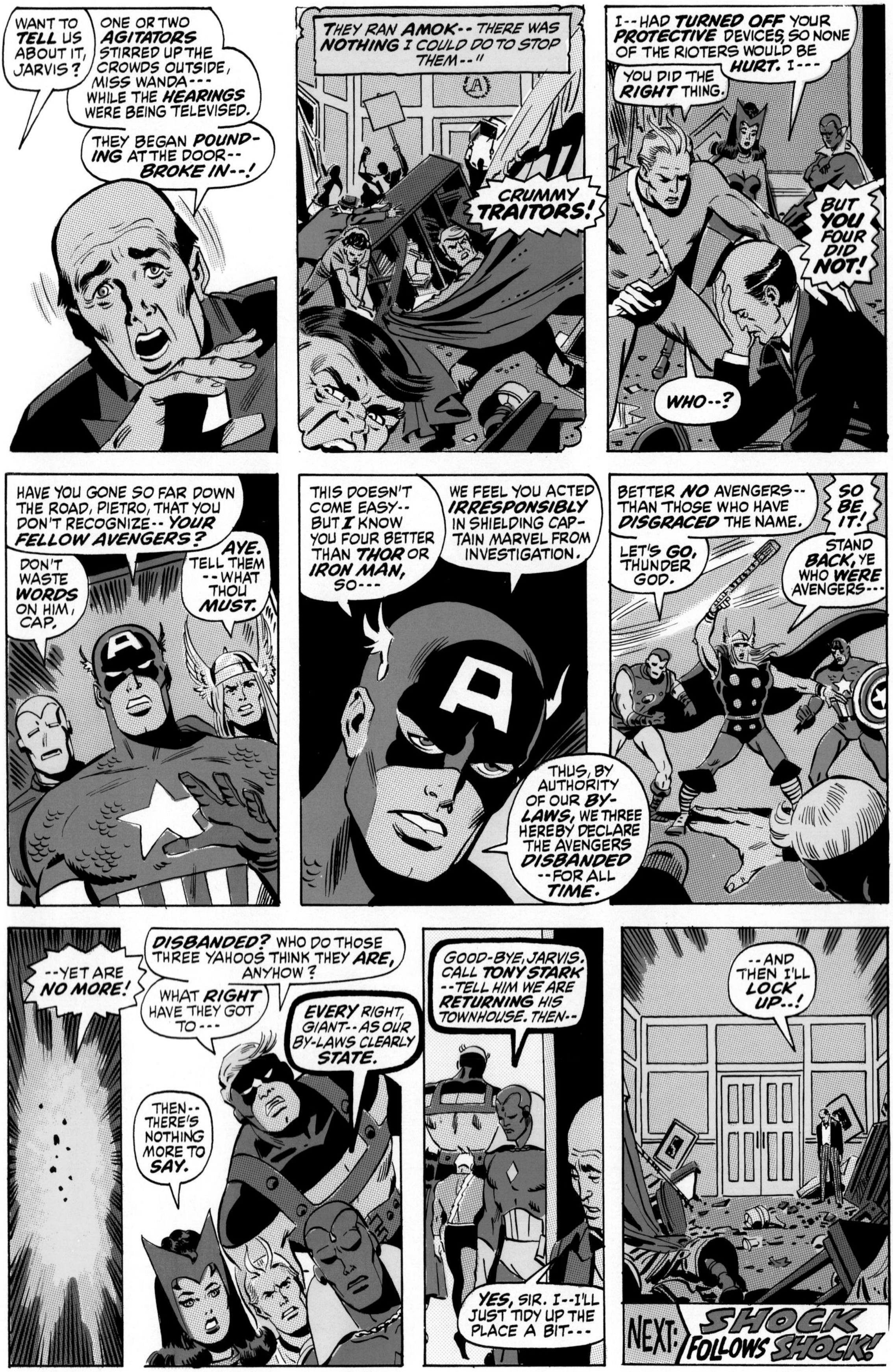

WANT TO TELL US ABOUT IT, JARVIS?
ONE OR TWO AGITATORS STIRRED UP THE CROWDS OUTSIDE, MISS WANDA--- WHILE THE HEARINGS WERE BEING TELEVISED.
THEY BEGAN POUNDING AT THE DOOR-- BROKE IN--!
THEY RAN AMOK-- THERE WAS NOTHING I COULD DO TO STOP THEM--"
CRUMMY TRAITORS!
I--HAD TURNED OFF YOUR PROTECTIVE DEVICES, SO NONE OF THE RIOTERS WOULD BE HURT. I---
YOU DID THE RIGHT THING.
BUT YOU FOUR DID NOT!
WHO--?
HAVE YOU GONE SO FAR DOWN THE ROAD, PIETRO, THAT YOU DON'T RECOGNIZE-- YOUR FELLOW AVENGERS?
DON'T WASTE WORDS ON HIM, CAP.
AYE. TELL THEM --WHAT THOU MUST.
THIS DOESN'T COME EASY-- BUT I KNOW YOU FOUR BETTER THAN THOR OR IRON MAN, SO---
WE FEEL YOU ACTED IRRESPONSIBLY IN SHIELDING CAPTAIN MARVEL FROM INVESTIGATION.
THUS, BY AUTHORITY OF OUR BY-LAWS, WE THREE HEREBY DECLARE THE AVENGERS DISBANDED --FOR ALL TIME.
BETTER NO AVENGERS-- THAN THOSE WHO HAVE DISGRACED THE NAME.
SO BE IT!
LET'S GO, THUNDER GOD.
STAND BACK, YE WHO WERE AVENGERS---
--YET ARE NO MORE!
DISBANDED? WHO DO THOSE THREE YAHOOS THINK THEY ARE, ANYHOW?
WHAT RIGHT HAVE THEY GOT TO---
EVERY RIGHT, GIANT-- AS OUR BY-LAWS CLEARLY STATE.
THEN-- THERE'S NOTHING MORE TO SAY.
GOOD-BYE, JARVIS. CALL TONY STARK --TELL HIM WE ARE RETURNING HIS TOWNHOUSE. THEN--
YES, SIR. I--I'LL JUST TIDY UP THE PLACE A BIT---
--AND THEN I'LL LOCK UP..!
NEXT: SHOCK FOLLOWS SHOCK!

CHAPTER FIVE

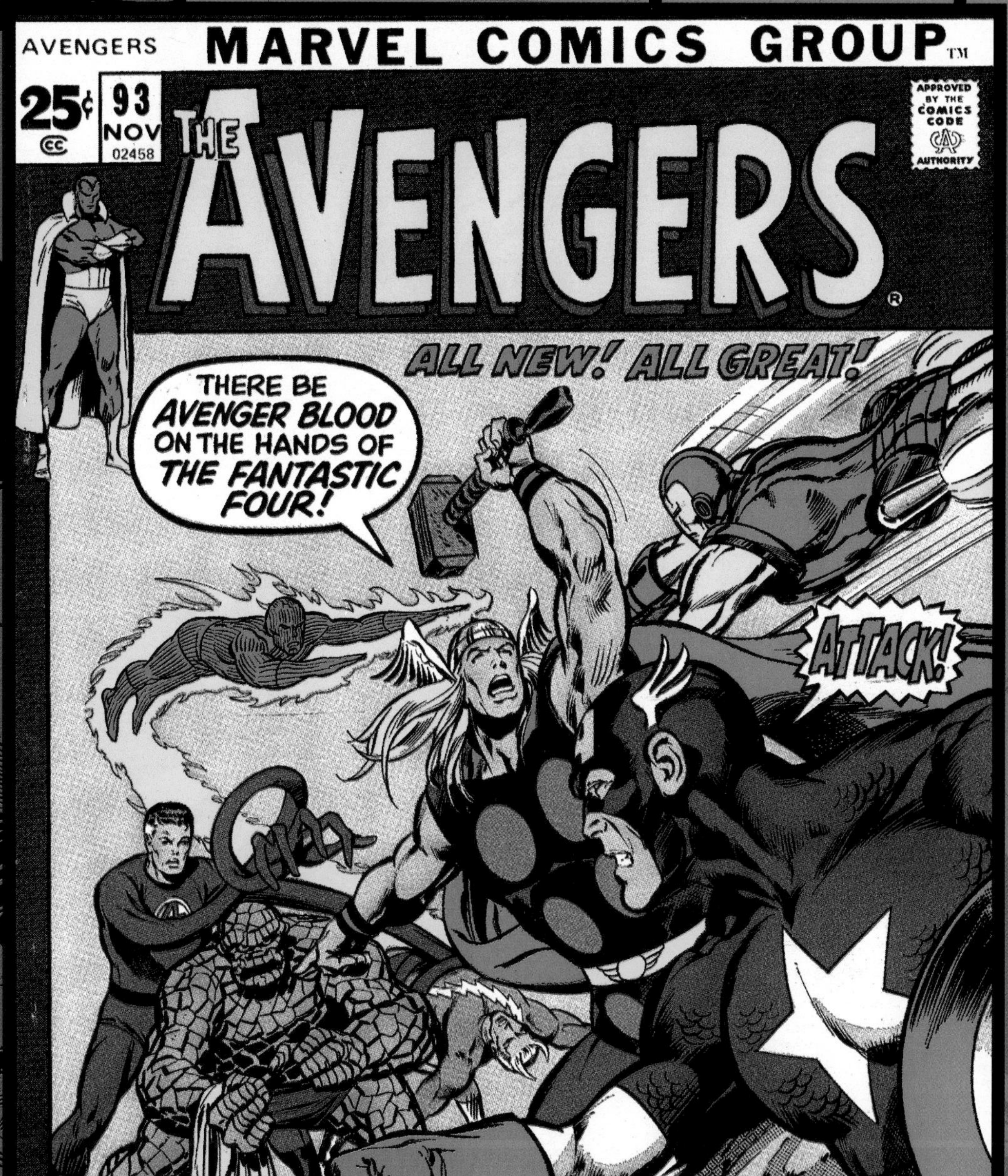
AVENGERS
MARVEL COMICS GROUP
25¢
93 NOV
02458
APPROVED BY THE COMICS CODE AUTHORITY
THE AVENGERS
ALL NEW! ALL GREAT!
THERE BE AVENGER BLOOD ON THE HANDS OF THE FANTASTIC FOUR!
ATTACK!
THE MIGHTY AVENGERS BATTLE THE FABULOUS F.F.··· OR DO THEY??
THIS BEACH-HEAD EARTH!

THIS BEACHHEAD EARTH

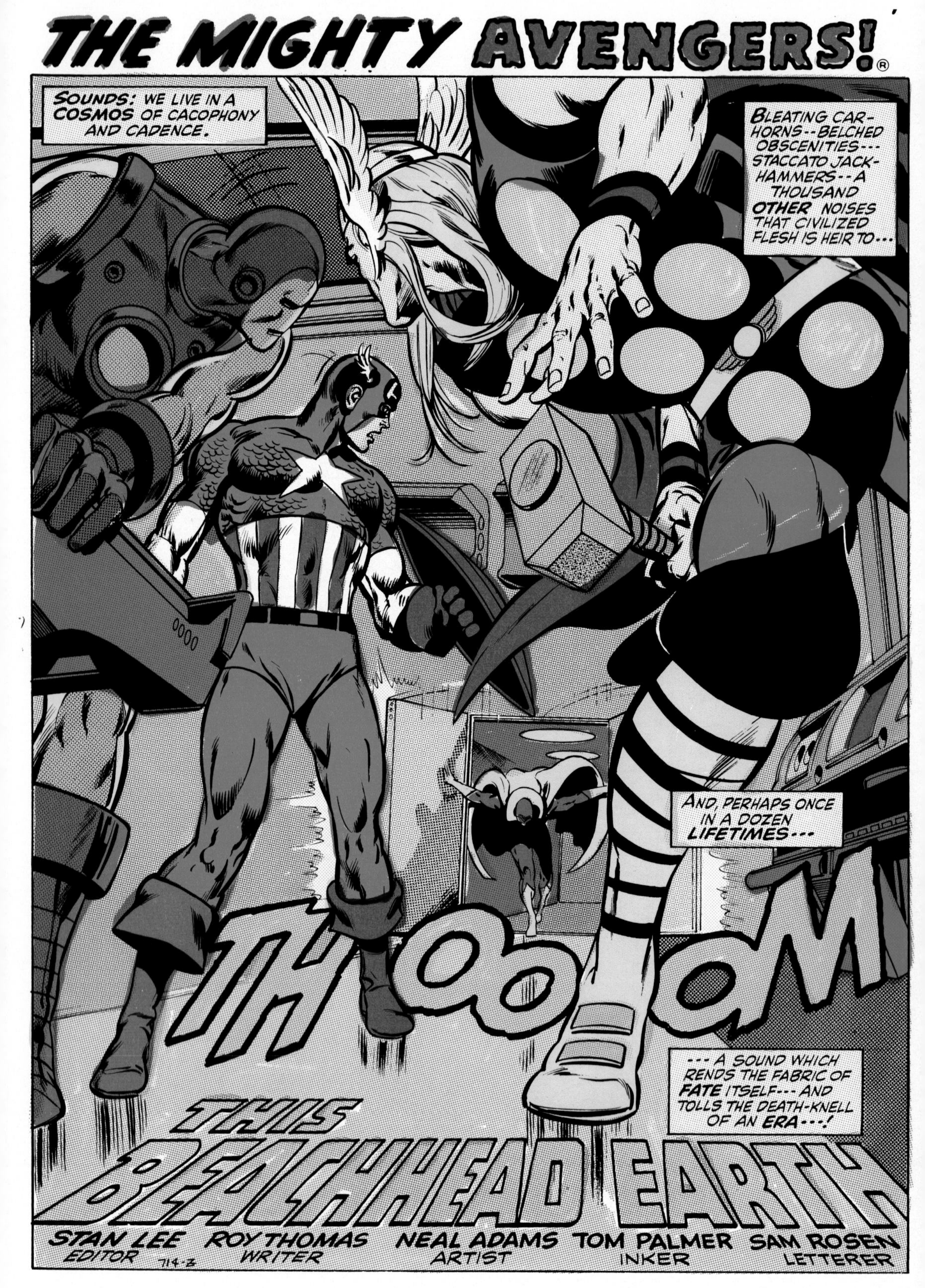
THE MIGHTY AVENGERS!®
SOUNDS: WE LIVE IN A COSMOS OF CACOPHONY AND CADENCE.
BLEATING CAR-HORNS--BELCHED OBSCENITIES---STACCATO JACK-HAMMERS--A THOUSAND OTHER NOISES THAT CIVILIZED FLESH IS HEIR TO---
AND, PERHAPS ONCE IN A DOZEN LIFETIMES---
THOOOM
---A SOUND WHICH RENDS THE FABRIC OF FATE ITSELF---AND TOLLS THE DEATH-KNELL OF AN ERA---!
THIS BEACHHEAD EARTH!
STAN LEE EDITOR
ROY THOMAS WRITER
NEAL ADAMS ARTIST
TOM PALMER INKER
SAM ROSEN LETTERER
714-3

HELP ME -- PLEASE --

HELP--- MEEEE--

WHUMP!

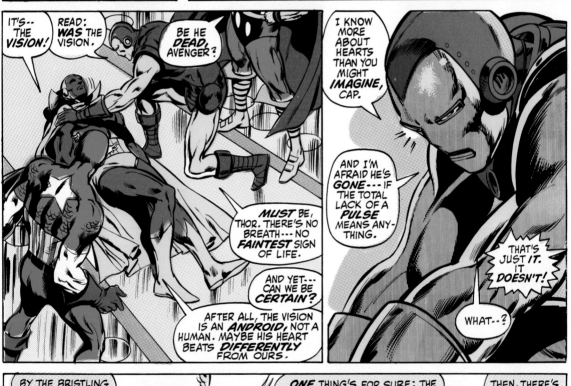

IT'S-- THE VISION!

READ: WAS THE VISION.

BE HE DEAD, AVENGER?

MUST BE, THOR. THERE'S NO BREATH--- NO FAINTEST SIGN OF LIFE.

AND YET--- CAN WE BE CERTAIN?

AFTER ALL, THE VISION IS AN ANDROID, NOT A HUMAN. MAYBE HIS HEART BEATS DIFFERENTLY FROM OURS.

I KNOW MORE ABOUT HEARTS THAN YOU MIGHT IMAGINE, CAP.

AND I'M AFRAID HE'S GONE--- IF THE TOTAL LACK OF A PULSE MEANS ANY-THING.

THAT'S JUST IT. IT DOESN'T!

WHAT--?

BY THE BRISTLING BEARD OF ODIN!

A VOICE-- ALMOST AT MY VERY SHOULDER --- YET NONE THERE BE TO CAST IT.

ONE THING'S FOR SURE: THE VISION DIDN'T SAY ANYTHING.

THEN, THERE'S A SPY-- RIGHT HERE IN AVENGERS MANSION!

2.

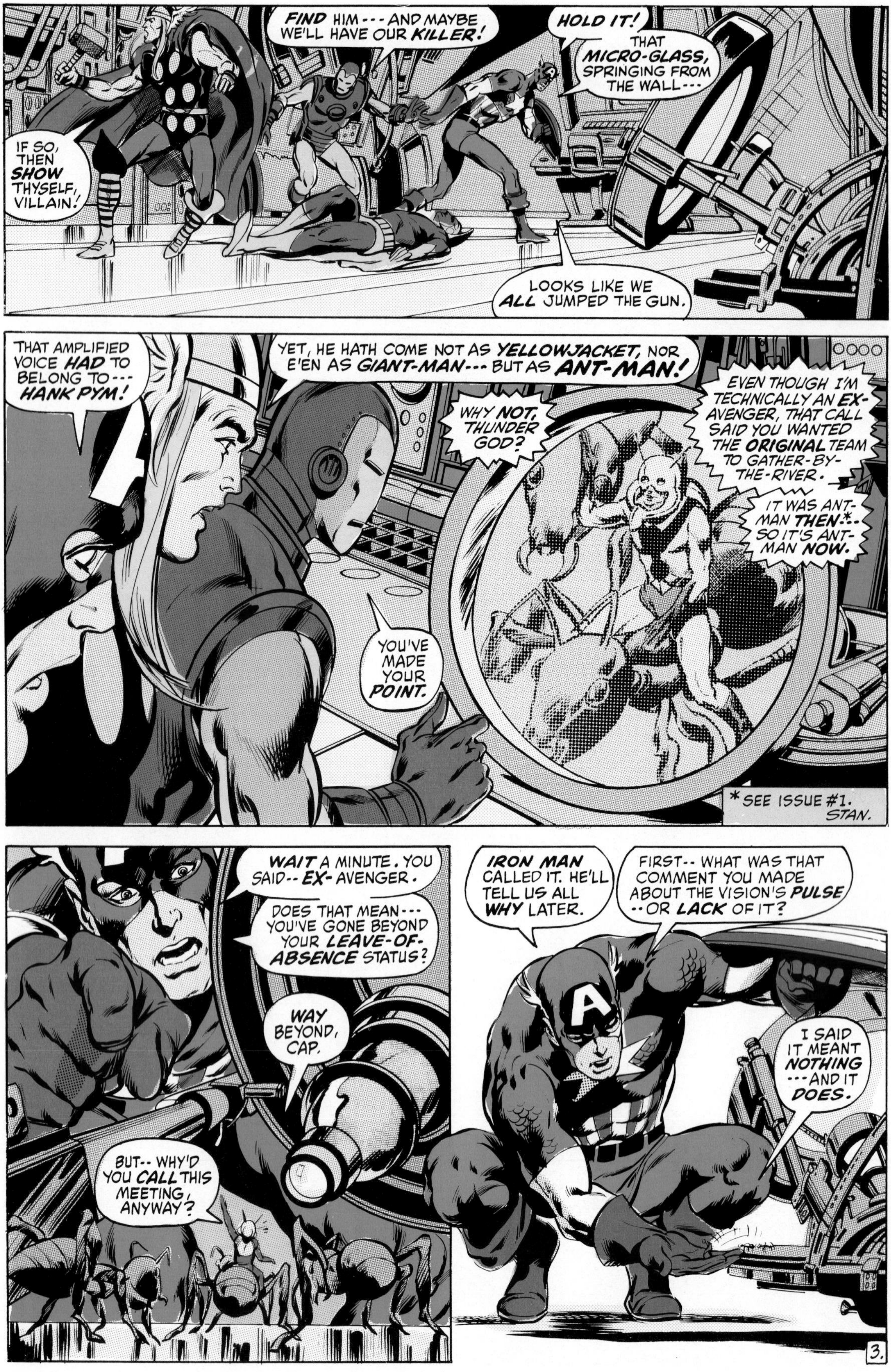
FIND HIM --- AND MAYBE WE'LL HAVE OUR KILLER!
IF SO, THEN SHOW THYSELF, VILLAIN!
HOLD IT!
THAT MICRO-GLASS, SPRINGING FROM THE WALL---
LOOKS LIKE WE ALL JUMPED THE GUN.
THAT AMPLIFIED VOICE HAD TO BELONG TO--- HANK PYM!
YET, HE HATH COME NOT AS YELLOWJACKET, NOR E'EN AS GIANT-MAN--- BUT AS ANT-MAN!
WHY NOT, THUNDER GOD?
EVEN THOUGH I'M TECHNICALLY AN EX-AVENGER, THAT CALL SAID YOU WANTED THE ORIGINAL TEAM TO GATHER-BY-THE-RIVER.
IT WAS ANT-MAN THEN*-- SO IT'S ANT-MAN NOW.
YOU'VE MADE YOUR POINT.
*SEE ISSUE #1. STAN.
WAIT A MINUTE. YOU SAID-- EX-AVENGER.
DOES THAT MEAN--- YOU'VE GONE BEYOND YOUR LEAVE-OF-ABSENCE STATUS?
WAY BEYOND, CAP.
BUT-- WHY'D YOU CALL THIS MEETING, ANYWAY?
IRON MAN CALLED IT. HE'LL TELL US ALL WHY LATER.
FIRST-- WHAT WAS THAT COMMENT YOU MADE ABOUT THE VISION'S PULSE --OR LACK OF IT?
I SAID IT MEANT NOTHING ---AND IT DOES.

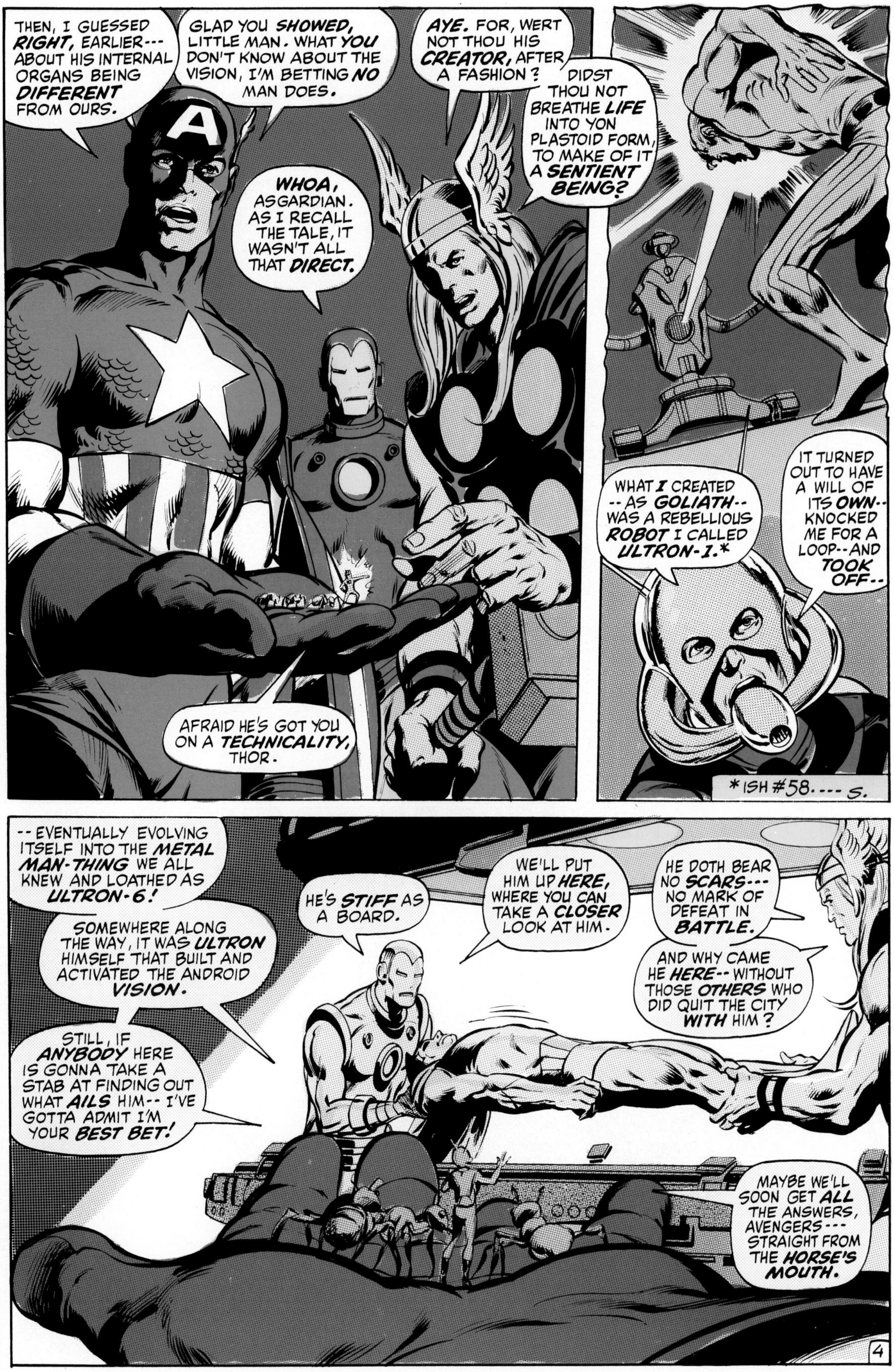
THEN, I GUESSED RIGHT, EARLIER--- ABOUT HIS INTERNAL ORGANS BEING DIFFERENT FROM OURS.
GLAD YOU SHOWED, LITTLE MAN. WHAT YOU DON'T KNOW ABOUT THE VISION, I'M BETTING NO MAN DOES.
AYE. FOR, WERT NOT THOU HIS CREATOR, AFTER A FASHION?
DIDST THOU NOT BREATHE LIFE INTO YON PLASTOID FORM, TO MAKE OF IT A SENTIENT BEING?
WHOA, ASGARDIAN. AS I RECALL THE TALE, IT WASN'T ALL THAT DIRECT.
AFRAID HE'S GOT YOU ON A TECHNICALITY, THOR.
WHAT I CREATED --AS GOLIATH-- WAS A REBELLIOUS ROBOT I CALLED ULTRON-1.*
IT TURNED OUT TO HAVE A WILL OF ITS OWN-- KNOCKED ME FOR A LOOP--AND TOOK OFF--
*ISH #58.--- S.
--EVENTUALLY EVOLVING ITSELF INTO THE METAL MAN-THING WE ALL KNEW AND LOATHED AS ULTRON-6!
SOMEWHERE ALONG THE WAY, IT WAS ULTRON HIMSELF THAT BUILT AND ACTIVATED THE ANDROID VISION.
STILL, IF ANYBODY HERE IS GONNA TAKE A STAB AT FINDING OUT WHAT AILS HIM-- I'VE GOTTA ADMIT I'M YOUR BEST BET!
HE'S STIFF AS A BOARD.
WE'LL PUT HIM UP HERE, WHERE YOU CAN TAKE A CLOSER LOOK AT HIM.
HE DOTH BEAR NO SCARS--- NO MARK OF DEFEAT IN BATTLE.
AND WHY CAME HE HERE-- WITHOUT THOSE OTHERS WHO DID QUIT THE CITY WITH HIM?
MAYBE WE'LL SOON GET ALL THE ANSWERS, AVENGERS--- STRAIGHT FROM THE HORSE'S MOUTH.
4

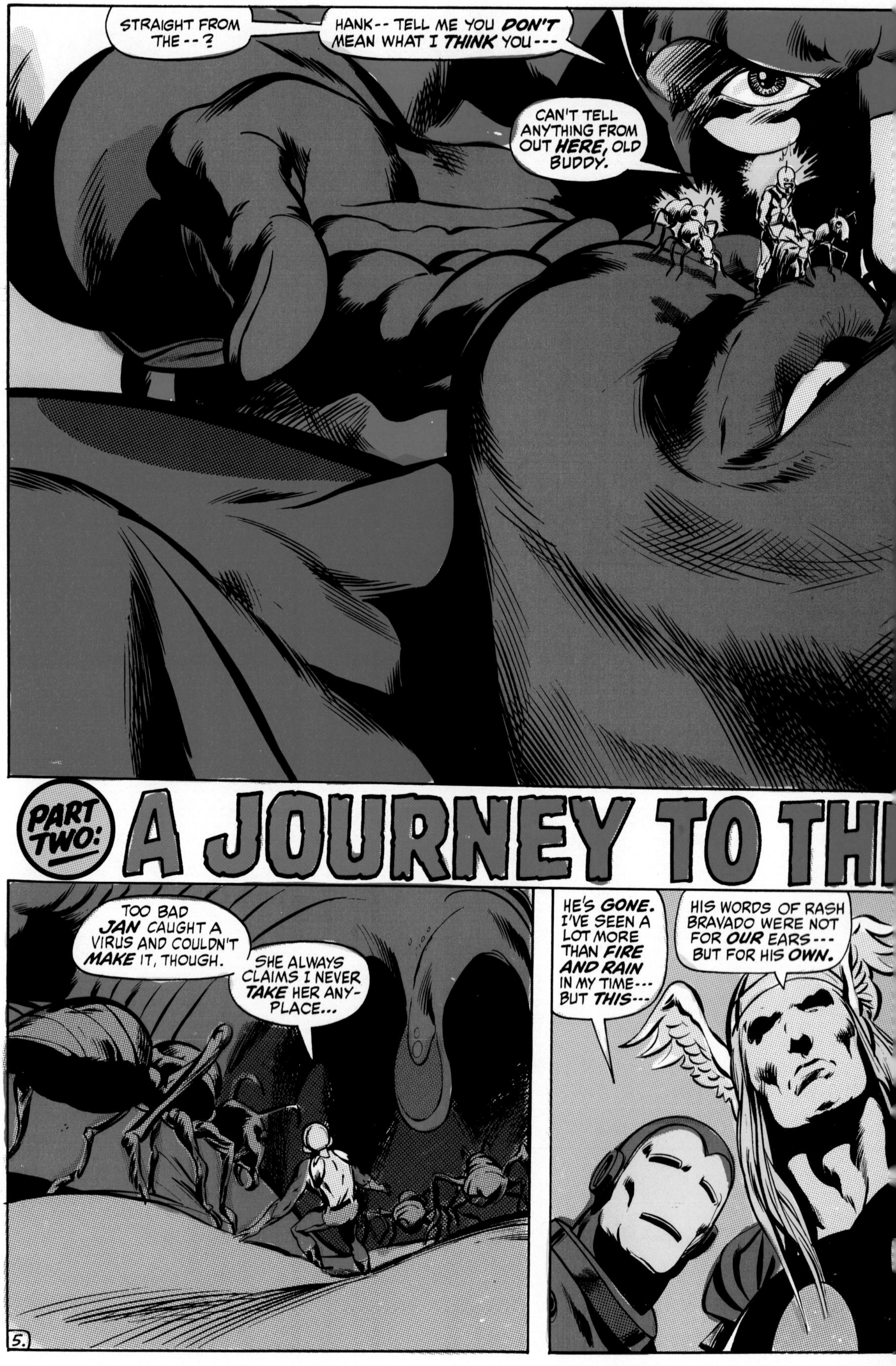
STRAIGHT FROM THE--?
HANK-- TELL ME YOU DON'T MEAN WHAT I THINK YOU---
CAN'T TELL ANYTHING FROM OUT HERE, OLD BUDDY.
PART TWO: A JOURNEY TO TH
TOO BAD JAN CAUGHT A VIRUS AND COULDN'T MAKE IT, THOUGH.
SHE ALWAYS CLAIMS I NEVER TAKE HER ANY-PLACE...
HE'S GONE. I'VE SEEN A LOT MORE THAN FIRE AND RAIN IN MY TIME--- BUT THIS---
HIS WORDS OF RASH BRAVADO WERE NOT FOR OUR EARS--- BUT FOR HIS OWN.
5.

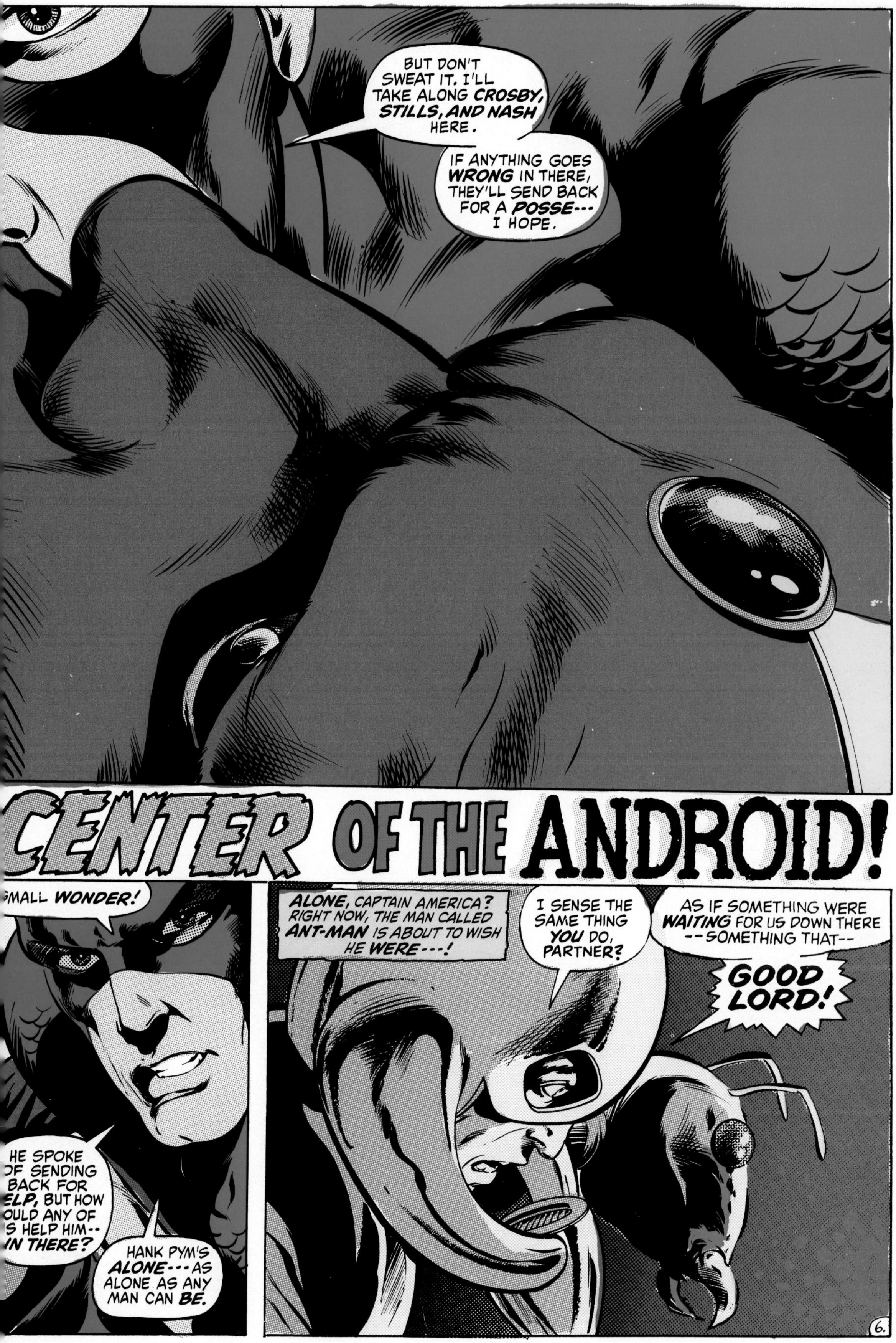

BUT DON'T SWEAT IT. I'LL TAKE ALONG CROSBY, STILLS, AND NASH HERE.
IF ANYTHING GOES WRONG IN THERE, THEY'LL SEND BACK FOR A POSSE--- I HOPE.
CENTER OF THE ANDROID!
SMALL WONDER!
HE SPOKE OF SENDING BACK FOR HELP, BUT HOW COULD ANY OF US HELP HIM-- IN THERE?
HANK PYM'S ALONE---AS ALONE AS ANY MAN CAN BE.
ALONE, CAPTAIN AMERICA? RIGHT NOW, THE MAN CALLED ANT-MAN IS ABOUT TO WISH HE WERE---!
I SENSE THE SAME THING YOU DO, PARTNER?
AS IF SOMETHING WERE WAITING FOR US DOWN THERE --SOMETHING THAT--
GOOD LORD!
6.

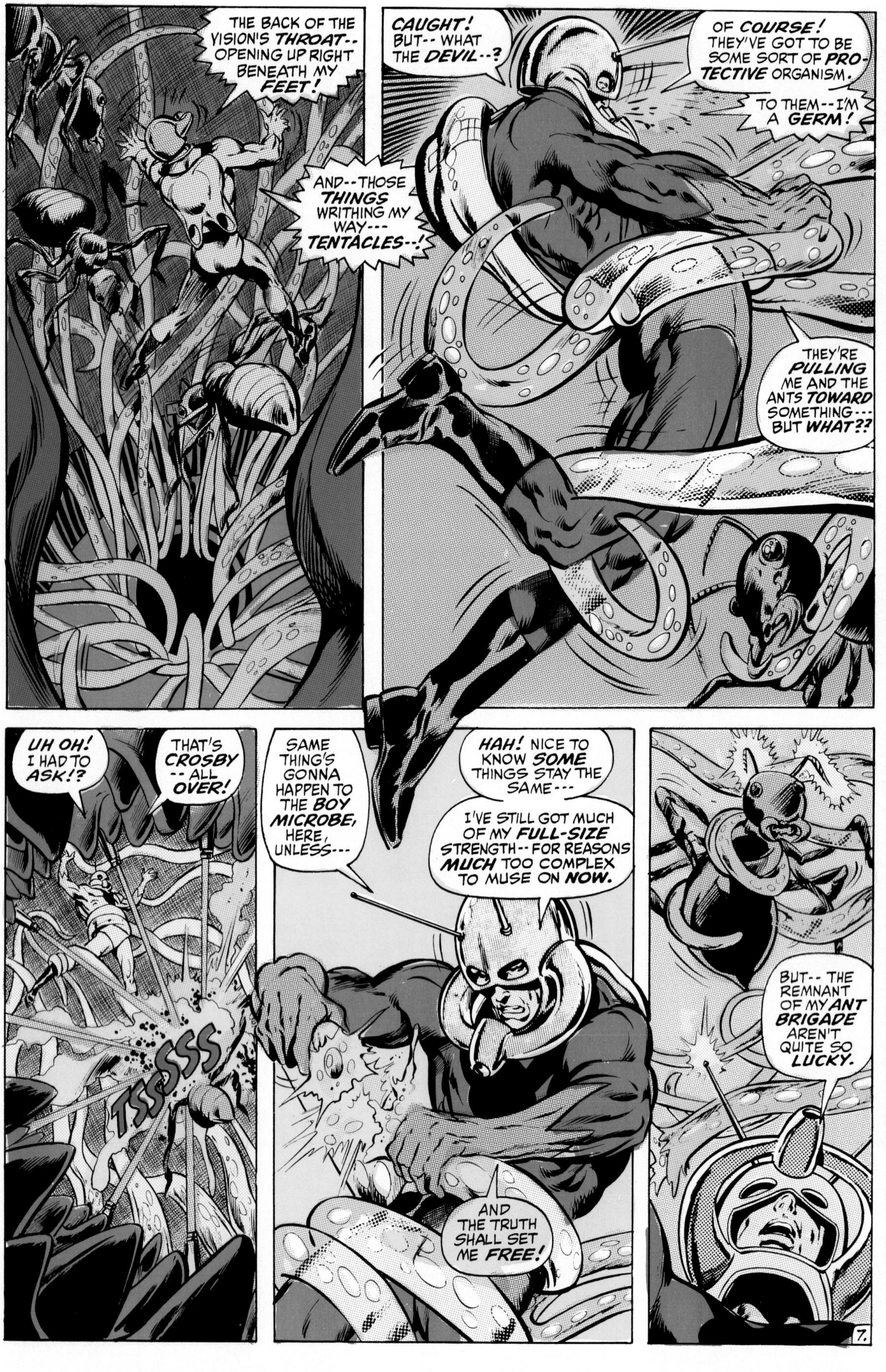

THE BACK OF THE VISION'S THROAT-- OPENING UP RIGHT BENEATH MY FEET!
AND--THOSE THINGS WRITHING MY WAY--- TENTACLES--!
CAUGHT! BUT-- WHAT THE DEVIL--?
OF COURSE! THEY'VE GOT TO BE SOME SORT OF PROTECTIVE ORGANISM.
TO THEM--I'M A GERM!
THEY'RE PULLING ME AND THE ANTS TOWARD SOMETHING--- BUT WHAT??
UH OH! I HAD TO ASK!?
THAT'S CROSBY -- ALL OVER!
TSSSSSS
SAME THING'S GONNA HAPPEN TO THE BOY MICROBE, HERE, UNLESS---
HAH! NICE TO KNOW SOME THINGS STAY THE SAME---
I'VE STILL GOT MUCH OF MY FULL-SIZE STRENGTH--FOR REASONS MUCH TOO COMPLEX TO MUSE ON NOW.
AND THE TRUTH SHALL SET ME FREE!
BUT-- THE REMNANT OF MY ANT BRIGADE AREN'T QUITE SO LUCKY.

HUMAN BEINGS ARE *FUNNY*-- THEY THINK NO LIVING THING *BUT THEMSELVES* CAPABLE OF FEELING *PAIN.*

THAT'S BECAUSE--- THEY'VE NEVER HEARD AN ANT *SCREAM.* WELL, *I* HAVE--

--AND IT'S A SOUND TO *HAUNT* A LIFETIME WORTH OF DREAMS.'

A SOUND LIKE LOST SOULS IN *TORMENT*-- OR THE WAILING OF A FORE-SAKEN *CHILD*---

--AND I DON'T *EVER* WANT TO HEAR THAT SOUND *AGAIN!*

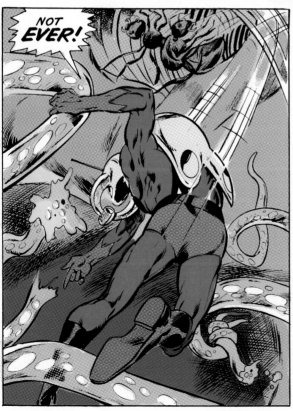

NOT EVER!

SO, *HEED* MY ELECTRONICALLY-BEAMED ORDERS, LITTLE FRIENDS -- AND *LEAVE* THE ANDROID'S BODY---*NOW!*

I CAN'T WATCH OUT FOR ONE BASHFUL *BIOCHEMIST* -- AND TWO *SIX-LEGGED* SIDEKICKS, TO BOOT--

WHERE *ANT-MAN* WALKS TODAY-- HE WALKS *ALONE!*

8

THAT BIT ABOUT "WALKING" WAS *FIGURATIVELY* SPEAKING, NATCH.

IN POINT OF FACT, IT'S TIME I GOT SOME USE OUT OF MY MINIATURIZED *BACK-PACK!*

STILL, I'VE *TIMED* THEM. THEY *BLAST AWAY* FOR FIVE SECONDS -- THEN *RECHARGE* FOR FIVE.

SO, WHILE IT'S *LULL-BEFORE-THE-STORM* TIME---

THOSE *SPRAYS* UP THERE ARE LIKE *ANTIBODIES*--- AND THEY'RE NOT GONNA TAKE *KINDLY* TO MY PASSING *THRU*---

ZZZZ

--- I MAKE MY MOVE!

VROOSH!

TSSSS

CLOSE -- BUT NO *CIGAR.*

HMMM-- IF ALL THE VISION'S BODILY PROCESSES ARE *INTACT*, THAT *PROVES* MY POINT.

THE ONLY WAY TO TRULY *KILL* AN ANDROID -- IS TO *DISMANTLE* HIM.

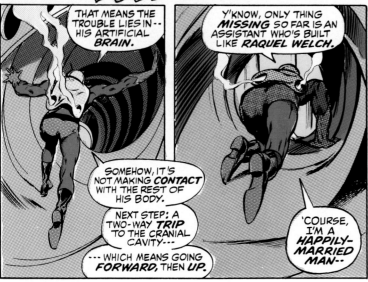

THAT MEANS THE TROUBLE LIES IN-- HIS ARTIFICIAL *BRAIN.*

SOMEHOW, IT'S NOT MAKING *CONTACT* WITH THE REST OF HIS BODY.

NEXT STEP: A *TWO-WAY* TRIP TO THE CRANIAL CAVITY---

--- WHICH MEANS GOING *FORWARD*, THEN *UP.*

Y'KNOW, ONLY THING *MISSING* SO FAR IS AN ASSISTANT WHO'S BUILT LIKE *RAQUEL WELCH.*

'COURSE, I'M A *HAPPILY-MARRIED* MAN--

BUT JUST THE *SAME*, I--

YEEEOWW!

ZOT!

9.

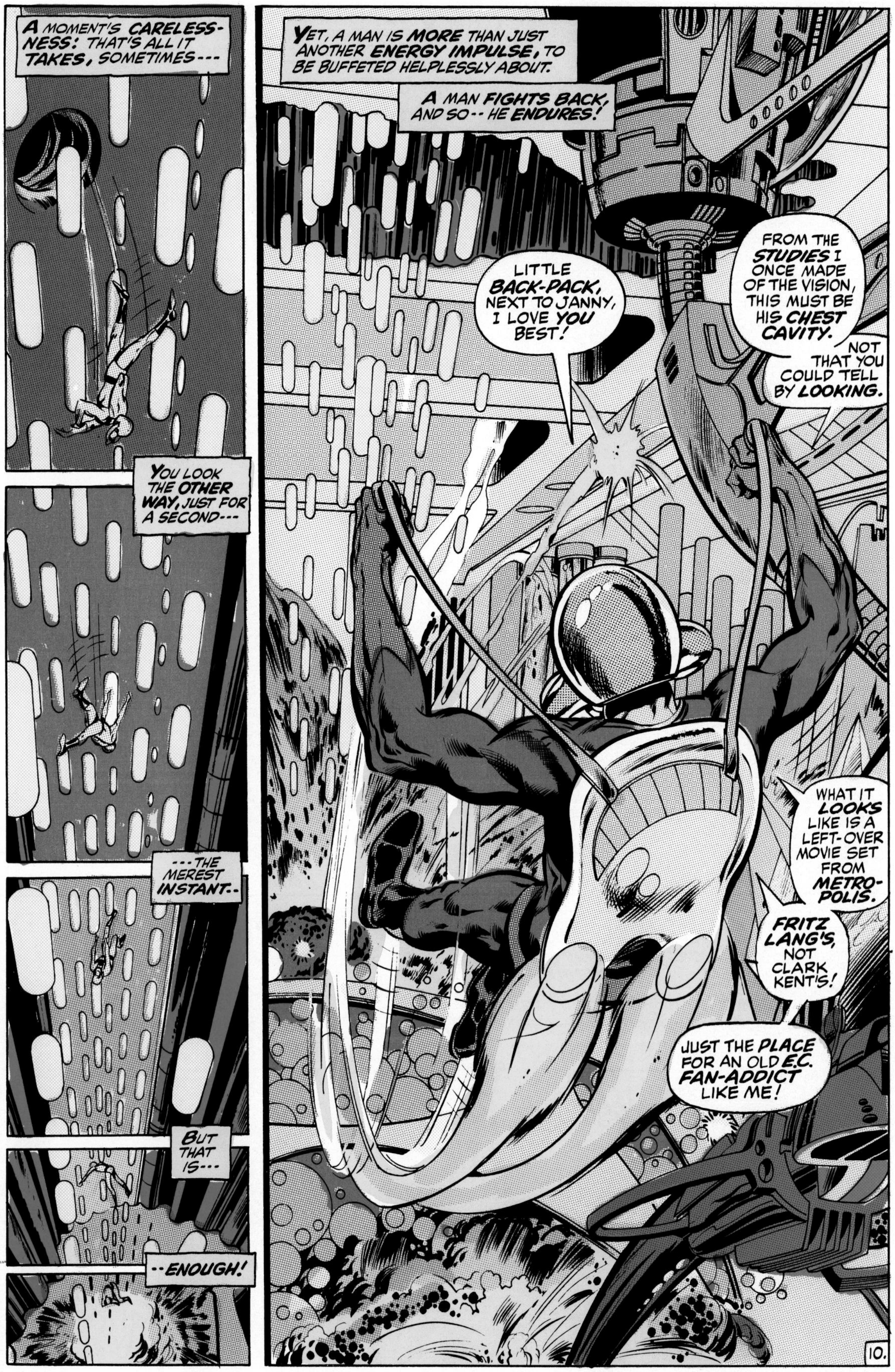
A MOMENT'S CARELESSNESS: THAT'S ALL IT TAKES, SOMETIMES---
YOU LOOK THE OTHER WAY, JUST FOR A SECOND---
---THE MEREST INSTANT--
BUT THAT IS---
--ENOUGH!
YET, A MAN IS MORE THAN JUST ANOTHER ENERGY IMPULSE, TO BE BUFFETED HELPLESSLY ABOUT.
A MAN FIGHTS BACK, AND SO-- HE ENDURES!
LITTLE BACK-PACK, NEXT TO JANNY, I LOVE YOU BEST!
FROM THE STUDIES I ONCE MADE OF THE VISION, THIS MUST BE HIS CHEST CAVITY.
NOT THAT YOU COULD TELL BY LOOKING.
WHAT IT LOOKS LIKE IS A LEFT-OVER MOVIE SET FROM METROPOLIS.
FRITZ LANG'S, NOT CLARK KENT'S!
JUST THE PLACE FOR AN OLD E.C. FAN-ADDICT LIKE ME!
10.

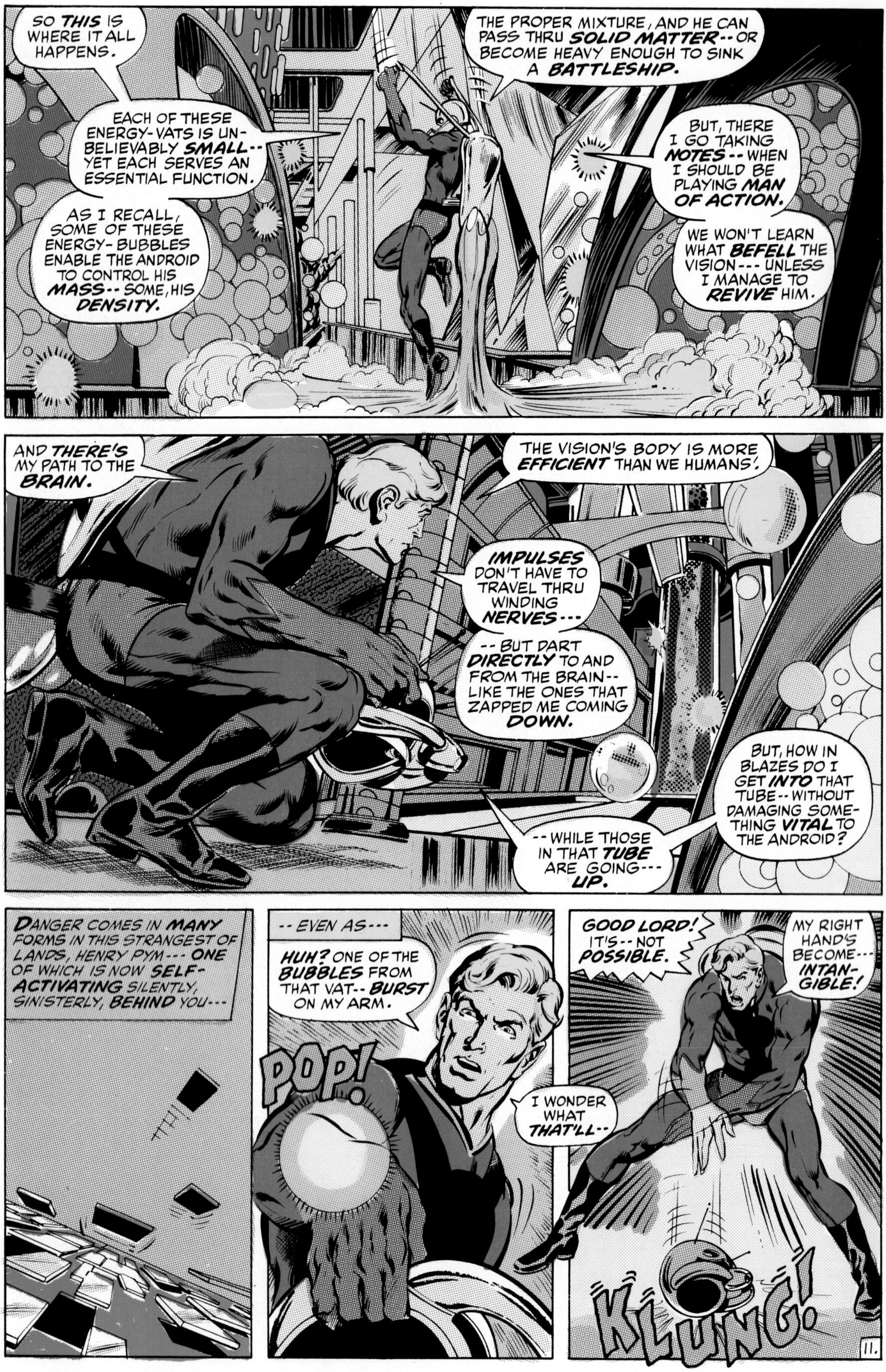
SO THIS IS WHERE IT ALL HAPPENS.
THE PROPER MIXTURE, AND HE CAN PASS THRU SOLID MATTER -- OR BECOME HEAVY ENOUGH TO SINK A BATTLESHIP.
EACH OF THESE ENERGY-VATS IS UNBELIEVABLY SMALL -- YET EACH SERVES AN ESSENTIAL FUNCTION.
AS I RECALL, SOME OF THESE ENERGY-BUBBLES ENABLE THE ANDROID TO CONTROL HIS MASS -- SOME, HIS DENSITY.
BUT, THERE I GO TAKING NOTES -- WHEN I SHOULD BE PLAYING MAN OF ACTION.
WE WON'T LEARN WHAT BEFELL THE VISION --- UNLESS I MANAGE TO REVIVE HIM.
AND THERE'S MY PATH TO THE BRAIN.
THE VISION'S BODY IS MORE EFFICIENT THAN WE HUMANS'.
IMPULSES DON'T HAVE TO TRAVEL THRU WINDING NERVES ---
-- BUT DART DIRECTLY TO AND FROM THE BRAIN -- LIKE THE ONES THAT ZAPPED ME COMING DOWN.
-- WHILE THOSE IN THAT TUBE ARE GOING --- UP.
BUT, HOW IN BLAZES DO I GET INTO THAT TUBE -- WITHOUT DAMAGING SOMETHING VITAL TO THE ANDROID?
DANGER COMES IN MANY FORMS IN THIS STRANGEST OF LANDS, HENRY PYM --- ONE OF WHICH IS NOW SELF-ACTIVATING SILENTLY, SINISTERLY, BEHIND YOU ---
-- EVEN AS ---
HUH? ONE OF THE BUBBLES FROM THAT VAT -- BURST ON MY ARM.
POP!
I WONDER WHAT THAT'LL --
GOOD LORD! IT'S -- NOT POSSIBLE.
MY RIGHT HAND'S BECOME --- INTANGIBLE!
KLUNG!
11.

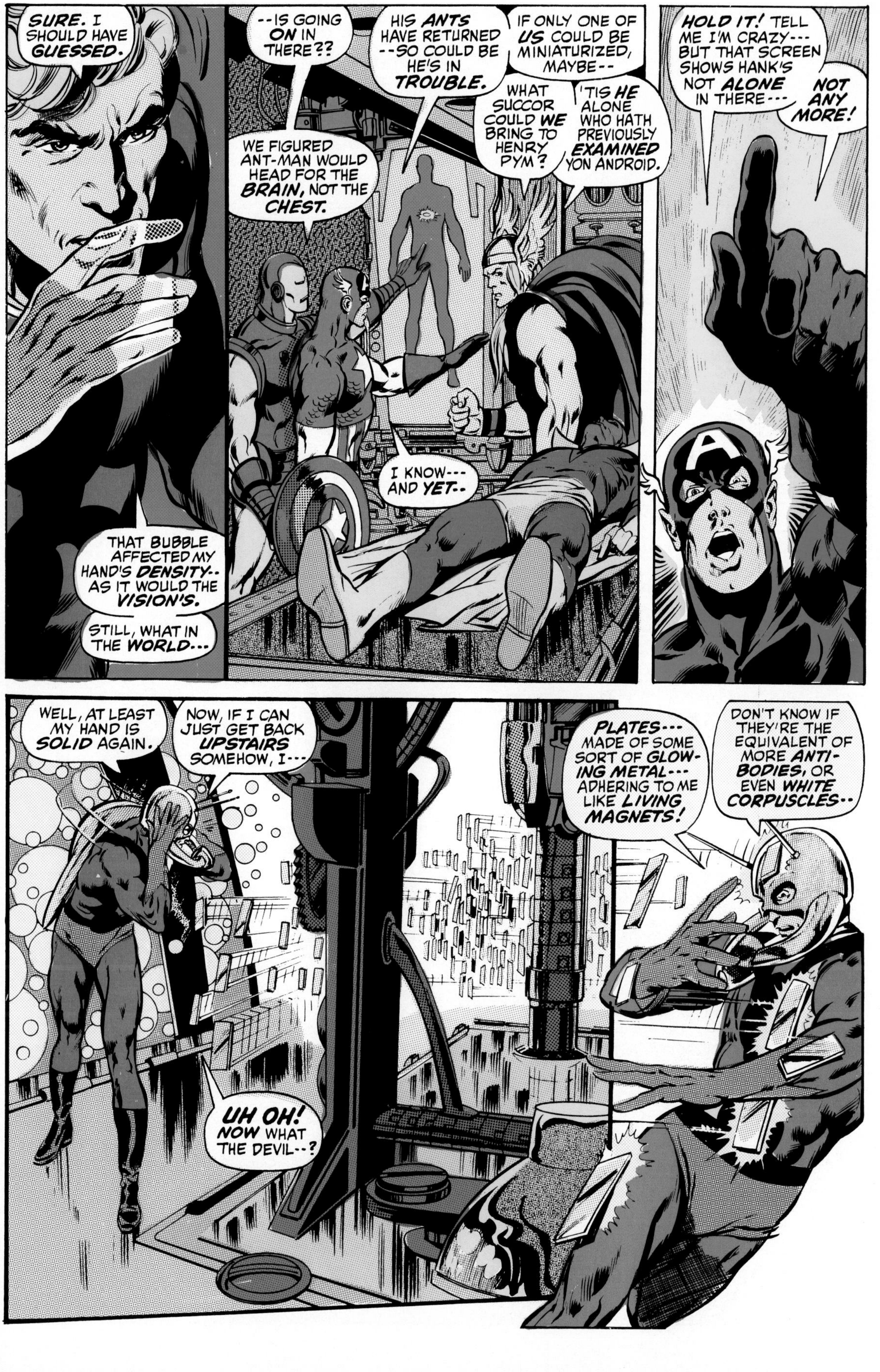
SURE. I SHOULD HAVE GUESSED.
THAT BUBBLE AFFECTED MY HAND'S DENSITY.. AS IT WOULD THE VISION'S.
STILL, WHAT IN THE WORLD...
--IS GOING ON IN THERE??
WE FIGURED ANT-MAN WOULD HEAD FOR THE BRAIN, NOT THE CHEST.
I KNOW--- AND YET--
HIS ANTS HAVE RETURNED --SO COULD BE HE'S IN TROUBLE.
IF ONLY ONE OF US COULD BE MINIATURIZED, MAYBE--
WHAT SUCCOR COULD WE BRING TO HENRY PYM?
'TIS HE ALONE WHO HATH PREVIOUSLY EXAMINED YON ANDROID.
HOLD IT! TELL ME I'M CRAZY--- BUT THAT SCREEN SHOWS HANK'S NOT ALONE IN THERE---
NOT ANY MORE!
WELL, AT LEAST MY HAND IS SOLID AGAIN.
NOW, IF I CAN JUST GET BACK UPSTAIRS SOMEHOW, I---
UH OH! NOW WHAT THE DEVIL--?
PLATES--- MADE OF SOME SORT OF GLOWING METAL--- ADHERING TO ME LIKE LIVING MAGNETS!
DON'T KNOW IF THEY'RE THE EQUIVALENT OF MORE ANTI-BODIES, OR EVEN WHITE CORPUSCLES--

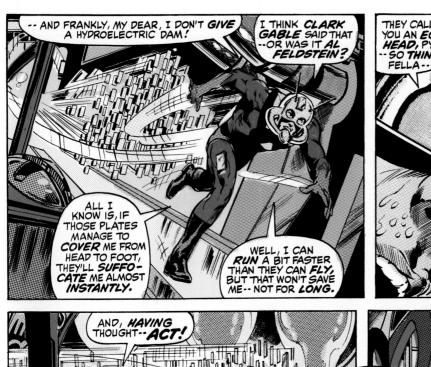

-- AND FRANKLY, MY DEAR, I DON'T *GIVE* A HYDROELECTRIC DAM!

I THINK *CLARK GABLE* SAID THAT --OR WAS IT *AL FELDSTEIN*?

ALL I KNOW IS, IF THOSE PLATES MANAGE TO *COVER* ME FROM HEAD TO FOOT, THEY'LL *SUFFOCATE* ME ALMOST *INSTANTLY.*

WELL, I CAN *RUN* A BIT FASTER THAN THEY CAN *FLY*, BUT THAT WON'T SAVE ME -- NOT FOR *LONG*.

THEY CALL YOU AN *EGGHEAD*, PYM -- SO *THINK*, FELLA...

THINK!

AND, *HAVING* THOUGHT -- *ACT!*

FIRST, YOU TAKE ADVANTAGE OF THE FACT THAT THEY'RE A *LOWER* ORDER OF SENTIENT CREATURE---

-- SO THEY CAN'T *CORNER* QUITE AS QUICKLY AS YOU CAN.

NOT *QUITE!*

THEN, YOU *USE* THAT EXTRA COUPLE OF SECONDS YOU JUST GAINED---

---TO TAKE YOUR FIRST *BUBBLE BATH* IN YEARS!

AND THAT GIVES YOU A FEW *MORE* PRECIOUS SECONDS, DURING WHICH YOU'LL BE VIRTUALLY *INTANGIBLE*---

13

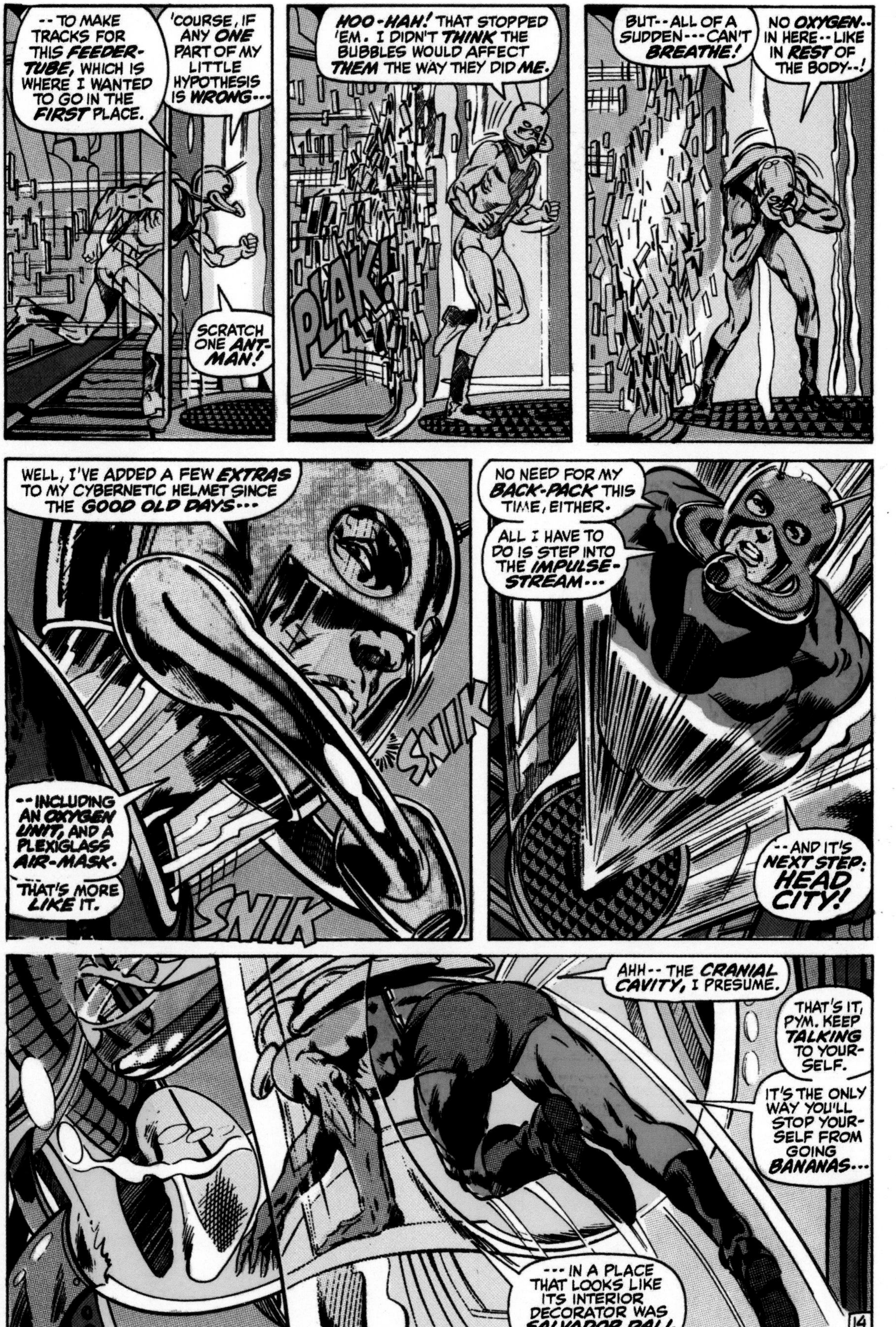

-- TO MAKE TRACKS FOR THIS FEEDER-TUBE, WHICH IS WHERE I WANTED TO GO IN THE FIRST PLACE.
'COURSE, IF ANY ONE PART OF MY LITTLE HYPOTHESIS IS WRONG...
SCRATCH ONE ANT-MAN!
HOO-HAH! THAT STOPPED 'EM. I DIDN'T THINK THE BUBBLES WOULD AFFECT THEM THE WAY THEY DID ME.
PLAK!
BUT--ALL OF A SUDDEN---CAN'T BREATHE!
NO OXYGEN-- IN HERE--LIKE IN REST OF THE BODY--!
WELL, I'VE ADDED A FEW EXTRAS TO MY CYBERNETIC HELMET SINCE THE GOOD OLD DAYS---
SNIK
--INCLUDING AN OXYGEN UNIT, AND A PLEXIGLASS AIR-MASK.
THAT'S MORE LIKE IT.
SNIK
NO NEED FOR MY BACK-PACK THIS TIME, EITHER.
ALL I HAVE TO DO IS STEP INTO THE IMPULSE-STREAM---
--AND IT'S NEXT STEP: HEAD CITY!
AHH--THE CRANIAL CAVITY, I PRESUME.
THAT'S IT, PYM. KEEP TALKING TO YOURSELF.
IT'S THE ONLY WAY YOU'LL STOP YOURSELF FROM GOING BANANAS...
---IN A PLACE THAT LOOKS LIKE ITS INTERIOR DECORATOR WAS SALVADOR DALI.
14

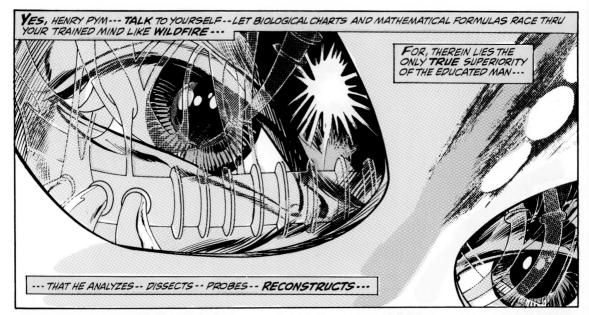

YES, HENRY PYM--- **TALK** TO YOURSELF--LET BIOLOGICAL CHARTS AND MATHEMATICAL FORMULAS RACE THRU YOUR TRAINED MIND LIKE **WILDFIRE**---

FOR, THEREIN LIES THE ONLY **TRUE** SUPERIORITY OF THE EDUCATED MAN---

---THAT HE ANALYZES-- DISSECTS -- PROBES-- **RECONSTRUCTS**---

--TILL THE PIECES OF A MADDENING MECHANICAL **PUZZLE** FALL NEATLY INTO PLACE---

---OR SO HE **HOPES!**

WELL, TIME TO **FISH**---

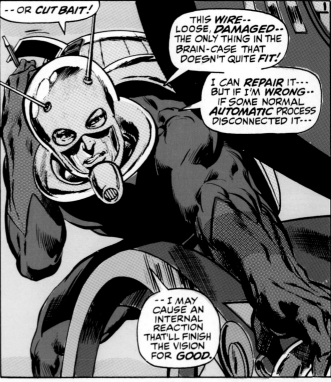

-- OR **CUT BAIT!**

THIS **WIRE**-- LOOSE, **DAMAGED**-- THE ONLY THING IN THE BRAIN-CASE THAT DOESN'T QUITE **FIT!**

I CAN **REPAIR** IT--- BUT IF I'M **WRONG**-- IF SOME NORMAL **AUTOMATIC** PROCESS DISCONNECTED IT---

-- I MAY CAUSE AN INTERNAL REACTION THAT'LL FINISH THE VISION FOR **GOOD.**

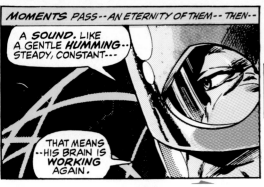

MOMENTS PASS--AN ETERNITY OF THEM-- THEN--

A **SOUND.** LIKE A GENTLE **HUMMING**-- STEADY, CONSTANT--

THAT MEANS --HIS BRAIN IS **WORKING** AGAIN.

THEN I'D BETTER **MOVE** IT, BEFORE-- **WHAT'S THIS??**

A MYSTERY WITHIN AN ENIGMA, ANT-MAN-- ONE OF WHICH OUR READERS MAY LEARN ONE DAY---

15

--- BUT NOT TODAY!

GOOD LORD!

THE *ANTIBODIES*-- OR WHATEVER-- COMING AT ME FROM THE *FEEDER TUBE!*

JUST TIME TO ACTIVATE THIS *TIMING DEVICE,* WHICH SHOULD *AWAKEN* THE ANDROID IN A FEW SECONDS---

--- THEN *RUN* LIKE THE DEVIL---

OTHERWISE, I'LL BE *TRAPPED* IN HERE WHEN THE VISION WAKES UP--

-- WHICH WOULD BE A DEFINITE *DISASTER.*

I MUST BE NEAR AN *ORIFICE.* THE HOT-PLATES ARE *TURNING BACK.*

-- AND PRAY THAT THIS REALLY IS THE *NASAL CAVITY* I *THINK* IT IS.

YEP-- EITHER THAT'S THE LIGHT OF *DAY* AHEAD---

-- OR ELSE THE VISION'S BEEN GOBBLING *FIREFLIES!*

THUS DO BRAVE MEN *JEST,* WHEN DEATH TURNS TAIL AND FLEES---AND THUS *ENDS* PERHAPS THE STRANGEST *RESCUE MISSION* IN HISTORY---

YET, IT MAY WELL BE THAT THIS HAS BEEN BUT A PALTRY *PRO-LOGUE* --- TO THE MOST *POR-TENTOUS* AVENGERS SAGA OF *ALL* ---!

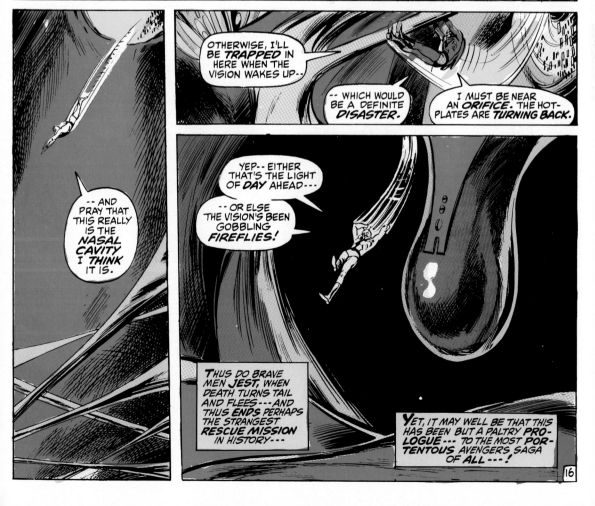

16

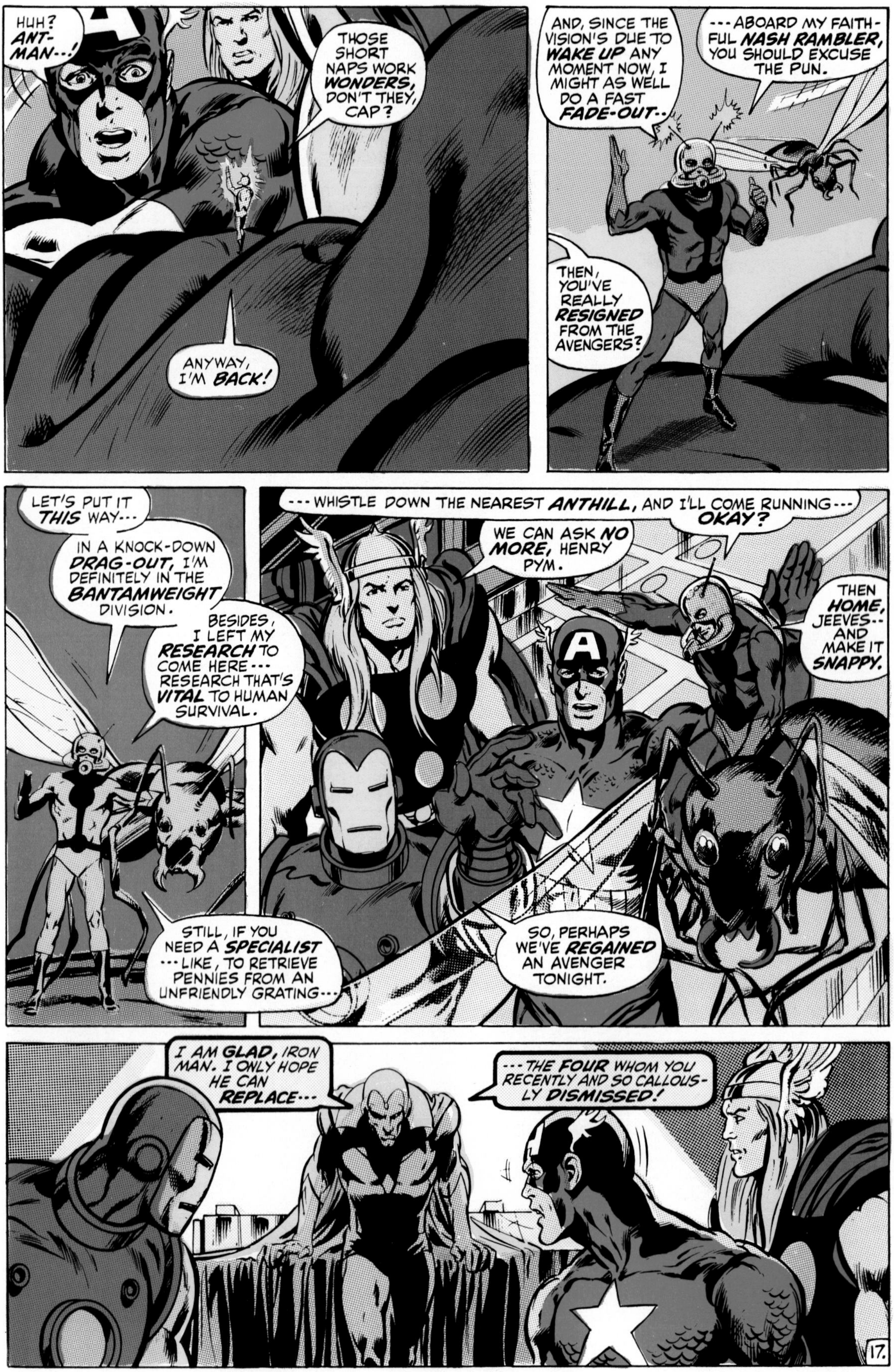

HUH? ANT-MAN--!
THOSE SHORT NAPS WORK WONDERS, DON'T THEY, CAP?
ANYWAY, I'M BACK!
AND, SINCE THE VISION'S DUE TO WAKE UP ANY MOMENT NOW, I MIGHT AS WELL DO A FAST FADE-OUT--
---ABOARD MY FAITHFUL NASH RAMBLER, YOU SHOULD EXCUSE THE PUN.
THEN, YOU'VE REALLY RESIGNED FROM THE AVENGERS?
LET'S PUT IT THIS WAY---
IN A KNOCK-DOWN DRAG-OUT, I'M DEFINITELY IN THE BANTAMWEIGHT DIVISION.
BESIDES, I LEFT MY RESEARCH TO COME HERE--- RESEARCH THAT'S VITAL TO HUMAN SURVIVAL.
STILL, IF YOU NEED A SPECIALIST ---LIKE, TO RETRIEVE PENNIES FROM AN UNFRIENDLY GRATING---
---WHISTLE DOWN THE NEAREST ANTHILL, AND I'LL COME RUNNING--- OKAY?
WE CAN ASK NO MORE, HENRY PYM.
THEN HOME, JEEVES-- AND MAKE IT SNAPPY.
SO, PERHAPS WE'VE REGAINED AN AVENGER TONIGHT.
I AM GLAD, IRON MAN. I ONLY HOPE HE CAN REPLACE---
---THE FOUR WHOM YOU RECENTLY AND SO CALLOUSLY DISMISSED!
17.

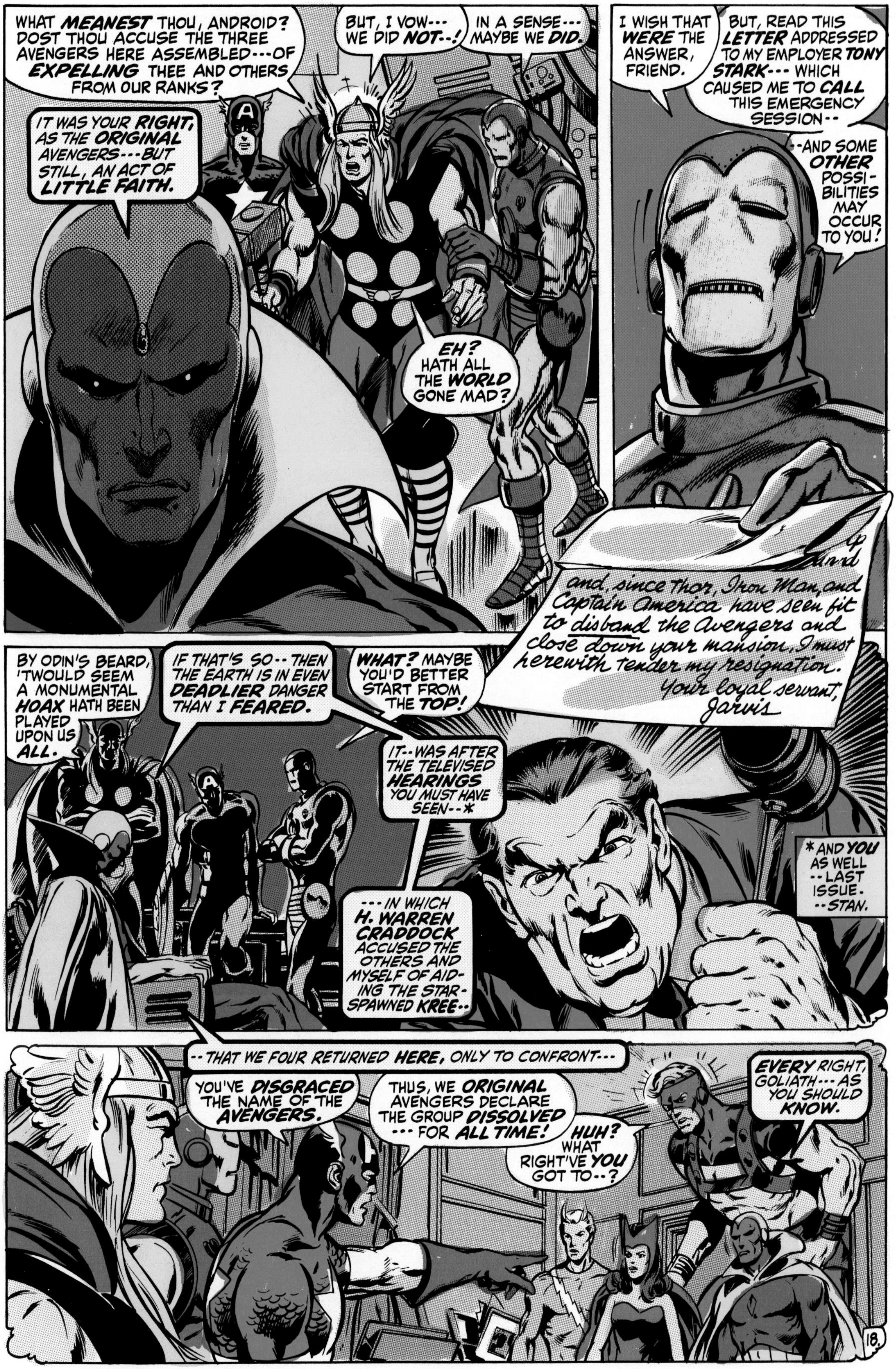
WHAT MEANEST THOU, ANDROID? DOST THOU ACCUSE THE THREE AVENGERS HERE ASSEMBLED---OF EXPELLING THEE AND OTHERS FROM OUR RANKS?
BUT, I VOW--- WE DID NOT--!
IN A SENSE--- MAYBE WE DID.
IT WAS YOUR RIGHT, AS THE ORIGINAL AVENGERS---BUT STILL, AN ACT OF LITTLE FAITH.
EH? HATH ALL THE WORLD GONE MAD?
I WISH THAT WERE THE ANSWER, FRIEND.
BUT, READ THIS LETTER ADDRESSED TO MY EMPLOYER TONY STARK--- WHICH CAUSED ME TO CALL THIS EMERGENCY SESSION--
--AND SOME OTHER POSSIBILITIES MAY OCCUR TO YOU!
and, since Thor, Iron Man, and Captain America have seen fit to disband the Avengers and close down your mansion, I must herewith tender my resignation.
Your loyal servant, Jarvis
BY ODIN'S BEARD, 'TWOULD SEEM A MONUMENTAL HOAX HATH BEEN PLAYED UPON US ALL.
IF THAT'S SO-- THEN THE EARTH IS IN EVEN DEADLIER DANGER THAN I FEARED.
WHAT? MAYBE YOU'D BETTER START FROM THE TOP!
IT--WAS AFTER THE TELEVISED HEARINGS YOU MUST HAVE SEEN--*
---IN WHICH H. WARREN CRADDOCK ACCUSED THE OTHERS AND MYSELF OF AIDING THE STAR-SPAWNED KREE--
*AND YOU AS WELL --LAST ISSUE. --STAN.
--THAT WE FOUR RETURNED HERE, ONLY TO CONFRONT---
YOU'VE DISGRACED THE NAME OF THE AVENGERS.
THUS, WE ORIGINAL AVENGERS DECLARE THE GROUP DISSOLVED --- FOR ALL TIME!
HUH? WHAT RIGHT'VE YOU GOT TO--?
EVERY RIGHT, GOLIATH--- AS YOU SHOULD KNOW.
18.

"THEN, YOU -- OR YOUR *IMITATORS* -- DEPARTED, AND WE DID *LIKEWISE* SOON AFTER---"

SHEESH! WHY COULDN'T WE AT LEAST TAKE ONE LOUSY *QUINJET?*

THOSE SHIPS WERE MERELY *LEASED* TO US, CLINT--- BY *TONY STARK.*

WE'RE JUST LUCKY MY *CREDIT CARD* GOT US THIS *CAR.*

"YET, EVERYWHERE WE WENT, DARTING GLANCES OF *SUSPICION* FOLLOWED US---FOR WERE WE NOT *ACCUSED* OF SHIELDING A PLANET'S *ENEMIES--?*

"AND, AMONG *HUMANKIND,* IS NOT *ACCU-SATION*---THE SAME AS *CON-VICTION--?*

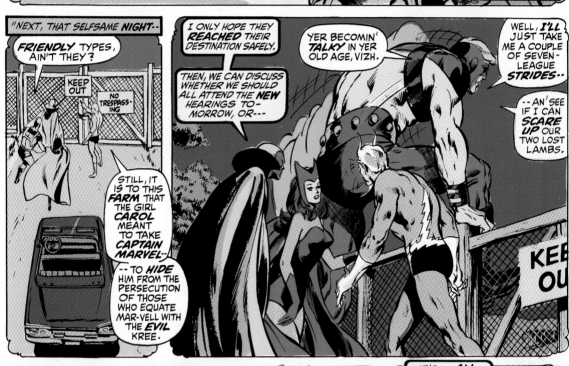

"NEXT, THAT SELFSAME *NIGHT*--"

FRIENDLY TYPES, AIN'T THEY?

STILL, IT IS TO THIS *FARM* THAT THE GIRL *CAROL* MEANT TO TAKE *CAPTAIN MARVEL*--

-- TO *HIDE* HIM FROM THE PERSECUTION OF THOSE WHO EQUATE MAR-VELL WITH THE *EVIL* KREE.

I ONLY HOPE THEY *REACHED* THEIR DESTINATION SAFELY.

THEN, WE CAN DISCUSS WHETHER WE SHOULD ALL ATTEND THE *NEW* HEARINGS TO-MORROW, OR---

YER BECOMIN' *TALKY* IN YER OLD AGE, VIZH.

WELL, *I'LL* JUST TAKE ME A COUPLE OF SEVEN-LEAGUE *STRIDES*--

-- AN' SEE IF I CAN *SCARE UP* OUR TWO LOST *LAMBS.*

KEEP OUT

NO TRESPASS-ING

KE OU

IF I CAN HELP *YOU* OVER, WANDA---

WHY, *THANK* YOU, VISION. I ---

NO!

MY SISTER NEEDS NO HELP FROM *YOU.*

PIETRO-- *WHAT*--?

FOR YEARS, WE HAVE DEPENDED ONLY ON EACH OTHER, AND ON *OURSELVES*--- WHICH IS HOW IT *SHOULD* BE.

IT'S --- *ALL RIGHT,* WANDA.

I --- UNDER-STAND--!

19.

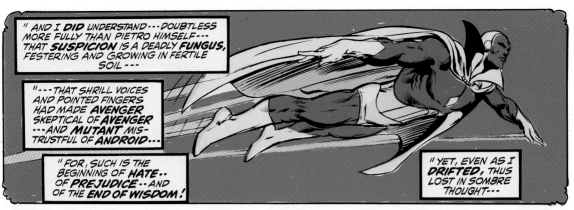

" AND I *DID* UNDERSTAND---DOUBTLESS MORE FULLY THAN PIETRO HIMSELF--- THAT *SUSPICION* IS A DEADLY *FUNGUS,* FESTERING AND GROWING IN FERTILE SOIL ---

"---THAT SHRILL VOICES AND POINTED FINGERS HAD MADE *AVENGER* SKEPTICAL OF *AVENGER* ---AND *MUTANT* MISTRUSTFUL OF *ANDROID*...

" FOR, SUCH IS THE BEGINNING OF *HATE*-- OF *PREJUDICE*--AND OF THE *END OF WISDOM !*

" YET, EVEN AS I *DRIFTED,* THUS LOST IN SOMBRE THOUGHT---

"-- I SUDDENLY PASSED THRU THE *GATES OF HELL*--!

AARR

ZZAKT!

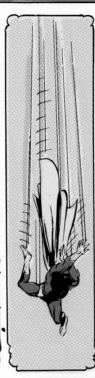

PIETRO -- THOSE *RAYS* WHICH STRUCK THE VISION DOWN! *WHERE* DID THEY--?

THEY SHOT OUT SO *SWIFTLY,* I COULDN'T *SEE!*

IT'S GOOD THAT HE LANDED AMONG THESE HARMLESS *CATTLE,* SO THAT---

" 'HARMLESS CATTLE!' THAT IS THE MOMENT, AS IF BY SOME SINISTER *CUE*---

"-- THEY BEGAN TO--- *CHANGE*---!

20

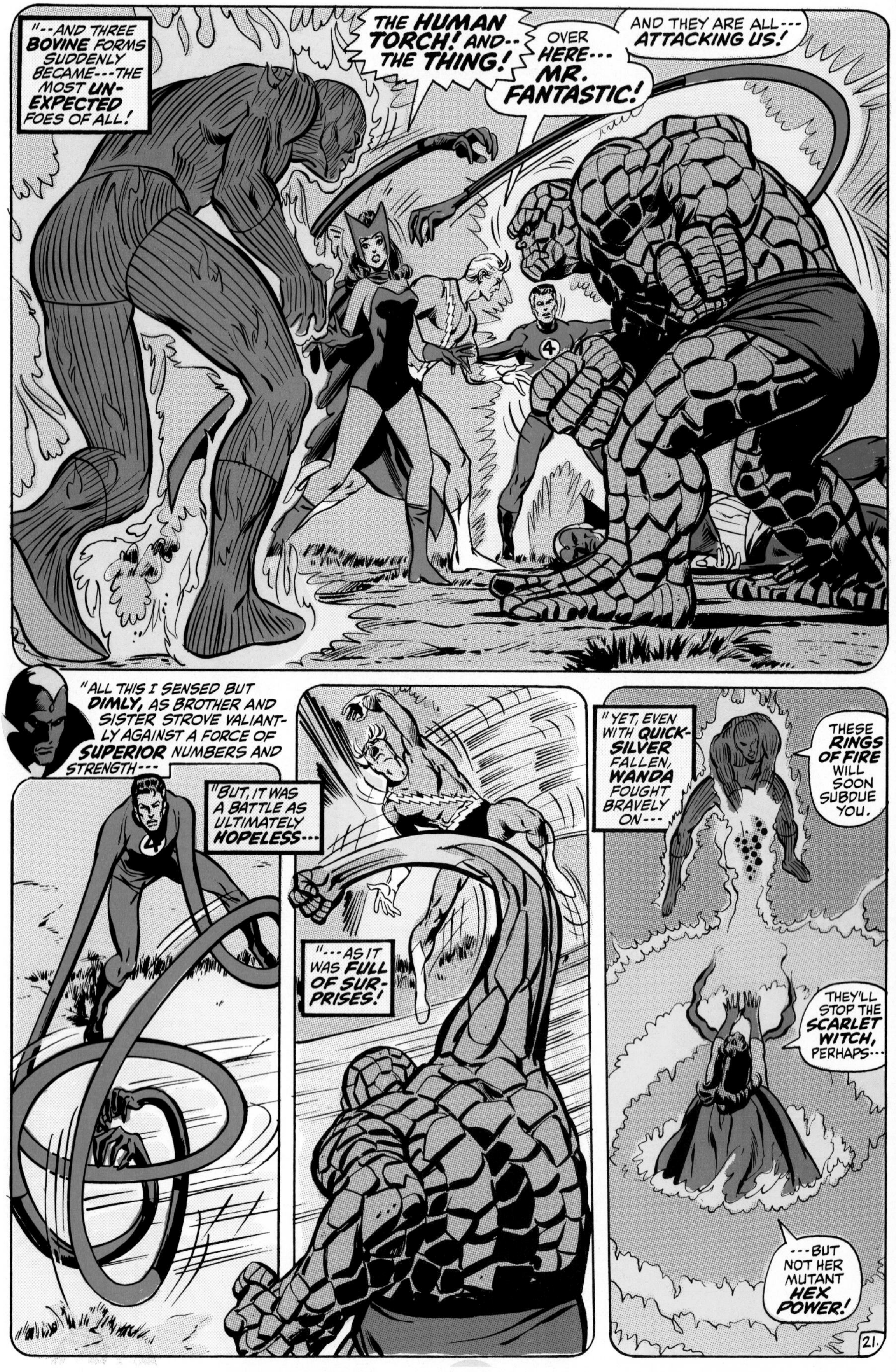
"--AND THREE BOVINE FORMS SUDDENLY BECAME---THE MOST UN-EXPECTED FOES OF ALL!
THE HUMAN TORCH! AND-- THE THING!
OVER HERE--- MR. FANTASTIC!
AND THEY ARE ALL--- ATTACKING US!
"ALL THIS I SENSED BUT DIMLY, AS BROTHER AND SISTER STROVE VALIANT-LY AGAINST A FORCE OF SUPERIOR NUMBERS AND STRENGTH---
"BUT, IT WAS A BATTLE AS ULTIMATELY HOPELESS---
"---AS IT WAS FULL OF SUR-PRISES!
"YET, EVEN WITH QUICK-SILVER FALLEN, WANDA FOUGHT BRAVELY ON---
THESE RINGS OF FIRE WILL SOON SUBDUE YOU.
THEY'LL STOP THE SCARLET WITCH, PERHAPS---
---BUT NOT HER MUTANT HEX POWER!
21.

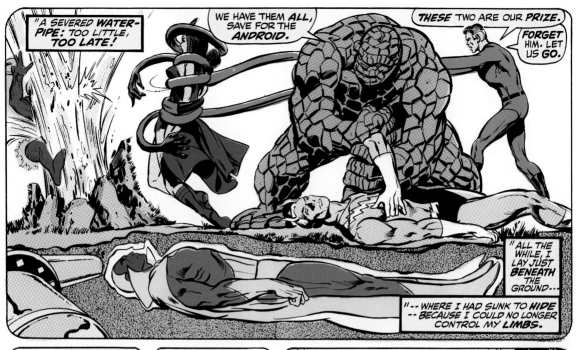

"A SEVERED WATER-PIPE: TOO LITTLE, TOO LATE!"

WE HAVE THEM **ALL,** SAVE FOR THE **ANDROID.**

THESE TWO ARE OUR **PRIZE.**

FORGET HIM. LET US GO.

"ALL THE WHILE, I LAY JUST **BENEATH** THE GROUND---

"-- WHERE I HAD SUNK TO **HIDE** -- BECAUSE I COULD NO LONGER CONTROL MY **LIMBS.**

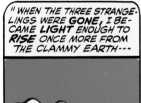

" WHEN THE THREE STRANGE-LINGS WERE **GONE,** I BE-CAME **LIGHT** ENOUGH TO **RISE** ONCE MORE FROM THE CLAMMY EARTH---

"-- THEN USED MY **LAST** DENSITY-CONTROL TO **STEER** MYSELF SLOWLY, **SURELY**---

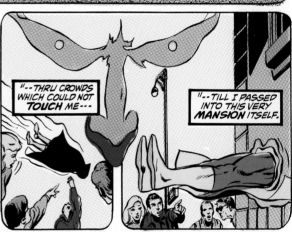

"--THRU CROWDS WHICH COULD NOT **TOUCH** ME---

"--TILL I PASSED INTO THIS VERY **MANSION** ITSELF.

AND NOW, I AM **WELL---FREE**--WHILE TWO COM-RADES LIE IN MORTAL **PERIL.**

I MUST **RETURN** TO THAT FARM--NOW!

BUT NOT ALONE--- **AVENGER.**

STILL--- **WHO** DID THEY FIGHT?

AYE! THAT, WE MUST AND **SHALL** LEARN.

FOR, THIS NIGHT HAVE WE A **WRONG** TO REDRESS ---A **NAME** TO **AVENGE!**

NOBLE WORDS. YET, **SOME** THINGS MAY LIE BEYOND REACH EVEN OF A **GOD**--!

22

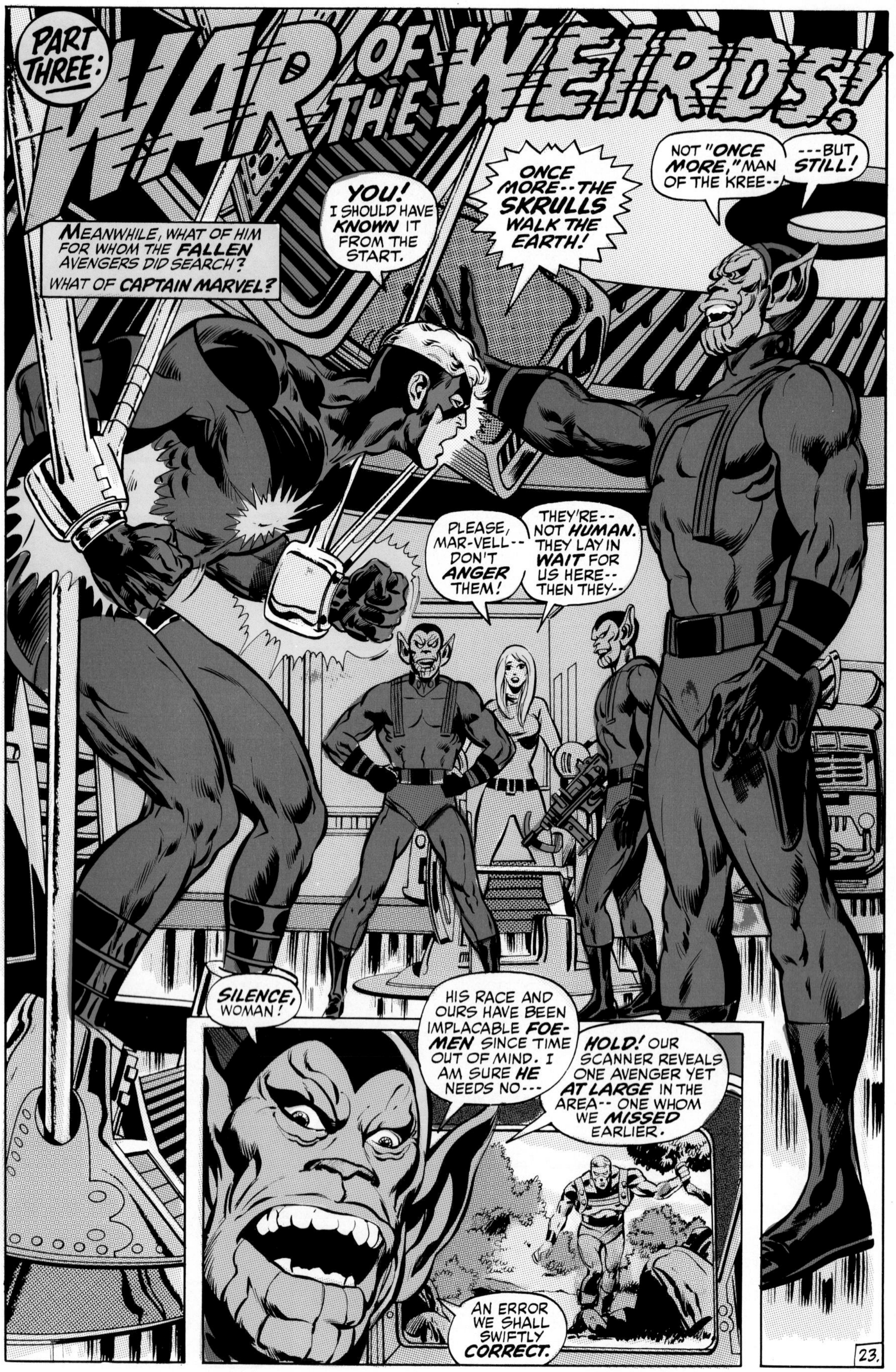
PART THREE:
WAR OF THE WEIRDS!
MEANWHILE, WHAT OF HIM FOR WHOM THE FALLEN AVENGERS DID SEARCH? WHAT OF CAPTAIN MARVEL?
YOU! I SHOULD HAVE KNOWN IT FROM THE START.
ONCE MORE--THE SKRULLS WALK THE EARTH!
NOT "ONCE MORE," MAN OF THE KREE--
---BUT STILL!
PLEASE, MAR-VELL--DON'T ANGER THEM!
THEY'RE--NOT HUMAN. THEY LAY IN WAIT FOR US HERE--THEN THEY--
SILENCE, WOMAN!
HIS RACE AND OURS HAVE BEEN IMPLACABLE FOE-MEN SINCE TIME OUT OF MIND. I AM SURE HE NEEDS NO---
HOLD! OUR SCANNER REVEALS ONE AVENGER YET AT LARGE IN THE AREA-- ONE WHOM WE MISSED EARLIER.
AN ERROR WE SHALL SWIFTLY CORRECT.
23.

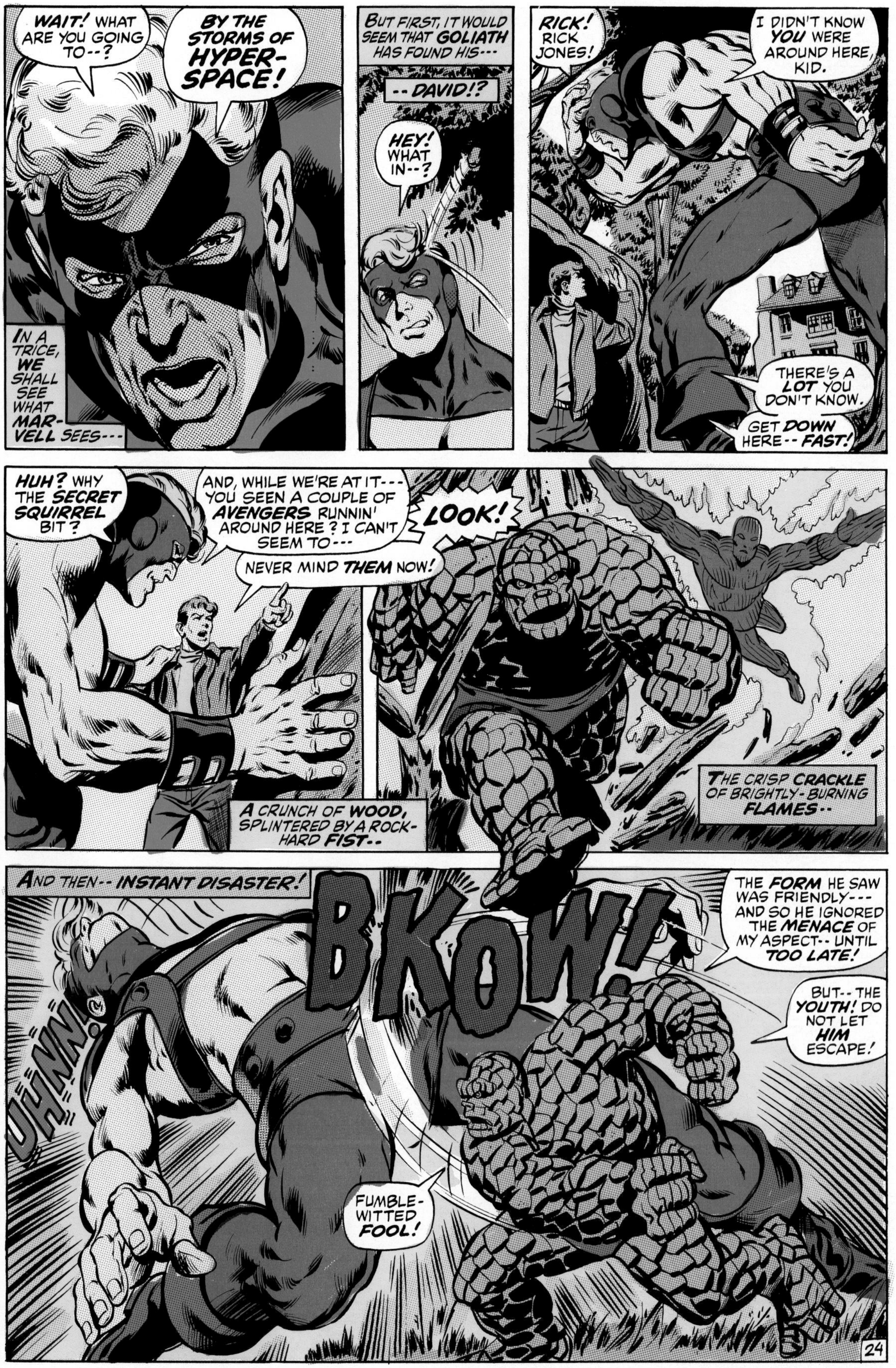
WAIT! WHAT ARE YOU GOING TO--?
BY THE STORMS OF HYPER-SPACE!
IN A TRICE, WE SHALL SEE WHAT MAR-VELL SEES---
BUT FIRST, IT WOULD SEEM THAT GOLIATH HAS FOUND HIS---
--DAVID!?
HEY! WHAT IN--?
RICK! RICK JONES!
I DIDN'T KNOW YOU WERE AROUND HERE, KID.
THERE'S A LOT YOU DON'T KNOW.
GET DOWN HERE--FAST!
HUH? WHY THE SECRET SQUIRREL BIT?
AND, WHILE WE'RE AT IT--- YOU SEEN A COUPLE OF AVENGERS RUNNIN' AROUND HERE? I CAN'T SEEM TO---
LOOK!
NEVER MIND THEM NOW!
A CRUNCH OF WOOD, SPLINTERED BY A ROCK-HARD FIST--
THE CRISP CRACKLE OF BRIGHTLY-BURNING FLAMES--
AND THEN--INSTANT DISASTER!
BKOW!
UHNN!
THE FORM HE SAW WAS FRIENDLY--- AND SO HE IGNORED THE MENACE OF MY ASPECT--UNTIL TOO LATE!
BUT--THE YOUTH! DO NOT LET HIM ESCAPE!
FUMBLE-WITTED FOOL!
24

DO NOT FEAR. I'LL SOON HAVE THE STRIPLING IN *HAND.*

YEAH? NOT IF *I* GOT ANYTHING TO SAY ABOUT IT, HOT STUFF!

AN' MAYBE I JUST *DO.*

THAT SHALLOW *STREAM* WILL NOT LONG PROTECT YOU.

IN MERE *MOMENTS,* MY FLAMES CAN TURN IT INTO A BUBBLING *CAULDRON.*

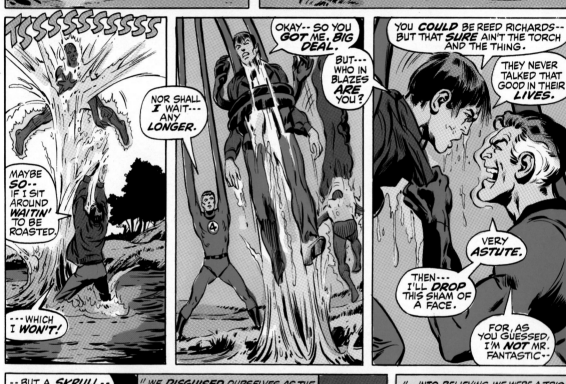

NOR SHALL *I* WAIT--- ANY *LONGER.*

MAYBE *SO*-- IF I SIT AROUND *WAITIN'* TO BE ROASTED.

---WHICH I *WON'T!*

OKAY-- SO YOU *GOT* ME. BIG *DEAL.*

BUT--- WHO IN BLAZES *ARE* YOU?

YOU *COULD* BE REED RICHARDS-- BUT THAT *SURE* AIN'T THE TORCH AND THE THING.

THEY NEVER TALKED THAT GOOD IN THEIR *LIVES.*

VERY ASTUTE.

THEN--- I'LL *DROP* THIS SHAM OF A FACE.

FOR, AS YOU GUESSED, I'M *NOT* MR. FANTASTIC--

--BUT A *SKRULL*-- ONE OF THE *FIRST* FEW EVER TO LAND UPON THIS PITIFUL PLANET. *

*AS TOLD IN (=ULP!=) F.F. #2!--STAN.

"WE *DISGUISED* OURSELVES AS THE FANTASTIC FOUR--- TO ABET OUR *CONQUEST* OF YOUR WORLD---

"BUT, CAPTURED, WE THREE WERE *HYPNOTIZED* BY REED RICHARDS---

"--INTO BELIEVING WE WERE A TRIO OF *CATTLE*--AND THUS WE *GRAZED,* FOR LONG, UNTOLD MONTHS---

"--UNTIL A SKRULL *HYPER-BEAM* FROM SPACE *REVIVED* US---

25

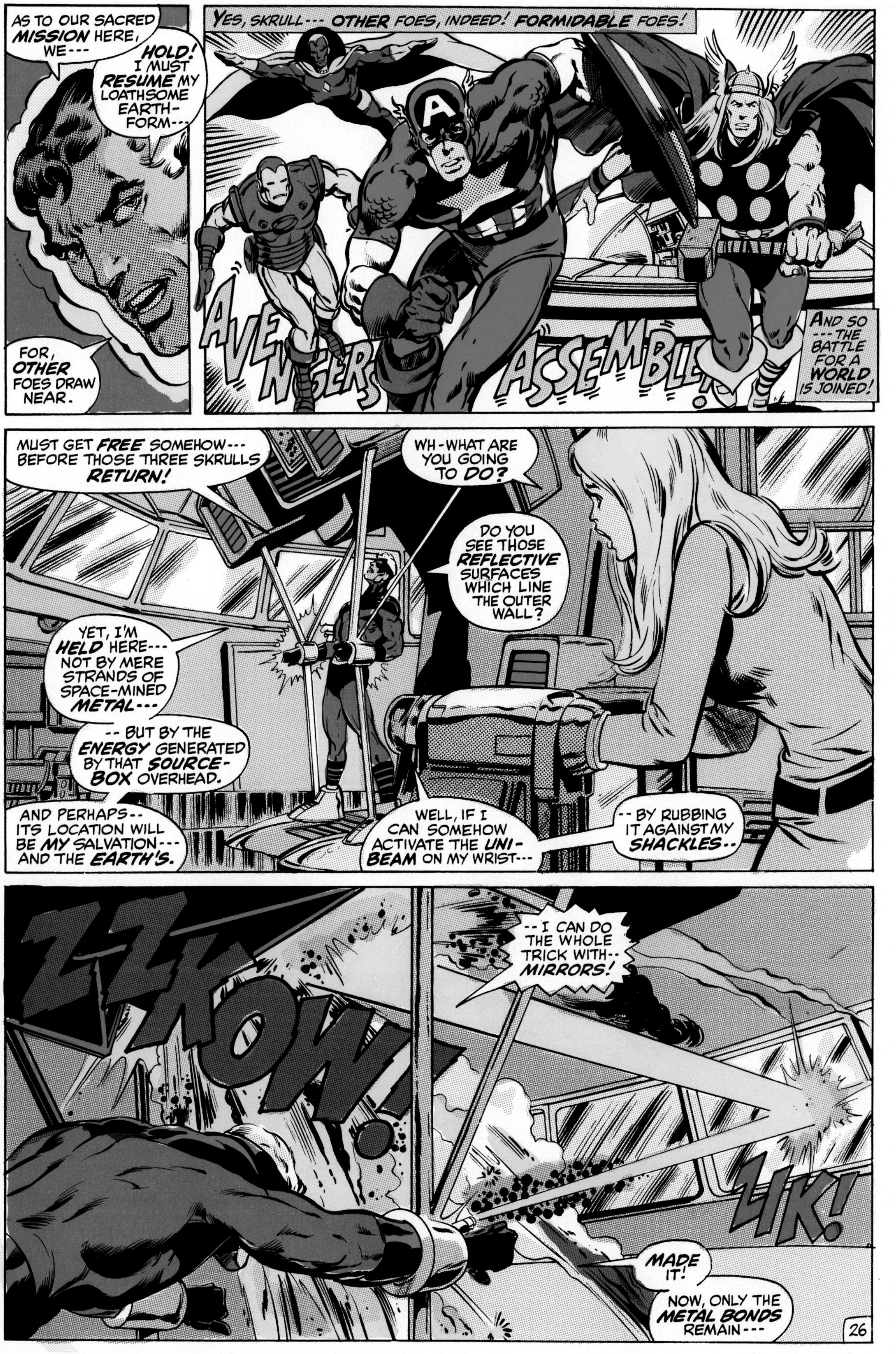
AS TO OUR SACRED MISSION HERE, WE---
HOLD! I MUST RESUME MY LOATHSOME EARTH-FORM---
FOR, OTHER FOES DRAW NEAR.
YES, SKRULL--- OTHER FOES, INDEED! FORMIDABLE FOES!
AVENGERS ASSEMBLE!
AND SO --- THE BATTLE FOR A WORLD IS JOINED!
MUST GET FREE SOMEHOW--- BEFORE THOSE THREE SKRULLS RETURN!
WH-WHAT ARE YOU GOING TO DO?
DO YOU SEE THOSE REFLECTIVE SURFACES WHICH LINE THE OUTER WALL?
YET, I'M HELD HERE--- NOT BY MERE STRANDS OF SPACE-MINED METAL---
-- BUT BY THE ENERGY GENERATED BY THAT SOURCE-BOX OVERHEAD.
AND PERHAPS-- ITS LOCATION WILL BE MY SALVATION--- AND THE EARTH'S.
WELL, IF I CAN SOMEHOW ACTIVATE THE UNI-BEAM ON MY WRIST---
-- BY RUBBING IT AGAINST MY SHACKLES--
ZZKOW!
--I CAN DO THE WHOLE TRICK WITH-- MIRRORS!
ZIK!
MADE IT!
NOW, ONLY THE METAL BONDS REMAIN---

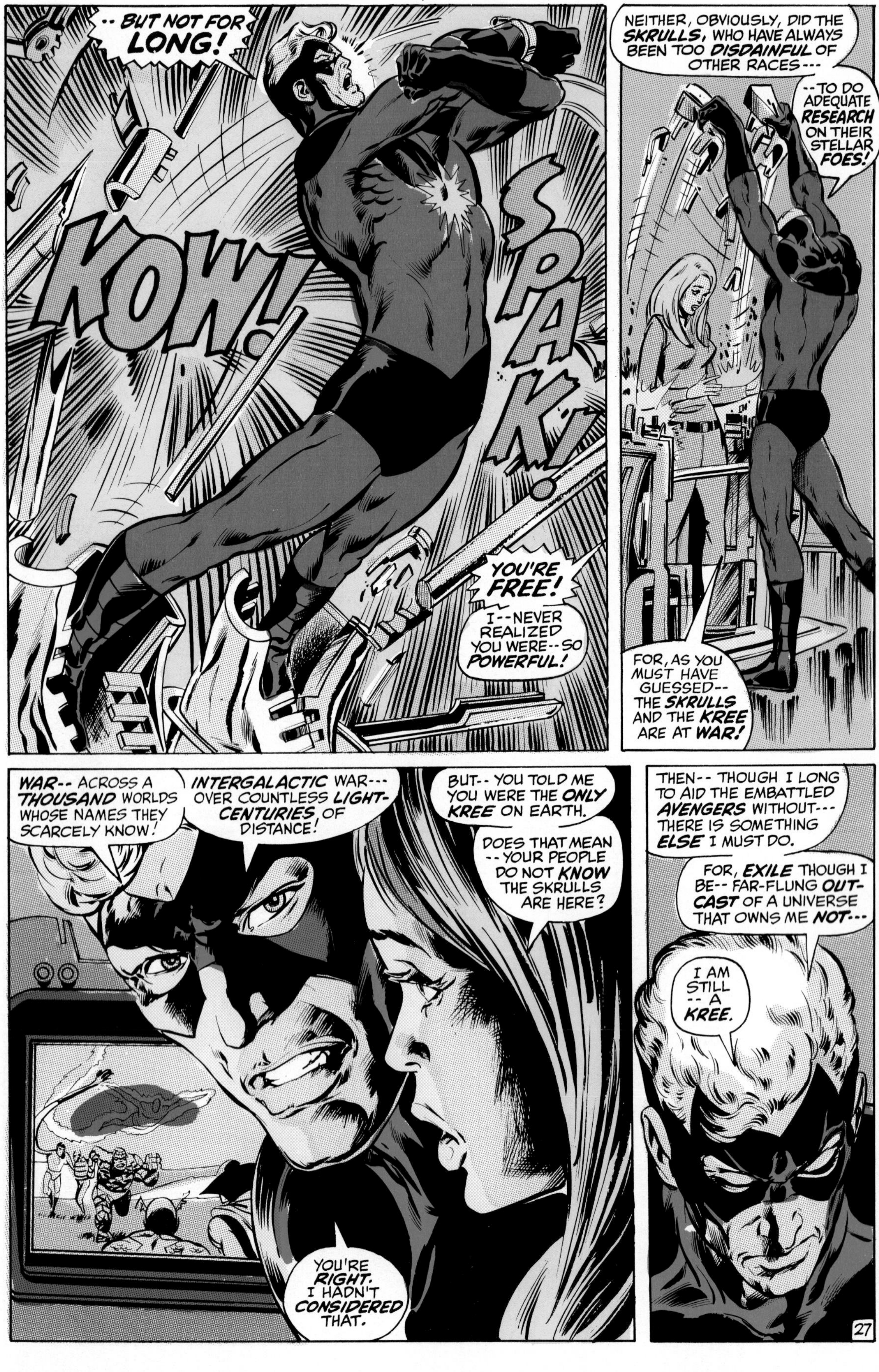

-- BUT NOT FOR LONG!
KOW!
SPAK!
YOU'RE FREE!
I--NEVER REALIZED YOU WERE--SO POWERFUL!
NEITHER, OBVIOUSLY, DID THE SKRULLS, WHO HAVE ALWAYS BEEN TOO DISDAINFUL OF OTHER RACES---
--TO DO ADEQUATE RESEARCH ON THEIR STELLAR FOES!
FOR, AS YOU MUST HAVE GUESSED--THE SKRULLS AND THE KREE ARE AT WAR!
WAR-- ACROSS A THOUSAND WORLDS WHOSE NAMES THEY SCARCELY KNOW!
INTERGALACTIC WAR--- OVER COUNTLESS LIGHT-CENTURIES OF DISTANCE!
BUT-- YOU TOLD ME YOU WERE THE ONLY KREE ON EARTH.
DOES THAT MEAN -- YOUR PEOPLE DO NOT KNOW THE SKRULLS ARE HERE?
YOU'RE RIGHT. I HADN'T CONSIDERED THAT.
THEN-- THOUGH I LONG TO AID THE EMBATTLED AVENGERS WITHOUT--- THERE IS SOMETHING ELSE I MUST DO.
FOR, EXILE THOUGH I BE-- FAR-FLUNG OUTCAST OF A UNIVERSE THAT OWNS ME NOT---
I AM STILL -- A KREE.

AN **OMNI-WAVE** PROJECTOR--- THAT IS THE **ONLY** ANSWER!

THAT ALONE CAN SEND AN **IN-STANTANEOUS** MESSAGE TO THE KREE GALAXY--ACROSS THE VOID OF **HYPER-SPACE!**

BUT-- WHY STAY **HERE**, ON THE SKRULL SHIP?

COULD AN EARTH-MAN BUILD A **RADIO** IF HE WERE STRANDED ON A **DESERT ISLE**?

ONLY **HERE** EXIST THE **TOOLS** FOR FORGING MY **UNI-BEAM** INTO THE PROPER FORM.

AND YET, THE SKRULLS WOULD GIVE **TEN PLANETS** FOR THE SECRET OF THE **OMNI-WAVE**.

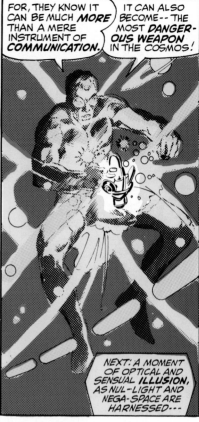

FOR, THEY KNOW IT CAN BE MUCH **MORE** THAN A MERE INSTRUMENT OF **COMMUNICATION.**

IT CAN ALSO BECOME-- THE MOST **DANGER-OUS** WEAPON IN THE COSMOS!

*NEXT: A MOMENT OF OPTICAL AND SENSUAL **ILLUSION**, AS NUL-LIGHT AND NEGA-SPACE ARE HARNESSED---*

⌐:COMPU-SYSTEMS PRIMED FOR BLASTOFF...

AMAZING! THESE GUYS CAN'T BE THE REAL F.F.!

AYE. BUT THEY **MATCH** OUR OLD FRIENDS--FOR POWER!

KRAK!

THOOM!

28.

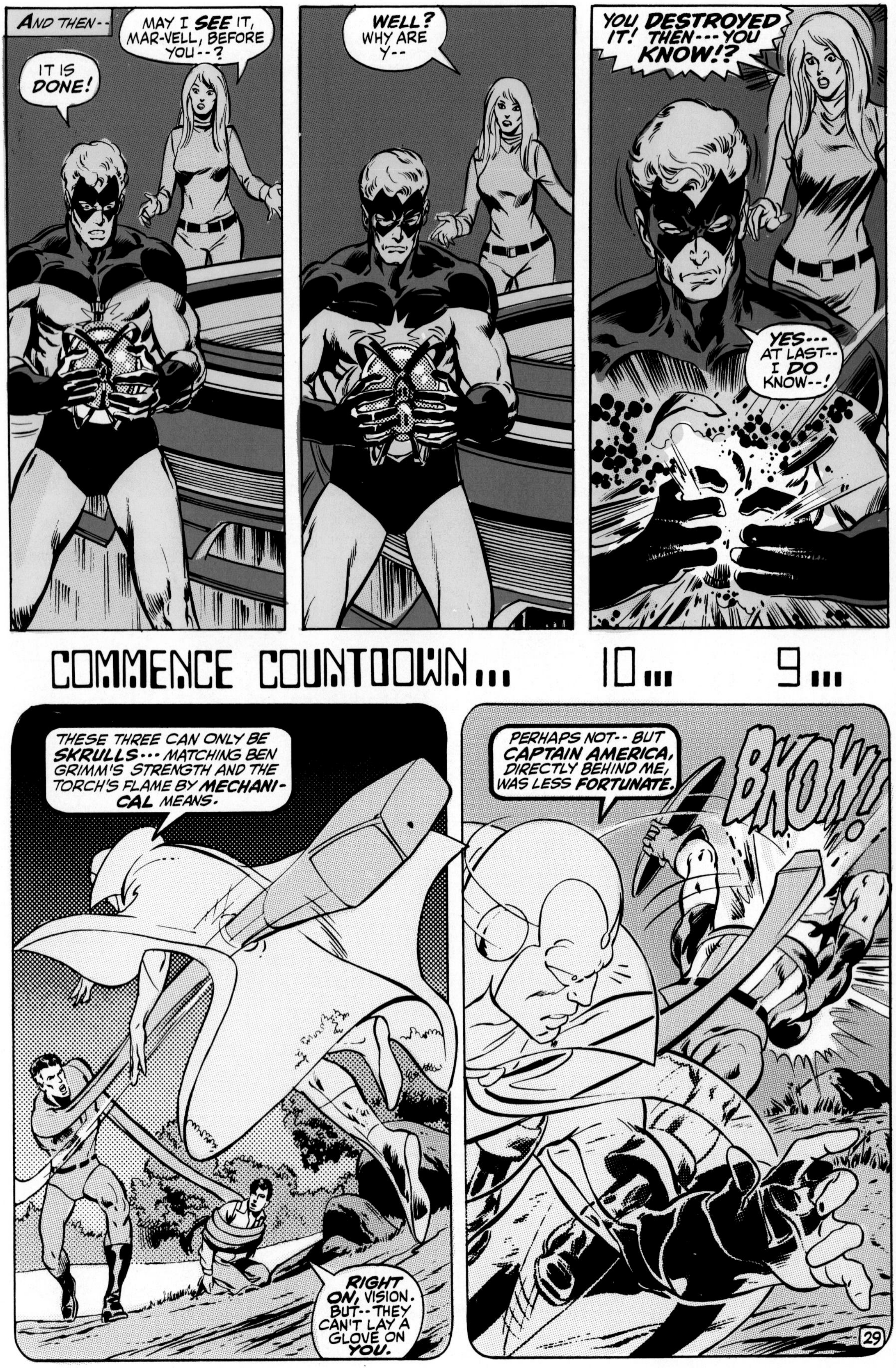
AND THEN--
MAY I SEE IT, MAR-VELL, BEFORE YOU--?
IT IS DONE!
WELL? WHY ARE Y--
YOU DESTROYED IT! THEN---YOU KNOW!?
YES--- AT LAST-- I DO KNOW--!
COMMENCE COUNTDOWN... 10... 9...
THESE THREE CAN ONLY BE SKRULLS--- MATCHING BEN GRIMM'S STRENGTH AND THE TORCH'S FLAME BY MECHANICAL MEANS.
RIGHT ON, VISION. BUT--THEY CAN'T LAY A GLOVE ON YOU.
PERHAPS NOT-- BUT CAPTAIN AMERICA, DIRECTLY BEHIND ME, WAS LESS FORTUNATE.
BKOW!
29

--- KNOW THAT YOU'RE **NOT** CAROL DANVERS--- BUT A **SKRULL!**

ONLY **THEY,** BESIDES THE AVENGERS, WOULD KNOW MY TRUE NAME WAS--- **MAR-VELL.**

I SHOULD HAVE REALIZED IT **BEFORE.**

NO **MATTER,** MAN OF THE **KREE---**

FOR, **NOTHING** WOULD HAVE SAVED YOU FOR LONG FROM ONE WHOM YOU KNOW **WELL--**

--- **I,** THE MOST **POWER-FUL** SKRULL OF **ALL!**

SPOW!

YOU'RE--- **SUPER-SKRULL!!**

8... 7... 6... 5...

DON'T COUNT ME OUT **YET,** AVENGER.

I CAN **STILL** TOSS A MEAN **SHIELD!**

UNGGH!

WAY TO **GO,** CAP!

WAK!

BUT-- LOOK AT **IRON MAN!**

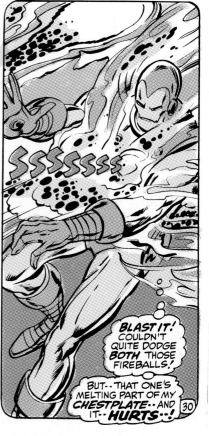

SSSSSSS

BLAST IT! COULDN'T QUITE DODGE **BOTH** THOSE FIREBALLS!

BUT-- THAT ONE'S MELTING PART OF MY **CHESTPLATE**-- AND IT-- **HURTS**--!

30

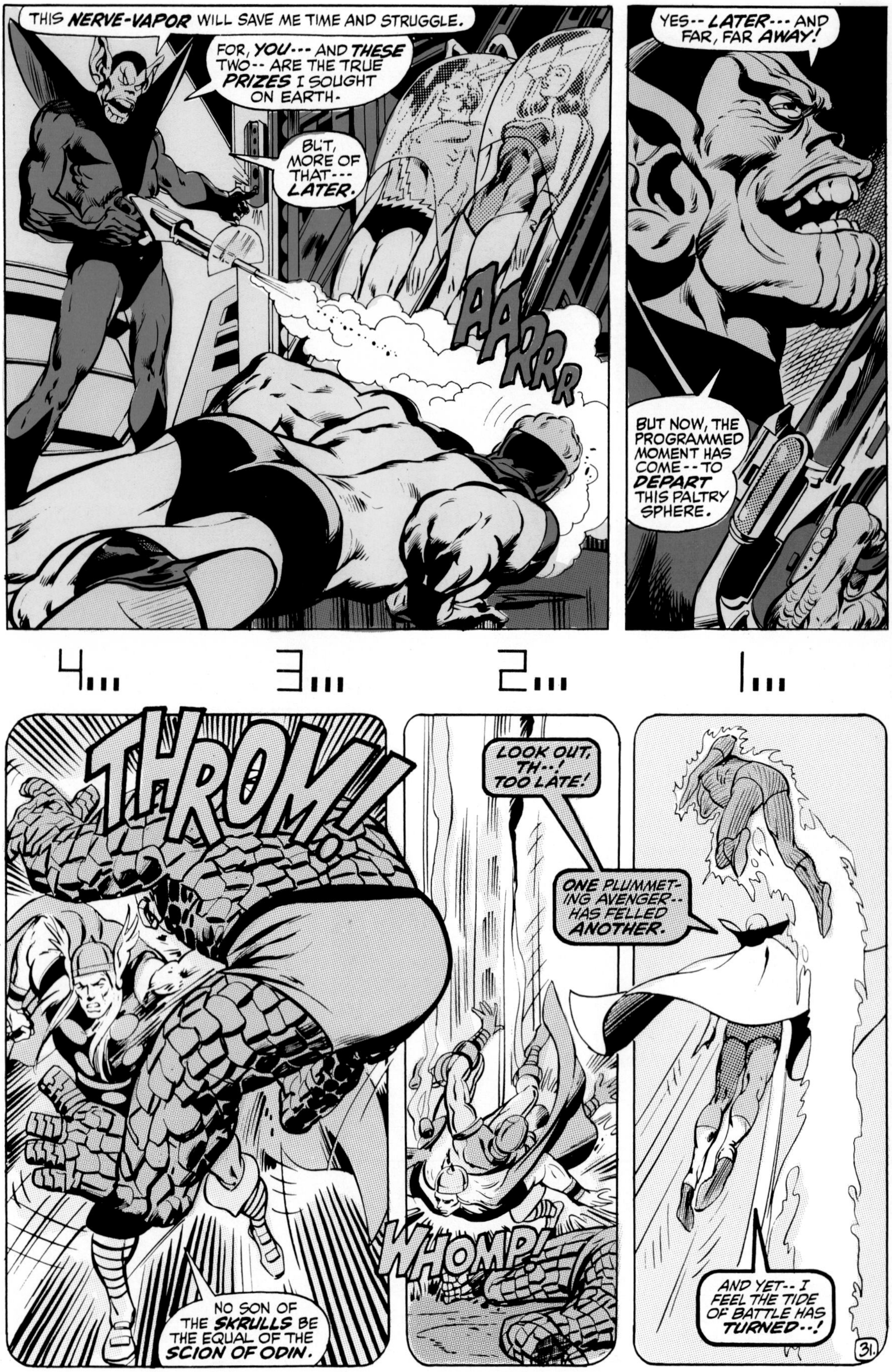

THIS NERVE-VAPOR WILL SAVE ME TIME AND STRUGGLE.
FOR, YOU--- AND THESE TWO-- ARE THE TRUE PRIZES I SOUGHT ON EARTH-
BUT, MORE OF THAT--- LATER.
AARRRR
YES-- LATER--- AND FAR, FAR AWAY!
BUT NOW, THE PROGRAMMED MOMENT HAS COME--TO DEPART THIS PALTRY SPHERE.
4...
3...
2...
1...
THROM!
NO SON OF THE SKRULLS BE THE EQUAL OF THE SCION OF ODIN.
LOOK OUT, TH--! TOO LATE!
ONE PLUMMETING AVENGER--HAS FELLED ANOTHER.
WHOMP!
AND YET-- I FEEL THE TIDE OF BATTLE HAS TURNED--!
31.

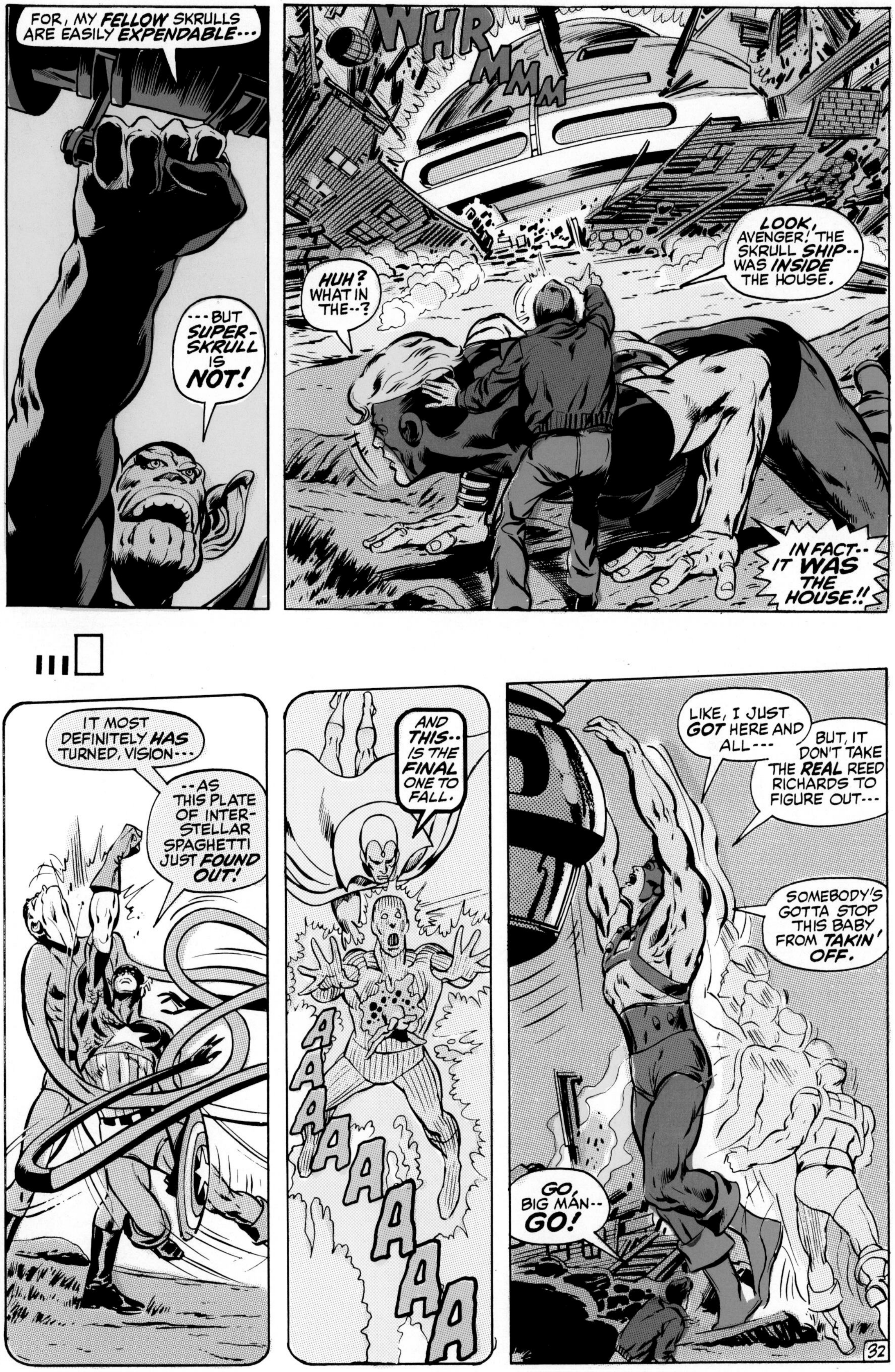

FOR, MY FELLOW SKRULLS ARE EASILY EXPENDABLE---
---BUT SUPER-SKRULL IS NOT!
WHRMMM
HUH? WHAT IN THE--?
LOOK, AVENGER! THE SKRULL SHIP-- WAS INSIDE THE HOUSE.
IN FACT-- IT WAS THE HOUSE!!
IT MOST DEFINITELY HAS TURNED, VISION---
--AS THIS PLATE OF INTER-STELLAR SPAGHETTI JUST FOUND OUT!
AND THIS-- IS THE FINAL ONE TO FALL.
AAAAAAAAAAAA
LIKE, I JUST GOT HERE AND ALL---
BUT, IT DON'T TAKE THE REAL REED RICHARDS TO FIGURE OUT---
SOMEBODY'S GOTTA STOP THIS BABY FROM TAKIN' OFF.
GO, BIG MAN-- GO!
32

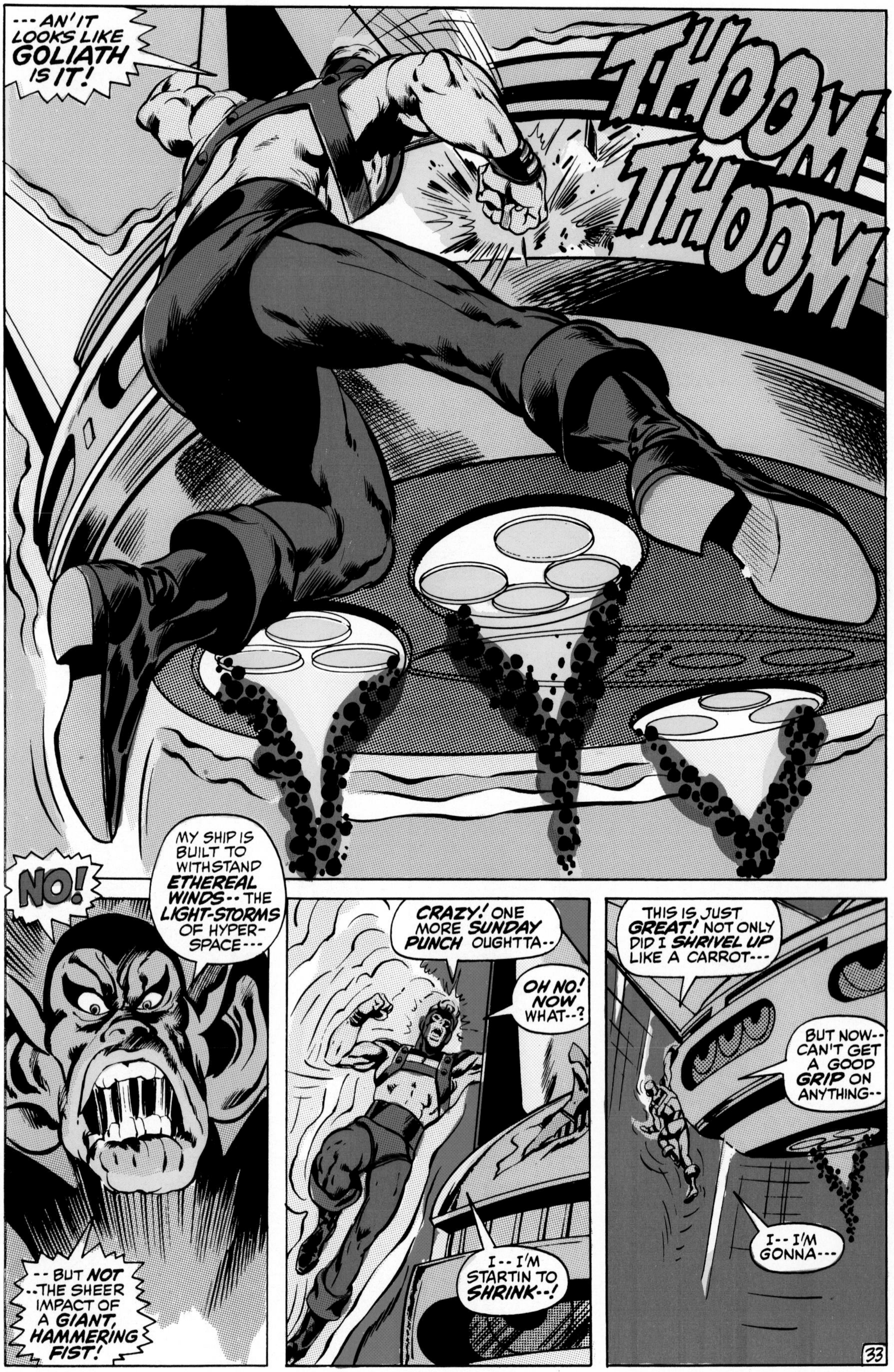

--- AN' IT LOOKS LIKE GOLIATH IS IT!
THOOM THOOM THOOM
MY SHIP IS BUILT TO WITHSTAND ETHEREAL WINDS-- THE LIGHT-STORMS OF HYPER-SPACE---
NO!
-- BUT NOT -- THE SHEER IMPACT OF A GIANT, HAMMERING FIST!
CRAZY! ONE MORE SUNDAY PUNCH OUGHTTA--
OH NO! NOW WHAT--?
I-- I'M STARTIN TO SHRINK--!
THIS IS JUST GREAT! NOT ONLY DID I SHRIVEL UP LIKE A CARROT---
BUT NOW-- CAN'T GET A GOOD GRIP ON ANYTHING--
I-- I'M GONNA---

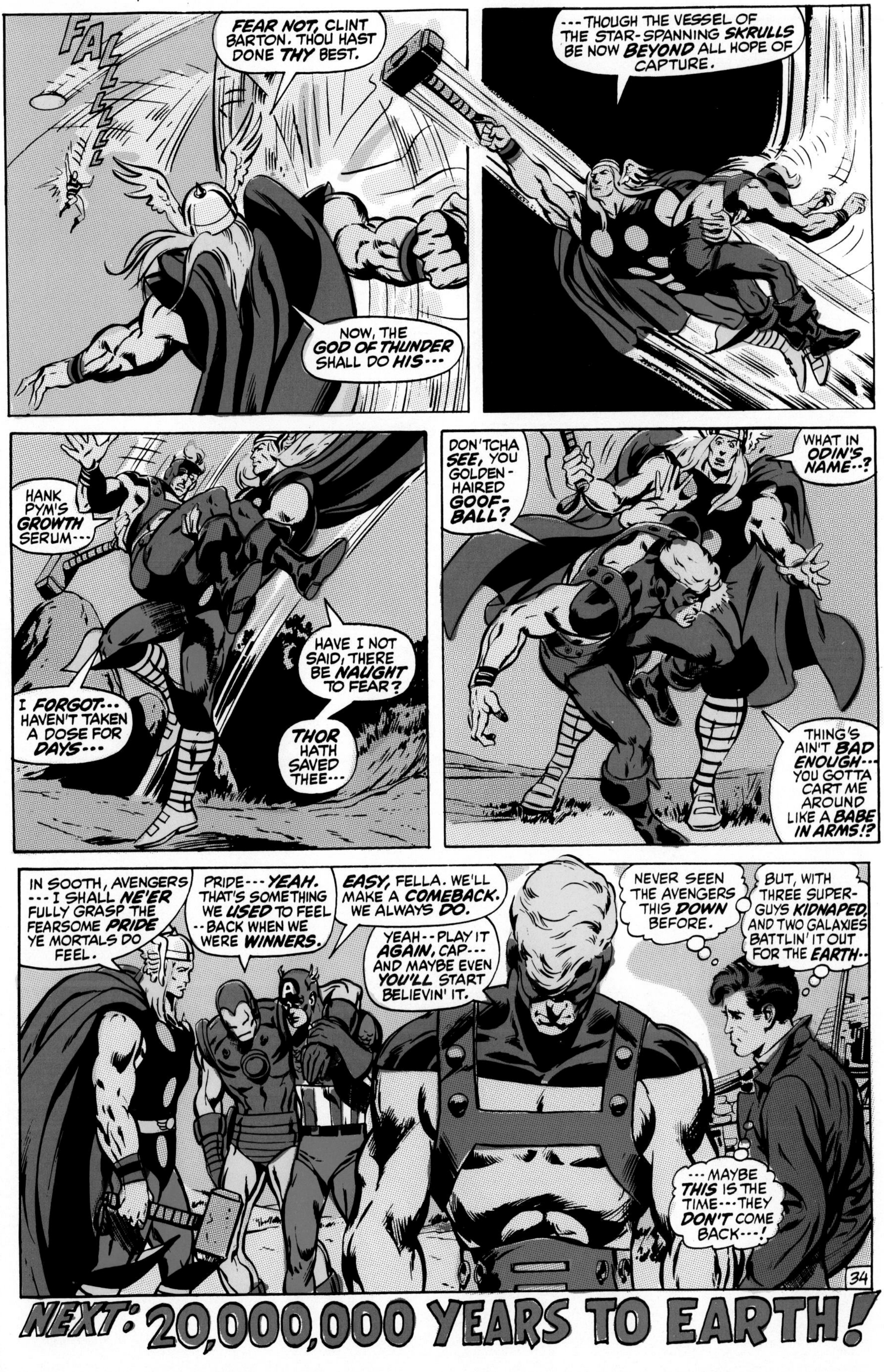
FALLLLLL
FEAR NOT, CLINT BARTON. THOU HAST DONE THY BEST.
NOW, THE GOD OF THUNDER SHALL DO HIS---
---THOUGH THE VESSEL OF THE STAR-SPANNING SKRULLS BE NOW BEYOND ALL HOPE OF CAPTURE.
HANK PYM'S GROWTH SERUM---
I FORGOT--- HAVEN'T TAKEN A DOSE FOR DAYS---
HAVE I NOT SAID, THERE BE NAUGHT TO FEAR?
THOR HATH SAVED THEE---
DON'TCHA SEE, YOU GOLDEN-HAIRED GOOF-BALL?
WHAT IN ODIN'S NAME--?
THING'S AIN'T BAD ENOUGH--- YOU GOTTA CART ME AROUND LIKE A BABE IN ARMS!?
IN SOOTH, AVENGERS --- I SHALL NE'ER FULLY GRASP THE FEARSOME PRIDE YE MORTALS DO FEEL.
PRIDE--- YEAH. THAT'S SOMETHING WE USED TO FEEL --BACK WHEN WE WERE WINNERS.
EASY, FELLA. WE'LL MAKE A COMEBACK. WE ALWAYS DO.
YEAH--PLAY IT AGAIN, CAP--- AND MAYBE EVEN YOU'LL START BELIEVIN' IT.
NEVER SEEN THE AVENGERS THIS DOWN BEFORE.
BUT, WITH THREE SUPER-GUYS KIDNAPED, AND TWO GALAXIES BATTLIN' IT OUT FOR THE EARTH--
---MAYBE THIS IS THE TIME---THEY DON'T COME BACK---!
34
NEXT: 20,000,000 YEARS TO EARTH!

CHAPTER SIX

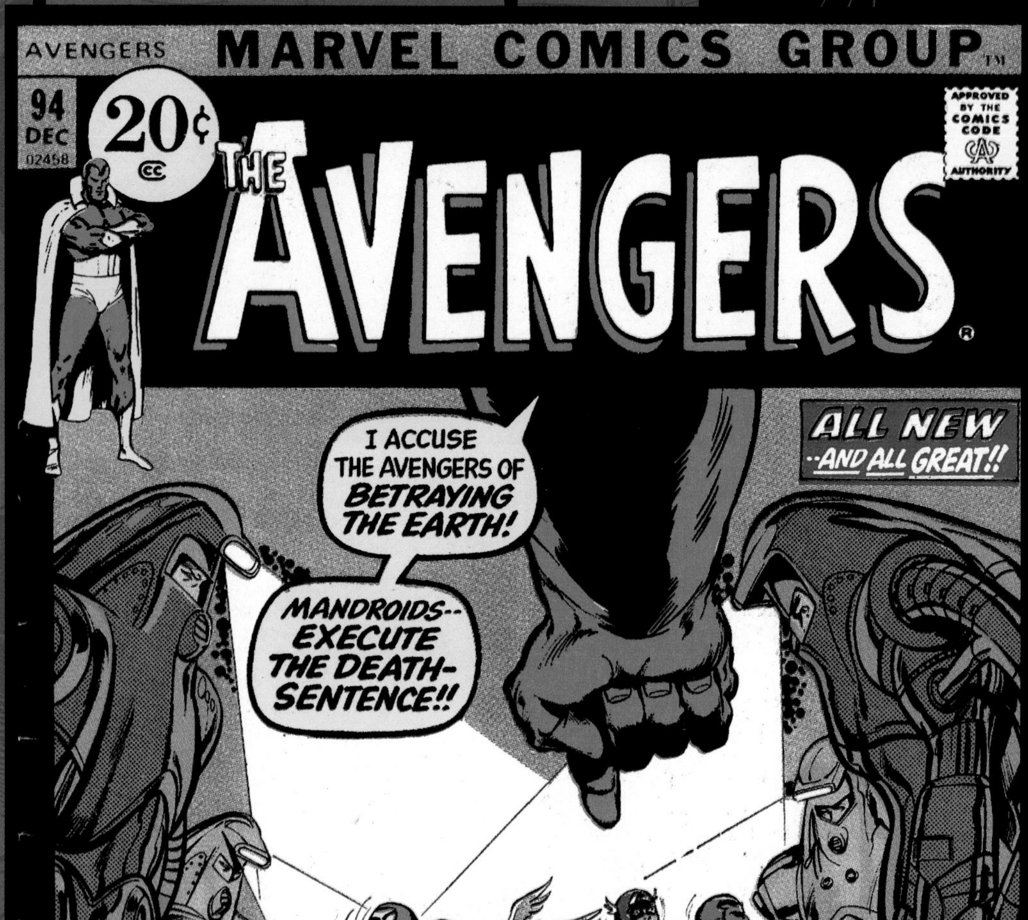
AVENGERS
MARVEL COMICS GROUP
94
DEC
02458
20¢
CC
APPROVED BY THE COMICS CODE AUTHORITY
THE AVENGERS
ALL NEW --AND ALL GREAT!!
I ACCUSE THE AVENGERS OF BETRAYING THE EARTH!
MANDROIDS-- EXECUTE THE DEATH-SENTENCE!!
BEHOLD THE MANDROIDS!

MORE THAN INHUMAN!

THE MIGHTY AVENGERS!®

STAN LEE EDITOR • ROY THOMAS WRITER • NEAL ADAMS ARTIST • TOM PALMER INKER • SAM ROSEN LETTERER

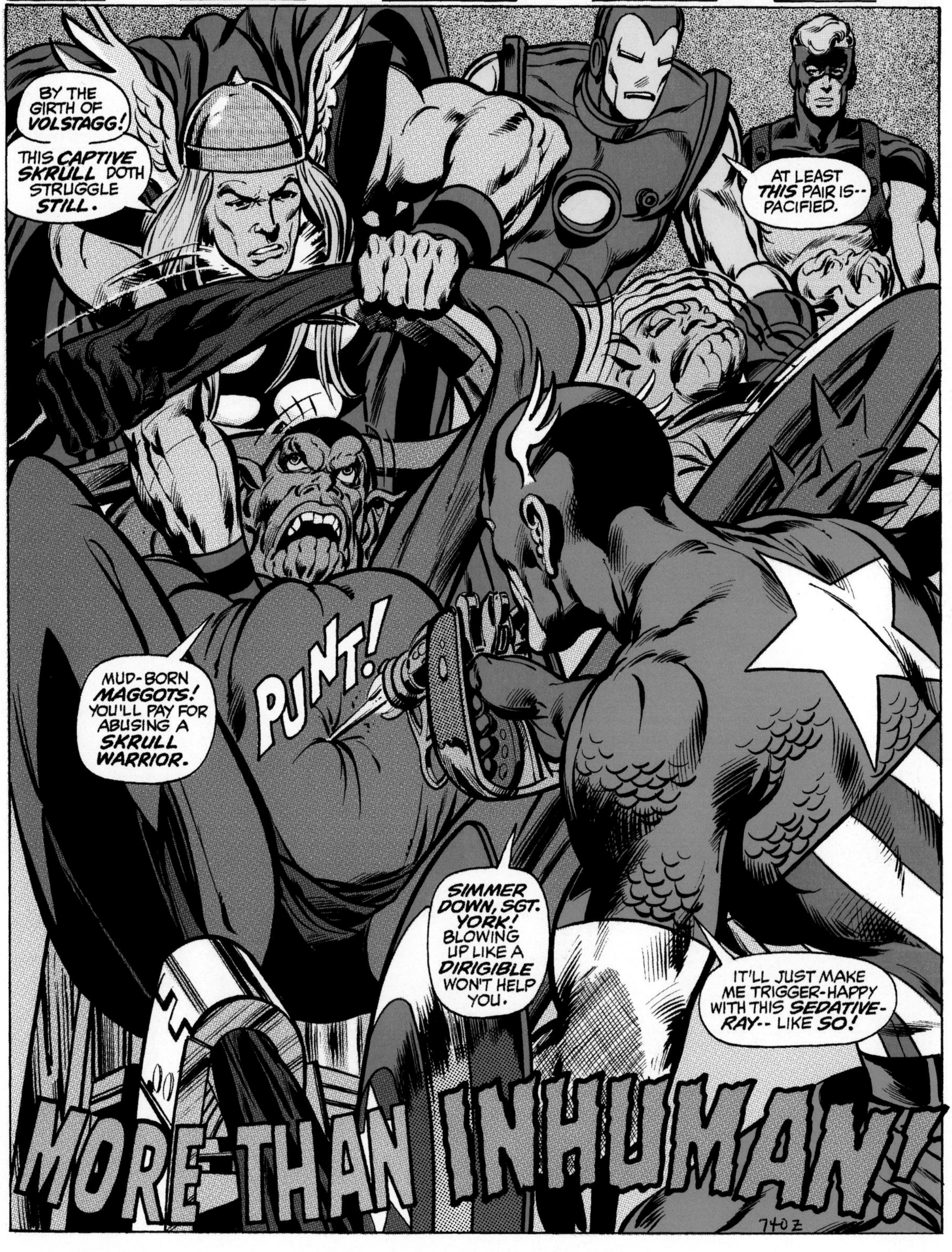
BY THE GIRTH OF VOLSTAGG!
THIS CAPTIVE SKRULL DOTH STRUGGLE STILL.
AT LEAST THIS PAIR IS-- PACIFIED.
PUNT!
MUD-BORN MAGGOTS! YOU'LL PAY FOR ABUSING A SKRULL WARRIOR.
SIMMER DOWN, SGT. YORK! BLOWING UP LIKE A DIRIGIBLE WON'T HELP YOU.
IT'LL JUST MAKE ME TRIGGER-HAPPY WITH THIS SEDATIVE-RAY-- LIKE SO!
MORE-THAN INHUMAN!

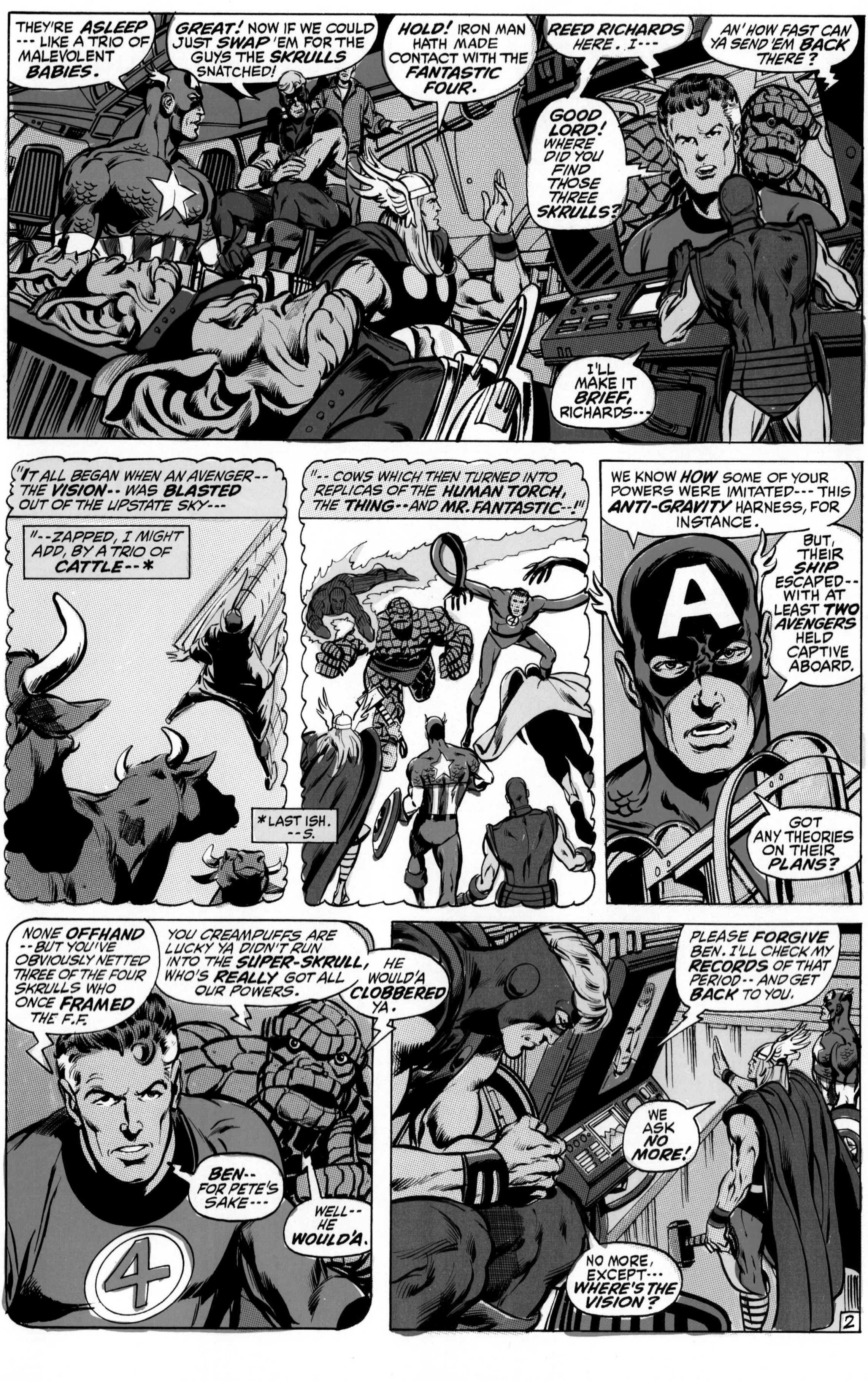
THEY'RE ASLEEP --- LIKE A TRIO OF MALEVOLENT BABIES.
GREAT! NOW IF WE COULD JUST SWAP 'EM FOR THE GUYS THE SKRULLS SNATCHED!
HOLD! IRON MAN HATH MADE CONTACT WITH THE FANTASTIC FOUR.
REED RICHARDS HERE. . I---
AN' HOW FAST CAN YA SEND 'EM BACK THERE?
GOOD LORD! WHERE DID YOU FIND THOSE THREE SKRULLS?
I'LL MAKE IT BRIEF, RICHARDS---
"IT ALL BEGAN WHEN AN AVENGER--THE VISION--WAS BLASTED OUT OF THE UPSTATE SKY---
"--ZAPPED, I MIGHT ADD, BY A TRIO OF CATTLE--*
*LAST ISH. --S.
"--COWS WHICH THEN TURNED INTO REPLICAS OF THE HUMAN TORCH, THE THING--AND MR. FANTASTIC--!"
WE KNOW HOW SOME OF YOUR POWERS WERE IMITATED--- THIS ANTI-GRAVITY HARNESS, FOR INSTANCE.
BUT, THEIR SHIP ESCAPED--WITH AT LEAST TWO AVENGERS HELD CAPTIVE ABOARD.
GOT ANY THEORIES ON THEIR PLANS?
NONE OFFHAND --BUT YOU'VE OBVIOUSLY NETTED THREE OF THE FOUR SKRULLS WHO ONCE FRAMED THE F.F.
YOU CREAMPUFFS ARE LUCKY YA DIDN'T RUN INTO THE SUPER-SKRULL, WHO'S REALLY GOT ALL OUR POWERS.
HE WOULD'A CLOBBERED YA.
BEN-- FOR PETE'S SAKE---
WELL-- HE WOULD'A.
PLEASE FORGIVE BEN. I'LL CHECK MY RECORDS OF THAT PERIOD--AND GET BACK TO YOU.
WE ASK NO MORE!
NO MORE, EXCEPT--- WHERE'S THE VISION?
2

"WHERE IS THE VISION?" AH, CLINT BARTON, IF YOU HAD BUT GLANCED UPWARD, ONE BRIEF *HOUR* AGO, AS THAT SKRULL SAUCER MADE ITS HASTY *ESCAPE* ---

--YOU MIGHT HAVE WITNESSED A GREEN-AND-GOLD *WRAITH*, LIGHTER THAN THE VERY AIR, SWOOSHING UPWARD *AFTER* IT--!

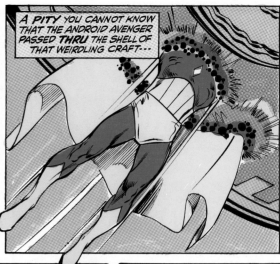

A *PITY* YOU CANNOT KNOW THAT THE ANDROID AVENGER PASSED *THRU* THE SHELL OF THAT *WEIRDLING* CRAFT---

--- WHERE ELECTRIC-CELL EYES BEHELD *THREE* HUMAN CAPTIVES, AND--- *THE SUPER-SKRULL!*

YOU THINK YOU HAVE *FOILED* MY MISSION, DON'T YOU, MAR-VELL, BY NOT YIELDING UP *KREE SECRETS?!*

BUT, I HAVE THESE TWO EARTH-BORN *SIBLINGS* AS WELL ---

--*MUTANTS*, WHOSE BRAIN-WAVES ONLY WE *SKRULLS* KNOW HOW TO TAP.

MMMMM

NOTE HOW THOSE BRAIN-WAVES *GUIDE* THIS AIR-VESSEL ---

--*LEAD* IT UNERRINGLY TOWARD A PLACE WHERE DWELL OTHERS, WITH *SIMILAR* BRAIN-WAVES---

--OTHERS, WHOM I MUST *DESTROY.*

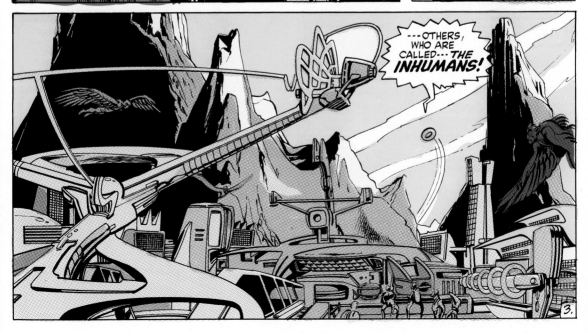

---OTHERS, WHO ARE CALLED--- *THE INHUMANS!*

3.

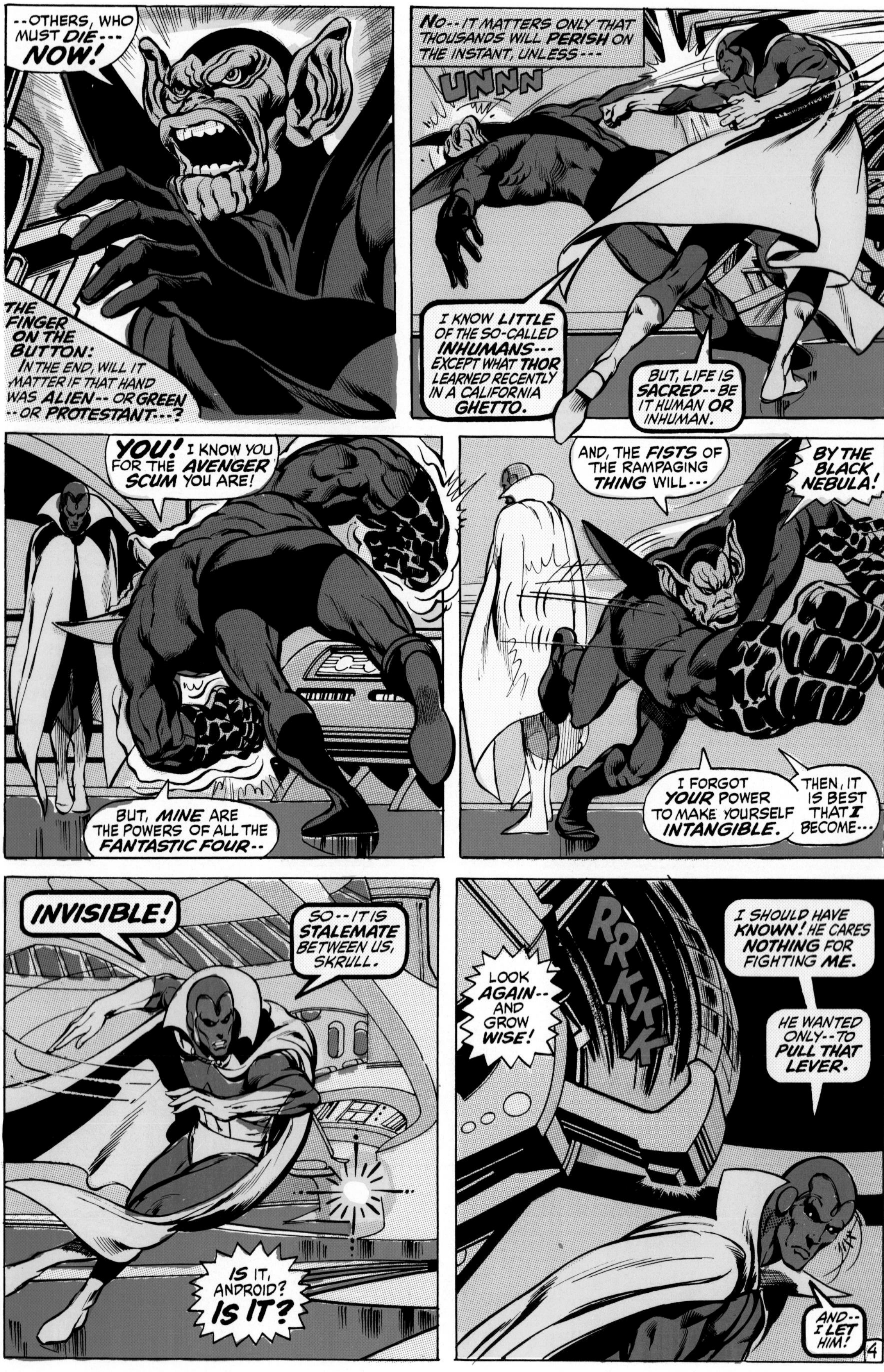
--OTHERS, WHO MUST DIE--- NOW!
THE FINGER ON THE BUTTON: IN THE END, WILL IT MATTER IF THAT HAND WAS ALIEN-- OR GREEN --OR PROTESTANT--?
NO--IT MATTERS ONLY THAT THOUSANDS WILL PERISH ON THE INSTANT, UNLESS---
UNNN
I KNOW LITTLE OF THE SO-CALLED INHUMANS--- EXCEPT WHAT THOR LEARNED RECENTLY IN A CALIFORNIA GHETTO.
BUT, LIFE IS SACRED--BE IT HUMAN OR INHUMAN.
YOU! I KNOW YOU FOR THE AVENGER SCUM YOU ARE!
BUT, MINE ARE THE POWERS OF ALL THE FANTASTIC FOUR--
AND, THE FISTS OF THE RAMPAGING THING WILL---
BY THE BLACK NEBULA!
I FORGOT YOUR POWER TO MAKE YOURSELF INTANGIBLE.
THEN, IT IS BEST THAT I BECOME---
INVISIBLE!
SO--IT IS STALEMATE BETWEEN US, SKRULL.
IS IT, ANDROID? IS IT?
RRKKK
LOOK AGAIN-- AND GROW WISE!
I SHOULD HAVE KNOWN! HE CARES NOTHING FOR FIGHTING ME.
HE WANTED ONLY--TO PULL THAT LEVER.
AND-- I LET HIM!
4

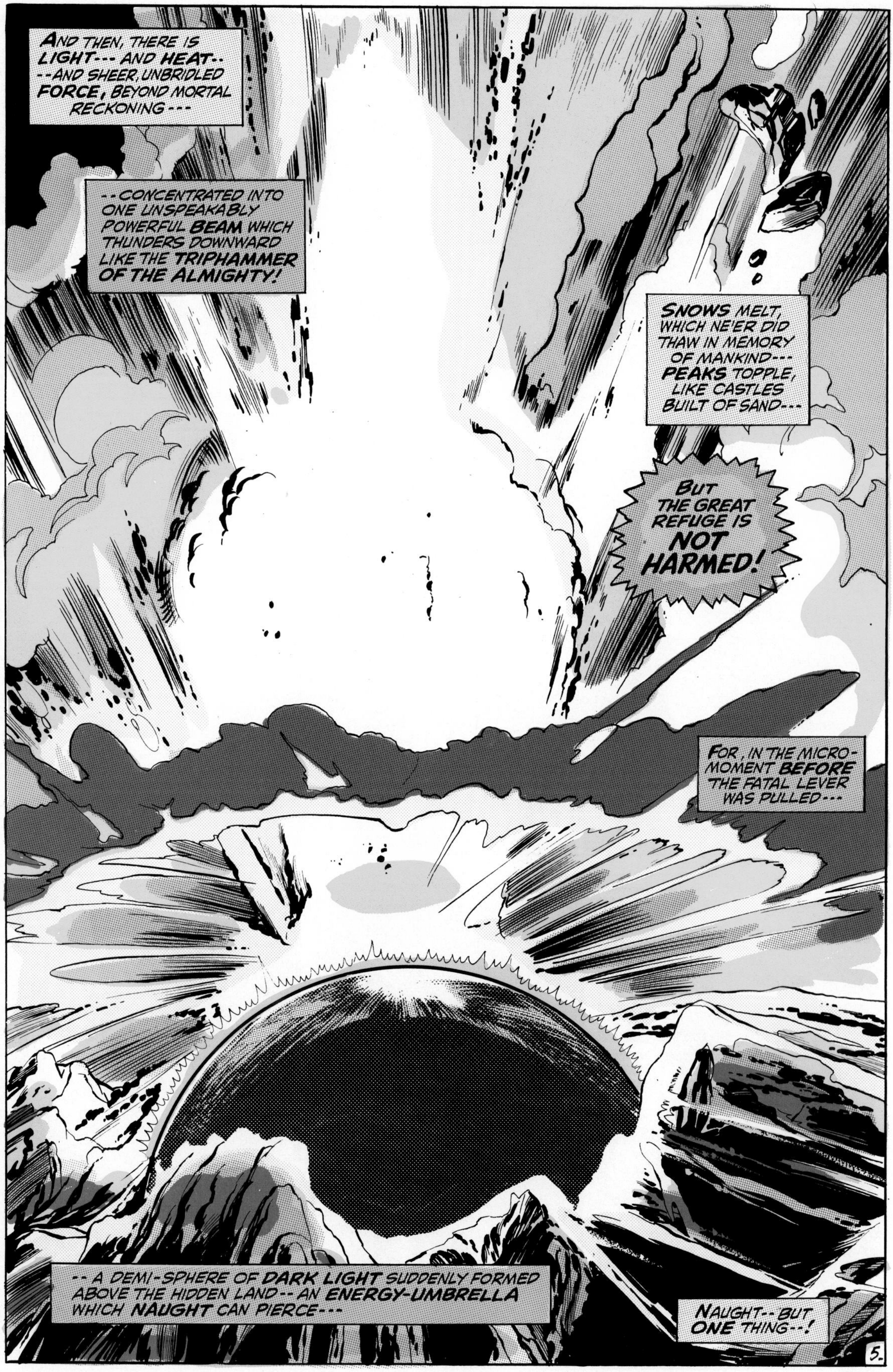
AND THEN, THERE IS LIGHT--- AND HEAT-- --AND SHEER, UNBRIDLED FORCE, BEYOND MORTAL RECKONING---
--CONCENTRATED INTO ONE UNSPEAKABLY POWERFUL BEAM WHICH THUNDERS DOWNWARD LIKE THE TRIPHAMMER OF THE ALMIGHTY!
SNOWS MELT, WHICH NE'ER DID THAW IN MEMORY OF MANKIND--- PEAKS TOPPLE, LIKE CASTLES BUILT OF SAND---
BUT THE GREAT REFUGE IS NOT HARMED!
FOR, IN THE MICRO-MOMENT BEFORE THE FATAL LEVER WAS PULLED---
-- A DEMI-SPHERE OF DARK LIGHT SUDDENLY FORMED ABOVE THE HIDDEN LAND -- AN ENERGY-UMBRELLA WHICH NAUGHT CAN PIERCE---
NAUGHT-- BUT ONE THING--!
5.

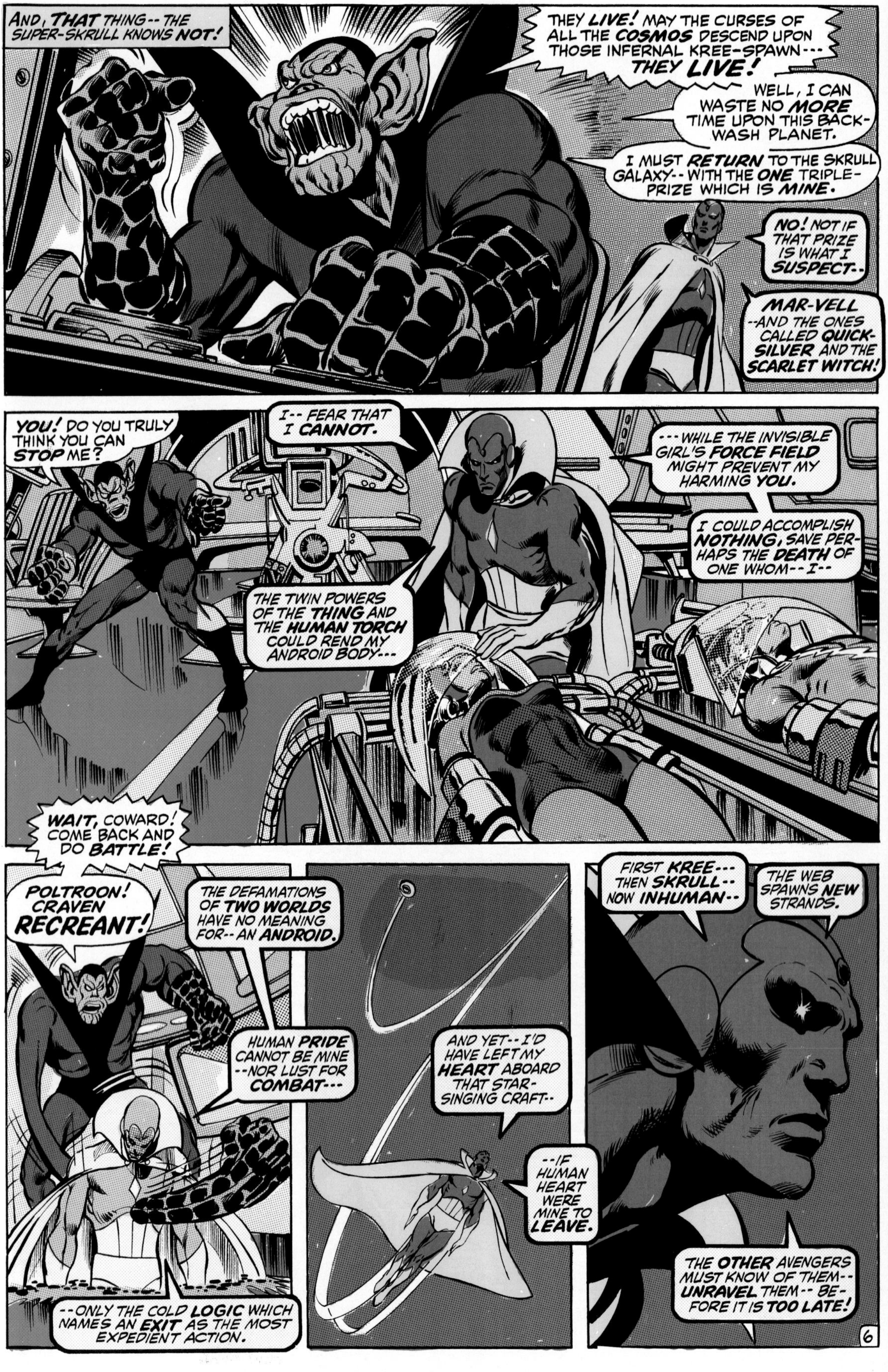
AND, THAT THING-- THE SUPER-SKRULL KNOWS NOT!
THEY LIVE! MAY THE CURSES OF ALL THE COSMOS DESCEND UPON THOSE INFERNAL KREE-SPAWN--- THEY LIVE!
WELL, I CAN WASTE NO MORE TIME UPON THIS BACK-WASH PLANET.
I MUST RETURN TO THE SKRULL GALAXY-- WITH THE ONE TRIPLE-PRIZE WHICH IS MINE.
NO! NOT IF THAT PRIZE IS WHAT I SUSPECT--
MAR-VELL --AND THE ONES CALLED QUICK-SILVER AND THE SCARLET WITCH!
YOU! DO YOU TRULY THINK YOU CAN STOP ME?
I-- FEAR THAT I CANNOT.
THE TWIN POWERS OF THE THING AND THE HUMAN TORCH COULD REND MY ANDROID BODY---
---WHILE THE INVISIBLE GIRL'S FORCE FIELD MIGHT PREVENT MY HARMING YOU.
I COULD ACCOMPLISH NOTHING, SAVE PER-HAPS THE DEATH OF ONE WHOM-- I--
WAIT, COWARD! COME BACK AND DO BATTLE!
POLTROON! CRAVEN RECREANT!
THE DEFAMATIONS OF TWO WORLDS HAVE NO MEANING FOR-- AN ANDROID.
HUMAN PRIDE CANNOT BE MINE --NOR LUST FOR COMBAT---
--ONLY THE COLD LOGIC WHICH NAMES AN EXIT AS THE MOST EXPEDIENT ACTION.
AND YET-- I'D HAVE LEFT MY HEART ABOARD THAT STAR-SINGING CRAFT--
--IF HUMAN HEART WERE MINE TO LEAVE.
FIRST KREE--- THEN SKRULL-- NOW INHUMAN--
THE WEB SPAWNS NEW STRANDS.
THE OTHER AVENGERS MUST KNOW OF THEM-- UNRAVEL THEM-- BE-FORE IT IS TOO LATE!

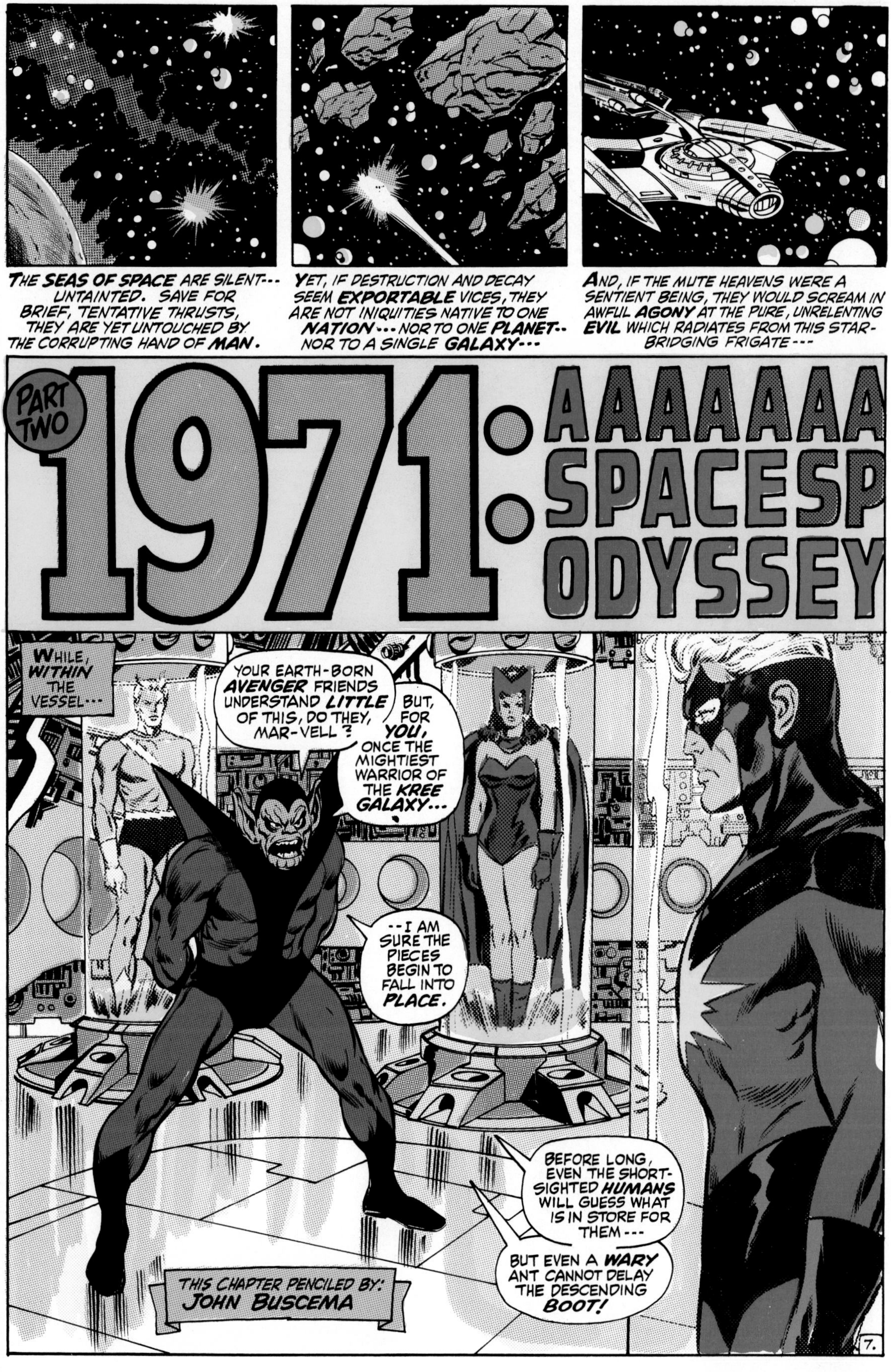

THE SEAS OF SPACE ARE SILENT--- UNTAINTED. SAVE FOR BRIEF, TENTATIVE THRUSTS, THEY ARE YET UNTOUCHED BY THE CORRUPTING HAND OF MAN.
YET, IF DESTRUCTION AND DECAY SEEM EXPORTABLE VICES, THEY ARE NOT INIQUITIES NATIVE TO ONE NATION--- NOR TO ONE PLANET-- NOR TO A SINGLE GALAXY---
AND, IF THE MUTE HEAVENS WERE A SENTIENT BEING, THEY WOULD SCREAM IN AWFUL AGONY AT THE PURE, UNRELENTING EVIL WHICH RADIATES FROM THIS STAR-BRIDGING FRIGATE---
PART TWO
1971: A SPACE ODYSSEY
WHILE, WITHIN THE VESSEL---
YOUR EARTH-BORN AVENGER FRIENDS UNDERSTAND LITTLE OF THIS, DO THEY, MAR-VELL?
BUT, FOR YOU, ONCE THE MIGHTIEST WARRIOR OF THE KREE GALAXY...
--I AM SURE THE PIECES BEGIN TO FALL INTO PLACE.
BEFORE LONG, EVEN THE SHORT-SIGHTED HUMANS WILL GUESS WHAT IS IN STORE FOR THEM---
BUT EVEN A WARY ANT CANNOT DELAY THE DESCENDING BOOT!
THIS CHAPTER PENCILED BY: JOHN BUSCEMA
7.

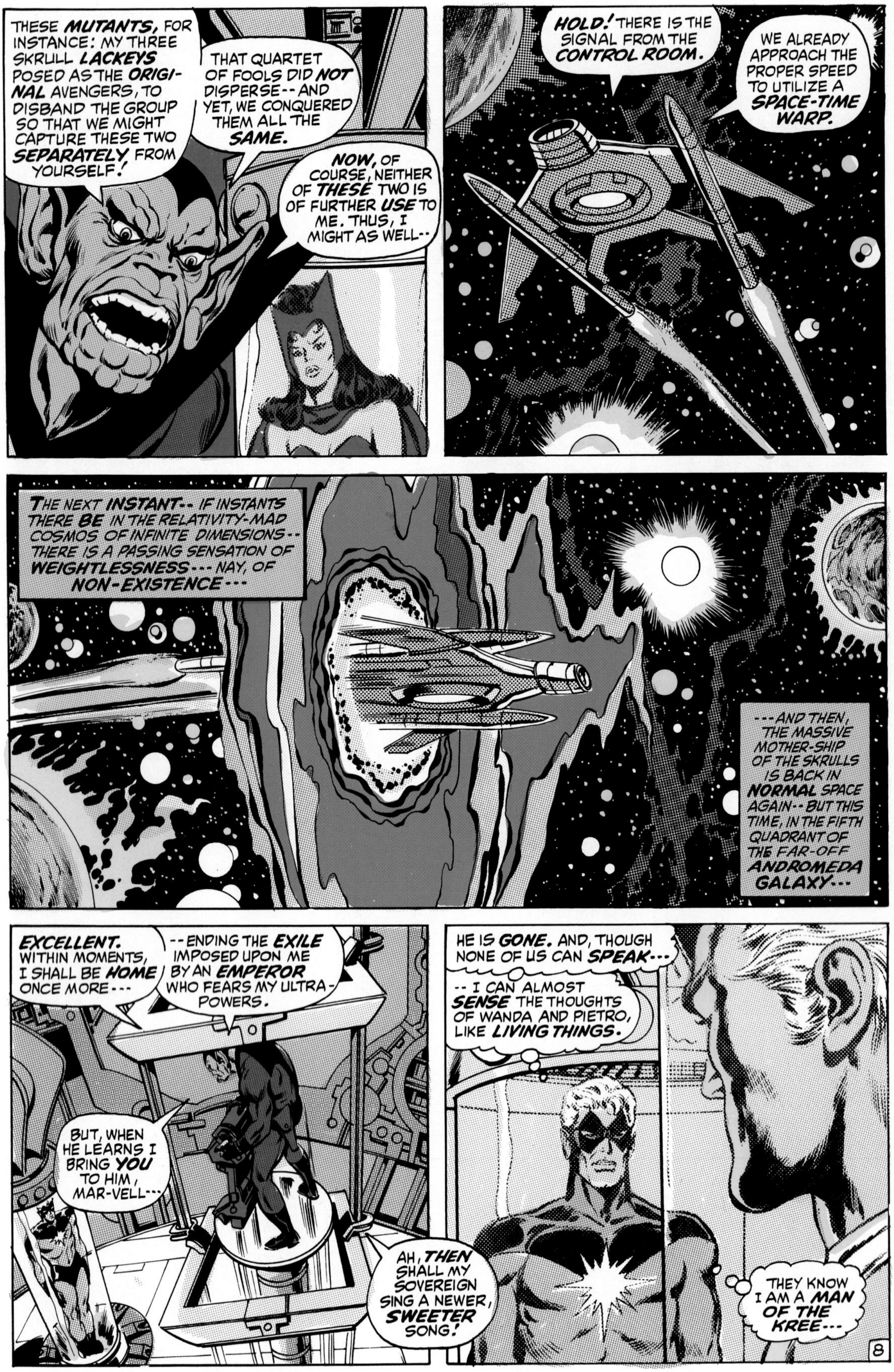

THESE MUTANTS, FOR INSTANCE: MY THREE SKRULL LACKEYS POSED AS THE ORIGINAL AVENGERS, TO DISBAND THE GROUP SO THAT WE MIGHT CAPTURE THESE TWO SEPARATELY FROM YOURSELF!
THAT QUARTET OF FOOLS DID NOT DISPERSE-- AND YET, WE CONQUERED THEM ALL THE SAME.
NOW, OF COURSE, NEITHER OF THESE TWO IS OF FURTHER USE TO ME. THUS, I MIGHT AS WELL--
HOLD! THERE IS THE SIGNAL FROM THE CONTROL ROOM.
WE ALREADY APPROACH THE PROPER SPEED TO UTILIZE A SPACE-TIME WARP.
THE NEXT INSTANT-- IF INSTANTS THERE BE IN THE RELATIVITY-MAD COSMOS OF INFINITE DIMENSIONS-- THERE IS A PASSING SENSATION OF WEIGHTLESSNESS--- NAY, OF NON-EXISTENCE---
---AND THEN, THE MASSIVE MOTHER-SHIP OF THE SKRULLS IS BACK IN NORMAL SPACE AGAIN-- BUT THIS TIME, IN THE FIFTH QUADRANT OF THE FAR-OFF ANDROMEDA GALAXY---
EXCELLENT. WITHIN MOMENTS, I SHALL BE HOME ONCE MORE---
--ENDING THE EXILE IMPOSED UPON ME BY AN EMPEROR WHO FEARS MY ULTRA-POWERS.
BUT, WHEN HE LEARNS I BRING YOU TO HIM, MAR-VELL---
AH, THEN SHALL MY SOVEREIGN SING A NEWER, SWEETER SONG!
HE IS GONE. AND, THOUGH NONE OF US CAN SPEAK---
-- I CAN ALMOST SENSE THE THOUGHTS OF WANDA AND PIETRO, LIKE LIVING THINGS.
THEY KNOW I AM A MAN OF THE KREE---
8

---AND THAT THE SKRULLS WANT STRATEGICAL **INFORMATION** FROM ME.

THEY DOUBT-LESS **SENSE** I WOULD NEVER BETRAY MY **HOMELAND**--- EVEN THOUGH I, LIKE SUPER-SKRULL, AM AN **EXILE!**

BUT WHAT IF THE SKRULLS WISH TO TRADE AN **END** TO THIS POTENTIALLY-CATACLYSMIC **WAR**--- FOR THE **DEATH OF THE EARTH?**

WHAT **THEN,** MAR-VELL?

HOW CAN YOU **ANSWER** THE AVENGERS' UNVOICED ACCUSATIONS---

---WHEN YOU **YOUR-SELF**-- DO NOT KNOW THE ANSWER---!?

WELL, SWINISH ONES? YOU ORBITED IN **SPACE,** WHILE **I** DID ALL THE WORK ON THE MUDBALL CALLED **EARTH.**

CAN YOU NOT BRING ME AT LEAST BEFORE THE **EMPEROR** WITHOUT THE SHIP'S **ROCKING** SO?

OUR CRAFT DOES NOT VIBRATE THUS OF ITS **OWN** ACCORD, MIGHTY ONE.

OBSERVE!

BY THE SARGASSOS OF SIRIUS!

WARNING BLASTS-- FIRED AT US FROM THE **PALACE ROYAL** ITSELF!

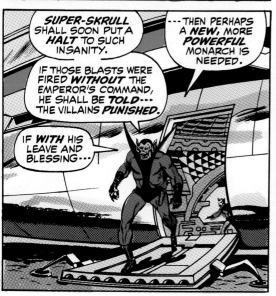

SUPER-SKRULL SHALL SOON PUT A **HALT** TO SUCH INSANITY.

---THEN PERHAPS A **NEW,** MORE **POWERFUL** MONARCH IS NEEDED.

IF THOSE BLASTS WERE FIRED **WITHOUT** THE EMPEROR'S COMMAND, HE SHALL BE **TOLD**--- THE VILLAINS **PUNISHED.**

IF **WITH** HIS LEAVE AND BLESSING---

HE COMES! HE COMES!

SO! THE TIME FOR **WARNING** BURSTS IS **PAST.**

FIRE, YOU MISERABLE **DUNG-DOGS**--- AND **FIRE TO KILL!**

9.

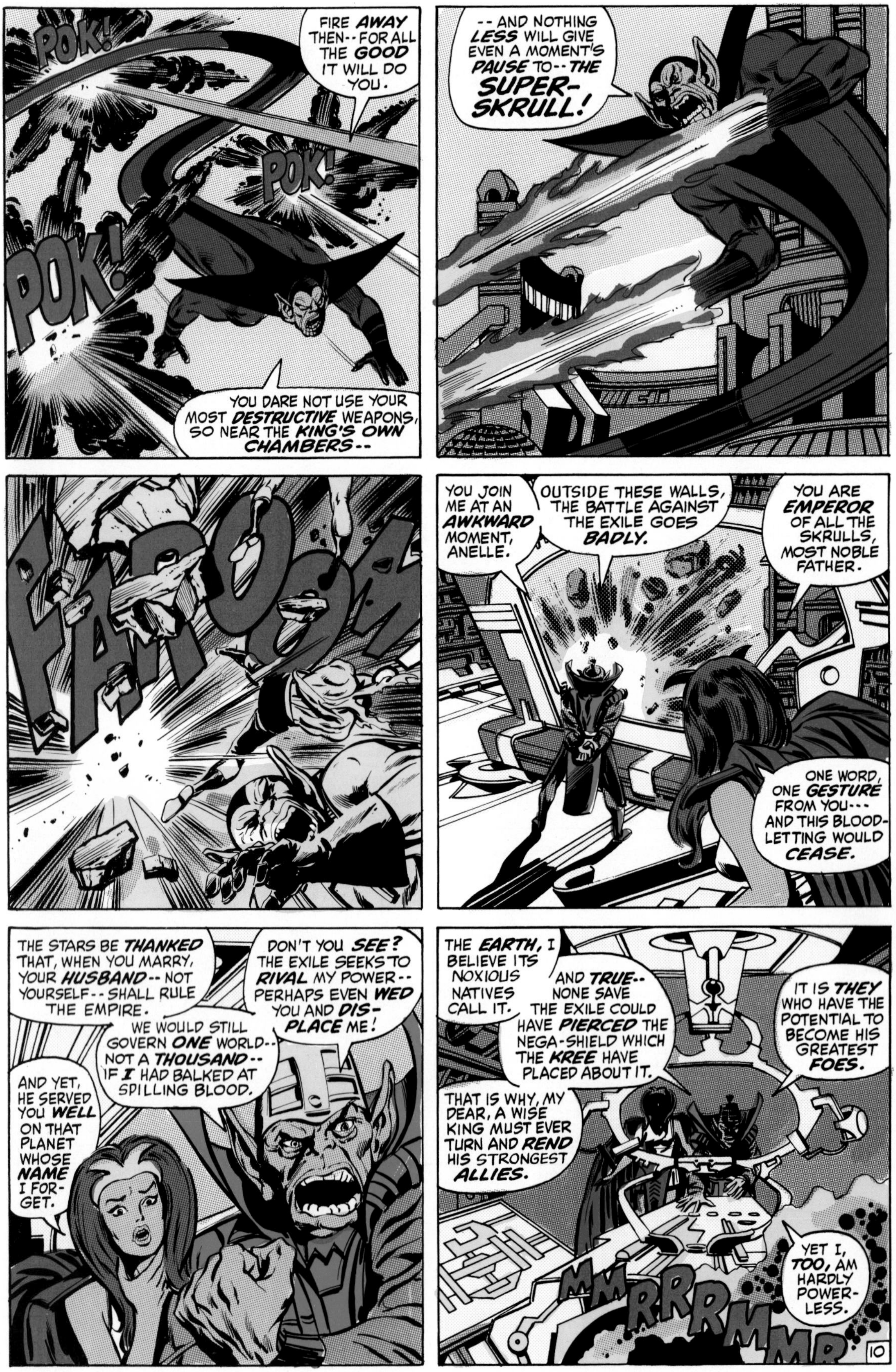

POK!
FIRE AWAY THEN-- FOR ALL THE GOOD IT WILL DO YOU.
POK!
POK!
YOU DARE NOT USE YOUR MOST DESTRUCTIVE WEAPONS, SO NEAR THE KING'S OWN CHAMBERS--
-- AND NOTHING LESS WILL GIVE EVEN A MOMENT'S PAUSE TO-- THE SUPER-SKRULL!
YOU JOIN ME AT AN AWKWARD MOMENT, ANELLE.
OUTSIDE THESE WALLS, THE BATTLE AGAINST THE EXILE GOES BADLY.
YOU ARE EMPEROR OF ALL THE SKRULLS, MOST NOBLE FATHER.
ONE WORD, ONE GESTURE FROM YOU--- AND THIS BLOOD-LETTING WOULD CEASE.
THE STARS BE THANKED THAT, WHEN YOU MARRY, YOUR HUSBAND-- NOT YOURSELF-- SHALL RULE THE EMPIRE.
WE WOULD STILL GOVERN ONE WORLD-- NOT A THOUSAND-- IF I HAD BALKED AT SPILLING BLOOD.
DON'T YOU SEE? THE EXILE SEEKS TO RIVAL MY POWER-- PERHAPS EVEN WED YOU AND DISPLACE ME!
AND YET, HE SERVED YOU WELL ON THAT PLANET WHOSE NAME I FORGET.
THE EARTH, I BELIEVE ITS NOXIOUS NATIVES CALL IT.
AND TRUE-- NONE SAVE THE EXILE COULD HAVE PIERCED THE NEGA-SHIELD WHICH THE KREE HAVE PLACED ABOUT IT.
IT IS THEY WHO HAVE THE POTENTIAL TO BECOME HIS GREATEST FOES.
THAT IS WHY, MY DEAR, A WISE KING MUST EVER TURN AND REND HIS STRONGEST ALLIES.
YET I, TOO, AM HARDLY POWERLESS.
MMRRRMMMR

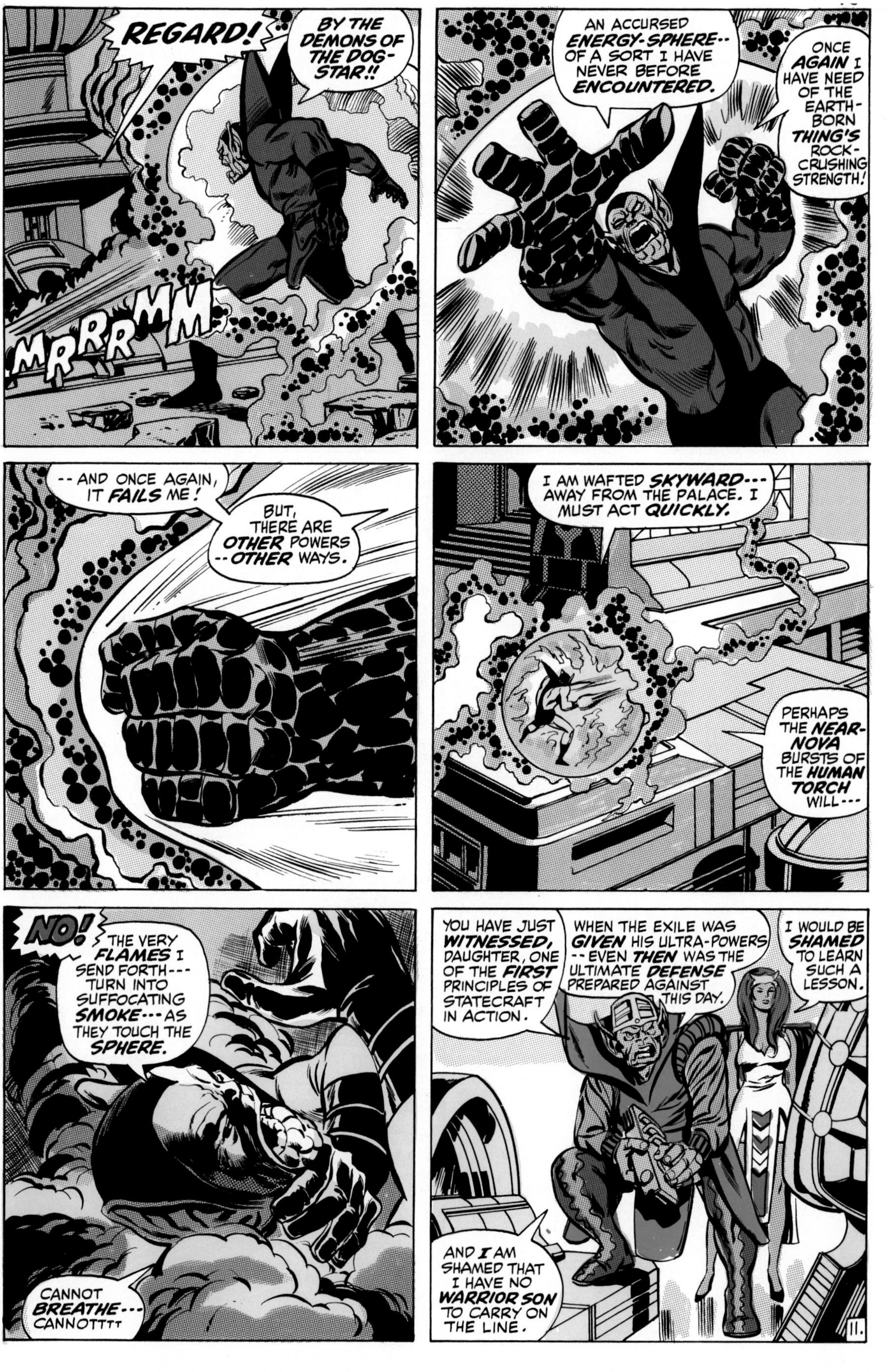
REGARD!
BY THE DEMONS OF THE DOG-STAR!!
MRRRMM
AN ACCURSED ENERGY-SPHERE-- OF A SORT I HAVE NEVER BEFORE ENCOUNTERED.
ONCE AGAIN I HAVE NEED OF THE EARTH-BORN THING'S ROCK-CRUSHING STRENGTH!
--AND ONCE AGAIN, IT FAILS ME!
BUT, THERE ARE OTHER POWERS --OTHER WAYS.
I AM WAFTED SKYWARD--- AWAY FROM THE PALACE. I MUST ACT QUICKLY.
PERHAPS THE NEAR-NOVA BURSTS OF THE HUMAN TORCH WILL---
NO!
THE VERY FLAMES I SEND FORTH--- TURN INTO SUFFOCATING SMOKE---AS THEY TOUCH THE SPHERE.
CANNOT BREATHE--- CANNOTTTTT
YOU HAVE JUST WITNESSED, DAUGHTER, ONE OF THE FIRST PRINCIPLES OF STATECRAFT IN ACTION.
WHEN THE EXILE WAS GIVEN HIS ULTRA-POWERS --EVEN THEN WAS THE ULTIMATE DEFENSE PREPARED AGAINST THIS DAY.
I WOULD BE SHAMED TO LEARN SUCH A LESSON.
AND I AM SHAMED THAT I HAVE NO WARRIOR SON TO CARRY ON THE LINE.
11.

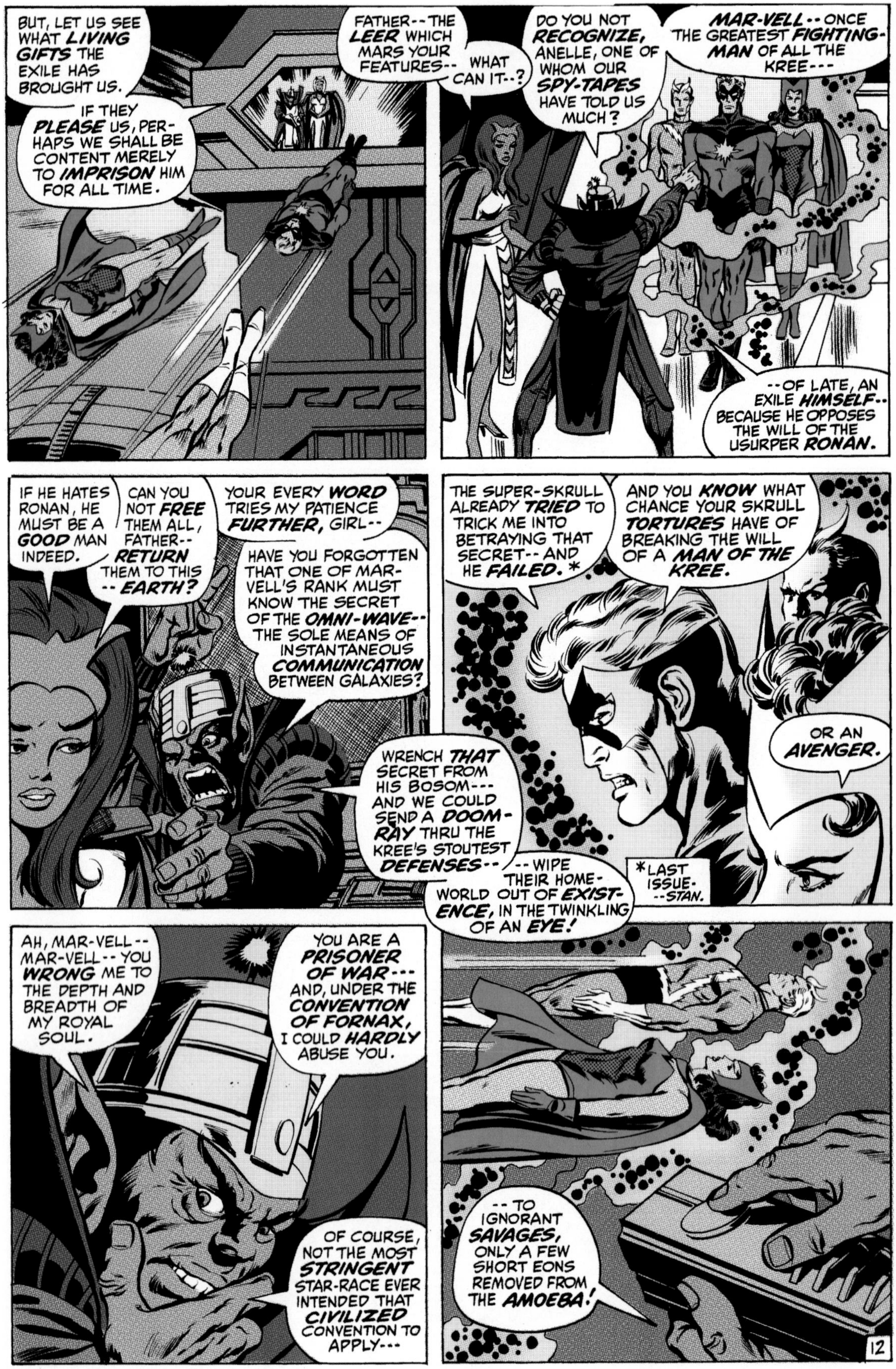
BUT, LET US SEE WHAT LIVING GIFTS THE EXILE HAS BROUGHT US.
IF THEY PLEASE US, PERHAPS WE SHALL BE CONTENT MERELY TO IMPRISON HIM FOR ALL TIME.
FATHER--THE LEER WHICH MARS YOUR FEATURES--
WHAT CAN IT--?
DO YOU NOT RECOGNIZE, ANELLE, ONE OF WHOM OUR SPY-TAPES HAVE TOLD US MUCH?
MAR-VELL--ONCE THE GREATEST FIGHTING-MAN OF ALL THE KREE---
--OF LATE, AN EXILE HIMSELF--BECAUSE HE OPPOSES THE WILL OF THE USURPER RONAN.
IF HE HATES RONAN, HE MUST BE A GOOD MAN INDEED.
CAN YOU NOT FREE THEM ALL, FATHER--RETURN THEM TO THIS--EARTH?
YOUR EVERY WORD TRIES MY PATIENCE FURTHER, GIRL--
HAVE YOU FORGOTTEN THAT ONE OF MAR-VELL'S RANK MUST KNOW THE SECRET OF THE OMNI-WAVE--THE SOLE MEANS OF INSTANTANEOUS COMMUNICATION BETWEEN GALAXIES?
WRENCH THAT SECRET FROM HIS BOSOM---AND WE COULD SEND A DOOM-RAY THRU THE KREE'S STOUTEST DEFENSES--
--WIPE THEIR HOME-WORLD OUT OF EXISTENCE, IN THE TWINKLING OF AN EYE!
THE SUPER-SKRULL ALREADY TRIED TO TRICK ME INTO BETRAYING THAT SECRET--AND HE FAILED.*
AND YOU KNOW WHAT CHANCE YOUR SKRULL TORTURES HAVE OF BREAKING THE WILL OF A MAN OF THE KREE.
OR AN AVENGER.
*LAST ISSUE. --STAN.
AH, MAR-VELL--MAR-VELL--YOU WRONG ME TO THE DEPTH AND BREADTH OF MY ROYAL SOUL.
YOU ARE A PRISONER OF WAR---AND, UNDER THE CONVENTION OF FORNAX, I COULD HARDLY ABUSE YOU.
OF COURSE, NOT THE MOST STRINGENT STAR-RACE EVER INTENDED THAT CIVILIZED CONVENTION TO APPLY---
--TO IGNORANT SAVAGES, ONLY A FEW SHORT EONS REMOVED FROM THE AMOEBA!
12

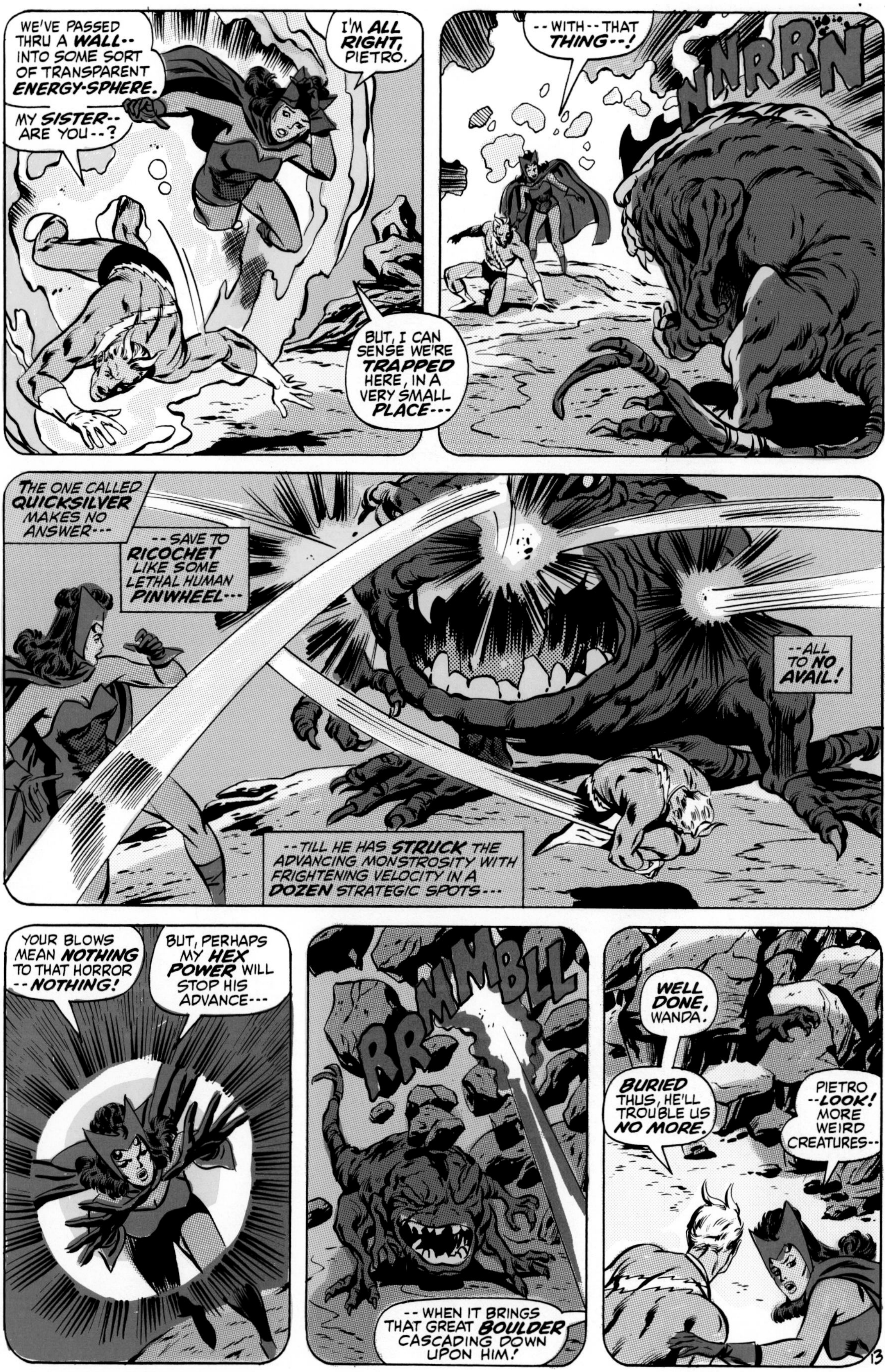

WE'VE PASSED THRU A WALL-- INTO SOME SORT OF TRANSPARENT ENERGY-SPHERE.
MY SISTER-- ARE YOU--?
I'M ALL RIGHT, PIETRO.
BUT, I CAN SENSE WE'RE TRAPPED HERE, IN A VERY SMALL PLACE---
--WITH--THAT THING--!
NNRRN
THE ONE CALLED QUICKSILVER MAKES NO ANSWER---
--SAVE TO RICOCHET LIKE SOME LETHAL HUMAN PINWHEEL---
--TILL HE HAS STRUCK THE ADVANCING MONSTROSITY WITH FRIGHTENING VELOCITY IN A DOZEN STRATEGIC SPOTS---
--ALL TO NO AVAIL!
YOUR BLOWS MEAN NOTHING TO THAT HORROR --NOTHING!
BUT, PERHAPS MY HEX POWER WILL STOP HIS ADVANCE---
BRRMMBLL
--WHEN IT BRINGS THAT GREAT BOULDER CASCADING DOWN UPON HIM!
WELL DONE, WANDA.
BURIED THUS, HE'LL TROUBLE US NO MORE.
PIETRO --LOOK! MORE WEIRD CREATURES--

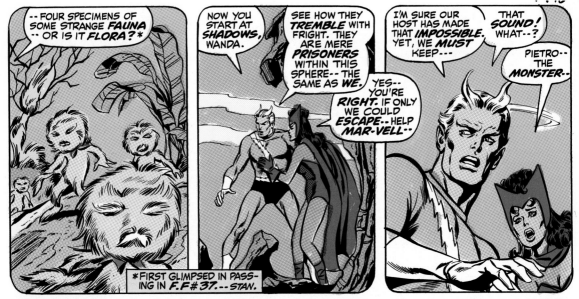

-- FOUR SPECIMENS OF SOME STRANGE *FAUNA* -- OR IS IT *FLORA*? *

NOW YOU START AT *SHADOWS*, WANDA.

SEE HOW THEY *TREMBLE* WITH FRIGHT. THEY ARE MERE *PRISONERS* WITHIN THIS SPHERE -- THE SAME AS *WE*.

YES -- YOU'RE *RIGHT.* IF ONLY WE COULD *ESCAPE.* -- HELP *MAR-VELL* --

I'M SURE OUR HOST HAS MADE THAT *IMPOSSIBLE.* YET, WE *MUST* KEEP --

THAT *SOUND!* WHAT --?

PIETRO -- THE *MONSTER* --

*FIRST GLIMPSED IN PASSING IN F.F. #37. -- STAN.

HE'S BREAKING *FREE!*

KRAKK!

DO YOU *SEE*, MAR-VELL? DOES THE FULL *IRONY* OF THE SITUATION PRESS IN UPON YOU?

IT *SHOULD* -- ALTHOUGH IT WILL DOUBTLESS *ESCAPE* THE MORE *PAROCHIAL* MINDS OF THE EARTHLINGS.

YOU'RE A *FIEND.* EVEN *RONAN* COULD NEVER BE MORE WANTONLY *CRUEL!*

FATHER --- *HALT* THIS BRUTAL MADNESS, BEFORE ---

IT IS IN THE *KREE-MAN'S* POWER TO HALT IT, ANELLE.

HE HAS BUT TO *PROMISE* ME THE SECRET OF THE *OMNI-WAVE.*

YOU'D HAVE ME *BARTER* THE LIVES OF TWO *FRIENDS* --- FOR THE SURVIVAL OF UNTOLD *MULTITUDES.*

I *CAN'T* DO THAT -- I *WON'T!* WANDA AND PIETRO --- WOULDN'T *WANT* ME TO!

THEN, YOU'VE *MADE* YOUR CHOICE.

LET THE GAME *CONTINUE* -- TO ITS *INEVITABLE* CONCLUSION.

STAND *BACK*, WANDA. WE HAVE BUT *ONE CHANCE!*

PERHAPS A WALL OF *SPEED* WILL MAKE THE MONSTER *DIZZY* -- GIVE US TIME TO *THINK* -- TO *PLAN.*

TAKE CARE, MY BROTHER -- *TAKE CARE!*

14

BUT, THE TIME IS *PAST* FOR CARE OR CAUTION---

-- OR FOR *ANYTHING* SAVE BLINDING *MOTION*---A WHIRL-WIND OF MADDENING *MOTION*---

--WHICH, BY SHEER *CHANCE,* SUCKS UP THE STRANGE *FLORA/FAUNA* INTO ITS IRRESIST-IBLE *VORTEX*---

-- AND *HURLS* THEM AGAINST THE ONCOMING *BEHEMOTH*---

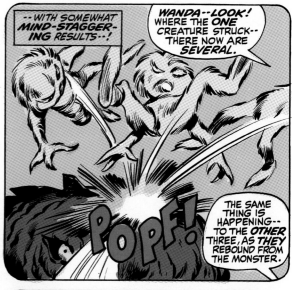

--WITH SOMEWHAT *MIND-STAGGER-ING* RESULTS--!

WANDA--LOOK! WHERE THE *ONE* CREATURE STRUCK-- THERE NOW ARE *SEVERAL.*

THE SAME THING IS HAPPENING-- TO THE *OTHER* THREE, AS *THEY* REBOUND FROM THE MONSTER.

POPF!

NOW-- THERE ARE *DOZENS!*

SECONDS AGO-- THERE WERE ONLY *FOUR* OF THEM.

ALREADY-- THERE IS SCARCELY ROOM TO *MOVE.*

AND-- THEY KEEP *MULTIPLY-ING!*

WE ARE *TRAPPED* WITH THEM-- TRAPPED IN THIS ENERGY-SPHERE, WITH NOWHERE TO *FLEE.*

SOON, WE'LL BE **CRUSHED**-- OR ELSE **SMOTHERED** ALIVE!

BUT, AT LEAST **MAR-VELL** WILL NOT HAVE BETRAYED HIS **PEOPLE**-- OR THE **EARTH**.

THINK OF THAT, MY **BROTHER**-- AS WE **DIE**!

RELEASE THEM, SKRULL!

THEY'VE DONE **NOTHING** TO ENDANGER YOUR **CRAVEN** RACE-- **NOTHING**!

'TIS NOT **I** WHO CONDEMNED THEM TO THEIR FATE, KREE-MAN-- BUT **YOU.**

YOU!

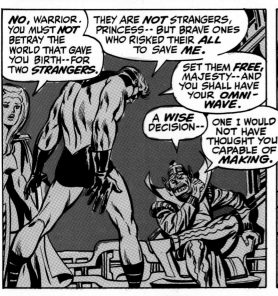

NO, WARRIOR. YOU MUST **NOT** BETRAY THE WORLD THAT GAVE YOU BIRTH-- FOR TWO **STRANGERS.**

THEY ARE **NOT** STRANGERS, PRINCESS-- BUT BRAVE ONES WHO RISKED THEIR **ALL** TO SAVE **ME.**

SET THEM **FREE**, MAJESTY-- AND YOU SHALL HAVE YOUR **OMNI-WAVE.**

A **WISE** DECISION--

ONE I WOULD NOT HAVE THOUGHT YOU CAPABLE OF **MAKING.**

AND YOU MADE IT-- WITH **MOMENTS** TO SPARE!

PIETRO-- **WHERE**--?

YOU ARE **SAFE** NOW, GIRL--- FROM ALL BUT THE ARROWS OF YOUR **CONSCIENCE.**

I-- **HAD** TO, WANDA. DON'T YOU **SEE**?

BUT, THAT MEANS-- **NO**, MAR-VELL YOU **COULDN'T** HAVE--!

BETTER FAR-- WE HAD **DIED**-- THAN CAUSE THE DEATH OF COUNTLESS **MILLIONS.**

AND DIE YOU YET **SHALL**, EARTH-SPAWN--

--IF YOUR FRIEND **BETRAYS** HIS VOW.

WELL, KREE-MAN?

BEGIN NOW TO WEAVE THE **DOOM-TAPESTRY**-- OF ALL THE **KREE GALAXY!**

16

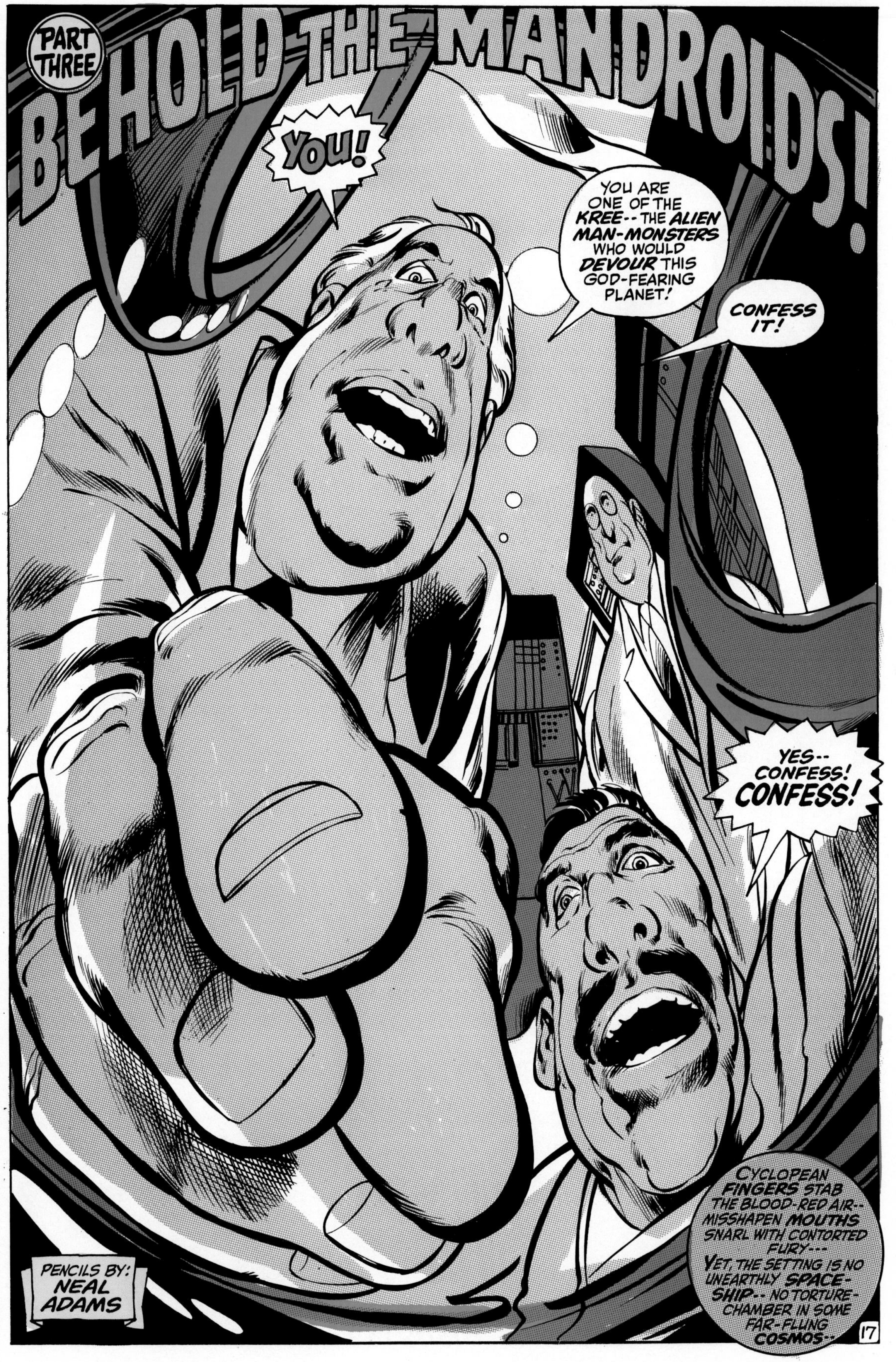
PART THREE
BEHOLD THE MANDROIDS!
YOU!
YOU ARE ONE OF THE KREE-- THE ALIEN MAN-MONSTERS WHO WOULD DEVOUR THIS GOD-FEARING PLANET!
CONFESS IT!
YES-- CONFESS! CONFESS!
CYCLOPEAN FINGERS STAB THE BLOOD-RED AIR-- MISSHAPEN MOUTHS SNARL WITH CONTORTED FURY--- YET, THE SETTING IS NO UNEARTHLY SPACE-SHIP-- NO TORTURE-CHAMBER IN SOME FAR-FLUNG COSMOS--
PENCILS BY: NEAL ADAMS

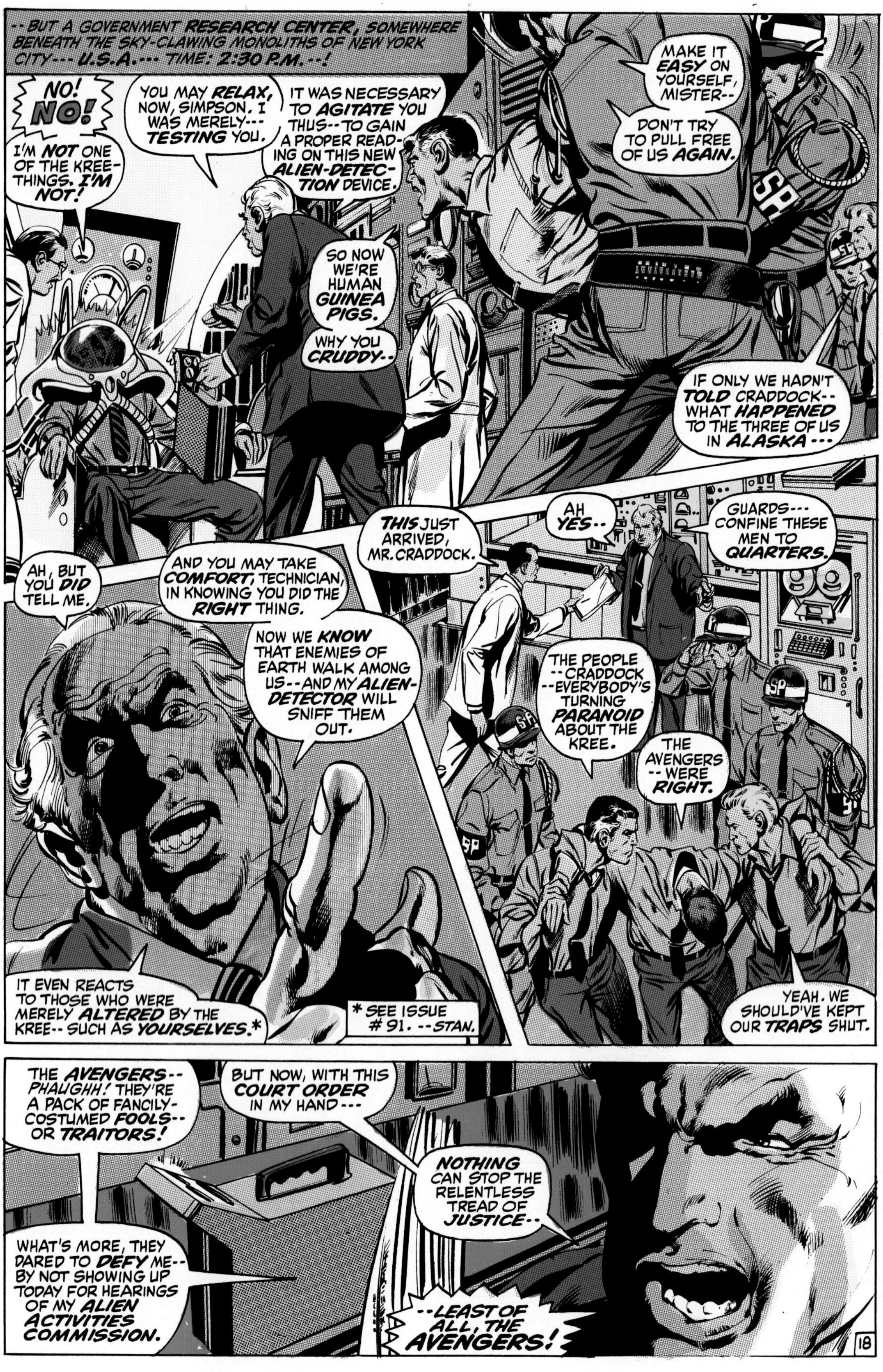
--BUT A GOVERNMENT RESEARCH CENTER, SOMEWHERE BENEATH THE SKY-CLAWING MONOLITHS OF NEW YORK CITY--- U.S.A.--- TIME: 2:30 P.M.--!
NO! NO! I'M NOT ONE OF THE KREE-THINGS. I'M NOT!
YOU MAY RELAX, NOW, SIMPSON. I WAS MERELY--- TESTING YOU.
IT WAS NECESSARY TO AGITATE YOU THUS--TO GAIN A PROPER READING ON THIS NEW ALIEN-DETECTION DEVICE.
SO NOW WE'RE HUMAN GUINEA PIGS.
WHY YOU CRUDDY--
MAKE IT EASY ON YOURSELF, MISTER--
DON'T TRY TO PULL FREE OF US AGAIN.
IF ONLY WE HADN'T TOLD CRADDOCK-- WHAT HAPPENED TO THE THREE OF US IN ALASKA---
AH, BUT YOU DID TELL ME.
AND YOU MAY TAKE COMFORT, TECHNICIAN, IN KNOWING YOU DID THE RIGHT THING.
NOW WE KNOW THAT ENEMIES OF EARTH WALK AMONG US--AND MY ALIEN-DETECTOR WILL SNIFF THEM OUT.
IT EVEN REACTS TO THOSE WHO WERE MERELY ALTERED BY THE KREE-- SUCH AS YOURSELVES.*
* SEE ISSUE # 91. --STAN.
THIS JUST ARRIVED, MR. CRADDOCK.
AH YES--
GUARDS--- CONFINE THESE MEN TO QUARTERS.
THE PEOPLE --CRADDOCK --EVERYBODY'S TURNING PARANOID ABOUT THE KREE.
THE AVENGERS --WERE RIGHT.
YEAH. WE SHOULD'VE KEPT OUR TRAPS SHUT.
THE AVENGERS-- PHAUGHH! THEY'RE A PACK OF FANCILY-COSTUMED FOOLS-- OR TRAITORS!
WHAT'S MORE, THEY DARED TO DEFY ME-- BY NOT SHOWING UP TODAY FOR HEARINGS OF MY ALIEN ACTIVITIES COMMISSION.
BUT NOW, WITH THIS COURT ORDER IN MY HAND---
NOTHING CAN STOP THE RELENTLESS TREAD OF JUSTICE--
--LEAST OF ALL, THE AVENGERS!
18

TIME: 5:17 P.M.---

NICK FURY! WHAT--?

JUST GIVIN' YOU A BUZZ, CAP, TO SEE IF ALL YOU AVENGER-TYPES WERE HOME.

Y'KNOW, THEY TELL ME ACAPULCO'S GREAT THIS TIME'A THE YEAR.

WELL, SEE YA.

NOW, WHAT THE DEVIL WAS THAT ALL ABOUT?

IT WAS ALMOST AS IF FURY WAS TRYING TO WARN US-- THAT WE SHOULD CLEAR OUT OF HERE.

PASSING STRANGE BE THE WAYS OF MORTAL MAN!

YET, 'TIS THE RESCUE OF THE CAPTIVE AVENGERS WHICH DOTH CONCERN US N---

EH? WHAT SHOUTS GOLIATH--?

THAT THERE AIN'T NO GOLIATH, PAL--- NOT ANY MORE!

THERE GOES THE LAST OF HANK'S GROWTH SERUM--- AND, AS FAR AS I'M CONCERNED--

HEY-- LOOK!

COMIN' THRU THE WALL--!

SPLINK!

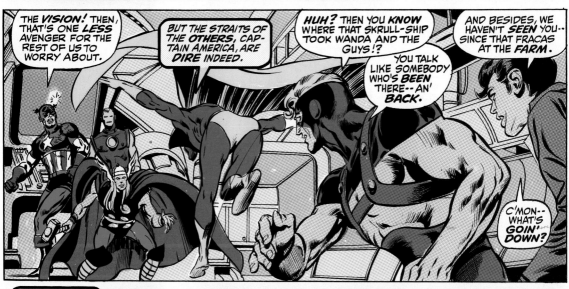

THE VISION! THEN, THAT'S ONE LESS AVENGER FOR THE REST OF US TO WORRY ABOUT.

BUT THE STRAITS OF THE OTHERS, CAPTAIN AMERICA, ARE DIRE INDEED.

HUH? THEN YOU KNOW WHERE THAT SKRULL-SHIP TOOK WANDA AND THE GUYS!?

YOU TALK LIKE SOMEBODY WHO'S BEEN THERE-- AN' BACK.

AND BESIDES, WE HAVEN'T SEEN YOU-- SINCE THAT FRACAS AT THE FARM.

C'MON-- WHAT'S GOIN' DOWN?

MANY THINGS, RICK JONES--- MORE THAN ANY OF US HAD DARED TO SUSPECT.

THE SKRULLS ARE INVOLVED-- YES, AND THE ETERNAL KREE---

--AND, IN SOME WAY I'VE NOT YET DIVINED-- SO ARE THE MYSTERIOUS INHUMANS OF WHOM THE THUNDER GOD HAS TOLD US. THEY--

ATTENTION, AVENGERS! ATTENTION, AVENGERS!

A LOUD-SPEAKER-- BLARING AT US FROM OUTSIDE--!

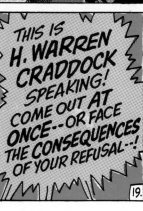

THIS IS H. WARREN CRADDOCK SPEAKING! COME OUT AT ONCE-- OR FACE THE CONSEQUENCES OF YOUR REFUSAL--!

19.

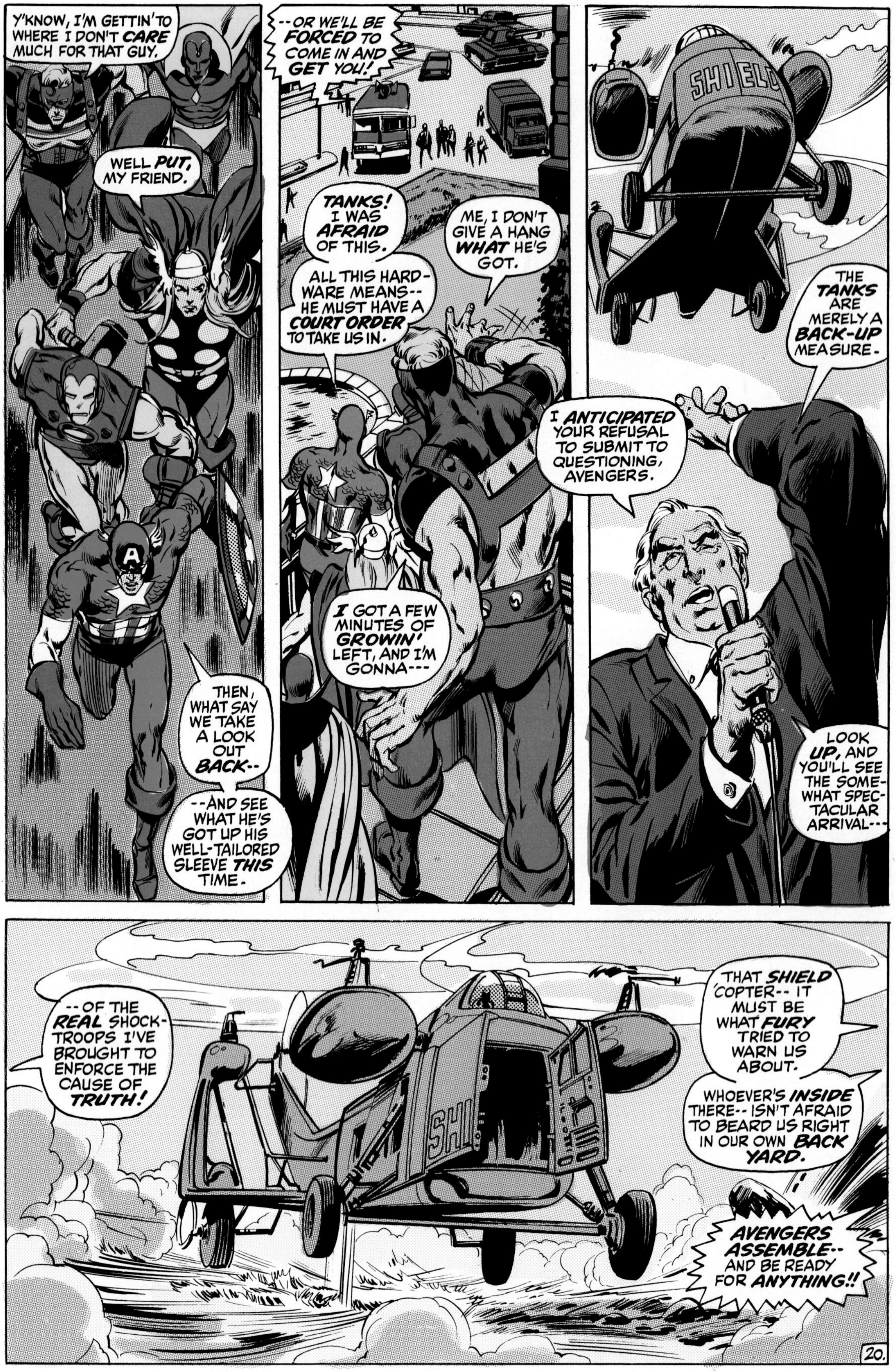
Y'KNOW, I'M GETTIN' TO WHERE I DON'T CARE MUCH FOR THAT GUY.
WELL PUT, MY FRIEND.
THEN, WHAT SAY WE TAKE A LOOK OUT BACK--
--AND SEE WHAT HE'S GOT UP HIS WELL-TAILORED SLEEVE THIS TIME.
--OR WE'LL BE FORCED TO COME IN AND GET YOU!
TANKS! I WAS AFRAID OF THIS.
ALL THIS HARD-WARE MEANS-- HE MUST HAVE A COURT ORDER TO TAKE US IN.
ME, I DON'T GIVE A HANG WHAT HE'S GOT.
I GOT A FEW MINUTES OF GROWIN' LEFT, AND I'M GONNA---
SHIELD
THE TANKS ARE MERELY A BACK-UP MEASURE.
I ANTICIPATED YOUR REFUSAL TO SUBMIT TO QUESTIONING, AVENGERS.
LOOK UP, AND YOU'LL SEE THE SOME-WHAT SPEC-TACULAR ARRIVAL---
--OF THE REAL SHOCK-TROOPS I'VE BROUGHT TO ENFORCE THE CAUSE OF TRUTH!
THAT SHIELD 'COPTER-- IT MUST BE WHAT FURY TRIED TO WARN US ABOUT.
WHOEVER'S INSIDE THERE-- ISN'T AFRAID TO BEARD US RIGHT IN OUR OWN BACK YARD.
AVENGERS ASSEMBLE-- AND BE READY FOR ANYTHING!!
SHI

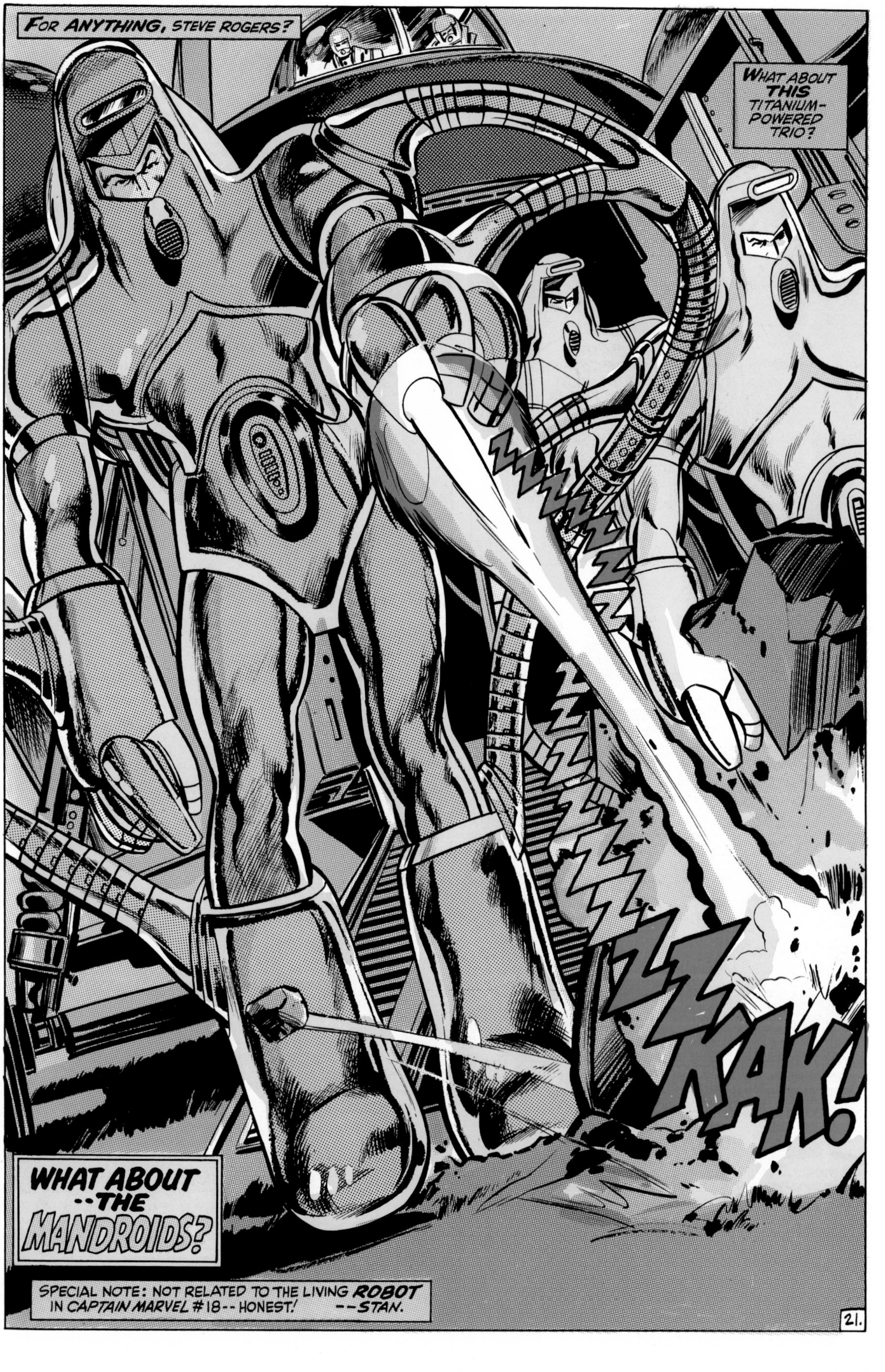
FOR ANYTHING, STEVE ROGERS?
WHAT ABOUT THIS TITANIUM-POWERED TRIO?
ZZZZZZZZZ
ZZKAK!
WHAT ABOUT --THE MANDROIDS?
SPECIAL NOTE: NOT RELATED TO THE LIVING ROBOT IN CAPTAIN MARVEL #18-- HONEST! --STAN.

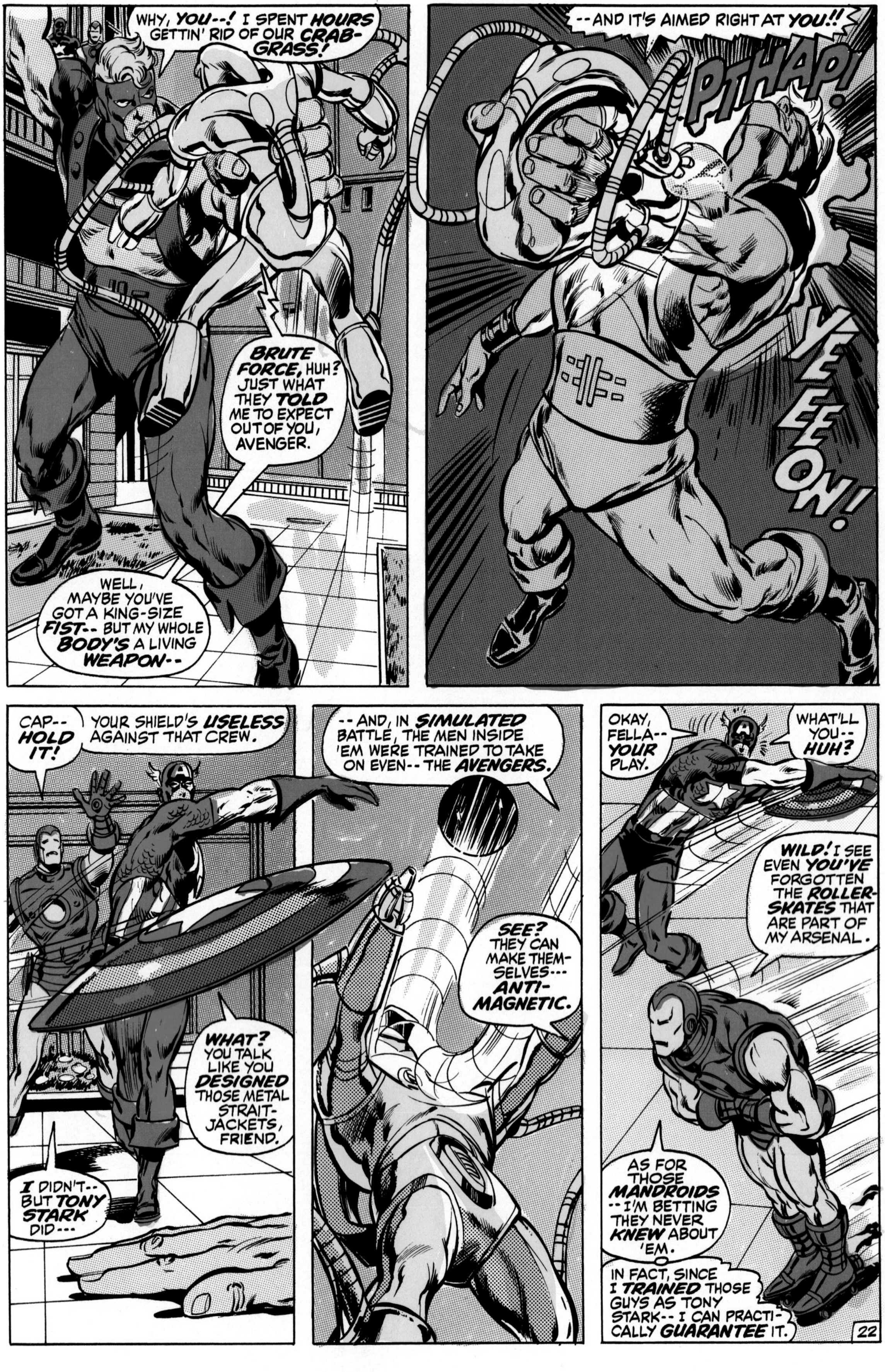
WHY, YOU--! I SPENT HOURS GETTIN' RID OF OUR CRAB-GRASS!
BRUTE FORCE, HUH? JUST WHAT THEY TOLD ME TO EXPECT OUT OF YOU, AVENGER.
WELL, MAYBE YOU'VE GOT A KING-SIZE FIST-- BUT MY WHOLE BODY'S A LIVING WEAPON--
--AND IT'S AIMED RIGHT AT YOU!!
PTHAP!
YEEEEOW!
CAP-- HOLD IT!
YOUR SHIELD'S USELESS AGAINST THAT CREW.
WHAT? YOU TALK LIKE YOU DESIGNED THOSE METAL STRAIT-JACKETS, FRIEND.
I DIDN'T-- BUT TONY STARK DID---
--AND, IN SIMULATED BATTLE, THE MEN INSIDE 'EM WERE TRAINED TO TAKE ON EVEN-- THE AVENGERS.
SEE? THEY CAN MAKE THEM-SELVES--- ANTI-MAGNETIC.
OKAY, FELLA-- YOUR PLAY.
WHAT'LL YOU-- HUH?
WILD! I SEE EVEN YOU'VE FORGOTTEN THE ROLLER-SKATES THAT ARE PART OF MY ARSENAL.
AS FOR THOSE MANDROIDS -- I'M BETTING THEY NEVER KNEW ABOUT 'EM.
IN FACT, SINCE I TRAINED THOSE GUYS AS TONY STARK-- I CAN PRACTI-CALLY GUARANTEE IT.
22

'COURSE, THAT WON'T SPARE ME A **COMPOUND FRACTURE**, IF ONE OF THESE SHIELD-BOYS **CONNECTS**.

BUT-- **NONE** OF THIS IS **GETTING** US ANY-WHERE.

IT'S THE **KREE** AND THE **SKRULLS** WE'VE GOT TO---

UH OH! GETTING **CARELESS**, TONY BABY.

THAT LASER-BLAST MADE **HASH** OUT OF THE CONCRETE, RIGHT IN **FRONT** OF---

RRAKKK!

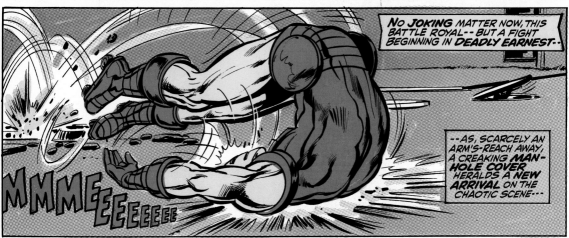

NO JOKING MATTER NOW, THIS BATTLE ROYAL-- BUT A FIGHT BEGINNING IN **DEADLY EARNEST**--

--AS, SCARCELY AN ARM'S-REACH AWAY, A CREAKING **MAN-HOLE** COVER HERALDS A NEW **ARRIVAL** ON THE CHAOTIC SCENE--

MMMEEEEEEEEEE

--A CREATURE FROM HALF A WORLD DISTANT --A CREATURE CALLED **TRITON**--

I AM **HERE**-- AT **LAST!!**

-- AND WHO CAN TELL IF HE BE FRIEND -- OR **FOE**--?

NEXT: AVENGER VS. INHUMAN -- AND WHY!

23

CHAPTER SEVEN

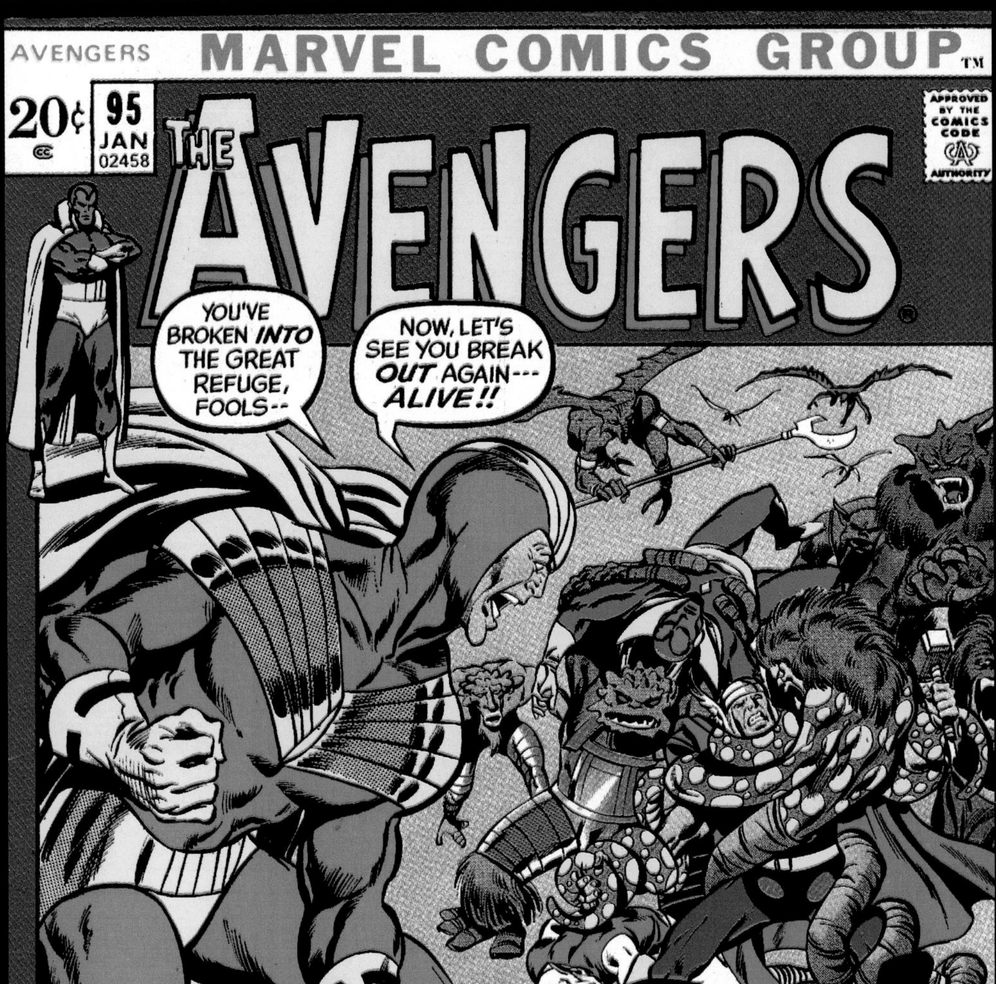
AVENGERS
MARVEL COMICS GROUP
20¢
95
JAN
02458
THE AVENGERS
APPROVED BY THE COMICS CODE AUTHORITY
YOU'VE BROKEN INTO THE GREAT REFUGE, FOOLS--
NOW, LET'S SEE YOU BREAK OUT AGAIN--- ALIVE!!
AVENGER VS. INHUMAN!
'NUFF SAID!

SOMETHING INHUMAN THIS WAY COMES!

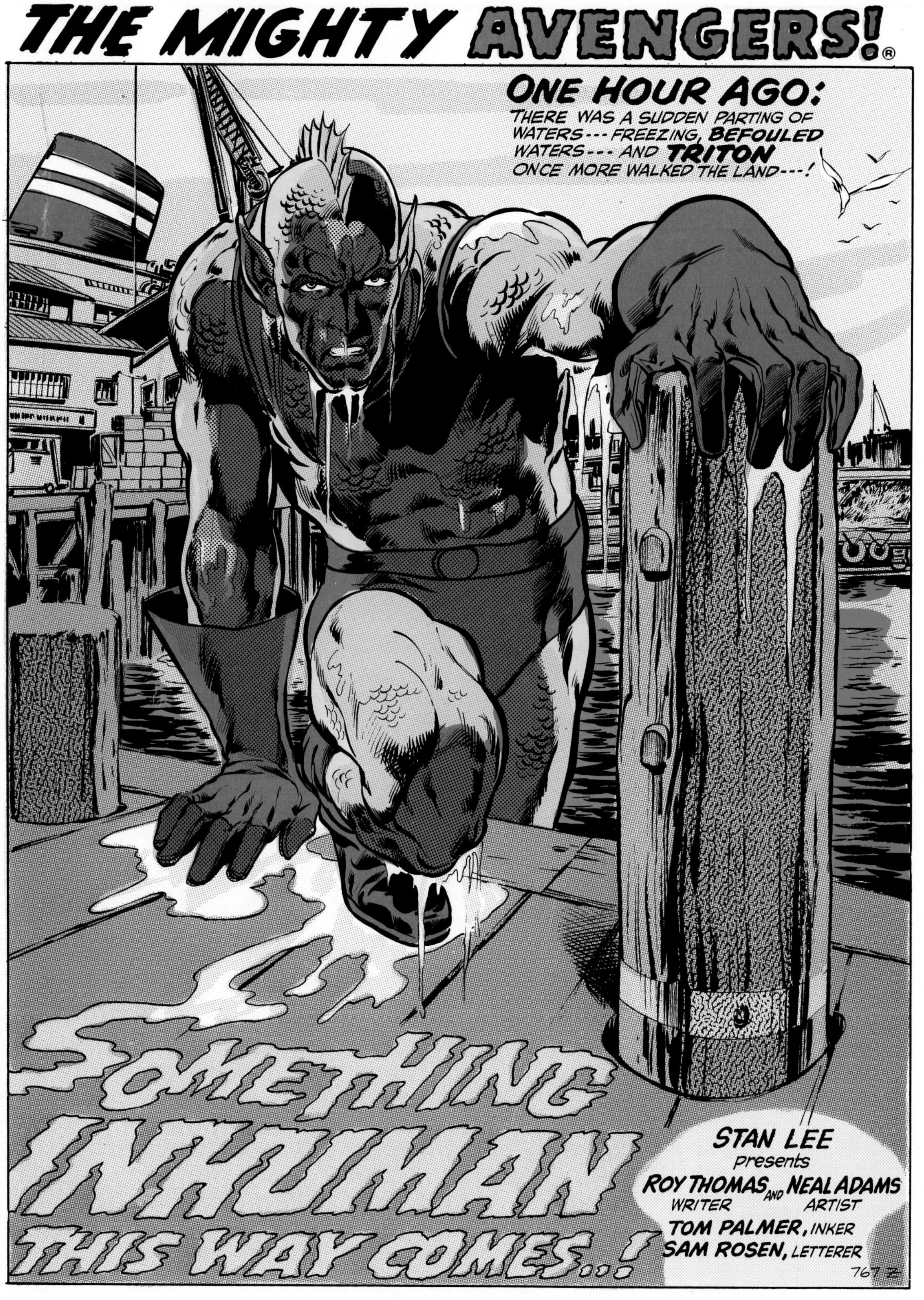
THE MIGHTY AVENGERS!®
ONE HOUR AGO:
THERE WAS A SUDDEN PARTING OF WATERS--- FREEZING, BEFOULED WATERS--- AND TRITON ONCE MORE WALKED THE LAND---!
SOMETHING INHUMAN THIS WAY COMES...!
STAN LEE presents
ROY THOMAS AND NEAL ADAMS
WRITER ARTIST
TOM PALMER, INKER
SAM ROSEN, LETTERER
767 Z

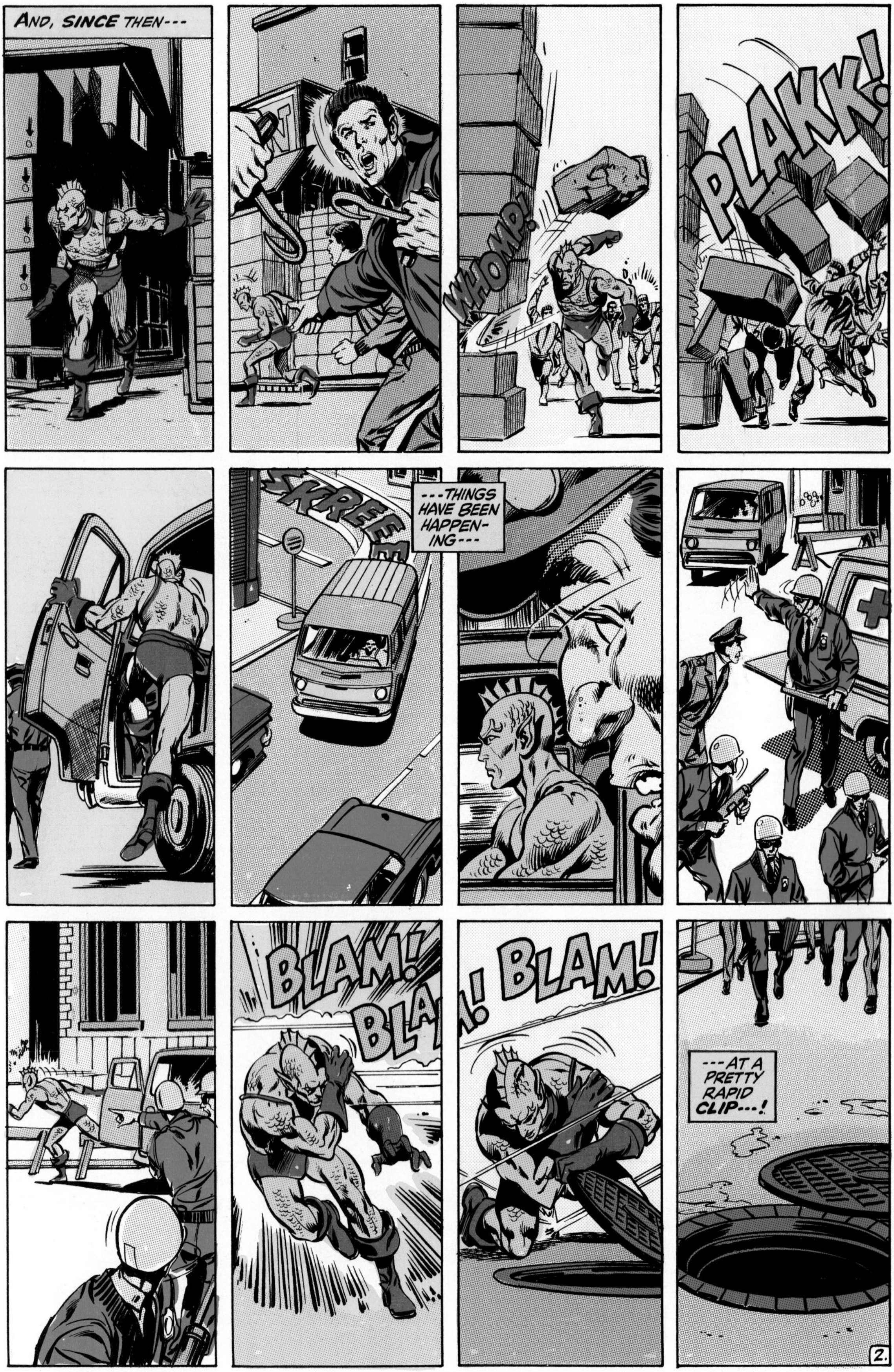
AND, SINCE THEN---
WHOMP!
PLAKK!
SKREEE
---THINGS HAVE BEEN HAPPEN-ING---
BLAM!
BLAM! BLAM!
---AT A PRETTY RAPID CLIP---!
2.

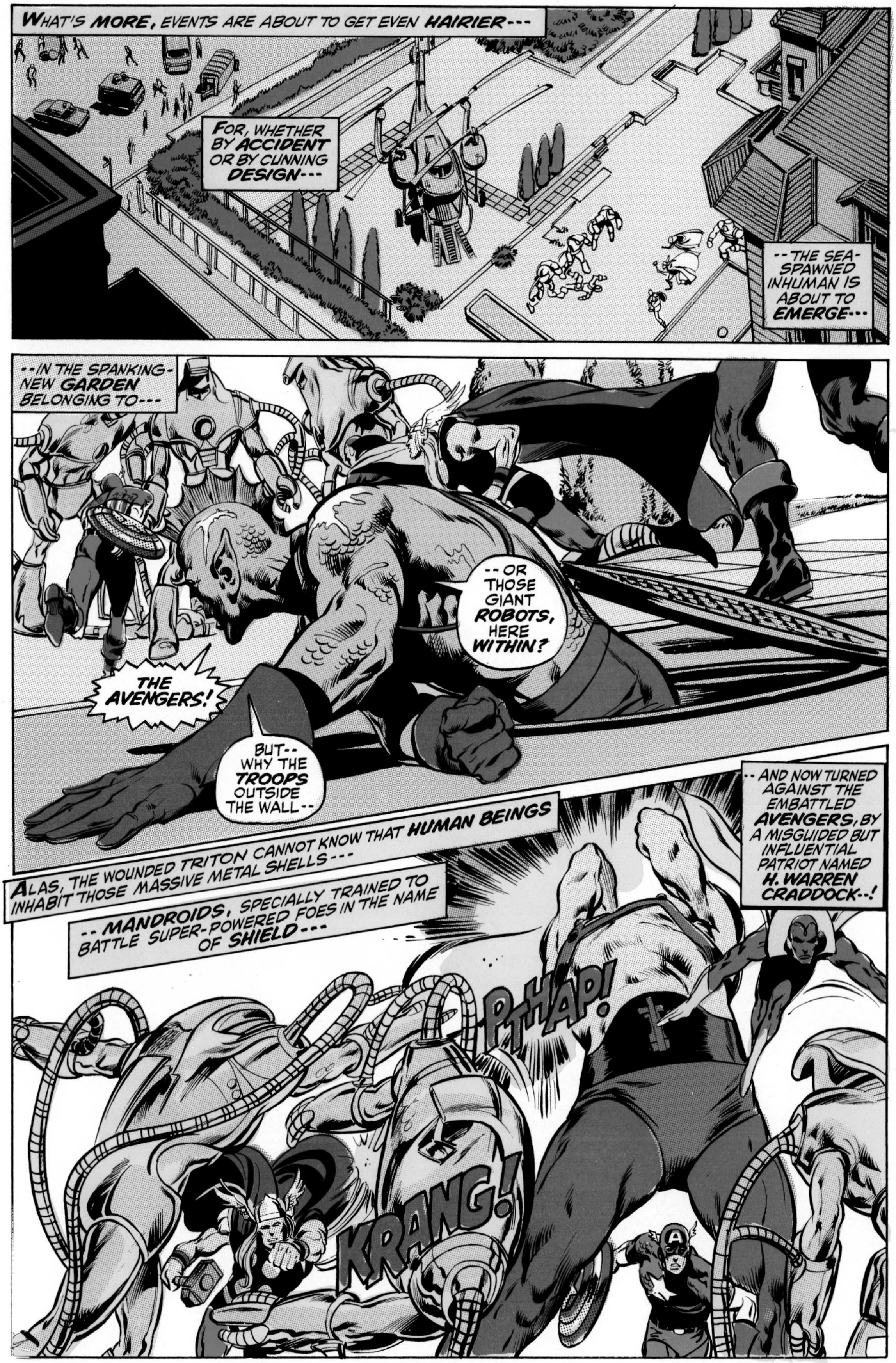
WHAT'S MORE, EVENTS ARE ABOUT TO GET EVEN HAIRIER---
FOR, WHETHER BY ACCIDENT OR BY CUNNING DESIGN---
--THE SEA-SPAWNED INHUMAN IS ABOUT TO EMERGE---
--IN THE SPANKING-NEW GARDEN BELONGING TO---
THE AVENGERS!
--OR THOSE GIANT ROBOTS, HERE WITHIN?
BUT--WHY THE TROOPS OUTSIDE THE WALL--
ALAS, THE WOUNDED TRITON CANNOT KNOW THAT HUMAN BEINGS INHABIT THOSE MASSIVE METAL SHELLS---
--MANDROIDS, SPECIALLY TRAINED TO BATTLE SUPER-POWERED FOES IN THE NAME OF SHIELD---
--AND NOW TURNED AGAINST THE EMBATTLED AVENGERS, BY A MISGUIDED BUT INFLUENTIAL PATRIOT NAMED H. WARREN CRADDOCK--!
PTHAP!
KRANG!

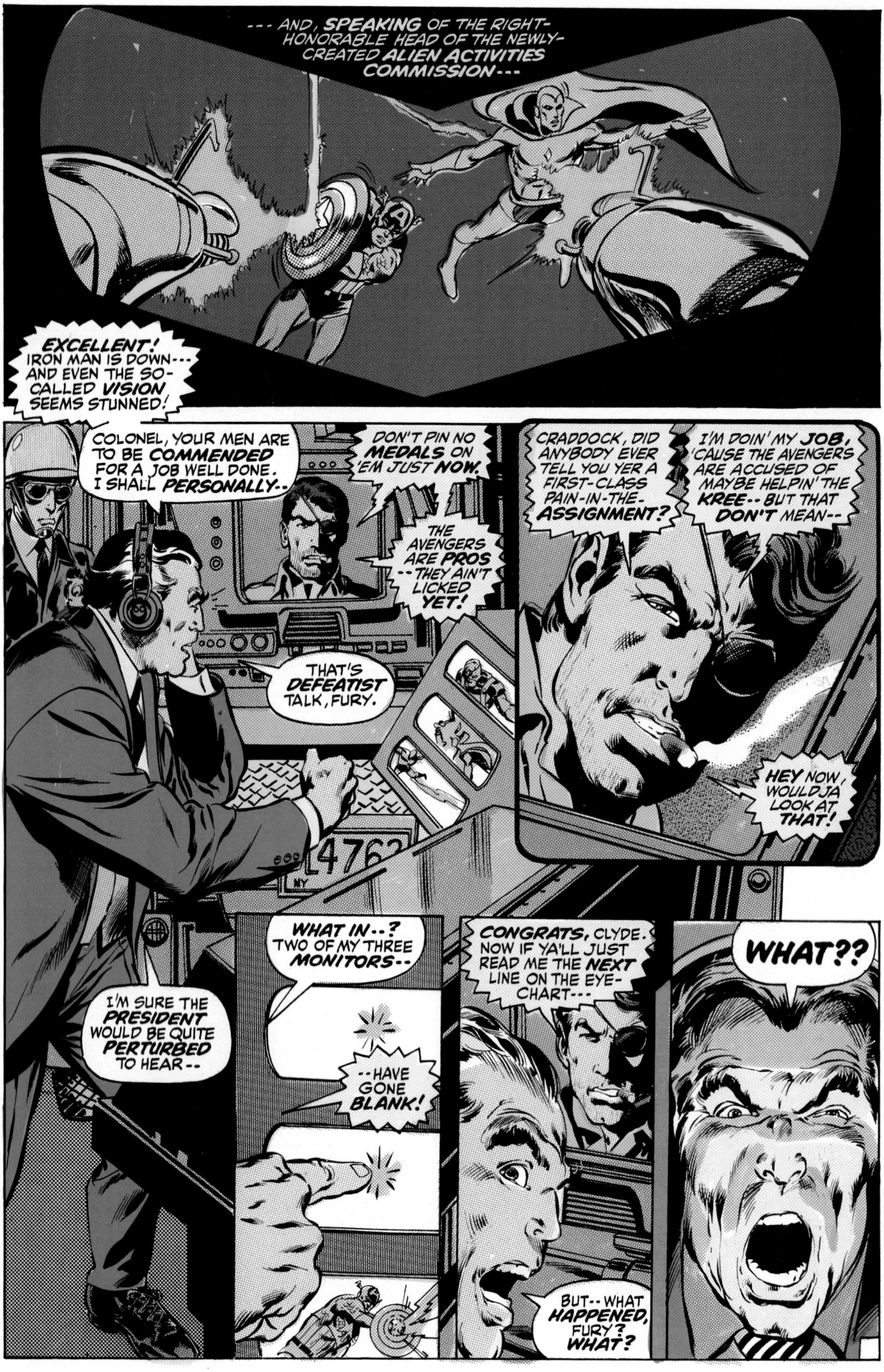
--- AND, SPEAKING OF THE RIGHT-HONORABLE HEAD OF THE NEWLY-CREATED ALIEN ACTIVITIES COMMISSION---
EXCELLENT! IRON MAN IS DOWN--- AND EVEN THE SO-CALLED VISION SEEMS STUNNED!
COLONEL, YOUR MEN ARE TO BE COMMENDED FOR A JOB WELL DONE. I SHALL PERSONALLY--
DON'T PIN NO MEDALS ON 'EM JUST NOW.
THE AVENGERS ARE PROS -- THEY AIN'T LICKED YET!
THAT'S DEFEATIST TALK, FURY.
I'M SURE THE PRESIDENT WOULD BE QUITE PERTURBED TO HEAR --
CRADDOCK, DID ANYBODY EVER TELL YOU YER A FIRST-CLASS PAIN-IN-THE-ASSIGNMENT?
I'M DOIN' MY JOB, 'CAUSE THE AVENGERS ARE ACCUSED OF MAYBE HELPIN' THE KREE -- BUT THAT DON'T MEAN--
HEY NOW, WOULDJA LOOK AT THAT!
L4762
NY
WHAT IN--? TWO OF MY THREE MONITORS--
--HAVE GONE BLANK!
CONGRATS, CLYDE. NOW IF YA'LL JUST READ ME THE NEXT LINE ON THE EYE-CHART---
BUT-- WHAT HAPPENED, FURY? WHAT?
WHAT??

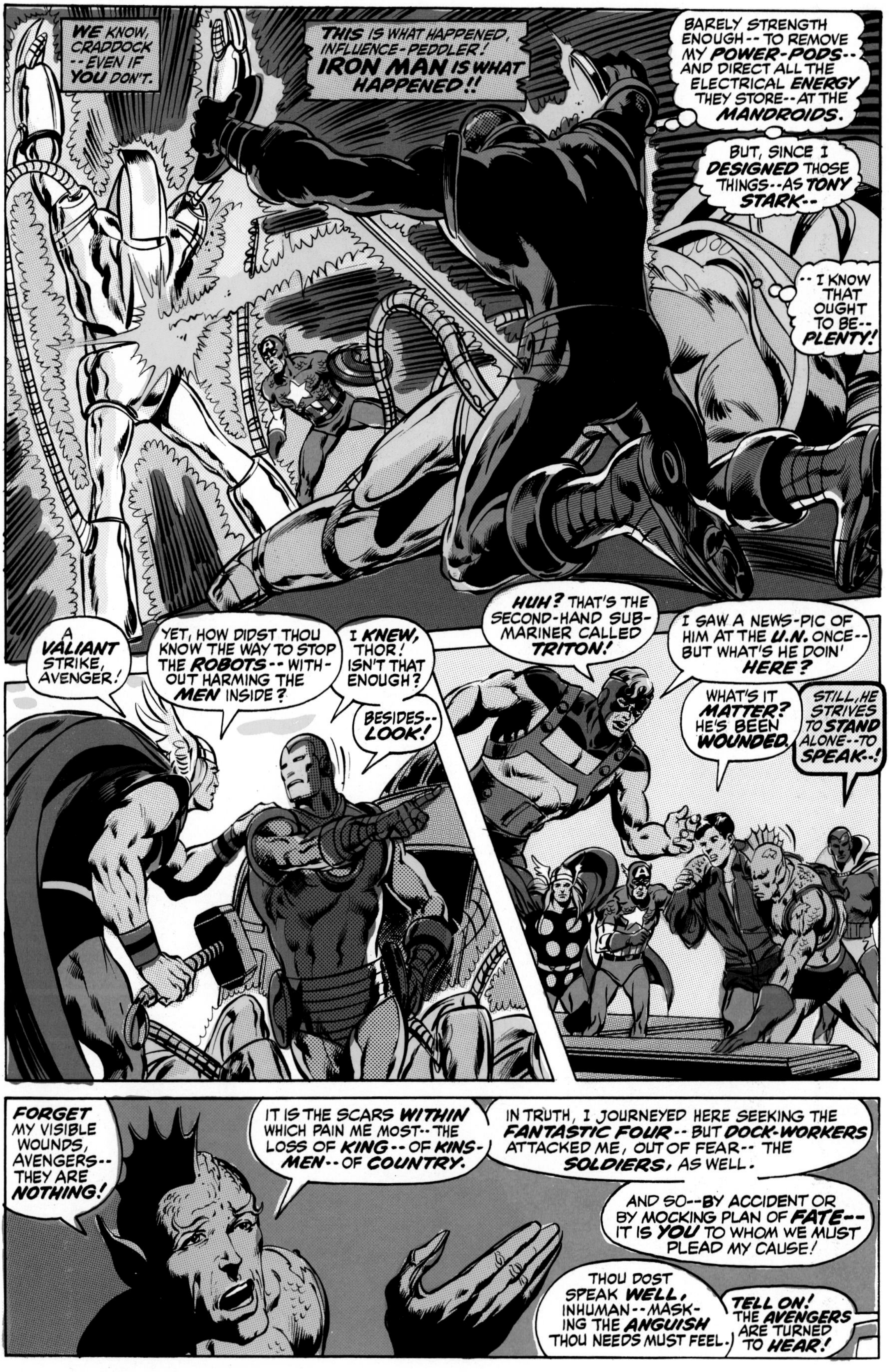
WE KNOW, CRADDOCK --EVEN IF YOU DON'T.
THIS IS WHAT HAPPENED, INFLUENCE-PEDDLER! IRON MAN IS WHAT HAPPENED!!
BARELY STRENGTH ENOUGH -- TO REMOVE MY POWER-PODS-- AND DIRECT ALL THE ELECTRICAL ENERGY THEY STORE--AT THE MANDROIDS.
BUT, SINCE I DESIGNED THOSE THINGS--AS TONY STARK--
-- I KNOW THAT OUGHT TO BE-- PLENTY!
A VALIANT STRIKE, AVENGER!
YET, HOW DIDST THOU KNOW THE WAY TO STOP THE ROBOTS-- WITH-OUT HARMING THE MEN INSIDE?
I KNEW, THOR! ISN'T THAT ENOUGH?
BESIDES-- LOOK!
HUH? THAT'S THE SECOND-HAND SUB-MARINER CALLED TRITON!
I SAW A NEWS-PIC OF HIM AT THE U.N. ONCE-- BUT WHAT'S HE DOIN' HERE?
WHAT'S IT MATTER? HE'S BEEN WOUNDED.
STILL, HE STRIVES TO STAND ALONE--TO SPEAK--!
FORGET MY VISIBLE WOUNDS, AVENGERS-- THEY ARE NOTHING!
IT IS THE SCARS WITHIN WHICH PAIN ME MOST-- THE LOSS OF KING -- OF KINS-MEN -- OF COUNTRY.
IN TRUTH, I JOURNEYED HERE SEEKING THE FANTASTIC FOUR -- BUT DOCK-WORKERS ATTACKED ME, OUT OF FEAR-- THE SOLDIERS, AS WELL.
AND SO--BY ACCIDENT OR BY MOCKING PLAN OF FATE-- IT IS YOU TO WHOM WE MUST PLEAD MY CAUSE!
THOU DOST SPEAK WELL, INHUMAN--MASK-ING THE ANGUISH THOU NEEDS MUST FEEL.
TELL ON! THE AVENGERS ARE TURNED TO HEAR!

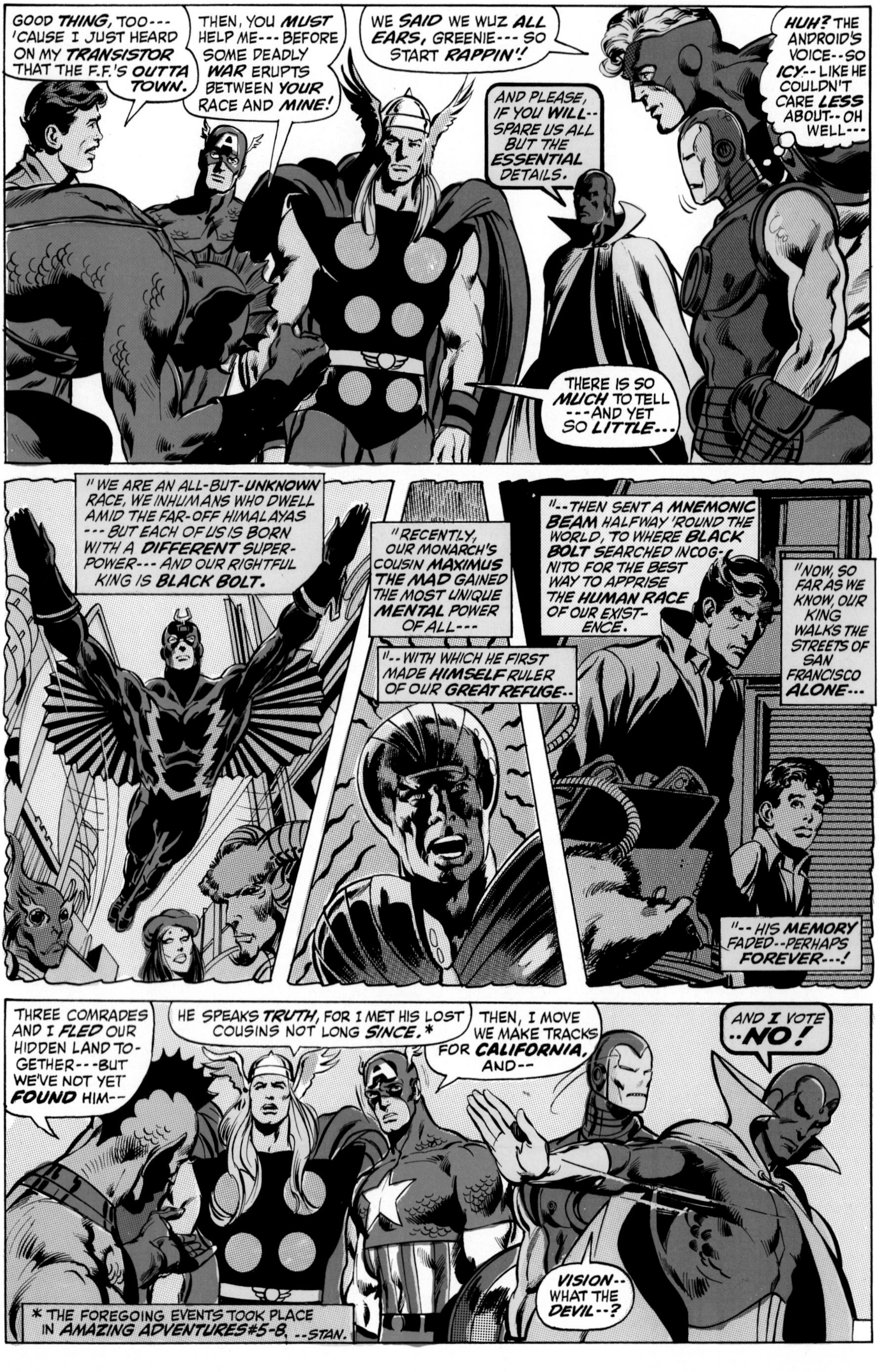
GOOD THING, TOO--- 'CAUSE I JUST HEARD ON MY TRANSISTOR THAT THE F.F.'S OUTTA TOWN.
THEN, YOU MUST HELP ME--- BEFORE SOME DEADLY WAR ERUPTS BETWEEN YOUR RACE AND MINE!
WE SAID WE WUZ ALL EARS, GREENIE--- SO START RAPPIN'!
HUH? THE ANDROID'S VOICE--SO ICY--LIKE HE COULDN'T CARE LESS ABOUT--OH WELL---
AND PLEASE, IF YOU WILL--SPARE US ALL BUT THE ESSENTIAL DETAILS.
THERE IS SO MUCH TO TELL ---AND YET SO LITTLE...
"WE ARE AN ALL-BUT-UNKNOWN RACE, WE INHUMANS WHO DWELL AMID THE FAR-OFF HIMALAYAS --- BUT EACH OF US IS BORN WITH A DIFFERENT SUPER-POWER--- AND OUR RIGHTFUL KING IS BLACK BOLT.
"RECENTLY, OUR MONARCH'S COUSIN MAXIMUS THE MAD GAINED THE MOST UNIQUE MENTAL POWER OF ALL---
"--WITH WHICH HE FIRST MADE HIMSELF RULER OF OUR GREAT REFUGE--
"--THEN SENT A MNEMONIC BEAM HALFWAY 'ROUND THE WORLD, TO WHERE BLACK BOLT SEARCHED INCOG-NITO FOR THE BEST WAY TO APPRISE THE HUMAN RACE OF OUR EXIST-ENCE.
"NOW, SO FAR AS WE KNOW, OUR KING WALKS THE STREETS OF SAN FRANCISCO ALONE...
"--HIS MEMORY FADED--PERHAPS FOREVER---!
THREE COMRADES AND I FLED OUR HIDDEN LAND TO-GETHER---BUT WE'VE NOT YET FOUND HIM--
HE SPEAKS TRUTH, FOR I MET HIS LOST COUSINS NOT LONG SINCE.*
THEN, I MOVE WE MAKE TRACKS FOR CALIFORNIA, AND--
AND I VOTE --NO!
VISION--WHAT THE DEVIL--?
* THE FOREGOING EVENTS TOOK PLACE IN AMAZING ADVENTURES #5-8. --STAN.

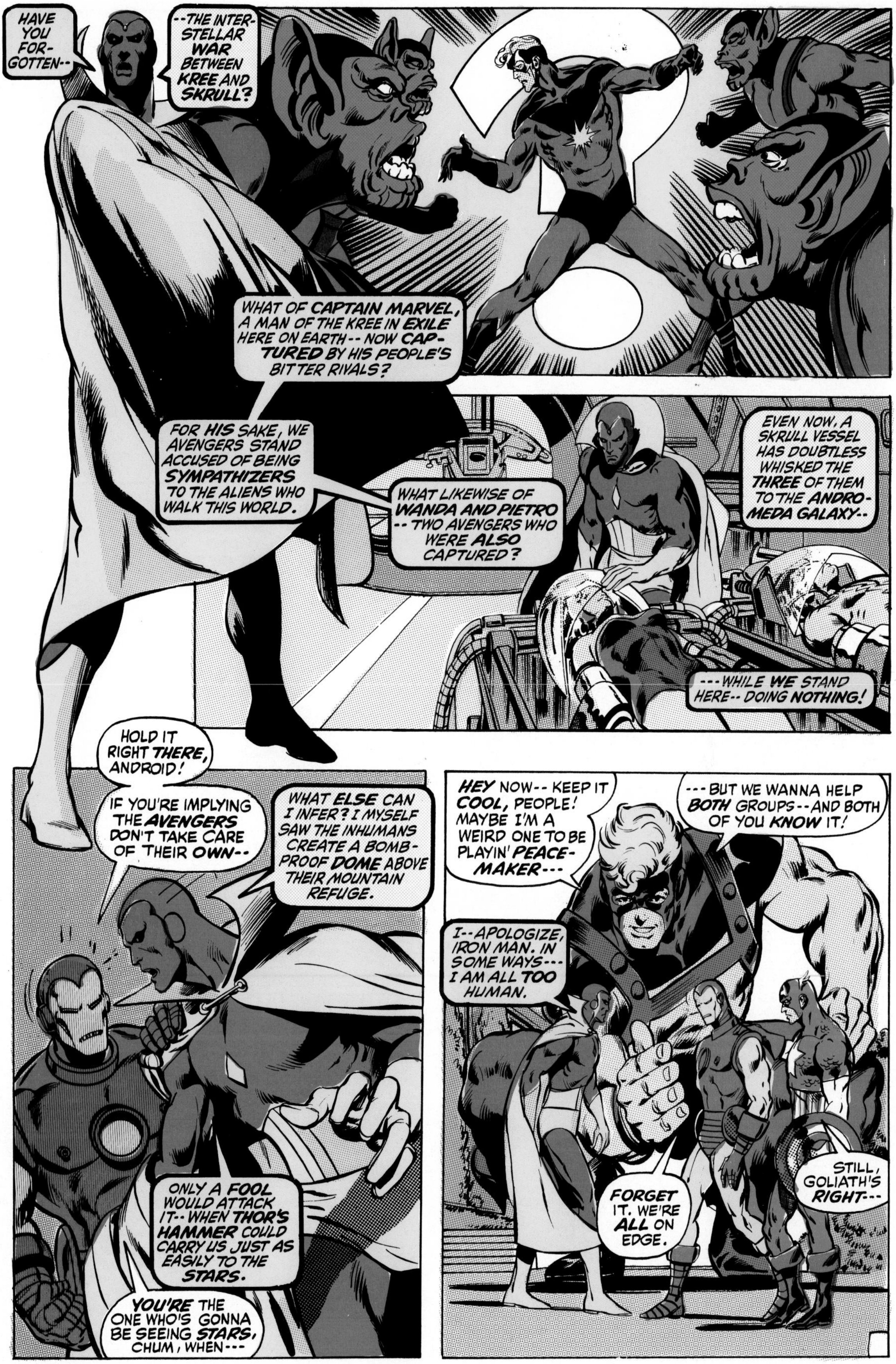

HAVE YOU FOR-GOTTEN--
--THE INTER-STELLAR WAR BETWEEN KREE AND SKRULL?
WHAT OF CAPTAIN MARVEL, A MAN OF THE KREE IN EXILE HERE ON EARTH-- NOW CAP-TURED BY HIS PEOPLE'S BITTER RIVALS?
FOR HIS SAKE, WE AVENGERS STAND ACCUSED OF BEING SYMPATHIZERS TO THE ALIENS WHO WALK THIS WORLD.
WHAT LIKEWISE OF WANDA AND PIETRO -- TWO AVENGERS WHO WERE ALSO CAPTURED?
EVEN NOW, A SKRULL VESSEL HAS DOUBTLESS WHISKED THE THREE OF THEM TO THE ANDRO-MEDA GALAXY--
---WHILE WE STAND HERE-- DOING NOTHING!
HOLD IT RIGHT THERE, ANDROID!
IF YOU'RE IMPLYING THE AVENGERS DON'T TAKE CARE OF THEIR OWN--
WHAT ELSE CAN I INFER? I MYSELF SAW THE INHUMANS CREATE A BOMB-PROOF DOME ABOVE THEIR MOUNTAIN REFUGE.
ONLY A FOOL WOULD ATTACK IT-- WHEN THOR'S HAMMER COULD CARRY US JUST AS EASILY TO THE STARS.
YOU'RE THE ONE WHO'S GONNA BE SEEING STARS, CHUM, WHEN---
HEY NOW-- KEEP IT COOL, PEOPLE! MAYBE I'M A WEIRD ONE TO BE PLAYIN' PEACE-MAKER---
---BUT WE WANNA HELP BOTH GROUPS--AND BOTH OF YOU KNOW IT!
I--APOLOGIZE, IRON MAN. IN SOME WAYS--- I AM ALL TOO HUMAN.
FORGET IT, WE'RE ALL ON EDGE.
STILL, GOLIATH'S RIGHT---

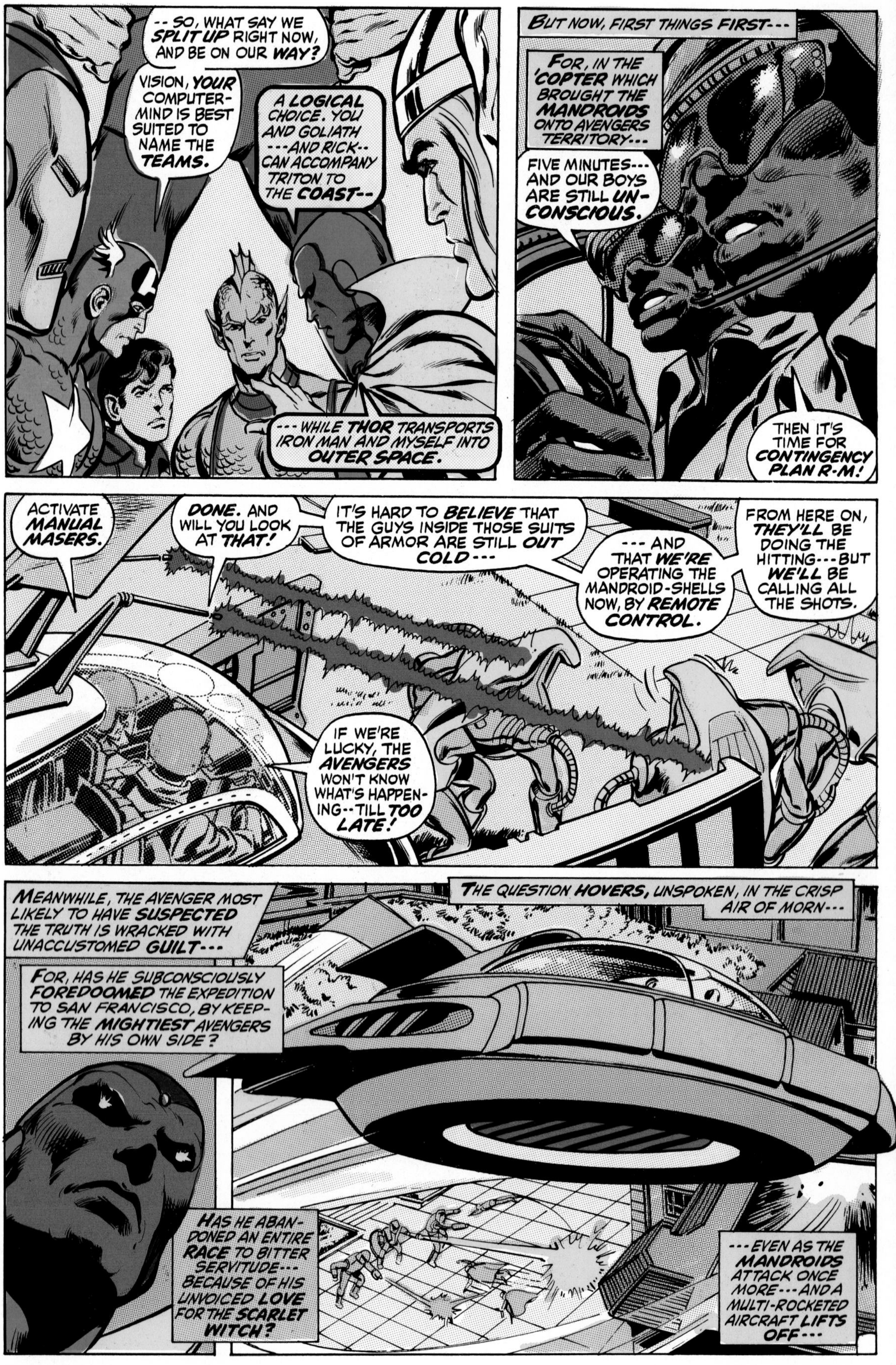

-- SO, WHAT SAY WE SPLIT UP RIGHT NOW, AND BE ON OUR WAY?
VISION, YOUR COMPUTER-MIND IS BEST SUITED TO NAME THE TEAMS.
A LOGICAL CHOICE. YOU AND GOLIATH ---AND RICK-- CAN ACCOMPANY TRITON TO THE COAST--
---WHILE THOR TRANSPORTS IRON MAN AND MYSELF INTO OUTER SPACE.
BUT NOW, FIRST THINGS FIRST---
FOR, IN THE 'COPTER WHICH BROUGHT THE MANDROIDS ONTO AVENGERS TERRITORY---
FIVE MINUTES--- AND OUR BOYS ARE STILL UN-CONSCIOUS.
THEN IT'S TIME FOR CONTINGENCY PLAN R-M!
ACTIVATE MANUAL MASERS.
DONE. AND WILL YOU LOOK AT THAT!
IT'S HARD TO BELIEVE THAT THE GUYS INSIDE THOSE SUITS OF ARMOR ARE STILL OUT COLD---
--- AND THAT WE'RE OPERATING THE MANDROID-SHELLS NOW, BY REMOTE CONTROL.
FROM HERE ON, THEY'LL BE DOING THE HITTING--- BUT WE'LL BE CALLING ALL THE SHOTS.
IF WE'RE LUCKY, THE AVENGERS WON'T KNOW WHAT'S HAPPEN-ING--TILL TOO LATE!
MEANWHILE, THE AVENGER MOST LIKELY TO HAVE SUSPECTED THE TRUTH IS WRACKED WITH UNACCUSTOMED GUILT---
FOR, HAS HE SUBCONSCIOUSLY FOREDOOMED THE EXPEDITION TO SAN FRANCISCO, BY KEEP-ING THE MIGHTIEST AVENGERS BY HIS OWN SIDE?
HAS HE ABAN-DONED AN ENTIRE RACE TO BITTER SERVITUDE--- BECAUSE OF HIS UNVOICED LOVE FOR THE SCARLET WITCH?
THE QUESTION HOVERS, UNSPOKEN, IN THE CRISP AIR OF MORN---
---EVEN AS THE MANDROIDS ATTACK ONCE MORE---AND A MULTI-ROCKETED AIRCRAFT LIFTS OFF---

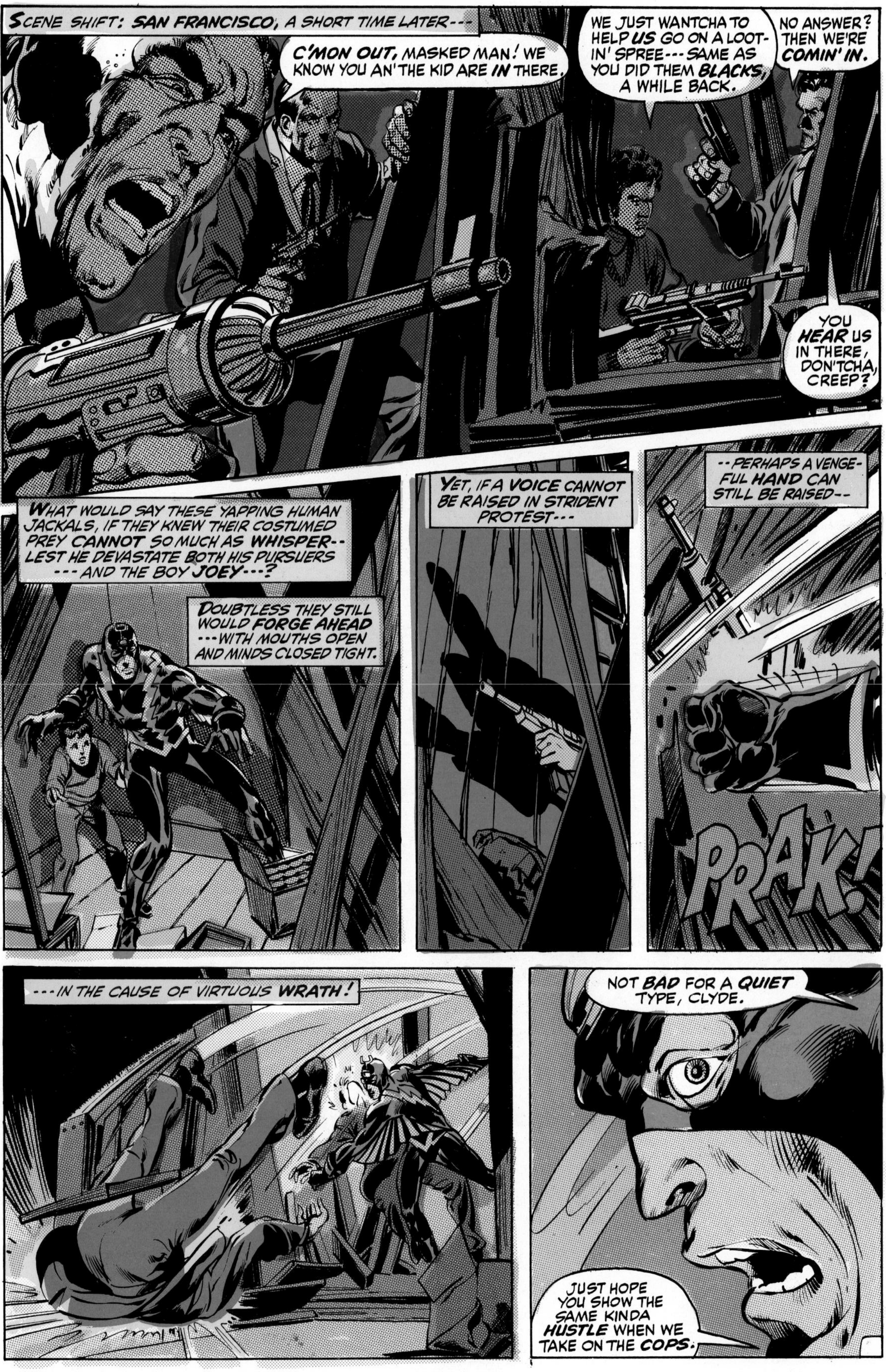
SCENE SHIFT: SAN FRANCISCO, A SHORT TIME LATER---
C'MON OUT, MASKED MAN! WE KNOW YOU AN' THE KID ARE IN THERE.
WE JUST WANTCHA TO HELP US GO ON A LOOT-IN' SPREE---SAME AS YOU DID THEM BLACKS, A WHILE BACK.
NO ANSWER? THEN WE'RE COMIN' IN.
YOU HEAR US IN THERE, DON'TCHA, CREEP?
WHAT WOULD SAY THESE YAPPING HUMAN JACKALS, IF THEY KNEW THEIR COSTUMED PREY CANNOT SO MUCH AS WHISPER--LEST HE DEVASTATE BOTH HIS PURSUERS ---AND THE BOY JOEY---?
DOUBTLESS THEY STILL WOULD FORGE AHEAD ---WITH MOUTHS OPEN AND MINDS CLOSED TIGHT.
YET, IF A VOICE CANNOT BE RAISED IN STRIDENT PROTEST---
--PERHAPS A VENGE-FUL HAND CAN STILL BE RAISED--
PRAK!
---IN THE CAUSE OF VIRTUOUS WRATH!
NOT BAD FOR A QUIET TYPE, CLYDE.
JUST HOPE YOU SHOW THE SAME KINDA HUSTLE WHEN WE TAKE ON THE COPS.

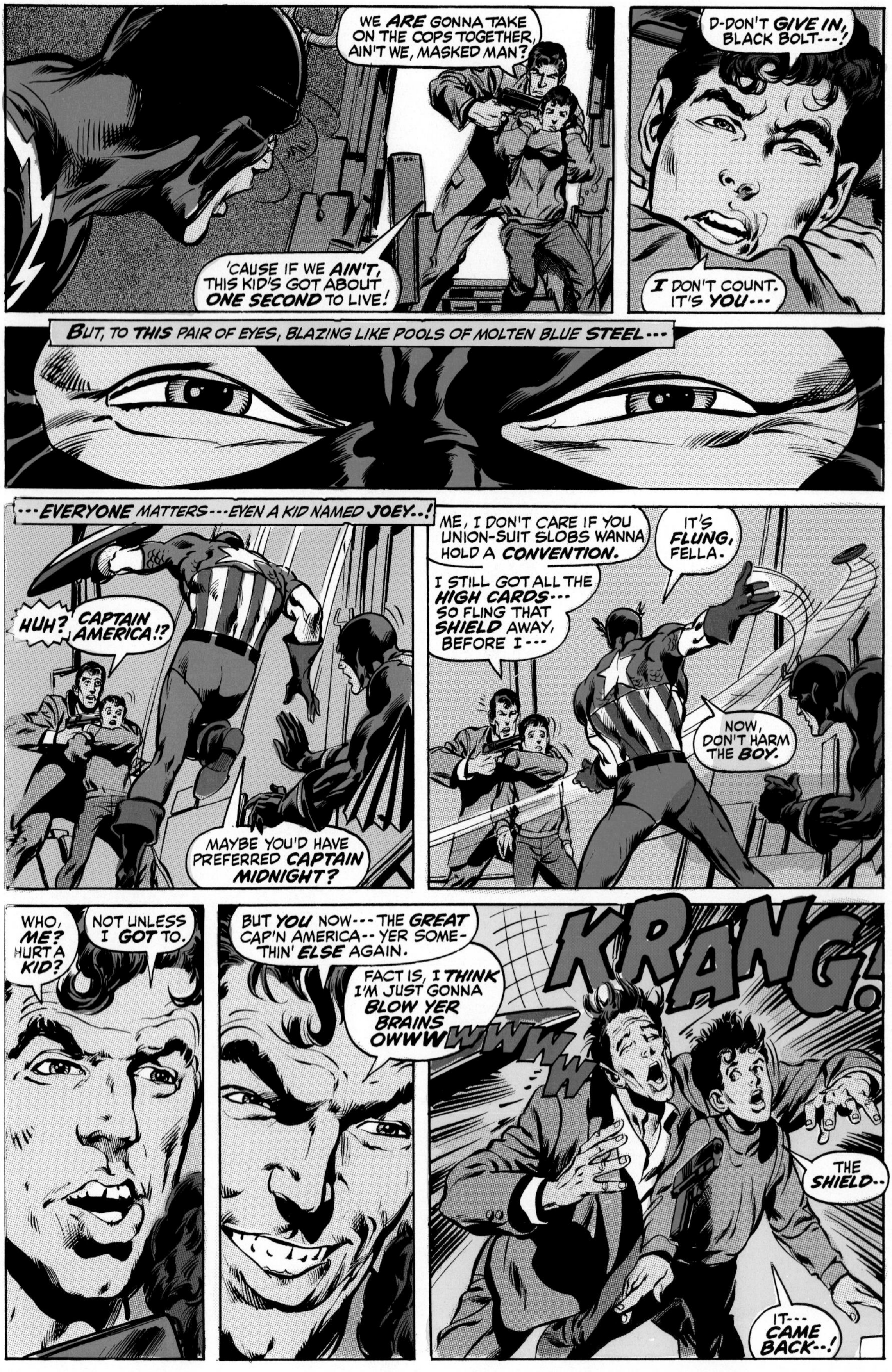
WE ARE GONNA TAKE ON THE COPS TOGETHER, AIN'T WE, MASKED MAN?
'CAUSE IF WE AIN'T, THIS KID'S GOT ABOUT ONE SECOND TO LIVE!
D-DON'T GIVE IN, BLACK BOLT---!
I DON'T COUNT. IT'S YOU---
BUT, TO THIS PAIR OF EYES, BLAZING LIKE POOLS OF MOLTEN BLUE STEEL---
---EVERYONE MATTERS---EVEN A KID NAMED JOEY--!
HUH?
CAPTAIN AMERICA!?
MAYBE YOU'D HAVE PREFERRED CAPTAIN MIDNIGHT?
ME, I DON'T CARE IF YOU UNION-SUIT SLOBS WANNA HOLD A CONVENTION.
I STILL GOT ALL THE HIGH CARDS--- SO FLING THAT SHIELD AWAY, BEFORE I---
IT'S FLUNG, FELLA.
NOW, DON'T HARM THE BOY.
WHO, ME? HURT A KID?
NOT UNLESS I GOT TO.
BUT YOU NOW--- THE GREAT CAP'N AMERICA-- YER SOME-THIN' ELSE AGAIN.
FACT IS, I THINK I'M JUST GONNA BLOW YER BRAINS OWWWWWWWW
KRANG!
THE SHIELD--
IT--- CAME BACK--!

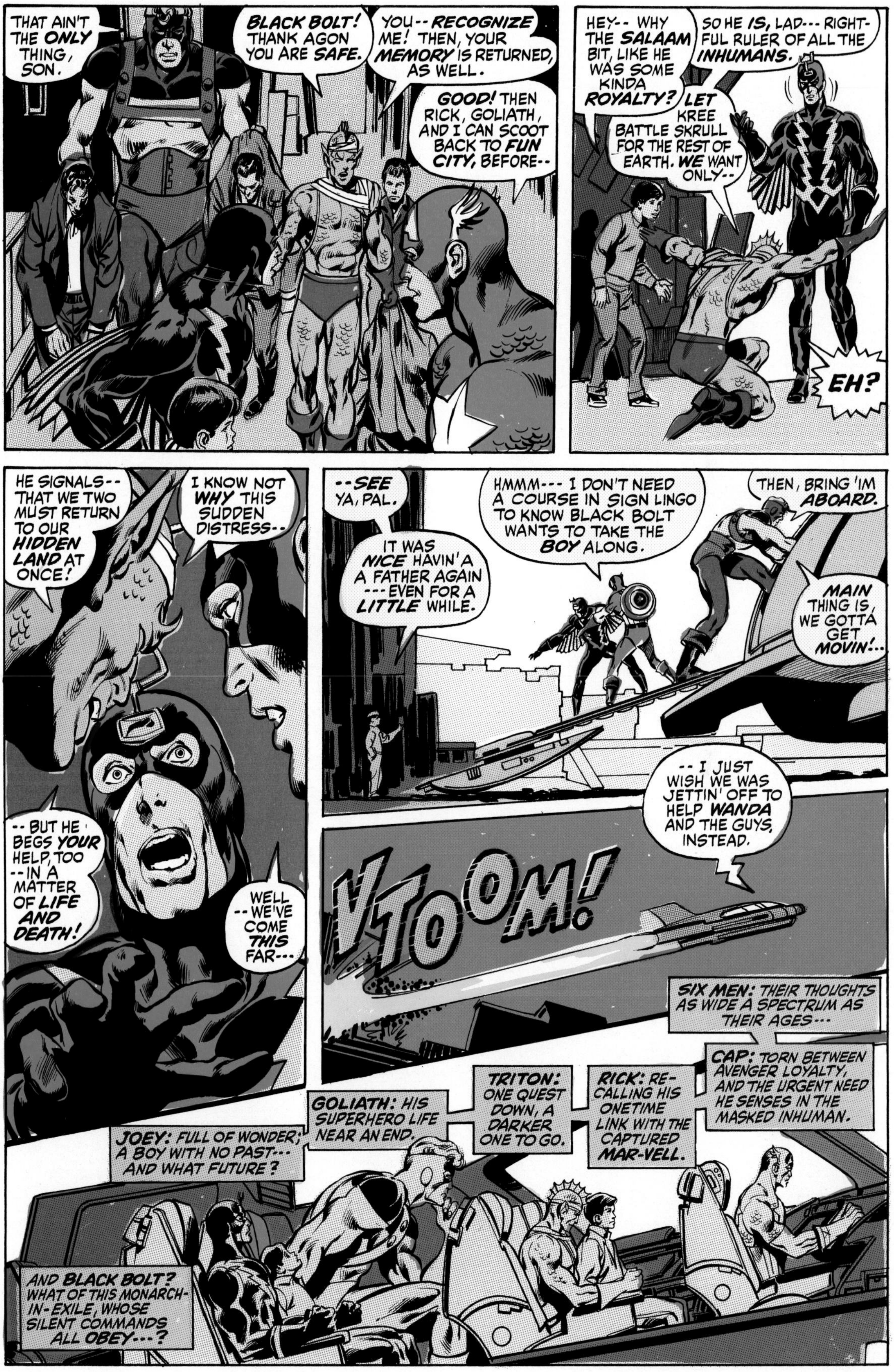
THAT AIN'T THE ONLY THING, SON.
BLACK BOLT! THANK AGON YOU ARE SAFE.
YOU -- RECOGNIZE ME! THEN, YOUR MEMORY IS RETURNED, AS WELL.
GOOD! THEN RICK, GOLIATH, AND I CAN SCOOT BACK TO FUN CITY, BEFORE--
HEY-- WHY THE SALAAM BIT, LIKE HE WAS SOME KINDA ROYALTY?
SO HE IS, LAD--- RIGHTFUL RULER OF ALL THE INHUMANS.
LET KREE BATTLE SKRULL FOR THE REST OF EARTH. WE WANT ONLY--
EH?
HE SIGNALS-- THAT WE TWO MUST RETURN TO OUR HIDDEN LAND AT ONCE!
I KNOW NOT WHY THIS SUDDEN DISTRESS--
-- BUT HE BEGS YOUR HELP, TOO -- IN A MATTER OF LIFE AND DEATH!
WELL -- WE'VE COME THIS FAR---
--SEE YA, PAL.
IT WAS NICE HAVIN' A A FATHER AGAIN --- EVEN FOR A LITTLE WHILE.
HMMM--- I DON'T NEED A COURSE IN SIGN LINGO TO KNOW BLACK BOLT WANTS TO TAKE THE BOY ALONG.
THEN, BRING 'IM ABOARD.
MAIN THING IS, WE GOTTA GET MOVIN'...
-- I JUST WISH WE WAS JETTIN' OFF TO HELP WANDA AND THE GUYS, INSTEAD.
VTOOOM!
SIX MEN: THEIR THOUGHTS AS WIDE A SPECTRUM AS THEIR AGES---
CAP: TORN BETWEEN AVENGER LOYALTY, AND THE URGENT NEED HE SENSES IN THE MASKED INHUMAN.
RICK: RE-CALLING HIS ONETIME LINK WITH THE CAPTURED MAR-VELL.
TRITON: ONE QUEST DOWN, A DARKER ONE TO GO.
GOLIATH: HIS SUPERHERO LIFE NEAR AN END.
JOEY: FULL OF WONDER; A BOY WITH NO PAST--- AND WHAT FUTURE?
AND BLACK BOLT? WHAT OF THIS MONARCH-IN-EXILE, WHOSE SILENT COMMANDS ALL OBEY---?

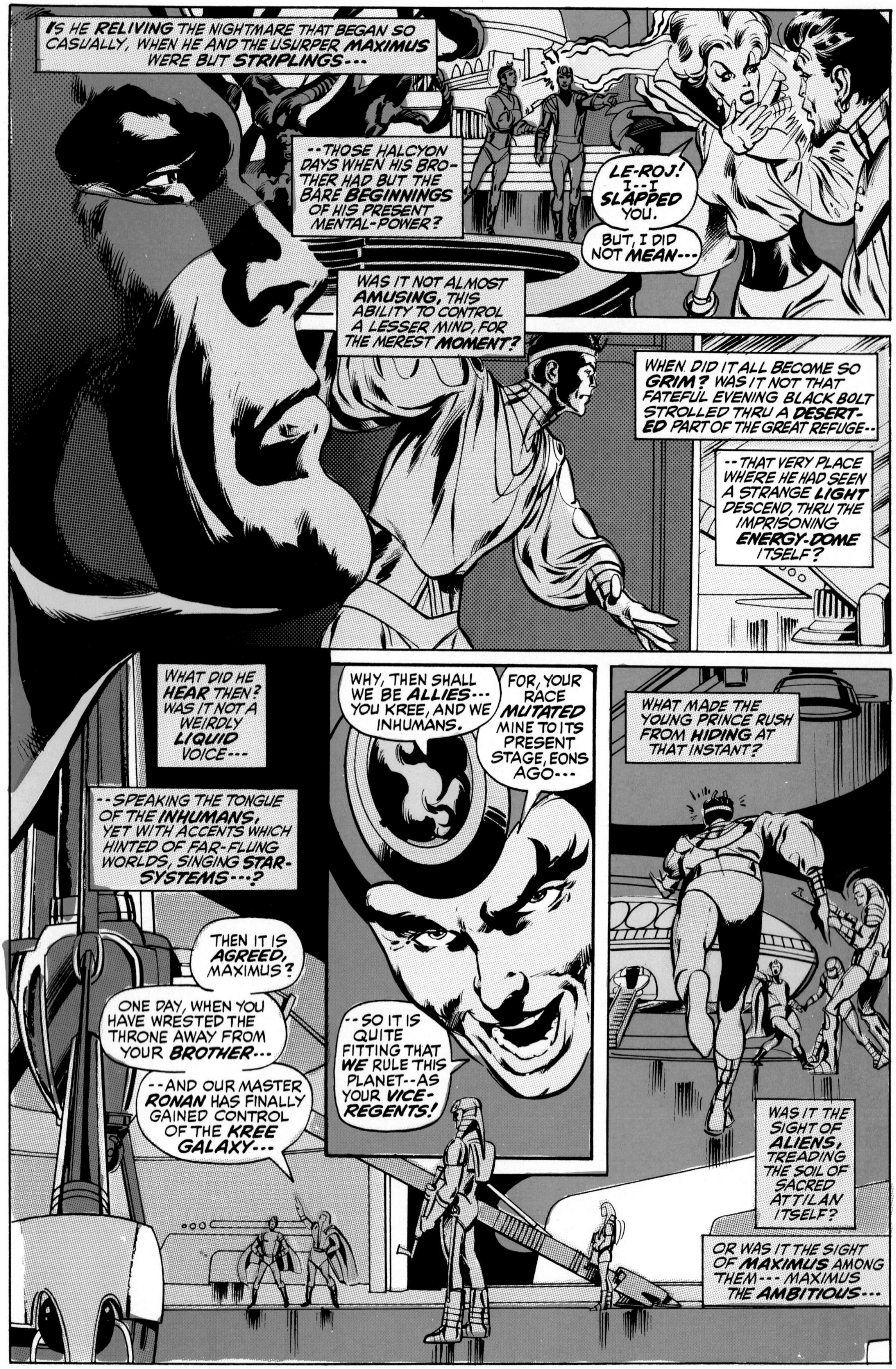
IS HE RELIVING THE NIGHTMARE THAT BEGAN SO CASUALLY, WHEN HE AND THE USURPER MAXIMUS WERE BUT STRIPLINGS---
--THOSE HALCYON DAYS WHEN HIS BROTHER HAD BUT THE BARE BEGINNINGS OF HIS PRESENT MENTAL-POWER?
LE-ROJ! I--I SLAPPED YOU.
BUT, I DID NOT MEAN---
WAS IT NOT ALMOST AMUSING, THIS ABILITY TO CONTROL A LESSER MIND, FOR THE MEREST MOMENT?
WHEN DID IT ALL BECOME SO GRIM? WAS IT NOT THAT FATEFUL EVENING BLACK BOLT STROLLED THRU A DESERTED PART OF THE GREAT REFUGE--
--THAT VERY PLACE WHERE HE HAD SEEN A STRANGE LIGHT DESCEND, THRU THE IMPRISONING ENERGY-DOME ITSELF?
WHAT DID HE HEAR THEN? WAS IT NOT A WEIRDLY LIQUID VOICE---
--SPEAKING THE TONGUE OF THE INHUMANS, YET WITH ACCENTS WHICH HINTED OF FAR-FLUNG WORLDS, SINGING STAR-SYSTEMS---?
THEN IT IS AGREED, MAXIMUS?
ONE DAY, WHEN YOU HAVE WRESTED THE THRONE AWAY FROM YOUR BROTHER---
--AND OUR MASTER RONAN HAS FINALLY GAINED CONTROL OF THE KREE GALAXY---
WHY, THEN SHALL WE BE ALLIES--- YOU KREE, AND WE INHUMANS.
FOR, YOUR RACE MUTATED MINE TO ITS PRESENT STAGE, EONS AGO---
--SO IT IS QUITE FITTING THAT WE RULE THIS PLANET--AS YOUR VICE-REGENTS!
WHAT MADE THE YOUNG PRINCE RUSH FROM HIDING AT THAT INSTANT?
WAS IT THE SIGHT OF ALIENS, TREADING THE SOIL OF SACRED ATTILAN ITSELF?
OR WAS IT THE SIGHT OF MAXIMUS AMONG THEM--- MAXIMUS THE AMBITIOUS---

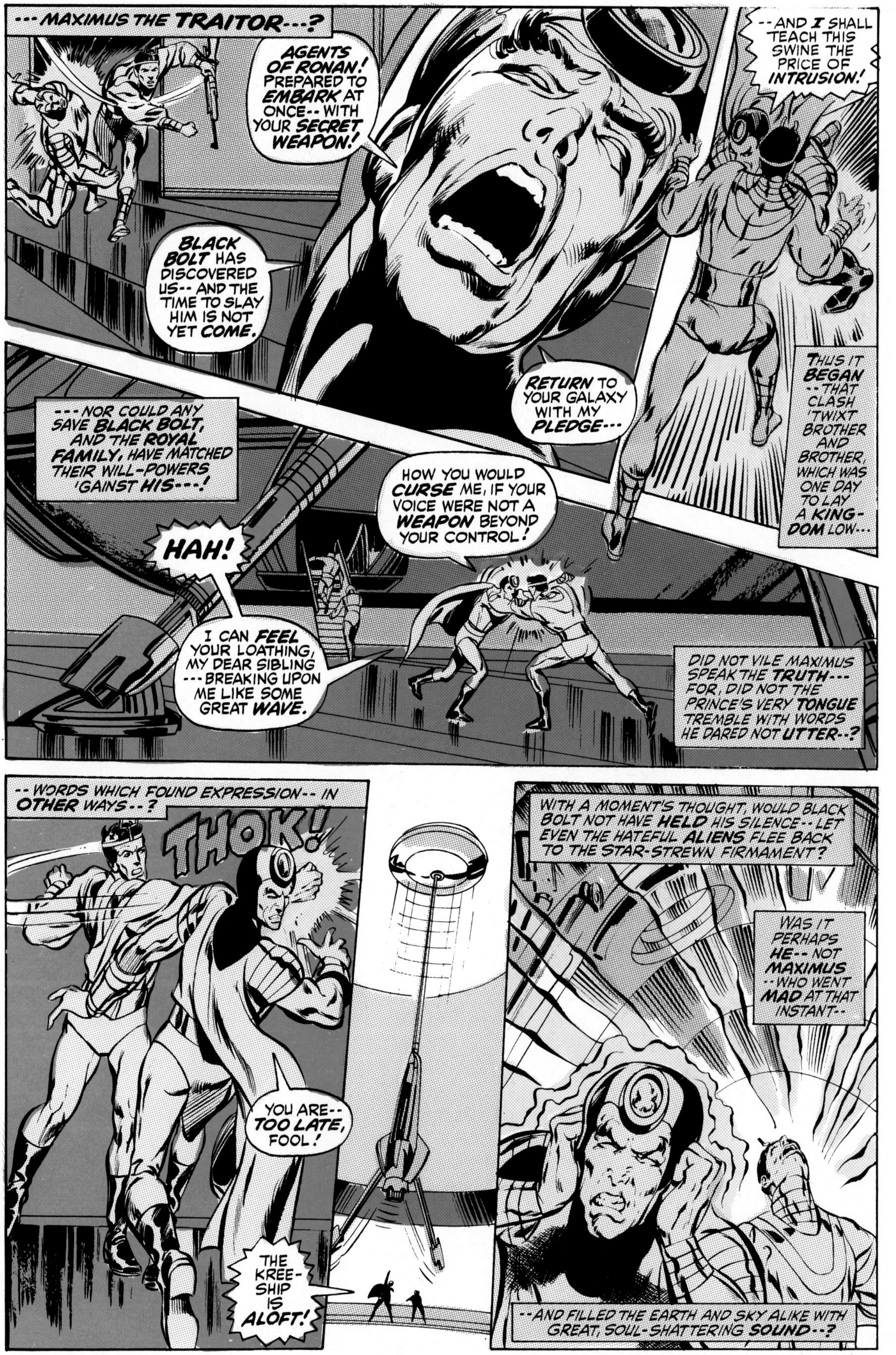

--- MAXIMUS THE TRAITOR---?
AGENTS OF RONAN! PREPARED TO EMBARK AT ONCE-- WITH YOUR SECRET WEAPON!
BLACK BOLT HAS DISCOVERED US-- AND THE TIME TO SLAY HIM IS NOT YET COME.
--AND I SHALL TEACH THIS SWINE THE PRICE OF INTRUSION!
RETURN TO YOUR GALAXY WITH MY PLEDGE---
THUS IT BEGAN --THAT CLASH 'TWIXT BROTHER AND BROTHER, WHICH WAS ONE DAY TO LAY A KING-DOM LOW---
---NOR COULD ANY SAVE BLACK BOLT, AND THE ROYAL FAMILY, HAVE MATCHED THEIR WILL-POWERS 'GAINST HIS---!
HOW YOU WOULD CURSE ME, IF YOUR VOICE WERE NOT A WEAPON BEYOND YOUR CONTROL!
HAH!
I CAN FEEL YOUR LOATHING, MY DEAR SIBLING ---BREAKING UPON ME LIKE SOME GREAT WAVE.
DID NOT VILE MAXIMUS SPEAK THE TRUTH--- FOR, DID NOT THE PRINCE'S VERY TONGUE TREMBLE WITH WORDS HE DARED NOT UTTER--?
--WORDS WHICH FOUND EXPRESSION-- IN OTHER WAYS--?
THOK!
YOU ARE-- TOO LATE, FOOL!
THE KREE-SHIP IS ALOFT!
WITH A MOMENT'S THOUGHT, WOULD BLACK BOLT NOT HAVE HELD HIS SILENCE-- LET EVEN THE HATEFUL ALIENS FLEE BACK TO THE STAR-STREWN FIRMAMENT?
WAS IT PERHAPS HE-- NOT MAXIMUS --WHO WENT MAD AT THAT INSTANT--
--AND FILLED THE EARTH AND SKY ALIKE WITH GREAT, SOUL-SHATTERING SOUND--?

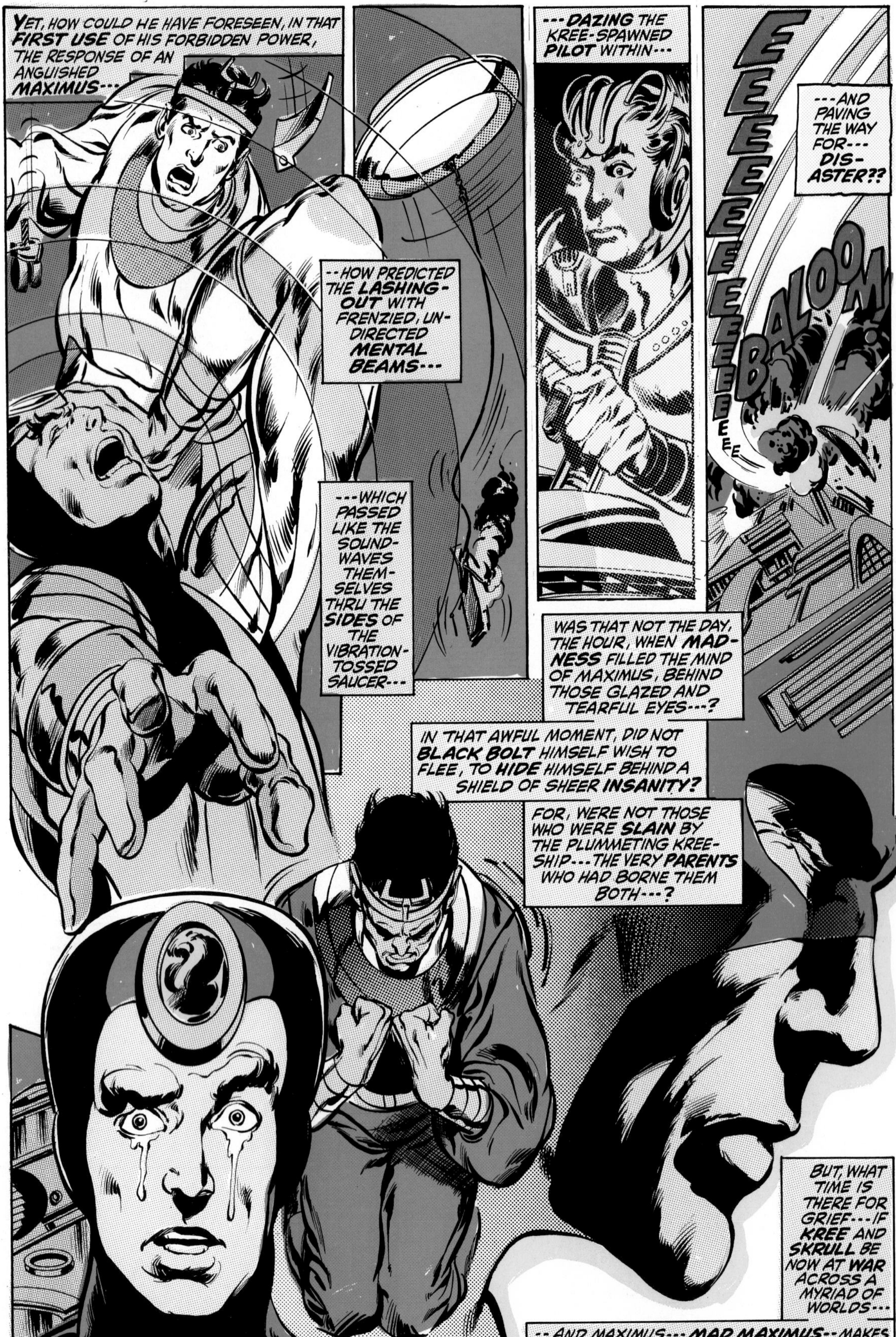
YET, HOW COULD HE HAVE FORESEEN, IN THAT FIRST USE OF HIS FORBIDDEN POWER, THE RESPONSE OF AN ANGUISHED MAXIMUS---
--HOW PREDICTED THE LASHING-OUT WITH FRENZIED, UN-DIRECTED MENTAL BEAMS---
---WHICH PASSED LIKE THE SOUND-WAVES THEM-SELVES THRU THE SIDES OF THE VIBRATION-TOSSED SAUCER---
---DAZING THE KREE-SPAWNED PILOT WITHIN---
EEEEEEEEEEEEEE
---AND PAVING THE WAY FOR--- DIS-ASTER??
BALOOM
WAS THAT NOT THE DAY, THE HOUR, WHEN MAD-NESS FILLED THE MIND OF MAXIMUS, BEHIND THOSE GLAZED AND TEARFUL EYES---?
IN THAT AWFUL MOMENT, DID NOT BLACK BOLT HIMSELF WISH TO FLEE, TO HIDE HIMSELF BEHIND A SHIELD OF SHEER INSANITY?
FOR, WERE NOT THOSE WHO WERE SLAIN BY THE PLUMMETING KREE-SHIP---THE VERY PARENTS WHO HAD BORNE THEM BOTH---?
BUT, WHAT TIME IS THERE FOR GRIEF---IF KREE AND SKRULL BE NOW AT WAR ACROSS A MYRIAD OF WORLDS---
--AND MAXIMUS---MAD MAXIMUS--MAKES READY TO HONOR HIS UNHOLY ALLIANCE--?

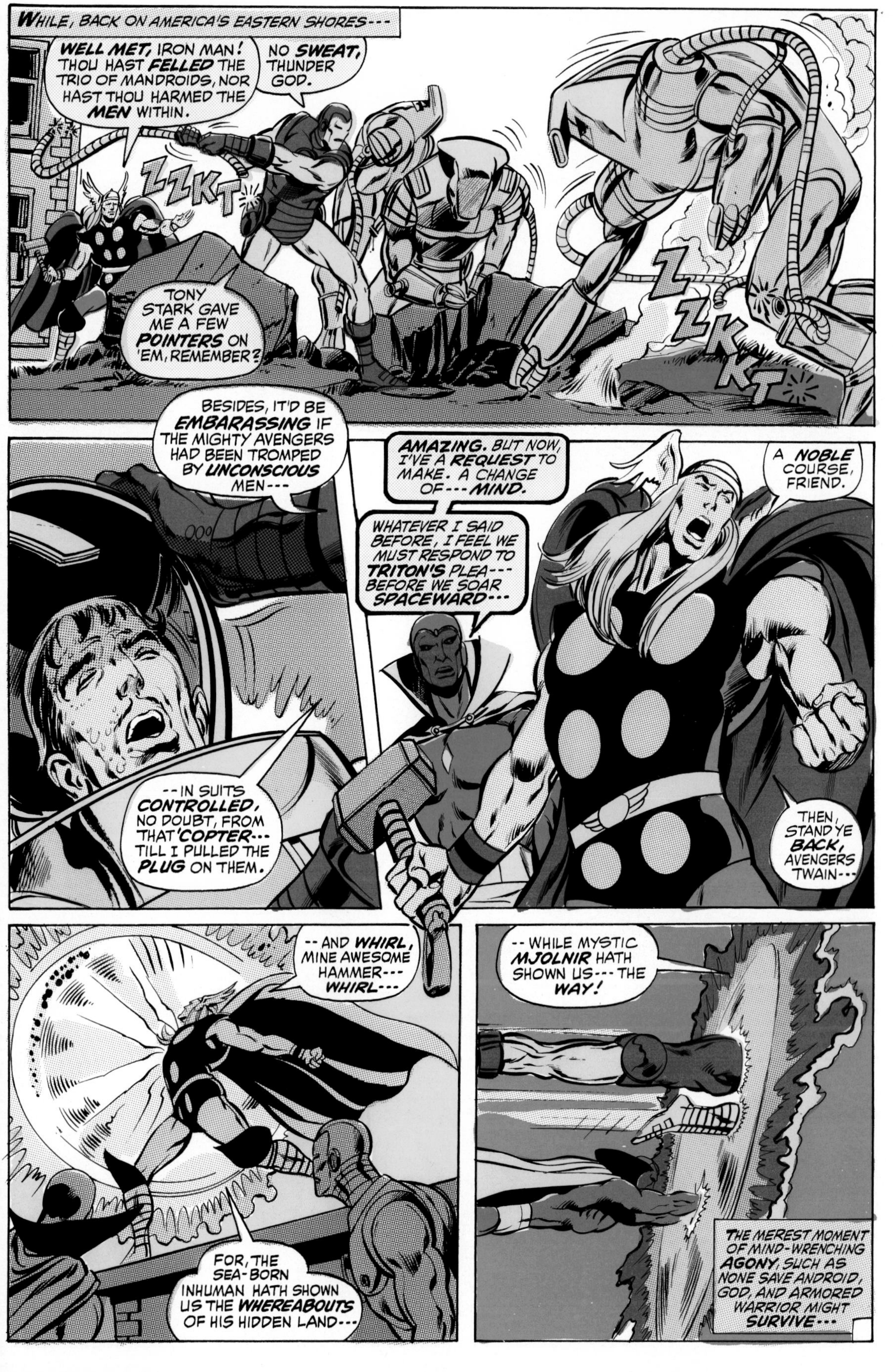
WHILE, BACK ON AMERICA'S EASTERN SHORES---
WELL MET, IRON MAN! THOU HAST FELLED THE TRIO OF MANDROIDS, NOR HAST THOU HARMED THE MEN WITHIN.
NO SWEAT, THUNDER GOD.
ZZKT
TONY STARK GAVE ME A FEW POINTERS ON 'EM, REMEMBER?
ZZKKT
BESIDES, IT'D BE EMBARASSING IF THE MIGHTY AVENGERS HAD BEEN TROMPED BY UNCONSCIOUS MEN---
--IN SUITS CONTROLLED, NO DOUBT, FROM THAT 'COPTER--- TILL I PULLED THE PLUG ON THEM.
AMAZING. BUT NOW, I'VE A REQUEST TO MAKE. A CHANGE OF---MIND.
WHATEVER I SAID BEFORE, I FEEL WE MUST RESPOND TO TRITON'S PLEA--- BEFORE WE SOAR SPACEWARD---
A NOBLE COURSE, FRIEND.
THEN, STAND YE BACK, AVENGERS TWAIN---
--AND WHIRL, MINE AWESOME HAMMER--- WHIRL---
FOR, THE SEA-BORN INHUMAN HATH SHOWN US THE WHEREABOUTS OF HIS HIDDEN LAND---
--WHILE MYSTIC MJOLNIR HATH SHOWN US---THE WAY!
THE MEREST MOMENT OF MIND-WRENCHING AGONY, SUCH AS NONE SAVE ANDROID, GOD, AND ARMORED WARRIOR MIGHT SURVIVE---

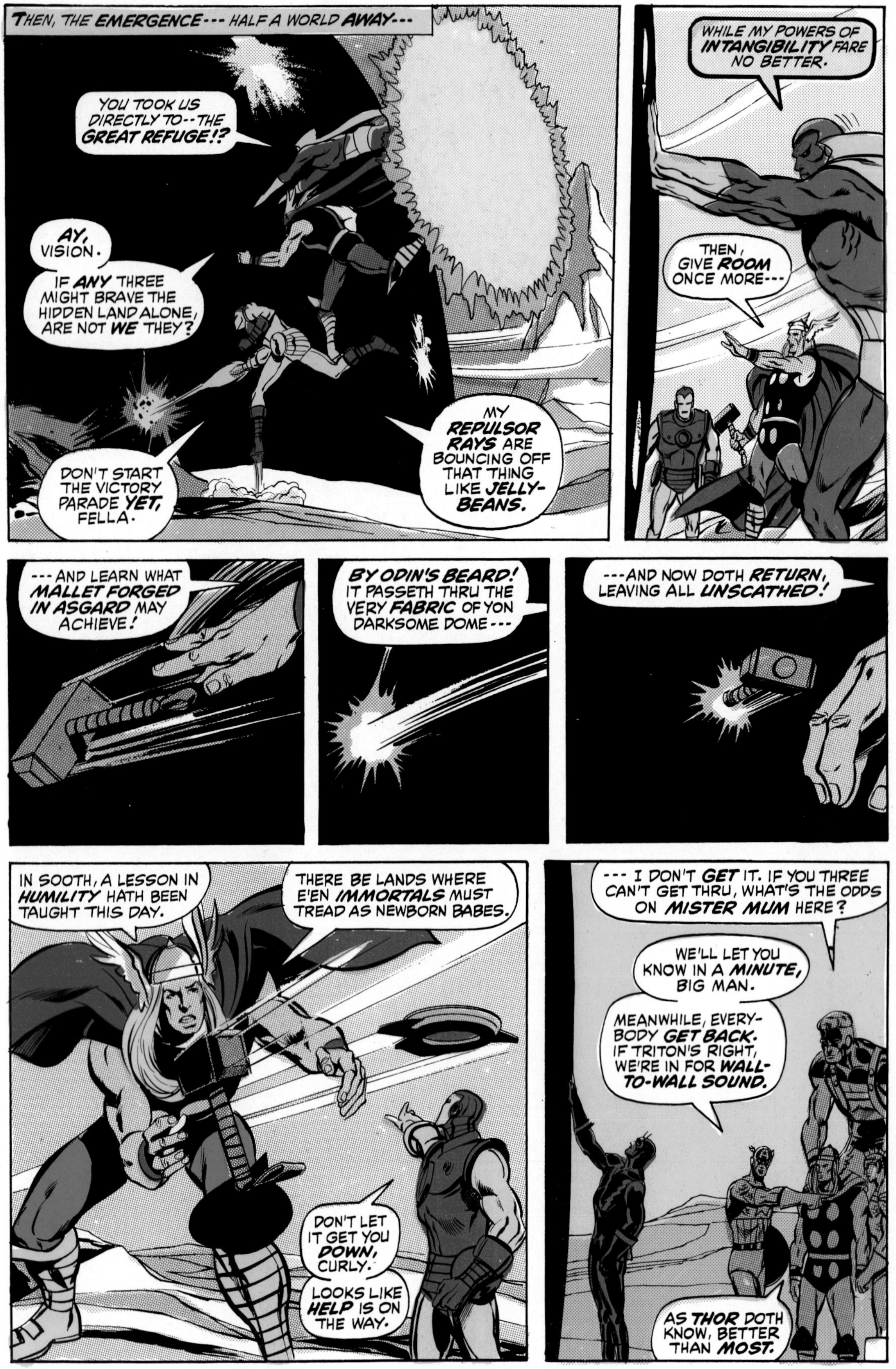

THEN, THE EMERGENCE--- HALF A WORLD AWAY---
YOU TOOK US DIRECTLY TO--THE GREAT REFUGE!?
AY, VISION.
IF ANY THREE MIGHT BRAVE THE HIDDEN LAND ALONE, ARE NOT WE THEY?
DON'T START THE VICTORY PARADE YET, FELLA.
MY REPULSOR RAYS ARE BOUNCING OFF THAT THING LIKE JELLY-BEANS.
WHILE MY POWERS OF INTANGIBILITY FARE NO BETTER.
THEN, GIVE ROOM ONCE MORE---
---AND LEARN WHAT MALLET FORGED IN ASGARD MAY ACHIEVE!
BY ODIN'S BEARD! IT PASSETH THRU THE VERY FABRIC OF YON DARKSOME DOME---
---AND NOW DOTH RETURN, LEAVING ALL UNSCATHED!
IN SOOTH, A LESSON IN HUMILITY HATH BEEN TAUGHT THIS DAY.
THERE BE LANDS WHERE E'EN IMMORTALS MUST TREAD AS NEWBORN BABES.
DON'T LET IT GET YOU DOWN, CURLY.
LOOKS LIKE HELP IS ON THE WAY.
--- I DON'T GET IT. IF YOU THREE CAN'T GET THRU, WHAT'S THE ODDS ON MISTER MUM HERE?
WE'LL LET YOU KNOW IN A MINUTE, BIG MAN.
MEANWHILE, EVERY-BODY GET BACK. IF TRITON'S RIGHT, WE'RE IN FOR WALL-TO-WALL SOUND.
AS THOR DOTH KNOW, BETTER THAN MOST.

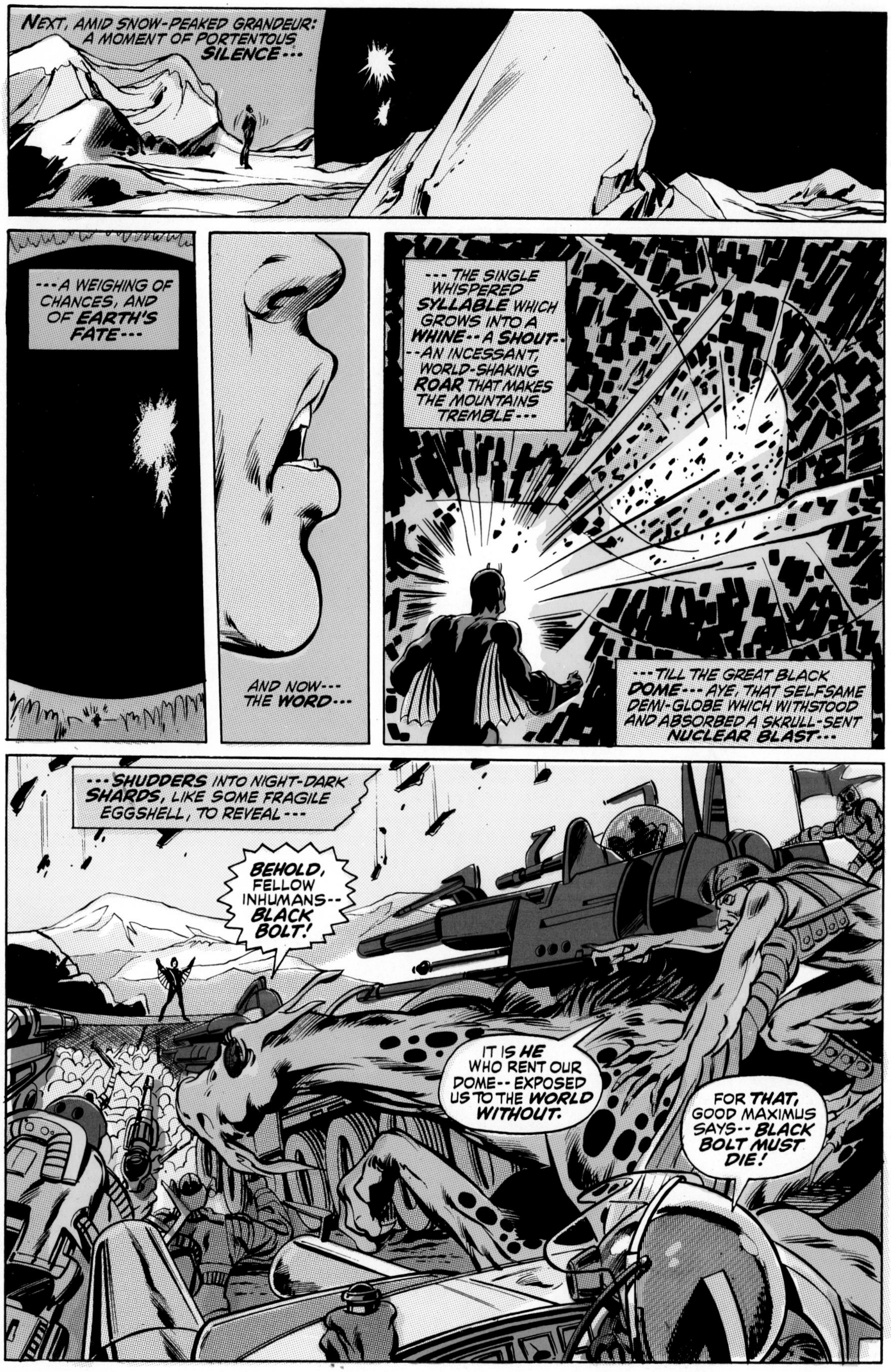
NEXT, AMID SNOW-PEAKED GRANDEUR: A MOMENT OF PORTENTOUS SILENCE---
---A WEIGHING OF CHANCES, AND OF EARTH'S FATE---
AND NOW--- THE WORD---
--- THE SINGLE WHISPERED SYLLABLE WHICH GROWS INTO A WHINE-- A SHOUT-- --AN INCESSANT, WORLD-SHAKING ROAR THAT MAKES THE MOUNTAINS TREMBLE---
---TILL THE GREAT BLACK DOME--- AYE, THAT SELFSAME DEMI-GLOBE WHICH WITHSTOOD AND ABSORBED A SKRULL-SENT NUCLEAR BLAST---
---SHUDDERS INTO NIGHT-DARK SHARDS, LIKE SOME FRAGILE EGGSHELL, TO REVEAL---
BEHOLD, FELLOW INHUMANS-- BLACK BOLT!
IT IS HE WHO RENT OUR DOME-- EXPOSED US TO THE WORLD WITHOUT.
FOR THAT, GOOD MAXIMUS SAYS-- BLACK BOLT MUST DIE!

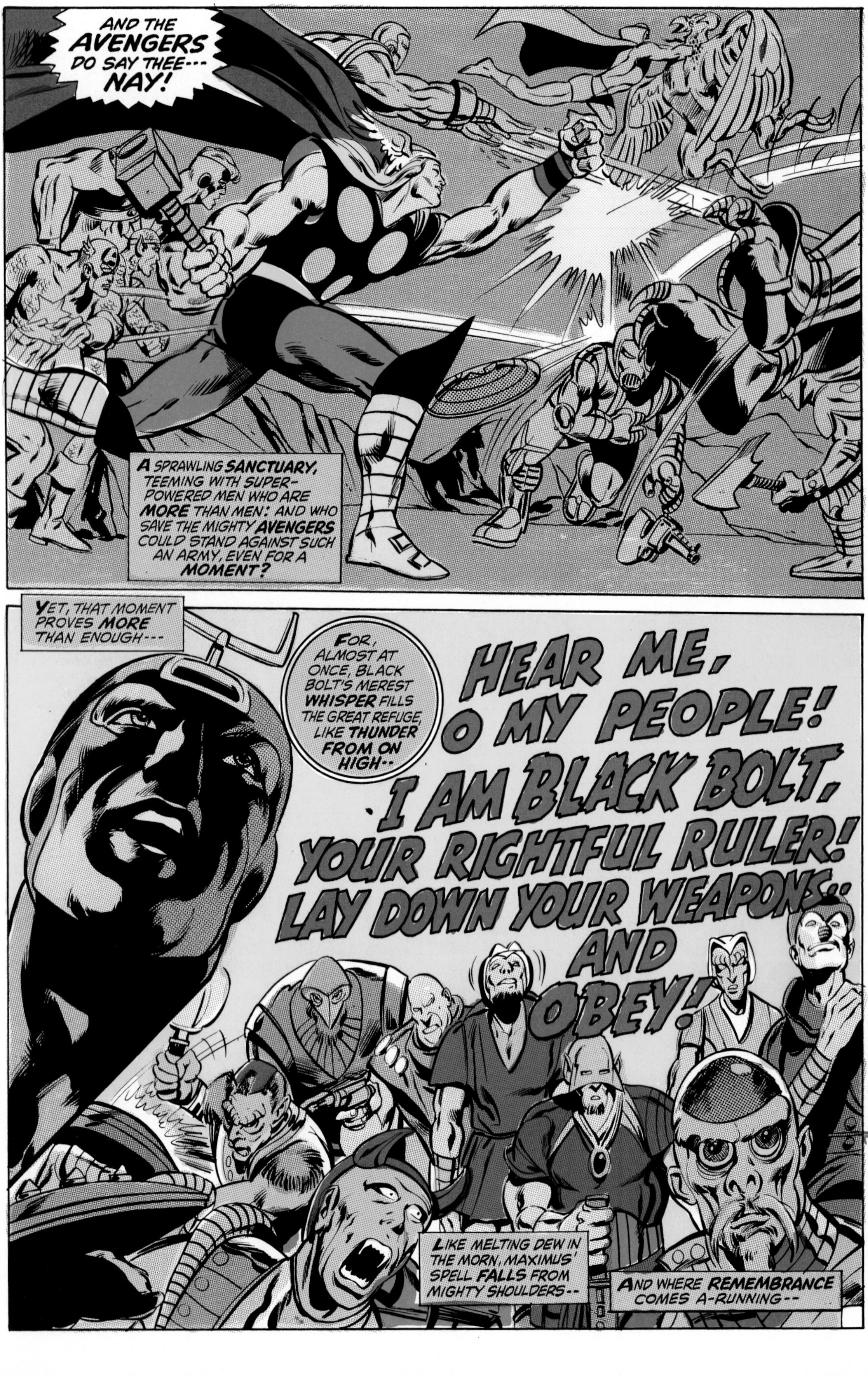
AND THE AVENGERS DO SAY THEE--- NAY!
A SPRAWLING SANCTUARY, TEEMING WITH SUPER-POWERED MEN WHO ARE MORE THAN MEN: AND WHO SAVE THE MIGHTY AVENGERS COULD STAND AGAINST SUCH AN ARMY, EVEN FOR A MOMENT?
YET, THAT MOMENT PROVES MORE THAN ENOUGH---
FOR, ALMOST AT ONCE, BLACK BOLT'S MEREST WHISPER FILLS THE GREAT REFUGE, LIKE THUNDER FROM ON HIGH--
HEAR ME, O MY PEOPLE! I AM BLACK BOLT, YOUR RIGHTFUL RULER! LAY DOWN YOUR WEAPONS.. AND OBEY!
LIKE MELTING DEW IN THE MORN, MAXIMUS' SPELL FALLS FROM MIGHTY SHOULDERS--
AND WHERE REMEMBRANCE COMES A-RUNNING--

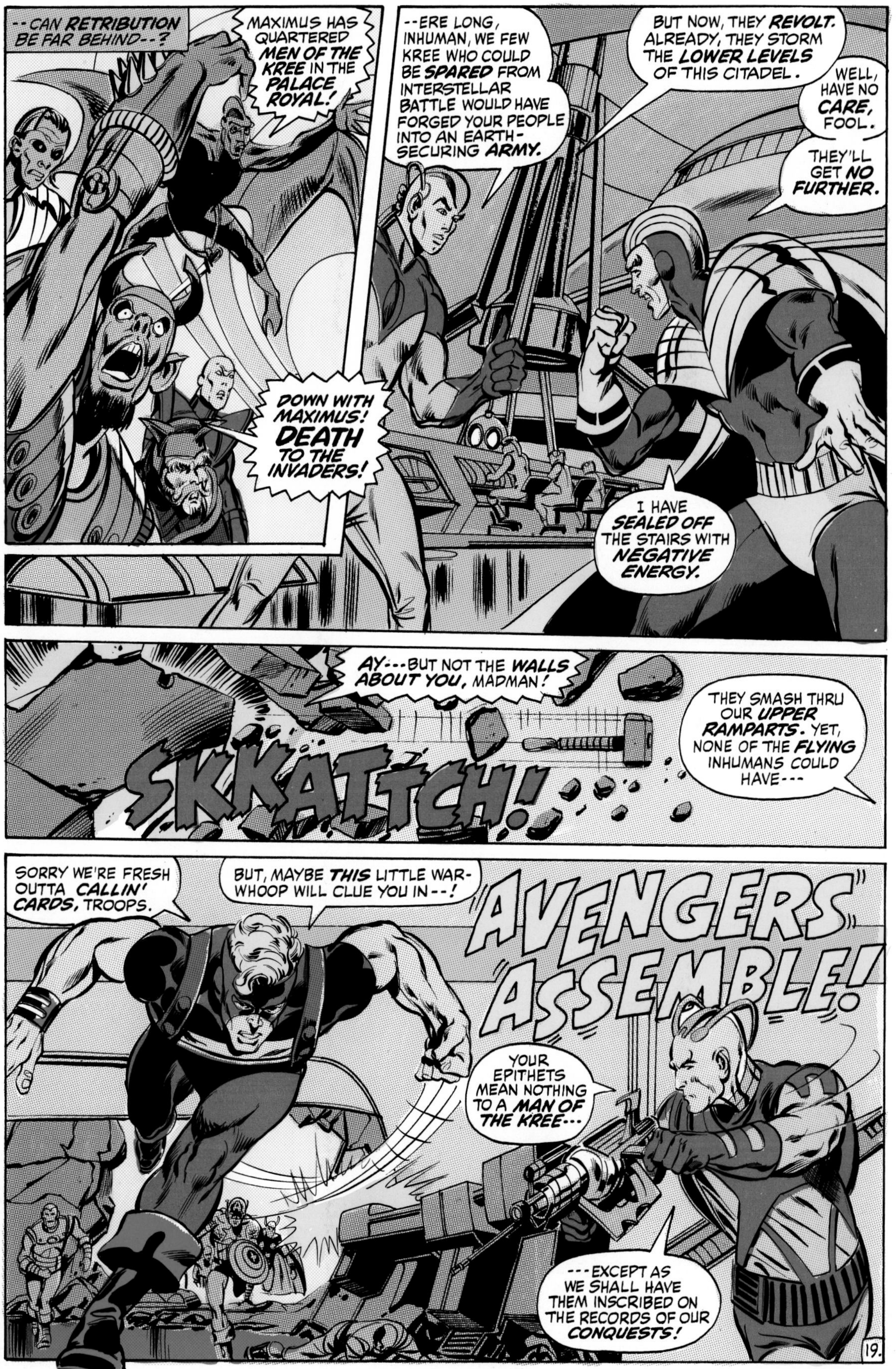
--CAN RETRIBUTION BE FAR BEHIND--?
MAXIMUS HAS QUARTERED MEN OF THE KREE IN THE PALACE ROYAL!
DOWN WITH MAXIMUS! DEATH TO THE INVADERS!
--ERE LONG, INHUMAN, WE FEW KREE WHO COULD BE SPARED FROM INTERSTELLAR BATTLE WOULD HAVE FORGED YOUR PEOPLE INTO AN EARTH-SECURING ARMY.
BUT NOW, THEY REVOLT. ALREADY, THEY STORM THE LOWER LEVELS OF THIS CITADEL.
WELL, HAVE NO CARE, FOOL.
THEY'LL GET NO FURTHER.
I HAVE SEALED OFF THE STAIRS WITH NEGATIVE ENERGY.
AY---BUT NOT THE WALLS ABOUT YOU, MADMAN!
SKKATTCH!
THEY SMASH THRU OUR UPPER RAMPARTS. YET, NONE OF THE FLYING INHUMANS COULD HAVE---
SORRY WE'RE FRESH OUTTA CALLIN' CARDS, TROOPS.
BUT, MAYBE THIS LITTLE WAR-WHOOP WILL CLUE YOU IN--!
"AVENGERS ASSEMBLE!"
YOUR EPITHETS MEAN NOTHING TO A MAN OF THE KREE---
---EXCEPT AS WE SHALL HAVE THEM INSCRIBED ON THE RECORDS OF OUR CONQUESTS!
19.

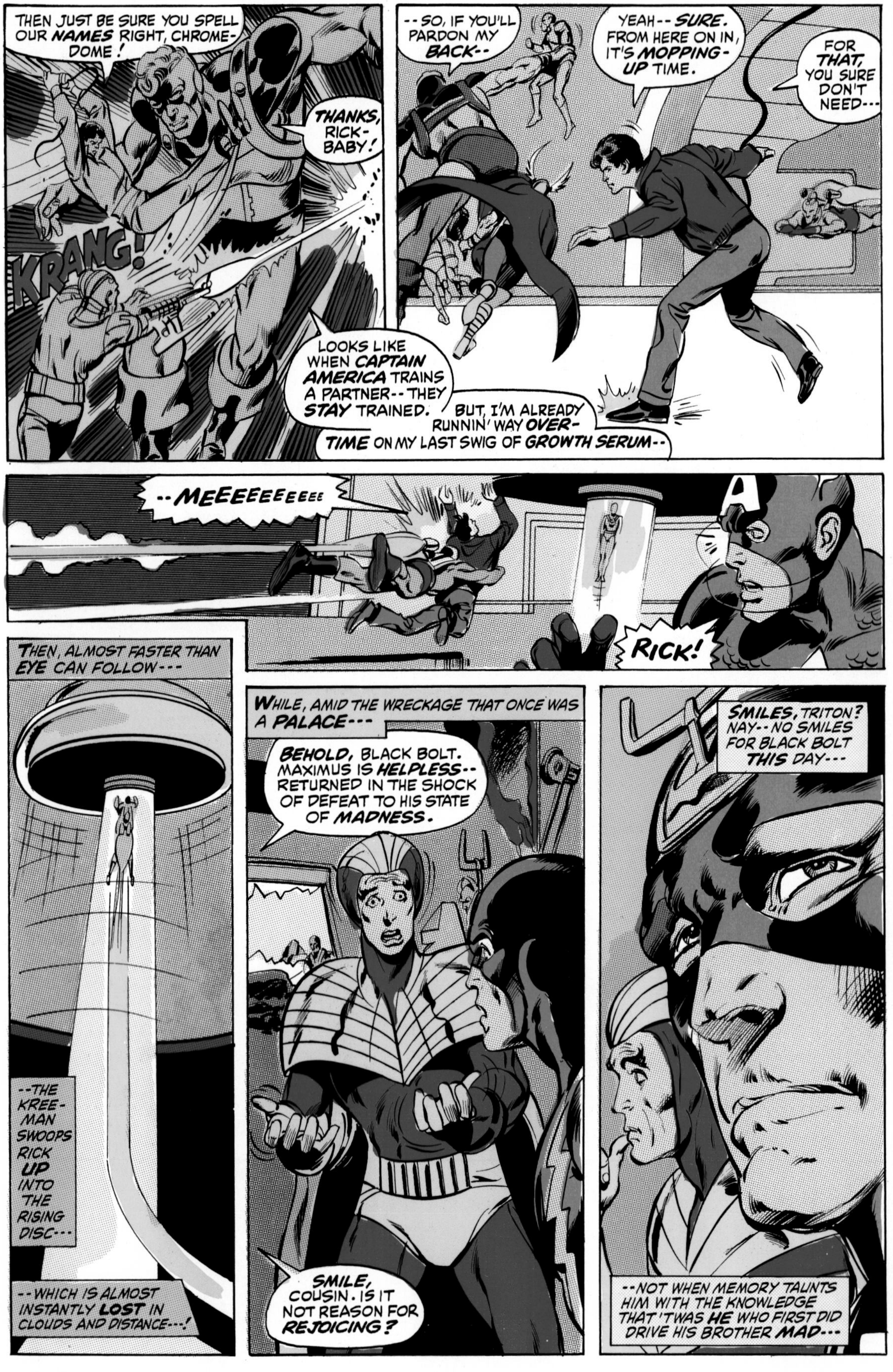
THEN JUST BE SURE YOU SPELL OUR NAMES RIGHT, CHROME-DOME!
THANKS, RICK-BABY!
KRANG!
LOOKS LIKE WHEN CAPTAIN AMERICA TRAINS A PARTNER-- THEY STAY TRAINED.
--SO, IF YOU'LL PARDON MY BACK--
YEAH-- SURE. FROM HERE ON IN, IT'S MOPPING-UP TIME.
FOR THAT, YOU SURE DON'T NEED---
BUT, I'M ALREADY RUNNIN' WAY OVER-TIME ON MY LAST SWIG OF GROWTH SERUM--
--MEEEEEEEeeee
RICK!
THEN, ALMOST FASTER THAN EYE CAN FOLLOW---
--THE KREE-MAN SWOOPS RICK UP INTO THE RISING DISC---
--WHICH IS ALMOST INSTANTLY LOST IN CLOUDS AND DISTANCE--!
WHILE, AMID THE WRECKAGE THAT ONCE WAS A PALACE---
BEHOLD, BLACK BOLT. MAXIMUS IS HELPLESS-- RETURNED IN THE SHOCK OF DEFEAT TO HIS STATE OF MADNESS.
SMILE, COUSIN. IS IT NOT REASON FOR REJOICING?
SMILES, TRITON? NAY-- NO SMILES FOR BLACK BOLT THIS DAY---
--NOT WHEN MEMORY TAUNTS HIM WITH THE KNOWLEDGE THAT 'TWAS HE WHO FIRST DID DRIVE HIS BROTHER MAD---

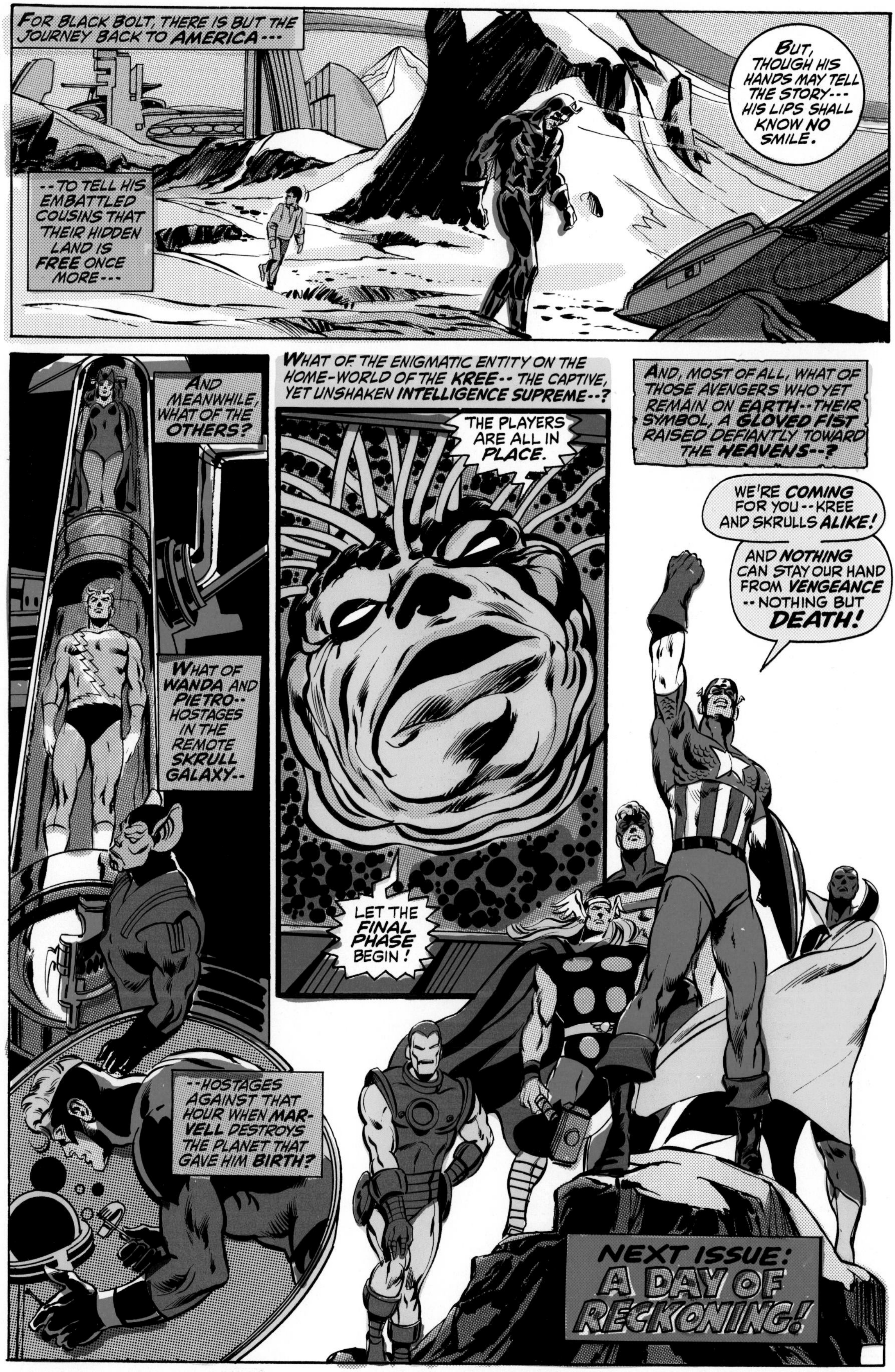
FOR BLACK BOLT, THERE IS BUT THE JOURNEY BACK TO AMERICA---
--TO TELL HIS EMBATTLED COUSINS THAT THEIR HIDDEN LAND IS FREE ONCE MORE---
BUT, THOUGH HIS HANDS MAY TELL THE STORY--- HIS LIPS SHALL KNOW NO SMILE.
AND MEANWHILE, WHAT OF THE OTHERS?
WHAT OF WANDA AND PIETRO-- HOSTAGES IN THE REMOTE SKRULL GALAXY--
--HOSTAGES AGAINST THAT HOUR WHEN MAR-VELL DESTROYS THE PLANET THAT GAVE HIM BIRTH?
WHAT OF THE ENIGMATIC ENTITY ON THE HOME-WORLD OF THE KREE-- THE CAPTIVE, YET UNSHAKEN INTELLIGENCE SUPREME--?
THE PLAYERS ARE ALL IN PLACE.
LET THE FINAL PHASE BEGIN!
AND, MOST OF ALL, WHAT OF THOSE AVENGERS WHO YET REMAIN ON EARTH--THEIR SYMBOL, A GLOVED FIST RAISED DEFIANTLY TOWARD THE HEAVENS--?
WE'RE COMING FOR YOU--KREE AND SKRULLS ALIKE!
AND NOTHING CAN STAY OUR HAND FROM VENGEANCE --NOTHING BUT DEATH!
NEXT ISSUE: A DAY OF RECKONING!

CHAPTER EIGHT

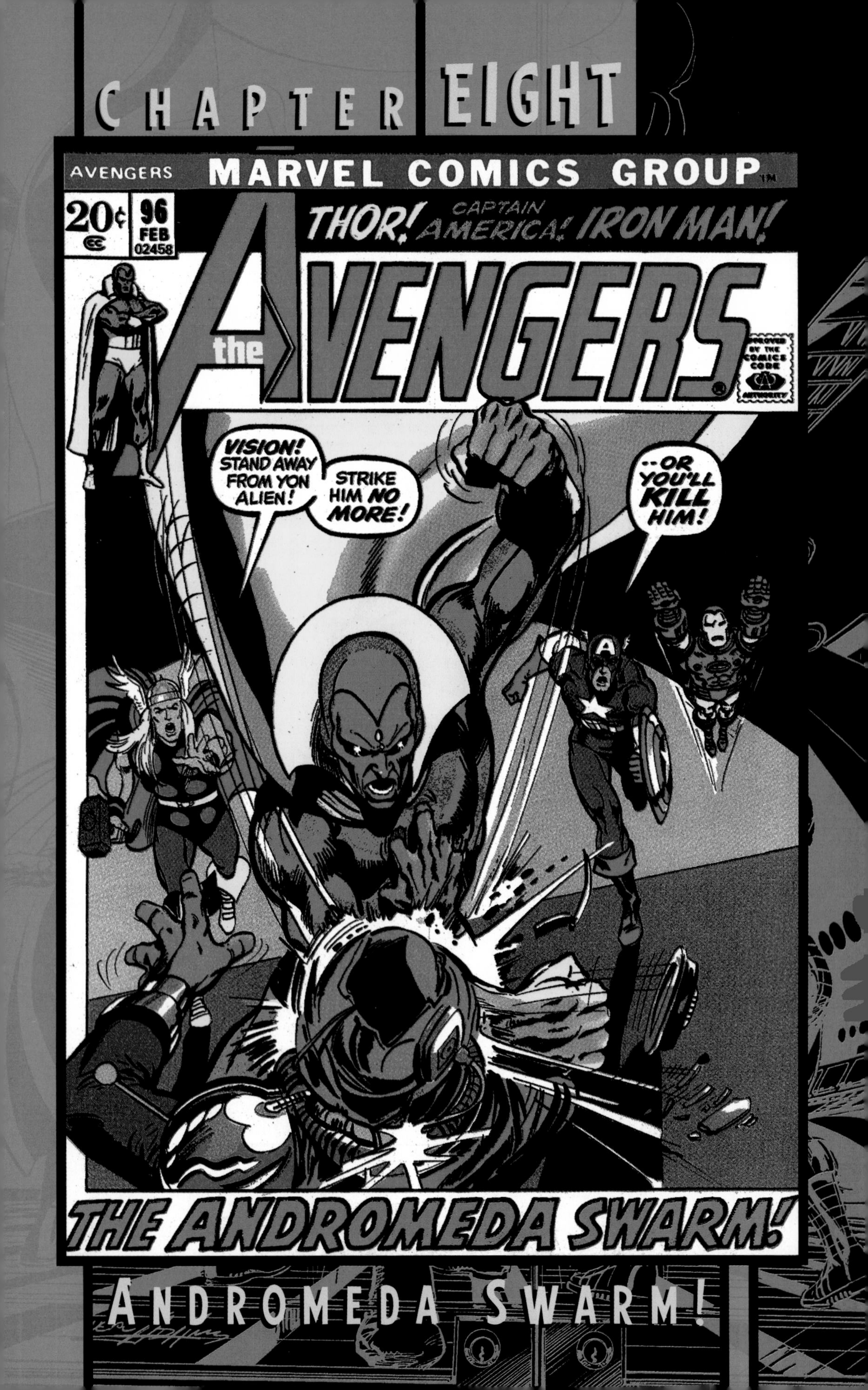
AVENGERS
MARVEL COMICS GROUP
20¢
96
FEB
02458
THOR! CAPTAIN AMERICA! IRON MAN!
the AVENGERS
VISION! STAND AWAY FROM YON ALIEN!
STRIKE HIM NO MORE!
--OR YOU'LL KILL HIM!
THE ANDROMEDA SWARM!

ANDROMEDA SWARM!

THE MIGHTY AVENGERS!®

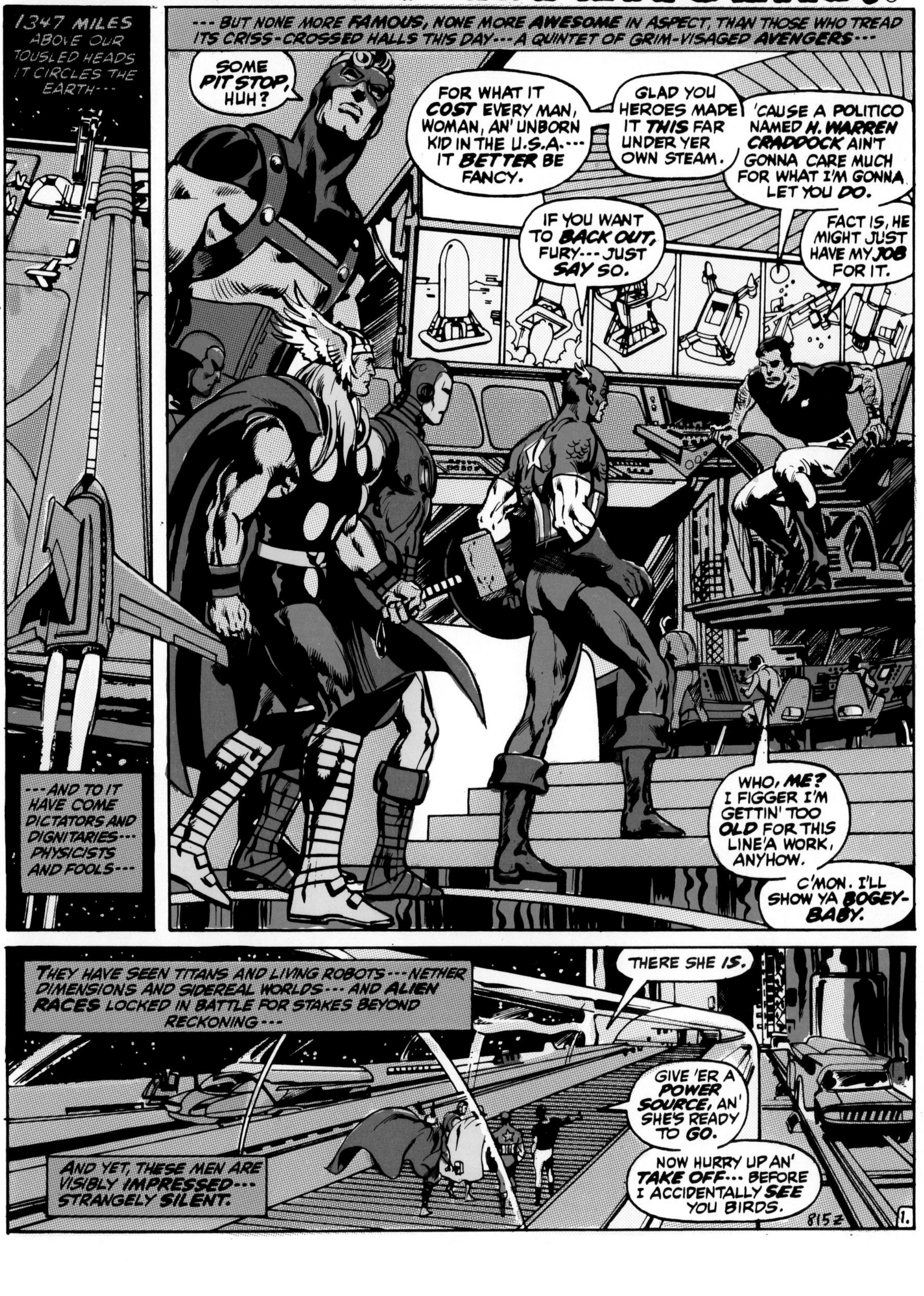

1347 MILES ABOVE OUR TOUSLED HEADS IT CIRCLES THE EARTH---
---BUT NONE MORE FAMOUS, NONE MORE AWESOME IN ASPECT, THAN THOSE WHO TREAD ITS CRISS-CROSSED HALLS THIS DAY---A QUINTET OF GRIM-VISAGED AVENGERS---
SOME PIT STOP, HUH?
FOR WHAT IT COST EVERY MAN, WOMAN, AN' UNBORN KID IN THE U.S.A.--- IT BETTER BE FANCY.
GLAD YOU HEROES MADE IT THIS FAR UNDER YER OWN STEAM.
'CAUSE A POLITICO NAMED H. WARREN CRADDOCK AIN'T GONNA CARE MUCH FOR WHAT I'M GONNA LET YOU DO.
IF YOU WANT TO BACK OUT, FURY---JUST SAY SO.
FACT IS, HE MIGHT JUST HAVE MY JOB FOR IT.
---AND TO IT HAVE COME DICTATORS AND DIGNITARIES--- PHYSICISTS AND FOOLS---
WHO, ME? I FIGGER I'M GETTIN' TOO OLD FOR THIS LINE'A WORK, ANYHOW.
C'MON. I'LL SHOW YA BOGEY-BABY.
THEY HAVE SEEN TITANS AND LIVING ROBOTS---NETHER DIMENSIONS AND SIDEREAL WORLDS---AND ALIEN RACES LOCKED IN BATTLE FOR STAKES BEYOND RECKONING---
THERE SHE IS.
GIVE 'ER A POWER SOURCE, AN' SHE'S READY TO GO.
AND YET, THESE MEN ARE VISIBLY IMPRESSED--- STRANGELY SILENT.
NOW HURRY UP AN' TAKE OFF... BEFORE I ACCIDENTALLY SEE YOU BIRDS.
815Z
1.

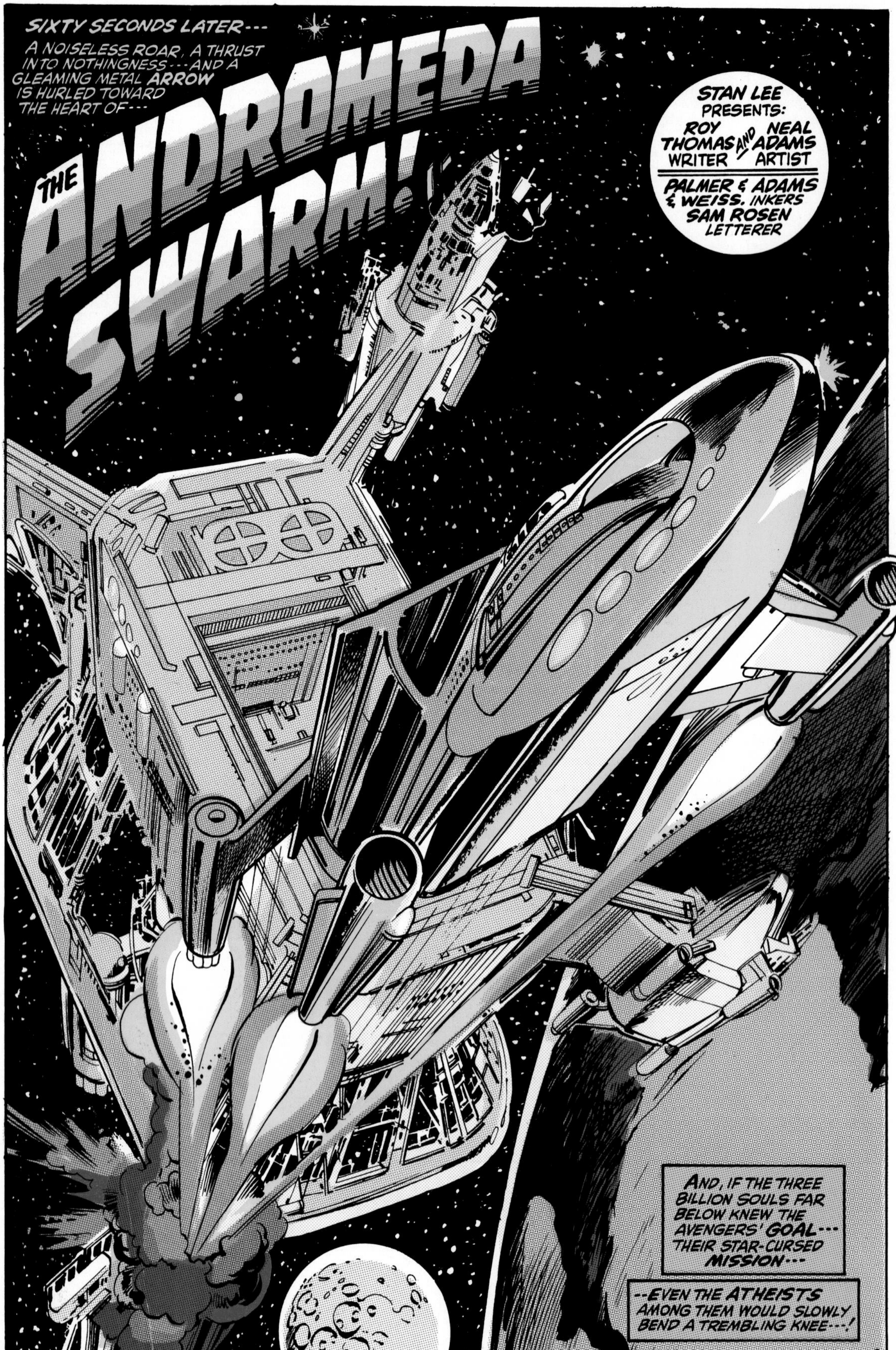
SIXTY SECONDS LATER---
A NOISELESS ROAR, A THRUST INTO NOTHINGNESS---AND A GLEAMING METAL ARROW IS HURLED TOWARD THE HEART OF---
THE ANDROMEDA SWARM!
STAN LEE PRESENTS: ROY THOMAS AND NEAL ADAMS WRITER ARTIST
PALMER & ADAMS & WEISS, INKERS SAM ROSEN LETTERER
AND, IF THE THREE BILLION SOULS FAR BELOW KNEW THE AVENGERS' GOAL--- THEIR STAR-CURSED MISSION---
--EVEN THE ATHEISTS AMONG THEM WOULD SLOWLY BEND A TREMBLING KNEE---!
2.

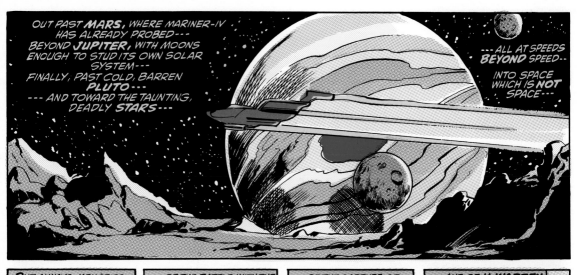

OUT PAST **MARS**, WHERE MARINER-IV HAS ALREADY PROBED--- BEYOND **JUPITER**, WITH MOONS ENOUGH TO STUD ITS OWN SOLAR SYSTEM--- FINALLY, PAST COLD, BARREN **PLUTO**--- --- AND TOWARD THE TAUNTING, DEADLY **STARS**···

--- ALL AT SPEEDS **BEYOND** SPEED··

INTO SPACE WHICH IS **NOT** SPACE···

BUT ALWAYS, MEMORIES OF **THREE FRIENDS**···

---HELD HOSTAGE BY THE **SKRULLS** IN THE **ANDROMEDA GALAXY**...

---OF THE BATTLE WITH THE **INHUMANS**, UNWILLING ALLIES OF THE SKRULLS' RIVALS, THE **KREE**···

--- OF THE CAPTURE OF **RICK JONES**, BY KREE-MEN FLEEING TO THEIR HOME WORLD···

---AND OF **H. WARREN CRADDOCK**, BAYING ETERNALLY AT THEIR HARRIED HEELS···

---HE WHO HAS NAMED THE AVENGERS **TRAITORS**, AND SWORN TO **HOUND** THEM TILL HE DIES---!

HO, VISION! THY MANNER BE FAR TOO **STERN**, E'EN FOR ONE WHO STANDS ON THE THRESHHOLD OF **ARMAGEDDON**.

FOR, SHALL WE NOT SOON **CLASH** WITH THOSE WHO HAVE SEIZED OUR FELLOW AVENGERS?

NOR COULD ANY CRAFT OF ANY NATION HAVE **SAILED** SO SWIFT, 'LESS POWERED BY SACRED **MJOLNIR**.

I'VE A HUNCH, THUNDER GOD, THAT THE **VISION** TAKES THE CAPTURE EVEN MORE--- **PERSONALLY**--- THAN **WE** DO. HE··

SLAP MY WRISTS FOR **INTERRUPTIN'** YA, SHELL-HEAD---

···BUT **LOOK!**

I **SEE** IT, GOLIATH.

AND, AT THIS STAGE-- I'M NOT SURE I'M **HAPPY** ABOUT IT!

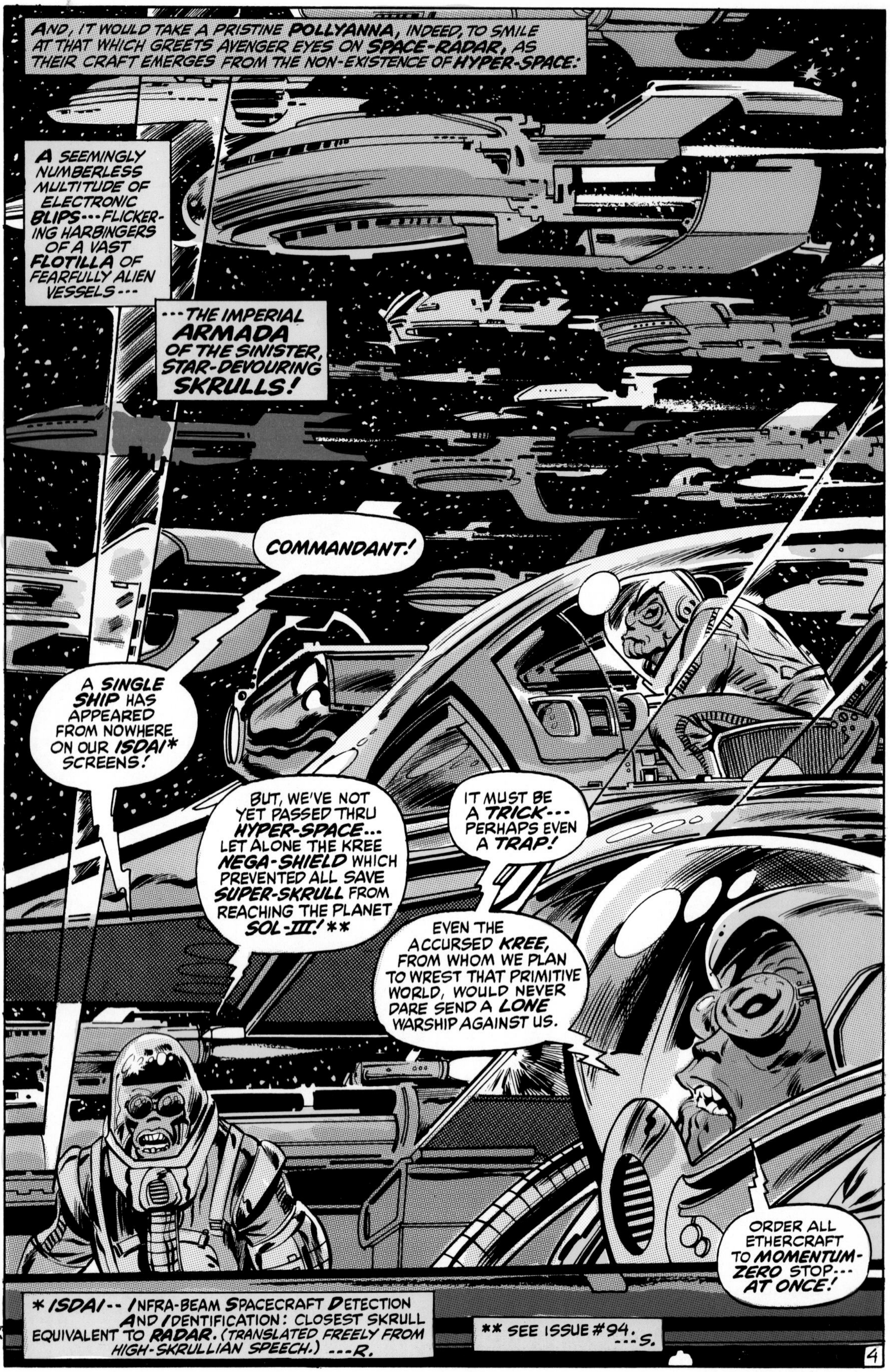
AND, IT WOULD TAKE A PRISTINE POLLYANNA, INDEED, TO SMILE AT THAT WHICH GREETS AVENGER EYES ON SPACE-RADAR, AS THEIR CRAFT EMERGES FROM THE NON-EXISTENCE OF HYPER-SPACE:
A SEEMINGLY NUMBERLESS MULTITUDE OF ELECTRONIC BLIPS--- FLICKERING HARBINGERS OF A VAST FLOTILLA OF FEARFULLY ALIEN VESSELS---
---THE IMPERIAL ARMADA OF THE SINISTER, STAR-DEVOURING SKRULLS!
COMMANDANT!
A SINGLE SHIP HAS APPEARED FROM NOWHERE ON OUR ISDAI* SCREENS!
BUT, WE'VE NOT YET PASSED THRU HYPER-SPACE... LET ALONE THE KREE NEGA-SHIELD WHICH PREVENTED ALL SAVE SUPER-SKRULL FROM REACHING THE PLANET SOL-III! **
IT MUST BE A TRICK--- PERHAPS EVEN A TRAP!
EVEN THE ACCURSED KREE, FROM WHOM WE PLAN TO WREST THAT PRIMITIVE WORLD, WOULD NEVER DARE SEND A LONE WARSHIP AGAINST US.
ORDER ALL ETHERCRAFT TO MOMENTUM-ZERO STOP--- AT ONCE!
* ISDAI -- INFRA-BEAM SPACECRAFT DETECTION AND IDENTIFICATION: CLOSEST SKRULL EQUIVALENT TO RADAR. (TRANSLATED FREELY FROM HIGH-SKRULLIAN SPEECH.) ---R.
** SEE ISSUE #94. ---S.
4

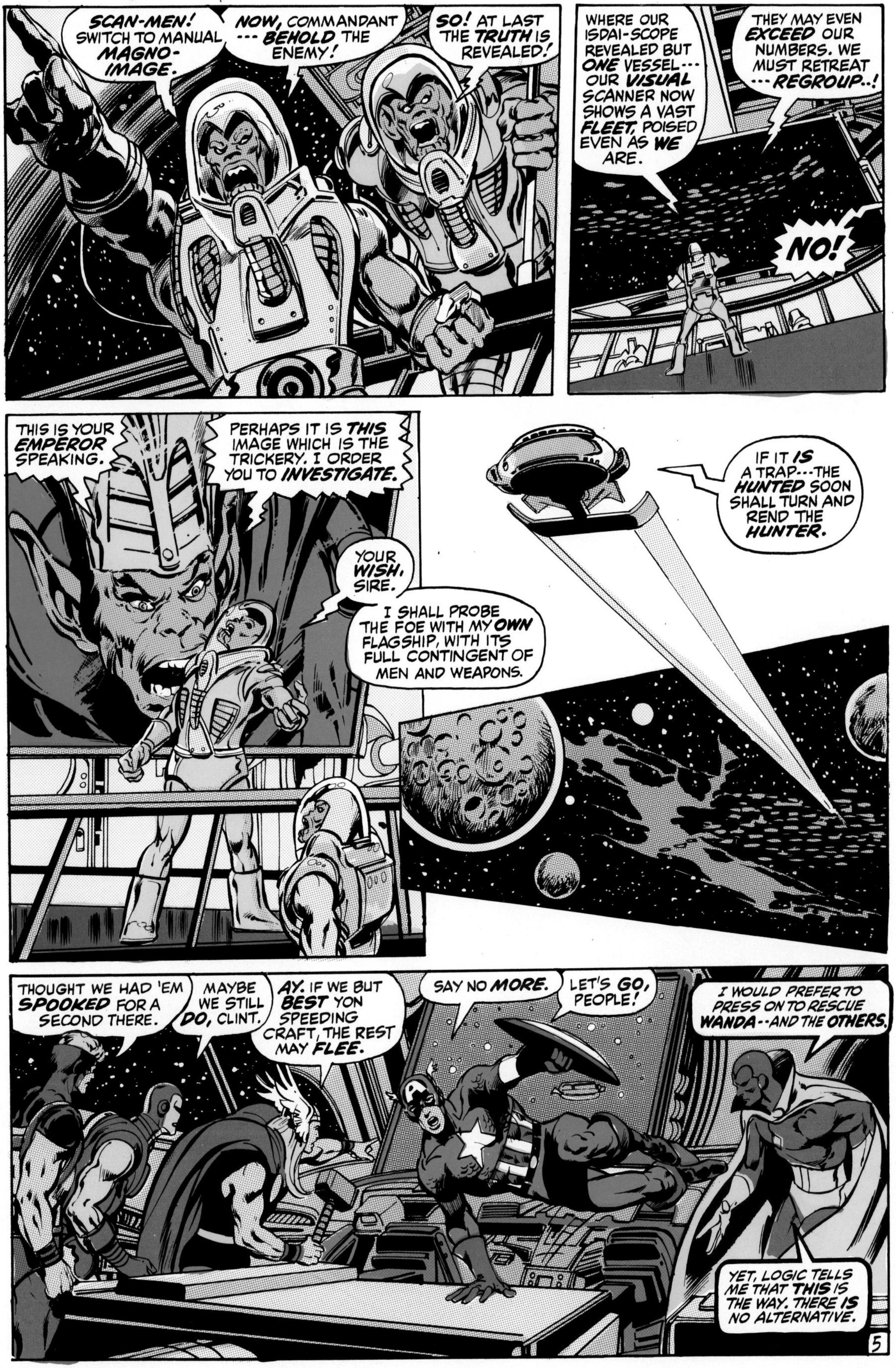
SCAN-MEN! SWITCH TO MANUAL MAGNO-IMAGE.
NOW, COMMANDANT --- BEHOLD THE ENEMY!
SO! AT LAST THE TRUTH IS REVEALED!
WHERE OUR ISDAI-SCOPE REVEALED BUT ONE VESSEL--- OUR VISUAL SCANNER NOW SHOWS A VAST FLEET, POISED EVEN AS WE ARE.
THEY MAY EVEN EXCEED OUR NUMBERS. WE MUST RETREAT --- REGROUP..!
NO!
THIS IS YOUR EMPEROR SPEAKING.
PERHAPS IT IS THIS IMAGE WHICH IS THE TRICKERY. I ORDER YOU TO INVESTIGATE.
YOUR WISH, SIRE.
I SHALL PROBE THE FOE WITH MY OWN FLAGSHIP, WITH ITS FULL CONTINGENT OF MEN AND WEAPONS.
IF IT IS A TRAP---THE HUNTED SOON SHALL TURN AND REND THE HUNTER.
THOUGHT WE HAD 'EM SPOOKED FOR A SECOND THERE.
MAYBE WE STILL DO, CLINT.
AY. IF WE BUT BEST YON SPEEDING CRAFT, THE REST MAY FLEE.
SAY NO MORE.
LET'S GO, PEOPLE!
I WOULD PREFER TO PRESS ON TO RESCUE WANDA--AND THE OTHERS.
YET, LOGIC TELLS ME THAT THIS IS THE WAY. THERE IS NO ALTERNATIVE.

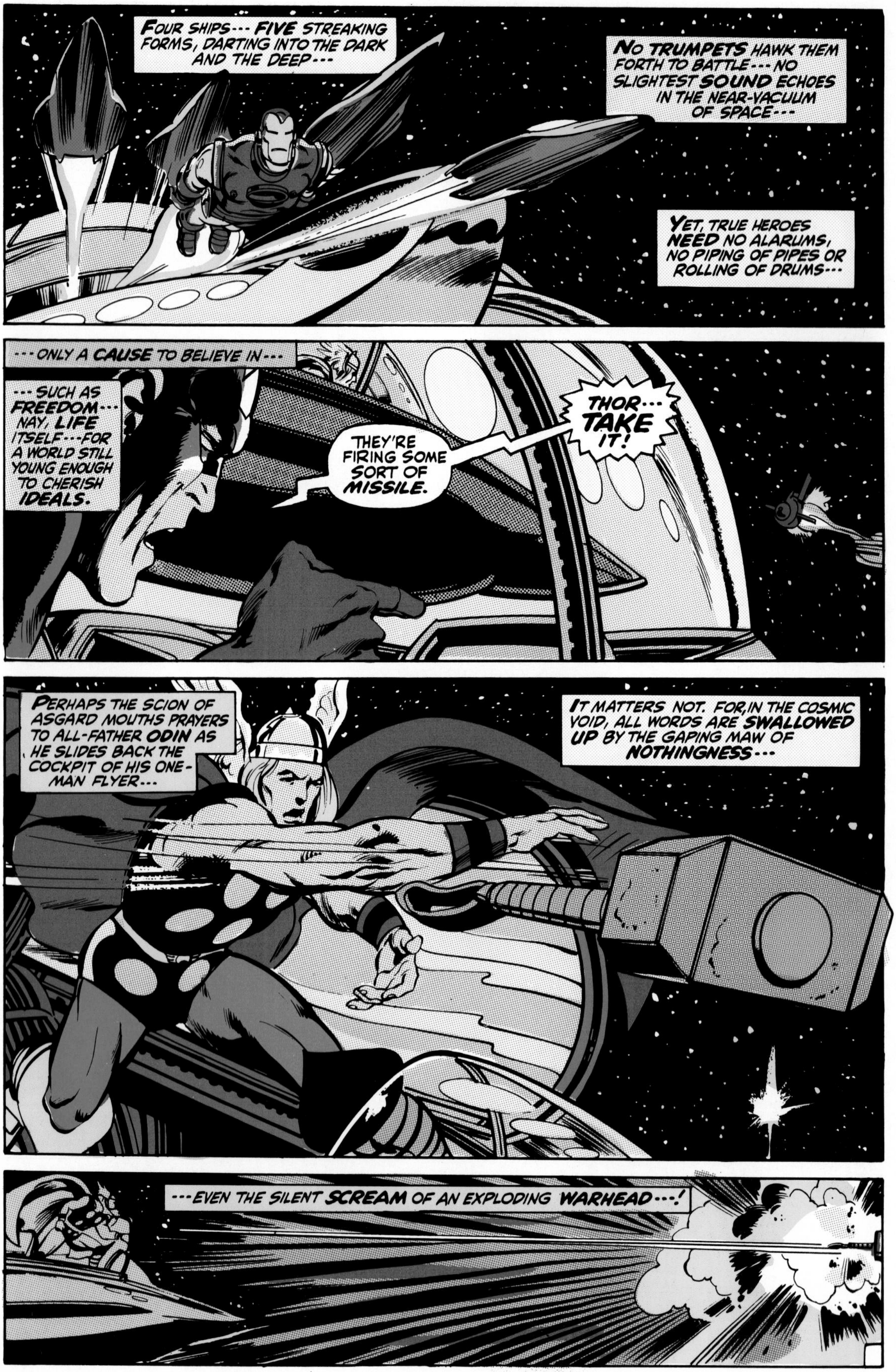
FOUR SHIPS--- FIVE STREAKING FORMS, DARTING INTO THE DARK AND THE DEEP---
NO TRUMPETS HAWK THEM FORTH TO BATTLE--- NO SLIGHTEST SOUND ECHOES IN THE NEAR-VACUUM OF SPACE---
YET, TRUE HEROES NEED NO ALARUMS, NO PIPING OF PIPES OR ROLLING OF DRUMS---
---ONLY A CAUSE TO BELIEVE IN---
---SUCH AS FREEDOM--- NAY, LIFE ITSELF---FOR A WORLD STILL YOUNG ENOUGH TO CHERISH IDEALS.
THEY'RE FIRING SOME SORT OF MISSILE.
THOR--- TAKE IT!
PERHAPS THE SCION OF ASGARD MOUTHS PRAYERS TO ALL-FATHER ODIN AS HE SLIDES BACK THE COCKPIT OF HIS ONE-MAN FLYER---
IT MATTERS NOT. FOR, IN THE COSMIC VOID, ALL WORDS ARE SWALLOWED UP BY THE GAPING MAW OF NOTHINGNESS---
---EVEN THE SILENT SCREAM OF AN EXPLODING WARHEAD---!

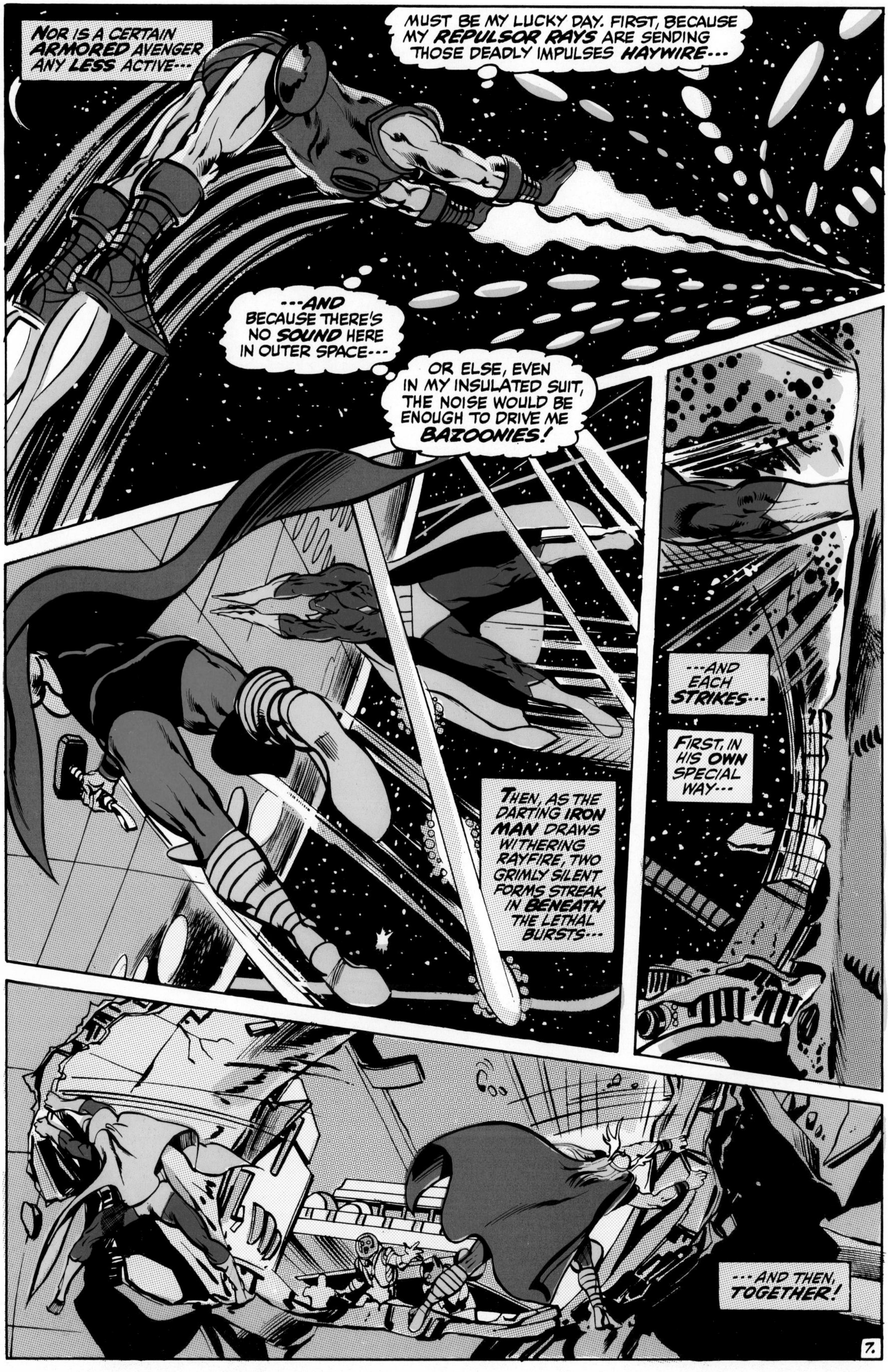
NOR IS A CERTAIN ARMORED AVENGER ANY LESS ACTIVE---
MUST BE MY LUCKY DAY. FIRST, BECAUSE MY REPULSOR RAYS ARE SENDING THOSE DEADLY IMPULSES HAYWIRE---
---AND BECAUSE THERE'S NO SOUND HERE IN OUTER SPACE---
OR ELSE, EVEN IN MY INSULATED SUIT, THE NOISE WOULD BE ENOUGH TO DRIVE ME BAZOONIES!
THEN, AS THE DARTING IRON MAN DRAWS WITHERING RAYFIRE, TWO GRIMLY SILENT FORMS STREAK IN BENEATH THE LETHAL BURSTS---
---AND EACH STRIKES---
FIRST, IN HIS OWN SPECIAL WAY---
---AND THEN, TOGETHER!
7.

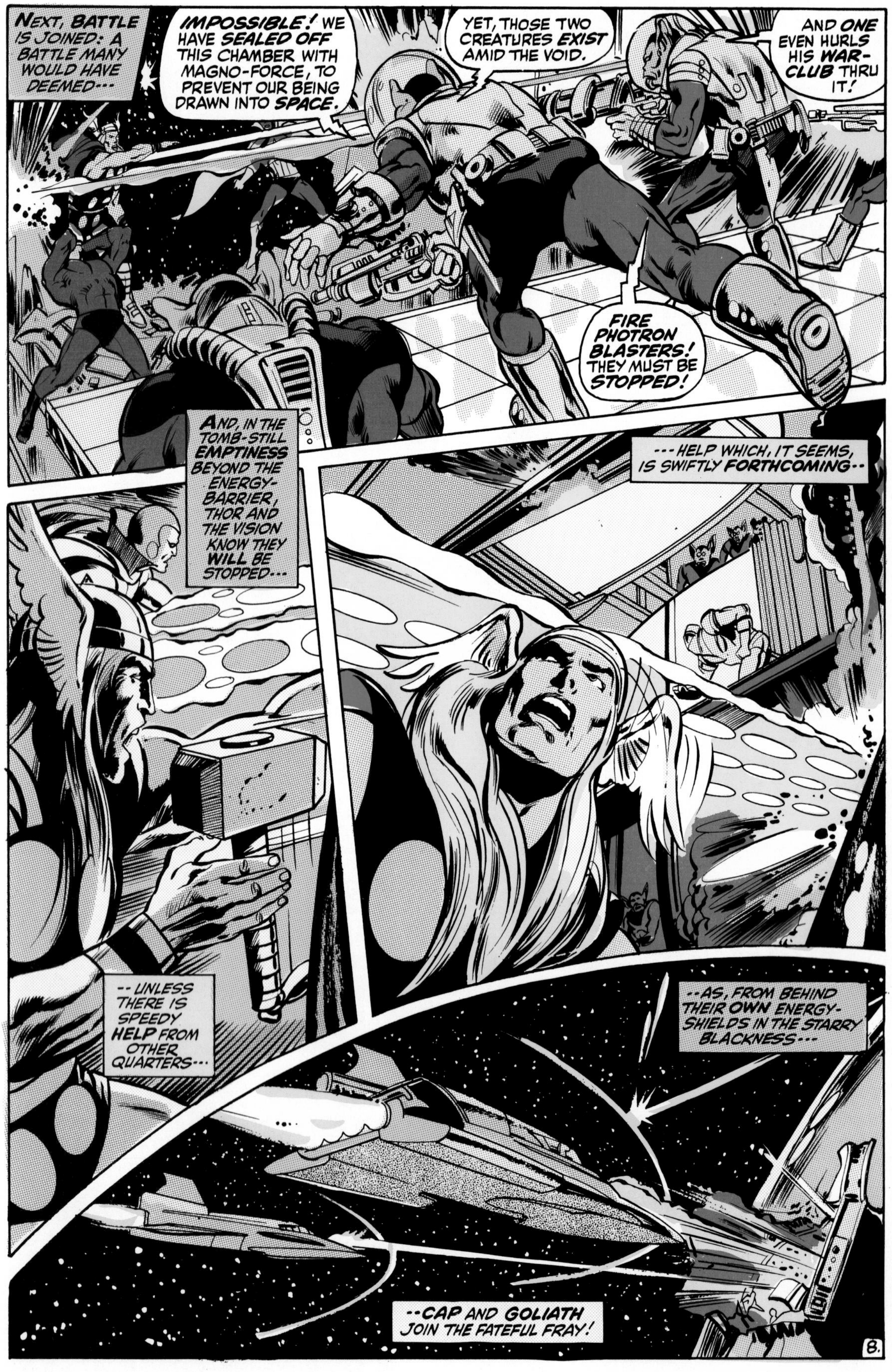
NEXT, BATTLE IS JOINED: A BATTLE MANY WOULD HAVE DEEMED---
IMPOSSIBLE! WE HAVE SEALED OFF THIS CHAMBER WITH MAGNO-FORCE, TO PREVENT OUR BEING DRAWN INTO SPACE.
YET, THOSE TWO CREATURES EXIST AMID THE VOID.
AND ONE EVEN HURLS HIS WAR-CLUB THRU IT!
FIRE PHOTRON BLASTERS! THEY MUST BE STOPPED!
AND, IN THE TOMB-STILL EMPTINESS BEYOND THE ENERGY-BARRIER, THOR AND THE VISION KNOW THEY WILL BE STOPPED---
--UNLESS THERE IS SPEEDY HELP FROM OTHER QUARTERS---
---HELP WHICH, IT SEEMS, IS SWIFTLY FORTHCOMING--
--AS, FROM BEHIND THEIR OWN ENERGY-SHIELDS IN THE STARRY BLACKNESS---
--CAP AND GOLIATH JOIN THE FATEFUL FRAY!

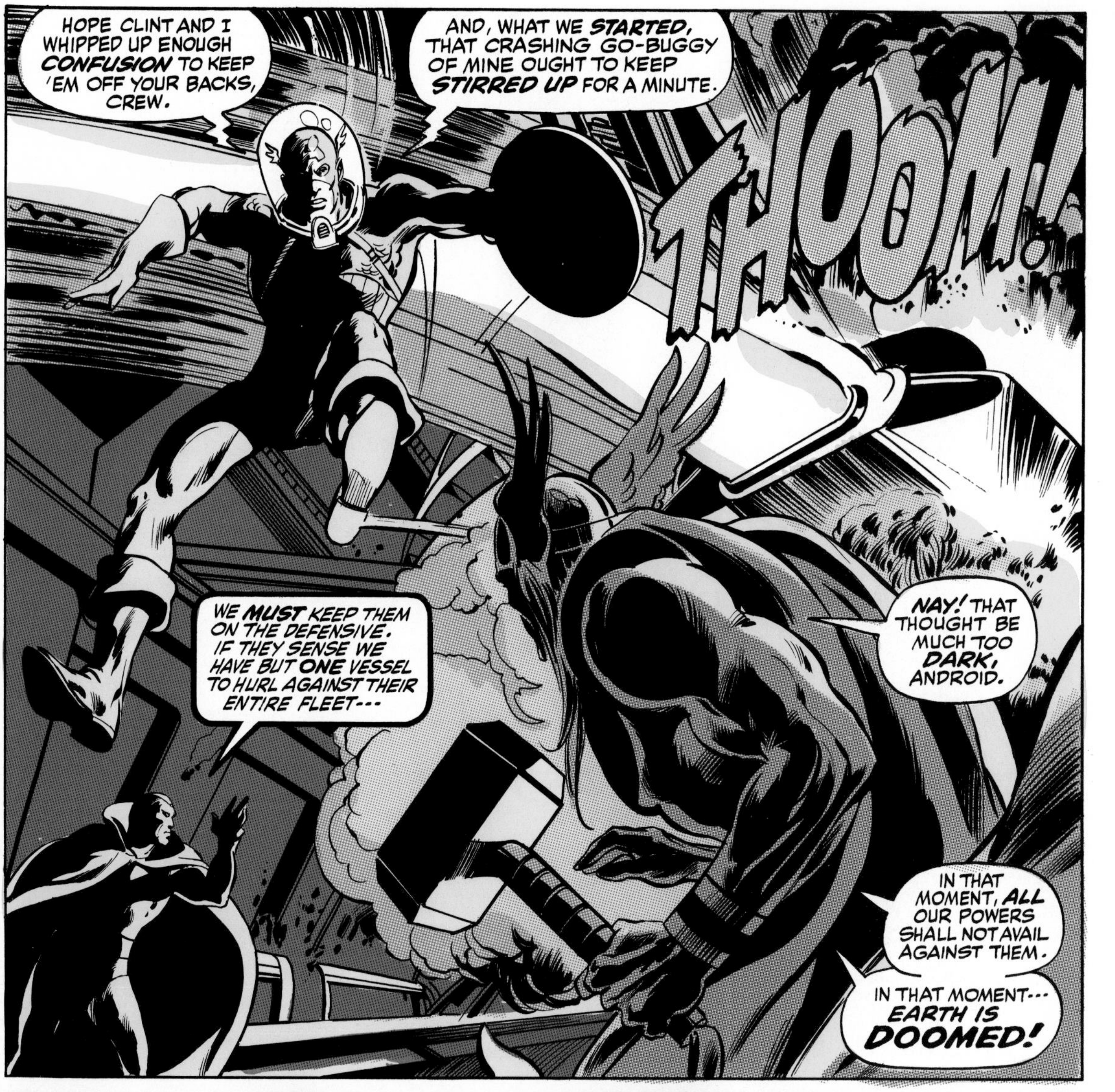
HOPE CLINT AND I WHIPPED UP ENOUGH CONFUSION TO KEEP 'EM OFF YOUR BACKS, CREW.
AND, WHAT WE STARTED, THAT CRASHING GO-BUGGY OF MINE OUGHT TO KEEP STIRRED UP FOR A MINUTE.
THOOM!
WE MUST KEEP THEM ON THE DEFENSIVE. IF THEY SENSE WE HAVE BUT ONE VESSEL TO HURL AGAINST THEIR ENTIRE FLEET---
NAY! THAT THOUGHT BE MUCH TOO DARK, ANDROID.
IN THAT MOMENT, ALL OUR POWERS SHALL NOT AVAIL AGAINST THEM.
IN THAT MOMENT--- EARTH IS DOOMED!

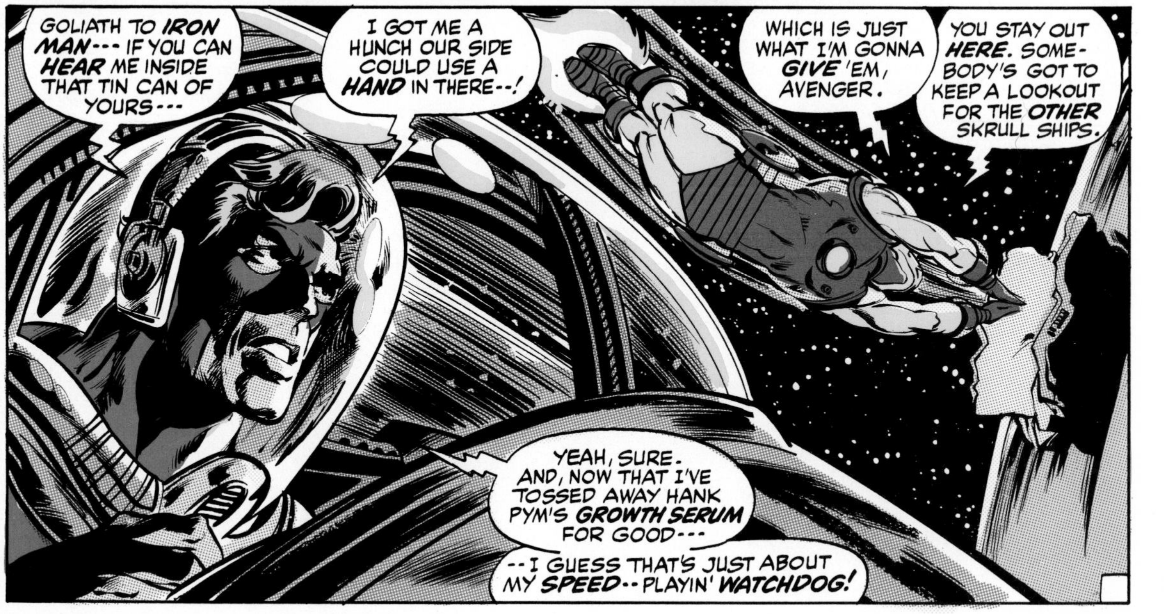
GOLIATH TO IRON MAN--- IF YOU CAN HEAR ME INSIDE THAT TIN CAN OF YOURS---
I GOT ME A HUNCH OUR SIDE COULD USE A HAND IN THERE--!
WHICH IS JUST WHAT I'M GONNA GIVE 'EM, AVENGER.
YOU STAY OUT HERE. SOME-BODY'S GOT TO KEEP A LOOKOUT FOR THE OTHER SKRULL SHIPS.
YEAH, SURE. AND, NOW THAT I'VE TOSSED AWAY HANK PYM'S GROWTH SERUM FOR GOOD---
--I GUESS THAT'S JUST ABOUT MY SPEED--PLAYIN' WATCHDOG!

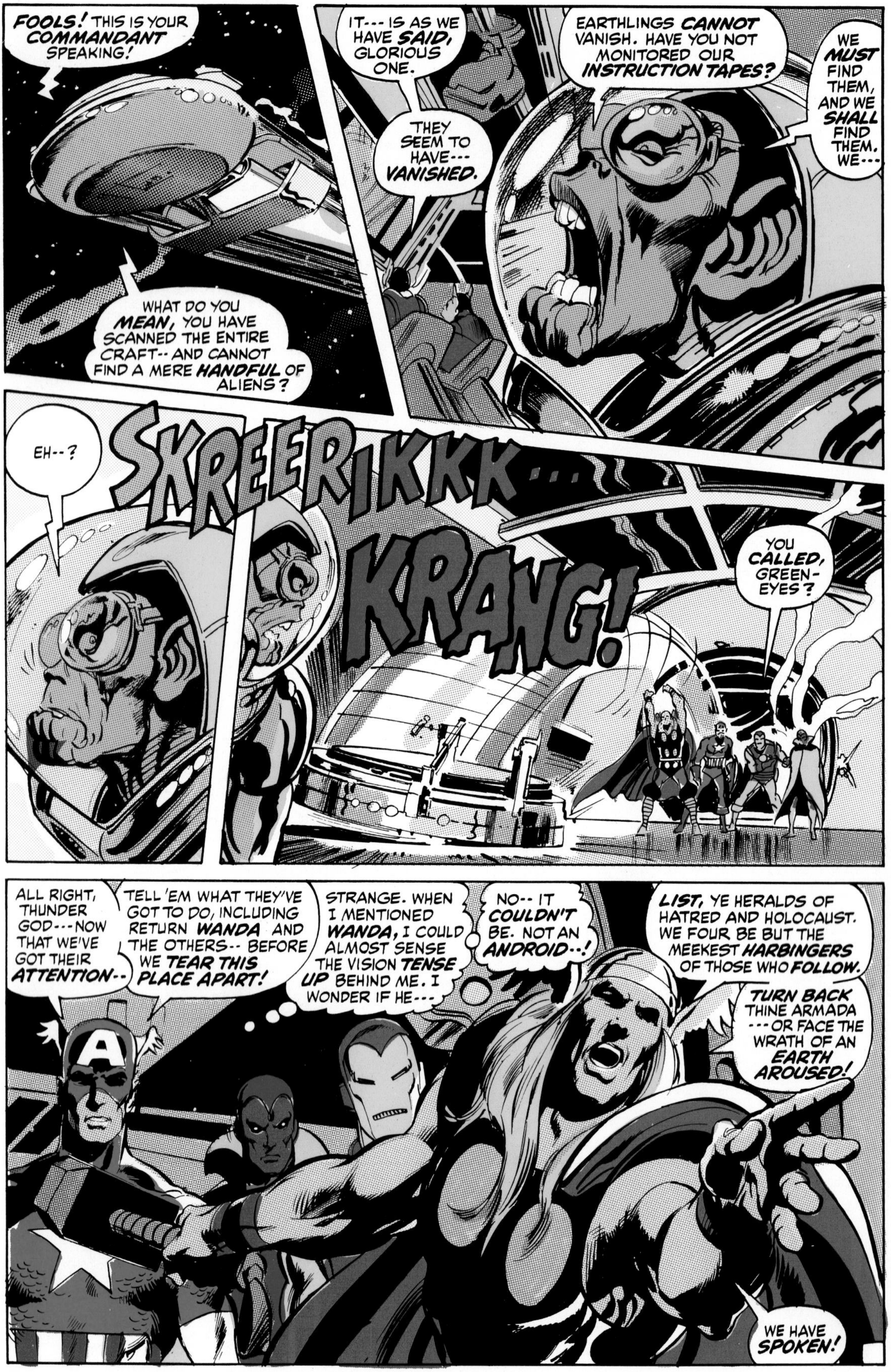
FOOLS! THIS IS YOUR COMMANDANT SPEAKING!
WHAT DO YOU MEAN, YOU HAVE SCANNED THE ENTIRE CRAFT-- AND CANNOT FIND A MERE HANDFUL OF ALIENS?
IT--- IS AS WE HAVE SAID, GLORIOUS ONE.
THEY SEEM TO HAVE--- VANISHED.
EARTHLINGS CANNOT VANISH. HAVE YOU NOT MONITORED OUR INSTRUCTION TAPES?
WE MUST FIND THEM, AND WE SHALL FIND THEM. WE---
EH--?
SKREERIKKK...
KRANG!
YOU CALLED, GREEN-EYES?
ALL RIGHT, THUNDER GOD---NOW THAT WE'VE GOT THEIR ATTENTION--
TELL 'EM WHAT THEY'VE GOT TO DO, INCLUDING RETURN WANDA AND THE OTHERS-- BEFORE WE TEAR THIS PLACE APART!
STRANGE. WHEN I MENTIONED WANDA, I COULD ALMOST SENSE THE VISION TENSE UP BEHIND ME. I WONDER IF HE---
NO-- IT COULDN'T BE. NOT AN ANDROID--!
LIST, YE HERALDS OF HATRED AND HOLOCAUST. WE FOUR BE BUT THE MEEKEST HARBINGERS OF THOSE WHO FOLLOW.
TURN BACK THINE ARMADA ---OR FACE THE WRATH OF AN EARTH AROUSED!
WE HAVE SPOKEN!

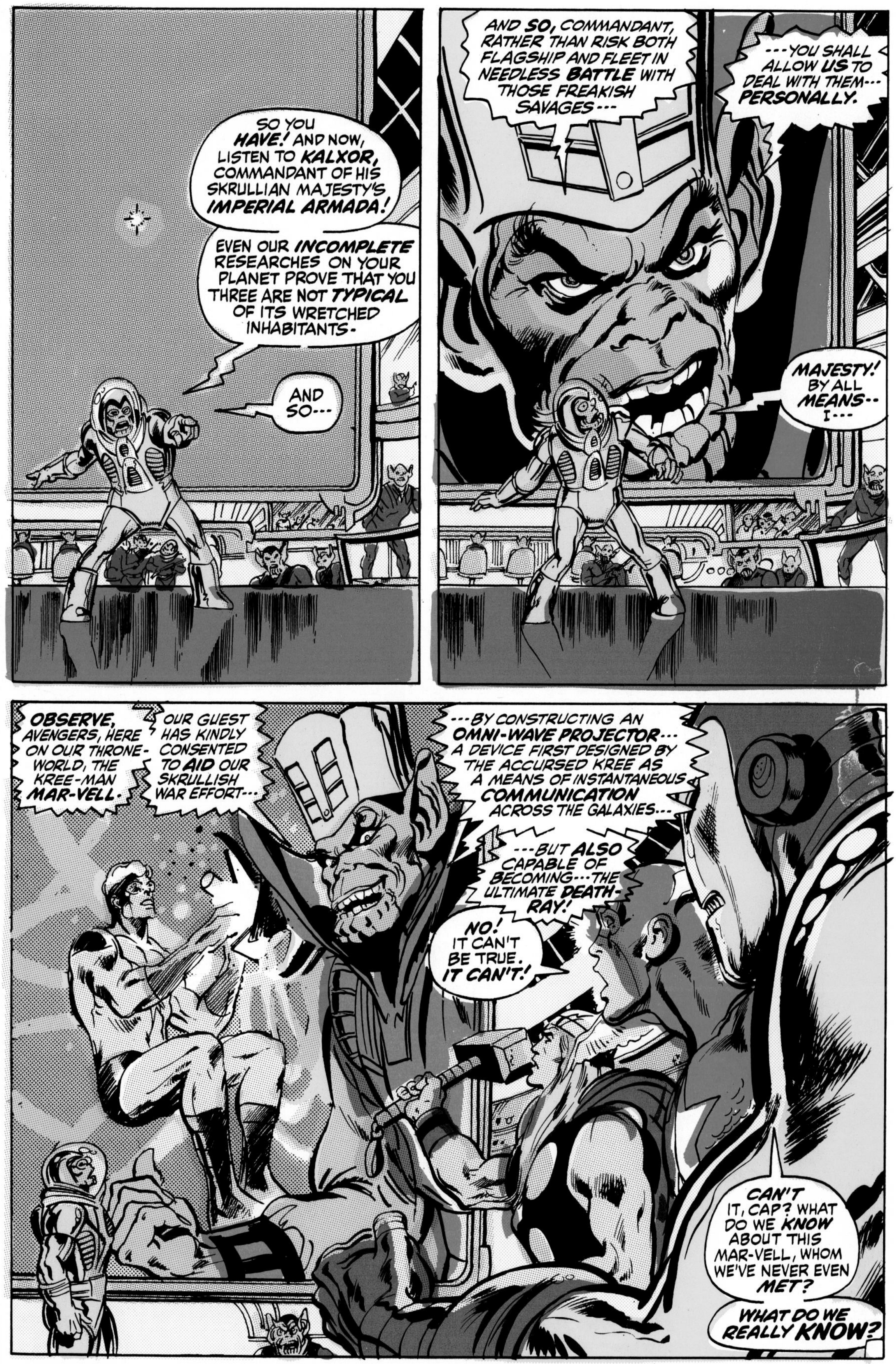
SO YOU HAVE! AND NOW, LISTEN TO KALXOR, COMMANDANT OF HIS SKRULLIAN MAJESTY'S IMPERIAL ARMADA!
EVEN OUR INCOMPLETE RESEARCHES ON YOUR PLANET PROVE THAT YOU THREE ARE NOT TYPICAL OF ITS WRETCHED INHABITANTS-
AND SO---
AND SO, COMMANDANT, RATHER THAN RISK BOTH FLAGSHIP AND FLEET IN NEEDLESS BATTLE WITH THOSE FREAKISH SAVAGES---
---YOU SHALL ALLOW US TO DEAL WITH THEM--- PERSONALLY.
MAJESTY! BY ALL MEANS-- I---
OBSERVE, AVENGERS, HERE ON OUR THRONE-WORLD, THE KREE-MAN MAR-VELL.
OUR GUEST HAS KINDLY CONSENTED TO AID OUR SKRULLISH WAR EFFORT---
---BY CONSTRUCTING AN OMNI-WAVE PROJECTOR--- A DEVICE FIRST DESIGNED BY THE ACCURSED KREE AS A MEANS OF INSTANTANEOUS COMMUNICATION ACROSS THE GALAXIES---
---BUT ALSO CAPABLE OF BECOMING--- THE ULTIMATE DEATH-RAY!
NO! IT CAN'T BE TRUE. IT CAN'T!
CAN'T IT, CAP? WHAT DO WE KNOW ABOUT THIS MAR-VELL, WHOM WE'VE NEVER EVEN MET?
WHAT DO WE REALLY KNOW?

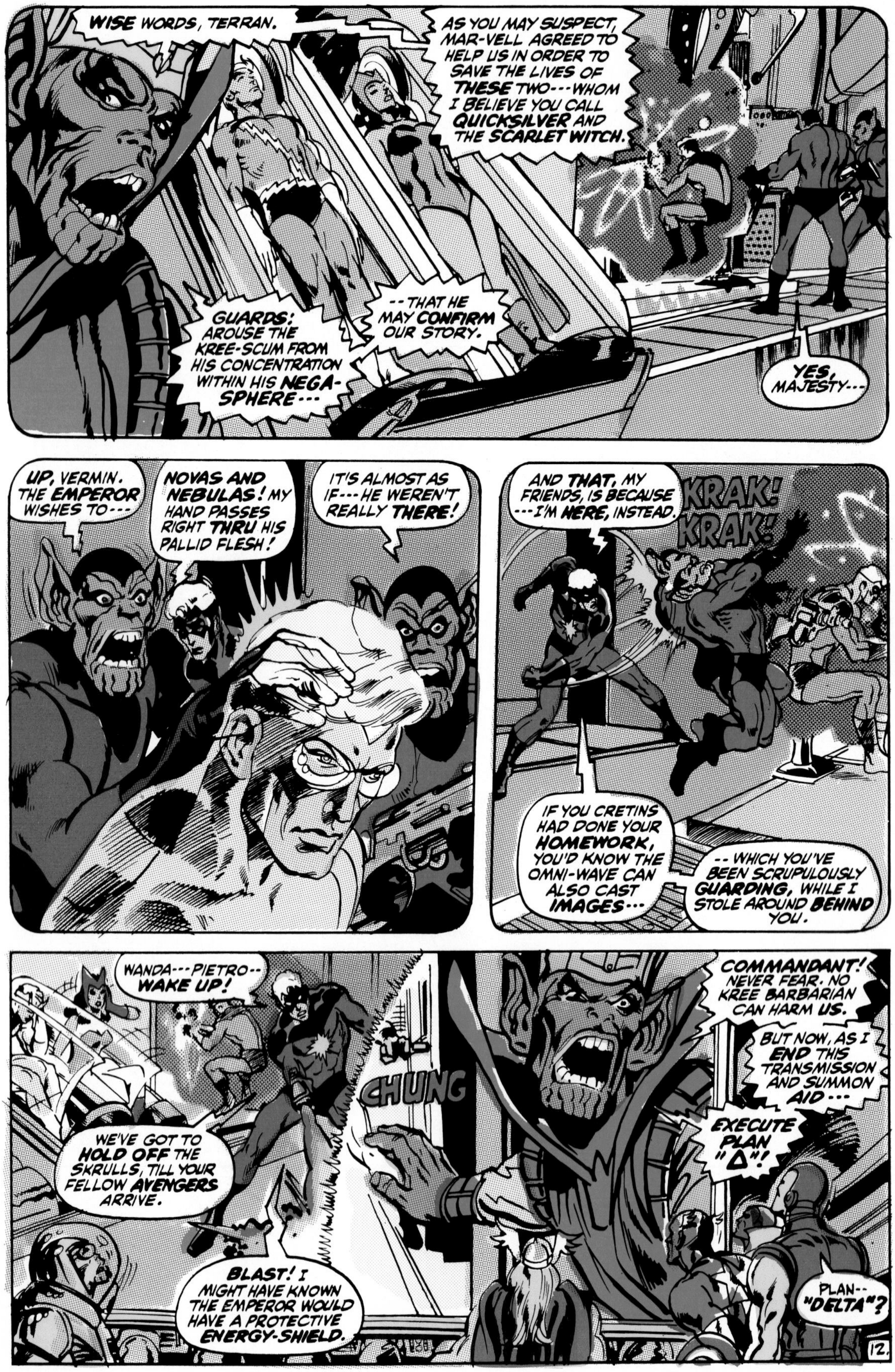
WISE WORDS, TERRAN.
AS YOU MAY SUSPECT, MAR-VELL AGREED TO HELP US IN ORDER TO SAVE THE LIVES OF THESE TWO--- WHOM I BELIEVE YOU CALL QUICKSILVER AND THE SCARLET WITCH.
GUARDS: AROUSE THE KREE-SCUM FROM HIS CONCENTRATION WITHIN HIS NEGA-SPHERE---
--THAT HE MAY CONFIRM OUR STORY.
YES, MAJESTY---
UP, VERMIN. THE EMPEROR WISHES TO---
NOVAS AND NEBULAS! MY HAND PASSES RIGHT THRU HIS PALLID FLESH!
IT'S ALMOST AS IF--- HE WEREN'T REALLY THERE!
AND THAT, MY FRIENDS, IS BECAUSE --- I'M HERE, INSTEAD.
KRAK! KRAK!
IF YOU CRETINS HAD DONE YOUR HOMEWORK, YOU'D KNOW THE OMNI-WAVE CAN ALSO CAST IMAGES---
-- WHICH YOU'VE BEEN SCRUPULOUSLY GUARDING, WHILE I STOLE AROUND BEHIND YOU.
WANDA--- PIETRO-- WAKE UP!
CHUNG
WE'VE GOT TO HOLD OFF THE SKRULLS, TILL YOUR FELLOW AVENGERS ARRIVE.
BLAST! I MIGHT HAVE KNOWN THE EMPEROR WOULD HAVE A PROTECTIVE ENERGY-SHIELD.
COMMANDANT! NEVER FEAR. NO KREE BARBARIAN CAN HARM US.
BUT NOW, AS I END THIS TRANSMISSION AND SUMMON AID---
EXECUTE PLAN "Δ"!
PLAN-- "DELTA"?
12.

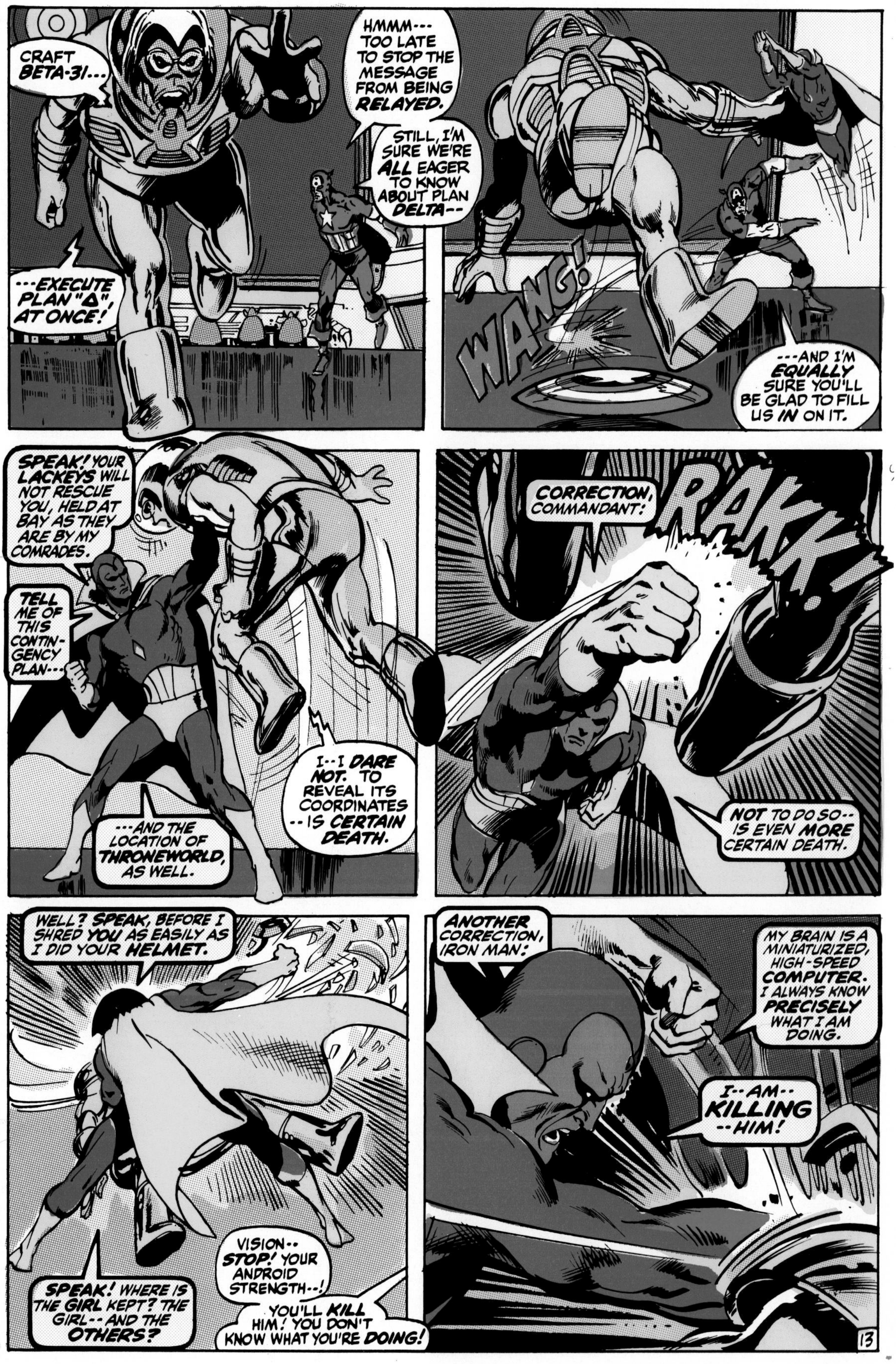
CRAFT BETA-31...
...EXECUTE PLAN "Δ", AT ONCE!
HMMM--- TOO LATE TO STOP THE MESSAGE FROM BEING RELAYED.
STILL, I'M SURE WE'RE ALL EAGER TO KNOW ABOUT PLAN DELTA--
WANG!
---AND I'M EQUALLY SURE YOU'LL BE GLAD TO FILL US IN ON IT.
SPEAK! YOUR LACKEYS WILL NOT RESCUE YOU, HELD AT BAY AS THEY ARE BY MY COMRADES.
TELL ME OF THIS CONTINGENCY PLAN...
...AND THE LOCATION OF THRONEWORLD, AS WELL.
I--I DARE NOT. TO REVEAL ITS COORDINATES --IS CERTAIN DEATH.
CORRECTION, COMMANDANT:
RAKK!
NOT TO DO SO-- IS EVEN MORE CERTAIN DEATH.
WELL? SPEAK, BEFORE I SHRED YOU AS EASILY AS I DID YOUR HELMET.
SPEAK! WHERE IS THE GIRL KEPT? THE GIRL--AND THE OTHERS?
VISION-- STOP! YOUR ANDROID STRENGTH--!
YOU'LL KILL HIM! YOU DON'T KNOW WHAT YOU'RE DOING!
ANOTHER CORRECTION, IRON MAN:
MY BRAIN IS A MINIATURIZED, HIGH-SPEED COMPUTER. I ALWAYS KNOW PRECISELY WHAT I AM DOING.
I--AM-- KILLING --HIM!
13

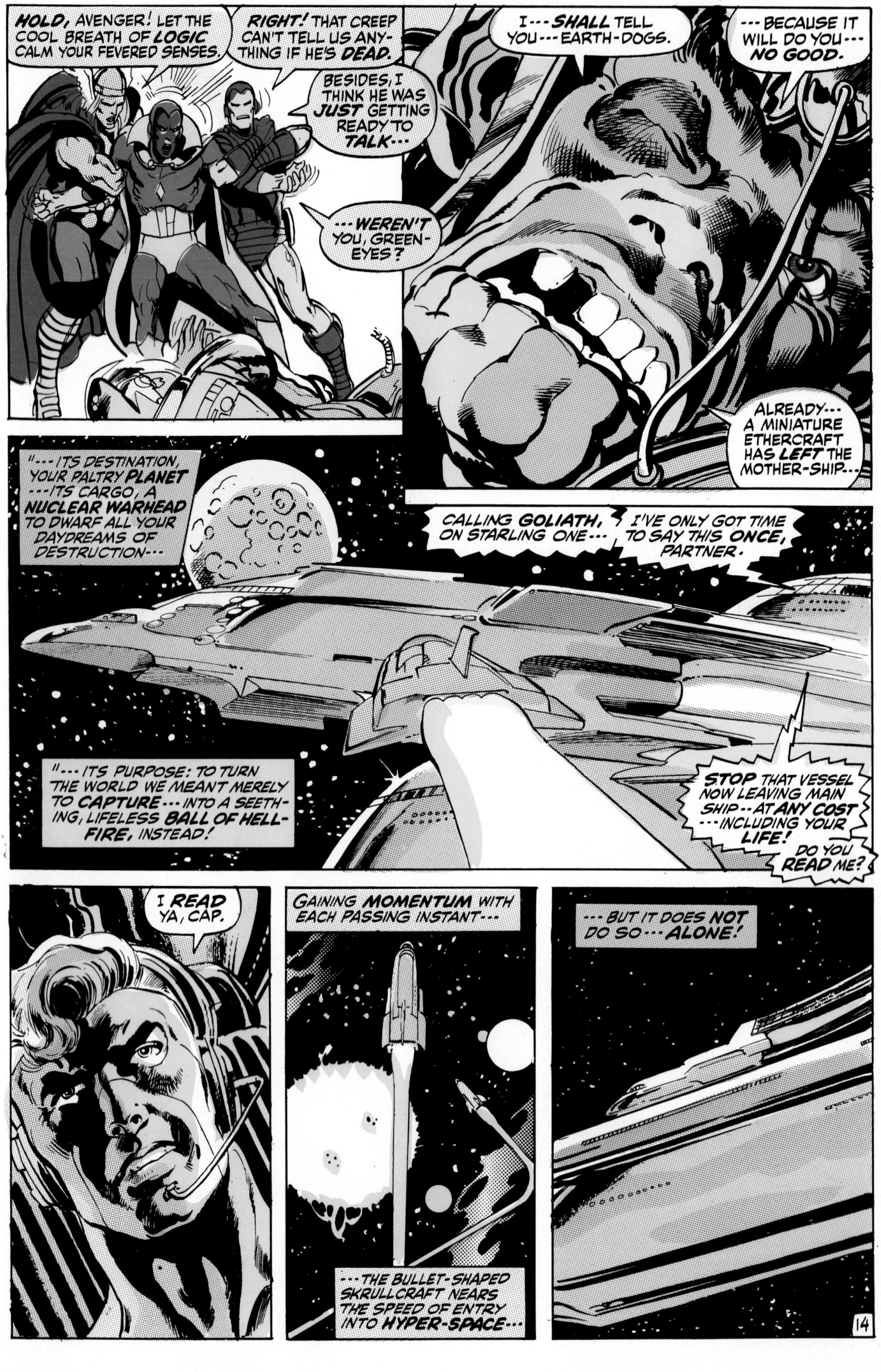
HOLD, AVENGER! LET THE COOL BREATH OF LOGIC CALM YOUR FEVERED SENSES.
RIGHT! THAT CREEP CAN'T TELL US ANYTHING IF HE'S DEAD.
BESIDES, I THINK HE WAS JUST GETTING READY TO TALK---
---WEREN'T YOU, GREEN-EYES?
I---SHALL TELL YOU---EARTH-DOGS.
---BECAUSE IT WILL DO YOU---NO GOOD.
ALREADY---A MINIATURE ETHERCRAFT HAS LEFT THE MOTHER-SHIP---
"---ITS DESTINATION, YOUR PALTRY PLANET---ITS CARGO, A NUCLEAR WARHEAD TO DWARF ALL YOUR DAYDREAMS OF DESTRUCTION---
"---ITS PURPOSE: TO TURN THE WORLD WE MEANT MERELY TO CAPTURE---INTO A SEETHING, LIFELESS BALL OF HELL-FIRE, INSTEAD!
CALLING GOLIATH, ON STARLING ONE---
I'VE ONLY GOT TIME TO SAY THIS ONCE, PARTNER.
STOP THAT VESSEL NOW LEAVING MAIN SHIP--AT ANY COST---INCLUDING YOUR LIFE!
DO YOU READ ME?
I READ YA, CAP.
GAINING MOMENTUM WITH EACH PASSING INSTANT---
---THE BULLET-SHAPED SKRULLCRAFT NEARS THE SPEED OF ENTRY INTO HYPER-SPACE---
---BUT IT DOES NOT DO SO---ALONE!
14

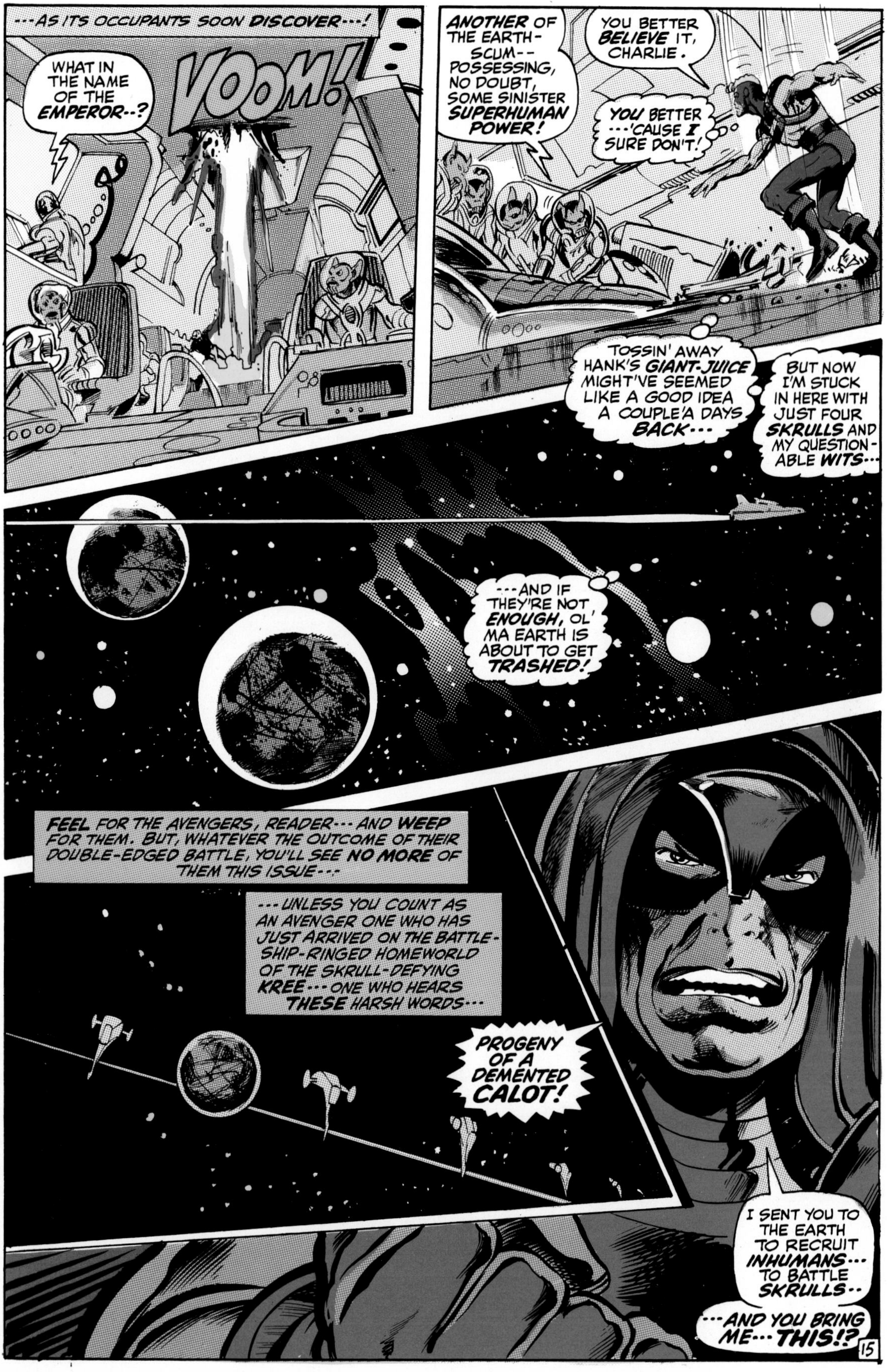

---AS ITS OCCUPANTS SOON DISCOVER---!
VOOM!
WHAT IN THE NAME OF THE EMPEROR--?
ANOTHER OF THE EARTH-SCUM--POSSESSING, NO DOUBT, SOME SINISTER SUPERHUMAN POWER!
YOU BETTER BELIEVE IT, CHARLIE.
YOU BETTER---'CAUSE I SURE DON'T!
TOSSIN' AWAY HANK'S GIANT-JUICE MIGHT'VE SEEMED LIKE A GOOD IDEA A COUPLE'A DAYS BACK---
BUT NOW I'M STUCK IN HERE WITH JUST FOUR SKRULLS AND MY QUESTION-ABLE WITS---
---AND IF THEY'RE NOT ENOUGH, OL' MA EARTH IS ABOUT TO GET TRASHED!
FEEL FOR THE AVENGERS, READER--- AND WEEP FOR THEM. BUT, WHATEVER THE OUTCOME OF THEIR DOUBLE-EDGED BATTLE, YOU'LL SEE NO MORE OF THEM THIS ISSUE---
---UNLESS YOU COUNT AS AN AVENGER ONE WHO HAS JUST ARRIVED ON THE BATTLE-SHIP-RINGED HOMEWORLD OF THE SKRULL-DEFYING KREE--- ONE WHO HEARS THESE HARSH WORDS---
PROGENY OF A DEMENTED CALOT!
I SENT YOU TO THE EARTH TO RECRUIT INHUMANS--- TO BATTLE SKRULLS--
---AND YOU BRING ME--- THIS!?

IF I'M TOO SCRAWNY FOR YA, RONAN, YOU'RE WELCOME TO THROW ME BACK.

SILENCE, WHELP! YOU KREE! WHICH OF YOU SALVAGED THAT LAMENTABLE SPECIMEN FROM THE JAWS OF DEFEAT--- AND WHY?*

I--- DO NOT KNOW, SUPREMOR- I SEIZED HIM ON--- A MOMENTARY IMPULSE.

THEN GIVE THANKS THAT YOUR LEADER STIFLES HIS IMPULSE TO---

HOLD! I HAVE SEEN THE EARTH-SPAWN BEFORE.

*LAST ISH, THE AVENGERS BLASTED A PLOT TO TURN THE UNCANNY INHUMANS INTO A KREE-DIRECTED ARMY. ---STAN.

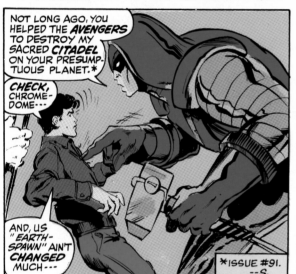

NOT LONG AGO, YOU HELPED THE AVENGERS TO DESTROY MY SACRED CITADEL ON YOUR PRESUMPTUOUS PLANET.*

CHECK, CHROME-DOME---

AND, US "EARTH-SPAWN" AIN'T CHANGED MUCH---

*ISSUE #91. --S.

-- RICK JONES STILL DON'T DIG BEIN' LEANED ON!

SKAK!

THERE! IF THAT DON'T MAKE MY POINT, THEN NOTHIN' EVER---

-- WILL.

16

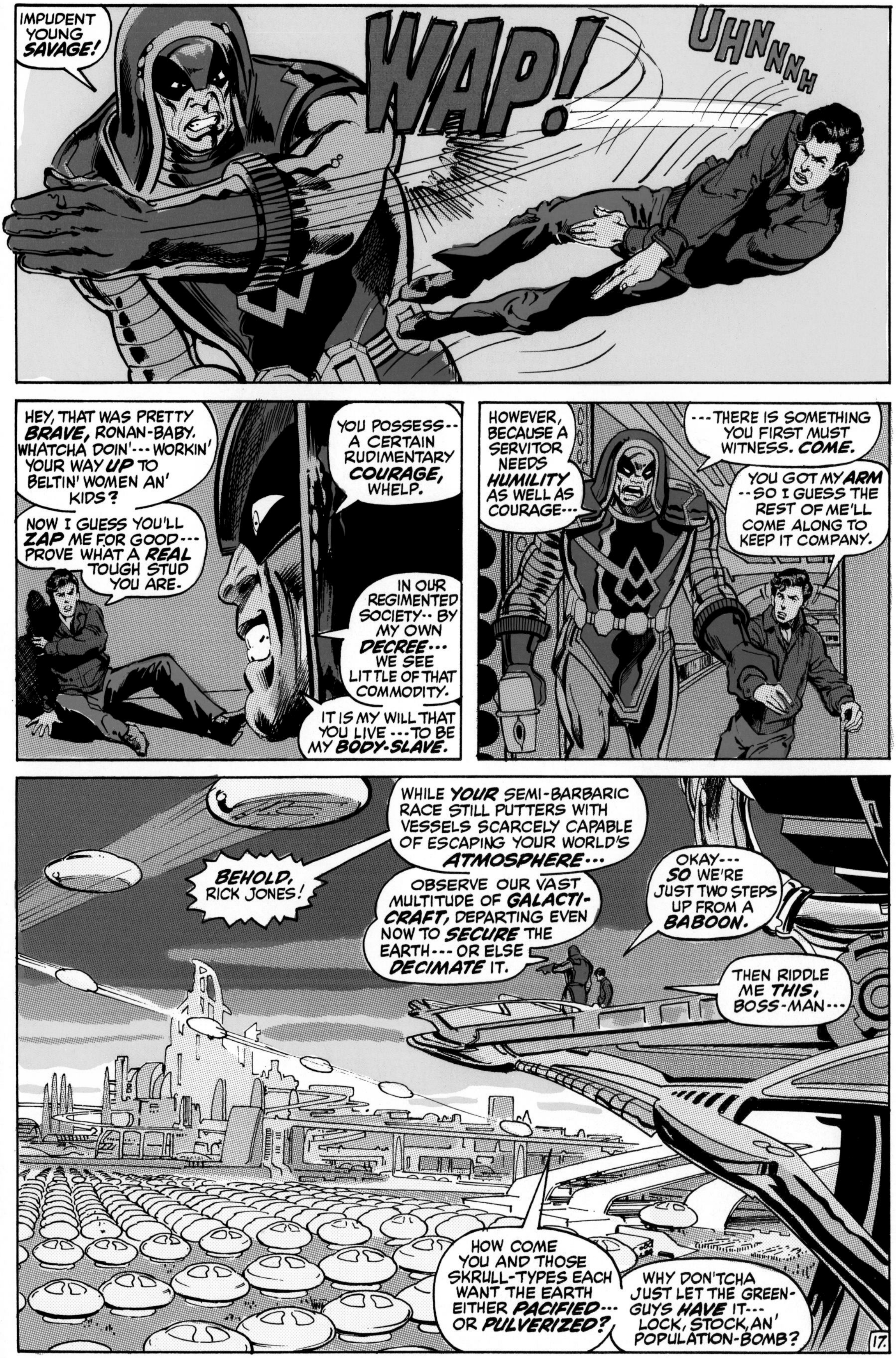
IMPUDENT YOUNG SAVAGE!
WAP!
UHNNNNH
HEY, THAT WAS PRETTY BRAVE, RONAN-BABY. WHATCHA DOIN'--- WORKIN' YOUR WAY UP TO BELTIN' WOMEN AN' KIDS?
NOW I GUESS YOU'LL ZAP ME FOR GOOD--- PROVE WHAT A REAL TOUGH STUD YOU ARE.
YOU POSSESS-- A CERTAIN RUDIMENTARY COURAGE, WHELP.
IN OUR REGIMENTED SOCIETY-- BY MY OWN DECREE--- WE SEE LITTLE OF THAT COMMODITY.
IT IS MY WILL THAT YOU LIVE---TO BE MY BODY-SLAVE.
HOWEVER, BECAUSE A SERVITOR NEEDS HUMILITY AS WELL AS COURAGE---
---THERE IS SOMETHING YOU FIRST MUST WITNESS. COME.
YOU GOT MY ARM --SO I GUESS THE REST OF ME'LL COME ALONG TO KEEP IT COMPANY.
BEHOLD, RICK JONES!
WHILE YOUR SEMI-BARBARIC RACE STILL PUTTERS WITH VESSELS SCARCELY CAPABLE OF ESCAPING YOUR WORLD'S ATMOSPHERE---
OBSERVE OUR VAST MULTITUDE OF GALACTI-CRAFT, DEPARTING EVEN NOW TO SECURE THE EARTH--- OR ELSE DECIMATE IT.
OKAY--- SO WE'RE JUST TWO STEPS UP FROM A BABOON.
THEN RIDDLE ME THIS, BOSS-MAN---
HOW COME YOU AND THOSE SKRULL-TYPES EACH WANT THE EARTH EITHER PACIFIED--- OR PULVERIZED?
WHY DON'TCHA JUST LET THE GREEN-GUYS HAVE IT--- LOCK, STOCK, AN' POPULATION-BOMB?
17.

A **SIMPLE** QUESTION, FROM A SIMPLE MIND. LOOK AT YONDER **WAR-VIZ**.

YOUR BACKWASH WORLD WAS OF **NO** IMPORT TO US---ALL BUT FORGOTTEN---UNTIL THE SKRULLS RENEWED OUR INTERMITTENT **WARFARE** IN EARNEST.

BY THE VAGARIES OF COINCIDENCE, EARTH LIES ALMOST **MIDWAY** BETWEEN THE ANDROMEDA GALAXY-- AND **OUR** GREAT COSMOS.

HENCE, YOU ARE NOW OF UTMOST **STRATEGIC** VALUE, AND MUST EITHER BE **OCCUPIED**, OR **ANNIHILATED**.

I HAVE **PERSONALLY** CALCULATED THE POSSIBILITIES OF EITHER **EVENTUALITY**... WITH THE AID OF **COMPU-MEKS**, OF COURSE---

---AND IT WOULD SEEM EARTH'S CHANCES OF SURVIVAL ARE **SLIGHT**.

ROUNDED OFF TO THE NEAREST DECIMAL, THEY ARE .00000327...

---OR, APPROXIMATELY **TWICE** THE ODDS IN FAVOR OF YOUR EVER **ESCAPING** THIS HOME-PLANET, **HALA**.

FRAPP!

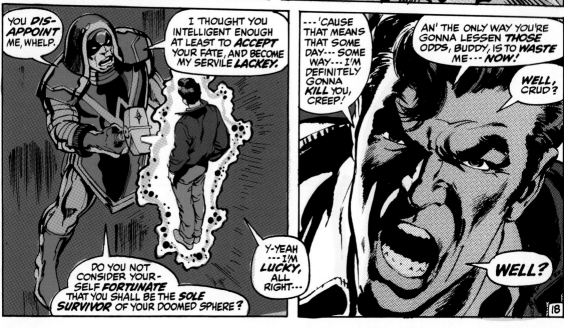

YOU **DIS-APPOINT** ME, WHELP.

I THOUGHT YOU INTELLIGENT ENOUGH AT LEAST TO **ACCEPT** YOUR FATE, AND BECOME MY SERVILE **LACKEY**.

DO YOU NOT CONSIDER YOURSELF **FORTUNATE** THAT YOU SHALL BE THE **SOLE** SURVIVOR OF YOUR DOOMED SPHERE?

Y-YEAH ---I'M **LUCKY**, ALL RIGHT...

---'CAUSE THAT MEANS THAT SOME DAY--- SOME WAY--- I'M DEFINITELY GONNA **KILL** YOU, CREEP!

AN' THE ONLY WAY YOU'RE GONNA LESSEN **THOSE** ODDS, BUDDY, IS TO **WASTE** ME--- **NOW**!

WELL, CRUD?

WELL?

18

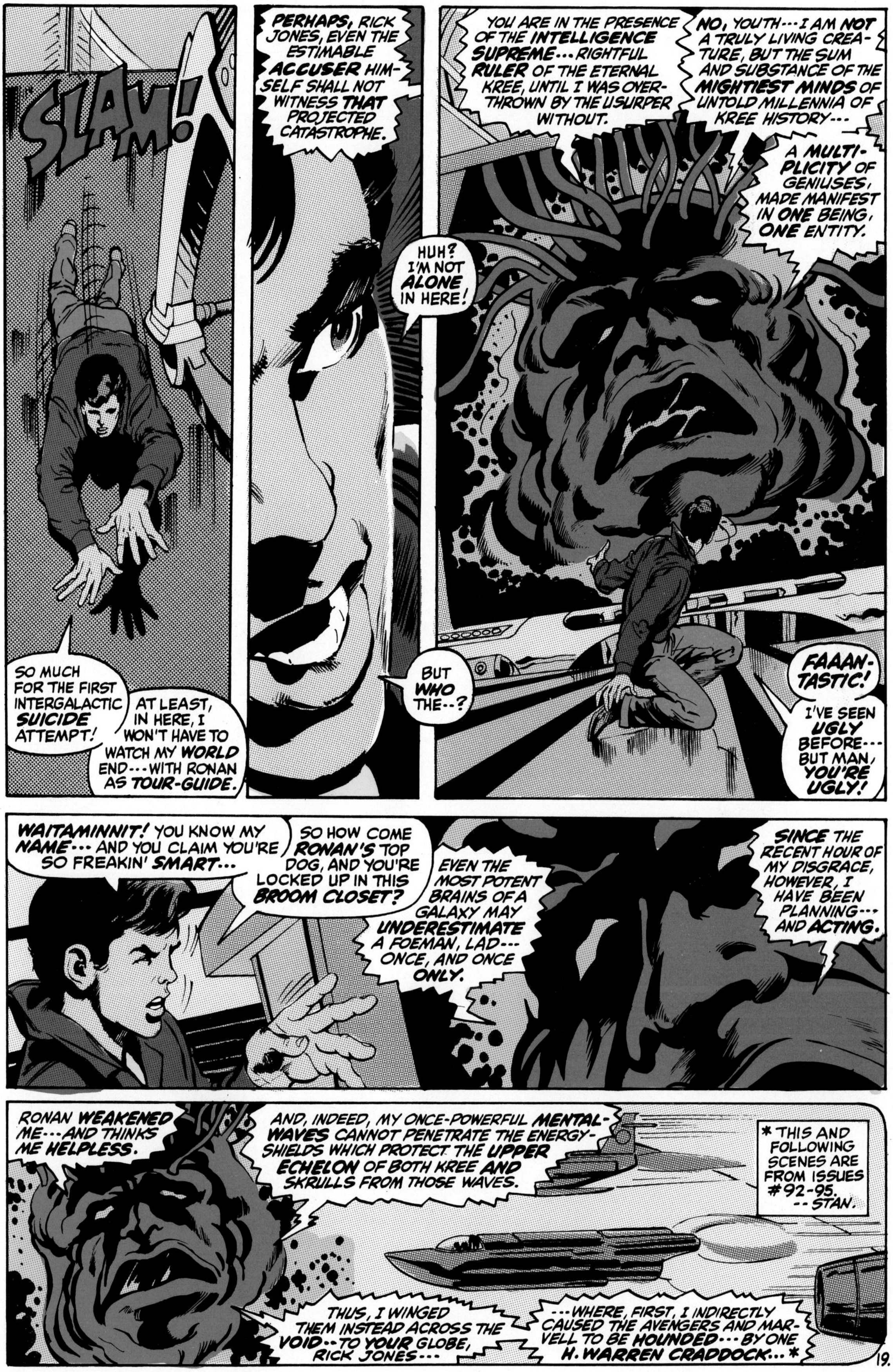
SLAM!
PERHAPS, RICK JONES, EVEN THE ESTIMABLE ACCUSER HIMSELF SHALL NOT WITNESS THAT PROJECTED CATASTROPHE.
HUH? I'M NOT ALONE IN HERE!
SO MUCH FOR THE FIRST INTERGALACTIC SUICIDE ATTEMPT!
AT LEAST, IN HERE, I WON'T HAVE TO WATCH MY WORLD END--- WITH RONAN AS TOUR-GUIDE.
BUT WHO THE--?
YOU ARE IN THE PRESENCE OF THE INTELLIGENCE SUPREME... RIGHTFUL RULER OF THE ETERNAL KREE, UNTIL I WAS OVERTHROWN BY THE USURPER WITHOUT.
NO, YOUTH--- I AM NOT A TRULY LIVING CREATURE, BUT THE SUM AND SUBSTANCE OF THE MIGHTIEST MINDS OF UNTOLD MILLENNIA OF KREE HISTORY---
A MULTIPLICITY OF GENIUSES, MADE MANIFEST IN ONE BEING, ONE ENTITY.
FAAANTASTIC!
I'VE SEEN UGLY BEFORE--- BUT MAN, YOU'RE UGLY!
WAITAMINNIT! YOU KNOW MY NAME--- AND YOU CLAIM YOU'RE SO FREAKIN' SMART...
SO HOW COME RONAN'S TOP DOG, AND YOU'RE LOCKED UP IN THIS BROOM CLOSET?
EVEN THE MOST POTENT BRAINS OF A GALAXY MAY UNDERESTIMATE A FOEMAN, LAD--- ONCE, AND ONCE ONLY.
SINCE THE RECENT HOUR OF MY DISGRACE, HOWEVER, I HAVE BEEN PLANNING--- AND ACTING.
RONAN WEAKENED ME--- AND THINKS ME HELPLESS.
AND, INDEED, MY ONCE-POWERFUL MENTAL-WAVES CANNOT PENETRATE THE ENERGY-SHIELDS WHICH PROTECT THE UPPER ECHELON OF BOTH KREE AND SKRULLS FROM THOSE WAVES.
* THIS AND FOLLOWING SCENES ARE FROM ISSUES #92-95. --STAN.
THUS, I WINGED THEM INSTEAD ACROSS THE VOID--TO YOUR GLOBE, RICK JONES---
---WHERE, FIRST, I INDIRECTLY CAUSED THE AVENGERS AND MAR-VELL TO BE HOUNDED--- BY ONE H. WARREN CRADDOCK...*

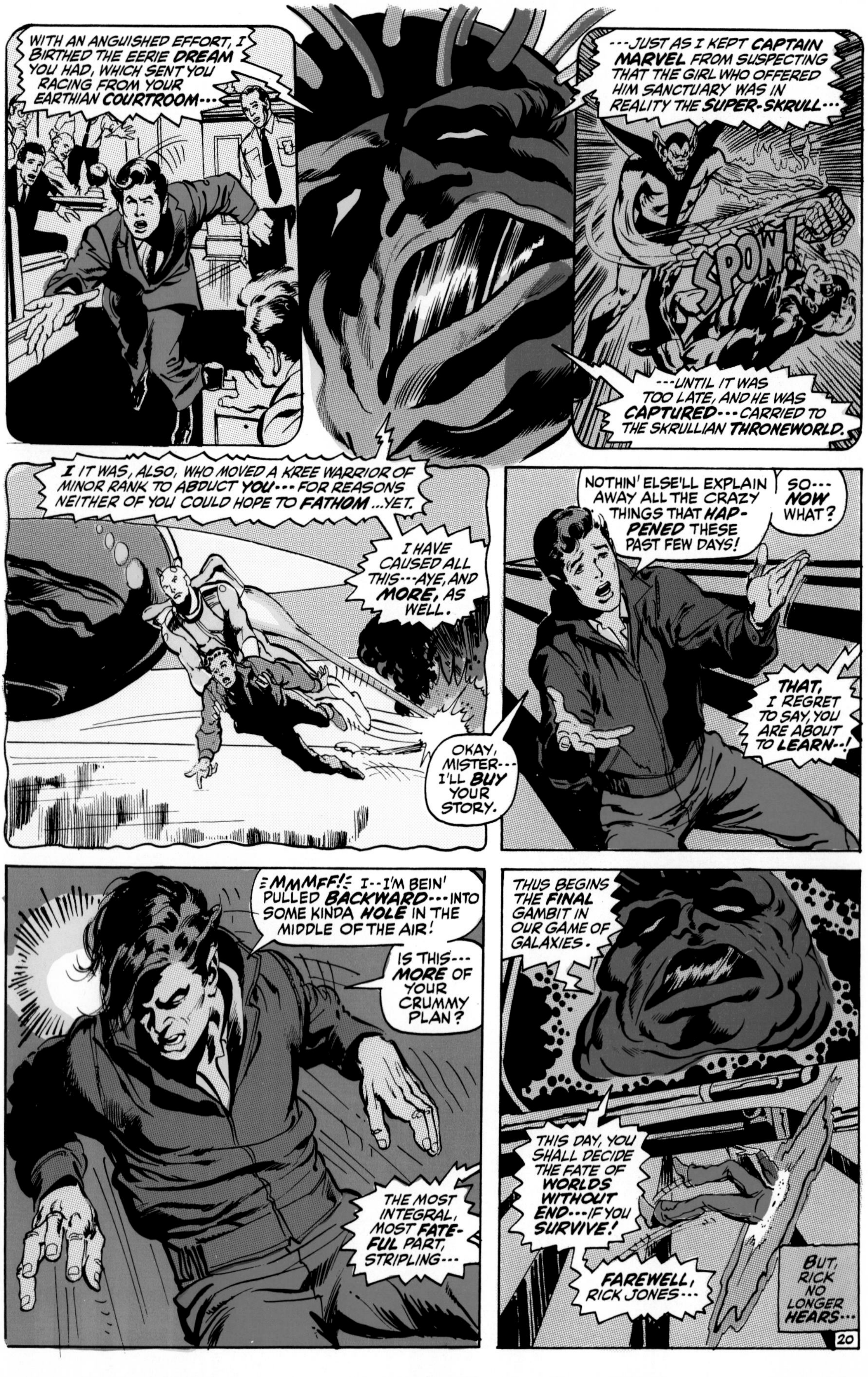
WITH AN ANGUISHED EFFORT, I BIRTHED THE EERIE DREAM YOU HAD, WHICH SENT YOU RACING FROM YOUR EARTHIAN COURTROOM---
---JUST AS I KEPT CAPTAIN MARVEL FROM SUSPECTING THAT THE GIRL WHO OFFERED HIM SANCTUARY WAS IN REALITY THE SUPER-SKRULL---
SPOW!
---UNTIL IT WAS TOO LATE, AND HE WAS CAPTURED---CARRIED TO THE SKRULLIAN THRONEWORLD.
I IT WAS, ALSO, WHO MOVED A KREE WARRIOR OF MINOR RANK TO ABDUCT YOU---FOR REASONS NEITHER OF YOU COULD HOPE TO FATHOM ...YET.
I HAVE CAUSED ALL THIS---AYE, AND MORE, AS WELL.
OKAY, MISTER--- I'LL BUY YOUR STORY.
NOTHIN' ELSE'LL EXPLAIN AWAY ALL THE CRAZY THINGS THAT HAP-PENED THESE PAST FEW DAYS!
SO--- NOW WHAT?
THAT, I REGRET TO SAY, YOU ARE ABOUT TO LEARN--!
MMMFF! I--I'M BEIN' PULLED BACKWARD---INTO SOME KINDA HOLE IN THE MIDDLE OF THE AIR!
IS THIS--- MORE OF YOUR CRUMMY PLAN?
THE MOST INTEGRAL, MOST FATE-FUL PART, STRIPLING---
THUS BEGINS THE FINAL GAMBIT IN OUR GAME OF GALAXIES.
THIS DAY, YOU SHALL DECIDE THE FATE OF WORLDS WITHOUT END---IF YOU SURVIVE!
FAREWELL, RICK JONES---
BUT, RICK NO LONGER HEARS---

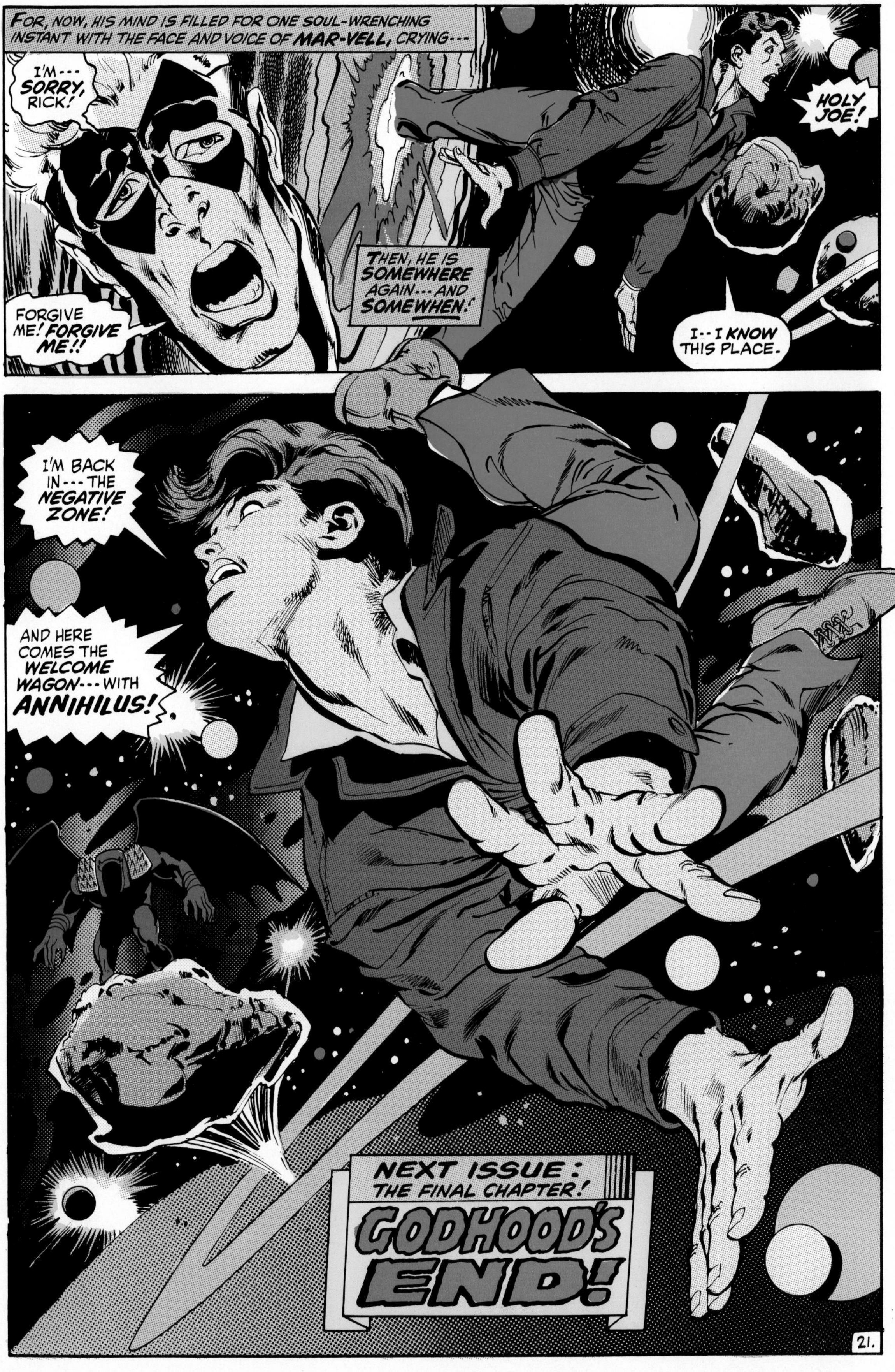

FOR, NOW, HIS MIND IS FILLED FOR ONE SOUL-WRENCHING INSTANT WITH THE FACE AND VOICE OF MAR-VELL, CRYING---
I'M--- SORRY, RICK!
FORGIVE ME! FORGIVE ME!!
THEN, HE IS SOMEWHERE AGAIN--- AND SOMEWHEN!
HOLY JOE!
I-- I KNOW THIS PLACE.
I'M BACK IN--- THE NEGATIVE ZONE!
AND HERE COMES THE WELCOME WAGON--- WITH ANNIHILUS!
NEXT ISSUE: THE FINAL CHAPTER!
GODHOOD'S END!

CHAPTER NINE

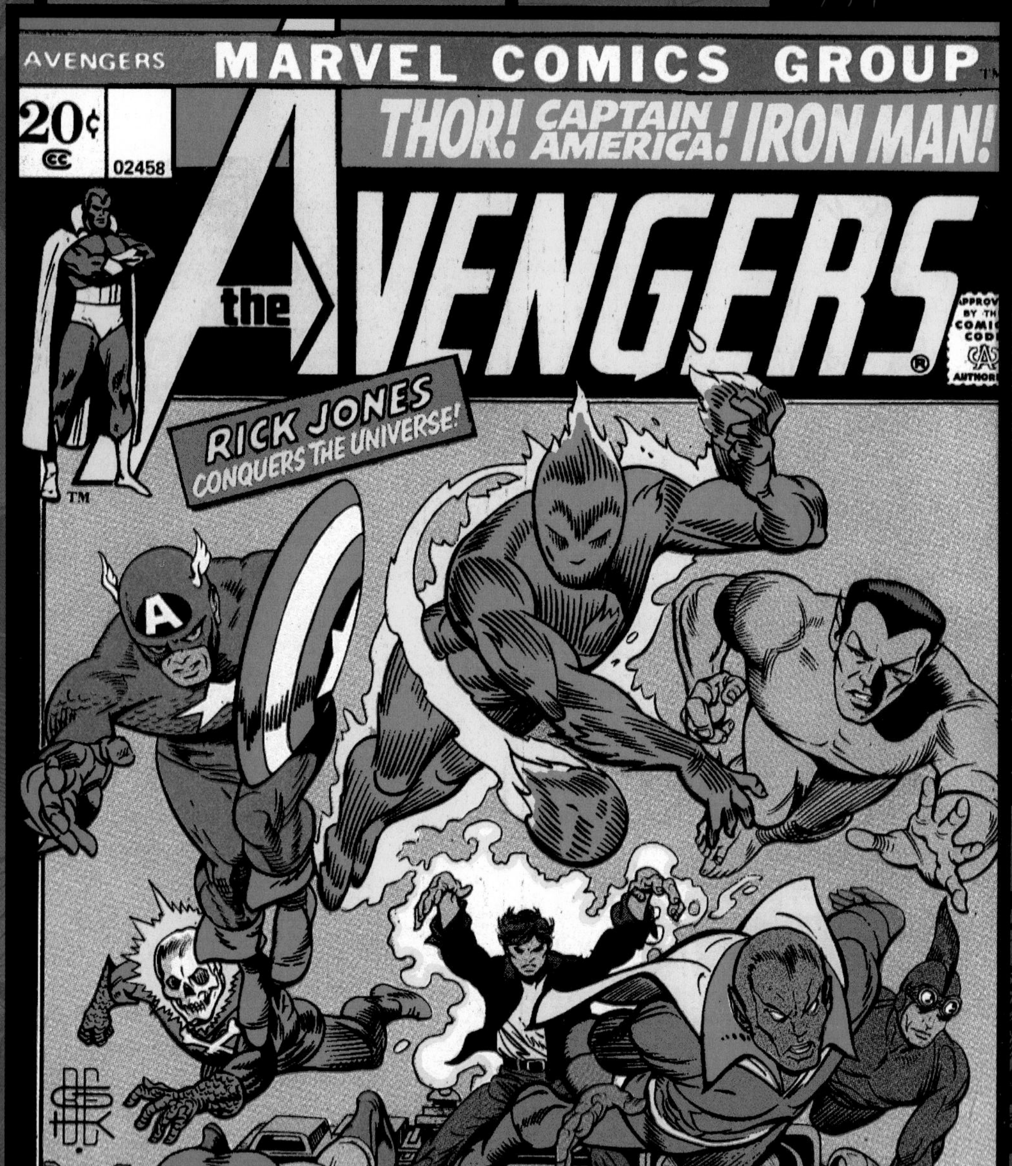
AVENGERS
MARVEL COMICS GROUP
20¢
02458
THOR! CAPTAIN AMERICA! IRON MAN!
the AVENGERS
RICK JONES CONQUERS THE UNIVERSE!
THIS IS IT! THE FEARFUL FINALE OF THE SKRULL VS. KREE WAR!!
GODHOOD'S END!

GODHOOD'S END!

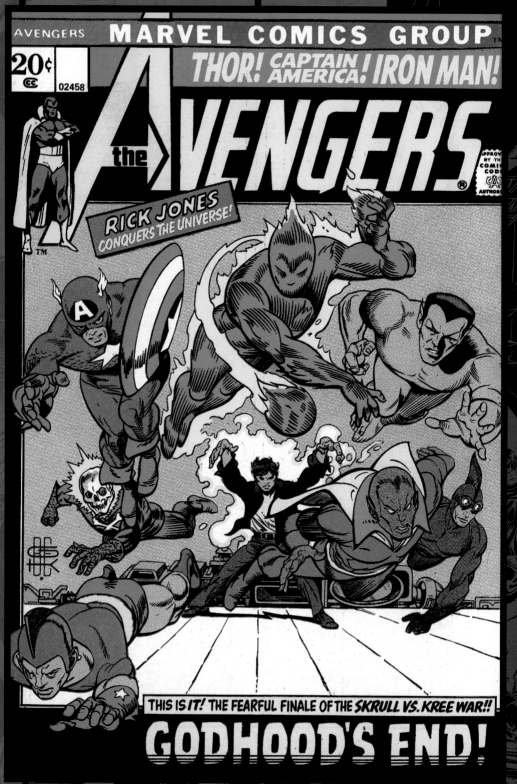

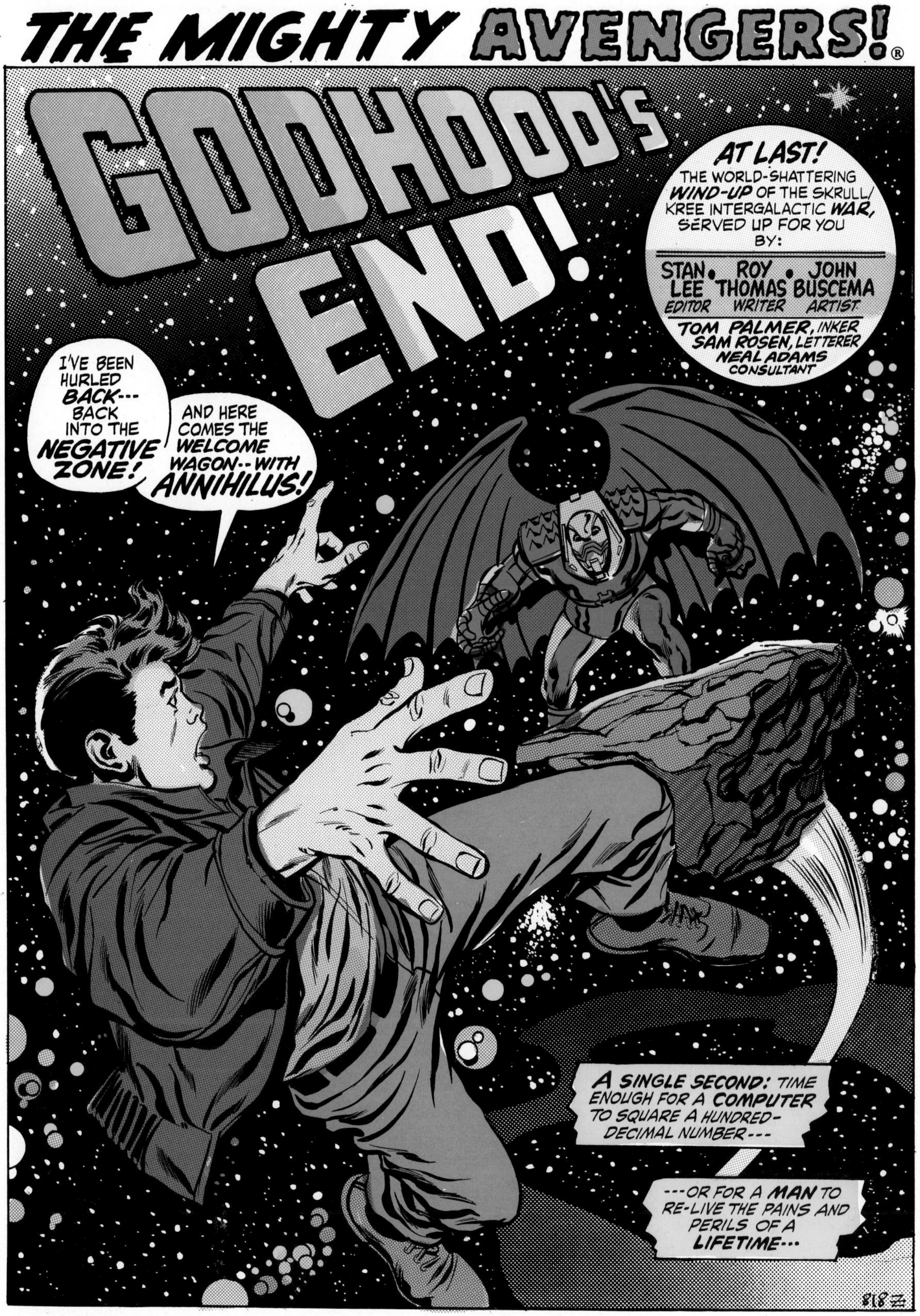
THE MIGHTY AVENGERS!
GODHOOD'S END!
AT LAST! THE WORLD-SHATTERING WIND-UP OF THE SKRULL/KREE INTERGALACTIC WAR, SERVED UP FOR YOU BY:
STAN LEE EDITOR • ROY THOMAS WRITER • JOHN BUSCEMA ARTIST
TOM PALMER, INKER SAM ROSEN, LETTERER NEAL ADAMS CONSULTANT
I'VE BEEN HURLED BACK--- BACK INTO THE NEGATIVE ZONE!
AND HERE COMES THE WELCOME WAGON--WITH ANNIHILUS!
A SINGLE SECOND: TIME ENOUGH FOR A COMPUTER TO SQUARE A HUNDRED-DECIMAL NUMBER---
---OR FOR A MAN TO RE-LIVE THE PAINS AND PERILS OF A LIFETIME...

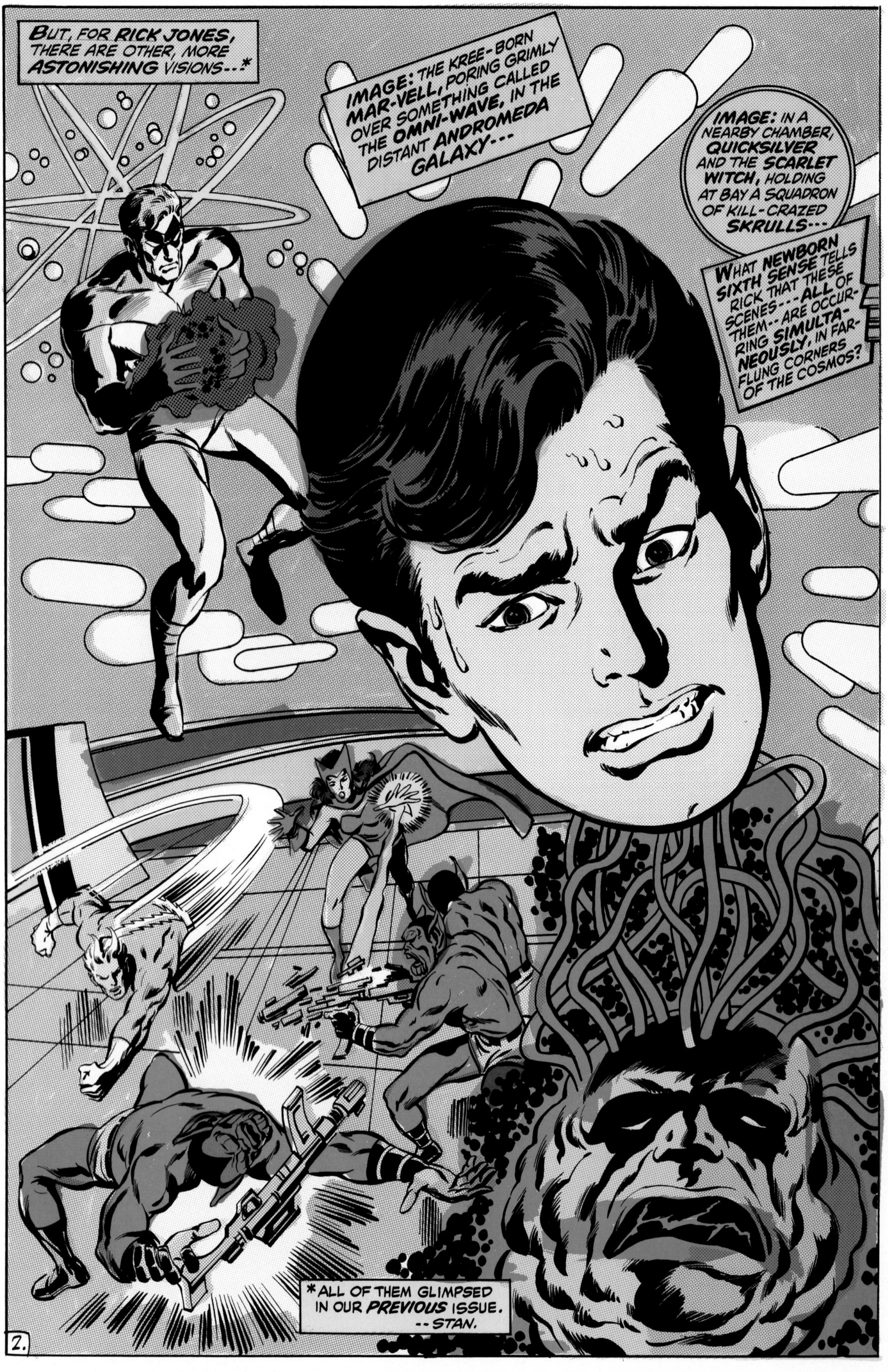
BUT, FOR RICK JONES, THERE ARE OTHER, MORE ASTONISHING VISIONS--.*
IMAGE: THE KREE-BORN MAR-VELL, PORING GRIMLY OVER SOMETHING CALLED THE OMNI-WAVE, IN THE DISTANT ANDROMEDA GALAXY--
IMAGE: IN A NEARBY CHAMBER, QUICKSILVER AND THE SCARLET WITCH, HOLDING AT BAY A SQUADRON OF KILL-CRAZED SKRULLS---
WHAT NEWBORN SIXTH SENSE TELLS RICK THAT THESE SCENES---ALL OF THEM--ARE OCCURRING SIMULTANEOUSLY, IN FAR-FLUNG CORNERS OF THE COSMOS?
*ALL OF THEM GLIMPSED IN OUR PREVIOUS ISSUE. --STAN.
2.

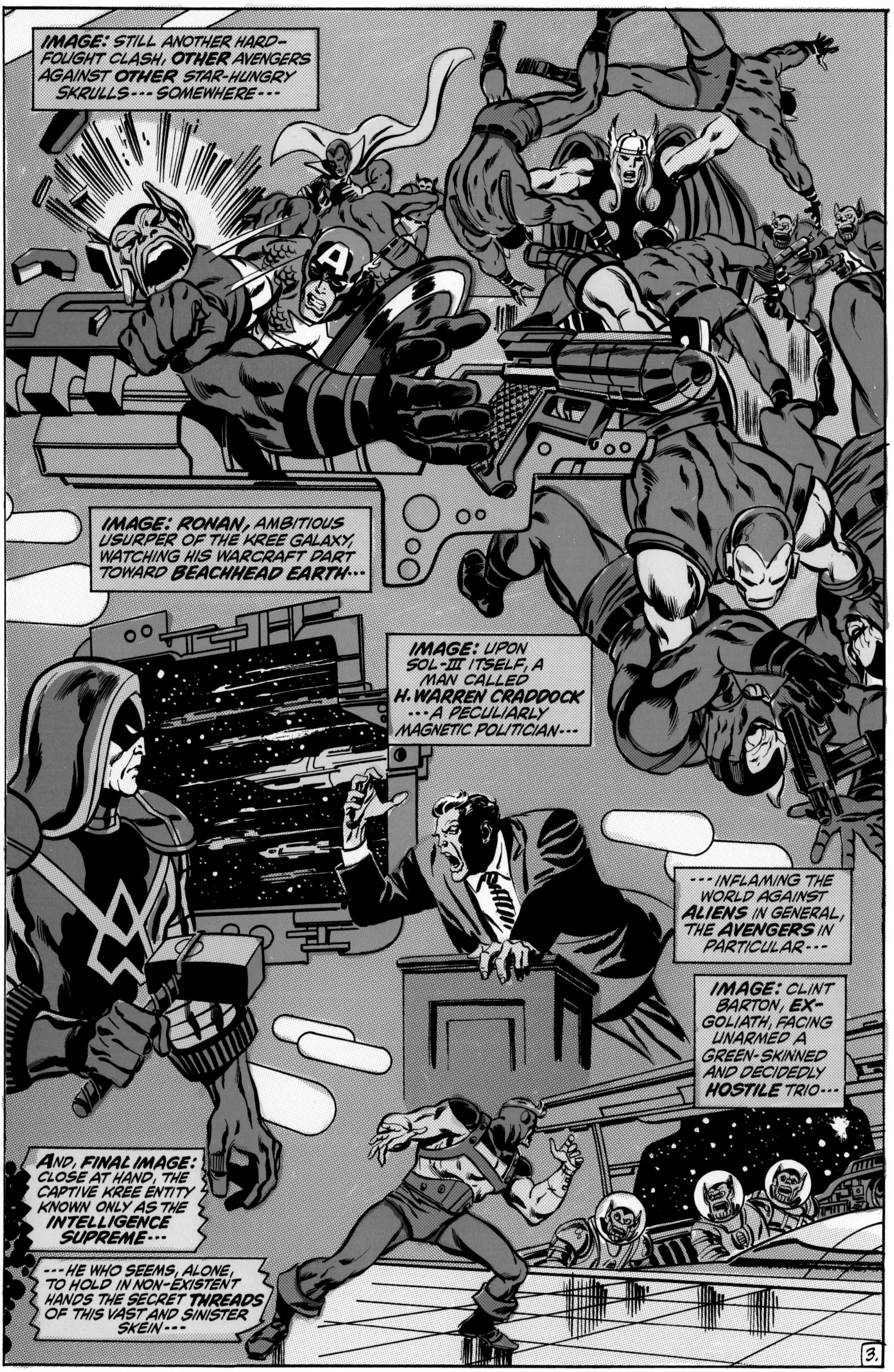
IMAGE: STILL ANOTHER HARD-FOUGHT CLASH, OTHER AVENGERS AGAINST OTHER STAR-HUNGRY SKRULLS--- SOMEWHERE---
IMAGE: RONAN, AMBITIOUS USURPER OF THE KREE GALAXY, WATCHING HIS WARCRAFT DART TOWARD BEACHHEAD EARTH---
IMAGE: UPON SOL-III ITSELF, A MAN CALLED H. WARREN CRADDOCK ---A PECULIARLY MAGNETIC POLITICIAN---
---INFLAMING THE WORLD AGAINST ALIENS IN GENERAL, THE AVENGERS IN PARTICULAR---
IMAGE: CLINT BARTON, EX-GOLIATH, FACING UNARMED A GREEN-SKINNED AND DECIDEDLY HOSTILE TRIO---
AND, FINAL IMAGE: CLOSE AT HAND, THE CAPTIVE KREE ENTITY KNOWN ONLY AS THE INTELLIGENCE SUPREME---
---HE WHO SEEMS, ALONE, TO HOLD IN NON-EXISTENT HANDS THE SECRET THREADS OF THIS VAST AND SINISTER SKEIN---
3.

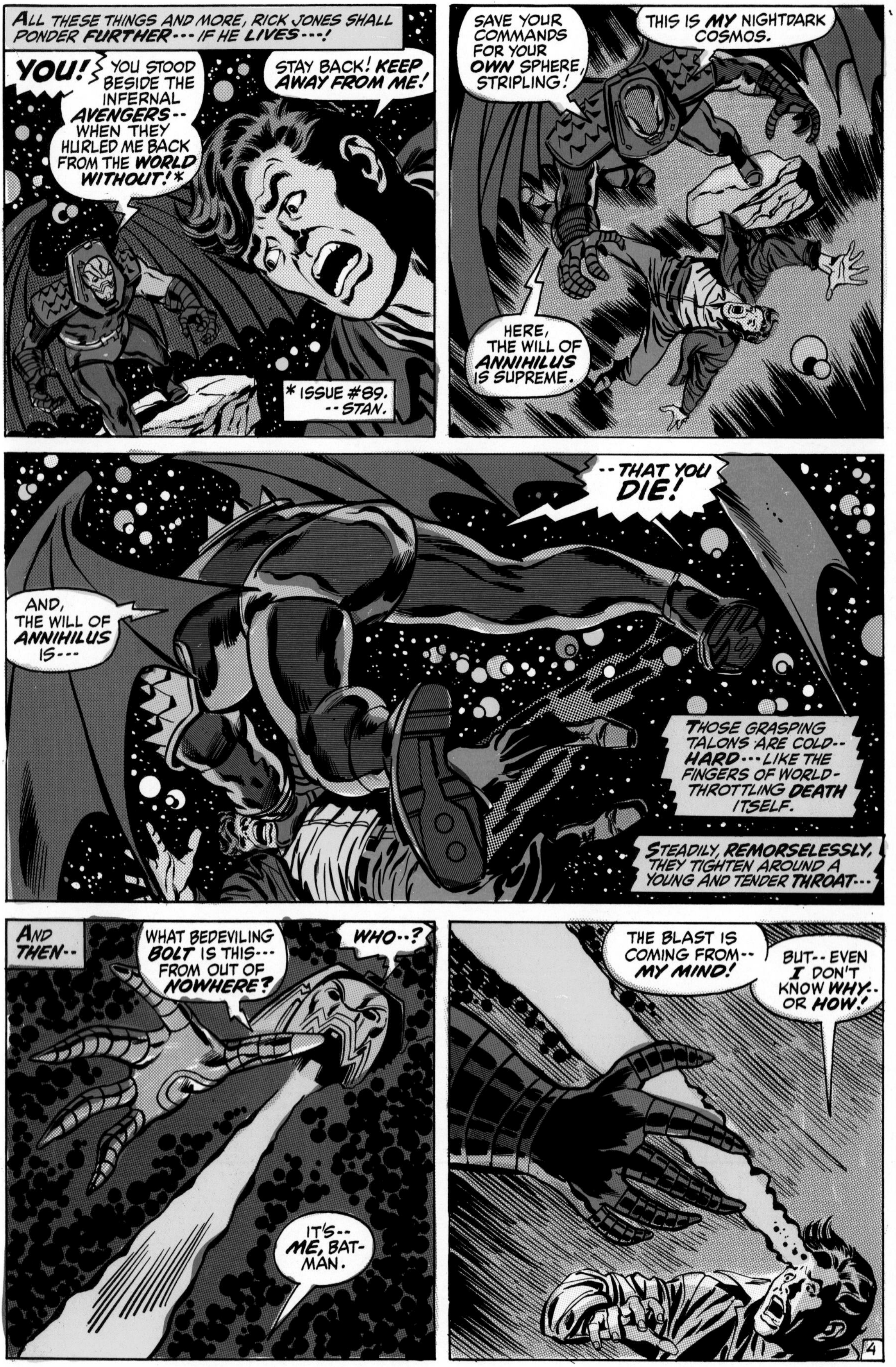
ALL THESE THINGS AND MORE, RICK JONES SHALL PONDER FURTHER--- IF HE LIVES---!
YOU! YOU STOOD BESIDE THE INFERNAL AVENGERS-- WHEN THEY HURLED ME BACK FROM THE WORLD WITHOUT!*
STAY BACK! KEEP AWAY FROM ME!
* ISSUE #89. --STAN.
SAVE YOUR COMMANDS FOR YOUR OWN SPHERE, STRIPLING!
THIS IS MY NIGHTDARK COSMOS.
HERE, THE WILL OF ANNIHILUS IS SUPREME.
AND, THE WILL OF ANNIHILUS IS---
--THAT YOU DIE!
THOSE GRASPING TALONS ARE COLD-- HARD--- LIKE THE FINGERS OF WORLD-THROTTLING DEATH ITSELF.
STEADILY, REMORSELESSLY, THEY TIGHTEN AROUND A YOUNG AND TENDER THROAT---
AND THEN--
WHAT BEDEVILING BOLT IS THIS--- FROM OUT OF NOWHERE?
WHO--?
IT'S-- ME, BAT-MAN.
THE BLAST IS COMING FROM-- MY MIND!
BUT-- EVEN I DON'T KNOW WHY-- OR HOW!
4

SPEECHLESS WITH SHOCK AND USELESS RAGE, ANNIHILUS IS SENT SWIFTLY, *VIOLENTLY* HURTLING AWAY---

--TILL HE IS *LOST* IN *DARKNESS* AND VAST *DISTANCE*---

--LEAVING A FLOATING, HELPLESS *RICK JONES* NO BETTER OFF THAN HE WAS BEFORE ---

--AND PERHAPS MUCH *WORSE!*

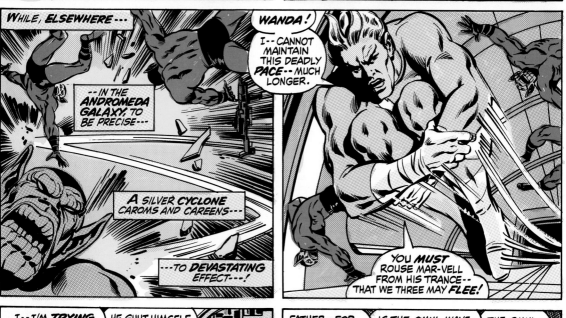

WHILE, ELSEWHERE...

--IN THE *ANDROMEDA GALAXY*, TO BE PRECISE...

A *SILVER CYCLONE* CAROMS AND CAREENS---

---TO *DEVASTATING* EFFECT---!

WANDA! I--CANNOT MAINTAIN THIS *DEADLY PACE*--MUCH LONGER.

YOU *MUST* ROUSE MAR-VELL FROM HIS TRANCE--THAT WE THREE MAY *FLEE!*

I--I'M *TRYING*, PIETRO. BUT EVEN MY *HEX POWER* HAS NO EFFECT.

HE SHUT HIMSELF AND THE *OMNI-WAVE* DEVICE WITHIN A SPHERE OF *NEGATIVE ENERGY*, AND--

--AND HE KNOWS HE SHALL *PERISH*, WENCH, THE INSTANT HE *EMERGES* THEREFROM!

FATHER--FOR THE FINAL TIME, I BEG YOU *HALT* THIS MAD ATTACK.

IS THE OMNI-WAVE--IS *ANYTHING*--- WORTH THE RISKING OF *STILL MORE* SKRULL LIVES?

THE OMNI-WAVE CAN BECOME, IN *MY* HANDS, THE *ULTIMATE* WEAPON AGAINST OUR FOEMEN, THE *KREE.*

ONCE WE WREST IT FROM MAR-VELL, *HE* SHALL DIE--AND THEN HIS GALACTIC *KINSMEN*--

--AS WOULD *YOU*, ANELLE, WERE NOT *YOU* THE SOLE OFFSPRING OF AN *EMPEROR!*

5

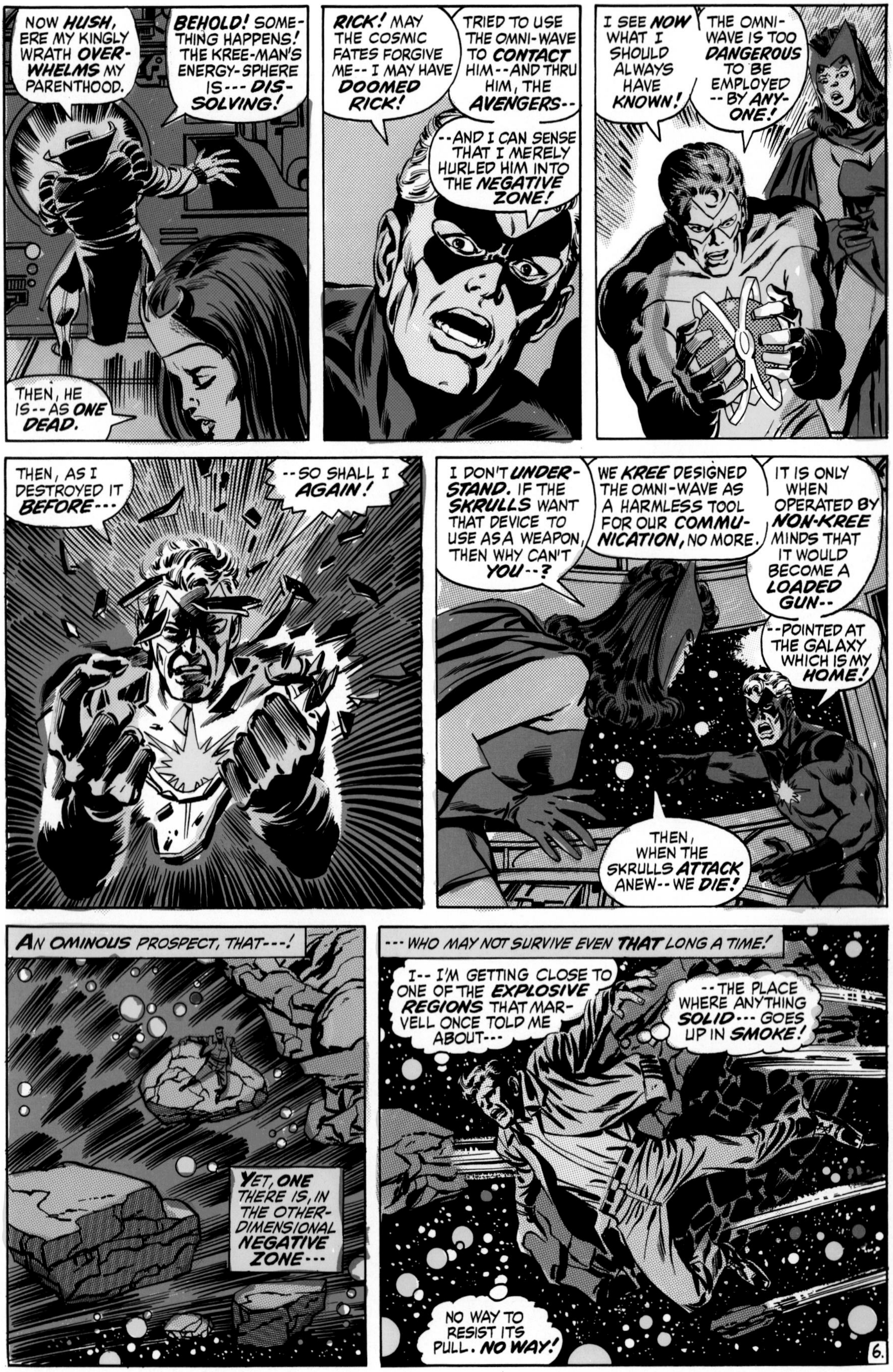
NOW HUSH, ERE MY KINGLY WRATH OVER-WHELMS MY PARENTHOOD.
BEHOLD! SOME-THING HAPPENS! THE KREE-MAN'S ENERGY-SPHERE IS--- DIS-SOLVING!
THEN, HE IS-- AS ONE DEAD.
RICK! MAY THE COSMIC FATES FORGIVE ME-- I MAY HAVE DOOMED RICK!
TRIED TO USE THE OMNI-WAVE TO CONTACT HIM--AND THRU HIM, THE AVENGERS--
--AND I CAN SENSE THAT I MERELY HURLED HIM INTO THE NEGATIVE ZONE!
I SEE NOW WHAT I SHOULD ALWAYS HAVE KNOWN!
THE OMNI-WAVE IS TOO DANGEROUS TO BE EMPLOYED -- BY ANY-ONE!
THEN, AS I DESTROYED IT BEFORE---
--SO SHALL I AGAIN!
I DON'T UNDER-STAND. IF THE SKRULLS WANT THAT DEVICE TO USE AS A WEAPON, THEN WHY CAN'T YOU--?
WE KREE DESIGNED THE OMNI-WAVE AS A HARMLESS TOOL FOR OUR COMMU-NICATION, NO MORE.
IT IS ONLY WHEN OPERATED BY NON-KREE MINDS THAT IT WOULD BECOME A LOADED GUN--
--POINTED AT THE GALAXY WHICH IS MY HOME!
THEN, WHEN THE SKRULLS ATTACK ANEW-- WE DIE!
AN OMINOUS PROSPECT, THAT---!
YET, ONE THERE IS, IN THE OTHER-DIMENSIONAL NEGATIVE ZONE---
--- WHO MAY NOT SURVIVE EVEN THAT LONG A TIME!
I-- I'M GETTING CLOSE TO ONE OF THE EXPLOSIVE REGIONS THAT MAR-VELL ONCE TOLD ME ABOUT---
--THE PLACE WHERE ANYTHING SOLID--- GOES UP IN SMOKE!
NO WAY TO RESIST ITS PULL. NO WAY!
6.

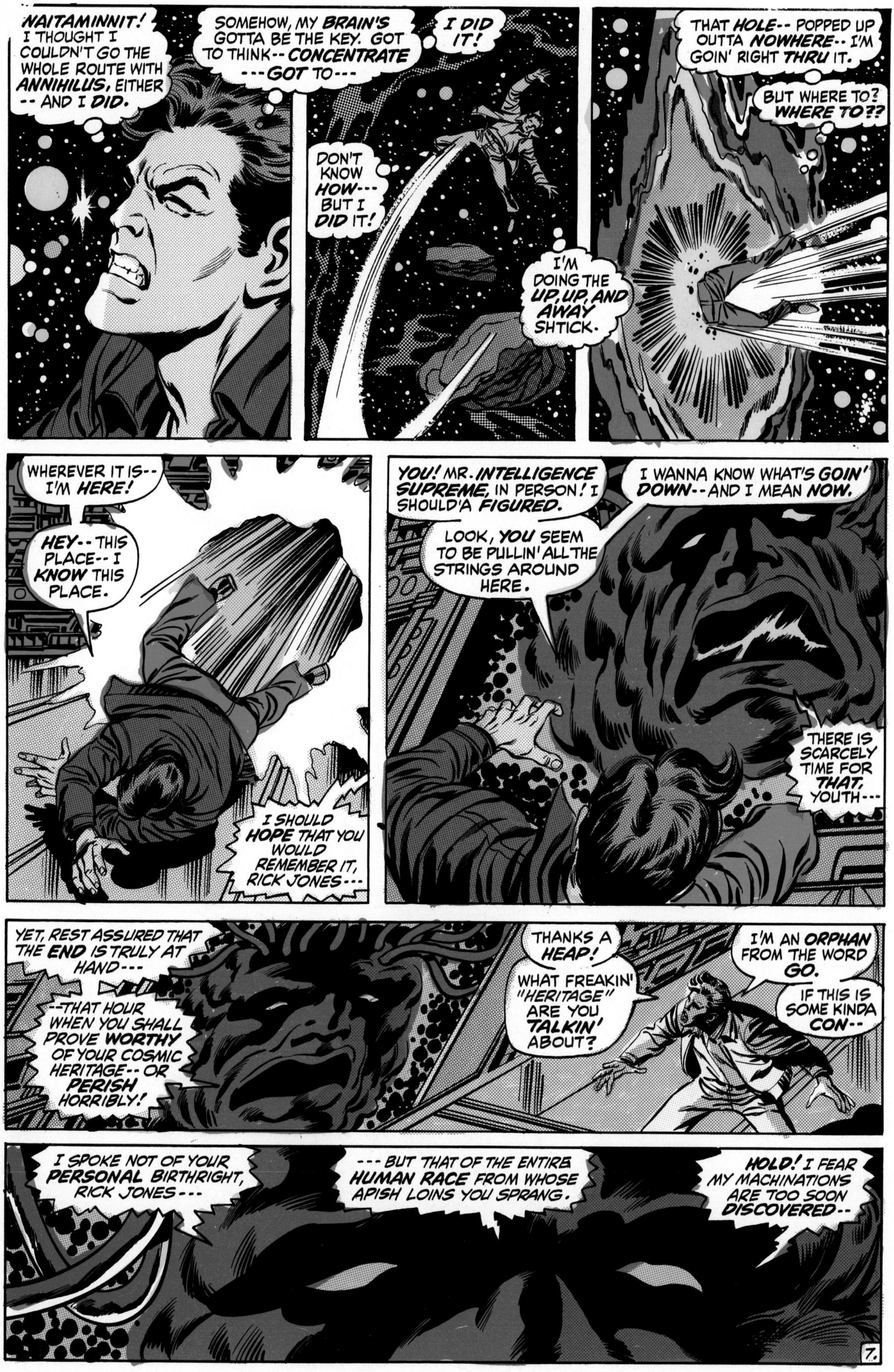
NAITAMINNIT! I THOUGHT I COULDN'T GO THE WHOLE ROUTE WITH ANNIHILUS, EITHER -- AND I DID.
SOMEHOW, MY BRAIN'S GOTTA BE THE KEY. GOT TO THINK -- CONCENTRATE --- GOT TO---
I DID IT!
DON'T KNOW HOW--- BUT I DID IT!
I'M DOING THE UP, UP, AND AWAY SHTICK.
THAT HOLE-- POPPED UP OUTTA NOWHERE-- I'M GOIN' RIGHT THRU IT.
BUT WHERE TO? WHERE TO??
WHEREVER IT IS-- I'M HERE!
HEY-- THIS PLACE-- I KNOW THIS PLACE.
I SHOULD HOPE THAT YOU WOULD REMEMBER IT, RICK JONES---
YOU! MR. INTELLIGENCE SUPREME, IN PERSON! I SHOULD'A FIGURED.
I WANNA KNOW WHAT'S GOIN' DOWN-- AND I MEAN NOW.
LOOK, YOU SEEM TO BE PULLIN' ALL THE STRINGS AROUND HERE.
THERE IS SCARCELY TIME FOR THAT, YOUTH---
YET, REST ASSURED THAT THE END IS TRULY AT HAND---
--THAT HOUR WHEN YOU SHALL PROVE WORTHY OF YOUR COSMIC HERITAGE-- OR PERISH HORRIBLY!
THANKS A HEAP!
WHAT FREAKIN' "HERITAGE" ARE YOU TALKIN' ABOUT?
I'M AN ORPHAN FROM THE WORD GO.
IF THIS IS SOME KINDA CON--
I SPOKE NOT OF YOUR PERSONAL BIRTHRIGHT, RICK JONES---
--- BUT THAT OF THE ENTIRE HUMAN RACE FROM WHOSE APISH LOINS YOU SPRANG.
HOLD! I FEAR MY MACHINATIONS ARE TOO SOON DISCOVERED--
7.

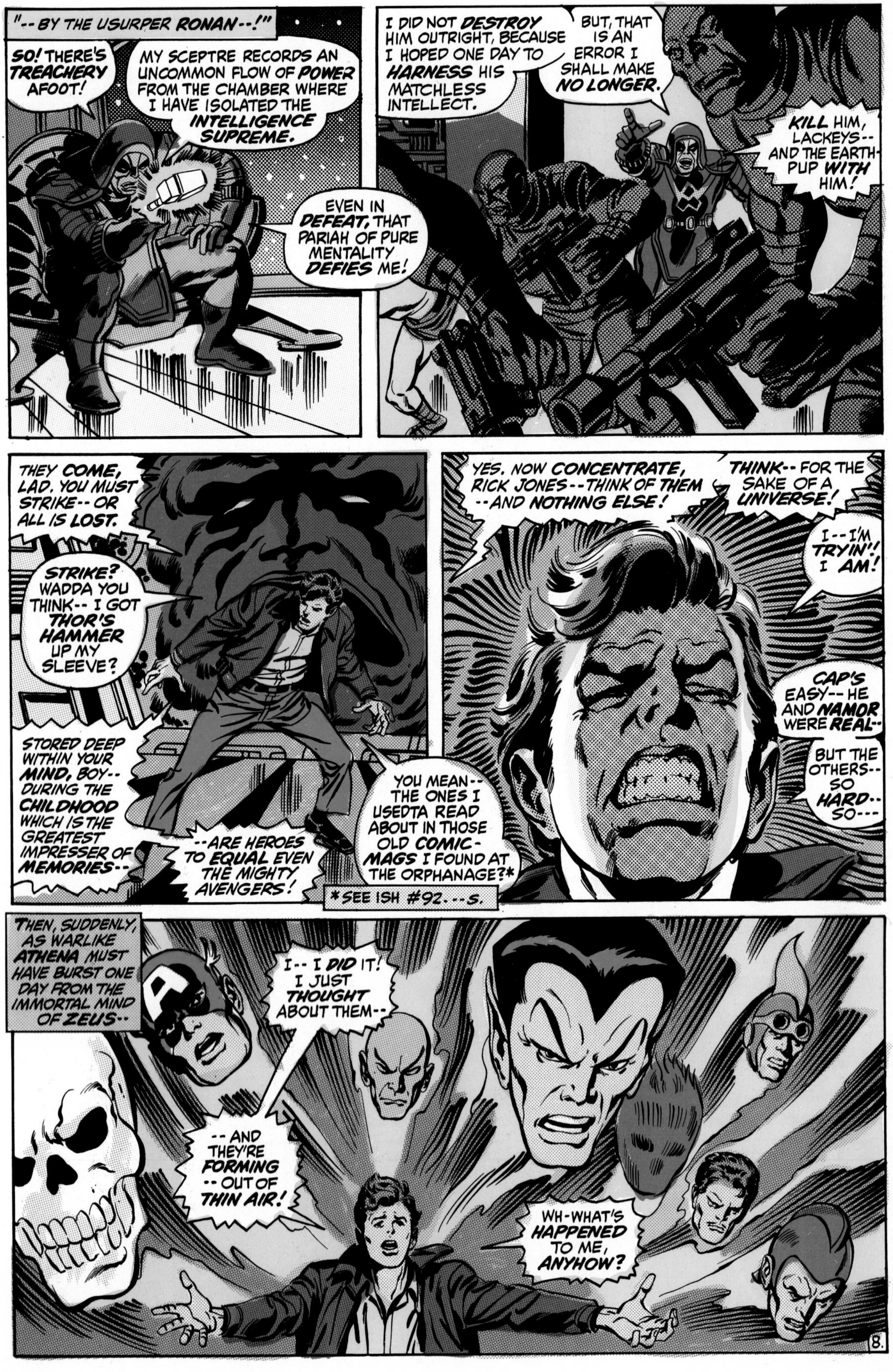
"-- BY THE USURPER RONAN--!"
SO! THERE'S TREACHERY AFOOT!
MY SCEPTRE RECORDS AN UNCOMMON FLOW OF POWER FROM THE CHAMBER WHERE I HAVE ISOLATED THE INTELLIGENCE SUPREME.
EVEN IN DEFEAT, THAT PARIAH OF PURE MENTALITY DEFIES ME!
I DID NOT DESTROY HIM OUTRIGHT, BECAUSE I HOPED ONE DAY TO HARNESS HIS MATCHLESS INTELLECT.
BUT, THAT IS AN ERROR I SHALL MAKE NO LONGER.
KILL HIM, LACKEYS-- AND THE EARTH-PUP WITH HIM!
THEY COME, LAD. YOU MUST STRIKE-- OR ALL IS LOST.
STRIKE? WADDA YOU THINK-- I GOT THOR'S HAMMER UP MY SLEEVE?
STORED DEEP WITHIN YOUR MIND, BOY-- DURING THE CHILDHOOD WHICH IS THE GREATEST IMPRESSER OF MEMORIES--
--ARE HEROES TO EQUAL EVEN THE MIGHTY AVENGERS!
YOU MEAN-- THE ONES I USEDTA READ ABOUT IN THOSE OLD COMIC-MAGS I FOUND AT THE ORPHANAGE?*
*SEE ISH #92. --S.
YES. NOW CONCENTRATE, RICK JONES--THINK OF THEM --AND NOTHING ELSE!
THINK-- FOR THE SAKE OF A UNIVERSE!
I--I'M TRYIN'! I AM!
CAP'S EASY-- HE AND NAMOR WERE REAL--
BUT THE OTHERS-- SO HARD-- SO---
THEN, SUDDENLY, AS WARLIKE ATHENA MUST HAVE BURST ONE DAY FROM THE IMMORTAL MIND OF ZEUS--
I-- I DID IT! I JUST THOUGHT ABOUT THEM--
--AND THEY'RE FORMING --OUT OF THIN AIR!
WH-WHAT'S HAPPENED TO ME, ANYHOW?
8.

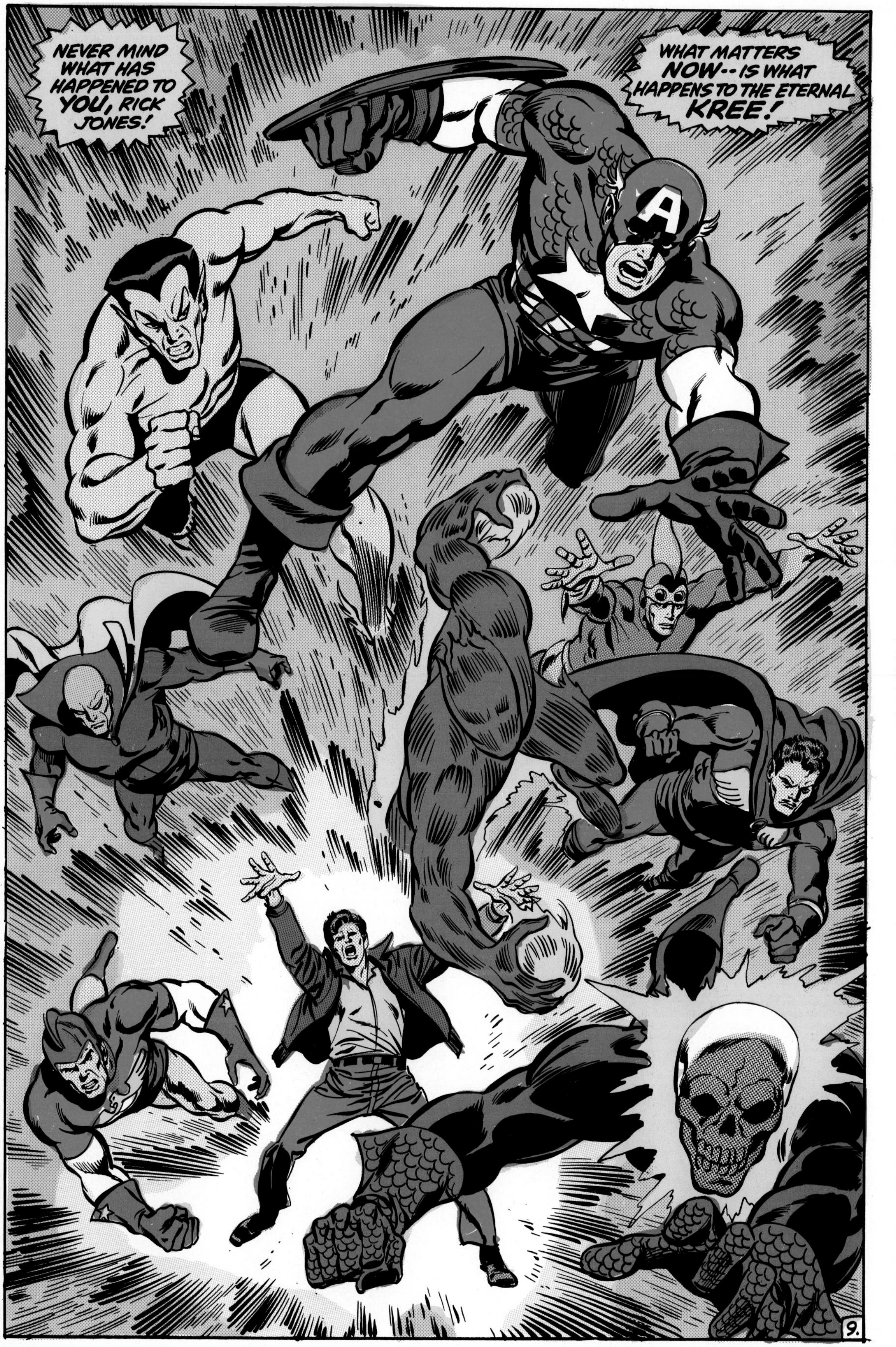
NEVER MIND WHAT HAS HAPPENED TO YOU, RICK JONES!
WHAT MATTERS NOW-- IS WHAT HAPPENS TO THE ETERNAL KREE!
9.

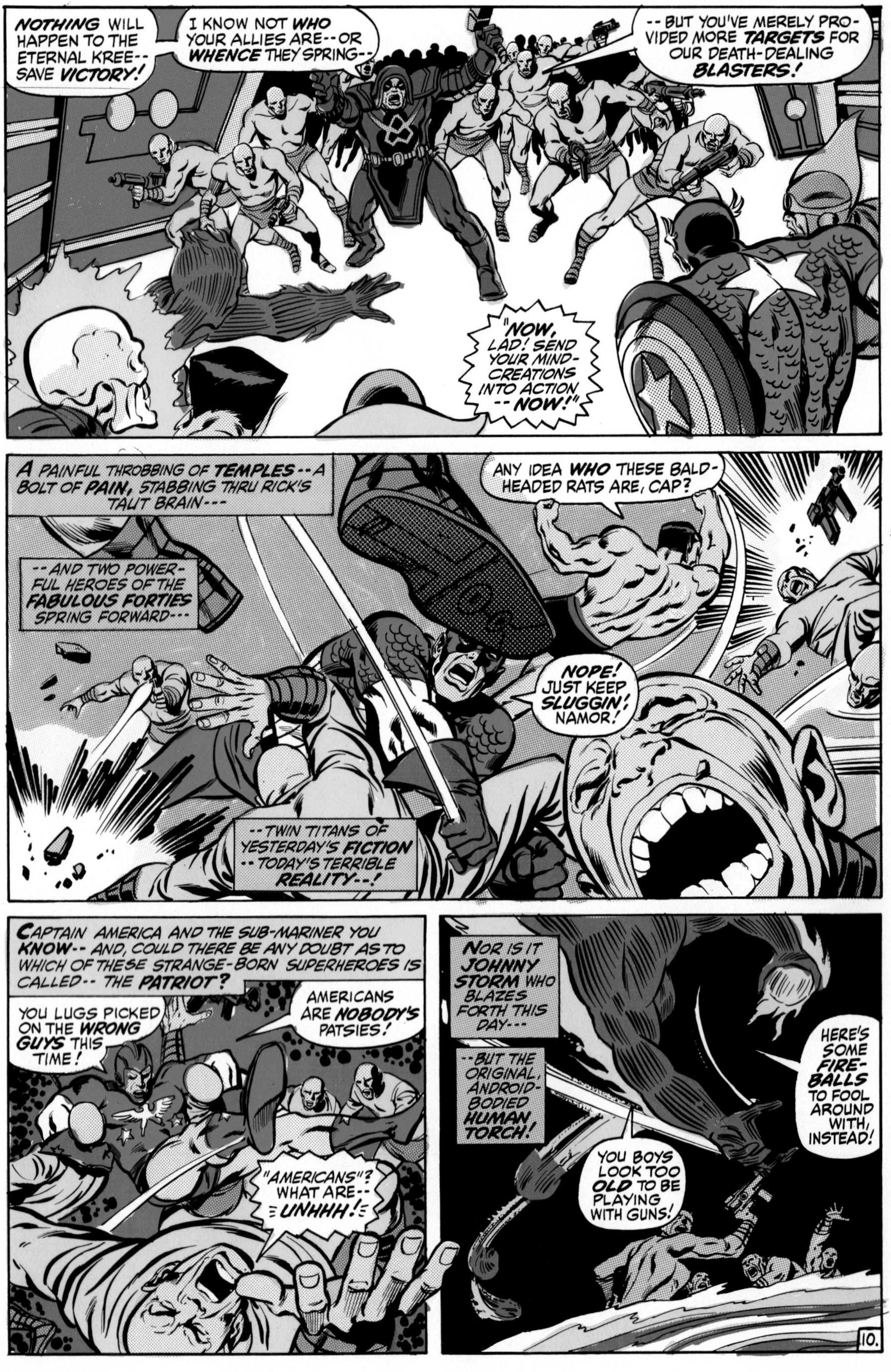
NOTHING WILL HAPPEN TO THE ETERNAL KREE-- SAVE VICTORY!
I KNOW NOT WHO YOUR ALLIES ARE--OR WHENCE THEY SPRING--
--BUT YOU'VE MERELY PROVIDED MORE TARGETS FOR OUR DEATH-DEALING BLASTERS!
"NOW, LAD! SEND YOUR MIND-CREATIONS INTO ACTION --NOW!"
A PAINFUL THROBBING OF TEMPLES--A BOLT OF PAIN, STABBING THRU RICK'S TAUT BRAIN---
--AND TWO POWERFUL HEROES OF THE FABULOUS FORTIES SPRING FORWARD---
ANY IDEA WHO THESE BALD-HEADED RATS ARE, CAP?
NOPE! JUST KEEP SLUGGIN', NAMOR!
--TWIN TITANS OF YESTERDAY'S FICTION --TODAY'S TERRIBLE REALITY--!
CAPTAIN AMERICA AND THE SUB-MARINER YOU KNOW-- AND, COULD THERE BE ANY DOUBT AS TO WHICH OF THESE STRANGE-BORN SUPERHEROES IS CALLED-- THE PATRIOT?
YOU LUGS PICKED ON THE WRONG GUYS THIS TIME!
AMERICANS ARE NOBODY'S PATSIES!
"AMERICANS"? WHAT ARE-- UNHHH!
NOR IS IT JOHNNY STORM WHO BLAZES FORTH THIS DAY---
--BUT THE ORIGINAL, ANDROID-BODIED HUMAN TORCH!
HERE'S SOME FIRE-BALLS TO FOOL AROUND WITH, INSTEAD!
YOU BOYS LOOK TOO OLD TO BE PLAYING WITH GUNS!
10.

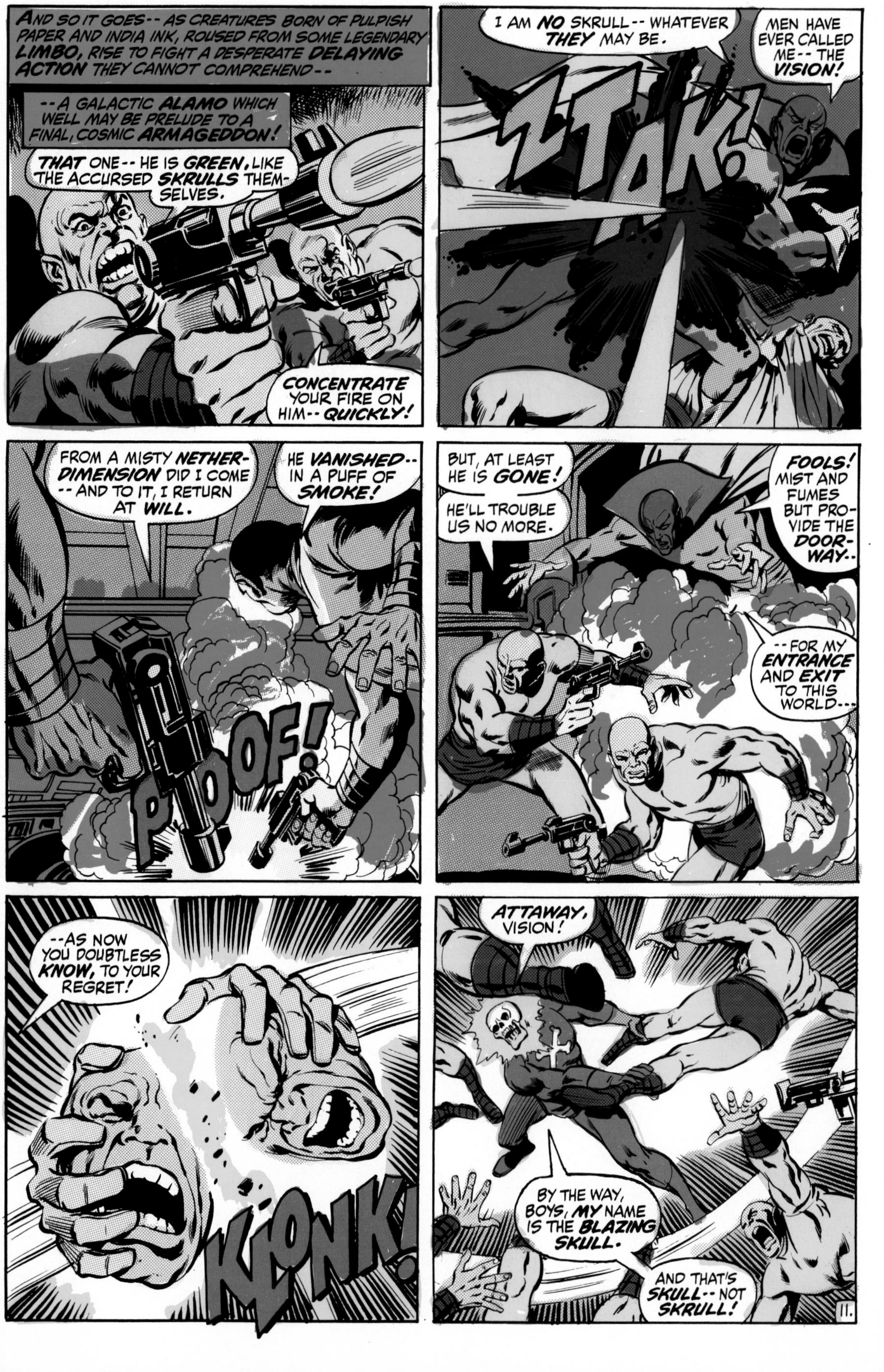
AND SO IT GOES -- AS CREATURES BORN OF PULPISH PAPER AND INDIA INK, ROUSED FROM SOME LEGENDARY LIMBO, RISE TO FIGHT A DESPERATE DELAYING ACTION THEY CANNOT COMPREHEND --
-- A GALACTIC ALAMO WHICH WELL MAY BE PRELUDE TO A FINAL, COSMIC ARMAGEDDON!
THAT ONE -- HE IS GREEN, LIKE THE ACCURSED SKRULLS THEMSELVES.
CONCENTRATE YOUR FIRE ON HIM -- QUICKLY!
I AM NO SKRULL -- WHATEVER THEY MAY BE.
MEN HAVE EVER CALLED ME -- THE VISION!
ZTAK!
FROM A MISTY NETHER-DIMENSION DID I COME -- AND TO IT, I RETURN AT WILL.
HE VANISHED -- IN A PUFF OF SMOKE!
POOF!
BUT, AT LEAST HE IS GONE!
HE'LL TROUBLE US NO MORE.
FOOLS! MIST AND FUMES BUT PROVIDE THE DOORWAY --
-- FOR MY ENTRANCE AND EXIT TO THIS WORLD...
-- AS NOW YOU DOUBTLESS KNOW, TO YOUR REGRET!
KLONK!
ATTAWAY, VISION!
BY THE WAY, BOYS, MY NAME IS THE BLAZING SKULL.
AND THAT'S SKULL -- NOT SKRULL!
11.

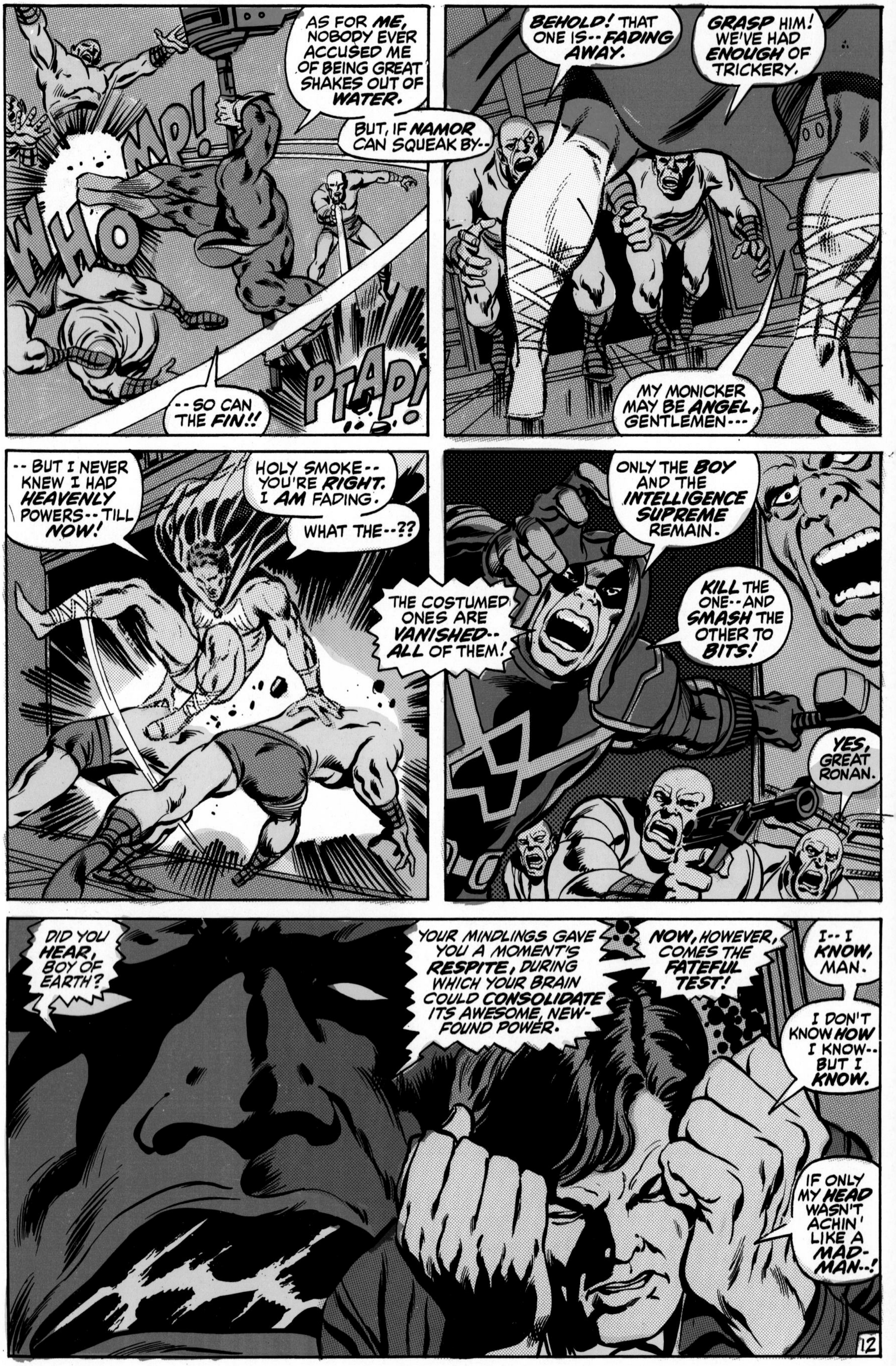
AS FOR ME, NOBODY EVER ACCUSED ME OF BEING GREAT SHAKES OUT OF WATER.
BUT, IF NAMOR CAN SQUEAK BY--
WHOMP!
--SO CAN THE FIN!!
PTAP!
BEHOLD! THAT ONE IS--FADING AWAY.
GRASP HIM! WE'VE HAD ENOUGH OF TRICKERY.
MY MONICKER MAY BE ANGEL, GENTLEMEN---
--BUT I NEVER KNEW I HAD HEAVENLY POWERS--TILL NOW!
HOLY SMOKE--YOU'RE RIGHT. I AM FADING.
WHAT THE--??
THE COSTUMED ONES ARE VANISHED--ALL OF THEM!
ONLY THE BOY AND THE INTELLIGENCE SUPREME REMAIN.
KILL THE ONE--AND SMASH THE OTHER TO BITS!
YES, GREAT RONAN.
DID YOU HEAR, BOY OF EARTH?
YOUR MINDLINGS GAVE YOU A MOMENT'S RESPITE, DURING WHICH YOUR BRAIN COULD CONSOLIDATE ITS AWESOME, NEW-FOUND POWER.
NOW, HOWEVER, COMES THE FATEFUL TEST!
I--I KNOW, MAN.
I DON'T KNOW HOW I KNOW--BUT I KNOW.
IF ONLY MY HEAD WASN'T ACHIN' LIKE A MAD-MAN--!

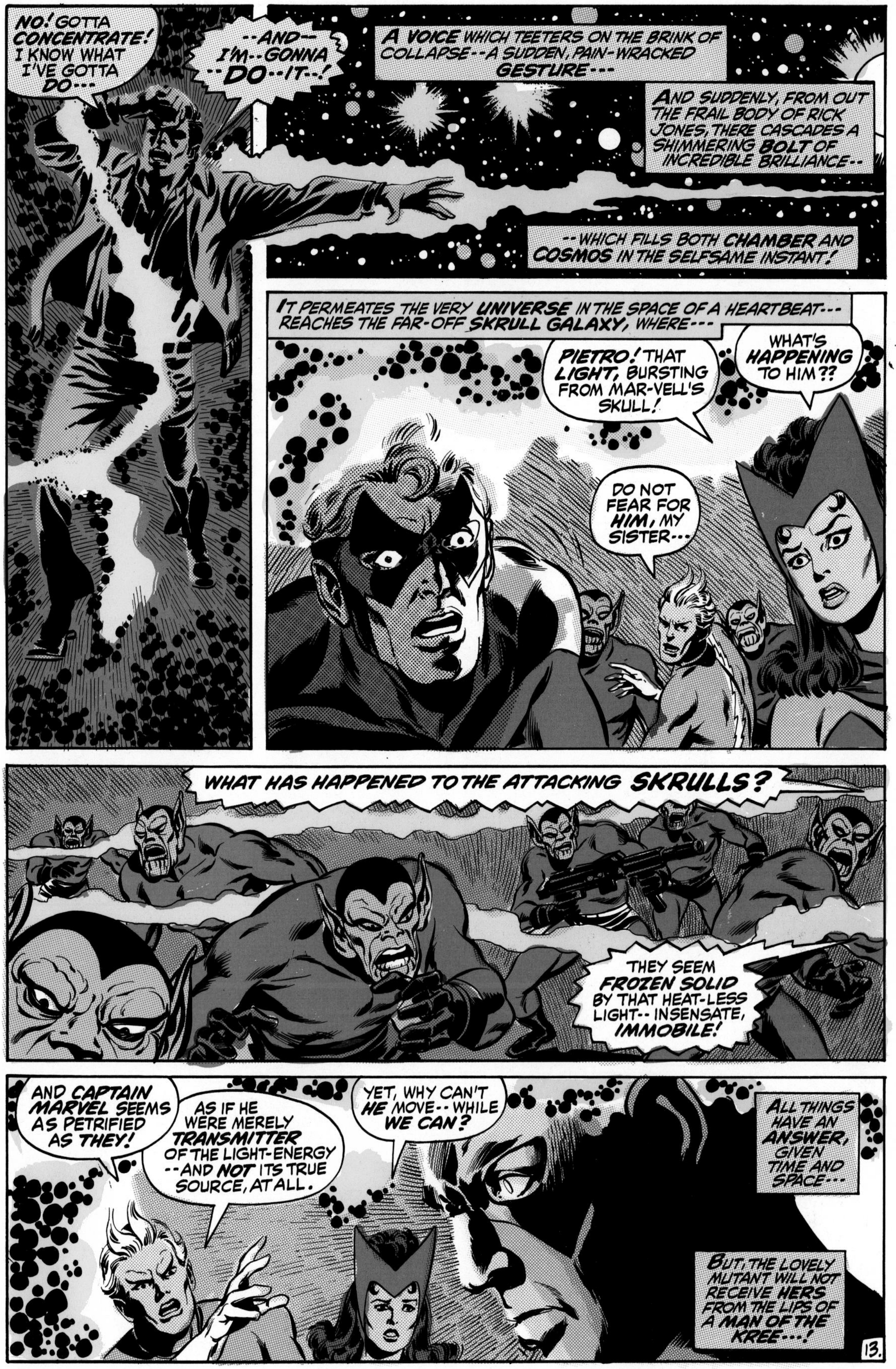
NO! GOTTA CONCENTRATE! I KNOW WHAT I'VE GOTTA DO---
--AND-- I'M--GONNA --DO--IT--!
A VOICE WHICH TEETERS ON THE BRINK OF COLLAPSE--A SUDDEN, PAIN-WRACKED GESTURE---
AND SUDDENLY, FROM OUT THE FRAIL BODY OF RICK JONES, THERE CASCADES A SHIMMERING BOLT OF INCREDIBLE BRILLIANCE--
--WHICH FILLS BOTH CHAMBER AND COSMOS IN THE SELFSAME INSTANT!
IT PERMEATES THE VERY UNIVERSE IN THE SPACE OF A HEARTBEAT---REACHES THE FAR-OFF SKRULL GALAXY, WHERE---
PIETRO! THAT LIGHT, BURSTING FROM MAR-VELL'S SKULL!
WHAT'S HAPPENING TO HIM??
DO NOT FEAR FOR HIM, MY SISTER---
WHAT HAS HAPPENED TO THE ATTACKING SKRULLS?
THEY SEEM FROZEN SOLID BY THAT HEAT-LESS LIGHT-- INSENSATE, IMMOBILE!
AND CAPTAIN MARVEL SEEMS AS PETRIFIED AS THEY!
AS IF HE WERE MERELY TRANSMITTER OF THE LIGHT-ENERGY --AND NOT ITS TRUE SOURCE, AT ALL.
YET, WHY CAN'T HE MOVE-- WHILE WE CAN?
ALL THINGS HAVE AN ANSWER, GIVEN TIME AND SPACE--
BUT, THE LOVELY MUTANT WILL NOT RECEIVE HERS FROM THE LIPS OF A MAN OF THE KREE--!
13.

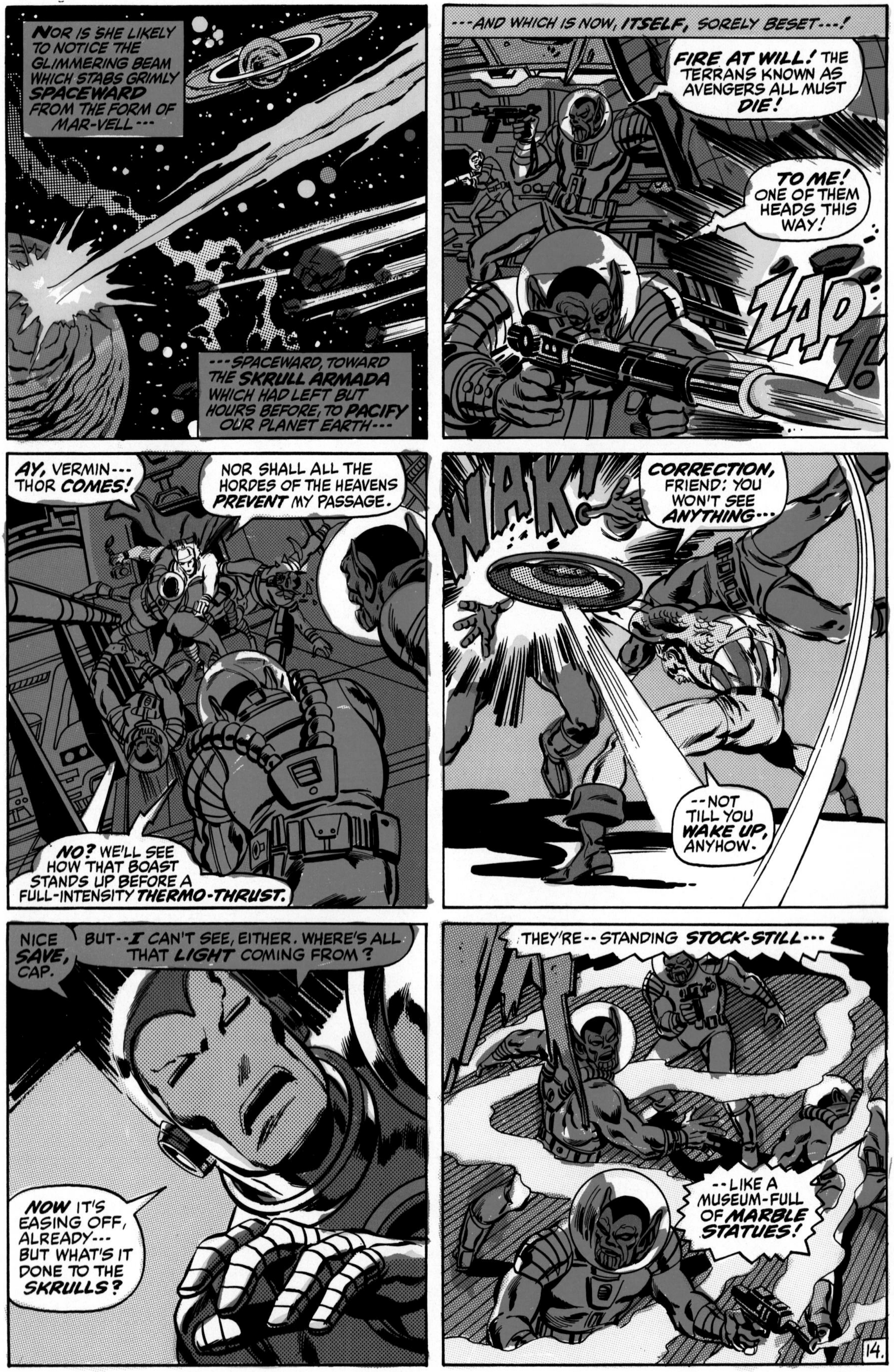
NOR IS SHE LIKELY TO NOTICE THE GLIMMERING BEAM WHICH STABS GRIMLY SPACEWARD FROM THE FORM OF MAR-VELL---
---SPACEWARD, TOWARD THE SKRULL ARMADA WHICH HAD LEFT BUT HOURS BEFORE, TO PACIFY OUR PLANET EARTH---
---AND WHICH IS NOW, ITSELF, SORELY BESET---!
FIRE AT WILL! THE TERRANS KNOWN AS AVENGERS ALL MUST DIE!
TO ME! ONE OF THEM HEADS THIS WAY!
ZAP
AY, VERMIN--- THOR COMES!
NOR SHALL ALL THE HORDES OF THE HEAVENS PREVENT MY PASSAGE.
NO? WE'LL SEE HOW THAT BOAST STANDS UP BEFORE A FULL-INTENSITY THERMO-THRUST.
WAK
CORRECTION, FRIEND: YOU WON'T SEE ANYTHING---
--NOT TILL YOU WAKE UP, ANYHOW.
NICE SAVE, CAP.
BUT--I CAN'T SEE, EITHER. WHERE'S ALL THAT LIGHT COMING FROM?
NOW IT'S EASING OFF, ALREADY--- BUT WHAT'S IT DONE TO THE SKRULLS?
THEY'RE--STANDING STOCK-STILL---
--LIKE A MUSEUM-FULL OF MARBLE STATUES!
14.

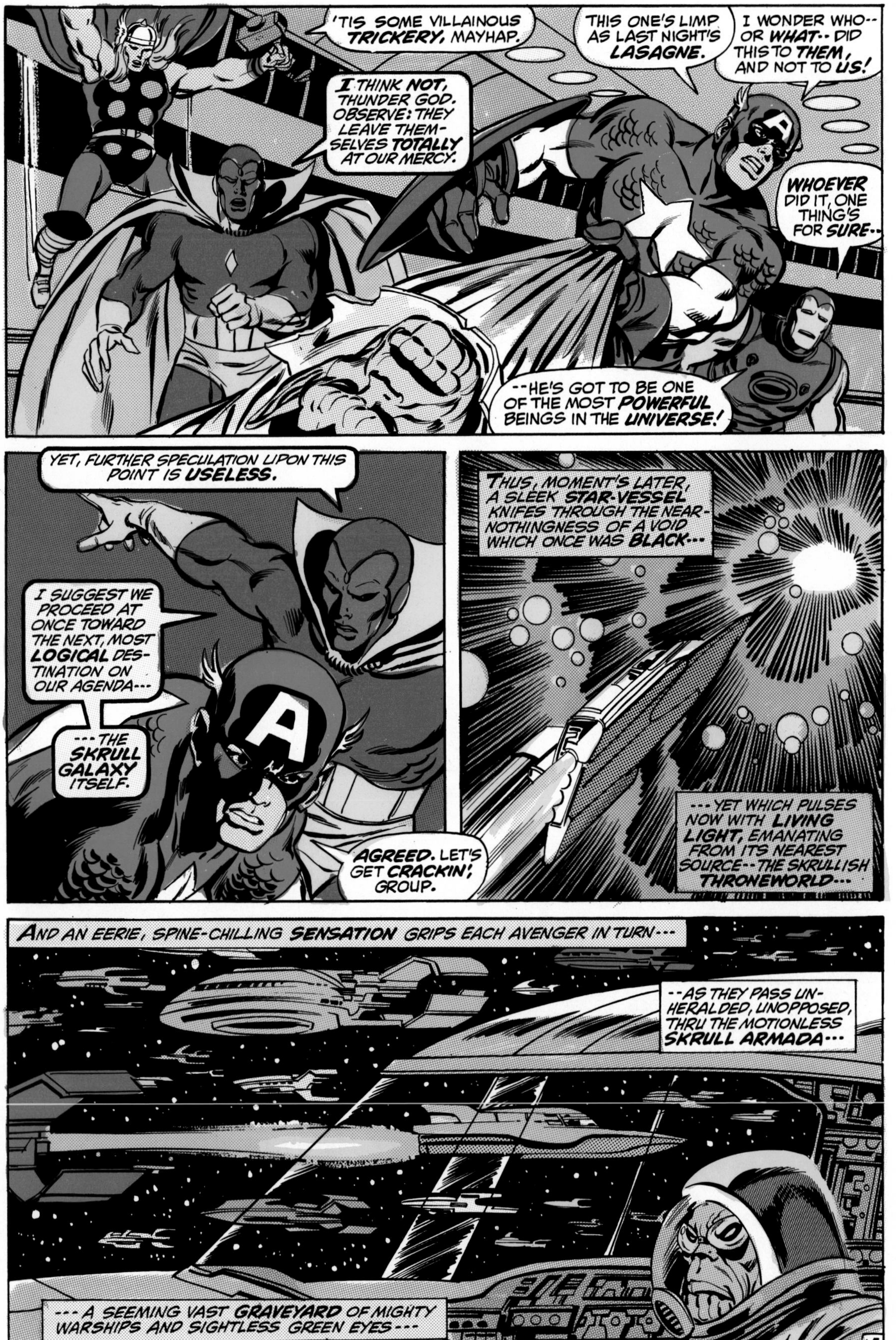
'TIS SOME VILLAINOUS TRICKERY, MAYHAP.
I THINK NOT, THUNDER GOD. OBSERVE: THEY LEAVE THEMSELVES TOTALLY AT OUR MERCY.
THIS ONE'S LIMP AS LAST NIGHT'S LASAGNE.
I WONDER WHO-- OR WHAT-- DID THIS TO THEM, AND NOT TO US!
WHOEVER DID IT, ONE THING'S FOR SURE--
--HE'S GOT TO BE ONE OF THE MOST POWERFUL BEINGS IN THE UNIVERSE!
YET, FURTHER SPECULATION UPON THIS POINT IS USELESS.
I SUGGEST WE PROCEED AT ONCE TOWARD THE NEXT, MOST LOGICAL DESTINATION ON OUR AGENDA---
---THE SKRULL GALAXY ITSELF.
AGREED. LET'S GET CRACKIN', GROUP.
THUS, MOMENT'S LATER, A SLEEK STAR-VESSEL KNIFES THROUGH THE NEAR-NOTHINGNESS OF A VOID WHICH ONCE WAS BLACK---
---YET WHICH PULSES NOW WITH LIVING LIGHT, EMANATING FROM ITS NEAREST SOURCE--THE SKRULLISH THRONEWORLD---
AND AN EERIE, SPINE-CHILLING SENSATION GRIPS EACH AVENGER IN TURN---
--AS THEY PASS UNHERALDED, UNOPPOSED, THRU THE MOTIONLESS SKRULL ARMADA---
---A SEEMING VAST GRAVEYARD OF MIGHTY WARSHIPS AND SIGHTLESS GREEN EYES---
15

WHILE, IN STILL *ANOTHER* GALAXY, FAR ON THE *OPPOSITE* SIDE OF PLANET EARTH---

I-- I DON'T *BELIEVE* IT!

A MINUTE BACK, THESE CLOWNS WERE COMIN' AT ME LIKE *UGLY* ON AN *APE!*

NOW THEY'RE ONE BIG *PETRIFIED FOREST,* WITH BIG DADDY *RONAN* AS HEAD REDWOOD!

WHAT *HAPPENED,* BIG BRAIN? YOU GOTTA *TELL* ME!

IF THE APPELLATION "BIG BRAIN" REFERS TO *THIS* ENTITY, LAD -- I *SHALL* TELL YOU---

FOR, I SEE NOW THAT YOUR *COMPREHENSION* HAS YET TO OVERTAKE YOUR *POWER!*

BUT FIRST, THERE IS *ONE* MORE SCENE WHICH YOU MUST WITNESS---

-- ONE WHICH JUST OCCURRED ON YOUR *OWN HOME WORLD* --

WHAT'RE YOU *DOIN'* TO ME? I -- FEEL --

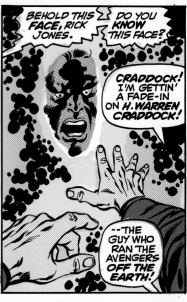

BEHOLD THIS FACE, RICK JONES.

DO YOU *KNOW* THIS FACE?

CRADDOCK! I'M GETTIN' A FADE-IN ON H. WARREN *CRADDOCK!*

-- THE GUY WHO RAN THE *AVENGERS* OFF THE *EARTH!*

"I SEE 'IM *CLEARLY* NOW, IN THE MIDDLE'A *NEW YORK,* AND --- *LORD!* I CAN EVEN-- *READ HIS MIND* --!"

-- THE *ALIENS* IN OUR MIDST MUST BE *FERRETED OUT* ...

THEY MUST BE *SMASHED,* I TELL YOU-- *DESTROYED!*

HAH! THE CROWD FOLLOWS ME LIKE *SHEEP* ...

LITTLE DO THEY SUSPECT THAT I OWE LESS TO MERE *ORATORY,* THAN TO UNIQUE POWERS OF *VERBAL HYPNOSIS.* I--

"HEY! THERE'S MY BIG BAD *BOLT* AGAIN-- THE ONE THAT CAME OUTTA MY *SKULL* .."

"IT'S *ZAPPIN'* CRADDOCK-- BUT *NOBODY ELSE!*"

=*AAARRRHH!*=

16

"HE-- SOMETHIN'S *HAPPENIN'* TO HIM -- RIGHT BEFORE MY *EYES*--!"

"HE'S *CHANGING*-- CHANGING INTO--"

"*FAAAN*-TASTIC! --INTO-- A *SKRULL*!!"

"AND--THAT HYPNOTIZED *CROWD* SEES IT, TOO!"

LOOK! THERE'S ONE'A THEM *ALIENS!*

CRADDOCK SAID THEY'RE OUT TO KILL US *ALL.*

WELL, *NOT* IF WE KILL THEM *FIRST!*

GET HIM! *GET HIM!*

SAVAGES! DO YOU THINK YOU CAN CAP-TURE A *SKRULL?*

I CAN *STRETCH* MY WAY TO SAFETY. I CAN---

NNOoo!

MY POWERS --*GONE!* CAN HARDLY *MOVE*--!

"*GOOD GRAVY!* HE-- HE'S LANDED RIGHT IN THE *MIDDLE* OF THE CROWD--"

"BUT, THEY'RE *NOT* JUST A CROWD-- NOT ANY *MORE.* CRADDOCK HAD TURNED 'EM INTO A *MOB* -- A FRIGHTENED, KILL-CRAZY *MOB!*"

"AND NOW-- HE'S *PAYIN'* FOR IT--THE *HARD* WAY!"

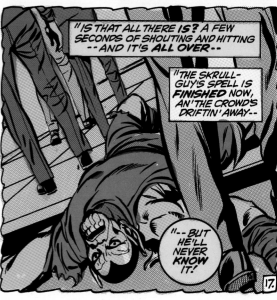

"IS THAT ALL THERE *IS?* A FEW SECONDS OF SHOUTING AND HITTING --AND IT'S *ALL OVER*--"

"THE *SKRULL-GUY'S* SPELL IS *FINISHED* NOW, AN' THE CROWD'S *DRIFTIN'* AWAY--"

"-- BUT HE'LL *NEVER KNOW* IT!"

17.

H-HE'S DEAD! AND, IN A WAY-- **I KILLED 'IM!**

IT WAS **HE** WHO LOADED HIS OWN DEATH-WEAPON.

YOU MERELY POINTED IT AT-- ITS PROPER **TARGET.**

BUT **HOW** DID I DO IT? HOW??

YOU **STILL** HAVE NOT SURMISED?

YOU KNOW RONAN **WEAKENED** ME-- SO I COULD NOT INFLUENCE THE MINDS OF THE **UPPER ECHELON** OF KREE AND SKRULLS.

YET, BY INDUCING **MAR-VELL** TO CONSTRUCT AND UTILIZE A KREE **OMNI-WAVE** DEVICE---

--I UNLEASHED POWERS WHICH LAY **DORMANT** WITHIN YOU.

FOR UNTOLD EONS, **SKRULL** AND **KREE** HAVE STALKED THE COSMIC CORRIDORS LIKE TWIN RACES OF MALEVOLENT GODS---

---NEVER KNOWING THAT **EACH** OF THEIR STAR-SPANNING CLANS HAS REACHED-- A **DEAD END.**

LIVE A **BILLION BILLION** YEARS, NEITHER WILL EVER ADVANCE ONE MORE **RUNG** UP THE LADDER OF EVOLUTION.

NOW, THEY CAN BUT **SNARL** AT EACH OTHER ACROSS THE SEA OF SPACE, HATING BOTH EACH OTHER--- AND THE **HUMAN RACE**---

---WHICH THEY SUB-CONSCIOUSLY **SENSE** TO BE THEIR ULTIMATE **SUPERIORS!**

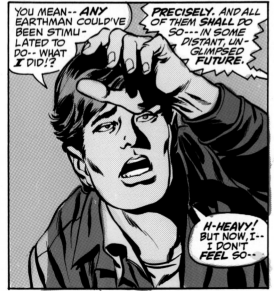

YOU MEAN-- **ANY** EARTHMAN COULD'VE BEEN STIMULATED TO DO-- WHAT **I** DID!?

PRECISELY. AND ALL OF THEM **SHALL** DO SO--- IN SOME DISTANT, UN-GLIMPSED FUTURE.

H-**HEAVY!** BUT NOW, I-- I DON'T FEEL SO--

RICK! RICK JONES!

18

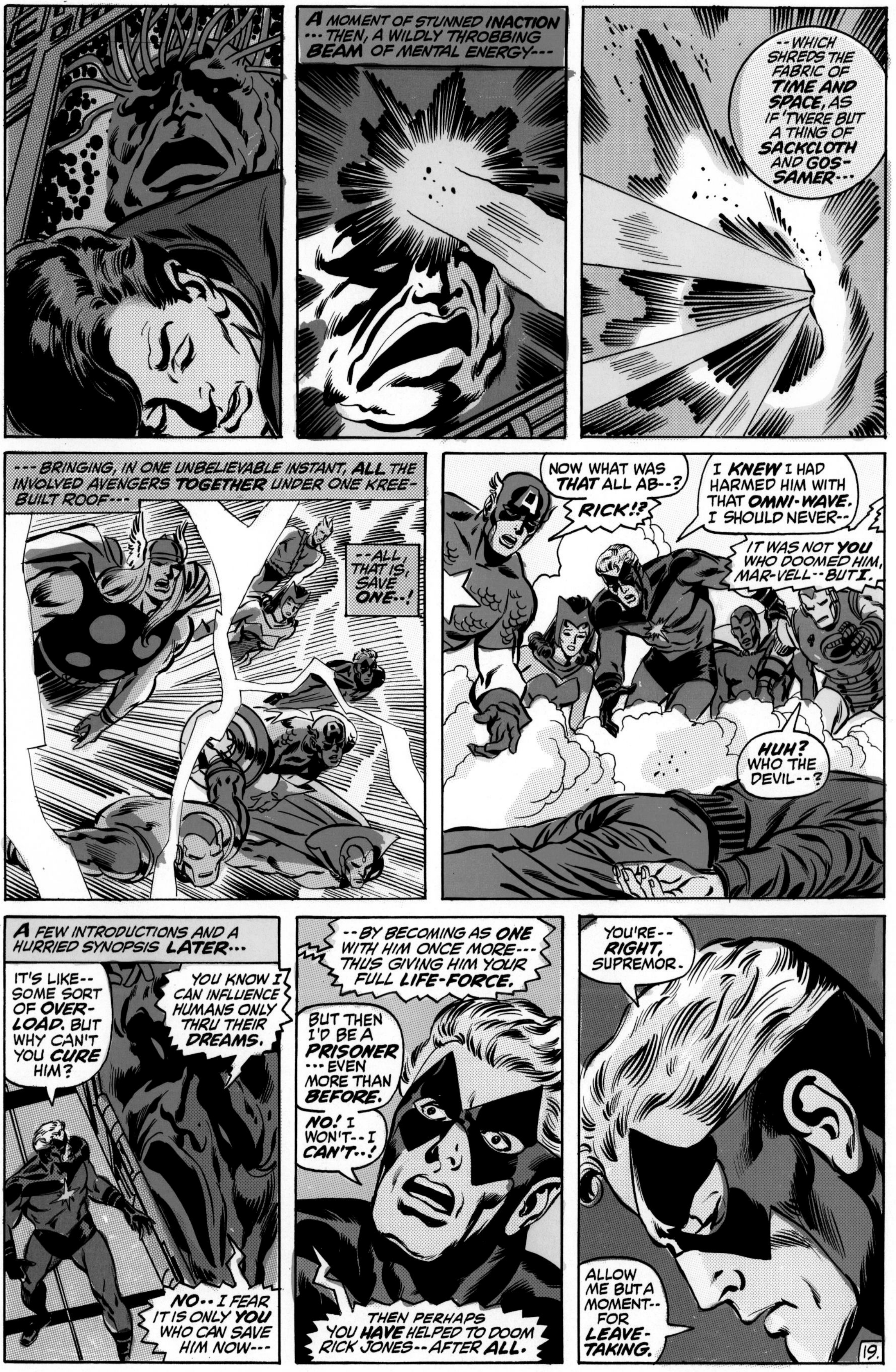
A MOMENT OF STUNNED INACTION --- THEN, A WILDLY THROBBING BEAM OF MENTAL ENERGY---
--WHICH SHREDS THE FABRIC OF TIME AND SPACE, AS IF 'TWERE BUT A THING OF SACKCLOTH AND GOSSAMER---
---BRINGING, IN ONE UNBELIEVABLE INSTANT, ALL THE INVOLVED AVENGERS TOGETHER UNDER ONE KREE-BUILT ROOF---
--ALL, THAT IS, SAVE ONE--!
NOW WHAT WAS THAT ALL AB--?
RICK!?
I KNEW I HAD HARMED HIM WITH THAT OMNI-WAVE. I SHOULD NEVER--
IT WAS NOT YOU WHO DOOMED HIM, MAR-VELL--BUT I.
HUH? WHO THE DEVIL--?
A FEW INTRODUCTIONS AND A HURRIED SYNOPSIS LATER...
IT'S LIKE--SOME SORT OF OVER-LOAD. BUT WHY CAN'T YOU CURE HIM?
YOU KNOW I CAN INFLUENCE HUMANS ONLY THRU THEIR DREAMS.
NO--I FEAR IT IS ONLY YOU WHO CAN SAVE HIM NOW---
--BY BECOMING AS ONE WITH HIM ONCE MORE--- THUS GIVING HIM YOUR FULL LIFE-FORCE.
BUT THEN I'D BE A PRISONER---EVEN MORE THAN BEFORE.
NO! I WON'T--I CAN'T--!
THEN PERHAPS YOU HAVE HELPED TO DOOM RICK JONES--AFTER ALL.
YOU'RE--RIGHT, SUPREMOR.
ALLOW ME BUT A MOMENT--FOR LEAVE-TAKING.
19.

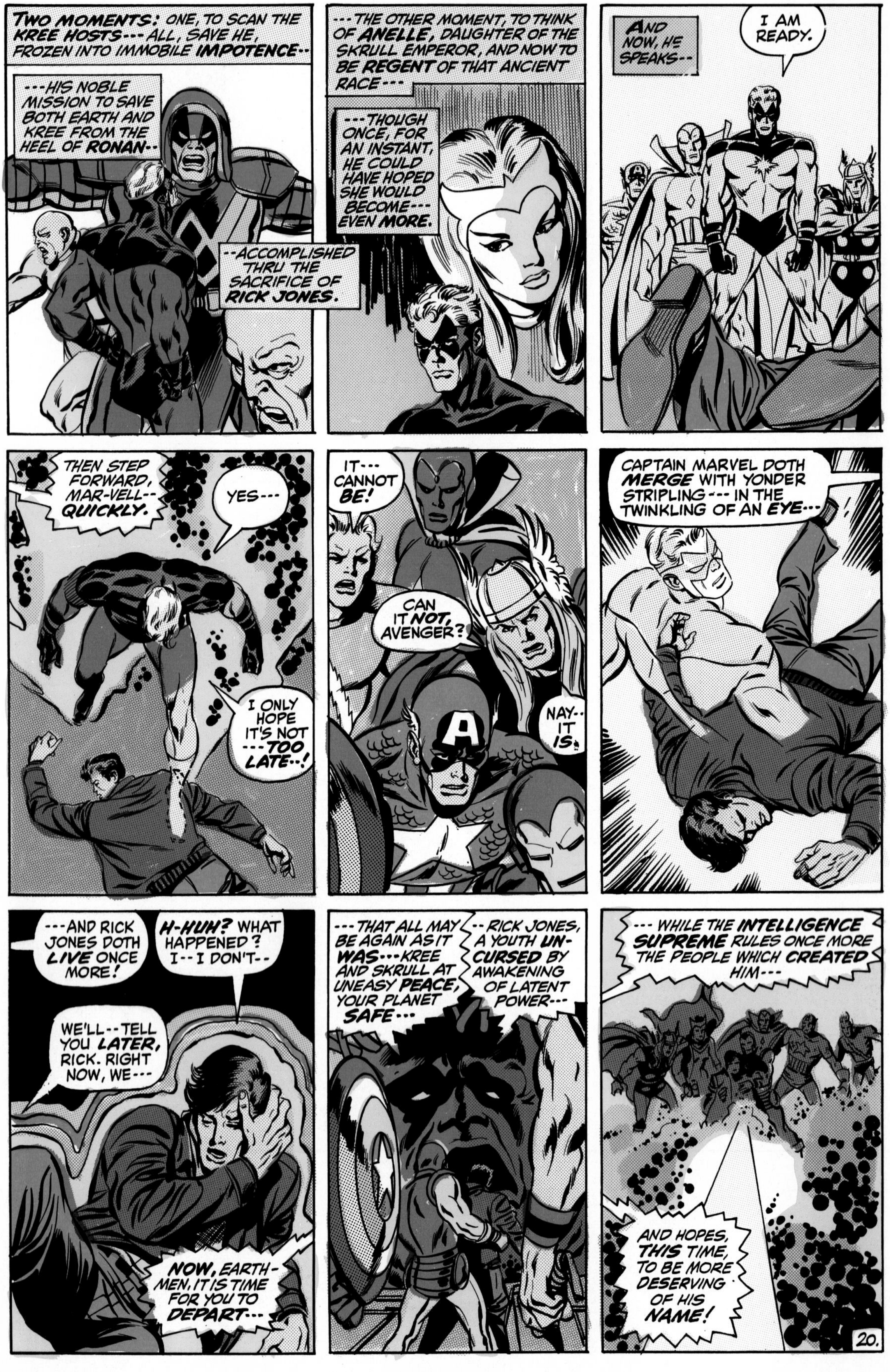

TWO MOMENTS: ONE, TO SCAN THE KREE HOSTS--- ALL, SAVE HE, FROZEN INTO IMMOBILE IMPOTENCE--
---HIS NOBLE MISSION TO SAVE BOTH EARTH AND KREE FROM THE HEEL OF RONAN--
--ACCOMPLISHED THRU THE SACRIFICE OF RICK JONES.
---THE OTHER MOMENT, TO THINK OF ANELLE, DAUGHTER OF THE SKRULL EMPEROR, AND NOW TO BE REGENT OF THAT ANCIENT RACE---
---THOUGH ONCE, FOR AN INSTANT, HE COULD HAVE HOPED SHE WOULD BECOME--- EVEN MORE.
AND NOW, HE SPEAKS--
I AM READY.
THEN STEP FORWARD, MAR-VELL-- QUICKLY.
YES---
I ONLY HOPE IT'S NOT ---TOO LATE--!
IT--- CANNOT BE!
CAN IT NOT, AVENGER?
NAY-- IT IS.
CAPTAIN MARVEL DOTH MERGE WITH YONDER STRIPLING--- IN THE TWINKLING OF AN EYE---
---AND RICK JONES DOTH LIVE ONCE MORE!
H-HUH? WHAT HAPPENED? I-- I DON'T--
WE'LL--TELL YOU LATER, RICK. RIGHT NOW, WE---
NOW, EARTH-MEN. IT IS TIME FOR YOU TO DEPART---
---THAT ALL MAY BE AGAIN AS IT WAS---KREE AND SKRULL AT UNEASY PEACE, YOUR PLANET SAFE---
--RICK JONES, A YOUTH UN-CURSED BY AWAKENING OF LATENT POWER---
--- WHILE THE INTELLIGENCE SUPREME RULES ONCE MORE THE PEOPLE WHICH CREATED HIM---
AND HOPES, THIS TIME, TO BE MORE DESERVING OF HIS NAME!

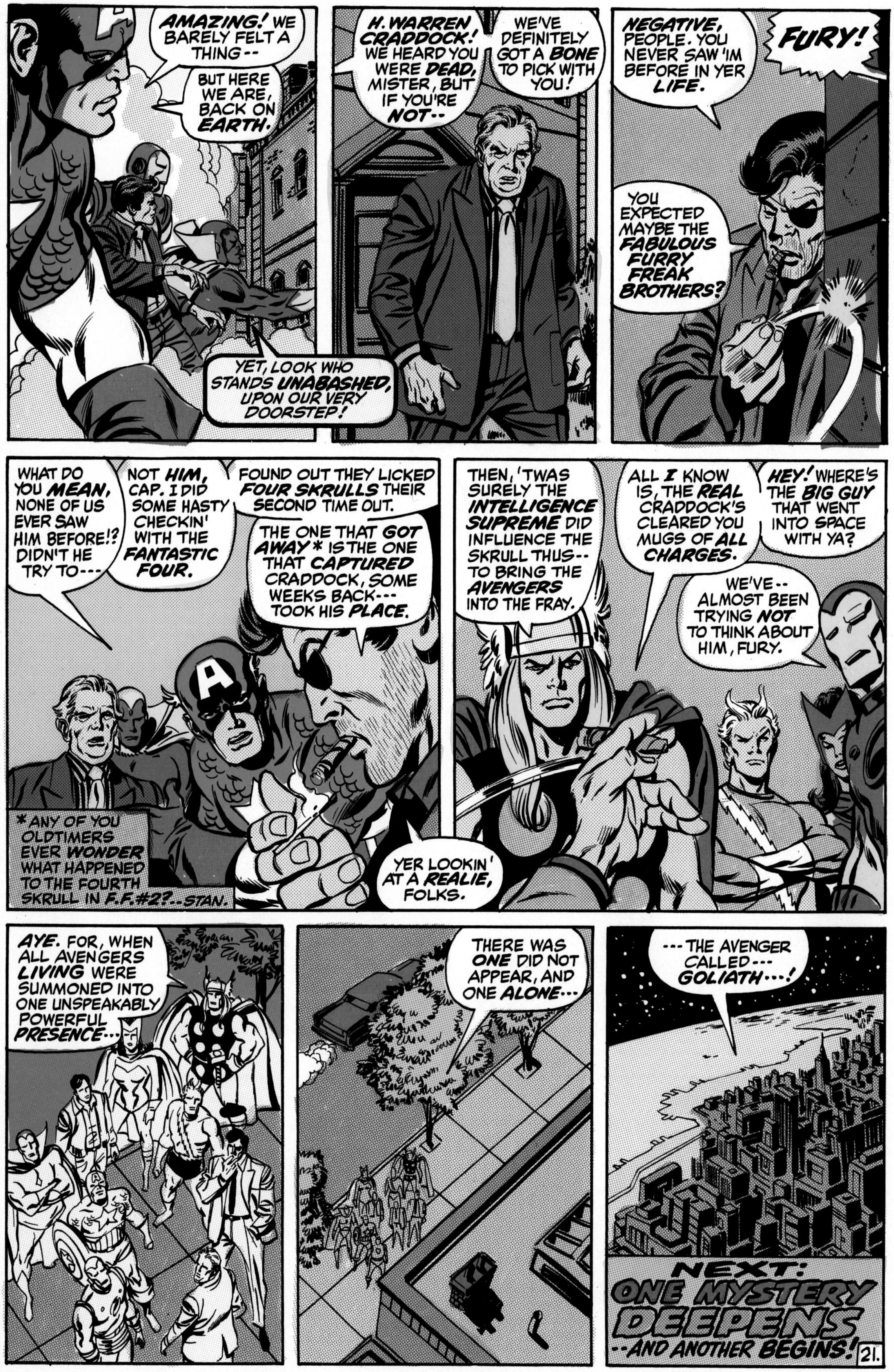
AMAZING! WE BARELY FELT A THING--
BUT HERE WE ARE, BACK ON EARTH.
YET, LOOK WHO STANDS UNABASHED, UPON OUR VERY DOORSTEP!
H. WARREN CRADDOCK! WE HEARD YOU WERE DEAD, MISTER, BUT IF YOU'RE NOT--
WE'VE DEFINITELY GOT A BONE TO PICK WITH YOU!
NEGATIVE, PEOPLE. YOU NEVER SAW 'IM BEFORE IN YER LIFE.
FURY!
YOU EXPECTED MAYBE THE FABULOUS FURRY FREAK BROTHERS?
WHAT DO YOU MEAN, NONE OF US EVER SAW HIM BEFORE!? DIDN'T HE TRY TO---
NOT HIM, CAP. I DID SOME HASTY CHECKIN' WITH THE FANTASTIC FOUR.
FOUND OUT THEY LICKED FOUR SKRULLS THEIR SECOND TIME OUT.
THE ONE THAT GOT AWAY* IS THE ONE THAT CAPTURED CRADDOCK, SOME WEEKS BACK--- TOOK HIS PLACE.
*ANY OF YOU OLDTIMERS EVER WONDER WHAT HAPPENED TO THE FOURTH SKRULL IN F.F.#2?--STAN.
YER LOOKIN' AT A REALIE, FOLKS.
THEN, 'TWAS SURELY THE INTELLIGENCE SUPREME DID INFLUENCE THE SKRULL THUS-- TO BRING THE AVENGERS INTO THE FRAY.
ALL I KNOW IS, THE REAL CRADDOCK'S CLEARED YOU MUGS OF ALL CHARGES.
HEY! WHERE'S THE BIG GUY THAT WENT INTO SPACE WITH YA?
WE'VE-- ALMOST BEEN TRYING NOT TO THINK ABOUT HIM, FURY.
AYE. FOR, WHEN ALL AVENGERS LIVING WERE SUMMONED INTO ONE UNSPEAKABLY POWERFUL PRESENCE...
THERE WAS ONE DID NOT APPEAR, AND ONE ALONE...
---THE AVENGER CALLED---GOLIATH---!
NEXT: ONE MYSTERY DEEPENS --AND ANOTHER BEGINS!
21.

A SPLENDID LITTLE WAR

The Kree-Skrull War was a happy not-quite- accident.

By the beginning of 1971 I'd been writing and editing for Smilin' Stan Lee for more than half a decade. Part of my job description, it often seemed, was to pick up the reins of whatever series Stan felt like dropping, be it MILLIE THE MODEL, SGT. FURY AND HIS HOWLING COMMANDOS, THE X-MEN, THE AMAZING SPIDER-MAN (briefly) -- or THE AVENGERS.

In fact, I'd already written more than fifty issues of THE AVENGERS by the time it occurred to me that the Skrulls and the Kree ought to go to war. After all, Marvel had no less than two rapacious, galaxy-spanning races out there knocking around in space, so it seemed to be an inevitability that they clash -- in fact, they were already long-standing enemies, and probably had been for ages. In Marvel terms, of course, the Skrulls had been around ever since FANTASTIC FOUR no. 2, though the Kree had debuted only two or three years before, in F.F. no.'s 64-65, and far less was known about them.

As Stan got busier with other things and wrote fewer and fewer comics, it was clear to me that he had no plans to get the Kree and Skrulls together; so, with his permission, I did it myself, in the pages of THE AVENGERS. And, since I had only recently revamped our Kree-born Captain Marvel (a.k.a. Mar-Vell), I used him as a starting point in AVENGERS no. 89.

Did I have some "master plan" when I started out? Not really. I simply knew that the Kree and Skrulls would be at war in the far reaches of space, and that their conflict would be threatening to spill over onto the Earth, turning our planet into the cosmic equivalent of some Pacific island during World War II. Here, I was unabashedly influenced by Raymond Jones' 1950s novel This Island Earth (but not, I hasten to add, by the god-awful movie made from it!).

The War started out slowly, as artist Sal Buscema and I moved our players into place. Then, about the time that we were ready to get moving in earnest, Neal Adams -- with whom I had already worked on much-acclaimed X-MEN and "Inhumans" series -- volunteered to draw THE AVENGERS. Sal moved on to other things, and the Kree-Skrull War (not yet so named) moved into high gear.

Neal and I had an almost symbiotic relationship over the next four issues -- so much so that, today, it would be impossible for the two of us to agree on who contributed what to the saga. Just to use one prominent example: I'm 100% certain it was my idea to bring back the "three Skrull cows" in Fantastic Four form; Neal is equally certain he suggested it to me.

Perhaps the most striking sequence in the whole epic, however -- even though it has virtually zilch to do with the actual War -- is the "Journey to the Center of the Android" segment in AVENGERS no. 93. That was Neal's idea, pure and simple. He told me he wanted to have Ant-Man return to the Avengers long enough to go inside The Vision -- and, being de facto editor as well as writer of the series, I told him to go for it. That issue contained, after all, a 34-page story, which is a lot of pages to fill... and Neal's notion sounded like a great way to fill it. And it was.

By the last issue of the story line (no. 97), due to deadline problems, I felt it incumbent to draft John Buscema (who had contributed one short chapter in no. 94) into finishing up the War. And, as I'd planned ever since no. 89, Rick Jones became the true hero of the piece, with images of Golden Age comic-book heroes emerging from his mind (like Athena from the brain of Zeus) to buy time for Captain Marvel and the Avengers.

Thus it was that, with the work of three excellent artists -- Neal Adams and the Brothers Buscema -- the Kree-Skrull War became one of the linchpins of the Marvel Age of Comics.

And, if I may be unabashedly immodest for a moment, I think it holds up fairly well.

My thanks to the good people at Marvel Comics for finally printing The Kree-Skrull War in its entirety. I've been holding a space open for it on my bookshelf for the past three decades.

ROY THOMAS · 6·2000

ROY THOMAS has written comics, often for Marvel, since 1965, and was Marvel's editor-in-chief from 1972-74. Besides THE AVENGERS, he is best known for his work with Neal Adams on X-MEN and with Barry Windsor-Smith and John Buscema on CONAN THE BARBARIAN. Over the years he has won Alley, Eagle, Shazam, Haxtur, and other awards for his scripting. Besides writing comics and screenplays, he currently edits Alter Ego, a magazine about the history of heroic comics.